Postmortems

Selected Essays Volume One

by Raph Koster

ALTERED
TUNING
PRESS

Ultima Online® is a registered trademark of Electronic Arts Inc.
Star Wars Galaxies® is a registered trademark of Lucasfilm Entertainment Company
  Ltd.

Published by Altered Tuning Press
12463 Rancho Bernardo Rd., #556
San Diego, CA 92128

ISBN-13: 978-0-9967937-4-2
ISBN: 0-9967937-4-7

Postmortems

Selected Essays Volume One

by Raph Koster

Also by Raph Koster

Books
A Theory of Fun for Game Design
Sunday Poems

Music
After the Flood

Contents

Foreword

The art form of computer games remains, I would argue, in its infancy... We are about 40 years in, and computer games have already grown to have more economic and arguably more social impact, than the industries of film, television, books, and other physical art forms combined, many times over. Yet, I say it's in its infancy, because so much about this art form is changing, so fast, that the art form has rarely stabilized into standards that can be observed and documented, much less built upon.

These days most all games are "online" in some way. Most games are downloaded, while only a few years ago, most games were purchased at a retail store. Multiplayer games are now common, and one of the best selling categories of games available. While this multiplayer dominance is a relatively recent phenomenon, multiplayer games go way, way back.

For about as long as there have been people using computers, people have been networking them together. Well before we published the Hall of Fame game *Ultima Online,* often credited as the first true Massively Multiplayer Online Role Playing Game (MMORPG), computer systems from PLATO to dial-up Bulletin Board Systems (BBS) were allowing people to play together online.

These early forays into online gaming may not have had the audiovisual bells and whistles that help sell the "Triple A" games of today, but they explored and refined techniques that are now being exploited and improved on by creators across the industry.

For years before Origin embarked on creating what would become the watershed *Ultima Online,* we watched the nascent evolution of early multiplayer games from text MUDs (Multi-User Dungeons) to graphical MUDs. We watched the development of head-to-head battle environments like Kesmai's *Air Warrior.* Yet year after year we waited, until near the end of the 1990's we saw the emergence of the World Wide Web and we knew this was the moment that everyone would soon be online, and finally truly massively multiplayer games would be possible.

Since no game of this style at this scale had been attempted, we sought out the expertise that existed before us. Raph Koster joined the founding *Ultima Online* team as its lead designer. He brought with him his years of experience in text MUDs, as we then all ran headlong into the future together.

MMORPG's are hard to make. They are basically Ernest Cline's Oasis from *Ready Player One,* with the state-of-the-art reality crafting that can be done with the day's technology. Crafting an alternate reality goes *far* beyond just the physics of a simulated world. Why are players there, what will keep bringing them back? What are the rules of interpersonal sharing of the experience, what can I do alone, when must I get help from another? How safe must the world be, or when could I backstab my partners, for fun or profit? All these aspects were new to me, new to the scale of product we were attempting, but not new to Raph.

Raph Koster is one of the few who not only lived through this period, but helped define how it grew. More importantly, he is one of the even fewer to create records of this evolution that should not just be of interest to any hoping to understand our medium, but to those who help to guide its future. I trust the readers of this book will grow in the knowledge, understanding and ability to work within and help advance the industry, just as I felt from spending years developing games with Raph Koster.

Richard "Lord British" Garriott
Creator of the Ultima *Series and the recent* Shroud of the Avatar

Dedication

This is dedicated to those builders of worlds whom I worked alongside, and who are no longer with us.

Ultima Online
- Brett Bonner
- Matt Crump
- Chuck Lupher
- Teresa Potts
- Joe Rabbitt
- John Watson

Origin
- Donavon Keithley
- Teresa Maxwell
- Brian Smith
- Paul Steed
- Clay Towery

Privateer Online
- Pete Shelus

Star Wars Galaxies
- Jeff Freeman
- Ben Hanson
- Wesley Haselden
- Andy Lamp
- Ethan Nason
- David Nevala
- John Roy

Sony Online
- Rick Johnson
- Steve Pierce
- Edwin Roselle
- Nathan Temple
- John Tessin

Metaplace
- Joe Skivolocke
- Adam Smith

Introduction

This isn't a memoir.

It may perhaps edge into that at times; it's hard not to start telling fun stories, once you are reminiscing! And I'm sure there are some who might be disappointed that this isn't a tell-all.[1]

This book strives to be what the title says: a collection of self-evaluative writings and lessons learned. It therefore has a hefty dose of history, but it's oriented around design, not salacious or behind-the-scenes tidbits. Oh, there are a few anecdotes here and there, but this book is intended to be something useful to working game designers and historians, and interesting to players of the various games discussed. With any luck, some of the lessons will be applicable to people working on any sort of connected online community.

When I started making online worlds, I sought out lessons from those who had done it before me: *The Lessons of LucasFilm's "Habitat,"*[2] the (at the time, new) paper by Dr. Richard Bartle entitled "Hearts, Clubs, Diamonds, Spades: Players who Suit MUDs."[3] There wasn't very much out there, but I did find an active community discussing how to push the state of the art forward, first on Usenet's[4] rec.games.mud.diku[5] and later on the fabled MUD-Dev[6] mailing list run by J. C.

---

[1] Catch me at a conference late at night, I'll fill your ears then.

[2] http://www.fudco.com/chip/lessons.html

[3] https://www.researchgate.net/publication/247190693_Hearts_clubs_diamonds_spades_Players_who_suit_MUDs

[4] Usenet is a bulletin board-style discussion group akin to today's web forums, that has existed on the Internet since 1980. Mostly forgotten these days, it once served the equivalent role to Facebook, Twitter, and countless discussion forums and comment threads as a way for so-called "netizens" to connect and communicate. And often flame one another.

[5] Google groups has archived all the traffic from this newsgroup, including many of the posts cited in the book, at https://groups.google.com/forum/#!forum/rec.games.mud.diku

[6] To quote from http://mud.wikia.com/wiki/MUD-Dev, "MUD-Dev (or MUD Development mailing list) was the principal mailing list concerned with the development of virtual worlds, including MUDs and other online games. Participants included the designers of *Dark Sun Online, EverQuest, Meridian 59, The Realm,* and *Ultima Online,* as well as many experienced hobbyist MUD developers/administrators,

Lawrence, in journals such as *Imaginary Realities*,[7] and amongst the early scholars who were exploring the possibilities in MUD, MUSHes, and MOOs.

I took that as a model. I strive to do my learning in public.

I've now been making games professionally for over twenty years, and I've been writing on my website for a very long time. The first writings there were put up sometime around 1996. I was actively posting on Usenet newsgroups and on the MUD-Dev mailing list in the mid-1990s. I've also made a lot of silly, often arrogant mistakes; had some successes; and along the way, tried to be honest with myself and others about both.

That's what this book is. There are writings in here that I cringe to read. Administrative practices that make me shudder, idealism that causes a wince, and design errors so glaring that I can't believe I missed them. But there are also a lot of hard-won learnings.

I've written far more about online game design than would fit in one book of this size; in fact, I'm working on a second collection like this one, that collects just the additional materials on virtual worlds ranging from MUDs to augmented reality games played on top of the real world, writings that aren't specifically about one world. After that, with any luck, will come another just related to general game design topics. But in the meantime, *Postmortems* focuses on specifically articles about games I led in some fashion. Some of them didn't even reach the public.

There aren't articles for every game I've worked on. Some games simply have more stuff to talk about. Some games have interesting design lessons, and others just have the sort of behind-the-scenes trivia that would no doubt interest a player, but don't have larger lessons to teach. That's fine. Every game developer's career is like an iceberg: there's far more that didn't ship, didn't matter much, than there is that made an impact.

To serve design historical purposes, there's quite a lot in here that simply just tries to capture contemporaneous material. In the early days of MMORPGs[8], a blog post written to the players of a particular game could turn out to be foundational enough to someday end up with a Wikipedia article of its own. I wrote a lot of essays and blog

---

and others. MUD-Dev served to facilitate the exchange of knowledge for the MUD community and the nascent MMORPG design community, and was notable for the rigor, detail, and usefulness of discussions." Archives of the traffic from the mailing list are still available on multiple locations including my website.

[7] Back issues are hosted at http://journal.imaginary-realities.com/

[8] "Massively multiplayer online roleplaying games," an unwieldy acronym for the virtual world games of the late 1990s. Soon abbreviated to just "MMO" as more forms of play became common.

posts specifically for players of the various games; those are in here too, just just retrospective views on it all. By and large, I have left these original writings intact. Any contemporary additions or commentary arising from more years to think on it are distinguishable by the use of a different typeface.

Enough time has gone by that I don't think it's reasonable for younger folks to even know of some of these older games, so there are pieces in here that I hope give readers the flavor of what it was like to walk around in a text MUD, what it was like to log into the worlds of *Ultima Online* or *Star Wars Galaxies* at launch, and what it was like to try making a small art game before the term even existed.

For many, I imagine the best way to use this book will be to simply jump to key essays. While most of the essays here are collected from my website, http://www.raphkoster.com, there are tens of thousands of new words written specifically for this volume, in order to provide that context and connective tissue from essay to essay. It's still a collection of individual pieces, and not a chapter book, but hopefully you can get a sense of the design story as we move forward through time.

Even if most people hop around, I do hope that at least some of you come along with me on the chronological journey through one point of view on the evolution of our connected lives. It's been a weird few decades, and the online worlds that form the bulk of this book were prefiguring our future in ways that only a few understood at the time.

Early days

In Peru

"If everything is designed, then design is everything" — the motto at Toulouse Lautrec.

I spent a large chunk of my childhood in Peru. It was there, in fact, that I first started to make games. I lived in Lima, in San Isidro, a relatively well-off neighborhood. It was the height of the Shining Path[9] terrorism period: *gringo* things were blown up with great regularity. The KFC. The Pizza Hut. The local arcade.

The art institute Instituto Toulouse Lautrec is launching the first ever game design program in Peru this year.[10] There are programs for 3d modelers, animators, and programmers there and elsewhere already. There's a small but thriving work-for-hire community that also does original game development. The time seemed right. When they asked me to come give a talk, it was an emotional moment — and the first time in almost thirty years that I had set foot in Lima.

I scheduled time with friends and relatives. Before I left, my mom pointed out, just as she did before I got the Online Legend Award,[11] that it's important to let people know that Latinos can manage a career in the industry. People don't think of me as Latino, and honestly, I don't tend to think of myself that way, most of the time.

It was a long flight over — San Diego to Atlanta, from there to Lima. I arrived at a bit past midnight. When the driver in the hotel shuttle heard that I used to live there, he took me the long way around, to show me the way that things had changed. It was

---

[9] A communist terrorist group known as Sendero Luminoso (Shining Path) began major guerrilla activity in 1980, shortly after I moved to Peru. They managed to take control of a decent chunk of the country. See https://en.wikipedia.org/wiki/Shining_Path

[10] This essay was posted to my website on February 5th, 2015.

[11] I was given the third Online Legend Award at the now defunct GDC Online Conference. This is a sort of lifetime achievement award for game designers working in the online game space. See the next chapter for a bit from the citation.

dark, but even in the middle of the night I could see the way development and careful in-filling had allowed the addition of a new highway on the coastal cliff from Callao to Miraflores. I fell asleep around 2:30am. Little did I know it would be the earliest bedtime I'd have during my stay.

It all began at 9am the next day. Breakfast with my oldest friend. Right after I was collected for a round of interviews and time to go over the proposed courses and syllabi for the game design program. I suggested a bit more on statistics, and wondered aloud about the amount of general traditional liberal arts education that could be offered within the context of the program. It's a vocational school, in a sense, but I strongly believe that traditional literature, arts, history, and humanities are vitally important for a game designer.

The IGDA party, all playing my boardgames

Then an IGDA[12] party. I had brought with me all the of the board game prototypes I have been making. We didn't get to try the newest one, but all the others were played quite a lot. I basically took over the IGDA party with play tests. Then off for dinner — at 1am.

I had been asked to run a workshop for the instructors there at the Institute the next day. It was 4½ hours straight of pacing and talking. We went over industry trends, team structures, that sort of thing — then a good solid 3 hours on what I am currently calling my "map of game." It's a diagram that encompasses all the fields, subjects, ways of looking at games, mapped onto the classic interaction loop. Reference books and cited articles, resources and ideas for further investigation — all in a giant infodump. It kind of underlined for me just how far we have come, and how much there is out there now, in terms of game studies.

---

[12] International Game Developers Association.

We drove by my old house. Second door, the dark one. Cops got suspicious when I kept taking photos.

Then another interview… This meant we didn't even tackle lunch until almost 3pm.

Then I had to go write my talk. At this point, it was all a stew in my head, and I decided to go with an autobiographical angle, because I had by then retold the story of how I grew up there dozens of times. I had thought about doing the Map of Game thing as the talk, but instead, all of these swirling emotions and thoughts came together in my head and I decided to just do a pure inspirational talk.

Here were all these enthusiastic kids, passionate about their fighting games or their Marios, wondering whether such a thing as a videogame career was even possible in a place like Peru. Here they were, wondering whether there could be a job for them

after they finished, wondering whether the country itself would have developed enough around them to make it possible.

Wondering, as Latin Americans often do, whether they are good enough, as they look around the history around them and think about the incredible resources the countries typically have, and the all-too-common wreck of things that have been made, via the legacies

of colonialism and the modern imperialism of market forces. People there just all too often think they're just not good enough, or else surely by now the country would have gotten on its feet? All too often when progress arrives, it's in the form of malls full of American and European brands, never anything local. Often, the history of South American countries makes them intensely proud of their culture, and totally unsupportive of it in any financial sense.

The Larcomar mall. I asked if there were any Peruvian franchises in it. The answer was no.

I just desperately wanted to tell them that yes, it can be done because all you need is a pencil and paper to get started. Yes it can be done because what you really need aren't game design programs but the passion to make yourself a lifelong learner. That yes, games matter despite what a culture might tell you about how they are for the lazy and the childish. That it's about putting one foot in front of the other.

We never stop wondering whether we're good enough. I stayed up until 4am another night, talking with Gonzalo Ordóñez, the Chilean artist known as Genzoman. We swapped stories of professional disappointments and how much of our work had never made it out into the world. The kids needed to know that this, too, is what success looks like.

The pun that serves as the title isn't easily translatable, alas. In Spanish, "carrera" is a career, a course of study (like a major, or a degree), and it also means a race, like a footrace. I moved freely across these three meanings as I spoke.

In the end, the best I can hope is that for some of these kids, it pointed a way forward.

Una carrera

This is adapted from a speech given in Spanish entitled "Una carrera," delivered at GameDay Peru in early 2015.

I was given the Online Game Legend[13] award at GDC Online[14] in 2010. The citation read in part,

> Raph Koster has led a prolific career. As the lead designer on *Ultima Online* and the creative director on *Star Wars Galaxies*, his contributions helped lay the foundation for the many massively multiplayer games that followed. Koster's professional credits span nearly every facet of game development, including writing, art, soundtrack music, programming and design.
>
> Raph Koster is considered a thought leader, as a frequent lecturer and published author on topics of game design, community management, storytelling and ethics in game development. His *A Theory of Fun*, published in 2004, is considered seminal by educators and members of the art game movement, as well as being one of the most popular books ever written about games…

I worry that people look at a career and see only this: the jobs, successes, awards and invitations to give talks.

But that's not how life is, and that's not what I feel like inside.

Upon hearing about the award, my mother asked me for a favor. "Please," she told me, "mention that you are Latino. People don't know, and you have a duty to encourage kids with dreams."

I lived in Lima, Peru, as a boy. Videogames were not common. Oh, I had played them in the States before arriving in Peru in 1979, and I continued to see them there

---

[13] See http://gdconlineawards.com/
[14] Variously known as Austin Game Conference, GDC Austin, and GDC Online, this was a long-running game development gathering focused on online games.

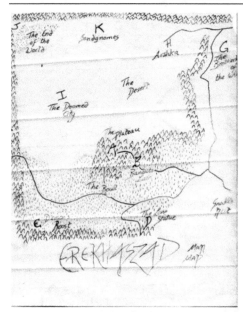

when I went back to spend summers with my dad. My dad also sent me a copy of *Dungeons & Dragons*, the red box Basic set, as a birthday present.

I already read like crazy: a book a day, usually science fiction or fantasy or murder mysteries. And I don't mean just Hardy Boys or kids' books — those, yes, but also Theodore Sturgeon and Isaac Asimov and Robert Ludlum. I was indiscriminate.

Of course, I started to create worlds, to draw little maps.

Thus began my course of study: I wanted to play those videogames that weren't making it to Peru. *Pengo* and *Q*Bert* and others weren't in the list of the ten or so games within a few miles of where I lived. In fact, there were so few that I can still recite the list of what was available: *Spider* at the rotisserie chicken place; *Asteroids, Gorf, Berzerk,* and *Star Castle* at the mall. On the bus we played the *Game & Watch* series — the dual screen *Donkey Kong* and *Donald & Mickey*. I had a Casio game watch, the one with the falling triangle blocks where you had to make a pyramid.[15]

With the help of videogame magazines, I made board game versions of the videogames I didn't have access to.

Porting a digital game to the world of tabletop play taught me the most basic thing: that games can manifest in many ways. *Pengo* could be decomposed into turn-based strategy. AI could be mimicked with dice or simple rules.

I started out like any other apprentice in the arts, by copying things. On my first original game, one called *Jungle Climb*, I basically took the ideas from the various *Donkey Kong* games, and drew a crude vertical platformer board. You moved a space at a time, and dodged just like you did on the LCD *Game & Watch* games… which was pretty dull pretty quickly, in a tabletop setting.

---

[15] This was the Casio GM-40, which today is a rare collectible worth hundreds of dollars.

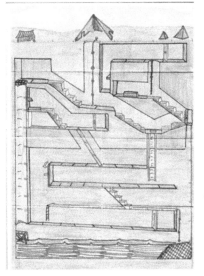

I then started to challenge myself on the visual front; *Egyptian Graverobber* required you to play against another player who controlled all the "AI" monsters, and try to get down to grab all the treasures and then escape. It still used basically the same mechanics.

It took several games, but eventually I took on the challenge of actually trying to create something with rules of my own invention. Based in part on the massive Gary Jennings novel *Aztec* (a decidedly mature read for someone who was probably thirteen at the time), *The Hunt for the Treasure of Quetzalcoatl*, spanned a dozen tall thin boards, with countless enemies, a randomized event generator from shuffled event decks, and a randomized quest order based on drawing cards from a separate deck. It took hours to play, and supported a bunch of kids all playing different creatures and monsters.

I look back on it now, and with hindsight, I say to myself "wow, it's almost as if I knew at age 12 that I was going to be a game designer as an adult." But that's a lie. I thought I was going to be a writer or teacher, you see. Everyone in my family had always told me so.[16]

I started to do things like take existing games and do revamped versions, to try to improve them. One in particular was a remake of TSR's *Dungeon!* I'm really not sure that my take was any better, but there it was. I rather quickly found to my dismay that my previous games had mostly just been about level design, map design, incident decks and movement rules. There was a whole new world at work in more sophisticated games — there was math, and statistics behind everything, stuff I just didn't understand.

---

[16] This book might indicate they were correct.

My try at a state-machine game based on sword fighting, creatively entitled *Swordplay*, was a miserable failure because just about everything led everywhere. I soon discovered the issue of "degenerate strategies" without knowing the term.

This basically led me to the library. I didn't think I was "studying." For me, reading up on this stuff was just part of the game of making games. By the time I hit high school I was researching ship-to-ship combat for a game called *Legal Pirates*, which was actually what I turned in for a class assignment in history class.[17] It came with an annotated bibliography; as it happens, this was not the last time I had a bibliography for a game design, even though it was never required of me again.

It was around when I was thirteen that I discovered that computers would actually let me make my own games. Oh, I had started playing with a *Pong* home console well before moving to Peru, and we had an Atari 2600 with quite a bunch of cartridges. But it was clear, from reading *Video Games* and *Electronic Games* and *Compute!* and *Creative Computing* that computer gaming was where the real action was. I started

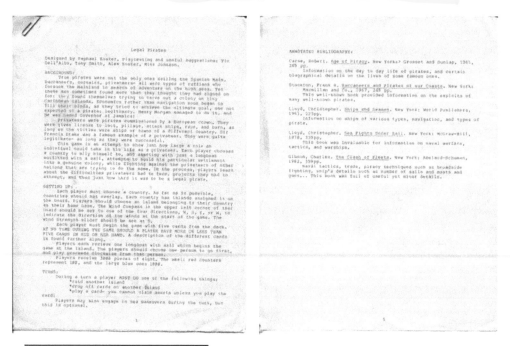

_____

[17] It was actually my second try at a naval game; I had done an enormous naval wargame that took up most of a dining room table when I was a younger teen.

learning some MS-BASIC on my dad's CP/M-based Osborne 1, hacking *Colossal Cave*[18] and playing ASCII versions of *Pac-Man* and *Wari*.

I begged and begged, and my great-uncle got me a 16K Atari 8-bit computer. I don't have that one anymore, because I upgraded three times before I was 16, ending up with the 130XE. I still have it, along with my collection of games on floppy disks.

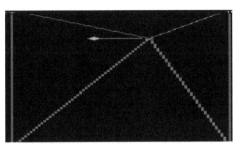

And so I threw myself into trying to create games again, just in a new medium.

My friends and I took ourselves very seriously. We actually called ourselves a company, and we put a copyright symbol by the company name (which is legally nonsensical, of course).

It took a few tries, but I made a game called *Orion*. And it was actually fun. It was imitative, for sure, featuring light cycles and spaceships. It consisted of linked games, so you could keep score of who won in each of the challenges. You can actually trace the progression of my programming skill over the course of the games; the first one was the light cycles; the second, I could move ships vertically but not freely; the third had free movement but not independent shots; and so on. I even had the brainstorm to bring in the kids' game of Capture the Flag into video game form.

After five linked games, I felt like I was a game developer. I wrote a second one, a pretty terrible one where you flew around over a moonscape and shot down aliens before they reached the ground, while dodging explosive satellites. We managed to sell a copy of that one to a friend, in a Ziploc baggie.

But then I stopped.

I finished high school.

I went to college.

I thought I would go be that writer, teacher, artist.

I studied poetry, and music, and art, but this time "for real." I even got an MFA in poetry.

A sheepskin doesn't make a poet, it turns out.

While in college, I ran a play-by-email roleplay campaign, but otherwise didn't really do much with game development. Macintosh computers were everywhere on campus—I was out of touch with programming and found the complexities of working with the newfangled graphical interfaces impenetrable. I could help fellow

---

[18] Also just known as *Adventure*, this was the granddaddy of all adventure games.

students with their Pascal homework, but I couldn't put a sprite on screen. I could max out the campus high score in *Crystal Quest*, but I couldn't make so much as a text adventure. My roleplay campaign was presented at a conference on academic computing by the head of the computer program, but all my creative energies went to writing.

I got pretty unhappy in grad school. There were academic politics. The writing that was in vogue felt utterly disconnected from most people's lived experiences to me, a sort of hermetic and self-referential body of work infatuated with other academic writers. I recall huge arguments over whether Stephen King was more important a writer than whoever we happened to be studying that week. I am pretty sure I was proven right by time.

But the Internet was starting to boom. To stay in touch with friends, we started using email. And after email, a friend pointed out that there were these crazy games, reminiscent of the D&D campaigns I had run as a kid, but run over the Internet. They were called MUDs.

MUDs were text-based virtual realities, but I didn't know that yet. I started out playing them, then in less than a year, making them. I could use the writing skills I had acquired for doing MUD development.

And MUDs were communities. Managing them, I had to study politics and

sociology. The result was that the industry knocked at my door.

And so I got lucky, helping lead *Ultima Online*, by the time I was 25.

I say luck, and it was indeed luck. But it also happened because we dreamt of fantastic worlds and the future of cyberspace. That wasn't something that we were equipped to build, but we tried anyway.

Even on a giant project like that, I still found myself drawing little maps with pencil. They don't look that different from the ones from grade school, if I am honest with myself. In some ways, it feels like I ran to stand still.

And as I ran, I ran with more ambition, because you have to challenge yourself, you have to beat the boss. By the time I did *Star Wars Galaxies,* I was inventing new technology around procedural generation techniques, to do something that wasn't quite possible: ship a 4 gigabyte game on a CD. I was teaching myself all the disciplines of all my colleagues, so I could do things like do all of the interface design for the game. I finally understood those mathematics behind everything, and now I was trying to turn them into magic, to allow other people to live improbable lives in impossible places.

I came to see games as gifts.

I have a daughter. She lives with Type I diabetes. When she was young, I made a videogame for her called *Watersnake*. The snake lives under the water, and the landscape scrolls by, all starfish with cute eyes and seaweed. The snake is always drifting down. If it hits the bottom, well, that's a seizure and coma and possible death

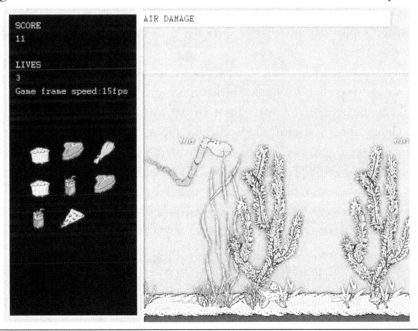

from a hypoglycemic event. If it goes up too high, it pokes above the water where it can't breathe, and suffers slow damage that can never be healed, equivalent to the slow damage caused by constant high blood sugars, the slow neuropathies and circulatory damage that occurs.

You have to toss food to the snake — cupcakes, steaks, pizza, fried chicken, juice boxes — kids' foods, things that she would want to eat herself. And you do it in order to pick up prizes under the water. Each food uses the real world glycemic index of that food to cause the snake to swim upwards, and them slowly come down. Fast carbohydrates cause the snake to shoot up to the surface and possibly the sky; slower proteins and fats cause gentle arcs.

Watersnake was a gift to my daughter.

I have a mother. She always worries that I will forget the cultures from which I sprang, my heritage. I made a game called *Andean Bird*, one of the very first "art games," for her. In it you fly over the littoral islands off the coast of Peru, in the form of a sea bird of some sort. You fly, and you experience the wind and the sunrise and the sunset, and you listen to music and you flap your wings and read a small poem about the ways in which our memories of cultures and heritages erode.

Andean Bird was a gift to my mother.

I realize now that games themselves have been my teachers, all this time. There came a moment when I realized it was my turn to teach. After all, you take turns in games. The result was a book called *A Theory of Fun for Game Design*, where I tried to share back what I had learned by ranging widely over other fields. My tools for making abstruse topics easy to swallow were the same little cartoons that I drew when I was twelve.

But now, of course, I take it all so so seriously. I have a tall shelf reserved just for books that are about games, for for fields that impinge directly on the sorts of games I make. Books about hypertext, books about virtual law. Books about industry history, and books about cultural anthropology. Books about the way in which virtualizing our world provides opportunities for constant surveillance, and books about how societies find ways out of pickles like that. Books about chance, and books about economics and books about cognition, and yes, still books about poetry.

Because games deserve to be taken seriously, and players deserve to be taken seriously, and most of the worst mistakes I have made over my career, the worst game design mistakes, have happened because I failed to do that.

Ultimately, what I do deserves to be taken seriously.

So I set out to help the world create their own games, without having to go through that study process. I created a platform called *Metaplace* which was intended to democratize the creation of online worlds, so that we could get back the creative explosion of them that had existed in the days before *World of Warcraft*. Spoiler: it didn't work. But working to create tools was yet another new design challenge, another new way to look at the problem.

Even though the platform didn't do what we hoped, people still made amazing things. Many of our best users are developers in the industry now, some of them on award-winning titles. The platform hosted a President speaking by video, arcade games and Nordic myth and lectures and parties and games about 9/11 and games about fuzzballs.

In the end, though, you really can't skip past the learning, I think. Those who seem to—say, lucky ones who lead a major title when they are 23—do so because they are learning in public, running forward like mad, because it is their passion. It's their art.

Yes, I said "art."

The world has changed a lot since I started. Now everyone plays games. I've made some for that "everyone," like *Island Life, My Vineyard,* and *Jackpot Trivia.*[19]

There is also now a bit of a science to making games; more is understood about verbs and loops and arcs and grammars, and I helped that to happen.

There are even classes inside virtual worlds, and you can go to a games program and learn how to make games from an actual teacher.

And if you want to get creative with games, you don't have to know how to make them yourself anymore. The games themselves are canvases and brushes, tools of creativity in their own right, and yeah, I helped make that happen too.

Lately, it has brought me all full circle. I'm back to working with cards and tokens and cluttered tabletops these days. It's fun and challenging to work with few moving parts, without the crutches, but also with a limitless field of possibility, the way it was when I was thirteen. It's fun to be able to go back to the prototype, back to experimentation, back to the heart of design. With a tad more confidence than before, perhaps, but never with too much. I know what pitfalls are out there now, after all.

But I also know that one learns from failures, from trying. That you dive into the thicket in order to understand it.

In the end, games connect us and teach us. They carry us from the simple to the complex; but only if we are willing to play.

Willing to play in our lives, willing to play with learning, willing to play and challenge ourselves.

---

[19] You can read about this game here: https://www.raphkoster.com/2015/03/10/jackpot-trivia/. It was not a substantial enough write-up to merit being a postmortem in this book, alas.

This is the race we run. We are our own opponent. It's not a bad thing to be a kid inside, if we never stop learning and never stop in that process of slowly growing up.

If we as game designers sometimes feel like we don't fit into society, well, it's because games form cultures, all the way in our youth, and sometimes someone is needed who can stand outside the culture and impart lessons. *That* is, in a sense, your cultural heritage.

You probably grew up with games. You can make them, and not be ashamed of it. You can love them, and not be ashamed of it. You can look at them, see their flaws, the ways in which people misuse them for exclusion, and work to make a change. Every year from now on, games will be a larger part of our world. They will change society as a whole. Learning to design them will prepare you for this new tech-mad planet.

It's a career. It's a long road.

You had better start running now.

My first game

The YouTube channel First Game Ever[20] started as a panel at PAX East one year. It then became a series of videos where developers shared their adventures in making their first game ever. I contributed a video,[21] and this is more or less a written version of what I sent.

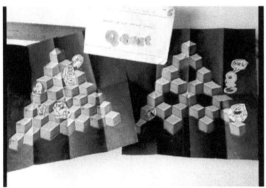

Hey there… my name is Raph Koster, and I'm probably best known for doing MMOs like *Ultima Online* and *Star Wars Galaxies*. I was asked to show you my first game…

I lived overseas as a kid. Arcades were rare, but I *loved* videogames. So I used to port my favorite arcade games to board games, because otherwise I couldn't play them at home. This one wasn't very successful… marking all the squares with little bits of paper that blew away was very fiddly.

Eventually, this led me to want to make my own games. I branded my little paper game company SUPERGAME and would sell copies to other kids during recess. Check it out, this one was so popular in 8th grade that I claimed it was "already a classic!"… in magic marker.

So I started to beg my mom for a computer. And eventually my brother and I got one as a gift from my great-uncle. It was an Atari 600XL, which was eventually upgraded to a 130XE. This one, in fact. I still have it in working condition.

[20] https://www.youtube.com/channel/UCskdg1doOBTkzIJhYu97dSA
[21] https://www.youtube.com/watch?v=3CK79TMoPCI

I of course immediately went nuts playing games on it: the classics like *Archon* and *M.U.L.E.* and the Infocom text adventures. But I also started to learn to program. I was 14, and I did it out of books like these – check out the introduction, written by a certain science fiction writer before he was famous![22]

And by typing in listings in magazines (which were also very hard to come by overseas!). And with this, I taught myself BASIC, and eventually a little bit of 6502 machine language which I have completely forgotten.

And that led to my first game, which we're going to boot up right now.

So, some friends and I started a little fake game company called Protocom. You can see we stuck copyright symbols on everything because we thought it was important. We sold games in Ziploc baggies with homemade labels, because we had heard that Richard Garriott got his start with *Ultima* that way. Who knew then that I would be working with him ten years later...

We had a cassette deck that we loaded games from before we had a disk drive. You could make the tape start to play anytime from code, which is why we had Van Halen's "1984" for the soundtrack. This loading screen is insanely slow, so I am going to let the video speed up... but it originally ran long enough so that you could hear the whole song, and then it would go into "Jump" for the first match. It wasn't slow because it was doing anything. It was slow because computers were slow. This game ran in like 8k of memory and was written all in BASIC on a 1.79MHz machine.

The first thing I did was make a clone of *Tron's* lightcycles. I couldn't clone anything else – that would have been too hard! Light cycles was easy. A big lesson: there is no shame in starting out cloning stuff. You learn a lot that way.

This was actually not one program – it was six of them, each loaded from disk while the victory screen played. And all of them were two player, because I had no idea how to write AI. In the second game, I tried having a ship on screen. They were stuck at the edges because I didn't know how to do collision detection, but I could check that they were at the same height, so that way

---

[22] The books in question were *COMPUTE's First Book of Atari Games* and *COMPUTE's Guide to Adventure Games.* The introduction to the former was written by Orson Scott Card.

I could tell when the shots hit each other. Oh, and the explosion animation sucked.

By the third one, you can see the ships move, but they flicker, because I was erasing and redrawing them every frame (yeah, that flicker is the framerate). But when you shoot, everything stops, because I didn't know how to make shots move independently of the main loop yet.

At least the explosion is more dramatic.

Then I had a brilliant idea. Why not adapt the playground game capture the flag? I probably should have patented that. I was used to asymmetric PvP design because in the board game adaptations, one player always had to play the computer.

This was also the first time I ever did procedural map generation. I've never stopped, still a go-to tool for me.

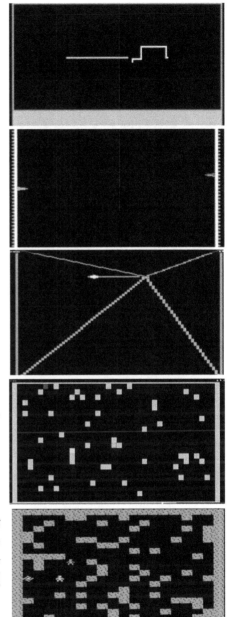

By the fifth game, I had learned how to replace the character set with custom graphics. So here we have an early deathmatch in a maze. This actually has a bug in it, you can end up with a starting map that traps you in the corner. You had to reset the machine to deal with it.

So at fourteen, I made all of the art and all of the music (except for "Jump," all of the graphics and all of the coding... Believe it or not, we played *Orion* for **months**.

In retrospect, it foreshadows a lot of my career doing *Ultima Online* & *Star Wars Galaxies*: multiplayer games full of PvP, insane technical overreaching, way way too many games stuffed into one box, tons of bugs... and more fun than they deserve to be.

The biggest thing it taught me is simple: it can be done.

We sold one copy. I consider it highly profitable.

MUDs

What is a MUD?

MUDs are the ancestral virtual worlds.[23]

Invented by Roy Trubshaw and Richard Bartle around 1978, MUDs are a multi-user version of old text adventures like *Zork* and *Colossal Cave*. Those games described where the player was standing in text, and let them perform commands by typing in pairs of words. When the game started, you'd see a *room description* like this, and interact with what was going on by typing commands:

```
You are standing at the end of a road before a small brick
building.  Around you is a forest.  A small stream flows out
of the building and down a gully.
> enter building
You are inside a building, a well house for a large spring.
There are some keys on the ground here.
There is a shiny brass lamp nearby.
There is tasty food here.
There is a bottle of water here.
```

MUDs worked the same way, except that *other people were playing the game at the same time.* You connected to a remote server,[24] and when other people happened to be in the same room as you, you could see it just like you saw the bottle of water and the tasty food in the above example. "Kaige is here." And if Kaige typed in

```
say hello
```

then you'd see

```
Kaige says, 'hello'
```

---

[23] There were several other virtual world platforms invented around the same time, as well as very important and influential ones that were created over the course of the 1980s. But MUDs have the most direct influence on the modern virtual world.

[24] Generally using Telnet, but also with dedicated MUD clients with names like tintin++ and TinyFugue.

Add pictures, and you'd get a graphical MUD. Add full immersive 3d graphics, and you'd get something like *World of Warcraft*. In fact, watching only the text box in a modern MMO is strongly reminiscent of playing a MUD.

MUDs spread all over the early Internet throughout the '80s, and by the late '80s and early '90s were speciating into a variety of sorts of virtual world: ones for hack 'n' slash combat like most MMOs today, ones dedicated to pure roleplaying where out-of-character behavior wasn't even allowed, ones just for hanging out and talking, and ones where users could actually build and change the world on the fly, much like *Second Life* now.

These various approaches to MUDs tended to go hand in hand with *codebases*, or varying versions of the server software that offered different capabilities based on what that particular world was about. Roleplayers tended to be on MUSHes,[25] the various MOO[26] codebases offered the most power for users who wanted to engage in online creation, and various sorts of MUD with names like LPMud, DikuMUD, and so on, were primarily game worlds.

Most of today's MMOs descend in a direct line from MUDs, and most of the early MMO developers were MUDders first.

---

[25] MUSH wasn't originally an acronym, but today is often decoded as Multiple User Shared Hallucination.

[26] MOO stands for *MUD, Object Oriented,* a reference to the technical architecture of the server code.

What is a Diku?

It's common to hear the word "Diku" tossed around, but many these days have no memory of where the word came from, or why some might call a game like World of Warcraft a form of Diku. This essay is from January 9th, 2009.

DikuMUD was derived from *AberMUD*,[27] which had similar mechanics, but had more of a scavenger hunt mentality in some ways.

At its core, it is a class-based RPG with the principal classes being fighter, healer, wizard, thief. (Later codebases added more). It was heavily based on the combat portion of *Dungeons & Dragons*. Advancement was handled by earning experience points through combat, reaching a set amount of points, returning to town and "levelling up," which unlocked new abilities. Classes were immutable (though eventually systems such as remorting,[28] etc were added). Rewards for killing things also included equipment, which affected your stats and damage capability. If you reached the maximum level, common cultural practice was that you were invited to become a game admin (this practice dates back to much earlier, and existed in some form in *MUD1*).

Combat was generally on a fixed rate, with "faster attacks" in cruder systems consisting of actually running the same attack multiple times in a row (so you could only do damage on multiples: 1x, 2x, 3x, 4x, 5x, 6x, 7x, 8x, 9x). More advanced systems added true variable interval attacks. Tactics were centered around controlling which target the mob was attacking, and using special state-affecting attacks that did things like trigger periods of indefensibility (stun), periods of damage multipliers, etc, using stances.[29]

Much of the gameplay consisted of moving about solo or in groups attacking

---

[27] See https://en.wikipedia.org/wiki/AberMUD

[28] The ability to take your character name and start over as a new class.

[29] These were usually termed "positions," as in POS_STUNNED, POS_STANDING, etc.

monsters for experience points[30] and loot. Grouping was a typical strategy because it was a large force multiplier, permitting players to kill targets much more powerful than they were alone. Because of this, an array of systems including level limits on equipment, on grouping,[31] and even on monster attacking were in place. A command called "consider" told you whether the monster was too easy or too hard.

Monsters spawned originally on time intervals called *resets*. At first, the whole zone reset at once, then resets evolved in Diku-derived codebases into per-monster timers. (A zone was a collection of world data, including rooms, monsters, and items — each zone could at first have 100 of each). There evolved the practice of "rare spawns" and eventually "rare drops" as well.

Weapons, potions, and the like were all based on simply on performing spell effects, in the fashion today referred to as a "proc.[32]" They were hardcoded back then, however. Players had the typical array of D&D stats, with the addition of "move points," which were literally spent by moving from room to room and based on the weight of stuff you were carrying and your strength. You had to rest to recover these.

Death in Dikus involved losing all your gear, because everything stayed in the corpse. It also could set you back levels, as it cost you a fraction of your experience points. You respawned back in town at the central spawn point, and in later codebases at your "guildhall" (a class-specific spawn point and levelling trainer). You then had to do a "corpse run" to get back to your body naked and reequip your gear. In an inheritance from aspects of AberMuds, you could scavenge gear from the "donation room" which was a place where excess gear nobody wanted (usually from outlevelling it or from trash drops) went when it was donated or "sacrificed" by other players.

This was not the only means of trying to keep the economy balanced. Every item had a cash value (the value for which it was sold in NPC[33] shops). In some Dikus, you got a fixed limit on what you could save with your character, said limit based on a maximum cash value. If you saved your character at a point where you were in excess of this limit, you were saved with nothing. In others, you simply could not save your character state. (State saving was manual, and you had to go to an inn to do it). There were also systems whereby your save time was limited, because you had to pay "rent"

---

[30] Earn enough experience points, and you gained a level.

[31] Grouping is a technical term for forming a group of players that were recognized as such by the server, as opposed to just standing near one another.

[32] The term comes from running a "spec_proc" or "special procedure" in the code.

[33] Non-player character, meaning the simplistic computer-controlled bots that were meant to look like other people in the game. Another common term is "mobiles," usually abbreviated to "mobs," which means *any* bot including animals or monsters.

at the inn where you logged out. The rent was proportional to the stuff you had, which drove people back to the game to keep earning gold.

Despite this huge sink, it was common for the economy to spiral out of control (termed "mudflation") and for the admins to wipe all items or even all characters. It was also common for the mud to crash, and corpses and stuff on the ground did not persist, since Dikus were a *character state* system.[34]

DikuMuds came with stock areas,[35] the best known of which is Midgaard, the main city. Many mudders from the time period would judge a DikuMUD based on whether Midgaard was the first thing they saw. Midgaard came to also feature stock tutorials called "mud school" which saw you through the first fight. Zones were built by editing text files, though eventually forms of online editing tools ("OLC," for "online creation") were added. Because map building was relatively easy, many Dikus were based on popular hack 'n' slash fantasy fiction such as *Forgotten Realms,* Fred Saberhagen, *Wheel of Time,* etc.

DikuMUDs did not come out of the box with any quests, because they were not a programmable game engine. They were about combat and levelling up. There was no crafting either. They did come with good chat features, grouping, etc. "Clans" were a common addition — you would call them guilds today, except that they were formed by admin command, not formed freely by players. (Honestly, I am not sure where free-form clan formation came from. I know we did it on *LegendMUD,* and we did it in *UO,* but I don't even remember which came first!)[36]

Believe it or not, Dikus *did* have simple pets out of the box (usually summoned and non-persistent). They also had hunger and thirst (with a requirement to eat and drink regularly for good health), containers, inventory, in-game messaging and bulletin boards, chat channels (at first just via "shout") and so on. They were quite sociable, because of the grouping requirements, the corpse mechanics, and the move rate factor. Towns tended to have fountains in them so you could drink and rest, for example, and people would gather there.

Eventually Diku games added questing engines, then scripting languages (see *Worlds of Carnage),*[37] etc, and diversity developed. Because they were functional games with content out of the box, many "stock muds" were created, which had little differentiation from one another. If you knew some C you could customize the game

---

[34] As opposed to "world state" systems, which persist the state of everything in the world.

[35] A set of rooms themed together was typically called an *area* or a *zone*. This latter usage has survived to this day to mean substantially the same thing in many MMOs.

[36] Like most innovations, it probably came from an LPMud rather than a Diku.

[37] See "Scripting languages in DikuMUDs," elsewhere in this volume.

some, and the single commonest means of doing so was to add more classes, more levels, and more player races. It got to be a common sight to see games advertising "20 classes, 30 races, and 500 levels!!!!!" without actually offering different gameplay.

It is important to realize that Dikus were the *least* flexible codebase at the time. The other dominant codebases were built to be programmable platforms out of the box: MUSH, MOO, and LPMuds[38] all had significantly greater capabilities and flexibility. They were "scriptable" out of the box, had online creation support rather than requiring you to create content in flat text files, and most importantly, the core rulesets for a game were written "in the platform," using the softcode tools that were available. Because of this, tracing the history of a given mud feature backwards will usually find that it didn't originate on Dikus.

That said, Diku codebases did eventually popularize many of the major developments in muds. Procedural zones had been done before; in Dikus, you saw 1,000 room procedural dungeons. Instancing, public quests, player housing (in the style we know today, as opposed to UGC systems),[39] the modern scripting system model, the modern persistence system, and aspects of zone-based PvP all were developed or hugely elaborated on DikuMUDs. In addition, once scripting hit, DikuMUDs arguably saw the flowering of quests to a level unseen in other codebases (this is of course, a matter of opinion!). Diku derivatives gained things that got going first on other codebases, like banks, auction houses, PvP systems, player-formed clans, moods systems, player government systems, overhead ASCII maps, and even tags for sound effects. Many Dikus had strict enforcement of rules regarding roleplaying, and even required players to stay in character at all times, or submit essays as *applications* to play. Despite this, the core remained hack n slash, with many terming Diku gameplay "roll-playing."

If Abers set the template, Diku was the root from which a huge portion of muds sprang, because they were so easy to get running (though hard to customize). As the initial code was released as open source (though not under what we would today call an open license),[40] many variants were made and also released, and many of these then

---

[38] See https://en.wikipedia.org/wiki/LPMud

[39] "UGC" stands for "user-generated content." Meaning, as opposed to systems where freeform building was a basic feature of the platform, such as in MOOs, or to use more modern examples, such as *Second Life* or *Minecraft* servers.

[40] The Diku license read:

```
DikuMud is NOT Public Domain, shareware, careware or the like!!

You may under no circumstances make profit on *ANY* part of DikuMud in any possible
way. You may under no circumstances charge money for distributing any part of
```

also resulted in derivatives, etc. When I did the tally in the late 90s, Diku-derived muds accounted for around 60% of all muds running. Considering there were at least three other major codebases and traditions with radically different architectures and significantly more power and flexibility, this was quite an achievement. By the end of their dominance, the Dikus were beginning to rival other codebases such as MOOs and LPMuds in flexibility, whilst still retaining a simpler core architecture than either.

Because they were template fill-in-the-blank muds, most of them were very similar, and had to differentiate solely on their world building and fiction. However, few altered the basic combat equation. Among other terms "tanking," "nuking" and the like were common.[41] (Thieves were sort of a nuker, in some ways — they were used to initiate combat with a "backstab" attack that did up to quadruple damage — they then they had to get out of the way! They were also used as scouts because they could move without triggering aggro). In fact, "kiting" also took place quite a lot, by leading high level aggressive mobs into low level areas.

EverQuest was created by players of DikuMUDs (specifically Forgotten Realms ones — *Sojourn, Toril, Duris),* and even had the same wording for many server-generated messages ("it begins to rain," which was completely superfluous for a 3d game!). It

---

dikumud – this includes the usual $5 charge for "sending the disk" or "just for the disk" etc. By breaking these rules you violate the agreement between us and the University, and hence will be sued.

You may not remove any copyright notices from any of the documents or sources given to you.

This license must *always* be included "as is" if you copy or give away any part of DikuMud (which is to be done as described in this document).

If you publish *any* part of dikumud, we as creators must appear in the article, and the article must be clearly copyrighted subject to this license. Before publishing you must first send us a message, by snail-mail or e-mail, and inform us what, where and when you are publishing (remember to include your address, name etc.)

If you wish to setup a version of DikuMud on any computer system, you must send us a message , by snail-mail or e-mail, and inform us where and when you are running the game. (remember to include your address, name etc.)

Any running version of DikuMud must include our names in the login sequence. Furthermore the "credits" command shall always cointain our name, addresses, and a notice which states we have created DikuMud.

You are allowed to alter DikuMud, source and documentation as long as you do not violate any of the above stated rules.

[41] Often referred to as "the Holy Trinity," tanks absorbed damage from attacking monsters, nukers dealt high damage to them, and healers kept the other two alive.

played so similarly to its inspirations that some wondered if it actually was a DikuMUD, with graphics added on, which was a (false) rumor.[42] *Meridian 59* had DikuMUD players on its team. *Ultima Online* had three Diku players on the original core team (and a couple folks from other codebases). Of the early MMORPGs, UO played the least like a Diku, whereas the line of inheritance from Diku to EQ and thence to *World of Warcraft* is completely undeniable.

In the end, the central elements of phase-based combat, combat states, cool-down based special attacks, tank-healer-nuker triad, and basic aggro management are what you play today in WoW. A Diku player from the late mudding period would feel completely at home if you just gave them slash commands and a text box. They'd be astonished by the number of quests, would think the crafting system was insane, and would think that the entire PvP system was either a rip from an EmlenMUD[43] or was teleporting you to *HoloMUD*,[44] in the case of the battlefields. Even raids would feel a lot like a "group of groups" tackling a level 50, albeit at a scale smaller; I recall participating in a "raidish" encounter on *Worlds of Carnage* against a dragon in a tower which nearly "wiped," consisting of a half dozen maxed out characters and an assortment of lower ones. My character, who was the lowest there by far, happened to get in the final blow and was the sole survivor, and gained five levels in one fell swoop.

While it is true that many of these core elements stretch back to *Advanced Dungeons & Dragons,* the fact is that as a pen and paper game, AD&D played quite differently when in the hands of an expert group. Similarly, even though there were plenty of of hack n slash tropes in place in AberMuds and various LPMud mudlibs (a mudlib is more or less a ruleset… that's a whole other article!), or in standalone games such as the *Wizardry* and *Might & Magic* series, there was a very specific "feel" to how Dikus played, and this remained even across all the many children codebases (the DikuMUD home page has a family tree[45] of these).

In the end, if you play modern MMORPGs, you are playing what to a veteran feels strongly reminiscent of what they saw when they headed out of Midgaard and towards Haon Dor to go kill giant spiders, in 1991.

---

[42] This was put to bed by the EverQuest developers signing a sworn statement stating that they had not used any Diku code. See https://en.wikipedia.org/wiki/DikuMUD#EverQuest_controversy

[43] Owen Emlen was a MUD designer who created several MUDs that experimented with various forms of player vs player combat. They were based on what today we would call *realm vs realm* systems, meaning that players were allocated into teams upon character creation, and the two teams killed each other on sight.

[44] A popular PvP MUD.

[45] https://web.archive.org/web/20150404111158/https://dikumud.com/family.aspx

Announcing LegendMUD

ARE YOU TIRED OF KILLING ORCS?
OF SEEING MIDGAARD?

OF MUDS THAT CONFINE YOU TO UNNATURAL CLASS SYSTEMS?

Announcing the Official Opening of LegendMUD, a classless mud with ALL NEW areas!

stimpy.washcoll.edu 4000 or 192.146.226.4 4000

LegendMUD is a history-based mud—instead of wandering in fantasy-land you get to explore the history of the Earth—not as it was, but as it was believed to be at the time. See where the legends came from as you visit Roman Britain, the Arabian Nights, and the Middle Ages. Be a Tai-Pan on the China Tea Trade in 1841, or help fight Rommel the Desert Fox in World War II North Africa.

Our classless system and dozens of skills allow you to build your character exactly the way you want based on a percentile stat system. Our stat system more accurately reflects the things you most need to know about your character. Our special practice system eliminates the cumbersome juggling of percentages you've become used to.

We have three eras of time with 1500 rooms open to the public, and more entering the game constantly. Our code is stable—no constant crashes or lags. And we're DIFFERENT: we promise to be a mud unlike any other you've played. Come learn our herb-based magic system, with over 100 possible affects and associated spells!

We research the historical periods for our areas in both fact-based and fanciful books. Our mobs are INTELLIGENT, with a wide range of reactions to what you say and do. Play blackjack with notorious criminal Big Jim Southland on the seamy side of London in the mid 19th century. Try to solve the riddle of the lamp and win Aladdin his princess!

LegendMUD is a school-sponsored mud located at stimpy.washcoll.edu 4000 (192.146.226.4 4000) and will be open to the public by 6 pm Valentine's Day. Come see what MUDs should have been all along! A challenge for the mind and the sword arm, a feast for the imagination, and of course, plain fun.

This ad promptly resulted in a flamewar on rec.games.mud.diku.[46] Among the participants is a young Damion Schubert, aka Heretic, later known for his work on Meridian 59, Shadowbane, *and* Star Wars: The Old Republic.

Amusingly, the flames started with the comment "*sigh* Why does EVERY dime-store mud programmer claim to be able to create 'intelligent' mobs? Trust me, if you could, you'd be rich and famous. Hell, I doubt any mud out there can even outdo ultima :)"

---

[46] https://groups.google.com/forum/#!search/legendmud/rec.games.mud.diku/YgfgLaFJ2-Q/dNo8NcSGg7sJ

A brief history of LegendMUD

This little essay appeared in the Legendary Times,[47] vol. 2, issue 2, on January 5th 1995.[48] The header of the issue wishes everyone "Happy Twelfth Night!" Among other topics, the issue also covers various roleplay dramas and tweaks to the combat system.

My name on LegendMUD was Ptah, the Egyptian god of time.

A Brief History of LegendMUD
by Ptah

People are always asking about the origins of *Legend*, so I thought I'd try to give a shot at recollecting how exactly we got started. Note that my memories may disagree just LOTS with those of other people! :)

The origins of *Legend* are almost certainly on the mud *Worlds of Carnage,*[49] where Kaige,[50] Charity,[51] and I met Sadist[52] and Flagg. Charity and Kaige and I had gone to college together, and Sadist and Flagg were roommates. We were all proceeding at a rapid pace towards immorting on that mud, and Flagg had actually immorted, when *Carnage* went down for an extended period of time.

Even before it went down Sadist and Charity had been talking about starting up a mud. Sadist wanted to try it as a coding challenge. During a Spring Break visit in early 1993, Charity came to visit us from college in Maryland and we spent a great deal of time with her discussing the possibility for a classless mud with groups of skills. The world design for that mud was going to be a fantasy one, based around the idea of an

---

[47] *LegendMUD's* emailed newsletter.

[48] https://www.legendmud.org/Community/lt_indices/Vol2/LTv2n2.html

[49] *Worlds of Carnage*, implemented by BadMood and DimWit, was historically important as the genesis of scripting languages in DikuMUDs. See the chapter by that name.

[50] Kristen Koster, née Johnson, my wife and design partner on *LegendMUD* and *Ultima Online*.

[51] Her real name is Sherry Menton.

[52] His real name is Rick Delashmit, and he went on to play a key role in many of the early MMOs, as well as pioneering MMO gameplay on mobile devices.

enormous city, a never-ending one. Areas of wilderness would simply be parks gone to seed or zoos or parts of the city left to crumble.

It was Charity, a history major, and Elessar, another friend from *Carnage*, who were the ones who finally came up with the idea of a historical mud. *Carnage* went down around May of '93 and stayed down until August or so, and during that time Sadist began coding work on what would become *Legend*.

Kaige and I however joined a couple of other friends from *Carnage* and became beginner immorts at a mud called *eXile*, which was composed of 'exiles.' This was also a straight fantasy mud. We had a few area designs that we had begun intending to use for *Carnage*, including a large area Kaige had begun to map out with an Arabian Nights theme, but we started work on new areas for them. We did an ocean with lots of underwater coral reef, and a Bremen Town, and found that nobody else was building anything, making progress on the code, or keeping the mud alive at all. The areas we REALLY wanted to build couldn't be done with the plain vanilla Merc or Diku code they were using.

What was to become Legend was up and running by around August, on our first site, stimpy.washcoll.edu. This was a Mac SE/30 with a dying hard drive. We began to do work with Legend when *eXile* stopped going anywhere. Arabia was the first area to go in—all 200 rooms at once. The lamp quest took six further months of development to get the bugs out though. :) Roman Britain was the next part to go in. The acts system was developed by Sadist as we went; each time we wanted to put in an effect, he extended the code. He's always had the policy of 'I'll make it possible' as far as coding goes.

Back in those days the immort staff was mostly people we knew from *Carnage*. Elessar ended up not following us over, and eventually quit *Carnage* as well. He's now an Implementor at *Renegade Outpost*. Early on Catalyst worked doing spells for us, but they were in a typical Diku format (lots of glowing colored auras) and we eventually ripped them out. Chocorua was with us as well, but eventually went on to immort at *Medievia*.[53] None of you guys know any of these people.

Around October or November the sysadmin at the site began asking for some sort of results. We were school-sponsored[54] as a history/computer project with some sort of academic justification. (You can get away with stuff like that at small liberal arts schools!) So in November we opened the mud to players located at washcoll.edu. Lirra

---

[53] A DikuMUD that later grew to be incredibly popular, but also deeply controversial due to its removal of the credits for the original DikuMUD authors. See https://en.wikipedia.org/wiki/Medievia

[54] At Washington College, in Chestertown Maryland, the school where Sherry, Kristen, and I all had gone for our undergraduate degrees.

is one of the players who dates back this far. We also invited a gang of players from Medievia (this was the early Medievia, average player load of 12, not yet infamous on the newsgroups). And So has been with us ever since, as one of the original gang that visited then.

For a long time the way to get between areas was to teleport. Every innkeeper and bartender in the mud would transfer you to any area just for the asking. It was only gradually that enough connective areas were added to permit walking between locations. Over the Christmas holiday I sat down and did London and the South Seas in about two weeks in order to try to provide a 'hub' for the mud. Even now it probably offers the best way to get anywhere else in a hurry, as I had to extend little bits of map everywhere to try to get in as many connections as possible.

By the end of January we were getting around 5-10 people playing the mud, gaining players purely by word of mouth. We decided on February 14th, Valentine's Day, as the day we'd open to the full net. Many things were done in a last minute rush at this point. Skills. A few areas. Help files. But we managed to get something open that actually worked and didn't crash all the time. And thus we had Legend's last playerwipe, and opened to the full net.

Stimpy was an unreliable site. We were always losing netlink, the lag was pretty bad, and the hard drive threatened to blow up at any moment. But we had it all to ourselves. When we opened we immediately generated a storm of controversy because a florid ad I wrote mentioned our "intelligent" mobs... we became the subject of a long-running thread on the newsgroups and by the end of the first week of being open had 6000 playerfiles[55] to deal with.

Some of our older players still recall those days fondly. There was no auction house. There was no OOC lounge. There were no spells at all. The fight messages were much simpler and boring. Fionn's "vorpal squirrels" killed literally hundreds of newbies on the road between Tara and the coast.

Players *started* with 2000 XP[56] and when they died as a newbie they found themselves 3K in the hole. That's right. 4K was level 2... The mud was *much* harder than it is now. There were only a fraction of the current skills available. No explore XP, no quest XP, few quests, far fewer areas. Back in those days, it was Arabia, Ireland, Roman Britain (and no way to walk from Roman Britain to Arabia), Nazca, Lima, Sherwood, the Abbey, Klein, the forest outside of Hell, Casablanca, and the

---

[55] A playerfile was a flat text file that stored the character record for a single player. There were no concept of "accounts" and multiple characters per account.

[56] Experience points; accumulate enough, and you advance to the next level. I know you probably know this, but just in case you're not a gamer...

London/South Seas skeleton. And many of these areas were smaller than they are now. No Andes. Bengal was only the docks. There wasn't a proper Norman castle of course; there was no rooftop on the Abbey; there were no moors in Ireland.

Personally, I like the way the mud is now, and better yet, I like what the mud will be as it keep growing and developing... Certainly this Valentine's Day we're going to have to have a party on LegendMUD, to celebrate one full year of being a place where all of you can come and meet the ghost of dead Frankish kings and Picts and German soldiers and Incas and Aztecs and of course, each other. Not just escape from the real world, but also learn something about it at the same time.

LegendMUD

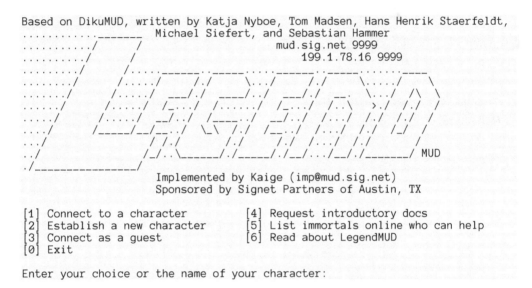

```
Based on DikuMUD, written by Katja Nyboe, Tom Madsen, Hans Henrik Staerfeldt,
.............._____     Michael Siefert, and Sebastian Hammer
........../    /            mud.sig.net 9999
........../   /....._____.._____.._____._____._____.____         199.1.78.16 9999
......../   /...../   /./    \.../    /./      \..../    \
......./   /...../   /___./../ ___/../ ___/./ __..  \.../ /\  \
....../   /...../ /_..../ /_..../../ /_..../ /..\   >./ /./  /
...../   /...../ __/./ /..... /_____./ __/../ /.../ /./ /./  /
..../   /_____/__../   \_\ /./   /_____/ /.../ /.../ /_/ /
.../    / /./    /./   /./     /./    /./   /./
../    /   /_/..\_____/./_____/./__/.../__/./_____/ MUD
./_____/
                    Implemented by Kaige (imp@mud.sig.net)
                    Sponsored by Signet Partners of Austin, TX

[1] Connect to a character        [4] Request introductory docs
[2] Establish a new character      [5] List immortals online who can help
[3] Connect as a guest             [6] Read about LegendMUD
[0] Exit

Enter your choice or the name of your character:
```

LegendMUD started out as a modified version of Merc 2.0b, which was itself a Diku-derived codebase. But it quickly developed in new directions, thanks to Rick Delashmit, aka "Sadist," rewriting most of the code.

It was founded sometime in the fall of 1993, and opened officially to the public on Valentine's Day, February 14th 1994. It was originally founded by Sherry Menton and Rick, and my wife Kristen and I joined right around when it was founded. Sherry used the handle "Charity," and she and another friend whose handle was Elessar were the ones who came up with the historical theme, which is still an unusual one among MUDs. Charity and Sadist were the only two Implementors at first — the highest rank in the game. Kristen and I were named Kaige and Ptah, respectively, and we eventually became Implementors as well, and took over the MUD completely on October 17th, 1994.[57] I stopped working on it when *Ultima*

---

[57] A fairly detailed article on LegendMUD can be found here:

Online consumed all of my time starting sometime in 1997-98, but Kristen kept on managing the game until the early 2000s.

All of us had been players on *Worlds of Carnage*, a MUD that featured the first embedded scripting system in a DikuMUD. This meant that there were quests and interactivity far beyond the norm in a typical Diku. On *Worlds of Carnage*, you even had a newbie sword that talked to you as a tutorial to introduce you to the game. We were determined to equal or exceed that level of interactivity, and so *LegendMUD* featured its own custom-designed scripting system. It also extended the basic capabilities of Dikus in all sorts of ways.

Most obviously, *Legend* was one of the first *classless* DikuMUDs; rather than choosing to be a fighter, mage, or thief, you instead chose one of the hometowns available scattered across three periods of history. If you started out in Tara in Ireland, or in Lima in Viceroyal Peru, or in London in the industrial period, it affected a set of statistics called *axioms* that in turn affected what sorts of things you could learn to do. Characters from the industrial time period couldn't learn magic, and characters from the ancient period couldn't learn how to use technology.

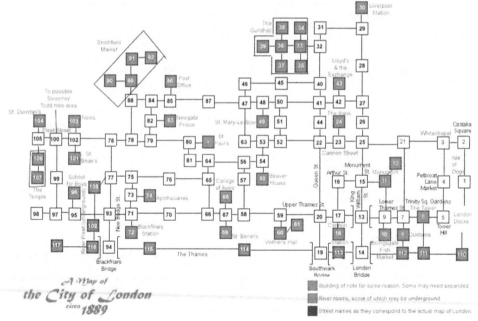

A map of the unfinished full London area.

However, all players could travel across all eras; many areas existed in more than one time period. For example, you could visit Ancient Roman Britain, Medieval

Sherwood Forest, or Industrial London, and go through a simple quest in order to travel through time. The theme was, more or less, "the world the way they thought it was." This meant that you could in fact find a vampire lurking in Victorian London, and would *definitely* encounter the sidhe in Ireland, or a djinn in the Arabian Nights.

Everything in *LegendMUD* was researched extensively. In fact, areas actually came with bibliographies and historical overviews accessed via help files. The maps of the areas were sometimes street-level accurate to the actual locations.

Because of the need for game systems that could reflect all these time periods, the server had an enormous amount of features. There was an herbalism system that allowed you to gather herbs and use them in poultices and tisanes, based on their actual historical uses. This also opened the door to a medical system, as opposed to only the magical healing you saw in pure fantasy games at the time.

The magic system accessed hardcoded spells via a syllabic magic system with words drawn from Sanskrit and Latin. You could haggle with shopkeepers. If you learned to play an instrument or speak eloquently, you could inspire, mesmerize, or calm opponents. This system could also affect the prestige of other players — a statistic that affected how much stuff you could save — using "praise" and "satirize."

You could cook food. Combatants could trade the loot they got from monsters on a global auction system. Druidic types could craft a staff made of living wood — an early example of the sort of crafting system that later appeared across all sorts of MMOs. Equipment was damaged over time, and could be repaired. Magical items were less susceptible to damage, but when were more vulnerable to it when in less magical areas. In the industrial era, you had guns with ammunition, which could fire into adjacent rooms. Players could specialize with various weapon types or learn a few simple martial arts moves, and rather than fights happening in simple slow rounds, they happened in more free-flowing "pulses" in order to allow very different attack speeds based on your specializations and the weight of your weapons. You could set up wary or aggressive fight styles, in order to arrange yourselves into crude "formations" within the room.

All of this was in service of a world that explicitly attempted to balance the major currents of mud play at the time: the combat and the roleplay, the player vs player fights and the social chatting.

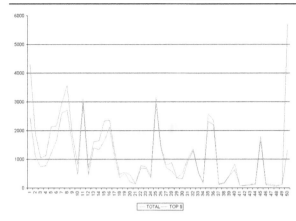

Combatants played in a system that was monitored by an early metrics system,[58] with careful game design setting statistics on all the monsters and creatures. The Implementors spent hours poring over graphs and attempting to eliminate "hell levels."[59]

For roleplayers, *LegendMUD* offered a truly extensive chat system, encompassing everything from the ability to create themed chat channels on the fly to the ability to define descriptions that others saw instead of your name as you moved around the game. Prose-like text parsing allowed logs of roleplay sessions to read more novelistically, and a "moods" system[60] gave far greater expressiveness to everyday actions in the game.

Playerkillers could join themed clans at first, and eventually create their own. Players could have housing of their own, including clan halls where they could hide from their opponents. *LegendMUD* even had temporary special events with dedicated areas for "recall tag," a special form of player vs player mini-game that had no repercussions on your character, so that those who wanted to participate in it occasionally could do without the long-term commitment implied by joining a clan.

For the purely social, the game offered an Out Of Character Lounge called the Wild Boar Tavern, where the bartenders were the Beatles, and lecture halls and wedding spaces and even a gift shop selling everything from birthday cards to naughty lingerie afforded activities for those taking a break from the game. The lecture series covered everything from cooking classes to descriptions of military life, talks by celebrity game programmers, and much more. Trivia nights, storytelling, and much more provided social outlets.

---

[58] In "A History of Game Analytics Platforms," (https://www.gamasutra.com/blogs/BenWeber/20180409/316273/A_History_of_Game_Analytics_Pl atforms.php) Ben Weber notes that "game analytics really started gaining momentum around 2009," but of course online games used metrics platforms much earlier, since they were connected systems.
[59] Levels with disprportionate experience point requirements, which therefore were exceptionally hard to complete.
[60] Later implemented wholesale in *Star Wars Galaxies*.

```
We've had some wonderful speakers. Thanks to all of them and all
who have attended! Still more good lectures upcoming including:

Sep 3 at 7pm Central: "How to Cook a Burkito" [RP Interview] - Tad

Sep 9 at 7pm Central: A lecture from Ultima's Head Programmer

Sept 17 at 7 pm Central: "Greek and Modern Olympics" - Greyscot

Sep 24 at 8 pm Central: "Comments on Mud Research" by Alan
Schwartz

Oct 1 at 7 pm Central: "Not-Quite-Gourmet Cooking" - Gail
[Reschedule]

Oct 8 at 7 pm Central: "Medicine in Ancient Times" - Croaker

Still others that are being considered, but not yet scheduled
include, a lecture by Richard Bartle, long-time mud administrator
and researcher; a lecture on Celtic myth from an Irish
Mythologist; a lecture on Icelandic myth including such rare tales
as "Nidud the Cruel" and "the Death of the Nornagest"; and a
lecture on alchemy. Keep watching the welcome board and the PR
board for more information. There may be guests on the mud who are
considering speaking from time to time, so please be polite to
them :)
```

And of course, all sorts of players enjoyed completing the game's many quests, some of which took as many as five or six hours to complete. These were complex puzzle tasks not unlike single-player games, and their like has arguably still not been seen in graphical MMOs to this day.

All of this had far-reaching consequences for the MUD's culture. *LegendMUD* was one of the earliest videogames to have what today are called "achievements,"[61] via something called *WHOIS strings:* titles you could acquire based on special deeds within the game. These were granted for roleplay, for questing, and much more. There was even a yearly awards ceremony called The Expies wherein players voted on awards in all these categories. When players retired, if they had managed to distinguish themselves enough, a version of their character might be implemented in the Hall of Legends and live on forever as a game character, complete with the player's original catch phrases and appearance.

All of this was actively managed by the admin staff. Easter Egg hunts, mud-wide games, a social calendar, and of course, chat moderation and even, sometimes,

---

[61] The Amiga game E-Motion is usually credited as the first, in 1990. They did not become widespread in videogames until 2005, with Microsoft's Gamerscore system. Legend didn't come up with this system independently — there was some other MUD I saw a similar system on, and I copied the basic idea and ran with it.

counseling players on their behavior and their real life problems. It was also one of the first muds to grapple with issues of player rights, following in the path of *LambdaMOO*.[62] It offered a player rights document by late 1994.

Everything that happened — from game patches to roleplay sagas to notable kills by expert playerkillers — was duly reported on in the Legendary Times, an email newsletter whose archives make for fascinating reading to this day.[63]

It was a world that privileged wit and skill both, a world where when your character slept, you might actually have their dreams shown to you, and they varied by where you were. Weather and seasons worked, in some places, and there was a Traveling Carnival that actually moved around the entire game. On April Fool's Day, you could expect to connect to a mud where perhaps all the directions were reversed, or where every creature was renamed.

Basically, *LegendMUD* was a place of whimsy, like many MUDs, but also one that pushed some of the boundaries of what a virtual world could be in the mid-90s; as, I hasten to add, did many other MUDs of the time. It was mostly built by naive college students, who wanted to explore what a virtual world could be. Never as popular as pure combat games or pure social games, it nonetheless attracted a healthy userbase, and more importantly, was influential on other MUDs, racking up a bunch of awards within the MUD community.[64] It also went on to be influential to the fledging MMO world, as at least five *LegendMUD* admins went on to work on MMOs such as *Meridian 59, Ultima Online, EverQuest, Star Wars Galaxies, Shadowbane, Star Wars: The Old Republic*, and more.

Not much like anything else at the time, and frankly, not much like anything else since.

---

[62] See Julian Dibbell's *My Tiny Life* for an in-depth exploration of that game.
[63] https://legendarytimes.org/index.php/Main_Page
[64] See https://www.legendmud.org/Overview/awards.html

Scripting Languages in Diku MUDs

A pair of newsgroup posts summarizing the state of the art in scripting languages on Diku-derived muds.[65]

January 25th, 1996

MobProgs in Merc 2.2 are based on the easyacts system in *Worlds of Carnage* and are acknowledged as such in the Merc documentation. *Carnage* had a policy of not releasing its acts system, but recently a second mud, *Cythera*, has started up using that system. The script functionality includes script attachment to objects, rooms, and mobiles, communication between same, many different types of triggers, alteration of attributes, and definition of new global flags. The scripts are read in with the area files, but I am not sure if they are stored in separate files like Merc's are. *Cythera* was begun by the fellow who was probably the top quest designer on *Carnage* (BadMood). Acts were written, as I understand it, by DimWit.

Stock MobProgs are conceptually derived from *Carnage*'s acts but are nowhere near as elegant. They require a separate file for each script, attach scripts only to NPCs, and were released with several major bugs including a memory leak. Several muds wrote patches in order to use the system, but I do not know whether they are available on the Net anywhere. I assume they are. MobProgs handle basic triggering capability and randoms and not much else.

Addendum in February 1998:

I recently learned that MobProgs were written by Satin, an immortal on Carnage who along with Damion Schubert, aka Heretic, formed a mud after Carnage went down in early 1992 for an extended period of time. The mud never got off the ground, but MobProgs were written in an attempt to emulate Carnage's acts system.

Damion went on to become a key designer on Meridian 59, and Satin for a time worked for him on that project as well. It's difficult to underestimate the impact that Worlds of

---

[65] The original thread on this topic can be found at
https://groups.google.com/d/topic/rec.games.mud.admin/RLqvkKYlFVs/discussion

Carnage had on the commercial mud arena, as key people from both Ultima Online and Meridian 59 started their serious mudding careers there.

DikuII's script system, DIL, as described in the web pages for *Valhalla*, is a very C-like script that makes use of things such as #defines in order to get global flagging. It has process monitoring and control, triggering, attribute altering, etc, and from the looks of it attaches to mobiles only, though I could be wrong. DIL has not been released to the general public. My personal opinion, in looking at it on the web pages, is that it is fairly cumbersome due to its close relationship with C. Powerful, but ease of use goes out the window. A big plus seems to be the ability to handle independent (i.e. not predefined) variables. You can see samples of DIL at:

```
http://valhalla.wtm.tudelft.nl/valhalla/dil-quest.html
```

DIL and mobile definition, as in the next example, are intimately related.

LegendMUD was founded by a set of players from *Worlds of Carnage*, and developed their own acts system back in 93 and 94. Scripts attach to mobiles or to rooms, and are loaded with the area file, in fact with each mobile or room as part of the basic definition of the mobile or room. They support pre-emptive and cooperative multitasking, inter-script messaging, global flags of several kinds, attribute alteration, map alteration, procedures, and many triggers including time-based ones for repetitive behaviors. They lack independent variables although these can be simulated with either flags or with setting and checking values in object, room, or mobile attributes. They also do not have a true process control system, and rely on use of the flags to handle it. *Legend*'s acts are also not available in the public domain. The web page at

```
http://www.legendmud.org/
```

has some descriptions of the acts system's capabilities, although it does not show any sample code. I'm a tad biased towards *Legend*'s code as I am an implementor there. It's more elegant than *Carnage*'s and although it lacks an important area of functionality in terms of lacking trigger attachment to objects, greater sophistication has been derived from it in the actual building. *Legend*'s acts were written by Sadist, who is now lead programmer on Origin's *Ultima Online* project.

Several other muds have cited having private script systems, many derived from MobProgs. I don't know anything about these other places, but would appreciate it if descriptions like the above were posted—I am rather curious.

January 27th, 1996

Got an email asking me to clarify some of the things I said in my earlier post about scripting languages. So below will be some clarification.

However, I've also had a bunch of people show up at *LegendMUD* asking for our acts system, and asking the other immortals (who didn't even know I had posted) to please give them samples or the actual code for the system. Sorry, but *Legend*'s code is not released to the public domain... I posted as part of my ongoing interest in mud design and in order to help out the guy who asked the original question, not in order to get the immorts at *Legend* pestered. :(

In any case, here's the requested clarification:

> MobProgs in Merc 2.2 are based on the easyacts system in Worlds of Carnage and are acknowledged as such in the Merc documentation. Carnage had a policy of not releasing its acts system, but recently a second mud, Cythera, has started up using that system. The script functionality includes script attachment to objects, rooms, and mobiles,

Meaning that you can have actions or such performed by any of those three things. In the case of *Carnage*, it means a newbie sword that talks to you and offers advice, rooms that can spring traps on you, and mobiles that can talk.

> communication between same,

So when you walk into a room, it makes a bunch of rats, then it tells the rats to go hug you. The rats get the message from the room and hug you.

> many different types of triggers,

Trigger being a thing you set up to react to a specific event happening. 99% of the time, what you are triggering off of is something someone said. So you the player say 'Hello' and your mobile has a trigger that when it hears hello, it says 'hiya, dope' back. There are dozens of possible things to react to–just in the case of speech, for example, you can have it react to any text, to questions only (ASK command), to whispers only (WHISPER), to tells, to emotes, to socials, etc.

> alteration of attributes,

Meaning setting of stats and values on PCs, NPCs, and objects.

> and definition of new global flags.

Meaning being able to define a new flag like KILLED_THE_HARPY when you kill the harpy, so that the vampire can check it and say 'You scum, you killed the harpy!'

> Stock MobProgs are conceptually derived from *Carnage*'s acts but are nowhere

near as elegant....MobProgs handle basic triggering capability and randoms and
not much else.

A basic action being of course the ability to randomly do things, such as every once
in a while hiccup.

DikuII's script system, DIL, as described in the web pages for Valhalla, is a very
C-like script that makes use of things such as #defines in order to get global
flagging.

#defines are a C thing. They are sort of global definitions you set up in advance in
order to establish 'ground rules.'

It has process monitoring and control,

Meaning that once you have the script going for the phoenix quest and players are
going through it, you can just check periodically to see if the phoenix quest code is
still running, and if it's been idle, set it all back to the starting point.

triggering, attribute altering, etc, and from the looks of it attaches to mobiles
only, though I could be wrong. DIL has not been released to the general public.
My personal opinion, in looking at it on the web pages, is that it is fairly
cumbersome due to its close relationship with C. Powerful, but ease of use goes out
the window. A big plus seems to be the ability to handle independent (i.e. not
predefined) variables. You can see samples of DIL at:

Meaning it looks like it can do math, and store numbers it arrives at, or store strings.
For example, say you are doing a quest that entails changing your strength. With DIL
you can store the old strength value, and then put it back later because your code
remembers what it was.

support pre-emptive and cooperative multitasking,

A given mob of room can have several scripts going at once, and set a priority on
them. In this case, you can have for example, a trigger on 'leaves north.' But if you set
the highest priority on it, it will happen before the person is even allowed to leave
north–it in effect happens before he left. You can have mobs who regularly walk a
particular trade route, but will still be able to converse with you while they are
walking.

inter-script messaging,

Like the rats above. You can also use this for recursion, using messages to the self
in order to keep triggering a script over and over again while certain conditions are
still met (this works because of the multitasking ability).

global flags of several kinds, attribute alteration, map alteration,

You can alter the exits and flags and so on of a room.

procedures,

You can set up routines that are global and callable by any room or any mobile.

and many triggers including time-based ones for repetitive behaviors.

Do something every hour, or only at 12 o'clock every seventh day…

They lack independent variables although these can be simulated with either flags or with setting and checking values in object, room, or mobile attributes.

Meaning *Legend* would not be able to 'remember' the strength you had before, though it could set up a thing whereby it uses a recursive routine to increment a value on a dummy object, thereby setting the strength as the number stored on that object, and later checking it by examining the object. Much more cumbersome.

They also do not have a true process control system, and rely on use of the flags to handle it.

Meaning that unlike DIL, you can't tell whether or not the quest is ongoing unless some mobile sets a flag on itself when the quest starts, so that you can check if it's set before allowing someone else to start the quest.

Hope this clarifies everything for those who might not have understood what I was trying to say.

LegendMUD scripting examples

These are some small examples of the sorts of behaviors that the LegendMUD scripting system, called ACTS, allowed.

A fawn sambhur

Tiny and scared, a young sambhur fawn looks up at you with pleading eyes.
This small Indian deer is the chief prey of jungle hunters.

```
ACT_RANDOM 50 {
  whimper
}
ACT_FIGHT 300 {
  cry
}
ACT_DEATH {
  _call_proc 666
  _emote_to $N looks at you one last time, and your heart melts.
  _emote_not_to $N looks at $N one last time as $N heartlessly kills $m.
  scream
}
```

A wild boar

A wild boar is here, about to charge!
This creature must be what hacked up the trees outside.

```
  // The longer a PC stays in the room with them the more they're
bothered
ACT_ARRIVE {
  _wait 2
  _get_vict PC
  _call_proc 666
  _call_proc 668
  _if [is_imm($N)] (
    _break
  )
  _set_variable $r get_agg_level $n
  _if ![is_valid($N)] (
    _if [hitcond($n) < 90] (
      _break
```

```
  )
  _if [is_aggressive($n)] (
    _math $r = $r * 5
    _if [eval_vs_constant($r) < 25] (
      _set_agg_level 75
      _aggressive // just turn it off
    )
    _set_agg_level $r // decrease agg level by 5
  )
  _break
)
_if ![is_aggressive($N)] (
  _quickcallback 30 CHECK_BOAR_BOTHER_LEVEL
  _break
)
_else (
  _math $r = $r + 5
  _if [eval_vs_constant($r) > 100] (
    _set_variable $r number 100
  )
  _set_agg_level $r // increase agg level by 5
)
}
ACT_CALLBACK "CHECK_BOAR_BOTHER_LEVEL" {
  _call_proc 11700 // common checks
  _if [hitcond($n) < 90] (
    _wander
    _break
  )
  _if [is_aggressive($n)] (
    _math $r = $r + 5
    _if [eval_vs_constant($r) > 100] (
      _set_variable $r number 100
    )
    _set_agg_level $r // increase agg level by 5
  )
  _if [eval_vs_constant($r) = 100] (
    emote stamps a foot angrily and looks ready to charge!
    _echo_adj You hear a loud, angry grunting sound from nearby!
    kill $N
  )
  _if ![is_aggressive($n)] (
    _aggressive // turn it on
    _quickcallback 30 CHECK_BOAR_BOTHER_LEVEL
    _break
  )
}
ACT_RANDOM 25 {
  _if ![is_aggressive($n)] (
    emote roots about in the brush, dirt goes flying everywhere!
    _echo_adj You hear a loud grunting sound from nearby.
    _get_vict PC
    _if [is_valid($N)] (
      _callback 1 CHECK_BOAR_BOTHER_LEVEL
    )
```

```
      _break
   )          .
   emote stamps a foot angrily and looks ready to charge!
   _echo_adj You hear a loud, angry grunting sound from nearby!
   _get_vict ABOVE_LVL 4
   _call_proc 666
   _if [is_imm($N)] (
      _break
   )
   kill $N
}
ACT_ACT
"(pokes|prods|taunts|beeps|honks|thumps|turns|spins|pats|pets|pinc
hes|tags|tickles|whaps) you" {
   _call_proc 33200 // common checks
   emote stamps a foot angrily and looks ready to charge!
   _echo_adj You hear a loud, angry grunting sound from nearby!
   _if [is_imm($N)] (
      _break
   )
   kill $N
   _if ![is_aggressive($n)] (
      _aggressive // turn it on
   )
}
ACT_RANDOM 5 {
   _if [hitcond($n) > 90] (
      _if [is_aggressive($n)] (
         _aggressive // turn if off
      )
   )
}
ACT_FIGHT 333 {
   _if ![is_aggressive($n)] (
      _aggressive // turn it on
      _set_agg_level 100
   )
   emote stamps a foot angrily and looks ready to charge.
}
```

The skeleton

```
The skeleton of the Maharajah moves uneasily on the throne!
The ivory bone is brittle and has been chewed by rodents. You cannot
tell what
holds it together.

ACT_LOAD {
   emote on the throne suddenly, startlingly, moves!
   emote bows.
   say Welcome to Oodeypore, home of great majesty.
}
ACT_ARRIVE {
   _call_proc 33200 // common checks
```

```
  _if [pcflag($N, CRIED_TREE_OODEYPORE)] (
    emote suddenly looks startled.
    _echo_room The green glow that was created in the gazebo gathers
around him!
    _echo_area All across the Cold Lairs, a vibrancy fills the air!
    _if ![pcflag($N, JUNGLE_QUEST1)] (
      _set_pcflag JUNGLE_QUEST1
      _call_proc 103
    )
    _mtell 33327 change
    emote is covered with a shimmer as translucent flesh covers him.
    _remove_pcflag CRIED_TREE_OODEYPORE
    _set_pcflag RESTORED_OODEYPORE
    _wait 4
    emote looks down at himself.
    sigh
    say The magic is not enough, we are too far gone.
    say I thank you anyway. In recompense, I tell you of my treasure
house.
    say It is under the greenhouse, and you need to be able to disarm an
old trap there.
    ponder
    say The guardian will ask for a token of me. Give him this.
    emote reaches up to his skull, and to your utter horror, pops it
off!
    _load o 33330
    _give skull
    _emote_to $N gives you an ivory skull.
    _emote_not_to $N gives $N an ivory skull.
    say Good luck, $N. And remember that ONLY YOU may cross the pit!
    cackle
    emote falls into a useless heap of bones.
    _goto 33200
    _mtell 33200 announce
    _slay $n
  )
}
ACT_DIRECTED_SPEECH "maharajah|king|ruler" {
  _call_proc 33200 // common checks
  emote chuckles drily.
  say Not a ruler of much worth ruling now, am I?
  _wait 2
  sigh
  talk $N It is sad to see the city so lifeless and in ruins. If only it
could be restored to its former majesty.
}
ACT_ASK "ankus quest treasure" {
  _call_proc 33200 // common checks
  emote looks at you with its eerie vacant eye sockets.
  say In whose name do you seek my treasure? I cannot trust you.
  emote lets its jaw drop in a parody of a grin.
  say I shall give you the key to my treasure room if you can restore
Oodeypore to life.
}
ACT_TEXT "restore life Oodeypore ruins" {
```

```
_call_proc 33200 // common checks
grin $N
say We have been dead for too long—it may not be possible to do it
fully.
sigh
say But if you can grow a tree from tears...
_echo_room With immense effort, the skeleton shifts on the throne.
say You must do it in the place where Oodeypore gazes over the world
it once mastered.
}
```

The quest to restore Oodeypore will, when completed, send messages to every ape of the Bandar-log and transform them into the citizens who once lived in the city. However, over time, the illusions will pop like soap bubbles, and Oodeypore will once again sink into ruin.

Beowulf

I mentioned in the comment thread for part one of "Do Levels Suck?[66]" that I ought to post one of the old *LegendMUD* quests I designed and implemented way back when.

So here it is, offered up as proof that I don't just do sandboxes.

This is the main quest in the Beowulf zone. Much of the zone is written in the style of the poem, with kennings and the like. You reach the zone by traveling south from the Viking area, or by crossing the North Sea from Anglo-Saxon Britain; you're almost certain to come from Britain, given that the Viking area is a dead-end.

Given that, your first experience of the invading Germanic peoples comes when you see a farmwife bemoaning her lost child, near the eastern shores of Britain. If you follow the trail, you will find the Saxons landing, holding the child prisoner. You can buy the child's freedom or kill the invaders. The Saxons want Roman armor, so you can either go kill legionnaires for them to get the pilum and lorica they want, or you can slay Eanmund, their leader, and free the boy. These have consequences, of course, for how further Saxons or Romans will treat you.

Your first hint that some large task exists is when you are sailing across the ocean to the area. Rugian fishermen ply the waters. If two of them get close enough to each other, you can overhear conversations like:

> 'Ho! How goes the trading?' says a Rugian fisherman to an Amber Coast trader.
>
> The captain of the other ship yells back, 'Well!'
>
> A Rugian fisherman hollers out, 'Have you any word if Hrothgar still huddles in Heorot afraid of his shadow?'
>
> The Amber Coast trader yells, 'He certainly does!' and laughs.

A short time before the player arrived in the area, Beowulf had a swimming contest with Breca (this is referenced in the "brags" portion of the poem, when Beowulf is giving his bonafides to the assembled in Heorot). Alas, in this world, Beowulf never surfaced. Many mobs in the area know this, and react with snickers when Beowulf's

---

[66] Found at https://www.raphkoster.com/2005/12/16/do-levels-suck/

name is mentioned, and discuss Breca's triumph. Breca himself believes that Beowulf was swallowed by a giant leviathan that lives under the sea.

Much of the area revolves around Modthryth, the spaewife or witch-woman. If you visit her, you will find a warrior, seemingly cowed and gone mad, huddling in the corner of her hut. Modthryth will attack you if you dare look into her eyes—that is why this poor warrior is suffering his penalty now. She is, however, wise in the ways of shapeshifting, and tells you that given the skin from an animal, you can enchant it and wear it to become that animal.

Throughout the area are wolves, birds, and even fish in the water whose shape you can take on. In this particular case, you'll want the pikeshape, since fish can survive underwater. If you have magical ability or items that allow underwater travel, you can use those too… either way, you will go in search of the leviathan.

The leviathan is a giant whale that lives in the waters between the lands of the Geats and Scyldings (Beowulf was a Geat). If you fight this whale, it has a random chance of swallowing you; if you show up as the pike, he'll eat you instantly. You literally get swallowed; you move to a room that is the gullet of the whale, and Beowulf is in there. There is no exit.

In the Belly of the Behemoth

It's very dark and very slimy in here. With every move the behemoth makes, you tumble and fall, sliding on the mucousy saltwater-slick flesh. Ribbed and strong, the gullet walls throb around you. Lucky for you that the monster breathes air; every once in a while a shower of droplets falls from far above, and fresh air rushes in like a tempest, tangling your hair. You see no way out of here whatsoever, except perhaps digestion.

While in the whale, you can chat with Beowulf, who says things like:

"Ah, what fair warriors, stouthearts indeed, have joined me in this dark intestine?"

"If only some great warrior, as strong as I, slew the whale! (wistful sigh)"

"I was on my way to rid Hrothgar's hall Heorot of the rimwalking fiend. (sigh)"

"(ponders) Perhaps I should have asked aid of the spaewife Modthryth before setting out."

"(grins) A fool's act, but perhaps we need to get the whale to sneeze us out."

You get out by tickling the whale's throat with a feather. The geese in the area (and probably other birds in the game) are a source of feathers. The normal path for first-timers here is not to know that they need the feather, and have to send a tell or chat for help. You can also just get the whale killed, but that's a significant job for a high-level group.

It's worth pointing out that thanks to the wonderful technology of text, the gullet of the whale is an unpleasant place to be—it shakes, it sploshes, it reacts to stimuli affecting the whale, such as whether it's being attacked outside.

Once you are sneezed out or the whale dies, you wash up on shore:

```
With a tremendous noise, the whale sneezes! In a tumult of water
and bile, you are thrown into the sea, losing consciousness, to
wake a while later…
```

Once on shore and conscious, you have a conversation with Beowulf:

```
Beowulf smiles. 'Indeed, you are of stout heart and wayfaring mind.
Henceforth, if any question your credentials, tell them on my
behalf! You are a Companion of Beowulf!'
```

```
Beowulf embraces you. 'But I cannot let this defeat, ignominious
end of battle, give me pause!'
```

```
Beowulf leaps back into the water to wrestle with the whale! After
a short pause, you hear a huge GULP, then all is still.
```

You are now a Companion of Beowulf, something that shows up in your profile when people check — on Legend, these are called WHOIS strings, since you can do a WHOIS FRED to read about their exploits. (I later put these into SWG and we called them 'badges.') This WHOIS string also required to visit the land of the Scyldings. When you attempt to enter their lands, you are stopped, and not allowed to pass unless you are proceeding in Beowulf's stead. (You can get past by other means, of course). The land of the Scyldings, of course, is afflicted by the attacks of the monstrous Grendel, who comes at midnight to attack the stout warriors of Hrothgar, the lord of the Scyldings.

When you arrive at Heorot, a herald actually stops you at the door, then marches in before you to announce you to the hall; the announcement of course varies depending on whether or not you are a Companion. If not, Grendel will not appear:

```
'Welcome to Heorot, Darniaq, to you and your thanes,' Hrothgar
says.
```

```
Hrothgar sighs. 'I had hoped you were Beowulf of the Geats, come to
save us.'
```

```
Hrothgar shrugs philosophically.
```

```
Hrothgar says, 'You may sleep here tonight, but I doubt me the
beast will appear.'
```

If you are a Companion, then he will show at midnight by the game's clock. All the thanes in the hall will go to sleep, and Grendel will come in, kill one of them, and if left undisturbed, leave after. If you attack Grendel, however, you can try to fight him. He's tough—a better solution is to arm wrestle him using the game's armwrestling skill, and rip off his arm, which happens in the poem. Then he will flee, leaving a trail of blood you can follow.

The blood trail leads through a perilous area. There are logs that you can slip off of and fall into freezing damaging water. There's a foul brackish pool you must swim under. The knowledge of shapeshifting with animal skins helps you get past these barriers—the birdshape, for example, will help you traverse the treacherous areas because you can't slip off a log if you are flying over it. You just need to kill an eagle, get its wing, and take it to Modthryth to fashion into a birdshape wearable for you.

Watch out with the wolfshape, though. Wearing it will make you warg, cursed outsider. You'll change on the who list and everywhere else to appear as a warg, your align will drop to max evil, and you will be reviled by everyone. And you can't take it off.

Alas, when you reach the pond and go under, you will find that Grendel's mother is basically undefeatable. You fight and don't seem to make a dent. That's when you will need to resort to Modthryth or other mobs in the area, who will tell you that it's going to take a sword crafted by the legendary Weland Smith to destroy her.

However, that cowering warrior held captive by Modthryth knows the story. According to legend, the last Sword of Weland to be seen in the area was owned by Fadhmir, a king of long ago who is buried in a barrow atop the cliffs. None will guide you there, however, because it is reputed to be haunted. The warrior's name is Wiglaf. He's essentially hypnotized, and believes that he is trapped in chains, even though he is not. Removing Modthryth from the picture and asking him about the sword will allow him to escort you to the barrows.

"Removing Modthryth from the picture" so you can free Wiglaf isn't done by killing her (though that is a shortcut, it's a dangerous one). When you ask her to free Wiglaf, she asks you to prove to her that the deeds done there, the heroic culture of her people, will live on. Since in *LegendMUD* you can travel in time, the solutions are to go to other eras and bring back artifacts. The sheet music to Wagner's Ring Cycle is in the piano bench in Casablanca, for example. A copy of Beowulf is available at the pawn shop on the Isle of Dogs in Victorian London, and so on. Bring her one of these items, and she will let Wiglaf go.

Guiding you along the way to the barrow, he will stop at a small cairn and tap at it three times and tell you 'remember that!' The cairn is known as a holy place—this is where you can pray to be relieved of wargshape.

At the barrow, Wiglaf leaves you, announcing that his love for Modthryth is such that he cannot resist gazing into her eyes. Off he goes to get locked up again, and you are left at the barrow entrance.

The barrow is dangerous—there are ledges that collapse and require groups to be by each other to catch each other when they fall, there's a lake of lava deep within, and so on. If you explore it fully, you will eventually find a blank wall which when tapped three times will reveal a secret room wherein resides Fadhmir's treasure, buried with him.

Fadhmir's Final Resting Place

```
Dark and oppressive, like the last breath from a lung bubbling with
blood, the air of this room hangs about you like sour cloth. Yet
the room is bright, bright, red and bright with the gold that lies
in molten hopeless piles about you, in rivers and lakes, in puddles
and mounds of melded coins and fused jewelry. The room dazzles with
red gold, the gold of the rivers, the gold granted men to make them
yearn for the heavens. For a moment the wod of greed takes hold of
you, and you hear the whisper of scales in your soul; but you are
deterred by the image of a man half-traced in gold melted onto
bones like candlewax. There lies Fadhmir, once thane over the
earth, and now a skeleton with chest caved in by the weight of the
wealth too great for one man to carry.
```

You can take the Sword, but as soon as you do, "a deep cavernous voice speaks in your mind! It says, 'Who disturbs my treasure?'" This is actually seen by *everyone* in the zone. That's because you have woken the greedy spirit of Fadhmir, who in the manner of Germanic legend, is a dragon because of his greed. This dragon will take up occupancy in the lava lake, and will periodically fly out over the land of the Geats from then on, attacking the village—everyone in the zone sees it happen, it's a fairly big deal.

But you have other fish to fry. You make your way back to the foul lake, swim underwater, and deal with Grendel's mom. This is tricky because unlike a normal fight, it isn't decided on gradually reducing hit points. Instead, you have to survive long enough to hit Grendel's mother a specific number of times with the blade. This shifts strategies a fair amount from the norm.

```
The last blow with the Sword of Weland bites deep into the
seawolf's heart, scattering her acid blood everywhere. The sword
dissolves in her blood, leaving only the hilt embedded in her
chest.
Grendel's mother tugs the hilt from her heart.
```

```
Grendel's mother drops the hilt of the Sword of Weland.
Grendel's mother staggers around the room, her acid blood hissing
on the rock.
```

Your wonderful magic sword is lost, and now you have but a hilt. You'll also find Grendel's dead body, bled to death from the lost arm. You can sever his head to carry back as evidence of your great deed. When you return to Heorot, you are announced as a savior, and given a new sword, Hrunting. Giving the head of Grendel to Hrothgar will also earn you a wondrous helm and a mail shirt.

I want to point out that you can abandon this quest at any point if you are satisfied with the rewards you have gotten. If you want the Sword of Weland (which has specific benefits and tradeoffs) then by all means, keep it and just don't do the rest of the quest. Hrunting has different benefits and tradeoffs.

All of the preceding ends the first leg of the Beowulf quest. But you have loosed a dragon upon the Geats, and they are not happy. All the conversations shift, and now all the talk is of the evil dragon Fadhmir who terrorizes the villages.

Off you go to learn the means of slaying a dragon… the first thing you learn is that again, your sword makes no dent in it. On top of that, it lives in the lava lake, and you can't stand in there to fight it, since the lava does massive damage to you when you touch it—ranged weapons, or better yet, some sort of flying or levitation ability are needed. Again the birdshape may come in handy.

But the real challenge is a weapon that can slay the dragon. Asking around will tell you that there is perhaps one smith whose work rivals that of Weland himself—the outcast dwarf Ragin, who for as long as anyone can remember has been smithing at his underground forge deep in the Geatish woods.

If you enter his forge the wrong way, you're liable to drop down his chimney and die instantly, and if you go too deep, you're going to find a world-spanning wyrm down there, so watch where you go.

Ragin is reluctant to help, but he'll offer to create a seithblade, as long as you can supply the deadliest poison made by magic. You'll want a high-level alchemist type now, who can make a vial of instant death potion. These are basically a rare commodity on the player markets. Give Ragin the vial and he will start forging for 24 game hours.

The seithblade that results is a poisoned weapon. But it still does nothing against the dragon. In fact, if you stomp on it, it will shatter into a zillion pieces. Ragin will shake his head sadly, and say that perhaps a sword quenched in blood in the old style would do the trick. As it happens, you were served blood pudding in Heorot, and the cook there has buckets of blood she will give you. By the way, while you're there, you might search around, find some letters in a chest by the warrior's hearth, ask the scop's apprentice, to translate them, and learn of a plot to assassinate Hrothgar.

Ragin forges away again, and sadly, when you stomp the blade, it shatters again. Perhaps, he says, what we need is sky-iron and magic. You do have that hilt of Weland's sword, so you give it to him. The sky-iron is tougher.

As it happens, meteorites of naturally occurring steel fall anywhere in the whole game from time to time. Sometimes they fall on a player and kill them, in fact. They are highly visible—everyone in the zone can see the meteor streak across the sky and crash into the ground. They are collectible, and rare—there can only be one such meteorite in the world at a time. The hunt for a meteorite can therefore span quite a while, but usually you can seek to buy one that someone else has found, or ask on chat channels for help.

Give the sky-iron and the hilt to Ragin, and he will craft the skyblade, greatest of swords that are within his power. Again, you could have settled for any of the intermediate swords, if you so chose. But when you stomp the skyblade, it bends and springs back. Now you can slay Fadhmir… it's a tough battle, and you probably want to bring friends, all of whom can survive in the lava lake.

Upon slaying the dragon, the depredations cease, of course. But Ragin the dwarf smith, who was Fadhmir's jealous brother (hence his willingness to help), will now try to take back the skyblade and Fadhmir's treasure, to rule in his stead. You will have to fight the very person who helped you defeat the dragon.

You return to town, where Wiglaf is once again under Modthryth's spell and all has returned to normal. But Wiglaf knows what you have done—and so does Modthryth.

```
A mighty flapping of wings can be heard… to your astonishment, a
majestic swan sails down from the skies before you and settles on
the ground at your feet. It bows its head to you like a servant.
The swan says, 'You have completed the great task, and are indeed a
hero fit for the meadhalls of Walhalla.'

The swan ducks its head, folds its wings, and with a wrench that
makes your guts twist, removes the swanshape and stands before you,
revealed as Modthryth—not Modthryth the spaewife, but Modthryth the
walkurja, shieldmaiden of Wodan.

Modthryth says, 'It has been years since I expected this to come to
pass. But it has. Praise be. You have earned a reward fit for
kings, yet I cannot grant such a thing. I may only hope that the
treasures you have earned are sufficient.'

Modthryth peers at her swancloak. 'And this, for I no longer have
need of it,' Modthryth says. Modthryth drops the swancloak.
```

The swancloak is a phenomenal item, of course. It gives you swanshape to fly, great armoring, and many other buffs.

Then everyone in the whole game can hear this announcement:

Hail, to one who shall forever be remembered as the slayer of Fadhmir the dragon, as the bane of the svart alfs, as the freer of a warrior-maiden under enchantment. Hail, all, to Darniaq, who has proven himself mightier than Beowulf, as mighty as any of the fabled heroes of old.

Much spamming of "grats!" on channels then ensues.

Modthryth curtsies. 'And now may I return to my barrow, to rest once more beside the quiet bones of my lord and husband, Fadhmir, who is now forever at peace.'

Modthryth bows her head, and her hair curtains her face. As you watch, her skin crumbles away from her bones, until she stands a gruesome skeleton.

The wind begins to rise.

Then she collapses in a heap of bones, flesh carried away by the wind, and before your eyes falls to ash, her remnants borne away by the swirling breezes and the sudden smell of spring flowers.

The End.

1950s and what a MUD could be

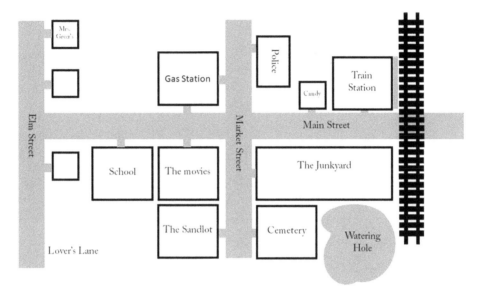

I worked extensively on an unfinished area for LegendMUD that was entitled "1950's Americana." The point of it was to do something quite different from the usual run of areas in the game; instead of a combat-centric area with rooms full of passive descriptions, this one would have what I termed an "impositional" flavor: an experience meant to immerse you in the vibe of the daydreamed 1950's... the one where The Blob might land, where girls sipped milkshakes at the local diner whilst sitting atop tall barstools, where there was a sock hop on Fridays and greasers racing for pinks on the back roads. But also where Catholics weren't quite trusted, and dark skin wasn't really welcome. I even planned to actually convert the players into young kids when they entered the area, with the NPCs commenting on their funny costumes when it wasn't even Halloween yet, my stars!

When I think of the sort of interactive worlds I want, I still think back to what I wanted this zone to make you feel.

It was set in an imaginary town named Springfield. You'd get there by catching a train from World War II New York...

On the Plane

It has been a tiring flight, as you leave behind the war-torn continent of Africa, leave behind the troubled fields of Europe, flying away from the insanities of the Third Reich. But now you are free of all that, heading to the United States. The plane touches down in New York, and after rushing through Customs and negotiating the labyrinth that is the airport, you are ready to catch a train into the heartland of the country. It seems odd, how so few here are talking about the War... almost as if it had already ended here, and was now the stuff of history books, consigned to libraries and classrooms. Oh well—west of you is the train station, and it is ready to leave. Perhaps you had better get on board.

> east

Go that way and you'll board a plane!

> west

Grand Central Station

You're far too busy managing your luggage to notice the grandness of this building—after all, transatlantic flights are a big deal. Between the concerns for tickets, and all the people getting on or off of the trains, your head feels stuck in a whirlwind. East lies the way to the airport, and of course merely sitting in a train means you will be whisked away out of the city and into the rolling hills.

> west

The tracks are over there. And you assume it's not too safe to walk on them.

Once you boarded the train, you lost control of your movements and were carried along willy-nilly.

On the Railroad

Chug a chug chug chug, CHUG a chug chug... whoo whoooo, here we go, the train a-pumpin' and tootin' its way across the countryside. This grand old country, which the pioneers traipsed over in bebooted and corned feet, which covered wagons rolled over on their big spoked wheels, zooms by under the clackerty-shlackerty wheels. Bumppd-dabump go the ties, and zinnnng go the rails, as the train roars its way across the hills. Sometimes kids race it on their bicycles, but mostly moo cows watch it go by, and just moo. They see it every day, and it just ain't as exciting the six thousandth ninety-ninth and a halfth time.

On the Railroad

Over the trestle, dropping bits of scattered metal, down the ravine and past the old watering hole—as you zoom on by the branches shiver and wiggle, all excited. The train is coming! whisper the leaves. It's coming fast! And every squirrel runs away and the deer make a point of not straying onto the tracks, and somewhere in the distance the kids who splash their summers away in the watering hole perk up their sodden heads and wonder what distances the old engine has crossed today... and the bravest, the ones who walked the trestle in the dark and laid precious pennies on the rails— why, they're watching for the wafer-thin sheets of copper to flap away on the wind, old Lincoln's nose longer than ever.

On the Railroad

Mountains of rust—it's a forest of gearshifts, a maze of chassis, a tangled and towering pile of delightful and toppling junk! The train zooms by it so fast you can hardly see the fragmented bits of motorcycles that greasy hair daredevils once rode too fast along river roads, the bits of Edsels consigned to their deserved fate, the vicious mean old dog that guards the place, the wrecking ball that fell off its cable a long time ago and never got the gumption to climb back up... and then it's gone, a blurred and fascinating picture, a graveyard of everything that could be made to rust, creak, whine, crackle, or collapse; the train zooms by it because it doesn't want to STOP here.

On the Railroad

Springfield is in view! Every roof is brown or red or faintly green, and every yard is green or faintly yellow, and every car is red or brown or blue or green or some other variant on solid colors. All in all, even though everything is some different combination of bright primary colors or sophisticated shades of pastel best left in the imaginations of the marketers, it all looks the same. Northwards the train station sits, a classic example of Industrial Americana, which is to say, a homely pile of bricks that looks like it got together by accident, partied too hard, and then forgot to go home in the morning.

> look west

That's where Main Street crosses the tracks.

> look east

It looks like typical small town America. The station is a homely collection of bricks piled up to greet the trains.

You automatically exited the train and found yourself in Springfield.

The Train Station Platform

Straight as an arrow, dirty as a hobo's backseat, the rails run inches past your feet on their clickety-clackety way into the horizon's depths. Sometimes trains zoom by, pushing the wind along with them in a great big rush of smells from faraway cities—maybe even New York City—and sometimes the trains carry with them the echoes of the sounds of distant places in their mournful whistles. A little something of the lonely lighthouse overlooking a slate sea, a little something of the spicy rhythms of a Spanish dance chattered along in the wheels. But when you look the other way, it is the regular brown roofs, the Levittown sameness, the suburban and similar lawns that you see. 'Welcome to Springfield,' says a sign in faded blue paint. 'America's Heart, Caring and True.'

> west

The Train Station

The paint seems eager to leave this place: eager in the same way that all those kids headed off to college are, eager like the faces of the traveling salesmen about to start another season of knocking door to door. The paint is so eager it is peeling off the walls in little patches of beige that slide along the reflective faux marble floor when you walk near them. A train schedule hangs on the wall, but most people around these parts know that the trains from Springfield just go to other places just like here.

> examine schedule

```
+--------------------------------------------------+
| Departures                         Arrivals      |
|   7:30am    New York City (express)  10:00am     |
|   9:45am    Hope                                 |
|  11:00am    Newton                               |
|  12:30pm    New York City            2:00pm      |
|   1:45pm    Chicago (sleeper)                    |
|   3:00pm    Pittsburgh (freight only)            |
|   5:30pm    New York City            8:00pm      |
|   7:00pm    Chattanooga TN                       |
+--------------------------------------------------+
```

> south

The heavy wooden door is closed.

> look door

Main Street lies past that heavy wooden door!

> open door

You open the heavy wooden door.

> south

Main Street Meets the Railroad Tracks

Good kids aren't allowed to go any further east. That's 'cause that's where the pavement stops for a bit and the ties start, where the railroad chops Main Street into tiny bits of gravel. After the tracks, it's not even Main Street anymore, it's some silly state route with a number on it. And good kids never ever EVER go traipsing down the tracks on warm nights, skipping to the rhythm of the crickets, no sirree! That's because once a small boy fell onto the tracks while playing marbles or something else dumb like that and was turned into mashed potato, just ask any mother in town! That's just the way of life here: Main Street ends at the tracks and only BAD kids go past it (or else good kids whose mommas don't know them very well...)

> `look east`

Onto the tracks? Are you CRAZY?

> `west`

The Bestest Part of Main Street

This is the bestest part of Main Street. And you can tell all the time, 'cause the smells are like sugar glazed on top of sticky buns! And the colors are the colors of tinny little wrappings painstakingly removed from chocolates. Ones just a BIT too soggy to be edible with the sort of propriety Grandma demands at the dinner table. This is the bestest part of Main Street, because right to the north is the door to Heaven! Not heaven like they say in church, 'cause they don't sell harps there, but they do have Superman and Batman and Wonder Woman even for the girls, and of course they have every delight known to mankind, because this is the bestest part of Main Street where the CANDY store is, except on Sundays after 5pm and weekdays after 7pm. Then it's boring.

> `north`

The Candy Store

Gumballs, bottom right. Chewing gum, first box with and second box without baseball cards. Milk duds. Lollipops for the little ones. Hard orange candy that stings your tongue when you suck on it too long. French creams. Necco wafers. Wax lips you can wear or eat. Rock candy that looks fresh-carved from a cave in the heart of Africa. Peppermint sticks to stick in lemons, up on the counter 'cause otherwise people would throw the lemons around. Red hots. Bazooka bubble gum for a penny, with the cartoons that are usually funny. Superman comics but that's boring 'cause he always wins anyway. Apples and oranges and ripe peaches with more fuzz on their cheeks than something that young has a right to. Oh! And the soda fountain with syrup and malteds and fizzy water and ice cream and floats and root beer and Coca-Cola and cherries and sarsaparillas and big curly straws and stools that spin ALL the way around and MOOooooOOM! Can't we just STAY here?

The soda jerk is here ready to take your order.

> look jerk

Pimply faced, this teenaged boy smiles happily back at you.

> ask jerk candy

The soda jerk says to you, 'Penny for gum. A dime for a lemon with a peppermint stick. A quarter for a pair of wax lips.'

The soda jerk polishes a glass dry and sets it back up on a shelf.

The soda jerk adds, 'And a nickel for any of the other kinds of candy.'

> give soda jerk 5 gold

The soda jerk examines 5 gold coins.

The soda jerk shrugs philosophically.

The soda jerk returns 5 gold coins to you.

> give soda jerk dime

The soda jerk gets lemon from a box and grabs a peppermint stick from a jar.

The soda jerk cuts a small hole in the lemon and inserts the peppermint stick.

The soda jerk hands a lemon with a peppermint stick to you.

The soda jerk smiles at you.

> south

> west

Main Street Meets Washington Square

This is where downtown really starts: the edge of Washington Square, with its big fountain in the middle, surrounded by polite little hedges that pretended to die every winter but always came back, and the bright red and yellow flowers that the little old ladies insist on planting every spring. The flowers never pretended: when they died, they MEANT it. At this end of Washington Square a white gazebo stands ready to hold whatever dorky band the Mayor picks for the parade this year. Last year it was Dixieland, and the old piano teacher Missus Greer was much affronted that some of the young ladies from the high school took it upon themselves to dress New Orleans!

> west

In Washington Square

Not that you'd ever think of setting foot in there, but north of you is where the Catholic kids all go to church. And that's all right, if you're a Catholic, say the various Methodist and Baptist and Episcopalian mothers in town, because it's not like they're really that different from us, but well, they are. (And the Baptists and the Methodists sometimes say the same about the Episcopalians because they sure do seem like Catholics sometimes.) And this ivy-covered wall here by the side of the street is where the caterpillars grow that the boys shove down the girls' dresses. They are the fuzzy orange and black kind—the caterpillars, not the girls, that is... best caterpillars in town. So sometimes the Catholic kids do get the best stuff, even if they have to go to their First Communion Sunday School Training and stuff while the rest of the kids play stickball on the sandlot. Oh well, the church is closed up anyway.

A fuzzy caterpillar inches along.

The town fountain is here.

> get caterpillar

Aww... it curls up into a ball when you poke at it.

> look fountain

The bluish fake marble of the fountain is chipped in places. The water is slightly greenish, and its cherubs seem just not-quite-cute-enough. Water sprays upwards from the spout and splashes down, sort of bored-looking, into the pool proper.

North Market Street and Washington Square

The Catholic church is over on the east side of the Square, and the fountain is to the south, and all the way over to the south side of the Square is the town clock which sits on the Methodist church, and there's the dinosaur logo on the Sinclair gas station, which makes it cool even though it IS just a gas station, and all in all, this is a quite decent little town square. Even if it is mostly inhabited by old people feeding bread crumbs to whatever living things venture too close to them. Northwards Market Street pretty much just ends at the police station.

Before the Sinclair Station

The dinosaur logo of the Sinclair filling station is overhead. Sometimes you wish it would come alive, preferably in better colors, and would careen around the downtown area, chomping miscellaneous people and stepping on the odd automobile. Maybe the first victims would be the obnoxious letter-sweatered senior high basketball team. And maybe the dinosaur would become your friend, and let you ride on its back, and yeah right, maybe pigs can fly and maybe the higher grade kids won't be such jerks next year and maybe you'll also win the lottery and get to stay up later and be allowed to listen to the music YOU wanna listen to (the stuff that barely comes through, that plays the Southern stuff with the beat that the preachers say is sinful).

At the right time, the dinosaur was indeed supposed to come to life, and stomp around the town wrecking everything.

> west

Main Street and Washington Square

The residential district starts to the west of here. So this is it, the boundary between downtown where the buildings at least pretend to look different, and the suburbs, where the houses seem to be terribly similar. It's not as bad as the Levittowns you hear are springing up outside of the big cities, where the houses are actually made of prefabricated pieces that get assembled to taste.

> east

> south

In Front of the Bijou

Oh Heavenly Paradise! Fount of all that is Hollywood! Source of copious quantities of ketchup-hued blood and interminable sissy kisses that elicit wolf whistles from the balcony! Dwelling place of the radioactively altered bees, ants, crabs, plants, pods, peaches, and poodles! Although you are here on the paved street, solid asphalt beneath your toes, merely gazing upon the space age chrome curve of the marquee makes this boring world dissolve and a much more intriguing world full of spies and lovers and cowboys and aliens appear in glorious black and white.

> south

The Lobby of the Bijou

Gold trim and lush wine velvet, everywhere you look. Those funny golden posts with knobby tops stand all over the place, segmenting the lobby with wine-colored velvet ropes—they all inevitably lead past one of two places: a snack counter full of the most ridiculously overpriced items (a chocolate malt, 15 cents?!?) or the station where the ticket taker stands, ready to make sure you aren't smuggling in your little brother hidden under your wide-skirted raincoat, or sneaking in a golden flask concealed in the inside pocket of your leather jacket. Movie posters hang from all the walls, and virtually every one has a city in flames at the bottom, and glaring yellow and red letters at the top, often the jaggy kind that make your eyes hurt.

> look poster

It's for Attack of the 50-Foot-Tall Radioactive Bug-eyed Ant Men.

> south

The Darkened Theatre

Dark and cavernous, the theater rises above you in Art Deco curves and shadows.

The seats face the screen in silent anticipation—even the popcorn butter and soda stains on the upholstery seem eager for the show to begin. Little lights glow along the aisles, like magical pathways into the wonderful black and white world that can fill the screen. Small exit signs glow a deep red (and flicker sometimes if someone stomps the floor too hard) at the front and back of the theater.

> stomp

You stomp around.
The exit lights flicker.

> watch movie

You needed the 3-d glasses. The seats buzzed periodically, and popcorn fell from the balcony above. And at a certain moment, as we described the movie playing, the ant-men (or spy movie, or Western) characters came out of the screen in full 3d, and came alive, and player could fight them off. When they succeeded, they returned to their seats.

> north

> north

> east

> south

Market Street

Market Street is a creaky old sort of a street. The kind with potholes that try to catch your ankles on purpose. The kind that still parades some of its faded beauty, like the mostly closed storefronts with Depression glass, the rowhouses with pseudo-Gothic cornices. It's like an old lady still proud of her moth-eaten feather boa. A sign of the way Market Street has fallen is the fact that much of what once made it great is now piled in the junkyard to the east.

> south

The End of Market Street

Market Street just sort of fades away, ending in abandoned railroad tracks and a high fence that nobody climbs because it's laced with barbed wire. Nothing much is left down here—it's the part of town that gave up the ghost, that grew up and moved away, that lost its hubcap. Am empty lot has been made over to serve as impromptu baseball field by the local kids who play down here, and the cemetery is over to the east: it's a perfect place to keep your dead, in the remnants of the town they once lived in that has since rearranged its heart and settled a bit farther north.

> look west

That's the sandlot where pickup baseball games get played.

You were supposed to be able to play baseball there.

> east

The Graveyard Entrance

Word has it that on odd-numbered dates on weekdays with six-letter names in winter when the moon is dark and a funeral has taken place within the last week, some of the gravestones in this cemetery have the names of those about to die. You can sneak past the creaky, rusty-hinged black gate, along the ridge where the larger mausoleums rest, down into the little gully where the ground is too wet to bury anyone for longer than a day, and into the center, where the gravestones have the names of children who died of tuberculosis during the Depression, and the names of Civil War veterans whose final breath came peacefully in their sleep, and see on a troublingly uncared-for and mossy stone your own name, carved by a hesitant hand, with the exact date of your demise immortalized forever. At least, so the sixth-graders say, and they should know, right?

> look gravestone

The succinct epitaph on the mossy gravestone was carved by a hesitant hand. It reads, 'Here lies [you], died of a broken neck after diving in the swimming hole.' After much frantic searching, you fail to find a legible date on the marker.

> east

By the Watering Hole

The grass demands bare feet: it wants to slip between your toes with its cool greenness and tickle. It wants to slide along the bulgy bone in your ankle and make it itch. Here in the shade of the great old trees that overhang the water deep and blue, the grass is soft and springy like the best old beds, made to be jumped on and rolled in. But it twitches away from the water itself, reluctantly conceding the shore to the mud that has been stomped and trampled into a cratered map of footprints. The water hole is enclosed by these trees, this grass, these reminders of past feet, running with their happy thud thud into the cool depths; it is fenced by this green, as if to keep it safe.

You could climb a tree, and swing on a rope out over the water, and jump in.

In the Watering Hole

From here in the water, the sun is like a thousand speckles of bright light, filtered through the leaves and dazzling off of the water. The leaves above rustle it into patterns like firecracker bursts on the Fourth of July. And the water is cool and silent, deep like a quarry and smooth like melting ice cream. It's chill like the breeze out of an ice box, and warm like the worn old blanket that lays on the back porch in the fall. When you move your arms through the water, it ripples, and deep in the water you can see the hidden treasures, golden and green, sea-changed somethings that nobody has ever been able to dive deep enough to reach. Not even if they swung from the old tire and jumped—not even if they kept going down until the water gripped their chest and their parents began to worry...

> west

> west

> north

> north

> west

> west

Main Street, In Front of Roosevelt Secondary School

Zebra crossings lay down ladders of white on the street pavement, and perky little yellow signs stand on the corners. It's all so terribly cheery! Bright colored construction paper cutouts sit in the windows of the lower grades, and so many of them portray kindly faces... and it's all a SHAM, a terrible hoax perpetrated by the establishment! For what resides within is no less than the ultimate penury, the exquisitely planned and orchestrated torture of endless meaningless classes, the grownup plot to keep all those young hormones in tight quarters and then tell them not to do anything, the holding pen for America's future! It's a jail, a prison, and the only reason to ever set foot inside is to see your friends again after the summer gets boring.

> look south

Aghhhh! The school! Horrors!

> south

The School Hallway

They must wax these floors every weekend, and maybe twice a week—lovingly going over every inch, polishing and scrubbing until every last speck of dirt is gone, until even the scratches shine, until you can see your reflection better than in your mirror at home—and it still means absolutely NOTHING. The halls are a scuffed and scrambled mess of walls the color of toothpaste and doors of institutional green, every pane of glass in a door crazed in that diamond pattern like a grid gone askew. Smears and splatters at your feet, and lockers the color of well-aged chewing gum, the illicit smell of tobacco drifting past your nose and the echoey lighting from the fluorescent bulb that can't quite hum along as it should: hello, Springfield High... you're looking good today.

There are school lockers here.

> east

The Principal's Office

Everything seems out of size here: the paddle hung on the back wall, like a somber reminder of buttocks past; the plaques and certificates claiming that the man behind the desk is somehow better and wiser than you, perhaps even than the teachers; the desk itself, huddled like a sleeping hippo in the middle of the room, piled high with papers and maybe even confidential school records. Somewhere in those drawers rest the remnants of everyone's third grade year, the year the teacher ignored them when they asked to go to the bathroom, and wouldn't give them a pass until the last minute, and they ended up, well, you know... and there's the notation of that time in fifth grade, when the incident with the frog and that obnoxious Suzie with the braids...

> look desk

There appear to be students records in there.

> read records

We would generate random records about the player themselves.

> west

> west

The Classroom

The air is redolent with the smell of paste glue and wood shavings: the aroma of sharpened pencils, made somehow heavier by the light falling through the large glass windows on one wall. Desks stand in disorderly rows, each shoving and pushing as if eager to get out the door. The desktops are scratched into a palimpsest of years of kids writing their loves and their hates and their favorite cusswords. On the walls are hung old class projects and maps of the world and the United States, yellowed away in visible spots where the sun hits them day after day.

> look projects

They were history reports on the other areas in LegendMUD.

> exit classroom

> south

The Gymnasium

This is a place of great drama. It was here that in 1949 Coach Bigelow led the Springfield Bigcats to their first and last county championship, and celebrated by bringing a keg of beer into the gym. It took a week to get the basketball court clean, and Bigelow was soon looking for a job, but the legend of that party has persisted across the years. It was here that only last year Johnny Moreland parked the old principal's car—upside-down. It was here that only last week Charlotte Martin told off Brian Boswell for leaving her all alone at the drive-in with his wanker friend Elmer, and it was here, at a football pep rally, that people first noticed that prissy Emily, the new Mrs. Hoffman, had a secret life, when she started to show. Oh yeah. They also play sports here sometimes.

This room changed dynamically, cycling between afternoon pep rallies to basketball games in the evenings.

One End of the Basketball Court

Above you hangs the hoop—regulation size, just perfect for a regulation ball of regulation size and weight. The net on the hoop isn't quite regulation, though, since Mrs. Randall knitted it one day after the old one started looking a little frayed. Somehow green yarn frays even faster than the ratty old cord that used to dangle there, victim of countless swishes. Some afternoons, kids play HORSE here and dream of playing for the Boston Celtics, or the Lakers, that team that moved from Minneapolis.

The Other End of the Basketball Court

ThUd-BumPPd. That's the sound a basketball makes here. ThUd-BumPPd. It echoed wildly against the wooden bleachers, under which some of the seniors go to smoke late at night, under which some of the cheerleaders go with the seniors, hoping against hope that the night janitor won't come in and interrupt (unless they WANT interrupted, of course, which does happen—those seniors can be SO insistent!).

```
> north
> north
> north
> west
```

Elm Street and Main Street

Here begins Home. Elm Street is where the people live. Where they tend their lawns and trim their shrubs, where they kneel down on loam and care for their rosebushes. Where they paint the trim on the windows and clean the leaves out of the gutter in the fall. Where garages gape cavernously, spilling out the accumulated junk of a marriage, occasionally engaging in a burst of glory, a rummage sale where people ooh and aah over that twelve-string guitar with the broken headstock, or the old set of china with the missing saucers, and even the twine-bound National Geographics from the 1930s. The houses line the street north and south, and face the gentle river on the west side.

> north

Elm Street

A quiet little house with a picket fence and frilly white curtains in the windows stands to the east of you, all decked out in its light blue paint. From behind it a nice big old tree looms, its canopy of leaves hovering protectively over it. The river runs quietly in its banks, green willow strands dangling into the water and little oak helicopters scissoring down from the treetops. It's all like being in a dream—one can only hope the dream does not go on too long, trapping you in a nightmare of perfect little houses full of Avon ladies and men with pipes in their mouths.

> south

> south

> south

Elm Street

Ah, suburbia. There is that je ne sais quoi about it; perhaps the sound of the vacuum cleaners waging their neverending war against grime and dust, perhaps the chiming of doorbells as Avon ladies and Kirby salesmen with better vacuum cleaners visit each house. One such house stands to the east of you, pretty and white, with nicely kept wooden steps in front and some well-tended rhododendron bushes by it. Of course, if you go any further down Elm Street, it becomes a terrible den of iniquity, a place of venial sins and tawdry nights.

There is a small mailbox here.

> look east

Hmm. On close inspection, and after much deliberation, you would have to say that that is a house. Definitely. A house, with a nice door, even. But assuredly just a house.

> open mailbox

The door appears to be ajar. You can't resist the urge to tamper with someone else's mail and take a quick peek inside. You see a leaflet inside.

> read leaflet

The leaflet has the following message written on it:

```
Welcome to Springfield.

Suddenly your eyes swim...

Welcome to Dungeon

You are in an open field west of a big white house with a boarded
front door. There is a small mailbox here.

> south
```

Lover's Lane

It overlooks the river. It's a muddy and rather dull river at this point, but with some effort one can imagine it glistening in the moonlight, small wavelets coursing in glowing rills along the current. This is where tongues lick ears, and fingers try buttons (and usually get slapped away). This is where countless prayers are made, and even answered. Where Going All The Way Actually Happens. There are handprints in the dirt where some fellows no doubt had to jump out and do pushups in order to settle down. There are also lost barrettes and pocket combs. It's the Land of Romance where Sweet Maidens (or not-so-maidens) and their Faithful Swains (or not so faithful) come when they want a little privacy from everyone except the other dozen or so couples.

```
> look river
```

Hmmm.. you don't see the submarines racing like the older boys were talking about in the school hallway.

```
> north

> east
```

A Living Room

The square windows look out upon a nice quiet little street. This living room is the site of countless family squabbles and countless reconciliations, of laughter and of tears. Right now it is mostly the site of a mess. Looks like some kid was playing and forgot to put away his toys. You have to walk carefully to avoid crunching toy soldiers underfoot. The kitchen is to the south, and you suppose that if the place were a little cleaner, it would look like a model home out of Good Housekeeping.

There is a dollhouse here.

```
> look dollhouse
```

It is big enough to sit in.

```
> sit dollhouse
```

In the Doll's House

You just barely fit in here. You're scrunching the kitchen table with one clumsy heel, and your eyes are the size of the window panes, peering out of the second story.

But it is in here, in the room concealed by the pink frilly curtains, where great events take place around the kitchen table. Young Philip leaves for school, and Mother bakes cookies for the PTA, and Daddy gets his briefcase and goes off to his office, and then Nancy sits in front of the window and daydreams the sort of thoughts that fill a teenaged girl's life... that is to say, the thoughts of a Girl Detective, wondering when her sidekicks Muffy and Brenda will show up so that they can go investigate the mysterious lights they've seen near the reported hideout of the diamond pirates! Why, all it would take for her to set off on her adventure would be to open that tiny little dollhouse door!

If you opened the door, poof, you became a Girl Detective, and kicked off a mystery quest across town.

> `> stand`

> `> south`

The Kitchen

This thoroughly modern kitchen is stocked with all the latest and greatest inventions of modern culinary science. There is a Deluxe Hobart mixer here, for example, and a shiny toaster that can handle FOUR slices of bread. It was not so long ago that kitchens like this were just in the dreams of housewives living in "cold water" flats. That was before the gentle rise of prosperity when it became apparent the Depression wasn't coming back, before Harry S. Truman inhabited the White House, and before there were quite so many kids born of the returning GIs and their wives to demand freshly buttered toast. The refrigerator is a wonderful brand new Frigidaire. Everything is spic and span, and a screen door leads out to the back yard.

There is a toaster here.

There is a Wonder Bread wrapper on the counter.

There are slices of bread in wrappers here.

> `> press toaster`

The toaster pops back up immediately since it is empty.

> `> get wrapper`

You get the Wonder Bread wrapper.

> `> put wrapper toaster`

You try to jam the Wonder Bread wrapper in, but it doesn't fit properly in the toaster and it ends up falling out and onto the counter.

> `> look wrapper`

There are bread crumbs in the wrapper.

> get bread

You take a slice of bread in a wrapper.

> open bread

There is a slice of bread inside the wrapper.

> get bread wrapper

> put bread toaster

> press toaster

The slices fall down into the slots and an orange glow emanates from the heating coils.

> wait

The toaster pops up.
You realize you should take out the toast before you burn it.

> press toaster

The slices fall down into the slots and an orange glow emanates from the heating coils.

> wait

The toaster pops up.
You realize you should take out the burned toast before you start a fire.

> press toaster

You think about putting the toast in for another cycle, but decide it is already ruined and set it on the counter.

> east

The Back Yard

It's amazing: the grass here is actually still alive. Between the beagle digging holes for his bones (watch out! almost stepped in one...) and the tromping of young feet, you'd think it would all have turned brown and blown away by now. The picket fence gives it a place to huddle against, though, a place to begin again as it tries to slowly edge the worst of the brown patches, covering up the discarded chewing gum wrappers and the forgotten plastic toy soldiers that are lost in the bushes. A huge cardboard box stands in the center of the yard, aluminum foil pasted over the brown, round windows clumsily cut out. A metal coathanger has been cleverly altered into a Mark VII Etheric Antenna and mounted on top, in order to catch any covert transmissions from the Galactic Overlord.

> sit box

Inside the Cardboard Box

This cardboard box is no mere box. It was not a simple, pre-Atomic Age refrigerator that came from within its depths. No, this is a hyperspatial MacMillan and Jones double-winged Jupiter 9 skimmer, with bifluxor engine and full complement of weaponry. Through its double-glassed windows and its neutrinic field shielding can be seen the stars of Andromeda, and the galaxies under the cruel fist of the Galactic Overlord, that foul being whose pirates and evil legions threaten Earth and its freeloving populace almost daily! If it were not for the Starblazers, an elite corps of highly trained superscientists who also happen to be athletic, mostly blonde, and not at all the sort to use a slipstick, the Milky Way would long since have been crushed under the heel of tyranny. And the Starblazers use ships just like these, ships started with the press of red buttons just like the one crudely drawn on the cardboard flap.

> `press button`

In Decontamination

The graceful curves and the shining silvery color of hypermagnetite alloys are everywhere. Decontam is severe and sterile despite its austere beauty, though, a place where magnetic fields vibrate the air and invisible hypoallergenic ultraviolet light beams strike surfaces and glance off, vaporizing every microbe and bacterium. Trays shoot out from the walls to take clothing and items and subject them to minute blasts of thorium radium electroauriomide so that they can be collected on the other side of the airlock.

> `press button`

The airlock dilates wide enough to climb through.

> `look airlock`

The airlock is to the east.

> `east`

The Airlock

Spacesuits line the walls, puffy like marshmallows, shiny like a dentist's tools, but a lot cooler-looking. The bubbles that are the helmets gleam without even the slightest spotting, and the hoses are all perfectly clean, their tight joints carefully screwed in so that none of that lifegiving, crucial air can slip out into the vacuum. Too bad this mission won't require their use! Instead, you just stand here as the WHOOSH and WHISTLE of the air cycling through the lock pulls impurities from the atmosphere and the quality of the air you breathe changes subtly.

> `up`

In the Cockpit of the Jupiter 9 Skimmer

It's hard to decide which is more interesting—the banks of buttons and glowing lights and sliders and gauges and glass globules full of glinting liquids that serve to calibrate gyros and the gaudy glyphs in twelve galactic languages—OR the vast blankness of space, dotted with pinpoint unwinking stars, each an unimaginable distance apart, steadily illuminating the darkness of infinite space, nestled within gauzy trails of nebulae, twirled in the Milky Way and tangled in Andromeda. Out there in that unimaginable black lurk the forces of the Galactic Overlord, who sees it as his destiny to crush opposition beneath his cruel heel... and you stand between him and the lives of billions of innocents, this ship and that daunting control panel your only hope...

> `look panel`

A fantastic assortment of colored lights, buttons, dials, switches, control knobs, sliders, and levers is arranged before you on the main control panel of the Jupiter 9 Skimmer.

From here, you could actually be given missions randomly. You could then return to the airlock, and cycle it open. If you weren't on the planet yet, you could space yourself (oops) unless you had a spacesuit. If you did have a spacesuit, you could come out on any of eight randomized planets where you could fight various aliens. As you killed them, they would flicker and return to their normal names: mailman, policeman, the family dog...

> `west`

> `north`

> `north`

> `north`

The End of Elm Street

Elm Street dissolves into a stand of trees here, circling tightly around and looping back into itself like the eye end of a needle. But you suppose that this part isn't really Elm Street anymore: Mrs. Greer probably thinks of it as her driveway! And that over there, that big wedding cake of a house with the gables and the arches and the windows that look like teeth, that would be where she lives. And the mysterious lights from the boarded up window in the middle of the night that you aren't supposed to know about and that none of the grownups admit exists, well, that would be the secret room where Mrs. Greer sits and gloats over whatever she got from the body she hides in the trunk. Not that anyone has seen it. And if you ask her about it, she'll probably just look at you over her glasses in that old folks' way, and tell you to get back to practicing your scales. And the fact that she is a wicked hard piano teacher has nothing at all, not at all, to do with the popularity of these conjectures among the grade school crowd.

> east

Mrs. Greer's Foyer

From the inside, Mrs. Greer's house is even more foreboding than from outside. The dust lays heavy on the places where she doesn't bother to dust: the tops of ornamented lintels and the intricate carvings on the legs of foyer tables. The floor is a rich parquet worn silky smooth by years of small feet marching in to their pianistic doom; for Mrs. Greer, horrible a hag as she may be when encountered in the street, as terrifying a harridan as she may be when chance met in the grocery store, is far, far worse when you come to her for your weekly piano lesson. And there lies the Pit of Doom, just over there to the south.

> south

The Piano Room

When young children come here for their piano lessons on the first day, the piano seems almost alive: an ungainly odd-bellied creature with ivory and ebony teeth, ready to clap down on small fingers at the first discord. The disturbing thing is that it still feels that way on the days afterwards. The lace doilies that flop over the edge seem like distraught hair, and the clawfooted legs look ready to scrabble away—a runaway piano, that's what it would be, bouncing down Main Street, doilies scattering and leaving a trail of sheet music. The rest of the room, all candles and rich wooden bookcases, just tries to be unobtrusive, just in case some afternoon when the day gets too hot and the air too still, the piano gets hungry.

The piano, of course, could indeed come alive and attack.

Mrs. Greer's Sitting Room

No room should have this much newsprint in it; the very floor sags from its weight, and the overstuffed and somewhat bursting old armchair (a natty gold once, but now more the color of old glass) is so ramshackle that were the piles of Life, Saturday Evening Post, and Reader's Digest not there, it might well collapse into separate little piles of back, arms, feet, and antimacassar. The windows are greasy enough to admit no real light, and at all times a lamp that makes a strange humming sound remains lit, casting light that flickers like candles. Stairs lead up, and if anything, it seems the shadows grow deeper there.

The humming of the lamp reaches an irritating level and then subsides again.

> up

The Top of Mrs. Greer's Landing

Here at the top of the landing is a quiet space; a small round window lets you glance out across the town, and it seems peaceful enough. No branches are close enough to the glass to go Tap Tap in the night; no mysterious lights dance inside ready to be seen by terrified girls in nightgowns outside, breathing half-giggly of ghosts to their slumber party friends. A small oval table has a single jelly jar, water long since dried out, and a dried yellow flower sits within it, as if it died there, straining towards the small sun the window might offer at midday. The wallpaper is green striped and peeling, interrupted only a pair of doors—one to the north, and another down the hall to the west.

> north

The Mannequin Room

Every step in this room raises small cloudlets of dust, dust that settles on the shelves and the haphazardly stacked boxes. It makes everything seem to move, as if you were in a geometric and ancient city. And then it is that the mannequins come alive: faces veiled, translucent silks draped across their perfect faces, hats twitching on the bald rounded heads... At night, you wonder if they turn to each other in the moonlight, and comment on each other's clothing, talk about the latest fashions from Paris, and daydream of the day when they earn legs taken from the pile of spare parts in the chest under the window...

At night, they did of course come to life too.

Mrs. Greer's Upper Hallway

A tall mirror sits at the end of the hallway, blocking what would otherwise be a view of Elm Street. Draped across the mirror are remnants of a bygone day: a feather boa, nailed to the frame and tattered far beyond its glory days; a Decca 78 suspended with a velvet ribbon, that might carry with it sounds of the Lindy Hop and the Scaramouche if you could but listen hard enough; a yellowed photograph of Mario Lanza, with what may have been the faintest autograph, and crowning it all, the shattered glass, spidered and spattered right where might sit a face, reflecting you into thousands of pieces on the wall and the floor. A doorway lies to the north.

> look mirror

The shattered glass, spidered and spattered right where might sit a face, reflects your face into thousands of pieces on the wall and the floor.

> look decca

The dusty, velvet ribbon hangs from one corner of the mirror, dangling a large phonograph record from it. The label is torn in half and the grooves are dusty and the surface scratched. It seems to be more a reminder of the past than fit for actual listening.

> look boa

It might have once been elegantly draped around a young woman's slender neck and shoulders. But now it appears to feed the moths and you aren't quite sure if it used to be pink or lavender for the thick coating of dust.

> look photo

Mario Lanza smiles back at you, but he looks a little worse for wear. A fold creases his left cheek in a horrible disfiguration and what appears to have once been an autograph is now faint and slightly smeared with age.

> north

Mrs. Greer's Bedroom

Red velvet ribbons tied to a heavy antique bedpost. Dust motes suspended in the air, like time isn't moving for fear of waking someone. Draped across the bed, the dresses: half-sewn, half torn, chiffon and lace and satin sleeves, musty and even moldy in places. Some have spilled to the floor, and bear the marks of heavy boots. A wardrobe stands ajar, and hangers sit empty, mute testimony to the source of the clothing. It is all a few decades out of style, with the perky hats meant to be worn over bobbed flapper hair. The four-poster bed itself seems to hunker down as if defying you, but sadder still in the small vanity, still kept clean with bright red lipsticks and rouges, violet eyeshadow and oily creams, Mrs. Greer's last bulwark against encroaching age.

> look dust

Tiny specks of dust float lightly on the air. They move so slowly you wonder if time is being altered somehow here in this room. You shake your head and quickly recognize that notion for the nonsense that it must be.

> look vanity

The vanity itself bears no dust or grime, sure signs of regular use. The variety of lipsticks, rouges, eyeshadows and creams would be enough to paint the faces of all the clowns at the circus that came through town last summer!

> look dress

These once beautiful dresses are now marred with time and age. A musty smell rises from them and you're sure those blotches aren't supposed to be there, but are just mold.

From here, the plan was that you could time travel, a common feature in LegendMUD areas. And when it was time to depart back to World War II, from whence you came, you'd catch the train, and head back to New York...

On the Plane

It's such a whirlwind of activity here: you had forgotten how industrious the citizens of New York seemed in time of war. Uncle Sam posters and little red, white, and blue ribbons in windows and Rosie the Riveter are everywhere, and the serious-faced young women who take your ticket smile at you when they see that you are heading for the African theater. It's a smile with a hint of wistfulness that not even all the swing music in the world can erase: perhaps their loved ones are there now, in cars or in caskets, driving for a general or slogging across the sand. And so you board the plane, sleep through the tiring flight, and land in Casablanca, where mystery meets war and directly east of you is a door into what may be the rest of your life.

Moods

A new roleplaying addition has been added into the mud.[67] It's 'moods' — essentially an adverb system for modifying your says, whispers, and talks.

What does it do?

Well, instead of the usual says that look like this:

```
Slasher says, 'Kill! I wanna kill!'
```

You might see any of the following:

```
Slasher says, eyes gleaming wickedly, 'Kill! I wanna kill!'
'Kill!' Slasher says, gibbering insanely. 'I wanna kill!'
'Kill! I wanna kill!' Slasher says, redfaced with anger.
```

The extra tags may or may not be there, but any of the different   placements of the speech tags might be.

How do I use it?

In order to speak says as listed above, you must have the eloquence skill. Once you have this skill, your says will automatically have the movable tags shown above. So will your whispers and your talks.

To add moods, you preface the regular say, talk, or whisper with a mood. For example:

You type:

```
SAD WHISPER JUJUBE I DON'T WANT TO DIE
```

They see:

```
'I don't want to die,' Slasher whispers sadly to you.
```

You type:

```
POUTING SAY YOU NEVER LIKE WHAT I SAY. YOU HATE ME.
```

They see:

---

[67] Moods were announced to the players on July 5th, 1995. See
https://www.legendmud.org/Community/lt_indices/Vol2/LTv2n28.html

```
'You never like what I say,' you say, lower lip trembling. 'You
hate me.'
```

You type:

```
SHY TALK CINDERELLA CAN I BE YOUR HERO?
```

They see:

```
Galahad says to you, eyes averted, 'Can I be your hero?'
```

That's a pain to type. Is there a shortcut?

Sure. Every mood abbreviates just like all other mud commands. You can simply cut it as short as possible so that it does not conflict with other commands, and it will work. Note that all regular mud abbreviations and socials have priority, so typing LOV will get you the love social, not the LOVING mood. For that you need to type LOVI at the least.

There's another shortcut, one which essentially adds over a hundred rather generic socials to the library.

You type:

```
DISTRACTED
```

They see:

```
PicnicBasket looks distracted.
```

Then you type:

```
SAY SORRY, SOMEONE TELLING TO ME.
```

And they see:

```
'Sorry, someone telling to me,' PicnicBasket says, mind clearly
elsewhere.
```

Using this method, the say will remember the last mood you entered.

Note! Either way, saying, whispering or talking clears the mood, and you have to enter it again if you want to use the same mood several times in a row. Which looks bad anyway.

If you use this two-part method, you can also do this:

```
ANNOYED
ANGRY ' HEY!
```

And they will see:

```
Huggermugger looks annoyed.
'Hey!' Huggermugger says angrily.
```

The latest mood will supersede the old one.

Cool! How many moods are there and how can I get a list?

There are currently 140 different moods. What's more, each mood has between one and three different speech tags that can be attached. To get a complete list of the moods, type MOOD. The full list is a little longer than a screen, so we advise you set SCREENLEN to something less than 23 to see it without getting spammed.

This is all ANNOYING. I hate it.

No problem! If you find yourself disliking this, just type MOOD OFF and you just won't see it anymore. :) You'll get the exact same messages you used to. Having mood off will also prevent your messages from being autocapitalized or punctuated for you.

People just entering the game may need to type MOOD ON to activate seeing it.

Help! Everything's getting split up into two sentences!

The punctuation marks that are read as ending sentences (? ! . and ...) are not interpreted as such when enclosed in () or "", so those of you who find stuff breaking in odd places may want to make use of the double quotes.

The interpreter will not split up stuff like ?!?!? or ??? but it may do it to really odd combos like !...!, and there's not much that can be done about it. :) Inventive typists can always find a way to defeat the system.

It DOES currently break, unfortunately, on Mr. and Mrs. and other abbreviations with periods after them. I suggest leaving off the periods. :) Maybe someday we can add a list to check for, but until we have the processor to ourselves I don't want to add that many if checks. :P

The double Huh? messages that those without eloquence are reporting will be gone soon.

So will the occasionally garbled messages that happen when there are many people in a room and someone uses talk with a mood to a specific other person (must be a given one in the order of who's in the room). In any case, that'll be fixed soon too. :)

Are there help files on this?

HELP ELOQUENCE explains how to use the basics.

HELP MOOD gives the syntax for the mood command.

Why can't everyone use this?

Because it's only for the eloquent, who have been waiting for some time for this skill to be useful.

Hey! Why can I be 'coy' but not 'flirtatious'? Can you add 'flirtatious'?

You can't be flirtatious because it's included in coy. There are a lot of adverbs you might want to use that are covered in others. We're not going to add 6 more synonyms for happy, when in practice the 4 or 5 that are there already cover 15 different ways of saying it. If you find a CATEGORY of emotion that is skipped (like, in the first version, I forgot completely about the many ways of being scared), please let me know and I will see if it can be added eventually. But don't ask for something that has a close parallel already.

Does this work with socials?

No, but who knows, it might work with some of them someday. Don't hold your breath.[68]

Why didn't you fix hellebore, add more spells, add more skills, write another area, or whatever else, instead of wasting time on a cosmetic thing like this?

Because this code wasn't for Legend but for a different project—I just happened to be able to port it. :) Count your blessings.

-Ptah

The other project was a virtual mall that Kristen and I developed on top of the LegendMUD codebase for our local Internet Service Provider in Tuscaloosa, dbTech. This was a MUD where you could walk around and visit virtual versions of real shops in the town. The hope on the part of the ISP was that they would be able to get their business customers to join the project and run virtual versions of the shops. Employees would sit online in the virtual shops and take orders there, or even receive them via MUDmail. Local citizens would be able to wander around the mall and get to know local businesses.

We built a bunch of the mall, and even some of the shop rooms. But it never launched, as far as I know. We did get comped free Internet services for quite a while, and I even did home tech support visits to help people get their modems set up for dial-up to dbTech.

The moods system, much later on, went into Star Wars Galaxies, *with the addition that it tied into the animations on your character.*

---

[68] It eventually did.

AFK chat

Which made me think back to a feature that I put into *LegendMUD* in 1995 or 96. We already had an AFK command. It used to be

```
> AFK
```

and when someone sent you a tell, they got

```
Ptah is away from the keyboard.
```

but then we added

```
> AFK Grabbing something to eat.
```

which relayed that status to the user.

But then we said "gosh, scrolling back through all of these missed tells is very annoying!" So we added a feature to record the tells you missed. When you came back, you typed

```
> AFK
```

and got back something like

```
While you were away, you got these messages:
Charity: Hey, we're thinking of dinner at Rudy's, wanna come?
Charity: Oh never mind, I see you ate. :)
```

At the time, I thought of this as an answering machine. Now it seems like a direct message in Twitter.

Perhaps a recipe for the next big viral technologies on the Internet is go through the various basic things that were present in muds, and figure out the HTTP-based versions of them that people would want in the sidebars of their browsers.

When we think of the Internet going virtual-worldy, it's going to be on the back of technologies like these, rather than our classic conception of what a virtual world is. It will be by absorbing all the features of virtual worlds except placeness, because placeness will be embedded rather than being the context.

=-=

DID YOU KNOW: Tips and tricks and little-used features

Hate to miss tells when you get up for a minute or your friends think you're ignoring their tells, when all you did was go grab some lunch? You can use the AFK command as a sort of "answering machine" for you when you need to go Away From the Keyboard. There is an 8K maximum on the messages you can save—any past that point will be lost. They are not saved from AFK session to session and renting also clears your buffer.

AFK <message> will set an automatic reply message for you and put you in AFK mode. While you are AFK, that status will be shown in your prompt. You can still use any commands while you are in AFK mode. But if you have set up an "outgoing message" those who send you tells will get that as a reply.

AFK used without any arguments when you are not already in AFK mode will put your character into a tell logging mode. This will log the messages like traditional AFK, but no outgoing message will be sent to the person sending you the tell.

AFK without a message takes you out of AFK state if you were in that state. Any messages you might have received via tell will then be reported back to you. We strongly advise that you turn screenlen on (see HELP SCREENLEN) or have backscroll enabled before turning AFK off. Otherwise, if you receive numerous messages, the report may scroll off your screen, resulting in their loss; similarly, some players with slower connections may find themselves disconnected by the barrage of messages.

Are you tired of seeing "You must clear your AFK buffer now. It is full."? Are your friends complaining about the spam you make when you need to check/clear/change your AFK messages?

AFK CHECK will show you your current AFK message is and any tells with the time they were received without deleting them.

AFK CLEAR is the same as typing AFK with no arguments except that you will remain in AFK mode with the same outgoing message if any.

AFK SET <message> will change it without having your AFK buffer sent to you.

You can always get more information about these commands online by checking out HELP AFK and HELP SCREENLEN.[69]

=-=

---

[69] Tips and Tricks article from the Legendary Times, Vol. 9, Issue 4, from Jan. 26, 2002.

Living with playerkilling

Playerkilling on LegendMUD required joining a clan. But even then, it wasn't that common early on, so people joined clans as social groups. Then we started to get the first players who were truly aggressive... and everything started to change. As you can see, we didn't understand what had happened, and instead urged the roleplayers to instead learn to live with it. Thus began the eternal conflict. This essay is from The Legendary Times of Feb 19th, 1995;[70] interviewing with Origin would actually start only a few months later.

Living with Playerkilling

by Ptah

Recently with the advent of Sylia and Bremmar as menaces to society and as playerkillers with few compunctions and even less remorse, there has been a great deal of argument and controversy over playerkilling (pk).

Let me start off by mentioning some of the things I have been asked to do in the last few days:

- delete Sylia and Bremmar on the grounds that they are mean
- restrict pk to 5 levels instead of 10
- not permit you to clan till 15th or else enable permadeath at 10th
- ban immortals from playing clanned characters
- ban immortals from playing mortals at all
- remove all penalties and rewards from pk—no XP loss or gain

---

[70] https://www.legendmud.org/Community/lt_indices/Vol2/LTv2n14.html

Some of the rumors I have had told to me:

- Bremmar cheated in a way that is not possible in the code
- immortals are in some sort of conspiracy to prevent players from levelling
- the mud officially encourages bullies

Let me start by assuring all of you that there is no such conspiracy, that we as immortals were indeed concerned with how stagnant and dull the clans had gotten, and to that end decided to liven things up with some roleplay. (Please note that Sylia is not an immortal's character). But immortals are not going on some pk rampage to destroy the playerbase. :P We have no reason whatsoever to do this.

The immortals of Legend are not particularly willing to change the pk system that has been working quite well till now. Most of the complaints center around the fact that a well-prepared high lvl character can ambush and defeat almost anyone. Unfortunately, this is true. Also unfortunately, this cannot be coded against, nor should it be really as it is how life works.

Likewise, someone ambushed is at a severe disadvantage in any fight, and there isn't much we can do about players getting killed because they were not alert enough, not prepared enough, or not expecting attack. It is part of the hazard of being pk enabled.

By my count we have the following conflicts going or near to going:[71]

- Sylia and Bremmar have killed several Bards
- Sylia and Bremmar have killed a Knight
- Edith, an Antipaladin, has killed a Bard
- Someone has attempted to kill Edith
- Some Hermetics seem to side with Sylia and Bremmar despite the alliances the Hermetics have with the Knights

All of the above are cases where the victim is someone with a substantial support group behind them. Now is the time for the clans to serve their defensive purpose; but it is not likely that the immorts will somehow code things so that they don't have to.

What I can do is help you work on fighting strategies that can help you survive the current violent climate.

1) remember, this is just a game

2) since you know who the violent people are, don't antagonize them unless you intend to back it up with a fight. This includes activities such as spying on them while invisible, guppy-bashing, or whatever else you think might set off a homicidal maniac

---

[71] It is rather hilarious today how *small* a problem this actually was!

3) never rest in the open where you are easily discovered, if you think you are or might be on a Hit List. I suggest to you that currently all Knights, Bards, and Antipaladins are on *someone's* hit list, as any of the attackers above have grounds to consider themselves in danger from the clans.

4) choose your ground. Don't fight in rooms with closeable exits. If you're a water mage, don't fight on land or indoors. Don't move farther away from your clan trans mob when someone is after you.

5) use your clan channels! This is the safest way to get in touch with your friends, fill them in on the situation, and not reveal your location.

6) if you know that whoever is after is strong and you cannot fight them toe to toe, make the tough call: honor or living to fight another day, perhaps dishonorably. if you truly regard the enemy as a homicidal maniac then they have no honor and you can feel free, I would think, to bash their heads in next time you see them sleeping, and think that you have done the world a favor. Maybe it'll get you expelled from your stuffy clan, but you will have saved the world... think about it

7) surveillance of dangerous people is a must. Use clan channel and tells to keep an eye out for likely killers. When you see them weakened, or fighting a tough mob, may be the best chance to do them in.

8) Blind. Entrance. Stun. Weaken. Idiocy. Steal. Clumsiness. etc. The weaker your opponent, the better chance you have of surviving.

9) Ambush, ambush, ambush. It is a military verity that the attacker has the advantage.

10) Leave your escape routes open but try to block theirs. Kill their clan trans mobs. Kill the innkeepers, if you can and dare. (Remember that this will affect other people and may just get you more enemies).

11) Don't do it alone. Get help. And make the help the sort that plays to your own weaknesses. Mages, find bards and tanks and healers. Warriors, look for magical help and healing. A well-organized team can take *anything*.

12) make good use of tactics like shooting them from another room, throwing things at them, etc, to lure them into places where you have the upper hand.

13) If you really can't handle the heat, rent. This may get you called names but you are *alive* and can fight another day.

There are countless other tactics and methods, this just scratches the surface. You could play friends, ask them to group with you in the Savanna, then assist the elephant. You could do the Seoni jungle quest with them and then leave them trapped in the tunnel. You could hire an assassin, be it of the Assassin clan or not.

What I would beg you not to do is to spread more rumors about how the immorts are out to get you, about how unfair the system is to the weak, and about how players who are simply playing the game with an eye towards capricious evil are necessarily jerks. Remember that the *player* and the *character* are not one and the same. Remember it's only a game, albeit one a lot like real life in some ways.

Just like real life, the strong can prey on the weak, until the weak get organized. This is why you have *clans* and aren't all rogues. It's time for the clans to take some action.

Fumbling around with bad behavior

You could earn a "string coupon" on *LegendMUD*. What this allowed was "restringing" an item — changing the text string that describes it, which effectively changed its appearance to anything at all. Players mostly did this to their weapons and armor to change it into looking like items that outright didn't exist within the game.

Coupons were mostly handed out for winning at games, such as recall tag or trivia; for doing something that an immortal thought was worthy of reward, such as maybe helping out a newbie; or for winning Expies, which were the in-game awards voted on by players. In fact, there was even an Expies category for most creative strings:

```
Best Strung Item

1994: K'MALA — a razor-sharp wit (a weapon)

1995: TAD — his various bits of dirt.

1996: ULRIC — Necronomicon

1997: BRONWYN — an irate-looking hedgehog (a weapon)

1998: MYRELLA — her cleavage (a container)

1999: VANDERVECKEN — the Flying Dutchman

2000: GRUNT — <above head> a dimly lit light bulb

WOLFRAM — <used as shield> nothing...real men use no shields

2001: FRAEGIS — delicately-sculpted demon

2003: DOMINGO — a badly-dented grey metal folding chair

2004: MCNUGGET — lethal levels of cholesterol[72]
```

Having a full set of strung gear was therefore a huge status symbol. Roleplayers who wanted to a complete a custom outfit head to toe would need 21 coupons to cover every single piece of visible gear (including rings, earrings, and so on). And if they were also players who took the combat aspect of the game seriously, they of course would want to only string the best items they had access to, since they wanted to maximize their combat effectiveness and *also* look stylish.

---

[72] https://www.legendmud.org/Community/expie.php

This all meant that coupons were the single most valuable thing in the entire game.

Coupons were eventually pretty easy to come by, and it was believed that relatively easy access to them helped roleplay by allowing players to really and truly customize their characters. However, stringing items wasn't something players could do; you had to call an immortal who had the power to do it, hand them the coupon, and recite what you wanted. In was quite a heavy "customer service" load.

A player suggested that maybe players themselves could be trusted with the text:

> Why be sooooo unreasonable about such a little detail! Let the players be responsible for their own stringing of items. Maybe a system could be set up that gave the players the right to change a strung's short description to whatever they liked.... a mob ooc could be used..or a command that would check for existing short desc's of in game items to make sure that item is in deed strung... after checking the player would just input the value of the short desc and it would be changed.... if the player abuses such a privilege and is caught wearing offensive items or uncalled for items, then these privileges could be revoked and either never be allowed to restring an item again, or have to go through an imm until the flag can be removed once trust is established again... I hate to say it, but we are being treated like children with a dangerous toy.

Today, of course, the idea of trusting players with the ability to customize absolutely anything in absolutely any way would horrify just about any customer service representative. The reaction "treated like children with a dangerous toy" would likely simply result in nods of agreement from most.

One of the most interesting aspects of reading discussions from this time period is the way in which hypothetical objections to "good enough" solutions were so often something I reached for. The reason has to do with the burgeoning flexibility that text MUDs were achieving, flexibility which I was interested in chasing.

For example, on *Legend* you could create an illusion. This was a command that let you type in absolutely anything, and make it look like what you typed was in the room, such as:

```
A cat is here.
```

Oh, someone with "detect illusion" or "detect magic" would see it as

```
An illusion of 'A cat is here.'
```

...But just picture the degree to which this could be used as a form of harassment! It was far more often used for silly pranks, for brief artworks, or as a tactic in competitive playerkilling. The Expies had a category for these too[73], and you can see

---

[73] https://www.legendmud.org/Community/expie_win.html

the range that other players found amusing enough to vote as favorites each year:

```
Best Illusion
1996: TERRORSPAWN's Santa runs you over with the sleigh DT.
1997: MAGIUS' [Auction]: Cuchullain's shield min bid 50k
1998: Agni tells you, 'Ah, so that's who your alt is....'
1999: TRAMPLE (???)
2000: The fight round in the 'Crossing the English Ocean' room
2001: PLAGASGRAW's grazing cattle
2002: RAEWYN's Carian Trag Castle
2003: AKIRA's imm corpses
2004: SPANISH-FLEA with Wren Traps
```

The winner in 2000 looked *exactly* like a complete fight happening in the room you were in — because, of course, the world was made of text, the fight messages were text, the other people were text. The winner in 1998 looked exactly like a private message that happened to arrive when you entered the room, and the one in 1997 just like an actual item for sale offered on the public auction channel (it was a highly context-dependent joke based on the rarity of that item).

More problematic were types of illusions that had physical concreteness if you didn't know they were an illusion. On *LegendMUD*, the most powerful of these were the various "wall" spells. You could create a wall of stone illusion that blocked an exit from a room, or a "wall of flames" that damaged anyone who moved through it — call it psychosomatic damage. If you could see through the illusion, the walls didn't work on you.

What did playerkillers do? They promptly walled up the doors to all the inns, so that their opponents couldn't run away and log off. This of course inconvenienced everyone, not just the intended victim. At first we had to create a policy that simply said "STOP walling up the inns, as we will dispel such walls as we come to them. We do this not to take sides but simply because it has become a real inconvenience for newbies and for the unclanned.[74]" (Eventually, the code was upgraded such that illusory walls obeyed the general PK rules and couldn't block non-PvP characters at all).

This sort of flexibility is what could lead to debates such as whether or not an "ignore" command could really work effectively on a sufficiently robust MUD. For example, consider this debate from Usenet in 1995 between myself and Brandon van

---

[74] https://www.legendmud.org/Community/lt_indices/Vol2/LTv2n23.html

Every[75]:

> Brandon:
>
> Algorithms can give people the power of an infallible
> @IGNORE, which in turn settles all disputes with
> terrible finality.

Me:

Incorrect assumption here that I had to point out. "All
disputes related to what one player can do to another
directly."

> Don't assume anything about what _I'M_ assuming. I'm
> talking about handling all the indirect, covert
> harassments as well. It's a technologically demanding
> problem, but it is definitely achievable.

Jerk kills NPC. You come looking for NPC. Its death is
tagged Jerk, so it didn't happen for you? Sorry, I do
not see how this is technologically achievable at any
PRACTICAL level under CERTAIN situations related to
game design. It's not an infallible cover-all-cases
solution, just a very very good one.

[What about] slanderous remarks that affect how others
deal with you?

> Much as in real life, you don't have to hang out with
> people who think badly of you. You can take what they
> say with a grain of salt, you can ignore them, or if the
> problem really disturbs you, you can @IGNORE them. In
> real life you can't jail people for having a bad opinion
> about you and saying so to others. ("Slander and libel"
> have very narrow legal definitions that we've already
> talked about, so don't bother bringing them up
> again.) MUDs are unusual in that they allow for such
> Thought Policing. Ordinary humans are expected to deal
> with such problems themselves. If you want to hang
> around with a bunch of lookey-loos who gossip about what
> a slut you are, that's your prerogative... most people
> find other circles to hang out and pay attention to.

---

[75] https://groups.google.com/d/topic/rec.games.mud.misc/M-mWcp1C3AA/discussion

To use the mimic example, someone mimics your actions and then zaps the mimic. No Jerk tag is left behind to show a trace, and there is nothing TO ignore except the bad word.

Yes, in RL we live with this, argue our side, ignore those who are jerks towards us on the basis of false info. Unfortunately, on a mud INFO IS REALITY because it's all you get. Large ethical dimension here... a log would 'prove' that it was you, you see, short of constant logging that would then need backtraced—proof could quite possibly come through email, for example. And since this is not an illegal action on anyone's part, someone's virtual life has been affected to a large degree on the basis of poor informational quality. And this may very well be an issue that affects them deeply, depending on their personal beliefs and principles.

[What about] alteration of the server environment in a manner that restricts play (changing around rooms or npcs, etc, countless possibles). That which affects the environment cannot be simply @IGNOREd.

> Not true! Here you assume too much. Let's say you've got a harasser named Jerk. You can tag all his actions with (origin Jerk). When these actions change the appearances of objects, then the data storage for those objects also gets the tag (origin Jerk). Every change of state that Jerk causes in the environment, directly or indirectly, whether through 1 intermediary or 5000, bears the fingerprint (origin Jerk). And thus the Jerk can be @IGNOREd by anyone.

When they alter exits in a location? A map that changes based on who you happen to ignore? Oh boy... What about the existence of loaded NPCs? Interactions of Jerk with other players, player whom you are NOT ignoring, interactions which may have relevance to you?

> Existing MUDs can't do this, but a from-scratch rewrite of a MUD server could. Processing and storage aren't as big a deal as you might think. Most players aren't Jerks, first of all.

It doesn't matter how many players are jerks—it only matters how many use @IGNORE for the side effects I am talking about to being to develop.

> Second, you can trace actions directly from Jerk as he performs them, so usually you don't have to store any object state. Third, if object state is really a problem, you could limit the number of game players to something modest like 128 players. If each player is represented by 1 bit, then that's only a 32-byte origin tag per object. Across 10,000 game objects that's only 320K of storage – not a bad price, for totally eliminating the need for admins. And since (origin Jerk) tags are expected to be infrequent, a simple origin list would probably yield better storage characteristics.

Again, this assumes simple alterations of the database, not anything with complexity. Which would depend on how much ability you place in the hands of players. I can see @IGNORE with not trouble in a Diku stock, and with major hassle on a MOO where anyone can extend the world. Consider a gaming system whereby you ignore Jerk, Jerk can make items, said items get used by others, perhaps against you? Where do you stop seeing his effects? If the items he makes cannot affect you, why then, ignoring everyone at strategic moments could prove most useful...

Other options apply including player systems of justice, since you seek to avoid admins. But i think discussion of that side of things is likely to get heated as well.

> Leaving it in the hands of humans is only so much politics and fallibility. I have nothing else to say on that matter.

So is RL :)

I'll say it again: on a mud the world is information. That means that ethics on a mud are informational. Blocking off information from unwanted sources is excellent in principle and on certain levels, but can be very pernicious depending on the amount of freedom the populace has.

Not objecting to the idea of an @IGNORE btw. :) I agree
with most everything you say. But you DO have certain
underlying assumptions here, and I'd be more interested
in hearing about the other design aspects (such as the
level to which players can impact the database) that
impact upon the discussion. Those are the assumptions
to which I was referring. :) What system is this mud
designed to be? An infallible backtracing ignore like
you describe could well wreak utter havoc on a
consistent [role-playing] world with player economy or
a gaming world, while working well on something else
with less player alteration or extension of database.

Over time, the answer to this and similar debates was in fact to reduce the power
that players had. No illusions, no stringing, no setting whatever title you liked on your
character, profanity filters everywhere, and eventually, no dropping items on the
ground, no collision between players, no trading of items, and so on. Just think: MUDs
didn't generally need a secure trade system![76]

LegendMUD around 1997 did add a "gag" command; what would today be called
"mute." Kristen implemented it. The syntax was simple, and only applied to private
messages ("tells"), a clear sign of how times have changed!

Syntax: gag	Lists people from whom tells will be ignored.
Syntax: ungag	Clears the list of people ignored.
Syntax: gag	Adds a name to your list, online or not.
Syntax: ungag	Removes a name from your list, online or not.

If you feel you are being harassed by another player through tells,
you can choose to ignore any and all tells from that player until
you remove them from your list. The list saves when you rent. The
administration still welcomes any and all reports of harassment,
but this command was added so players could take some defensive
action themselves.

Repeated use of these commands against a particular player or
character will result in an investigation by the admin department
as all uses of these commands are logged.

---

[76] It is common on MMOs for a trading system to include a custom interface in which both players
place their proposed items or valuables to trade in a sort of "escrow" window, and the trade does not
take place until both participants have had the chance to mutually verify what the other players are
giving. Then the swap happens instantly and simultaneously when both sides approve. Any change to
the contents automatically negates previous apprvals to force players to verify the exchange again.
On MUDs, you had "give <item> <person>."

A couple of months after it went in, we got this complaint on the game's discussion boards:

> hmm ... till now this mud was rather friendly, but that command will cause that it will become unfriendlier ... as soon as more people will ignore people coz they are ignored...[77]

Today, of course, the idea that being able to mute offensive players would make an environment *less* friendly sounds ludicrous. But that's the sort of difference that scale made, and a tight community. The gag command was often used between people who were actually *friends* but were just exasperated with one another, not too dissimilar from how people might ignore your texts today.

As an example, at one point a random troll showed up on the MUD and started pestering everyone. The incident was notable enough to be written up in The Legendary Times. It also prompted an editor's note that gives an idea of to what degree immortal fiat was not considered the right approach to solving problems:

```
Legend is a place with a mature atmosphere and we'd like to keep it
that way. We realize that telling YOU this instead of the Net is
sort of preaching to the converted, but it's better than not
telling anyone. :) You guys manage to make an enjoyable place to be
thanks to your polite and considerate natures. It is because we
enjoy such a range of ages and professions and walks of life on the
mud that we ask that people not behave in manners that are rude.
Thank you for respecting the beliefs of others and please do let us
know if you feel someone has been personally insulting towards you
(as a player, not as a character, that is). Of course, this can
get hard to determine in cases of roleplaying, in which case we
encourage you to go to the OOC and hash it out. That's what "Out of
Character" is for.
```

Another case called "The Joe6 incident" was met with not only site-banning the entire Internet service provider for the troll, but letters were written to the service provider requesting that they take action against the individual in question. Yes, you could "lose your right to Internet" over bad behavior on a MUD.

LegendMUD eventually even had a "Roll of Shame," which functioned very much like a police blotter.[78] Players could read about infractions of the rules, with names redacted, to get a sense of how much "crime" was going on. By 1997, players could actually type WARN to see a list of all the warnings they might have accrued if they violated policies — sort of like seeing their criminal record.

---

[77] From https://www.legendmud.org/Community/discuss/discussion_98/disc_98_012.html
[78] The first example appears to be in November of 1996.

And yet, the playerkilling debates, and even political protests against the admins using playerkilling as the method (read this as "wholesale slaughter of everyone they could kill," as a means of protest), meant that the game continued to shed veteran players who were simply exasperated by what had been a friendly environment changing into a ruthless one. One admin who was already largely inactive was fired for supporting this protest using a regular character, rather than discussing the issues with fellow immortals. We never took the step of barring immortals from playerkilling, but probably should have; it took quite a while to get around to barring them from having their immortal character online at the same time as a clanned character, in fact.

A few years further on, I was in a debate (once again on Usenet) with Ultima Online players over the feasibility of a PK switch. In it, I argued that a PK switch had simply never been done without it causing huge admin load. I advanced the hypothetical scenario of a non-PvP player hiring a playerkiller to kill a third (playerkill-enabled) target.

> -PvP hires PvP A to kill PvP B. I've listed this one many many times before, and people just answer with "well, PvP B is PvP, he knew what he signed up for." Which is an invalid answer— the -PvP player broke the rules. But there is no recourse in code and no way of detecting it.
>
> …You start getting really weird things whereby PvP+ groups can send in a character marked PvP- through blockades to take indirect action, etc. Say you have a guildhall. You can't keep the -PvP guy out, and he is actually a member of a PvP guild who will let the others in once you leave… etc.

Players by and large didn't see any issues with this:

- This is perhaps the most illogical and silly response I've seen. Who exactly in your example [cough] is the aggrieved party ? PvP A broke NO rules.
- How did he break the rules? What rules? Remember, the PVP victim *knew* he could be killed by other players. He didn't have the switch on.
- -PvP doesn't directly kill PvP B. A PvP is attacking another PvP which is not an exploit. if 10 PvP's attack PvP B does it make it an exploit? no that's just tough life in the PvP Environment and asking for recourse is absurd. The playing field still maintains it's same amount of fairness vs anything else. In order for PvP B to be attacked it must be by a another PvPer regardless of the motives. I wouldn't consider that an exploit, A trivial one at best.
- Most of this can already happen with blue players/non-guild players/throwaway characters - just res and keep moving.

- This is called hiring an assassin... which has perfectly good role-playing foundations, and imho is acceptable, and doesn't affect the pvp switch.
- How is this breaking the rules?? PvP A is role-playing an assassin. He is hired for a job and completes it. <gasp> They were role-playing. How dare they?? PvP A actually killing someone for a reason instead of randomly killing the first innocent player he comes across.
- Nonsense. He paid someone to take a risk. If the person wins great. If not the guys is out all his stuff, and pvp- guy lost his cash for no reason.

My response was, "you are assuming that it is fair for a member of group A to harm a member of group B, but NOT for the reverse to happen. PvP B does indeed have a legitimate complaint—he is being discriminated against.[79]" This was a point of view driven by trying to fit all the types of players in one game, of course, and according them equal value — driven by past experiences on *LegendMUD* where engaging in player vs player was basically a sports-like activity, rather than a griefing one.

Leaving aside that argument, was I wrong about the scenario coming to pass? Only sort of. Here is a description a year later of a set of fixes to the code includ[80]ing a whole host of weird edge case workarounds:

> In the new update being published as we speak, criminals cannot resurrect nor use the bank (tackling bank thieves and tag team thieves there), a whole bunch of UOE/UOP tricks are fixed, the potions-with-bow thing is fixed (common PK tactic), monster gating is disallowed (also common PK tactic), ordering pets and hirelings to be friends with inanimate objects (blue PK trick), vended items outside of vendors (PK trick), arrow dupe, moving with res menu up (house break-in), and various rep system flagging problems are fixed...

Later on we would see challenges in *EverQuest* around the practice of "training mobs" — meaning, attacking a high level mob thereby making it angry, then leading it to a location where there were low level players, and letting it wreak havoc.

Most concretely, the higher end gameplay in the famously unfriendly space MMO *EVE Online* is strongly driven by exactly the example I gave, with entire huge guilds falling prey to undercover characters and characters who turn out to be secretly working for opponent PvP guilds[81]. The stories make for great narratives, and perhaps

[79] https://groups.google.com/d/topic/rec.games.computer.ultima.online/CxSmS_RuyIw/discussion
[80] https://groups.google.com/d/topic/rec.games.computer.ultima.online/LEDhQX_qbkU/discussion
[81] See "The EVE upset," https://www.raphkoster.com/2009/02/11/the-eve-upset/. "For the uninitiated: there was a huge aliance named Band of Brothers. There was another clan named GoonSwarm who hated them (*edit: well, everyone, really*) and worked against them, but was not nearly as big or powerful. GoonSwarm would recruit BoB members in order to scam them. A BoB member joined under these false pretenses, but then chose sides and rather than be scammed, asked to join for real — and offered up

can be extrapolated out to the issues we see today in terms of moderation on social media.

This freedom versus friendliness debate would continue to be recapitulated over the course of virtual world history. *Second Life* would allow scripting and importation of art, and the result would be a swarm of flying penises attacking someone. Game worlds with huge customer bases would disallow dropping items on the ground or even trading them, because of the damage players could do to one another with the most basic interactions. You haven't been able to collide with a player in another virtual world probably since around the year 2000.

By that same year my views had firmed up:

> Raph, is it really worth trying to reform grief players?

```
No, I'd rather ban them. I want to reform the people
who WOULD [not] be grief players [but] are acting out
because they can't find any other way to have fun
because the games are too limited.
```

And for that matter,

> But on the switch—well, I was around three feet away from the lead developers of both AC and EQ when they said, "If I had to do it over again, I would not do a PK switch" to an audience of 300 people at GDC... Both of them were saying they'd just ditch PvP entirely. They wouldn't bother with a switch because of the headaches it causes versus the reward of having it.[82]

How much of what was left after all these changes could be called "a virtual world" remains as open question, to my mind. After all, quite a lot of the magical power that they afforded was sucked out of them, in the process of making them safer. I still miss strung items and illusions and yeah, even the tactical combat afforded by player-to-player collision. But the trade-off was, and continues to be, between a rich virtual world with a lot less people in it, and large scale with something noticeably poorer. Something that, in the end, is more of a plain old game that happens to have other people in it.

BoB as his price of entry. He was a high-level admin of BoB, and he basically disbanded the whole thing, destroying it from within, and GoonSwarm made piles of virtual money."

[82] https://groups.google.com/forum/#!original/rec.games.computer.ultima.online/pxNCYp-UKCk/TcKjMlTWMA8J

An Open Forum on the Future of LegendMud

The following is a highly edited log of an open forum on "the future of the mud" held the night of 7/8/95. The original log can be found at https://www.legendmud.org/Community/lectures/future.html.

The first half of the discussion that was trimmed away focuses on the issue of roleplaying. The second half of the discussion, reproduced here, was on the issue of the mud as a virtual society and community, and how to (and whether to) establish rules of behavior and facilities for thinking of it in that way.

PTAH: OK, now, because this other subject is near and dear to both my heart and his, I'm going to ask Bay_El-Lor to speak first, but let me frame the questions. I dunno how many of you have read Seph's interview of me in the LT?[83]

Crowe nods his agreement with you. A sea-worn mariner nods solemnly.

PTAH: Half of it anyway.

Seph smiles at a sea-worn mariner. Seph is avoiding recognition Farslayer claps for Seph approvingly. Seph grins evilly. Crowe applauds Seph's quick thinking and good judgement. Wraith applauds Seph's quick thinking and good judgement. A sea-worn mariner cheers for Seph – huzzah!

PTAH TO SEPH: Too late.

Wraith smiles at Seph. Seph blushes bright red.

PTAH: OK. so let me get to the actual subject. I tend to think of muds in general and especially this mud as being not just games and not just rp environments, but also societies.

---

[83] The full interview can be found on my website at https://www.raphkoster.com/games/interviews-and-panels/ptah-god-of-the-mud/. At the time of this log, half of it had been published in the Legendary Times; the other half would be posted the following week.

Crowe nods his agreement with you. A lithe wild-eyed girl nods solemnly.

PTAH: You've heard me rant about ethics in a mud framework, I'm sure.

Ptah chuckles politely. Farslayer nods solemnly. A lithe wild-eyed girl giggles. ParticleMan nods solemnly.

PTAH: And about countless other things as well.

A tall muscular Swede with piercing eyes hasn't but...

PTAH: I think this third side of the server (I am shifting off of the term mud purposely here), the social side, which includes the educational side, etc, is very important.

A man wearing a #23 Bulls jersey applauds Ptah's quick thinking and good judgement.

PTAH: If we talked about MUDs and MUSHes before, this is MUCK territory here. Not only this meeting but others, and earlier events ranging from the Halloween scary stories night held around a bonfire right here, to Dominic's excellent talk on military life as a medic, are about that social aspect. And of course the mud's theme lends itself to this aspect as well.

Seph nods solemnly.

PTAH: In the interview I make the point that in a sense a mud society cannot evolve a very long way because it relies upon immortals, upon imps, who perforce administer, maintain, and extend the system. All major changes must be filtered through them, and it is not an elected position. Here, anyway.

A tall muscular Swede with piercing eyes chuckles politely.

SEPH: Uh oh.

A tall muscular Swede with piercing eyes is having that problem on his mud. Seph cringes while pondering what is coming next.

PTAH: So my question to you is, how effective is this side of the system, from mud parties to ethics of interaction (are there any other kind of ethics?), and how might it develop further given that limitation? I'd like to ask Bay_El-Lor to speak first.

Ptah grins evilly at a sea-worn mariner. A sea-worn mariner looks up into the sky and ponders. Ptah lobs a slow easy one at ya. A lithe wild-eyed girl sighs loudly. A sea-worn mariner wishes he hadn't been sipping rye all night.

PTAH: Yes, I actually spend waking hours thinking of this sort of thing.

You snicker softly. Seph chuckles politely at your feeble witticism. A tall muscular Swede with piercing eyes thinks Ptah has too much spare time.

BAY_EL-LOR: I don't know what to say, rightly .. Except the forum here is underused ... We have an environment where, educationally, theoretically, we can do most anything ... Clans are confined to mages, thieves, warriors ... What if they proposed tougher challenges?

Crowe looks very confused.

BAY_EL-LOR TO CROWE: Crowe ... I know you're something of a detective .. What if every knight had to undergo a serious knight training quest?

NHOJ: Hmm...

BAY_EL-LOR: What if every secretive had to really learn something?

CROWE: Is this rhetorical or direct?

BAY_EL-LOR: What if the interaction between our groups .. Was more than casual .. Colleges play at model UNs .. Here we have the chance to play that game with real loves and lives .. Because when we can't agree, someone dies.

Ptah mentions that the design for the new martial arts system will be detailed enough and specific enough that you will perforce learn about the differences between karate and tai chi, whether you want to or not :)

BAY_EL-LOR: I don't know what you were looking for from me Ptah ...

PTAH TO BAY_EL-LOR: Thoughts, any thoughts. :)

KEIKO TO BAY_EL-LOR: Ethics...

BAY_EL-LOR: But as an interactive system, this seems to me to be way beyond anything we played with in high school .. Or college .. Or graduate school..

Crowe smiles happily.

BAY_EL-LOR: A chance to make from nothing something.

SEPH TO PTAH: There aren't THAT many of us ...why don't you open the forum enough crowe can ask questions, or answer?

KEIKO TO BAY_EL-LOR: For example the council you wanted to establish...

CROWE: Well...

A sea-worn mariner nods his agreement with a lithe wild-eyed girl.

Ptah mentions that as a society, you do not NEED our permission to create social constructs

CROWE TO BAY_EL-LOR: First of all, i think things such as you mentioned regarding challenges for clans are really up to the GM. You could make every secretive learn things, if you wanted.

A sea-worn mariner shakes his head.

BAY_EL-LOR: I can't ...

CROWE TO BAY_EL-LOR: Why not?

A sea-worn mariner holds his tongue A sea-worn mariner looks up into the sky and ponders. Crowe shrugs helplessly.

BAY_EL-LOR: May I speak?

CROWE: Go ahead.

BAY_EL-LOR: Simply because I'm in a world, and I need the support of other GMs .. It's like a single employer paying employees more—it can't work alone.

KEIKO: But it can.

A man wearing a #23 Bulls jersey looks up into the sky and ponders.

CROWE TO BAY_EL-LOR: It really does depend on how you run things.

KEIKO TO BAY_EL-LOR: By setting a good example and strengthening one clan, the others will follow or fall.

BAY_EL-LOR TO KEIKO: We would hope so, wouldn't we?

KEIKO: Very much so.

PTAH: Um, I might mention that social structures are not limited to clans, or to unofficial rp clans, or such.

CROWE TO BAY_EL-LOR: The Knights DO only clan those that fit the knight profile, and have proven themselves in our eyes.

WRAITH: What if GMs could ostracize members as a punishment instead of just pkilling or kicking them out?

PTAH: We might as well discuss why nobody else volunteered for talks in this room after Dom did his.

A lithe wild-eyed girl peers at Crowe, looking him up and down. A sea-worn mariner peers at Ptah.

KEIKO: I thought you arranged the one with Dom, and wasn't it supposed to be first in a lecture series... Oh I'd like to say something else...

PTAH: Yes, it was. But despite an open call for more talks, nobody felt they could or would.

PTAH TO WRAITH: I'd add, why hardcode something that people can do themselves without code?

A lithe wild-eyed girl can't imagine what she'd talk about. A tall muscular Swede with piercing eyes will talk on multi-culturalism or languages any time.

PTAH TO KEIKO: Real life herbs? Programming? Your rp world?

KEIKO: Oh. Well ok.

PTAH: ANYTHING.

WRAITH: Because you could enforce the punishment without having to rely on members to follow through.

PTAH: We are talking about a chance for interaction far beyond the scope offered at even a university, in some ways.

A sea-worn mariner nods his agreement with Ptah.

PTAH TO WRAITH: Then is it a valid punishment?

KEIKO: So you are talking about use of ooc as a meeting place beyond the game?

Ptah shifts to Socratic method and cackles.

WRAITH: There's a poor communications system right now too.

SEPH: Why don't you give some examples Ptah.

PTAH TO KEIKO: Am I? My point is that WE define this.

A tall muscular Swede with piercing eyes nods his agreement with Ptah.

KEIKO TO PTAH: Oh ok well I want to say something.

SEPH: Our imaginations are limited.

WRAITH: You can't just post it on a board that so-and-so is to be ignored.

Ptah would actually rather people had their own examples.

CROWE TO PTAH: Thing is, just like RP, the players have to WANT that level of society. While most people do, there are those that really are just here to kill mobs.

PTAH TO WRAITH: Why not? It works in rl.

PTAH TO CROWE: Is that an obstacle for the rest of us?

CROWE: Not at all.

Ptah is quite serious about Socratic method here

PTAH TO CROWE: Then why is that an objection?

A tall muscular Swede with piercing eyes agrees with Crowe. Crowe didn't say it was. Crowe chuckles politely.

WRAITH TO PTAH: Because mortals can't post right now, they would have to use email which is outside of the MUD and not everyone would want to give out their email address.

PTAH: Well. Let me tell you that as a teacher,[84] some of the most FUN times for me online have been talking about things.

CROWE: But there are many subtle levels of motivation.

PTAH: I've gotten a name for lecturing.

Ptah hangs his head. Seph nods solemnly.

PTAH: But I think that it is VALUABLE.

SATSU: I'll talk for a while on something...

PTAH: And in fact as valuable as the game.

SEPH: Er about fun times from talking.

PTAH: As valuable as the fantasies of rp.

Satsu nods his agreement with you. Seph has yet to leave ooc and is still having fun.

SATSU: But its only valuable to you.

PTAH TO SATSU: Is it? What do you think?

SATSU: What I mean by that statement is.. Different people place different values on different things.

PTAH: Hopefully, unless I am a totally pompous windbag, it's valuable to others as well.

SATSU: You and I may consider that of paramount importance.

PTAH: Oh, most assuredly. So my question then becomes the following:

SATSU: But to Maimer the Newbie, he may not care.

BAY_EL-LOR TO SATSU: Is the mud here to satisfy the Maimer?

CROWE TO SATSU: I think Ptah's point is, those that DO place it in high priority have tremendous opportunities here.

PTAH: Do we regard it as valuable enough for enough people, that we wish to

---

[84] I was a graduate student during this time period, and teaching various English literature classes.

encourage it and the parallel things of ethics in gameplay and personal relations, and so on; if so, how do we encourage it.

KEIKO: The mud is here to give back what you put into it.

SATSU TO BAY_EL-LOR: I'm not under the impression that the mud is here to satisfy any particular group of people ONLY..

SEPH: Why do you think the social aspects are being under-utilized?

PTAH TO SATSU: Correct. It is not. So another question I'd ask is, does the game aspect preclude this?

SATSU TO BAY_EL-LOR: I thought it was here for all.. That is why we are having this discussion in the first place, is it not?

Crowe nods his agreement with Seph. A sea-worn mariner nods his agreement with Satsu.

SATSU TO PTAH: Thats a good question.

PTAH TO SEPH: The last time this room was used for a public meeting that was not rp was last October.

BAY_EL-LOR TO SATSU: But preserving it for Maimer does not mean freezing it as it is.

KEIKO TO PTAH: In some cases I think so.

PTAH: Oh... There was an herbalism meeting in... February?

SEPH TO PTAH: But public meetings are not the only kind of social function

KEIKO TO PTAH: Some people will come here with the premise that this is entirely a game, and that is fine for them.

SATSU TO BAY_EL-LOR: I TOTALLY agree... You have to foster the environment of rp, but not force it down everyone's throats.

Seph notes there are usually lots of people in ooc.

SATSU TO BAY_EL-LOR: Oops... You have to foster that environment but not force it down everyone's throats.

PTAH: How many of them are hiding from pkill? Or going to talk privately one on one? Or here for the gift shop? We don't know.

BAY_EL-LOR TO SATSU: *nod* there is a difference between force and creative availability.

A sea-worn mariner nods his agreement with Ptah. Crowe thinks most people who

WANT such things already practice them for the most part.

PTAH: Let me pose some examples and questions then.

KEIKO TO PTAH: They won't care about the rest of the aspects of the mud. The only problem is when their view causes trouble with others'

SATSU TO BAY_EL-LOR: I think it important to foster this vulnerable environment..But not at the ...*shrug* I'm at a loss for words.

PTAH: 1) do you think the mud as a society needs more evolution or not, and is it ethical to foster such evolution at all.

2) would addition of features such as say online library reading and so on be detrimental or an example of such fostering.

CROWE TO PTAH: I believe the coming and going of people all the time is a kind of evolution in itself...

BAY_EL-LOR: Asking about evolving means we have already.

SEPH: I would like on-line library.

KEIKO: I think it can't help but continually evolve.

PTAH: 3) how much does this factor impinge upon thing like gameplay and rp which perforce depend on the bending of what we consider ethical.

Satsu nods his agreement with a lithe wild-eyed girl.

SEPH: And i agree with Crowe - it evolves on it's own.

SATSU: What is the definition of evolution? Its simple.

Ptah leads up to his punchline here.

SATSU: You can't stop evolution. It happens on its own.

Satsu thought about it.

PTAH: I'd ask, what's the definition of SENTIENCE—which is, self-awareness.

A sea-worn mariner peers at Satsu, looking him up and down.

PTAH: And that is why I raise this issue.

Seph nods her agreement with Satsu. Satsu thought it would be best not to make a joke.

KEIKO: It's an interactive environment based on too many other peoples definitions of reality to avoid constant adaptation and mutation.

PTAH: Because I wondered how many of you were aware of this dimension at all.

BAY_EL-LOR TO SATSU: You can impede evolution—and what we're asking is if we will ...

Crowe was. Seph nods her agreement with a lithe wild-eyed girl.

SEPH: Of the social dimension?

SATSU TO BAY_EL-LOR: Yes, you can.

Seph would be surprised if anyone wasn't.

PTAH: I think everyone is aware of it in a sort of plain way. E.G. we get to meet and talk. But how many think of it literally as a society?

SATSU: So then we're asking not if we should Foster evolution but if we should impede it.

BAY_EL-LOR: Legend is alive Ptah ..it's too late.

KEIKO: But see as an entity its going to have all aspects present to some degree or another. Classify them as whatever archetypes as you want to.

PTAH: Too late? Too late? It's never too late.

SEPH: Lots of them Ptah.

SATSU: It'll grow/evolve with or without fostering.

WRAITH: The nation of Legend!

Seph rolls around on the ground with laughter. A lithe wild-eyed girl giggles. Wraith whistles innocently to himself. Satsu rolls around on the ground with laughter. Seph smiles at Wraith.

PTAH: No—that is NOT actually ludicrous.

Seph hugs Wraith.

CROWE TO PTAH: I find that a person's level of RP and their social behavior go hand-in-hand. In other words, the extent to which they play their RL selves influences how much they use the MUD as a social tool.

PTAH: If we think of it in that way, then we need to think about things that have begun to happen. Like, the recent trial for example.

KEIKO TO CROWE: RL selves or rp selves?

PTAH: Until THAT, I never thought that this place was truly attempting to become a society.

SEPH: What trial?

CROWE TO KEIKO: Both.

KEIKO TO SEPH: Multiplaying trial.

ParticleMan looks up into the sky and ponders. Seph missed everything.

PTAH: Recently some players actually got a judge and a jury and held a trial with witnesses and a court over another player's alleged multiplaying.

Seph smiles at a lithe wild-eyed girl. Seph gasps in astonishment.

SEPH: Wow - outcome?

PTAH: If anything, the desire for a government, which is what that implies, means that this society is becoming self-aware.

KEIKO TO PTAH: Which I think was silly in some ways because I see other people do it all the time and never get nailed.

PTAH: And that means that it NEEDS to think NOW about what it wishes to be. Which is why I have been so focused on ethical issues lately.

Satsu nods his agreement with you. Seph nods solemnly.

WRAITH TO KEIKO: You have to get caught first.

PTAH TO KEIKO: Feel free to help us nail em.

Seph puts the discussion more in perspective.

KEIKO TO WRAITH: Caught by an imm?

Seph smiles at Crowe.

KEIKO TO PTAH: I have a moral obligation that somewhat precludes me from judging other people.

A sea-worn mariner bonks a lithe wild-eyed girl on the head!

WRAITH TO KEIKO: I think that might be best, it's hard to go just on hearsay.

SEPH TO CROWE: Missing info makes a difference... If the players don't run to the immorts for judging, what does that mean?

BAY_EL-LOR TO KEIKO: Oh you do not ..

PTAH: Well, that's a very good thing to know, and it means that an issue is whether that is a general feeling on the mud or not.

KEIKO TO WRAITH: Hearsay or witnessing it...

PTAH: Because that implies a very specific thing for the culture.

KEIKO: I think it is outright wrong. But I also think that players snitching on players is not a good environment to encourage.

A sea-worn mariner grumbles.

BAY_EL-LOR: Hearsay is bad—but hearsay by trial is better than executive authority
..

A lithe wild-eyed girl hates overstepping bounds of authority established for herself.

PTAH: Well, then perhaps the society to foster is one of "I'm too stinkin' PROUD to cheat'?

Seph nods her agreement with a sea-worn mariner. A lithe wild-eyed girl nods her agreement with a sea-worn mariner.

SEPH: Very interesting development.

BAY_EL-LOR: That's what Ptah is talking about ..the creation of society ..

KEIKO: Yes that would be utopic.

PTAH: Ah, hell, let's BE utopic.

Crowe thinks the MUD definitely does not lack for pride as it is.

BAY_EL-LOR: We're not good yet—but we evolved ..for a moment.

Ptah grins evilly.

SEPH: And almost possible in the mud world. This place discourages those who want it easy anyway.

Satsu notes that this is LEGEND mud, which is pretty close to UTOPIA mud.

KEIKO: It does discourage them, but it doesn't preclude that behavior.

Seph smiles at Satsu.

PTAH: Let me state that one reason why I state this is because I DO encounter many different attitudes towards the mud from different people.

SATSU: I can vouch for that Seph.

SEPH: No, but it does convince them to go away. And can more so.

SATSU TO SEPH: It discourages people who want an easy ride.

PTAH: And given a diverse populace, we need to have some sort of structure within which they can exist, be it by setting one attitude in primacy over others, or not.

Seph nods her agreement with Satsu.

SATSU TO PTAH: You're talking about defining peoples opinions.... Can you do that?

A lithe wild-eyed girl peers around the room intently.

PTAH: The other day a member of the community, one who is a citizen in long standing, made the statement that nothing on the mud could hurt anyone's feelings.

CROWE: A sort of structure of that nature already exists really.

A lithe wild-eyed girl looks at Ptah, boggled.

PTAH: That attitude is so incredibly alien to me and my impression of what can happen on muds, I was flabbergasted.

SATSU: That person is...Looney. But.. They exist!

Seph learned the hard way how much people on muds care.

KEIKO: Well you see they take it that way and project their perception enlightened or not onto the general populace.

A sea-worn mariner nods his agreement with Seph.

PTAH: And then we get people who will quit the mud over hurt feelings.

Satsu has had that several times on his mud.

PTAH: This mud gets VERY loyal players.

SATSU: Totally!

BAY_EL-LOR: it's alive! dammit! It's alive!

PTAH: And I can say that almost uniformly, we lose players to only three causes.

SEPH: Everyone needs to grow up some ways, some times.

KEIKO TO PTAH: You see it is enlightened in some ways to perceive this as a game and to be able to keep separate the game world from the personality. And to view it as an outlet for some aspects of a personality.

SATSU: Loyal players...And if you hurt someone's feelings, sometime's they'll quit over it.

PTAH: One, a very very few have quit from boredom. Two a lot have moved or last access.

KEIKO TO PTAH: But it is unenlightened for them not to perceive that some people do not fully divest themselves when playing.

PTAH: The vast majority of people who leave Legend do so out of disgust with other people's attitudes.

A lithe wild-eyed girl nods solemnly.

PTAH: Either over cheating, over rp, over hurting feelings, whatever.

Satsu nods solemnly. Seph looks up into the sky and ponders.

PTAH TO KEIKO: Then THAT is a social precept we need to instill.

BAY_EL-LOR: And in this, Legend is like real life .. Only you can't leave rl when it pisses you off.

KEIKO TO PTAH: But then you chose to transcend the bounds of game entirely.

Crowe shrugs philosophically.

PTAH TO BAY_EL-LOR: Tough philosophical question. Does that make leaving here more cowardly? Less so? Make this less of a commitment than RL? More of one?

SATSU TO PTAH: None of the above.

A sea-worn mariner sighs loudly.

SATSU TO PTAH: It's different.

BAY_EL-LOR: More .. much more.

KEIKO TO CROWE: In a way too many people get emotionally involved too much and in a way not enough get involved at all.

SEPH: Stay aware for awhile and then see how you feel.

Seph grins evilly.

SATSU TO PTAH: I think you're trying to compare apples and orange..

PTAH TO SATSU: Can you say the feelings are different? Disgust is disgust, hatred is hatred, love is love?

CROWE TO KEIKO: Everyone is different.

KEIKO TO CROWE: Rightfully so.

PTAH: Let me give you a situation.

Crowe nods his agreement with a lithe wild-eyed girl.

SATSU TO PTAH: Sure, they're both fruit, but they also are quite different.

PTAH: This includes juicy good gossip.

A sea-worn mariner bows before Satsu. Seph listens in fascination.

KEIKO: Oooh.

BAY_EL-LOR TO SATSU: You are an admirable foil ..I salute you,

A lithe wild-eyed girl peers around the room intently.

PTAH: The other day I got very very angry with a player that I regard as cheating. Others do not feel he was cheating.

Satsu salutes a sea-worn mariner briskly.

PTAH: He himself was the one who made the remark that it won't hurt anyone's feelings.

Satsu guffaws.

PTAH: Other immortals got very upset with me.

SEPH: And who should decide how other people *should* feel?

PTAH: Anyway, I was accused by other immorts of being high on my hobbyhorse.

A lithe wild-eyed girl chuckles politely. Satsu looks confused. Seph giggles.

PTAH: I was told that in this case the cheating was not cheating for one technicality or another. And I was also told that others had done the same thing in the past and I had not objected, and therefore I was hypocritical. All of which made me madder, of course.

KEIKO: Ptah it is still a game and it is far too natural for people to desperately and creatively try to exploit the system. It's a big puzzle.

Satsu nods his agreement with a lithe wild-eyed girl.

PTAH TO KEIKO: I have not reached the punchline... this isn't ABOUT that.

SEPH: Now i wanna know what KIND of cheating.

KEIKO: The goal is to figure out the best way to put the piece together.

Satsu listens carefully.

PTAH: What this is about is the mail I got later from someone.

A lithe wild-eyed girl waits patiently. A sea-worn mariner looks cautious.

PTAH: I quit out in anger, you see, saying that to my mind, anything that made someone play under a different system from his peers was cheating, and if it was done purposely and we ignored it, we were condoning the equivalent of theft. That we were legitimizing the attitude that if nobody is watching, steal. And I said that I did not know that I wanted to play somewhere where that was a prevalent attitude. And quit out. The email I got said in its first few lines, basically, 'If you are going to keep this up, maybe you SHOULD quit.'

A sea-worn mariner is completely boggled.

PTAH: And argued that the mud would never be a perfect game nor a perfect society, so I should stop turning the mud into an armed camp over it.

Satsu is feeling the same as Bay.

PTAH: I was most angered over the accusations of hypocrisy.

A lithe wild-eyed girl sighs loudly.

SATSU: It would anger me also...

PTAH: But finally concluded that they were CORRECT. I am still here, you see.

SATSU: I disagree.

A lithe wild-eyed girl chuckles politely.

PTAH: I value the continuation of this society MORE than I value the principles that led me to make that statement. And therefore I am sacrificing those principles to stay on and keep working on the mud.

A sea-worn mariner hugs you.

KEIKO: Don't you see tho, you've sort of set yourself up as an aspect of the superego or conscience of the mud.

PTAH: If I were sticking by my guns, I would have resigned two days ago.

Seph hugs you.

SATSU: We're glad you didn't Ptah.

PTAH: Well, so am I.

A sea-worn mariner sweeps you into a romantic waltz.

SEPH: Please don't leave.

KEIKO TO PTAH: And as such you tend to go to the extreme for your principles.

SATSU TO KEIKO: I totally agree with you.

BAY_EL-LOR: Nietzsche said I want a god who dances ...

Satsu nods his agreement with a sea-worn mariner.

SATSU TO BAY_EL-LOR: He did.

SATSU TO PTAH: What Keiko just said is vitally important.

PTAH: Well, then, the reason I tell this story is to illustrate that regarding the mud as a society is the ONLY reason to choose to sacrifice the principles.

KEIKO TO PTAH: I'm not judging (I never do that if I can avoid it) But you do need to learn to see things from the other points of view to remain sane. Not give in, not be a hypocrite, just get a better understanding of perspective.

PTAH: Yes, I know it is.

SATSU TO PTAH: You've set yourself up.

PTAH TO KEIKO: I hate to say it, but I do that more regularly than anyone I know. Otherwise, I would not have compromised the many OTHER times this same situation has arisen. I have set myself up, yes.

KEIKO: Then you need to find someone willing to share the responsibilities of that particular role.

SEPH: I disagreed with you about immorts not needing people-savvy.

PTAH: So my challenge to the mud if it is to develop as a society that I have just made that monstrous commitment to is this.

SEPH: I think if you weren't here to be the mud's conscious....

PTAH: Shouldn't there be some superego in all of you? Why do we rely on the executive fiat?

KEIKO TO PTAH: You can't be good at what you've chosen to do until you can perceive the other viewpoints.

SEPH: It would have disintegrated.

PTAH TO SEPH: Who would be?

KEIKO: I have plenty of superego silly.

PTAH: Ah, there's the rub. If it would have disintegrated, is it worth saving?

A lithe wild-eyed girl sighs loudly.

SEPH: Yes!

PTAH: If it would have disintegrated, have I made my commitment erroneously?

SATSU: No you haven't.

PTAH: Because I DO NOT intend to be a superego all my life.

SEPH: Why should you think so?

KEIKO: I don't think it would disintegrate but it very well may reach a level of decay that you wouldn't be happy with personally

PARTICLEMAN: But doesn't every society have a central point that it revolves around???

PTAH: Most specifically—I came here very annoyed over a debate over the future of the mud.

SEPH: I said would have... I don't think it would now...it's much bigger than a year ago.

PTAH: It hits home because I may have a full-time-plus job in a month. I ain't gonna be your central point no more. You will have to be. And that means that you all need to think about your society a little more.

SATSU: A central point doesn't have to be here all the time...:)

A sea-worn mariner sighs loudly. Seph sighs loudly.

PTAH: And I need to think about it a little less.

SATSU: Again we come to hierarchy..

PTAH: Or at least write up articles about this issue and make a name for myself.

Ptah grins evilly. A lithe wild-eyed girl chuckles politely.

BAY_EL-LOR: Or a - hierarchy ..

Satsu nods solemnly.

KEIKO TO PTAH: That's it, find a way to turn this into a livelihood. For all of us.

SEPH: It would help if people outside the immort system were not threatened with losing what they can input.

BAY_EL-LOR: Order need not be executive ..

PTAH: Again, there cannot be NO hierarchy. It's inhuman, for one, and for another, on the net as yet not possible.

A lithe wild-eyed girl sighs loudly.

SEPH: For example, the www and lt and discussion list.

SATSU: Bah HUMBUG. There is a hierarchy in ALL things.

PTAH TO SATSU: That is what I just said

SATSU TO PTAH: Right down to Nature... There is always hierarchy.

A sea-worn mariner chuckles politely at Satsu's feeble witticism.

BAY_EL-LOR TO SATSU: Structuralist.

PTAH TO SATSU: My point was that on a mud in particular there is a hierarchy imposed by the necessity for tech people to keep the game running, for coders and designers to expand the system...

Crowe chuckles politely.

SATSU TO BAY_EL-LOR: Realist is what I am.

WRAITH: Even with true communism?

PTAH: It is a hierarchy imposed by the demands of the medium.

A lithe wild-eyed girl is completely boggled.

PTAH: Even with true communism, you're gonna get an alpha male leading the pack. Or alpha female :)

SATSU: No.

A lithe wild-eyed girl attempts to crush her anarchistic self for a moment. A lithe wild-eyed girl peers at Ptah.

SEPH: Somebody has to be in charge - but that doesn't mean that the contributions of those outside the hierarchy can't be accepted and valid.

SATSU: A hierarchy is not imposed by the demands of the medium... It is imposed by nature and man's need to participate in nature.

PTAH TO KEIKO: Anarchy just means the strongest one eventually wins out. Anarchy never lasts for very long.

A sea-worn mariner holds Ptah's head under water until he admits there's no alpha :) A lithe wild-eyed girl chuckles politely. Ptah rolls around on the ground with laughter. Seph giggles.

KEIKO TO PTAH: An anarchy of true equals is nice though.

Satsu giggles.

PTAH: Hate to say it, but if there were no alpha, you guys would not be in this room.

A lithe wild-eyed girl giggles.

WRAITH TO SATSU: I'd have to say it was the system.

PTAH TO KEIKO: Find two true equals.

A lithe wild-eyed girl peers around the room intently.

SATSU TO WRAITH: I disagree. I think that .. Hierarchies exist everywhere.

KEIKO TO PTAH: Well it's a matter of perspective. One is on the sofa next to me asleep. You are one also. The world is filled with them.

SATSU TO WRAITH: They are neither the cause, nor the effect of the medium... They merely exist.

KEIKO TO PTAH: I'm one of those neutral sorts that attempts to transcend judgment.

PTAH TO KEIKO: That is discussion in the abstract. I am sure that there are things that you do better than they, and vice versa. All that remains is creation of a context favoring one or the other of you, and one will perforce be the leader.

A sea-worn mariner sighs loudly.

A lithe wild-eyed girl stifles the part of herself that says but of course I'll lead.

PTAH TO SATSU: When the server crashes and nobody is around to put it up, THAT'S what I mean by an imposed hierarchy.

WRAITH TO SATSU: If you didn't have immortals controlling what was being added to the MUD you would have chaos as each tries to dominate the others by making more powerful items and mobs.

A lithe wild-eyed girl chuckles politely at Wraith's feeble witticism.

PTAH: The fact is, the people who lead a mud are NOT required to be good leaders.

BAY_EL-LOR: Leadership requires economic and social imbalance—the Mud precipitates hierarchy necessarily.

Seph nods her agreement with Wraith. Seph has seen that mud.

PTAH: There is a hierarchy imposed by other needs.

Crowe giggles at Seph.

SATSU TO PTAH: You've reverted to the MUD per gaming hierarchy... There is a hierarchy within the social aspect.

Ptah nods solemnly. A lithe wild-eyed girl nods her agreement with Satsu.

PTAH: Yes, there is.

Seph smiles at Crowe.

PTAH: Of course, there's no social aspect with no server.

You chuckle politely.

SATSU: True, when the mud crashes, that requires one of you guys.

Satsu chuckles politely at your feeble witticism.

PTAH: Well, then, who has final say on the whole shebang? You are arguing for input.

SATSU: We are limited by the confines of the server... But..

SEPH: You, dad-blast it.

PTAH: That ONLY happens when the leadership permits it. OK, well, you've all known muds where THIS talk isn't going to happen, correct?

WRAITH TO SATSU: Even MUDs which claim not to have 'gods' still have people who fill that function.

KEIKO: Well if the leadership didn't permit it do you think we'd stick around and play?

SEPH: Bleh

SATSU TO WRAITH: I agree.

PTAH TO KEIKO: A statement I made in the interview...

Satsu nods his agreement with a lithe wild-eyed girl.

PTAH: "There are any number of people willing to live under jerks"

A sea-worn mariner peers at Ptah.

KEIKO: Well fine they make that decision.

SEPH: I disagree.

Seph nods her agreement with Satsu. A sea-worn mariner wonders how to write a Mud .. Ptah shrugs philosophically.

PTAH: I can easily find examples.

KEIKO: People are perfectly capable of being responsible for their own actions

SEPH: You don't realize how much modifying value the rest of you have had.

Seph smiles at Wraith. A sea-worn mariner giggles at Satsu. A lithe wild-eyed girl peers at Satsu, looking him up and down.

SATSU TO PTAH: I'm sure you can.. But those people aren't people participating in a talk like THIS.

PTAH: Do you need one like my high school, Iraq, or Medievia?

KEIKO TO SATSU: What?

SEPH: High school is not choice

SATSU TO KEIKO: What?

PTAH TO SATSU: My point is that these people are here because I encourage and permit and even demand it.

SEPH: Would you stay at Iraq or medievia?

PTAH: One must fight for such freedoms, they are not generally handed to one.

PTAH TO SEPH: I have a friend who lives in Peru. I lived there too, and cordially, it sucks.

BAY_EL-LOR TO PTAH: We're here because we're challenged, silly ..

PTAH: He is my equal in every way I can think of.

Seph thought you meant a mud

PTAH: He stays because he loves the country. I do not, I can leave.

KEIKO TO BAY_EL-LOR: That's for sure, we're challenged alright.

SEPH: Living places are not necessarily choice either.

Satsu nods his agreement with Ptah.

Ptah points to an analogous situation he described just a little ways back involving him and hypocrisy.

PTAH: Well, so here's the question. I'll pose it to Crowe.

SATSU: I have lived in Mexico, France, Spain, Russia, Canada, and Japan... And let me tell you...

PTAH TO CROWE: You really care so little about this place that you'd quit if the leadership changed?

SATSU: I have met all kinds of people that live places that I will NEVER go back, that love it there.

PTAH TO SEPH: Or you?

BAY_EL-LOR TO SATSU: Imagine a revolution, a civil rights movement, on a mud...

PTAH TO KEIKO: Or you?

PTAH TO SATSU: Or you?

Greebo looks up into the sky and ponders.

SEPH: That's not fair Ptah.

WRAITH: The leader can have a great impact.

CROWE TO PTAH: No, I care so MUCH about it that I would quit under someone like that.

PTAH: Do you see why this is NOT an idle question?

KEIKO: I stay as long as my friends are here.

PTAH: Ah!

SEPH: Yeah i prolly would leave if you did... I don't think that counts.

PTAH: Then you've made the first steps towards a mud society, and I am happy.

Seph sighs loudly.

SATSU TO PTAH: I agree with crowe.

Greebo wonders if he can interject an idea.

PTAH: But if you believe that, of course, then you make every effort to prevent it.

Satsu nods his agreement with Ptah.

PTAH: And that implies instilling the same attitude in others... And we come full circle.

Satsu sighs loudly.

PTAH: Which is why I held this talk in the first place and raised these issues. You know what my reply said? To that email?

SATSU: We've now run ourselves in one GIANT circle.

Seph looks confused and unhappy.

GREEBO: If no option remained, I would leave. But before that, if this mud were under leadership which I disagreed with, I would make every effort to make life as miserable as possible for the new leader.

Satsu bonks Greebo on the head!

PTAH: "Yes, I care for this mud. I care too much to shut up." Shut up about society, about ethics, about cheating, about whatever. About ideas for expanding and extending the game. Shut up about CONTRIBUTING. And that there, that alone, is what I would hope is the social goal here.

Satsu looks confused.

PTAH TO KEIKO: Even if it means snitching for the greater good. Or at least trying to get the criminal to grow up and accept the same idea.

A sea-worn mariner hugs Ptah. ParticleMan nods solemnly.[85]

---

[85] ParticleMan in particular is an interesting case, because of an incident that came to light in April of 1996, as reported in an LT issue found at
https://www.legendmud.org/Community/lt_indices/Vol3/LTv3n6.html

> As most of you know from a recent Legendary Times Special Bulletin, the imms recently discovered a cheating ring, wherein players were crashing the mud in order to duplicate rare and/or "old" gear (gear with given stats that no longer exists

KEIKO TO PTAH: I'd sooner confront them and appeal to their sense of dignity.

WRAITH: If no-one contributes, won't it stagnate?

PTAH TO KEIKO: Please do.

A lithe wild-eyed girl sighs loudly.

PTAH TO WRAITH: Haven't you seen that here in the past?

KEIKO TO PTAH: I already told a god.

Wraith nods solemnly.

PTAH: I won't start my civics lecture on relating this to your RL :)

Ptah cackles gleefully. A lithe wild-eyed girl thanks you heartily.

PTAH: Partly because I don't volunteer anywhere, nor do a damn thing. I think this is enough.

SATSU: It is.

PTAH: Hopefully this gets people thinking at any rate.

WRAITH: I remember Sadist stating, when the mud first opened, that Legend would never leave beta stage.

PTAH: About everything from how you answer a newbie to what you do with a

---

in the code). Those involved were deleted. If you'd like a copy of that Special Bulletin, please e-mail Rusalka at lt@mud.aus.sig.net.

In connection to the cheating ring, ParticleMan's player asked that we re-print the letter that he posted on the welcome board:

Seems I got word from ParticleMan asking me to post this note to the MUD. Here it is verbatim from ParticleMan:

```
To the MUD, I apologize to each and every one of you, even those not involved in
what happened that fateful day. Seems a few of us had found a crashing bug and
decided to capitalize on it.  Seems I even logged on as another character to do
the dastardly deed. Seems I got caught doing my first illicit(sp) activity in my
long and not so glorious time on the MUD. so to those of you who lost eq due to
the crash, I give you my most humblest apologies, to those of you whos trust I
broke I apologize for that too.  To the Immorts, Heros, Angels and Imps, I
apologize to you all for breaking your trust in me, and putting you all in a
position to have to delete multiple characters. I know thats not an easy job.
To everyone, take notice of this post. I cheated ONCE in over a year, and all
the time and patience it took for me to make it to level 50, the long hours of
work and all the friendships built up, all went to nothing in the blink of an
eye all went to nothing in the blink of an eye because I wanted to get ahead
illegally. Remember what happened to me and 4 other great characters all because
we wanted to cheat.  So please learn from our screwups, I'd hate to see others
end up the same way.  And please accept my deepest apologies. ParticleMan the
disgraced (and deleted)
```

multiplayer and whether or not to hold a trial.

A lithe wild-eyed girl sighs loudly. Seph STILL looks confused and unhappy and is not sure what the point was.

PARTICLEMAN: And I thought rl was hard...

PTAH: Simply this, Seph.

A lithe wild-eyed girl chuckles politely at Seph's feeble witticism. Crowe comforts Seph.

PTAH: I would hope that the social goal of Legend is to try to make life here better. Period.

BAY_EL-LOR TO PARTICLEMAN: This is real life ..

Seph smiles at Crowe. ParticleMan smiles happily. Crowe smiles at Seph.

PTAH TO BAY_EL-LOR: Exactly my point.

GREEBO: Uhm... Better than?

KEIKO TO GREEBO: Heh.

PTAH: Than it was five minutes ago.

Ptah chuckles politely.

SEPH: Didn't you already think it was?

SATSU: We're evolving people.

GREEBO: That should be the goal, whether it's virtual or r/l (refer to my essay).

A lithe wild-eyed girl shudders. Greebo grins evilly. A lithe wild-eyed girl sighs loudly. Seph doesn't think she's ever seen her, or Dylan, or Dr. make a suggestion that wasn't in hopes of making this world a better place - even the bad ones.

KEIKO: I still haven't written an essay.

SATSU: The mud will gradually make itself better. We're just trying to foster that process.

PTAH: And with that, I'll leave you, making two points. One, you all really missed out by not taking any of my classes, huh.[86]

Crowe smiles at Ptah. A sea-worn mariner nods solemnly.

KEIKO TO PTAH: I'll take yours if you take mine. Hah!!!

---

[86] I wince every time I read this.

SATSU TO PTAH: You're a teacher?

A sensuous beauty giggles. A lithe wild-eyed girl throws her head back and cackles with insane glee!

GREEBO: Drive on out to Baltimore and educate me, Ptah. :)

PTAH: And two, I've put up with a hell of a lot of abuse, esp in the last few days, over this attitude, and I don't care if it is overly righteous, but this reasoning is the ONLY reason why I put up with it.

New Immortal Structure

Within a few months, LegendMUD began to institute changes such as having an Immortal whose job was "player ombudsman." Immorts were assigned jobs, and Charity and Sadist, the original Implementors, stepped down. Eventually this culminated in attempting to move to "the rule of law."

A new immort structure was rolled out to the LegendMUD admins after a period of comment, in May of 1996. As you will see, it was built around a strict permissions system that curtailed the godlike powers given to different sub-specialties of game admin. Prior to this, all admins had all powers.

The reason for these changes were to try to address a series of major administrative issues that had developed. The players were complaining that admins played favorites, that there were abuses of power. The changes to the game had slowed, and it was falling into a bit of rut. New players would join the game, and not stick very long, causing the game to develop a reputation as unfriendly.

It all came to a breaking point when one of the immortals was accused of misbehavior by another, and two groups lined up to take sides. The game was in danger of having up to one third of its staff quit. The solution was to professionalize.

The division of admins into formal groups for the purposes of game administration was not a common pattern in MUDs at the time (though of course far more common in the commercial systems).

Sometime in the next few days, the following system will go into effect. It is a combination of the elements of the various systems suggested by all of you who posted, plus input from various other sources.

The job system

There will be four "wizbit" sets which are as follows:

- Builder: in charge of all aspects of area maintenance and of area building.
- Coder: in charge of programming tasks and debugging server code.
- Admin: in charge of discipline, rules administration, and paperwork stuff.

- PR: in charge of making the mud fun with aspects beyond the game proper.

Commands are distributed among the wizbits with an eye towards permitting them to do their jobs with the bare minimum of commands necessary. This means that some of you if not all of you *will* lose commands. However, you are not limited to having only one wizbit.

A few new commands have been added as well though not all are as yet fully debugged. One we know works and will be in: string (for stringing objects only).

The new level system

Level 51: "inactive" immort

This level is for those who do not have a "job" wizbit set, or who are not present on the mud enough to work within one of the wizbit jobs. They have access to the following commands:

wizhelp	disconnect	notell	goto
file	holylight	invis	poofin
poofout	think	shout	qsave
fly	muzzle	unmuzzle	seename
cc	bandwidth		

Duties/responsibilities: none really, though they may move into a wizbit with approval of the other members of that wizbit. As they have muzzle, they can and should monitor channels for abuse and language. As they have disconnect, they may handle requests for that as well. And as they have cc, they may make and remove conferences if they see the need.

Level 52: "newbie" imm or assistant in a wizbit.

This level is for people who do not have a given wizbit as a primary job, or who are newly immorted and do not yet know all the ropes involved in a given job.

The commands gained at this level, broken down by job, are:

Builder:	Coder:	Admin:	PR:
stat	memory	glue	find
lflags	profile	transfer	whozone
census		clanset	register
navigate		where	string
evaluate		find	echo
			where

Duties/responsibilities: vary by job, but in a nutshell:

- PR: handle stringing requests, run trivia games, recall tag, roleplaying competitions, and most importantly of all, help ALL new players, ideally going to them as they enter the game and offering to assist them in getting the hang of the mud. Generally, promote goodwill among the players towards the immorts and towards others on the mud.

- Coders: learn the mud code and tackle easy debugging tasks and simple additions.

- Builders: work on their first area and work on simple bugfixes and area maintenance.

- Admins: handle the daily clanning requests, handle simple disciplinary issues, etc.

Level 53: full immort.

This level is where you become a "full builder" or whatever else. It is not expected that someone will get full immort in multiple disciplines necessarily, though there is no reason why it is not possible. Full immorts within a specialty are going to have ongoing tasks to keep them busy.

The commands gained at this level, broken down by job, are:

Builder	Coder	Admin	PR
Set	None new	Stat	Clear
Rtell		Load	Announce
Mtell		Users	At
Switch		Snoop	Snoop
Echocatch		set	Load
Force			Switch
Load			transfer
At			
transfer			

Duties/responsibilities: the full immorts in each area will be performing ongoing tasks to keep the mud moving forward. Examples:

- PR: running the Legendary Times, weekly trivia contests, expanding and enhancing the web pages, handling advertising and pr, running weekly or monthly tinyplots, holding periodic Expies awards, sponsoring theatre productions in the OOC, roleplaying competitions, flag hunts, and other activities.

- Coding: commenting the entire server code, optimizing it for speed, consistency, and stability, increasing code flexibility, adding new features and capabilities, increasing the capabilities already present.

- Building: maintaining *ALL* areas regardless of who the builder was, including all quest and area maintenance, bugfixes, typos, etc. Revising all areas to include any and all new features such as local weather, titles, extra descriptions, _give and other new acts features, etc. Working on new areas as well. Also serve as the peer review board for all new areas. Any area put in the mud will be considered fully complete or it will not be installed. Builders of already installed areas may work with the building staff to ensure that the original intent of the area is preserved, but should note that they are NOT the final arbiter of content.

- Admin: monitor incidents of harassment, multiplaying, cheating, etc. Handle the task of distributing the issues that arise such as bugs to the appropriate people for fixing. Serving as general resource for things like archiving, area bugs that caused altered stats or lost practices, etc.

Level 54: head of job.

Four people are at level 54, and their principal task is to coordinate projects and set agendas for all issues related to their wizbit. These four people have basically all the imp commands save the ability to make new immortals. They have promotion and demotion authority for those within their wizbit; admin has promotion and demotion authority for any wizbit. They have the ability to set job wizbits.

NOTE! These four positions are not decided purely on merit or longevity on the mud. They are decided based on who can do the job. There is absolutely no stigma attached to stepping down from this position (unless they are demoted for cause), nor should there be considered to be a great honor attached with taking on all the hassles and responsibilities these jobs imply.

Commands available to all heads:

allow	ban	wizlock	advance
reboot	shutdown	slay	playerdelete
restore	clear	snoop	jobset
pcflag	rtell	purge	force
mtell	announce	peace	set
load	switch	users	invbag
at	profile	glue	census
memory	clanset	navigate	transfer
find	system	lflags	echo

echocatch	register	string	where
whozone	notell	goto	evaluate
disconnect	invis	poofin	file
holylight	shout	qsave	poofout
think	unmuzzle	seename	fly
muzzle	wizhelp		cc
stat			

Duties and responsibilities:

Administrating everything under their purview; serving as "deputy" imps and handling emergencies or issues that require high-level access to commands.

Level 55: implementor.

The job here is split in two; Ptah will be trying to set the direction for the mud's future, and Kaige will be trying to make sure that what is here (and what is coming) actually works and works towards that end. They have all commands, plus the ability to make new immorts with immortalize.

What is this all for

What follows below are the long-term goals for each of these wizbits, including particular aspects that are going to be addressed. The tasks below are what the department heads will be prioritizing and assigning as ongoing tasks to those with wizbits in that specialty.

Player relations:

LONG TERM GOAL: to make this the friendliest mud on the Net, with a welcoming atmosphere, a rich diversity of people, a mature atmosphere, and a depth of social context unmatched anywhere.

- weekly Lecture series events with interesting guest speakers from OUTSIDE Legend
- promote and encourage roleplaying
- promote Legend's OOC aspects as a community of players with similar interests and goals
- promote Legend's IC aspects as a community of characters with extremely different (and changing) goals and interests
- find ways to acknowledge imm and mort accomplishments better
- extend the OOC to support a library, additional lounge areas, a trophy room, and immort offices

- roleplaying impromptu competitions
- regularly scheduled trivia with a standings board
- regular meetings with players, including weekly feedback on reported bugs and fixes in progress, on development of new features, and acknowledgment of those who submit or report bugs and ideas.
- immort-sponsored tinyplots and pkill tourneys on a regular basis

Builders:

LONG TERM GOAL: to make Legend capable of supporting 150 players, that takes full advantage of the code and showcases it to best effect, and that all areas are cohesive, well-designed, and balanced.

- make sure all areas use all code features
- work with coders to ensure comprehensive and accurate docs
- maintain all areas and fix all problems found
- add extra descriptions and exit descriptions to every area and every room
- add increased detail in all acts and conversations, quest hints where appropriate, and greater interactivity
- make all hometowns for skill trees into acceptable hometowns
- attempt to balance all hometowns
- supervise the overall balance of the mud, redistributing access to stat quests and items as necessary
- revise the stock areas (limbo, wobble, clan) into something more flexible and usable
- place generic low level mobs in limbo and make sure they are used consistently across the mud
- generate highly specific and useful building guidelines, including for distribution and access to stat boost items
- create firm standards of area proposal and acceptance
- revise areas command so that it gives details and credit
- standardize learning and costs of skills
- create a set of quest templates
- help files for all areas

- devise widely applicable procedures, including fight strategies for mobs
- establish the rule that every new area installed implies an overhaul of an old area
- local weather everywhere
- greater attention paid to the Americas

Coders:

LONG TERM GOAL: to get the mud code in good enough shape to release publicly as a code base for other muds. To make it flexible, efficient, stable, expandable, and configurable.

- fix all memory bugs (highest priority!)
- polish skill trees
- identify and fix bugs in the code
- return the mud to the cutting edge of server design
- a working mud economy
- hardcoded guidelines flags that show when areas are loaded
- better area file reader that is more flexible and also does not permit loading of out of guideline areas, and is less cryptic with error messages
- fully commented code
- ACT_TALK system for generic conversation AI
- moods integrated into socials and personally settable moods
- configurable prompt
- threaded board system
- temperature and effects in local weather
- MOTD and NEWS to become boards accessible from anywhere
- Macintosh and DOS testmud ports
- ability to run on as many flavors of Unix as possible

Admin:

LONG TERM GOAL: to have a mature, professional staff to set a good example for the players.

- enforce guidelines for behavior among immorts and players

- make immorts more accessible to mortals, including a series of immort offices located in the OOC
- fix the help files
- organize the revamping of the proposing process
- handle desc requests in conjunction with PR
- handle clanning requests
- handle archive requests
- handle monthly playerfile purges
- handle player housing

What The New System Means For You

The following four people are being made level 54 and given departments to head:

- Rusalka: player relations.
- Rufus: building. He is reimmorting for this purpose.
- Chocorua: administration.
- Ganelon: coding. He is being immorted for this purpose.

The following two individuals are being immorted directly into the new structure at the level of assistant builder. Until they are more familiar with the setup they will not be moving beyond that job: Sandra and Sabella.

The following two individuals have been approached about being immorted as well: Joule and Spencer. It is quite likely that others such as Baca and Sharpe and Tad will also be approached in order to make use of the talents of committed long-term players for the betterment of the mud.

Where do you fit? Where you feel most comfortable and competent; and where you are suited. You will all be showing as Inactive Imm until you have jobs set on you once the code is installed. You will need to contact the head of the job you are interested in to get your job set. Note that they may well turn you down because they feel it is not what you are best suited for and they think your talents would be best utilized elsewhere.

How Are Decisions Made From Now On?

Issues that are restricted to a single job are decided within that job and by the imps. Issues that cross boundaries and are significant enough are voted upon by the imm staff. If an issue falls under the jurisdiction of more than one specialty, all affected specialties have full votes.

Votes are weighted as follows:

0   inactive immorts have no vote
1   immortals not within the specialty (have no wizbit in that area)
2   immortals within the specialty and job heads when outside their specialty
4   head of specialty in their specialty
6   implementors, with flat veto and line-item veto as well

(Vetoes can only be done if both imps agree).

It is expected that with delegation, minor issues will not come up for vote. It is also expected that people who do not vote in a timely manner do not care; and that everyone who has a vote is a productive member of the staff. Dropping to inactive is no crime; leaves of absence, vacations, etc, are quite normal and expected.

New Immorts

This system is designed for a much larger staff than we have presently. We are going to set about getting that staff. We do not want to rob the playerbase of all its best players; nor do we wish to lower standards for immorting—if anything, we wish to raise them. However, one may immort directly into a specific specialty, in which case the abilities of the person *in that specialty* are most important. Votes for immorting into a given specialty are conducted as an issue central to that specialty, but affecting the whole staff, using the weight system given above.

The level for proposing to immort has been lowered to level 45 effective immediately. A new structure for proposing is not completely settled yet, but it will be on a job-to-job basis.

A Few Extra Comments...

1. Sadist has already given his permission to release the code
2. This is a last-ditch effort to rescue the mud from the mediocrity it has become. Thus the emphasis on new blood, on increased hierarchy, on ongoing tasks, and on player relations
3. If you don't like it, you are welcome to leave; this IS happening no matter what
4. If you leave and your area has been installed, it is considered part of Legend and we will not release it to you
5. a mud that does not evolve and change is a mud that dies; the basic premise of this

is to get people caring enough again to see Legend grow

6. Read and understand the immort code of conduct. Immortals *and their morts* will be held to a higher standard than players are. The slate of past offenses is wiped clean, effective immediately. The code of conduct is also in effect immediately.

–Ptah and Kaige

To modern eyes, the commands possible even in this more constrained system seem ridiculously trusting of admins, and something that could never scale beyond a trusted group. Admin commands were all logged, but these sorts of powers, distributed to a larger, less trusted group, led to immense issues on Ultima Online later on.

Some of what these powers did:

- *Allow and ban: ban users and then allow them back in.*

- *Reboot: restart the whole game server.*

- *Restore:*

- *Pcflag: see, and set, flags on the players for quests and the like.*

- *Mtell: activate code triggers on creatures and mobiles (mobiles are all creatures and NPCs).*

- *Load: create items on the fly.*

- *At: perform an action at an arbitrary location without having to go there.*

- *Memory: monitor the server's memory load.*

- *Find: locate items, creatures, or NPCs in the game's database.*

- *echocatch*

- *Whozone: see who was in an area.*

- *Disconnect: Forcibly disconnect a player from the game.*

- *Holylight: toggle light that allowed visibility even in the darkness or when blind.*

- *Think: the private admin chat channel.*

- *Muzzle and unmuzzle: remove the ability to chat or speak from a player.*

- *Stat: see all the stats associated with a player, object, or mobile.*

- *Shutdown: shut the game down.*

- *Clear: remove flags from a player or mobile.*

- *Rtell: activate code triggers on a room.*

- *Announce: send an anonymous global message visible to everyone in the game (a system message).*

- *Switch: possess the body of a mobile — or a player!*

- *Profile: pull up statistics on server performance.*

- *Clanset: used for managing the guild system.*

- *System: more server commands.*

- *Register: Create a new guild.*

- *Notell: turn off the ability to send private messages.*

- *Invis: go invisible to all mortal players.*

- *Shout: Shout loudly enough to be heard game-wide.*

- *Wizhelp: the help system for all immortal commands.*

- *Wizlock: Lock the game to all mortals, so only admins can get in.*

- *Slay: Instantly kill anything or anyone.*

- *Snoop: Monitor the network traffic of someone. This literally let you see everything they saw, as if you were them.*

- *Purge: delete every object in the room.*

- *Peace: Instantly stop combat in the room.*

- *Users: Get a list of online users including their network information.*

- *Glue: Freeze a player or mobile in place so they could not move at all.*

- *Navigate: give you the path to any point in the game.*

- *Lflags: list flags on someone or something.*

- *String: change the textual appearance of something.*

- *Goto: Teleport around the game.*

- *Poofin and poofout: change the messages shown to others when you teleported in or out.*

- *Qsave: quit and save.*

- *Seename: strip away personal descriptions so you could see the actual names of players.*

- *Advance: move a player up in level, used for making someone an immortal.*

- *Playerdelete: delete a player's character permanently.*

- *Jobset: assign an immortal into a job.*

- *Force: forcibly cause a mobile or a player to input and perform whatever commands you wished.*

- *Set: change any statistic on anything.*

- *Invbag: see everything carried by a player.*

- *Census: get statistics on everything in the whole MUD.*

- *Transfer: Teleport anything or anyone to you.*

- *Echo: generate text seen by everyone in that room that looked exactly like system output. With this, you could make it look like absolutely anything at all had happened.*

- *Where: find anyone or thing in the game.*

- *Evaluate: another way to look at stats.*

- *File: a special form of inventory that let immortals file away in game email.*

- *Fly: allowed immortals to walk on water (or lava, or in the air...)*

Player Code of Conduct

It may be interesting to compare the LegendMUD Player Code of Conduct to the modern versions of TOSes and EULA's on social media sites, now that administrators of online communities have largely abdicated actually moderating the spaces they run. Among other things, it features strong restrictions on any form of harassment or doxxing; extremely clear tiers of punishments; and strict enforcement of language standards against cursing, even. And perhaps most importantly, it is also accompanied by a statement of player rights.

For some time now, the staff of *LegendMUD* has been working on developing a coherent and consistent document that could serve as a player code of conduct. The reason for this document is simple: the controversies and debates over whether or not certain standards were rules, whether or not certain matters of etiquette were official, whether or not standards of punishment were codified, and on so on, had reached a point where even simple enforcement of basic rules was becoming counterproductive.

A major effort was made to gather together all the many rules, suggestions, standards, and policies into one document, for easy reference and to once and for all end the debate as to whether a given behavior was illegal or not.

It is important to emphasize that there is nothing NEW in this document. Rather, this is just a formalized version of the rules under which all the players already live and play with really, very few problems. Yes, it seems like a huge, daunting list, but really, the vast majority of it is common sense, and the document you are about to read tends to over-explain even the most basic things so that there is a definite reference to point to.

Where will this Code go?

The rules overview will be placed in HELP RULES, which replaces HELP CHEAT as the basic file to refer to for guidelines. There are also individual help files for each of the 12 rules (yes, there are only twelve rules). In addition, all new characters will get shown these twelve rules as part of the character creation process, so that even a casual spammer who wanders in cannot say that they were ignorant of the rules.

In addition, the code of conduct will be placed on the welcome board, and it will remain there permanently, so that it is easily referred to by players by that method as well. And of course, the help files are accessible by anyone. On top of THAT, it'll also be on the web site.

Reasons why you shouldn't freak out

"Oh no! The evil immortals are imposing more of their moral judgements upon us! Agh! I must flee!"

Hardly. So relax. As I said above, there are only twelve rules. They cover the basic stuff that you all already know quite well, like multiplaying, abusing bugs, and harassment. All we've done is gather them together and formalize them. From now on, if you get punished for something that is not in this document, you've got a great case in your defense; on the other hand, we're not perfect, and probably missed something. Because of that, we expect this to be a "living document" that evolves and changes over time.

Another major reason why you should not freak out is really a simple one. The rules are designed primarily to protect the players, and not to circumscribe them. In order for that to be perfectly clear, there is commentary interspersed below that describes the rationale for each rule. Frankly, none of them are very controversial.

Where to discuss the code of conduct

Since this is a living document, player input is always welcome. Although the welcome board has the code posted on it, it is not really the best forum for discussing it. Rather, discussion and debate related to the code of conduct is best posted on the discussion board in the Out of Character Lounge.

Please do not flood the Legendary Times address with comments about the code.

The following is HELP RULES, the overview of the twelve rules. This file is also sent to newbies during character creation.

Rules

LegendMUD has few rules, but the following activities are unwelcome here. Players caught engaging in these activities will be dealt with on a individual basis, but the basic violations listed below all potentially call for character deletion. Punitive actions can also include any and all of the following: removal of equipment or gold, alteration of stats, denied access to mud commands (e.g. being muzzled or glued), denied access to a character, forced clanning, demotion of level status, or banning of a site if repeated violations occur.

Generally, first offenses will result in your name being noted in a log of offenders and perhaps the loss of some skill, stat, privilege, or equipment. Upon a second offense, the log will be updated, you will be reminded that you were warned, and you will lose one half of your experience; other punishments—loss of stats, equipment, gold, or privileges—may also be imposed. A third offense warrants deletion, and your site will be noted in the log. A fourth offense may result is siteban. (See HELP VIOLATIONS, HELP RIGHTS)

All players are held responsible for understanding and following the rules set forth below, and violations will not be less severely punished because a player claims to have not known he or she was breaking a rule. For additional information, see individual help files or immorts with the 'Admin' flag.

- Multiplaying (logging in more than one character at a time) and trading equipment among your characters (or using one of your characters to benefit another of your characters in any way) are prohibited; additionally, only one player may play a particular character. (See HELP MULTIPLAY).

- Harassing other players is prohibited; harassment may include, but is not limited to, out of character threats, sending unwanted tells when asked to stop, using offensive language, making unwanted out-of-character attacks or comments, or using in-character justifications for what are really out-of-character assaults. (See HELP HARASSMENT).

- Sexually explicit language, cursing, and slurs are not permitted over public channels—like chat, auction, and info—or in other public fora like illusions or character names/titles; such language may be prohibited even in 'tells' to the extent it amounts to harassment. (See HELP HARASSMENT).

- Non-clanned players may not interfere in the general activities of clans or player-kill. 'Interference' may involve, but is not limited to, using skills, spells, or other in-game functions to assist a pkiller or impede his or her opponent, either directly or by using skills, spells, or other in-game functions against other mobs or the mud environment. (See HELP PKILL).

- Non-clanned players may never loot the corpse of a clanned or non-clanned character, except anyone may remove items from the corpse of a character at that character's request to assist in corpse recovery, so long as he or she does not thereby involve an non-clanned character in pkill. (See HELP LOOTING).

- Asking or getting immorts to reveal or change your stats is not permitted, nor is getting or asking them to load items or mobs for you or to confer any other unfair advantage. (See HELP IMMORTS, HELP CHEAT).

- If you find a bug, you must report it by using the BUG command or mudmail to an immortal or even email to imp@mud.aus.sig.net. Taking advantage of a bug or using it to crash the mud is not permitted. (See HELP CHEAT).

- Intentionally placing a character over rent by loading him or her with excessive equipment is not permitted. (See HELP CHEAT).

- Experience may not be 'given' away by clanned characters permitting others to pkill them; repeated deaths will attract the attention of immorts. (See HELP CHEAT).

- In-game information (such as mob or item stats, quest solutions, etc.) may not be placed on public channels or boards (including clan boards). (See HELP CHEAT).

- Making false accusations under these rules is itself a punishable offense.

- There are also several rules that we have catalogued under 'etiquette.' Violations of these rules may not necessarily call for character deletion, but repeated violations may call for one of the lesser penalties listed above. Adherence to them will help to ease your relationships with other players on LegendMUD. (See HELP ETIQUETTE).

See generally, HELP MULTIPLAY, HELP HARASSMENT, HELP PKILL, HELP ETIQUETTE, HELP RIGHTS, HELP VIOLATIONS, HELP IMMORTS, HELP CHEAT, HELP LOOTING.

What follows are the individual help files referred to above. Each one is prefaced with a brief explanation of why the behavior is deemed undesirable.

Violations

Every law must have its penalties for when it is broken. Because this is an area in which so many have felt unfairly treated, we are going with a very straightforward system. This system has been in use by the admin department ever since the wizbit system went into effect.

Immorts maintain a log of violations in order to allow graduated punishment against repeat offenders. In the event of violations of the above policies:

- First Offense: a stern talking to, being written up in the offenders file, and possibly muzzling or revocation of other privileges or wrongfully acquired equipment or gold (tell, chat, etc.).

- Second Offense: a reminder that you have been warned, an append to the offenders file, plus the loss of half of your experience and, when relevant, loss of other equipment, stat, or right.

- Third Offense: character deletion and notation in the offenders file of the site from which you are logging.
- Fourth Offense: siteban is very possible.

The administrators reserve the right to upgrade the punishments based on the severity of the offense, and punishments may be more closely tailored to the specific violation (loss of gold or equipment or some other benefit wrongly acquired). Again, by entering the mud, you have agreed to abide by its policies and will be held responsible for them. We have very few problems on LegendMUD, as a whole, and the players themselves tend to uphold these rules as stringently as the immortals do. So please help keep this mud as nice a place as it has been for the last few years. See HELP RULES for basic guidelines and a list of related help files.

Multiplaying

Multiplaying not only gives an advantage to those players who run mud clients, but it also causes problems for the mud design itself. When a player uses multiple characters at once, the efficiency of monster-killing goes way, way up. The result is that there is less available for players to do. A mud with 60 multiplayed characters has to be larger than a mud supporting 60 separate characters. We prefer to sustain the maximum amount of people possible, rather than cater to fewer players. In addition, having 60 real people instead of 20 people and 40 robots also makes for a more interesting gaming session for the players themselves, as they get to interact with more people and have more varied experiences.

Players may make as many characters as they like, but they may connect only one at any given time. The rule against multiplaying is designed to put players on, as much as possible, an equal footing: to ensure that every item or advantage gained by a character was really gained by him or her or in grouping with other players. Where you have any doubt whether or not a particular activity constitutes multiplaying, ask yourself if the benefit your character is about to enjoy could have been gained if he or she were the first character you had ever made on LegendMUD.

In its most obvious form, 'no multiplaying' means you may not connect two characters at once, whether those characters are grouped or not grouped or for any other purpose. But 'no multiplaying' also means you may not use one of your characters for the advantage of another of your characters: you may not get equipment with one your characters to be given to another of your characters (either directly, by leaving it for the other to pick up, by giving it to another player to deliver, or by any other means). Multiplaying also includes dropping link, not completely renting out a character before logging on another character.

In the spirit of the rule against multiplaying, LegendMUD also asks that no more than one person play any given character. You may give away an non-clanned character, but please do not permit other people to play one of your characters. Sharing your character password is always a bad idea. No exceptions to the rules will be granted because a player claims that someone else was playing his or her character.

See HELP RULES for basic guidelines and a list of related help files.

Harassment

It seems odd to have to justify a rule against harassment, but there you go. :) As the help file explains, Legend has attracted a wide range of players of all ages and nationalities. A game is only fun as long as most of the players get along most of the time. At times, people get angry or upset, but that doesn't justify personal attacks that would not be permissible in real life either. In the past, the staff at Legend has had to resort to real-life action against those who have engaged in harassment, because this sort of behavior is frowned upon in general by law enforcement around the world.

In a different vein, the language restrictions are simply because polite society demands a higher standard of discourse than conversation among friends does. The public channels on LegendMUD are public venues, and people do not have a way to partake in the good aspects of them while filtering out the bad. Therefore we try to maintain a minimum standard on the public channels. It is worth noting that the restrictions given are far less stringent than what the Congressional Decency Act defined—and that the CDA is *not* defeated but merely in dispute and not currently enforced. Legend supports free speech, and believes that you have every right to state your opinion in a mature manner, but we also don't want the mud to be sued or shut down on obscenity charges. :)

In the area of harassment, we are concerned primarily with two topics: language used over public channels (general harassment) and harassment of particular persons or groups (specific harassment).

Language

LegendMUD has had players ranging from the age of seven on up. Therefore, we strictly enforce the following restrictions on language:

- No sexually explicit or strong cursing language on public channels. This includes CHAT, INFO, AUCTION, clan channels, and on public boards. Upon occasion a chat conference that has the tag [adult] may be created by an immortal, and [adult] conferences may make use of stronger language. [Adult] conferences must be explicitly joined by the individual, and hence listening to one implies acceptance of the language there.

- Said language is also not permissible in private communication—for example in mudmail, using the TELL command, or on clan boards—if it is unwelcome or someone hearing or receiving said language has asked you to stop.

- Said language is also not permissible as part of a character name or title, or in illusions.

Harassment

- Derogatory comments directed at the player operating a character are outside the bounds of LegendMUD and therefore have no place here. Real life threats are not only unwelcome on LegendMUD, they are illegal in real life.

- A pattern of extreme rudeness toward a specific character or player that is judged to exist outside the framework of the game and roleplay will not be tolerated. If harassment persists, we will go so far as to contact the systems administrator at your site and request that punitive action be taken, such as restricting access to our port, Internet service, or even that school disciplinary or criminal charges be filed.

- Likewise, a pattern of aggressiveness that has the above characteristics will not be tolerated, particularly if the aggressor carries it across multiple characters. OOC harassment masquerading as IC roleplaying is impermissible.

- Using unwanted and intimate socials on another character may be harassment. If he or she asks you to stop, then stop. In other circumstances, use your good judgment and remember that there is a person behind the character in the game.

- 'Spamming,' or the practice of sending repeated strings of text, is not allowed. Spamming a particular individual in tells will be considered harassment as will spamming over public channels.

- Racist or sexual slurs or slurs against any group are not any more permissible than the personal attacks forbidden above. Sexual harassment, including unwanted advances, is also not tolerated, including in names, titles, on public channels, in illusions, etc.

- Asking players repeatedly for help—spellword locations, equipment stats, skill advice, etc.—may be considered harassment in certain cases.

- In general, if a player asks you to leave him or her alone, you would be advised to comply.

See HELP RULES for basic guidelines and a list of related help files.

Playerkilling

This is probably the touchiest part of the rules, and the most controversial. At the same time, in many ways it is the most necessary. The players of Legend are essentially on an honor system when it comes to good behavior with playerkilling. None of what follows is new, but hopefully seeing it all laid out will help. The reasoning behind the playerkilling and clanned/unclanned rules is simply that there is so much potential for bad blood with the current system. Players and immorts do not favor going to a pkill-free mud nor an all-pk mud, and therefore we've collectively saddled ourselves with these rules.

Pkill is the exclusive prerogative of pkill-enabled characters, who must actively choose to become pkill-enabled. You may have only one pkill-enabled character at a time. Once a character is clanned, you may only unclan that character by either permanently retiring that character through deletion, permadeath, or petitioning to be included in the Hall of Legends, or by reaching 100,000,000 experience.

Characters who are not pkill-enabled may not interfere with pkill. In other words, while only pkill-enabled characters are actually able to kill another character, non-pkill-enabled characters might be able to find ways to interfere (for instance, by healing a participant in pkill, making him or her invisible or providing detect invisibility ability, repairing equipment, putting up walls, killing innkeepers or trans mobs, etc.)—such activities confer the excitement and fun of pkill without any of the risk.

Likewise, non-clanned characters may not ask a clanned character to kill another clanned character, or loot anything from the corpse of a clanned character. In other words, clanned characters may not accept a 'contract' on another clanned from a non-clanned character.

Therefore, any direct or indirect interferences, by a non-pkill-enabled character, even if the action is on behalf or otherwise representing a clanned player, will result in forced clanning of the non-pkill-enabled character (and the consequent deletion of any other clanned character belonging to the player); if the interference was solicited by a pkill-enabled character, he or she will also be subject to punishment.

Non-pkill enabled characters should generally refrain from giving any assistance that might be of use to pkill-enabled characters if there is any doubt about whether the pkill-enabled character is presently engaged in a running pkill battle. In other words, if you are grouped with a pkill-enabled character and saw him or her get wounded by the lion, you are of course free to heal him/her. But if that same character appears by you, leaking guts, and begs a heal (or any other help), it is your responsibility to be certain you are not interfering with pkill; when in doubt, it is your responsibility to make sure you are not interfering with pkill.

LegendMUD encourages grouping, and nothing in the rules concerning pkill should prevent clanned and non-clanned players from grouping. But, as a general rule, when pkill ensues, if you are an non-clanned character grouped with pkillers, you may not assist. Nor may you, alerted to the situation through your non-clanned character, run to get your clanned character to assist, since this would be multiplaying.

See HELP CLAN and HELP RULES for basic guidelines and a list of related help files.

Etiquette

This is a catch-all grab bag of minor rules and tips. Mostly tips. Often etiquette and social conventions on Legend are mistaken for hard and fast rules when they are not. But in many ways, conventions are more binding than rules (for one thing, usually everyone enforces them, not just the immort staff). You will see the term "officially discouraged" below. It refers to behaviors that in general are considered "twinkish" or poor sportsmanship, but which are unenforceable as rules. They'd likely get you kicked out of someone's living room, but won't get you kicked out of the mud unless they escalate into an illegal behavior. They WILL get you sermonized against, yelled at, and quite possibly discussed as an example of how Legend's playerbase is going to pot (hey, it's happened plenty before...) One of the main things to keep in mind about these sorts of etiquette rules is that they have arisen out of PLAYER concerns more than out of immort concerns, and have become so entrenched that we often get requests that they be officially enforced. They are not the immorts' rules so much as they are your own.

Society has many, often unspoken, rules of conduct that it relies upon for smooth operations. Newcomers to mudding are often unaware of mud etiquette. The tips that follow are a crash course in the most serious 'don'ts' of life of *LegendMUD*.

- Purposely attempting to put someone over rent is illegal.
- Please refrain from using all caps, in any circumstance. It is considered shouting.
- Please think carefully about the language and socials that you use (see help harassment). *LegendMUD* has an elaborate system of 'socials' that allow you to perform everything from a bow to a lick, but not every 'social' is appropriate in every situation or with people you have just met. When in doubt, ask yourself if you would presume to do x in real life... and, if not, then refrain.
- The general consensus on the mud is that multiple kills of another player are

bad form. They will be frowned upon, and will make the perpetrator an immediate target for permanent death among other pkill-enabled players. Multiple kills are not illegal; they are officially discouraged.

- The Out of Character Lounge is to be considered a place separate from the main mud. Please do not drag in-character conflicts into that area. Sitting in the OOC and taunting opponents is considered very bad form, as is hiding there from opponents. Again, it is not illegal; it is officially discouraged.

- Never lie to an immortal; always be fully co-operative with them, as they are trying to do a tough job. Do not assume they have all the information they need, and be as helpful as possible to them so that they can respond appropriately.

- Treat every character as a separate individual, and do not play 'across characters' ('crossplaying'). Do not give out the names of a player's other characters, do not ask for them, and do not reveal any information about their real life, including sites from where they connect, email addresses, etc. Real life stops as soon as you see the title screen—leave it there.

- Requests for help will generally be answered—demands for help will be ignored or flamed. Be polite and people will generally be polite in response.

- Do not place in-game information such as the stats on equipment, mobs, other players, quest steps, etc., on public channels or boards, including clan boards.

- Be reasonably polite and helpful to others on the mud. This includes things like not stealing their kills, not sitting by a mob and claiming you are 'reserving' it, not looting others' kills, etc.

- Before asking for help, take advantage of the FAQs and extensive help files that LegendMUD provides.

See HELP RULES for basic guidelines and a list of related help files.

Player rights

You were wondering, I'm sure. :) The player rights section attempts to correct some oddball myths about Legend—like the weird notion that we log everyone all the time—as well as make clear to what extent you have freedom there. The rights are really the foundation for all the other rules. Harassment rules would not exist if it were not for the right to enjoy "a mature atmosphere in which to play" (as it is described below). In that sense, this is the most important section of the rules.

Rights

- You have a general right to privacy. LegendMUD does not log your activity except for a log of failed saves for the purpose of tracking reimbursals. Snooping your activity only takes place during the course of an investigation into a violation of the rules, or with your explicit permission.

- You have the right to a mature atmosphere in which to play and enjoy yourself, and freedom from harassment.

- You have freedom of expression insofar as it does not harass anyone or violate the game rules or the rules of conduct.

- You have the right to professional treatment by the immortals. They have a much stricter code of behavior than players do, which may be read on the welcome board.

- You have the right to have your complaints heard. Please keep in mind that you should be ready to provide evidence or witnesses for complaints.

- Players with a complaint or those accused of any rule violations have a right to know who is accusing them and what they are being accused of; they have a right to defend themselves before the immort involved, explaining their take on events, what happened, and why; they have a right to have the immort making the decision explain his or her decision and the punishment imposed. Generally, these rights will attach before an immort takes any action against you; in extreme situations (as where someone is intransigently chatting obscenities), immorts reserve the right to act first and make inquiries after.

See HELP RULES for basic guidelines and a list of related help files.

Looting

The following rules are really related back to the clanned and unclanned rules. Nothing in either of them is particularly surprising. One thing to note is that changes to corpses with the new skill trees may make some of them obsolete, by literally not permitting some of these actions to occur.

Looting

- In general, looting of player corpses is only allowed if both the victim and the looter are clanned. This means that non-clanned characters may not loot the corpses of clanned characters or of non-clanned characters. Clanned characters may not loot the corpses of non-clanned characters, but they may loot the corpse of any clanned character (realizing, of course, that looting another pkiller's kill is likely to direct his or her attention to you).

- The one exception to the looting rule occurs in the case of assisting in corpse recovery. Clanned or non-clanned characters may loot the corpse of any character, at that character's specific request, in order to help that character recover his or her equipment, so long as this does not impermissibly involve an non-clanned character in pkill.

See HELP RULES for basic guidelines and a list of related help files.

Cheating

The reason why the following things are not allowed is simple: we want the mud to stay fun. A game where all the solutions are handed out to you in advance is a game where there is no challenge, fewer surprises—and in the long term, a lot less players. Hence rules restricting the public dissemination of stats, solutions, and so on. This doesn't mean that you can't help out your friends, of course. It just means that going about it in a very public manner is counterproductive. Instead of helping those people, you are actually limiting their enjoyment. If ever in doubt, think back to when you first managed to solve some particularly tricky quest, or discovered that awfully cool item—and ask yourself why you'd want to deny that same thrill to another player.

- If you see a bug, you are obligated to report it (SEE HELP BUG) and not to take advantage of it, for the sake of the mud's balance and the enjoyment of other players. We typically give small rewards for reporting bugs. Exploitation and concealment of a bug is regarded as cheating. Any advantages you gain from a bug will be stripped if it is discovered you have been making use of one.

- Purposeful crashing of the mud will result in immediate deletion of all characters involved.

- Offering quest solutions, mob or equipment stats, locations of skill teachers or spell words, or any other 'secret' in-game information over public channels (info, chat, etc.) or by posting on public or clan boards is cheating. We officially discourage the posting of such information on web pages or through clan mailing lists.

See generally, HELP RULES, HELP MULTIPLAY, HELP HARASSMENT, HELP PKILL, HELP ETIQUETTE, HELP RIGHTS, HELP VIOLATIONS, HELP IMMORTS, HELP LOOTING.

Immorts

In case you were feeling like the immortals had it easy in this whole thing, here's this section to show otherwise. The immort staff is obligated to follow *ALL* the rules that apply to players, only to an even higher standard. They are often not allowed to even help their friends *with their mortal* in a way that would be perfectly legal if they were not immort. In general, being an immort is treated as a volunteer job, complete with progress reports, bosses, and deadlines. It is never a way to help your mortals advance—in fact, as a rule you can expect your mortal characters to stagnate as all of your time gets taken up with immort duties. :)

- Immorts are not permitted to give in-game help. Attempting to get an immort to give in-game assistance or information is illegal, especially information about other players' characters, sites, etc. Repeated attempts may be considered harassment.

- Immorts are not permitted to use their status as immortals for the benefit of their other characters. Immortals must generally log out their immort before logging in a pkill-enabled character.

- Immorts are not permitted to use their status as immortals to abuse or harass players; they may not use their abilities to help players outside the realm of their immort duties.

- Immorts are governed by a strict code of conduct. If you believe you have been wrongfully treated by an immort, inform an Admin Immort or one of the Implementors, Kaige or Ptah at imp@mud.aus.sig.net.

See HELP RULES for basic guidelines and a list of related help files.

The Immort Code Of Conduct

One thing which may strike you about the imm code of conduct is that it isn't fair towards the immorts. It outright states that "this doesn't cover everything, and it doesn't matter. If you do something wrong that violates the spirit of these rules, you're still in very hot water." That is not the case with the player code of conduct, which will get amended to cover new situations as they arise. Immorts are held to a much higher standard, and the rules are consequently more vague.

Immort Code of Conduct

The following Code of Conduct was rolled out to LegendMUD along with the new immort structure. In it you can see early steps towards later key ideas such as the notion that as servants of the online community, immortals are more restricted in their behaviors than ordinary players are. It also strongly emphasizes the notion that immortals are bound by strict ethics rules that curtail their ability to use the godlike powers that their position affords them. It was a common practice on many MUDs for admins to use their powers for their own amusement; the first person I ever fired was in fact a MUD admin on LegendMUD who considered it a perk of the job to spy invisibly on couples having virtual sex in their private rooms.

General Principles

- the immortals are here to improve the mud
- the immortals are here to make the experience of being on Legend enjoyable for everyone, not just your friends
- use your head! if you have to stop to think whether an action is illegal, it's better not to do it, and ask someone, than to chance it
- respect the players—they are why we are here
- do nothing to harm the growth of the mud

Punishment structure

- First offense: warning
- Second offense: demotion (stripping of wizbits and/or level)
- Third offense: deletion

This means that if you are given a warning for command abuse and are then caught harassing a mortal or another immort you will be demoted. This is a very strict punishment system but should be easy enough to live with if we all behave like adults.

Warnings remain on record for six months, so you can screw up once every six months until someone catches on to the pattern.

Command Abuse

Using your immort powers to give benefit to **any** mortal (yours or others') beyond the scope of your normal immort duties, is considered abuse of immort powers. Likewise, using your immorts' skills and spells to benefit **any** mortal is abuse.

Examples of some things not to do:

- transfer a player from anywhere but OOC unless within the scope of your job
- attack or kill a player by any means
- snoop or otherwise spy upon a player or other immortal
- heal a player
- use immort knowledge or commands for in-game benefits such as telling another player where an item or mob or player is
- revealing anyone's site or other characters to anyone
- steal from a player
- load or otherwise obtain objects for players
- alter or affect a character's attributes or equipment
- transferring mobs
- registering unapproved descriptions
- stringing items without a coupon
- etc

This is a pretty small list of possible offenses. It represents the **spirit** of the rules. If you violate the spirit of the rules, you will be held as accountable as if you violated the letter of the law.

There is a small list of things that may seem counter to these rules that are permissible **if** you have the appropriate wizbit. Ask your Dept. Head about them.

Harassment

An immortal harassing a mortal in any way has no place on Legend, and may result in summary demotion or deletion.

Immortals harassing other immortals will be considered on par with any other offense.

Information and actions as a mortal

An immortal may not give out any information beyond hints or explanations of why something happened. If you do not know why something happened, **say so**. Do not simply tell players, "You must have done something wrong."

At all times, be as helpful as possible within the rules. The mortals of immorts are held to the same standard, which means they must not give out quest solutions, teacher locations, skill information, item stats, etc.

Similarly, immortals' morts may not engage in playerkilling or stealing without extremely clear in-context reasons that are clearly evident to the victim. If the victim is not aware of the reason, then the immortal is at fault. Yes, this limits the scope of an immorts' actions as a mort, but all immortals **must** serve as an example of ideal player behavior, or the credibility of all immortals is undermined. It may also serve to help immortals broaden the scope of their actions and roleplay, rather than falling back on the typical mortal behaviors.

Summary

All of the above are intended to do the following:

- encourage trust in the immort staff
- encourage the immort staff to take a more creative and helpful role in the development of the mud
- encourage a more mature and polite atmosphere

If you do not feel comfortable with the principles embodied in the above, it is suggested you depart from the immort staff as quickly as possible.

MUD Influence

As part of the ongoing raking over the coals of Richard Bartle for saying the obvious[87] (yes, you can tell what side I am on in those debates!), Steve Danuser says over at Moorgard.com » Sacred Cows[88]:

> I get tired of people implying that today's MMOs owe their entire existence to the MUDs of yesteryear. Sorry, I disagree. The gameplay style of EQ or WoW is obviously influenced by MUDs, but I propose that MMOs would have evolved anyway.

And Ryan Shwayder posts in comments saying

> *Ultima Online* is a direct descendant of what MUD? I'm not saying it isn't, I'm just saying that I don't know what particular MUD had a profound influence on that game. It seems like the MMO industry was born of different influences; *EverQuest* from DikuMuds, *Ultima Online* from Ultima games. Not all MMOs have a lot of direct comparisons to MUDs, so I think he's right that they'd exist whether MUDs did or not.

Well…

There's little doubt that MMOs would have evolved anyway. In fact, they actually DID evolve anyway. MMOs were created simultaneously and independently by a dozen groups at once. The folks doing *Meridian 59* did not know about the folks doing *Kingdom of the Winds*, and so on. Not to mention older antecedents like *Habitat*. MUDs, in fact, were also invented independently at least four times, as Bartle himself has stated many times over.

That said:

- The early *EverQuest* developers played Diku derivatives in the form of *Sojourn* and children muds such as *Duris* and *Toril*.

---

[87] Dr. Bartle had given at interview at Massively (https://web.archive.org/web/20080705121755/http://www.massively.com:80/2008/06/20/richard-bartle-on-how-hed-make-world-of-warcraft-better/) which caused some controversy among MMO bloggers.

[88] https://web.archive.org/web/20080705193828/http://www.moorgard.com/?p=235

- Early folks on *Meridian 59* played Diku derivatives such as *Worlds of Carnage*.

- The original core team on *Ultima Online* was a mix of two LP Mudders, a MUSH/MOOer, and a few Diku-folks. And one *Ultima* guy.

- I could go on — *The Realm* and many others also had those sorts of antecedents.

The result? Today's MMOs are mostly reskinned muds. It is very very hard to find an MMO that **doesn't** have a direct comparison to a text world. Yes, even *EVE*, even *A Tale in the Desert*.

And, I must point out, even today much of the leadership behind the MMOs today is *still* from that "old guard" (though not necessarily from the mud world) — the designers and executives of the mid-to-late 90's *are still the ones determining what you play* in many ways, from Mark[89] over at Mythic/EA to Damion, Rich, and Gordon over at Bioware,[90] to Kim Taek-jin and the Garriotts at NCSoft…

If they had been invented independently, **they would be different**.

What did MMOs **really** bring to the table, design-wise?

- Greater sense of spatiality. This mostly affected aggro management, and it did make combat significantly richer.

- More advanced raiding — it existed, but it lacked all of the support infrastructure that eventually popped up.

- Much heavier use of instancing — it was a very unusual and rare technology back then.

- Lots of cool support features — like, adding quest logs to quests, for example.

- Dancing.

- Pictures.

In the recent discussions, a lot of folks have cited stuff like WAR's upcoming public quests as new, or the Tome of Knowledge. These people have clearly never played *MUME*.[91] Or maybe not *EverQuest*, which had public quests too. Or…

I think it's easy to be dismissive of history, and say that it's not relevant. I'm pretty sure I have heard a quote somewhere about the consequences of that. Moving forward without knowledge of the past is far more likely to result in going in circles. **MMOs have *removed* more features from MUD gameplay than they have added**, when you look at the games in aggregate.

---

[89] This would be Mark Jacobs.

[90] Damion Schubert, Rich Vogel, and Gordon Walton, who were working on *Star Wars: The Old Republic* at the time.

[91] Multi Users in Middle Earth, a very popular Tolkien-themed MUD. See http://mume.org/

The fact that people can cite things like "big boss battles in a public zone" or "really rich badge profiles and player stat tracking" as truly differentiating features mostly speaks to how narrow the scope of the field has gotten in the public's mind. This is like arguing over whether scalloped bracing in acoustic guitars is a defining characteristic for all of music, when in fact it has zero relevance to MIDI controllers. By analogy, Bartle, like many of us, is arguing from the perspective of all music — all virtual worlds. And his detractors are people who only listen to indie rock from the Athens, GA, area circa 1989. All Richard is asking for is for someone to *please play some jazz.*

Failure to evolve more radically isn't a flaw — in that sense, I agree completely with Moorgard. But then, I tend to think that **all** the current MMOs in the game industry are already the Old Guard relative to the new webby folks. I think the mudder crew is already the Older Guard anyway. So in a sense this is kind of like an argument between art rockers and disco musicians.

Leaving Legend

Many classic issues of MMO design manifested on MUDs, but they all tended to have a much more personal flavor precisely because the populations were much smaller. Here is a little log showing what it looked like to be Ptah, the immortal "Implementor" on LegendMUD.

Among the things coming up in this brief session — probably around half an hour — were dealing with in-bound questions for a player who had lost their real life cat and whether a virtual memorial could be created for it. There is also a discussion with the creator of the first full quest walkthrough site for LegendMUD ever put up on the web; Legend, like many MUDs of the day, had a policy against disclosing quest solutions to other players as it was considered cheating.

This log has had about half the text cut, mostly stuff that was admin messages showing the arrival and departure of every player on the system. It was also edited and in some cases re-ordered chronologically to be easier to follow.

You tell Beam, 'If you're going to leave the page up (and we can't really stop you) you should at least check it before putting it up to make sure it doesn't invade people's privacy like that...'

You tell Beam, 'you can certainly expect a lot of flak from the bards whose encyclopedia you posted...'

Mika bounds up and licks you.

Beam tells you, 'well the quest page is gone now'

Beam tells you, 'but i need to remove some things'

Beam tells you, 'i will edit it'

You tell Beam, '*sigh* I can't tell you how lousy having the page exist at all makes us feel, like it's not worth working on the mud anymore :P'

Beam tells you, 'what if it just had an eq list would that be bad?'

You tell Beam, 'honestly, yes :P'

Beam tells you, 'ok'

You tell Beam, 'for example, say we wanted to make identify useful. We wouldn't be able to, because of that page. The only way to make it useful would be to randomize the bonuses on eq'

Mika whines.

You tell Beam, 'say we wanted to write quests, the only way to make ones that people wouldn't know the answer to would be to make random goals'

Clutch tells you, 'if and when i remember to write Rufus about putting in my office, can i have a pet? :)'

Beam tells you, 'ok i will remove it'

Mika gives you a big, wet, slurpy kiss.

You tell Beam, 'which means very simplistic quests'

Mika sniffs around you, looking for a handout.

You tell Beam, 'I understand that you are trying to create a fan web page—I also understand that you want to give help to those who want to play well. :(But I don't know how to go about it in a way that doesn't make a cheat sheet'

Beam tells you, 'hmm'

You tell Clutch, 'a pet is usually every builder's first project.'

Clutch tells you, 'ahhhh...'

Beam tells you, 'what about just a list of quests and hints how to start them'

Mika barks once loudly.

Clutch tells you, 'so only builders have pets?'

You tell Clutch, 'well, used to be every imm was a builder, see. :)'

You tell Clutch, 'So I don't know what the policy would be now, or whether we have room to put them in the OOC'

Clutch tells you, 'yah, i know :)'

Clutch tells you, 'i guess just no non-builders have asked until now... :)'

You tell Beam, 'Hints are a lot better than full solutions, certainly, and lists sort of exist already in the whois'

Clutch tells you, 'i guess i should talk to Rufus?'

[Chat] Somar: *wishes the amulet quest was repeatable

Mika gives you a big, wet, slurpy kiss. :)

You tell Clutch, 'I guess :)'

Beam tells you, 'ok i will stick to general advice and stuff'

[Chat] Bulk: *wishes the token quest was repeatable ;)

You tell Beam, 'You could also go to a tiered system, where in each quest you had to go through a bunch of web pages to get specific info (like a hint book... one general advice, then after that more specific, after that more details, etc)'

Clutch tells you, 'cool...i've had a couple requests for memorials...Ryssa's cat died, and my friend's ran away from home...'

You tell Clutch, '*nod*'

Clutch tells you, 'maybe i SHOULD be a builder :)'

[Chat] Somar: *wishes the seoni quest was repeatable*

[Chat] Bulk: actually. a repeatable HP quest would b nice :P

[Chat] Somar: *wishes every quest was repeatable*

[Chat] Fatale: *wishes the spirit quest was repeatable because she only needs spirit to join the naked mage club*

[Chat] Tabitha: is glad that the quests aren't repeatable because newbies would never get a chance then

[Chat] Ptah: *wishes no quests were repeatable because they went away after being solved a new one was automatically created*

Beam tells you, 'ok'

[Chat] Sandra: yay Ptah!

[Chat] Truth: What Ptah, so only ONE person does a quest?

[Chat] Fatale: then another quest takes it place.

[Chat] Ptah: Sure, an ever-changing world, where you can't do the same thing twice because time has moved on, the city was restored, the dragon was dead, and something else entirely took its place

```
[Chat] Clutch: *cheer* Ptah
[Chat] Somar: is that coming in with skilltrees?
[Chat] Bulk: i like repeatable quests. they make you
feel smart ;)
[Chat] Clutch: i think it was wishful thinking...
```

Ryssa tells you, 'can you make The Imp like your Mika?'

```
[Chat] Ptah: no, it's not coming in anytime that I know
of.
[Chat] Ptah: Not unless you want us to shut down this
mud and start a new one—in which case, see ya in two
years
```

Mika whines.

```
[Chat] Bulk: uhm. no.
```

You tell Ryssa, 'The Imp?'

Drakkon tells you, 'what program did you make this mud with?'

Ryssa tells you, 'my cat that died :('

You tell Drakkon, 'it is written in ANSI C. We started out with a Merc code base but rewrote it from scratch'

```
[Chat] Coldfire: <—wants to know WHEN the skilltrees are
coming
[Chat] Green2Guest: skill trees ?
```

```
[Chat] Ptah: well, at this point, Kaige and I are
ending our 9th successive week of working 12 hour
days... you can imagine that the imp's time for doing
skill trees is rather limited :P
[Chat] CLeo: a new way to learn skills...
[Chat] CLeo: therefore there will be more required
skills to learn others… something like that
```

Drakkon tells you, 'cool I'm making one right now with a program called make zones fast'

You tell Drakkon, 'Oh, that's just an area editor for room files...'

You tell Drakkon, 'we use a text editor :)'

Mika runs off to play elsewhere.

Drakkon tells you, 'ahhh how do you do that is it hard?'

```
[Chat] Ptah: GreenGuest, there is a lengthy FAQ on
skill trees on the web page and on the welcome board.
basically it is a skill-based usage system with twice
as many skills and many more possible professions…
         [Closing link to Green2Guest.]
[Chat] Ptah: oh well, he lost link :P
```

You tell Drakkon, 'Not really, the area parser is one of the things we rewrote :)'

Beam tells you, 'ok its being removed now'

CLeo tells you, 'hey btw did you ever tried my recipe? The dolmathes?'

Beam tells you, 'did you get my note about wimpy triggering'

```
         [Chat] Bulk: skilltrees is a mere legend ; )
[Chat] Ptah: is not, there's a working copy of the code
on this machine. Two, actually (one has configurable
prompts and the other doesn't).
```

You tell CLeo, 'No :('

Drakkon tells you, 'It's pretty fun making zones and weapons and items and stuff on mzf:)'

CLeo tells you, ':) well try it :)'

You tell Beam, 'Yes, I did, but we're going to have to look at the code to see why. Dropping link, btw, never did change the initiative thing… only renting out did'

Ryssa tells you, ':(please?'

CLeo tells you, ';)'

```
         [Chat] Truth: Wonder which comes out first Macintosh
         System 8.0 (Copeland) or skill trees?
         [Chat] Panzer: so thats why its always so lagged? your
         running a background mud?
[Chat] Ptah: no, Panzer, we do not run a background mud
all the time :P
```

Beam tells you, 'it did for pkill'

Beam tells you, 'put you on top of wholist'

Beam tells you, 'not on mobs tho'

[Chat] Panzer: bug! bug! bug!

You tell Ryssa, 'There is a mob called The Imp that is your cat?'

Ryssa tells you, 'I was wondering if you could make one like Mika...'

You tell Ryssa, 'You'll have to ask Rufus about adding in your cat... but I know Clutch was asking about it too, so maybe you'll get it :)'

You tell Beam, 'you made the changes very quickly. :) Thank you'

Drakkon tells you, 'your making another mud, whats it called?'

You tell Drakkon, 'Ultima Online :)'

You slowly vanish into thin air.

Alright guys!

Alright guys!

Ptah, Kaige, Rufus, Sadist, and many others have been working on this game for a LONG time...the pre-alpha test is already long gone.....now the beta is here!!

Those of you who dreamed of a real graphical MUD may want to take a look at this....and perhaps about 1000 other players will be on at the same time. The system requirements are fairly steep, however, and here goes for the WIN95 version:

8 megabytes of RAM (prefers 32)

486DX4/75 CPU (prefers 133Mhz Pentium)

VLB or PCI video with 1 Megabyte of RAM(prefers 2 MBs with PCI)

50 MEGS of HD space(prefers 150MBS)

2X CDROM(prefers 4XCDROM)

16-bit soundcard

.....and a REALLY GOOD MOUSE:)

You can register at www.owo.com(I think) and you will find more info there)

you must send $2 check to cover cost of CD and postage

See you online!(beta tests prolly start sometime in the fall...)[92]

---

[92] From the Legendary Times, July 30th, 1996.
https://www.legendmud.org/Community/lt_indices/Vol3/LTv3n9.html

Ultima Online

Ultima Online is Fifteen

Today was the fifteenth anniversary of the launch of *Ultima Online*.[93] Here's something that I think no one has ever seen. My wife and I were driving from Alabama (where we were in grad school) to Austin, to visit friends there — Sherry Menton and Rick Delashmit. All four of us worked together on *LegendMUD*.

Kristen and I had been talking about making another mud, one with deeper simulation elements. We talked about having abstract properties running behind things, instead of hard-coding every quest. How much cooler would it be, we thought, if the NPCs were simulated entities, rather than merely responding to player actions?

We took notes on a pad of paper, as we drove. We took turns, which is why the handwriting in these images changes:

---

[93] Thi is from a blog post posted on Sept 25th, 2012.

series of "polar" attributes that define characters
limited scale   not all polar
... uses fiction to define behavior

✦ spells — completely component attribute based
major kinds of power necessary to
control spell

det
are away from
temperature   crush to crush
weather   ⎬ area info
topography   ⎬ elevation in the rooms

ACT_DATE "Month day" or ACT_DATE x y z

closed economy = limited number of each item
in the space
technology? up to crossbow? limit total gold also
basic motorized vehicles — maybe?

perhaps precious
items melted
down into
coins.

languages — "hometown" based

.... to some sort of scale
long stretches of "not to scale" places world
used to talk passage of some sort

Place an important role in world.

everyone is still enabled and dead → dead
corpses track who killed them
most mobs hate people who come in and start killing randomly
level ≠ greater ability
familiarity imparts abilities

Name mobs & players upon creation with
set of syllables & masculine/fem endings
title = nickname
manufacture of items ONLY from raw materials

define what provides sustenance room or obj
to create a food chain
mear Resets based on # supportable   gradually
skills until that # met   loaded or

Generic fauna in generic file
and equipment

begin w/trading/frontier outpost near
a lake for fishing

say should take arguments
say (annoyed)
(testy)
plus also analogues — let mutter, grumble,
etc give messages.

"Generic description system" — a new section
of the area file, #GENERIC or something.
Fires generic descs by num. In a room's
desc, it can [#vnum] and it is assumed
that it uses the generic desc, followed by specs
The move_char routine calls a special
do_look that checks that the new room &
old room have different generic descs —
and if they don't, show all; if do, just
fire " "You are still <room title>.

corpses — short — the corpse of a ____

long — a dead ____ is here.

multiples RACE   or ~~names~~

Number ~~s~~ are here.   • the corpse of — is here.

vary unless multiples.

generic "growls at you, is here" message
is based off the RACE flags
so birds etc don't growl—very silly!

MOBS "homeroom" isn't "room loaded to" but
a room where mobs return to to
sleep and heal.

Currency = gp, sp, cp? or what?

Coins Gold of course weighs! Can you pick up
partial piles of gold?

No inventory other than hands. figure # by

SIZE = VOLUME   kg can get

You can do certain things to items
in the dark — perhaps another
light level. DARK < PITCH-BLACK (?)

Objects have a line of values which indicate
what you need to produce them.
new mobonly command —produce or
—manufacture vnum' if you give them
a component they will see if they
can make it and if so will. (used with
                                        ACT_GIVE
shopkeepers will keep producing so can't
new items as long as they have the manufact
raw materials. Maybe reboot loads   just a
them with X number of item to sell and item
Y number of components.

                              ; height
Mobs/Chars have a weight which , I guess
is influenced by race & "con",
determines corpse weight so you could

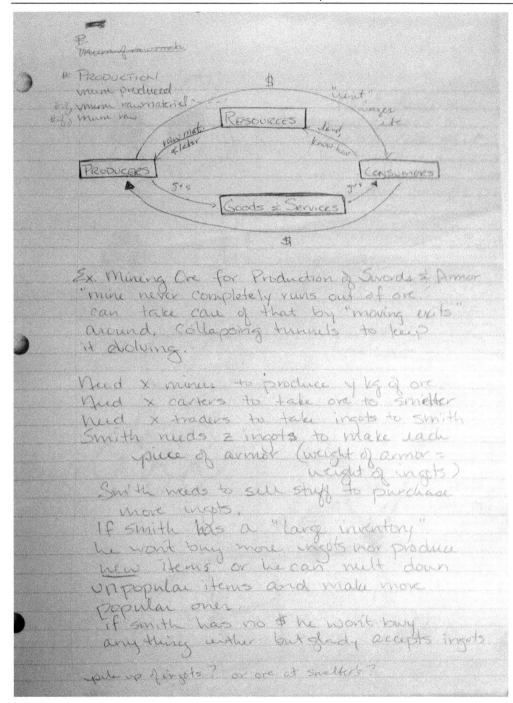

Ex. Mining Ore for Production of Swords & Armor
"mine never completely runs out of ore.
can take care of that by "moving exits"
around. Collapsing tunnels to keep
it evolving.

Need x miners to produce y kg of ore
Need x carters to take ore to smelter
Need x traders to take ingots to smith
Smith needs z ingots to make each
      piece of armor (weight of armor =
                        weight of ingots)
Smith needs to sell stuff to purchase
   more ingots,
If smith has a "large inventory"
he won't buy more ingots nor produce
new items. or he can melt down
unpopular items and make more
popular ones.
if smith has no $ he won't buy
anything either but gladly accepts ingots

pile up of ingots? or ore at smelter's?

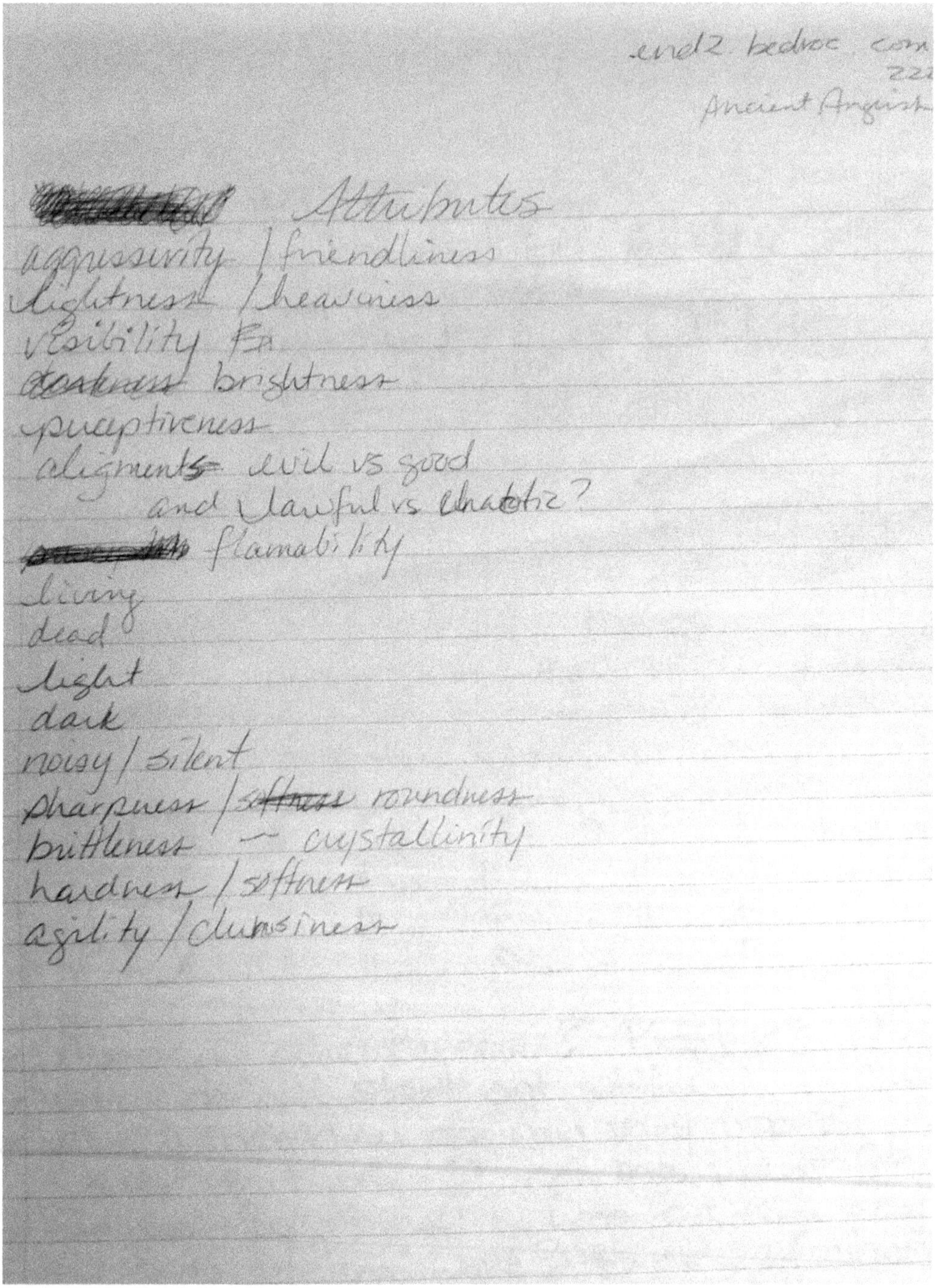

end2 bedroc con
zz
Ancient Anguish

Attributes

aggressivity / friendliness
~~lightness~~ / heaviness
visibility Fa
~~darkness~~ brightness
perceptiveness
~~alignments~~ evil vs good
    and lawful vs ~~chaotic~~?
~~_____~~ flamability
living
dead
light
dark
noisy / silent
sharpness / ~~softness~~ roundness
brittleness — crystallinity
hardness / softness
agility / clumsiness

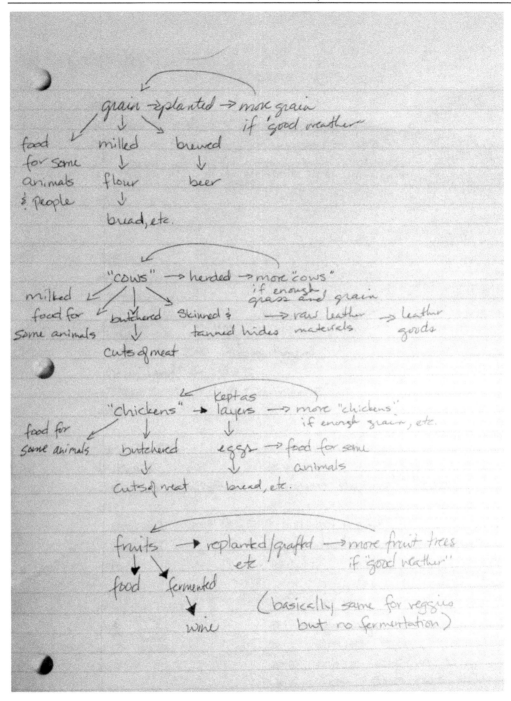

#RESETS
#ticks to check & begin update
M vnum areanum maxnum (in area)
O vnum rnum (if ground item) maxnum
B vnum dir [1] in previous item maxnum
   rnum
S
#0

#SHOPS
#vnum SHOPKEEPER
 #produced
vnum1 vnum2 vnum3 etc.
 initial initial
markup markdown
0 24 2 4 24 store hours
min "level" to shop
"RACES that can patronize"
#0

#GROUPS   # ANTIGROUPS
#vnum   # vnum
 vnum assists   vnum naturally hates
#-1   #-1
 vnum1   vnums that
 vnum2   mutually hate each other
#0   #0

#WEATHER   #SYLLABLES
#1 better   #1 ~~beginning~~ consonant beg.
    same
#2 better   #2 vowel beg.
    same
    worse
#3 "   #3 masc. endings
#4 "   #4 fem endings
#0   #5 punctuation
                           #0

Skills hunt doesn't work off of whole area
but rooms keep track of last ✖ people
in it. Higher Traffic = loss of trail
checks rooms in all dir and gives
directional messages for ~~highest number~~
~~one~~ one next in path to person?
Or one with "highest/most recent pass by?

dowsing – creates a timed spring.

water & elevation. – RAIN RUNS DOWN HILL &
     if "bad" or long enough weather can
     create rivers, flooding & mud!?!
A Lot of which can be done in procedures
~~Rooms~~ ~~can ha~~

Fountains can dry up!
   water ones may be can be replenished with
                              rain water
you can empty items into fountains & others
   as well so you could fill a tub from
   the stream or other water source

can fill in water rooms but depending
on room flag depends on water type
   fresh to salt
   ~~water~~ 2 new ROOM FLAGS SALT_WATER,
              and FRESH_WATER
timer on FOUNTAIN TYPES maybe shows
        when puddles dry up
   and add a value so marble/more
   Perm structures dry up but are empty

One of those pages has the old address of *Ancient Anguish*, a mud we were checking out. It's still up.[94] As you can see, a lot of the heavy lifting was done by my wife, the economist. Some of this stuff ended up making it into *LegendMUD* — the weather stuff, for example. You also see there the notes on the genesis of the moods system that was first in *Legend*, then eventually in *Star Wars Galaxies*. It wasn't until '05 that I was able to do the water flowing downhill stuff, as part of an R&D project at SOE that was never used for anything. It worked, though.

Here was born the resource system.[95] When we were asked to submit design samples, the resource system is what we sent in. It was more elaborated than this, much closer to what was eventually built for the game. Then they asked us to submit quest samples. They had sent us some sample code, to ask if we could read and understand it. We could… and we weren't very impressed by it. I sent in the Beowulf quest from Legend as my sample…

Jungle art

An anecdote: We're all meeting over the fact that we're short on artists. It meant that we might lose the entire jungle biome.

I said to Starr, "If I can have a Wacom tablet, I can probably draw plants."

Starr turned to Rick and said "Is he any good?"

Rick shrugged. "Yeah, he's not bad."

I got a Wacom tablet. And I did all of these. They were all drawn from issues of *National Geographic* that I brought in from home… that's why there are several specifically Hawaiian plants there. Later, poor Chuck Crist had to go through and painstakingly remove the black edging from them — I hadn't done them on a transparent layer.

---

[94] At http://ancient.anguish.org/
[95] See a few chapters ahead!

That was far from the only art stuff I did on UO. All the design materials for UO went off to the lawyers when the lawsuit hit. It was a six foot tall stack of paper. I don't actually think it ever came back. There was a printed out record of every patch. Design specs for everything. Detailed maps of every section of the world. For all I know, it is sitting in a legal file folder at EA somewhere… But I do have a few things from a sketchbook.

A lot of the time we were trying to solve problems like stairs, or buttresses. For those who recall the Mage Tower in Britain, I created the templates for arches and flying buttresses just for that building. Trinsic was the reason we got sloping walls at all. I also created the templates for how to do stairs, and later, sloping terrain.

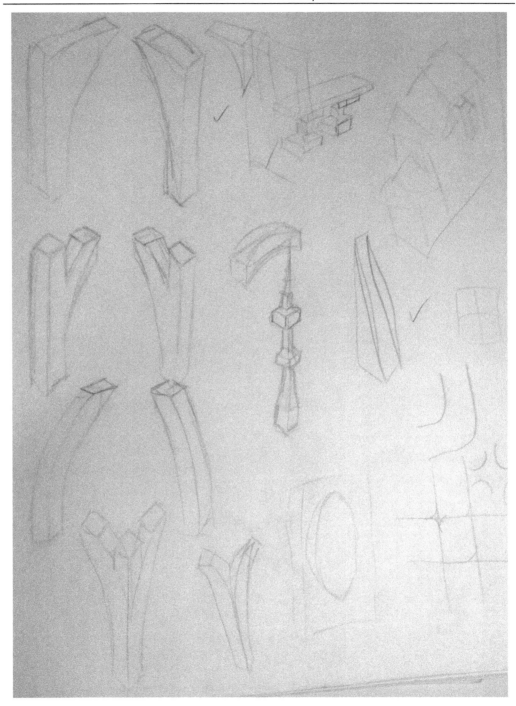

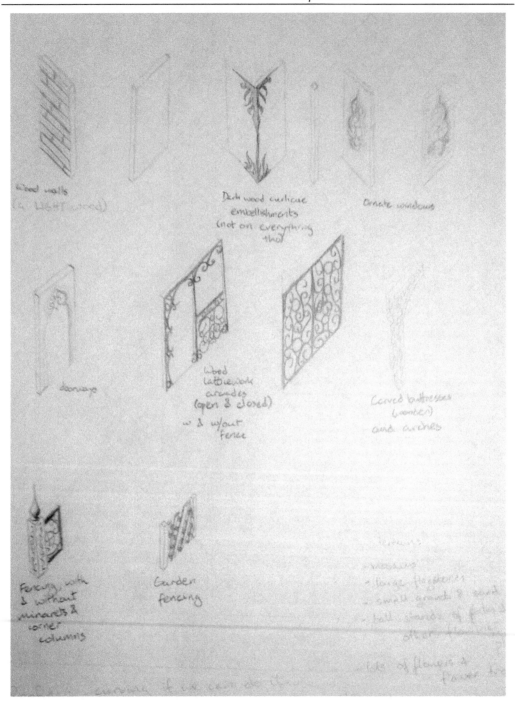

Wood walls
(& LIGHT wood)

Dark wood curlicue
embellishments
(not on everything
tho)

Ornate windows

doorways

Wood
latticework
arcades
(open & closed)
~ & w/out
fence

Carved buttresses
(wooden)
and arches

Fencing with
& without
minarets &
corner
columns

Garden
fencing

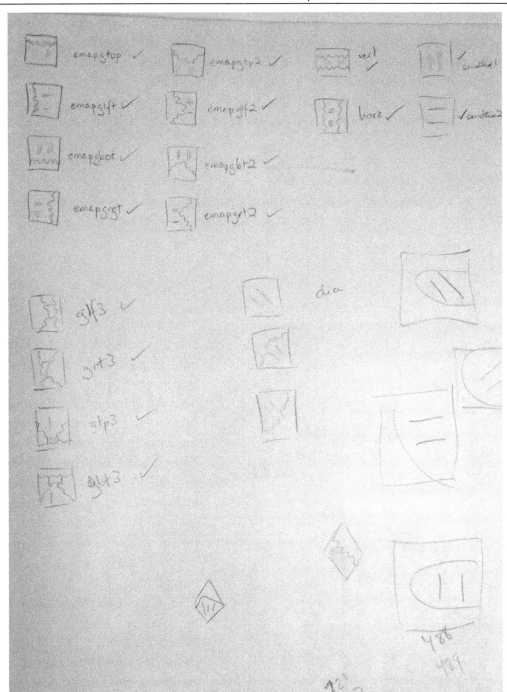

The embankments, as we called them, were an interesting challenge. We had experimented with doing height as pure optical illusion… I had worked up a faked set of terrain tiles which just had lighter and darker sides and were impassable, to suggest slopes. The whole thing made the ground look ziggurat-like.

Then Rick Delashmit said he could probably actually give us texture-mapped terrain. But we needed a way to signal ravines and other slopes that were impassable… in particular, along the shorelines.

The result were the embankment texture sets — the fourth image above is presumably where I worked them out…

I used to actually draw isometric versions of structures, and even whole cities (I did for Serpent's Hold) in order to plan out exactly where everything would go…

Launch

Eventually, of course, the game launched. And with it came a lot of press. I would be given faxed-in copies of articles from all over the world by the PR folks. Almost all of the reviews were middling to bad. 6 out of 10 was a pretty common score. (We did also get a pile of awards, including a couple for special achievement. We never got to see any of the trophies. They all went to EA HQ. I hear they are now all at Mythic).

In one of these pics you can see the faxed-in cover of *Computer Games* magazine… I had been slaving for weeks over a very cool and much more elaborately built environment called Teratha. It was a spider-worshipping culture that built its city around a volcano. It became the cover image for the magazine article — and was cut from the game a little while later. I was devastated... but we had to make a *lot* of cuts... I mean, three whole continents were the first to go...! I remember sketching stuff out for the cultures of the Lands of the Dark Unknown — I think some of this eventually became stuff used in the Lost Lands and in Elikki and some other locales in Britannia. So if you ever wondered where these extra islands and whatnot came from... like Ocllo... well, now you know.

I also got a dozen or so emails and letters from fellow developers across the game industry — from Meridian 59, from Blizzard, from LucasArts and Bioware, full of praise. I printed them out and tacked them up on my office door. Marketing folks then asked me if they could use them in press materials and I told them no, they were never meant for the public. I still have those print-outs — and I am still not sharing them with you.

During the early days of UO, when PKing was rampant, we notice a major issue in servers hosted along the Pacific Rim — much higher rates of PKing, harassment complaints, etc. We dig in, and it turns out that we were seeing lots of warfare and animosity between players from Asia and players from the US.

Hong Kong servers suffered for a while from triad gang wars being imported into UO. Guilds would form that matched the gangs, and the streets of Britain would run with simulated real-life blood.

Years later, I visit China, and I am surprised that anyone even knows who I am, since China never officially got a UO release. I was told that UO servers running either pirated servers or gray shard servers probably hit as many as 400,000 players across China.

And then, of course, came the lawsuit.

The lawsuit was, as I recall, over the fact that the game was advertised as being available 24/7. But it was crashing, and therefore not always available. So a lawyer who went by the game handle "Bunboy" sued us. And his lead plaintiff, amazingly enough, was someone that I already knew: a *LegendMUD* player who had been an administrative challenge for years. In short, a problem player from one game had followed us to another game!

By then, Kristen was staying home with our second child. We had brought our first born, our daughter, into the offices with us. Every single person on the UO team had either quit, moved back to *Ultima IX,* or moved over to the already begun *Ultima Online 2.* I was the only person left.

Origin asked us for an expansion. We had to use the empty space left on the edge of the map. All that would fit was a small chunk that I sketched out to

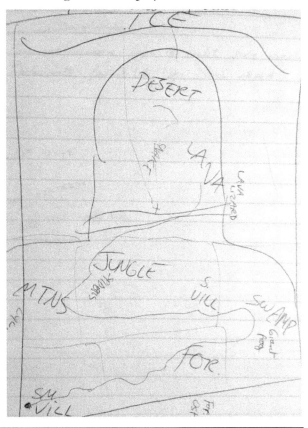

mimic a portion of Ambrosia from *Ultima III*. We hired a few new folks — Chris Mayer (Faceless), Runesabre (Kirk Black)… I think it was a team of six, plus some of the folks who had quit working on contract, and we made *The Second Age* in three months.

The EA lawyers were very unhappy with me over a quote from that newspaper article in the pic. I ended by saying UO was "a grand experiment."

They said "don't you realize that's the sort of thing they will use in court against us?"

But it was. Grand.

Random UO Anecdote

There used to be an ad agency on the fifth floor of the Origin building, back when it was off of 360. I can't remember what it was called, but after they moved us from our cramped offices where we were packed in three or four to an office, we were moved up there. It was very early in UO's actual development, but long after Rick Delashmit had  done the initial prototype — maybe a month or two in from what I think of as the start of the "real" UO, which was in September of 1995. We had to go by the receptionist, who always wondered who those scruffy guys in t-shirts were who ducked past them to go into the nondescript corner of the floor.

A red sign made by Micael Priest hung there. It read "Multima" in the classic Ultima lettering, and it was shaped like an arrow. I still have it. You went in a door behind a security badge access, and in there was the UO team, in cramped space. Two artists in the hallway. Four programmers in one office, working off of folding tables. Starr Long & the original lead designer each had an office of their own. Kristen and I shared something that may once have been a largish storage space — it was long enough to put two desks side by side, but too narrow to put much of anything else. There was one more office, for Micael and another artist.

We were there during the winter. The development servers were directly under the temperature sensor for the AC unit in that four-programmer office, so the AC blew nonstop. We all wore gloves inside the office space, because it was too cold to type otherwise.

The ad agency moved out, and Origin took over the whole floor. They needed to redo the layout, so they gutted it. The elevator surfaced onto the fifth floor, and you were there, in December, with the wind blowing right through the whole floor. It was bare concrete and pilings, and if you walked to the edge of the floor, you could jump off the building through the window or the big chute they set up for disposing of trash. The Multima sign still hung, fluttering in the wind, on the outside of the one section of drywall that remained: our offices, the only part of the floor that wasn't gone.

We had little clue of the goings-on at the rest of the company. We ran our own game website on OWO.com, a domain that I am not sure Origin quite knew we had. The website was served from one of those machines that kept everything freezing cold. We didn't have any art yet, so the original UO FAQ had on it some llamas and a "happy butthole" logo, which was from a practical joke war being played between Richard Garriott and his ex-girlfriend. Eventually, we added the original logo, which didn't survive contact with the marketing department.

The marketing department barely knew we existed at the time. Up on the fifth floor, we were pretty isolated. One day a marketing guy showed up and said "We're trying to give previews for *AH-64 Longbow* (I think — could have been some other

game) and the press guys only want to know about this Multima thing. What is it?" When we told him they probably saw the website and the FAQ, he was horrified. Another time Richard came up to gauge our reaction to the fact that an entire production group had been cut — we all shrugged and said "who?" I think he was a little nonplussed, because apparently the rest of the company was all agog and freaked out.

Original alpha textures on the Bardic Conservatory were made by me, sourced from photographs of wooden shingles. I also made the other shingles, the benches you see here, and the flagstones and flowers. Much of this was redrawn, but the flowers are in UO to this day.

We made most of the pre-alpha there. We saw Richard once a month or so. One of the times he came up was to complain about the art, and Micael pointed out that most of what he was complaining about was actually stuff that Kristen & I had put in there, scavenged off the web, because we needed to do some building and little of the architecture was done yet. I think the walls in the above screenshot were ones that we took from photo source of roof shingles. I think I drew those plants in the upper right corner, too.

That period, to me, is the quintessential UO development time, even though it was relatively short. The fifth floor was mostly finished, and we were moved downstairs so they could finish up. I scavenged the Multima sign before it was taken away. It was not too long after that that the UO team lost its skunkworks unity as more people came onto the team, eventually including the entire *Ultima IX* team. But at that time, we were punk kids (even Micael, an old kid) doing stuff in the attic, and our parents had no idea what we were up to.

Richard Garriott got involved on several specific systems — for example, he came in and redid the whole UI at one point. But during this early phase, he wasn't around that much. I do remember a big conflict over the conversation system — I think that happened shortly after the move. Later on, he was in a bunch of the design meetings. But he was never on the team in a day to day fashion.

The prototype that Rick Delashmit did that I mentioned in the post was done on top of the Ultima 6 engine. I believe that a few aspects of the U6 engine survived into the early client.

Origin Culture

What was the workplace culture like at Origin Systems during the development of Ultima Online?[96]

I hesitated over answering this, because the question was about the culture of Origin during the development of UO. And for the most critical periods of development of UO, it was a skunkworks project that was rather peripheral to Origin. So really, Mr Mike's [Mike McShaffry] answer is far more thorough for what Origin's culture was — because the UO core team had its own, different culture.

UO started with a few Origin vets — Ken Demarest, Jim Greer, Starr Long, Andrew Morris. But the bulk of the actual dev team was all new to OSI.[97] Ken and Jim left a week after I got there. Andrew left a year (?) later. We had myself, fresh out of grad school at age 24. My wife, grad school dropout at age 26. Jeff Posey and Scott Phillips, right from high school. Rick Delashmit, college dropout. Edmond Meinfelder was older, I think. And we had Micael Priest (young at heart). Soon after we got Clay Hoffman as an artist as well, also fresh out of school.

A few weeks before we got to Origin, my wife and I were told "You absolutely do not want to work there. It's a sweatshop." We laughed nervously, and went on anyway.

All of the programmers and designers except Andrew came from text muds. There was a *big big* gap between them and the Origin vets, most of whom did not play online games. This absolutely led to piles of tension later on when the U9 team was pushed onto the project.

But before that — sheesh, UO was run out of a couple of rooms on a different floor of the building. You had to walk through an ad agency lobby or something to get to it. The artists had to sit in the hallway because there was no room. And later, when the ad agency left and they did a buildout, there was a period where the rooms where

---

[96] This was an answer to a Quora post written in 2012. See https://www.quora.com/What-was-the-workplace-culture-like-at-Origin-Systems-during-the-development-of-Ultima-Online

[97] OSI was a common shorthand for "Origin Systems Interactive."

we were were the only drywall standing on that floor. You had to walk across the bare concrete to get to the door labelled "Multima" — labelled with a color-printed sign tacked up with tape. You could literally WALK OFF THE BUILDING AND FALL TO YOUR DEATH.

The prototype server sat under the thermostat, so it was always freezing. We used to bring fingerless gloves to work to be able to type. We rarely saw the rest of the company. When Warren's entire group was dismantled, Richard came up to tell us, and said "as you have probably heard, we did huge layoffs today" and we all looked at each other in perplexity. We had not heard. We were skunkworks.

This was the period where we did things like launch our own marketing website, logo, and even beta program that cost $, kinda without letting marketing know. :)

This isolation continued after we moved downstairs back into the main LB productions area. And that's where tensions got uncomfortable. I mean, our team loved things like the Lego or PlayDoh sculpting contests just as much as anyone else at Origin did. Or the prank wars — constant and hilarious. But there was a lot of tension there around questions of technical competence (cut both ways, I think), online vs single player design, and a big dose of the "FOR" factor.

"FOR" meant "friend of Richard." It's hard to judge these things now with greater distance on it all, Richard and I get along well, and I don't think any of this necessarily reflects on him. But there was always chatter in the halls about the degree to which the right friendships helped your career. I gather it was just as true for "friend of Chris" [Roberts] and so on. The fact is that there were fault lines in the company. They went between studios, as Mike articulated...[98] there could be actual hostility if you went down the wrong hallways sometimes. But also within teams.

These things had big impacts on the UO product, after the U9 merge. When Andrew was gone, we had Brian Martin and Joye McBurnett (at the time, different name now) as managers over the design team. I was "creative lead" but I did not have the authority to tell anyone from the U9 team what to do (well, authority to tell *anyone*, but original-UO folks would listen to me). Systems were redesigned, or original designs ignored, etc. Sometimes this was for the good. Sometimes it was for the bad.

One way in which the UO team was different, I suspect, was actually in attitude towards shipping and towards engineering. A lot of hackers on the UO team. Lots of trying crazy stuff... But it was also very practical, in a way — I mean, prototype with Rick was, I guess, something like March–Sept 95. The pre-alpha was built between

---

[98] This is in reference to another answer to the question, by Mike McShaffry, available at the same URL.

Sept 95 and May 96. Then most everything was rewritten, and beta dev was May to May 97. And then we shipped in September 97.

As a contrast (sorry Mike! ;)) when we showed up for work in Sept 95, we were shown an isometric *Ultima 9*. U8 had shipped in March of 94. UO interrupted U9 for well over a year. But it didn't ship until 99.[99] That sort of delay was a huge factor in the eventual demise of the studio... and it was a huge source of the tensions between different production groups. To my mind, some of this also explains the eventual fate of UO2.

To me, the takeaway (which has only been reinforced for me over the years) is that skunkworks really works. UO was a skunkworks project, through and through. I am fairly sure that if we had not been stuck in the "closet" on the top floor, that it would not have been made.

I should emphasize that this also means we were lucky it worked at all, and it was held together with chewing gum. I don't mean to paint the team as heroes. We were young, arrogant, and blinkered to consequences of our choices.

All that said — what emerged from all that was that Origin was like a big, extended, fractious family. When you ended up working with someone from "the other side" (whichever one it was!), especially later, you bonded over the fact that it had been the same for everyone. All the vets told you when you got there "Oh, Origin is nothing like it used to be before EA..." But there's still signs of a lingering Origin culture to this day, permeating the Austin game dev scene. A sense of family, a sense of craziness, a sense of ambition... and a lot of projects that slip. ;)

---

[99] Mike pointed out in a comment that "One thing you should know tho - Crusader enjoyed the bulk of the the U9 team for much of the time between March 94 and the following year, and then most of that team stayed with Tony [Zurovec], and never returned to U9. So, U9 only had a skeleton crew on it for that time, doing design work and investigating how we could bring 3D to Britannia."

The Technology Stack

What was the technology stack driving the original Ultima Online servers?[100]

My memory on all this is fuzzy, so caveat emptor.

The gameserver was a custom C or C++ server (don't remember which), running on Solaris.[101] Some kind of crazy Sparcs I think. We had a small office or closet we converted to a server room with a fan in it. We used to hover a beachball over the exhaust.

Each shard (the term sharding probably originated with UO) was actually multiple game servers that pointed at one persistence DB, and that did data mirroring across the boundaries. The load balancing within a shard was statically determined by config files, and was simply boxes on the map — nothing fancy. Race conditions here led to most of the dupe bugs, by the way.

Game static DB from flat text files (creature & item definitions). We edited these in vi.

Maps and object placements stored in binary files (.MUL files). These were edited using the "god client." The file format is out there now, reverse-engineered for the gray shards. These were taken and placed on the game disc.

Most developers ran a copy of the server on Linux right there, so they could do dev work. Then everything was merged in.

---

[100] Another Quora answer, found at https://www.quora.com/What-was-the-technology-stack-driving-the-original-Ultima-Online-servers

[101] Per Ruben Cortez, from the original ops team: "Those original servers were Sun Ultra II's running Solaris. If I remember correctly, it was a dual proc box (rare in those days), 300mhz, with 256MB of ram (which we subsequently upgraded to 512MB for a boat load of cash). The server weighed a ton, and certainly wasn't rack mountable. and they cost about $30k each, making one UO shard cost about $150k (not including external storage), which is a ridiculous amount of money these days for a single shard." Chris Mayer commented, "The hardware [by the time of *Second Age*] was a mix of different types (SPARC and Intel) and operating systems (Solaris and Linux), so we had to distribute the source code out to the machines to be compiled during a publish. This added a lot of time to our publish and deploy process since we could not distribute binaries. Once we were able to unify the servers and had them all running on Intel architecture and Linux, we were able to stop shipping source out to all the end points and distribute binaries only."

Two scripting languages. The main one was called Wombat, homegrown. An event-driven C-syntax language with its philosophy derived architecturally from MUD scripting languages in DikuMUDs, specifically *Worlds of Carnage* and *LegendMUD*. This basic scripting architecture is kind of the industry standard now, actually. All object interactivity, most game logic, most AI, etc, was written in Wombat. Exceptions included movement, combat, and all the "common" AI.

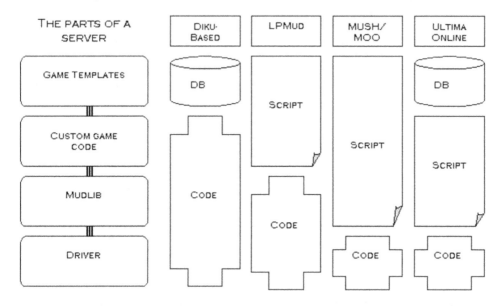

AS CAN BE SEEN FROM THE DIAGRAM, THE BASIC TYPES OF MUD SERVER DIVIDE UP NEATLY BASED ON HOW THEY HANDLE THE DIVIDING POINT BETWEEN DRIVER, MUDLIB, AND GAME-SPECIFIC CODE. THE LEAST FLEXIBLE OF THE MAJOR CODEBASES, DIKU, USES A DATABASE FOR ITS TEMPLATE DATA, AND HARDCODES EVERYTHING ELSE. LPMUDS WRITE DRIVERS AND MUDLIBS IN CODE, AND THEN THEIR TEMPLATES LEVERAGE THE SCRIPT LANGUAGE FOR GREATER FLEXIBILITY. MUSHES AND MOOS, BEING MORE OBJECT-ORIENTED, HAVE JUST A BAREBONES DRIVER IN CODE, AND EVERYTHING ELSE IS HANDLED IN SCRIPT. THIS RESULTS IN A CONFLATION OF THE CONCEPTS OF TEMPLATE AND RUNTIME DATABASES. LASTLY, *ULTIMA ONLINE* ATTEMPTED TO MERGE THE EASE OF USE OF DIKUS WITH THE FLEXIBILITY OF LPS AND MOOS. THIS PROVED VERY SUCCESSFUL.

The other was hacked in overnight the night or so before we launched the pre-alpha, called **escript**. Without it, we wouldn't have finished the map in time. It literally read off disk and parsed as it went. It was specifically for doing large-scale procedural edits to the map. It had loops, random, query tile, set tile, spawn object, and that was about it. The syntax was horrible — every command with @@ around it, every variable with ## around it, that sort of thing. I eventually (*Second Age* period) wrote a script that served as a front-end to it to do the commonest things (fill with trees, raise/lower/flatten areas, place the transition tiles between different tilesets... this last one because terrain alpha blending was not in the engine).

I honestly do not remember about the runtime database.[102]

For a picture of how this all fit together, see here:

Client written in C.

Network protocol was custom handcrafted packets designed to save every byte.[103] Our low end was a 28.8 modem, so we aimed for 400 bytes per second, if I recall correctly. We ran over TCP. Changing a packet meant coordinated updates of the client and server.[104]

Source control was SourceSafe on the PC and CVS for server data.

Dunno about stuff like the billing

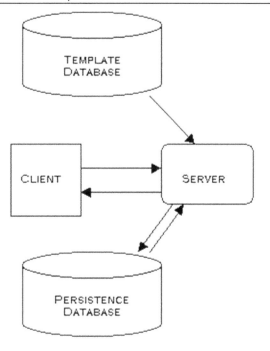

HOW A SERVER COMMUNICATES

---

[102] Brian Crowder, programmer on UO Live, adds, "As Raph also notes, there were no databases originally involved in the storage of game state or player data for UO (disregarding analytics here), everything was kept in flat files. Backups worked by flagging a moment in time where no one was allowed to cross server-boundaries -- during that moment, each areaserver was commanded to fork(), essentially duplicating itself in memory (it's more complicated than this, thanks to Copy-on-Write, but let's simplify). After everyone had fork()ed, the "lock" preventing boundary-crossing was cleared. Then each areaserv began to dump out its huge chunk of memory-state into a file on an NFS server. Those files were then all tarred together and kept as a "backup" of the state of the server. These heavyweight backups happened at half-hour intervals, I believe."

[103] Brian Crowder added a comment later saying "In terms of communication, the protocol was all TCP. As Raph suggests, the data riding on top of TCP was tuned byte-by-byte, but not otherwise encrypted in any way, at least not initially. Linux at that time (and Solaris, too, iirc) had a limit of file descriptors per process, capping out at 256! And that, only if you closed STDIN, STDOUT, and STDERR. That limitation required the deployment of "player servers", a kind of load balancer (connection load, though, not server load, alas), which did some very simple sanitization, and beyond that did nothing more than manage hundreds of connections (253 or so, iirc, per playerserv, with many playerservs per shard -- enough for a few thousand players), tunneling traffic back and forth."

[104] Ruben again: "I think where we revolutionized administration of a distributed MMO was on the network side, specifically via the VPN, which was very new at that time. Short of ordering PTP circuits all over the country and world, we used a software VPN to create those tunnels over our public internet connection at the time (a SINGLE DS3 -- it wasn't until late 1998 that we had a second

DB, and there was some sort of login server in front. You could run a client config file to point at alternate servers though.[105]

[Edit: I really need to add that all credit for the above should go to, first and foremost, Rick Delashmit, who probably wrote 80% of the code for the client and server; and Scott Phillips, Ed Meinfelder, Jeff Posey, & Jason Spangler from the original core team. After that, a giant pile of more programmers contributed — check the credits.]

_____

circuit!) to allow for login handoff, administration, backups, publishes, etc. our hub and spoke VPN design and subsequent fully-meshed design were what made distributing shards economically feasible… Credit to Mark Rizzo for the architecture and buildout of the UO's backend."

[105] Mike McShaffry added, "The backend database for logging in and game analytics was a Microsoft SQL server, version 6."

"Sharding" Came from UO?

What an odd term — "sharding." Why would a database be described that way?

So I started reading a bit about it. It basically means running a bunch of parallel databases and looking into the right one, rather than trying to cram everything into one.

Near as I can tell, a quick Google seems to say that the term came about because of a guy who worked at Friendster and Flickr[106]. Wikipedia has only had an article[107] for a little while. In the comment thread at Lessons Learned, there's mention of the term being used in 2006.

Flickr, of course, was born as an MMO called *Game Neverending*. In fact, I was quoted in Ludicorp's business plan, and Stewart Butterfield had asked if I could be an advisor, but I couldn't do it at the time because of my contract with Sony. Sigh. Anyway, I would be *shocked* if the term "shard" hadn't been thrown around those offices… because in MMOs, of course, "shards" has a very specific meaning and history.

It means database partitioning — of worlds. Parallel worlds each running the same static template database source, but evolving different runtime databases. But these were just called "servers" — like, *Meridian 59* had bunches of them, and they had numbers instead of the common practice of names that is in use today.

No, "shards" came about specifically because when we realized we would need to run multiple whole copies of *Ultima Online* for users to connect to, we needed to come up with a fiction for it. I went off and read a whole mess of stuff about early Ultima

---

[106] http://highscalability.com/unorthodox-approach-database-design-coming-shard
[107] https://en.wikipedia.org/wiki/Shard_%28database_architecture%29

A snippet from the UO intro movie.

lore and tried to come up with a fictional justification.[108] What I ended up with is that the evil wizard Mondain had attempted to gain control over Sosaria by trapping its essence in a crystal. When the Stranger at the end of Ultima I defeated Mondain and shattered the crystal, the crystal **shards** each held a refracted copy of Sosaria.

It was a very very specific word chosen because, well, it was a piece of a crystal, which was a completely fictional invention. If Mondain had captured Sosaria on a parchment or in a painting, I would have said "a tatter" or a "fragment" or some such. But in the original U1, it specifically said he had used a crystal to gain power. We even talked about terms like "multiverse" and the like at the time and dismissed them as comic-book geeky and not really Ultima-flavored… so "shard" it was.

Now, from there time kept marching forward as each parallel Sosaria evolved in tandem. (UO was supposed to be between U3 and U4, in terms of chronology). The difference is, some of them got the Avatar (sent by the Time Lord) and some didn't. Some of them were captured by The Guardian, and we invented the notion that Shadowlords were essentially evil beings created from shards he had captured. In fact, the beta test shard eventually was captured in this way — if you read up on it, you'll find that really, there should be a fourth Shadowlord running around now.

(Originally, the landmass of *Second Age* was supposed to be Ambrosia from Ultima III, and there's actually a spot up north that is where Exodus is supposed to go. We even made the art for the whirlpool that is supposed to go there, and then just never put it in. But that's a whole other story…)

(Oh… and then why does the Stranger in the original UO intro movie have an Ankh on his chest? Because U9 was in development already, and nobody had time to make a new model. So it's the same 3d model as was used in U9, which didn't ship until *years* later. So expedience led to a fictional glitch.)

In any case, we called parallel servers "shards" and it became a term used occasionally though not universally as a term of art within the field. You'll hear folks who worked on MMOs in the 90s use server and shard interchangeably — sometimes saying "shard"

---

[108] Richard may have provided the core concept; I honestly don't remember anymore.

to reference a parallel server cluster rather than a physical server.

So, did this database term come from a doc that I dashed off one afternoon in 1996? Umm… I am not sure. Seems like an interesting coincidence, if not.

I wonder if I still have that doc…

Original planned UO map, photo by Cory Doctorow, CC BY-SA

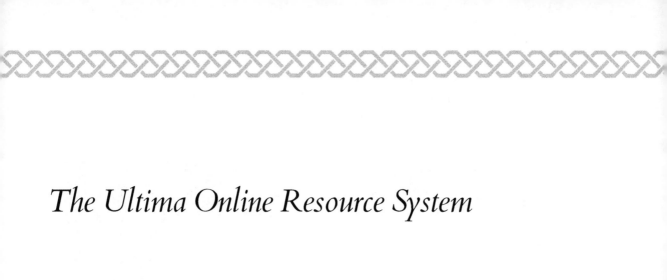

The Ultima Online Resource System

Part 1

Recently, some readers asked for posts that were more game-design centered. Since there was talk recently of the virtual ecological modeling that a Second Life user created,[109] I thought I might talk a little bit about how the original resource system in *Ultima Online* worked. It's more virtual world design than game design, but it has a lot of implications for game systems. Pretty much everything I am writing here has been published before in one place or another, but a lot of the old UO interviews and articles are not on the Internet, so it's all been lost, and I imagine folks newer to the whole virtual world thing may never have heard about it.

This will be long, so I'll break it into a few posts, probably.

A bit of background

I've written before, albeit briefly, about how the system came to be.[110] Kristen and I conceived of it in rough form during the long car drive from Tuscaloosa to Austin, or on the way back — I can't recall which. Somewhere, I still have the notebooks for it all; we were talking at the time about how to make a new MUD with a better form of crafting.

This was in early 1995. Neither *The Sims* nor *Thief* had come out yet, but for those of you who have played those games, much of the underlying design principle is the same, even though the game mechanics wrapped around them are radically different.

The way crafting had worked in the earlier Diku-derived muds, and in fact still does in many of them, is via a recipe system. First, understand that a given item in a typical MMO system will be identified by its template name or number, which is a unique identifier for the "master copy" of an item. All actual items are spawned by creating an object with the characteristics of the master copy. The master copy will

[109] https://www.raphkoster.com/2006/05/31/way-cool/
[110] See "Playing to Bake Bread" a few chapters ahead.

sometimes have random factors in it.

A recipe simply says "if you have any of the item IDs in list A, and any of the item IDs in list B, you can use them up to create an item from list C." List A may be a set of things like kindling, logs, lumber, or planks; list B may be nails, screws, metal rods, and metal bands; and list C will have in it things like chairs, tables, barrels, and so on.

Generally, each possible item in list C must have its own custom recipe designed, specifying which item templates can be used and in what amounts. If someone adds a new type of wood building material — such as wood blocks — then every recipe that uses wood must be updated to permit that as a new ingredient.

There the system generally stops; it's used for the purpose of creating craftables, after all. There's no applications towards larger-scale systems such as AI.

Abstracting properties

The core of what Kristen and I had talked about on that road trip was putting abstracted properties onto objects. Rather than building a recipe out of the item ID numbers for every object that worldbuilders had made that was "raw wood," we would instead track that the object was *made* of wood. And then the crafting code could just query, "is this wood?" and if so, do things with it.

In the end, we ended up with slightly more than that. Big kudos here go of course to the rest of the original core UO team, who all contributed to one degree or another on these concepts.

We ended up saying that a given object (which was still defined in a template) could have as part of it, a set of resources. A resource was just a label — nothing more and nothing less. (Much later, in SWG, that team would introduce the concept of resources with stats, but that's a post for another day.) The server had a list of the resources that existed in the world, and designers could create new ones fairly readily. Resources were things like Metal, Wood, and Cloth. But they were also things like Magic and Player and other such abstract qualities.

A given object was capable of treating resources in the following ways:

1. It could have a **PRODUCTION** of a resource — as many as it needed to. This meant, effectively, that the object was "made of" this stuff. Each production entry consisted of the resource tag, the current

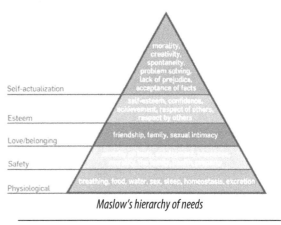

Maslow's hierarchy of needs

amount of it, the max amount, and the regrowth rate. If there was no regrowth rate, then the object would not replenish itself when the resource was removed. If there was, then it would grow back that resource should it be consumed in some manner. All objects, pretty much, produced something. The other three types of resource fields were mostly only used by AIs.

2. It could have a list of **FOOD** resources. The foods had a stomach size, a bite size, and a minimum amount that could catch its interest. Basically, it would try to find objects with the resource it wanted to eat, as long as the amount there was above its interest threshold; then it would eat away at it at a rate based on the bite size, until it had so much that the stomach was full. If the object in question was alive (eg, a mobile and not just an object or a corpse) it would attack it first and kill it, then eat. If it ate all the resources on something, we would actually delete the object.

3. It could have a list of **SHELTER** resources. The desired behavior for SHELTER was that it just hung around near the object producing stuff. The parameters on this one were basically like food, but there was one other wrinkle. Instead of a stomach size, it had a "home" flag, which meant that once it found a shelter that satisfied it, it would remember where it was and go back there. In the case of many monsters, I had hoped that once they picked a lair, they would actually drop whatever goods they had acquired somewhere near their lair.

4. Lastly, there were **DESIRES**. Again, there was a total amount of a resource they wanted, there was a minimum amount they would try to get in one go, and then there was a flag called "aversion." If they found something that was

big enough to want, and they still wanted more, they would try to pick it up. If they couldn't pick it up, then they would just hang around near it. If the aversion flag was there, then the opposite would occur — they'd be scared of it, and try to stay away.

You'll notice that this is darn close to ripped straight out of Maslow's Hierarchy of Needs. And in fact, AI attempted to satisfy its FOOD needs first, followed by its SHELTER, followed by its DESIRES, just as in Maslow. Alas, we didn't get around to allowing our AIs to have self-actualization.

A rabbit, then, might look like:

- **PRODUCE** FUR in a small amount, and doesn't regrow it; and MEAT
- **EAT** GRASS, FLOWER, and VEGETABLE, up to a small stomach size, in small nibbly bites.
- **SHELTER** in GRASS or BUSH, but treat BUSH as home if they're a decent size
- **DESIRE** nothing, but have an aversion to anything that produces CARNIVOREMEAT

Conversely, a wolf might be

- **PRODUCE** FUR in a medium amount, and doesn't regrow it; and CARNIVOREMEAT
- **EAT** MEAT, up to a small stomach size, in medium bites.
- **SHELTER** in TREE or CAVE, but treat CAVE as home if they're a decent size
- **DESIRE** nothing, but have an aversion to anything that produces CARNIVOREMEAT

Stuff like pack behaviors were layered on top of this, so wolves, being pack animals, could have a DESIRE to be near other wolves. When animals were in a pack, they were supposed to add up their needs, so that a pack of wolves would start ignoring bunny rabbits and start being willing to tackle bigger game.

Lastly, the (in)famous dragon example:

- **PRODUCE** SCALES in a medium amount, and doesn't regrow it; and a huge pile of CARNIVOREMEAT
- **EAT** MEAT or CARNIVOREMEAT, up to a huge stomach size, in big bites.
- **SHELTER** in MOUNTAIN or CAVE, but treat CAVE as home if they're a decent size

- **DESIRE** GOLD, GEM, and MAGIC

I'll post later about how this was supposed to work in terms of AI behaviors, the way the world populated its data, and why it all didn't work.

Ironically, the first version did work as expected. But that version didn't survive alpha, because it was, well, alpha-level code. The second version, which is what we tried to get working during beta, is what failed. And we never did do a third try.

It's been a while, but my recollection is that the alpha version had all of the above data structures, but maybe not the pack behavior. It had creature skill advancement, and it had AI hunting and stuff. I don't think the full lair behavior ever worked. It did have the desires, even down recursive container searching — orcs would kill you for gold you had hidden in a backpack. It did not have spawning as described in the second post.

The beta version had more or less the same functionality, but it had the "spontaneous generation" spawning and the closed economy loop. But it also had creatures in sleep mode, and incredibly slow behaviors (I distinctly recall watching the programmer show me a demo of a bear seeking honey and shelter — and watching it take multiple minutes to find the honey that was right there on screen with it).

Part 2

Last time I wrote about the basic structure of how the resource data worked in the original design for Ultima Online. Now I'll talk a bit more about applications of that data.

A world with properties

The UO world was a tile-based environment broken up into "chunks" that were 8×8 tiles. The map was static data — there was no way to modify it, and it was built by assembling the tiles, which were fairly small, one at a time in a worldbuilding editor. We had an assortment of tools to ease this process, that allowed us to "paint" grass or trees or even outline buildings quickly and easily, roofs included. We ended up writing an assortment of additional tools in the game's scripting language as well, to speed up the process.

Static items had some big advantages — they did not need to be streamed down because they were replicated on the client, and they didn't incur significant server-side storage. However, since the world was static, that meant that each tile and each tree was merely a lookup into an art table. They couldn't have properties, including any resource data, and they couldn't run scripts. This meant that we had gone to all that effort to make trees be made out of wood, but then the trees we built the world with couldn't store that fact.

The solution the programmers came up with was "chunk eggs." Basically an invisible dynamic object sat in each chunk. When the world came up, this egg analyzed the static art that resided in that chunk, and set itself to produce the resources that this art would have produced were it made of "real" objects and not just set dressing. If there were nothing but grass tiles there, then the chunk egg produced grass to the tune of 64 grass tiles' worth. If there were trees, then it also produced wood, and so on.

We used this to make every bit of exposed rock in the world produce ORE, which was the first step in refining metal in the crafting system, and to make every bit of water produce WATER, and so on.

The downside to this, of course, was that there weren't actually five trees in a chunk — there was one invisible one. Trying to harvest wood from any of the trees actually harvested it from the chunk egg. This was why you could harvest a lot of wood from one tree, and find that you had exhausted all the adjacent ones. This later led to "8×8 macroing" and various other clever adaptations to the environment.

Dynamic objects didn't have all these troubles, and in fact, there were parts of the world which were dynamic objects. Fruit trees, for example, were "real," and were hand-placed trees with scripts on them. As I recall, this script was bugged pretty much my entire tenure at Origin, and for years after, which is bad because I wrote it. It simply checked when the tree was clicked on; if the tree had sufficient FRUIT resource on it, it would create a fruit of the appropriate type for what tree it was, and move the resources off the tree and onto the new fruit. Thus you could harvest apples from the apple trees in Lord British's garden. The FRUIT resource on the tree had a regrowth rate, so you could pick all the apples from it, but eventually they would grow back.

This sort of process, of moving resources from one thing to another, is the core strength of the resource system. You could look at an object and treat it abstractly. Not too long after, a very similar system was used in *Thief*, permitting water arrows or buckets of water or indeed anything that had the WATER property to douse fires.

This sort of thing would have permitted many cool effects that we refrained from putting in. For example, a fireball could easily have caught every wooden or cloth possession on fire. A rust monster could have destroyed all of your metal objects with every hit.

Some of the examples of moving resources from thing to thing were truly nuts. The craziest script was perhaps the "bladed" script. This was attached to everything with a sharp edge on it: axes, knives, swords, whatever. If it was used on wood, it would chop wood away. If it was used on cloth, it would cut it up into strips and then bandages. If it was used on a carcass, you would dress the carcass and get fur and meat. Cut up the meat further and you could get filets.

The most extravagant use of this was when Dan Rubenfield extended the bladed script to work on cutting up corpses into a rather disturbing array of bits, including allowing the harvesting of skulls. This ended up being removed when the game launched in Europe, but not before some of the battle-hardened playerkillers had engaged in cannibalism (MEAT was MEAT after all) and the collecting of their victims' ears.

Applications for AI

I already described the basics of how this system interacted with AI. It began at the first first level, with spawning. UO's spawning system originally worked based on there being a surplus of resources in the world. If there was a lot of GRASS laying about, then it would select from the list of templates that ate GRASS. If there was then an abundance of MEAT, it would spawn MEAT-eaters. In other words, it worked by the scientifically discredited mechanism of abiogenesis,[111] or "spontaneous generation," as opposed to being defined by static spawn locations.

To help shape the world, invisible boxes were drawn on it that could each have their own list of what sort of things spawned in it. The list of GRASS-eaters in the jungle could therefore be different from the list of GRASS-eaters in a pine forest. Alas, there was no concept of temperature, humidity, or other such natural variables in the original system, or else climate alone could well have taken care of this.

This "spawn region" system eventually took over all the spawning in the game, ignoring the resource system altogether for reasons I will talk about later. Spawn regions have an advantage of their predecessor system of spawn points, of course, because they can span larger areas and make spawning a little less predictable — yet can be made as small as is needed for replicating the purpose of a spawn point.

Originally, the new objects (for things like resources, wheat and other crops, and the like, were also spawned this way) were actually withdrawn from a "resource bank." This meant that when the bank was overdrawn of MEAT, nothing that used MEAT could spawn until some of the MEAT in the world was destroyed and therefore returned to the bank. This "closed economy" was famously written about by Zach Simpson, where he rightfully identified it as a core problem with UO's economic system. In retrospect, should more have kept spawning, it would not have mattered, because the resultant plants and animals would have starved to death without sufficient food anyway.

The famous dragon example that got so much press when UO was in development went something like this:

> Nearly everything in the world, from grass to goblins, has a purpose, and not just as cannon fodder either. The "virtual ecology," as Starr Long, the game's associate producer calls it, affects nearly every aspect of the game world, from the very small to the very large. If the rabbit population suddenly drops (because some gung-ho adventurer was trying out his new mace) then wolves may have to find different food sources – say, deer. When the deer population drops as a result, the

---

[111] See https://en.wikipedia.org/wiki/Spontaneous_generation

local dragon, unable to find the food he's accustomed to, may head into a local village and attack. Since all of this happens automatically, it generates numerous adventure possibilities.[112]

Rabbits were GRASS eaters. They spawned, thereby bringing a small amount of MEAT into the world. They ate grass, and meanwhile, also resulted in spawning wolves, which are there to eat their MEAT.

However, players are also after the rabbits, so the wolves end up hungry. Some would die off. But all animals in the original UO design levelled up just like players; a wolf who had been in a lot of scrapes could get tougher. (This led to some truly amusing early alpha experiences whereby players who let bunnies escape would effectively train up Pythonesque killer rabbits; I watched these lay waste to entire packs of wolves — and newbies! — which mistook them for easy prey.)

Normally, a single wolf would not attack a deer, because the deer was too big a hunk of meat for its "bite." However, put more wolves together and they summed together their "bite," making them willing to attack fairly large things. So if players harvested the bunnies, the wolves were going to move on to attacking other, larger bits of meat. Players included.

Originally, there was no concept of "aggro" in the game. Hunger or greed was the only reason why creatures attacked. This was overruled by some of the other folks on the team, who felt that from a game experience point of view, certain creatures should always be dangerous.

Should the wolves clear out the deer, then whatever ate the deer would then need to find other prey as well. "Bite size" imposed a lower threshold on what something would go after as well. A dragon, with a large stomach size, eating MEAT in big gulps, would not be willing to hunt down rabbits. But it might well find a human a tasty snack if it came across one.

Dragons would not normally be right next to player cities, of course. But if the deer that normally existed in between the players and the dragon's lair were gone, the dragon's search radius away from its home might well carry it to the village…

Most of this is actually fairly straightforward, in terms of AI implementation. The basic AI behavior of a creature was

1. If I'm hungry, search for items that produce stuff on my FOOD list, and attack or eat them. Wander as far as needed to accomplish this.

2. If I am not hungry, then start looking for a home base. If I already have one,

---

[112] From a preview here: http://uk.videogames.games.yahoo.com/pc/previews/ultima-online-6a2baa.html

then go there. If I get hungry while doing this, go back to hunting for food.

3. If I am sheltered and not hungry, then look around for stuff that I just like. If I can pick it up, bring it to my shelter. If not, just hang around there — until I get hungry.

At one point, we had effects like beggars who had desires for GOLD, and thus followed rich players in the street. We had bears who would hang out in their cave, but would wander over to hang around near beehives. All that stuff worked. The problem was that the constant radial searches were incredibly expensive, and so was all the pathfinding.[113]

One of the first things to go was the search frequency. Next, the step was taken to put every creature to "sleep" when players were not nearby. This change alone really ruins the large-scale ecological applications completely. On top of that, the issues with spawning "overdrawing" the bank were not foreseen; in practice, it wasn't MEAT that resulted in creatures not spawning. It was all the FUR and whatnot that ended up hoarded by players that prevented the deer and rabbits from returning.

The last big element, however, was that there were a fair amount of team members who saw the whole system as a boondoggle, and not worth pursuing. Alas, one of them also ended up in charge of implementing it in beta. By beta time, systems that used to work in alpha no longer did.

This meant that we never got to the *second* stage of implementation on it, which would have been hooking it into quests.[114] But I will talk about that next time.

---

[113] *The Sims* ended up addressing the radial searches by simply reversing the model: instead of the entities constantly doing searches, the entities instead broadcast their production values to things nearby.

Pathfinding, alas, still costs a ton, because of the increased complexity of the environments.

One approach that may be fruitful is again demonstrated by *The Sims* — having a fine grid with fall-off from broadcast sources. Then the pathfinding can fall back from A* to simple hillclimbing.

Why hasn't something like this been implemented since? I think the answers are inertia, complexity, lack of seeing the benefits, and desire by players for predictability.

[114] Nothing really precludes handcrafted content from being layered on top of a system like this, or tailoring as much of the experience as you care to above a system like this. The point is more that the underlying structures permit the developers more choices and — I think — even better handcrafting, if they choose to make use of the data.

Part 3

I've now written two posts that were far lengthier than I anticipated, about the way that UO's resource system was originally intended to work. The first dealt with underlying data structures, and the second with applications of those data structures to the actual world. I want to talk a bit about future directions that we didn't get to pursue.

Cool ways to use what we already had

The mining system in UO was an example of "transmutation" in action. We placed ORE in the chunk eggs based on the presence of rocks and the terrain rock texture. We mined ORE out by clicking on rocks or the rock texture and transferring the ORE to the new "pile of ore" object.

When I added in the varieties of metals to the system, the way I did it was by adding a dynamic variable to the chunk egg. They were called "object variables" or "objvars" in UO parlance, and they were essentially flags with values that could be attached to any dynamic object. You could tag someone as "BEAT_THE_HARPY" with a value of "TRUE" and then use *hasObjVar(target, "BEAT_THE_HARPY")* to see if the objvar was present, or *val = getObjVar(target, "BEAT_THE_HARPY")* to get that value into a variable for script use. These objvars were persistent, so you could build complex systems out of them.

I simply attached a little script to every chunk egg that checked to see if it had an objvar that defined a metal type. If it didn't, then it randomly chose a metal type and set the objvar to that value. This meant that after this script was updated, every chunk in the world bore a different kind of ore. I weighted some to be rare and others to be more common.

When the ORE was mined, I had the mining script transfer that variable to the new object along with the ORE resource. I also had it tint the ore graphic based on a standard lookup table, dependent on what the value of the objvar was. And thus colored armor was born — we simply had each step transfer the variable along.

This worked even when we actually recycled the ORE and conjured up METAL out of thin air instead. This was the step of refining the ore into ingots. You could also combine ore — I don't recall how we handled this, but it was probably by picking the commoner of the two types. It would have been fairly easy to add new metal types that were not minable but were only available as alloys, too. In a more modern system, we would have instead had types of METAL such as IRON or COPPER that inherited from the base type — and that is in fact how SWG worked.

This sort of transmutation, where you query the amount of RESOURCE1, delete it, and then create a corresponding amount of RESOURCE2, permitted the concept of "refinement" of one type of quality into another. COTTON or FLAX into CLOTH is a similar thing, only with the wrinkle that it permits two different initial sources to become the same sort of thing in the end.

I mention this example just to point out that there were a lot of possibilities for the use of transmutation of one resource type to another; for example, a stone mage could use up ORE as resources and turn it into MAGIC; really, we should have made one's mana pool be literally how much MAGIC resource they represented. A druid could have instead drawn power from the amount of GRASS or TREE that was around. And a necromancer — well, every time something died, it could have added DEATH to the chunk egg based on what was killed; a necromancer would then be able to "mine death magic" from spots where many things had been killed. Had we done this, I am sure we quickly would have had necromantic sacrifice altars, and they would have intentionally herded players (who of course would carry much power!) to those places to die. Temple of Doom, here we come...

Other applications based solely on what was already present:

- You could do real tracking, based on things leaving traces in the chunk eggs.
- You could have NPCs or creatures who collected or desired items with specific resources.
- You could easily do a nice "detect magic" or really, "detect anything" sort of informational spell, with strength of the glows dependent on the amount of the resource present
- You could create secret or transmutation paths — mix MAGIC and METAL to make MITHRIL or something, regardless of what the item looked like originally.
- You could do "melting down" of materials.
- You could create greater or lesser susceptibility to damage based on conditions. It's easy to imagine a HUMIDITY value stored on a chunk egg — it could even move around. And then it could affect the growth rate of GRASS or the decay

rate of METAL.

- This also reflects the whole "dragon fire breath actually sets things on fire" thing.

Player actions could affect resources on them, such as reputations with certain groups, karma, and so on. They could acquire the "scent" of things they worked with often, for example. This would then replace a typical stats system, which would need to be hardcoded to interact with every other data type in the game.

This could, for example, allow a disease to be transmitted invisibly across the game, affecting only, say, magical reagents — and players could be the carriers without knowing it, unless it was detected by a spell or skill.

Most obviously, had we chosen to incur the cost of streaming the chunk eggs, we could have actually made the rendering of the chunks *change* based on what the chunk egg represented. As the grass is eaten, bare dirt is left behind. As the ore-bearing rock is reduced, change the rock tile to gravel. As the temperature changes, draw dead grass or even snow. And so on.

I could go on; suffice to say that even with just an abstract property system and no real AI work, there's lots of potential for a lot of interesting and fresh gameplay.

What we didn't have: causality

But the real issue with something like the dragon example is, "how do I know that the dragon is hungry, and not just a random spawn?" In other words, there needs to be a sense of purpose to what is going on.

The reason why it matters that the dragon is hungry and not just a random spawn is because it suggests multiple ways to solve the problem. You could kill the dragon. You could also feed it to get it to go away. Herd deer in between you and the village, let's say. The problem is, maybe there is no reason. How can the player tell?

Let's take the simpler case of some rabbits who eat the lettuce out of a farmer's garden. What you **really** want is for the farmer to tell you "I's gots me some rabbit issues; filthy buggers're eatin' muh lettuce! I'll pay ye ta 'sterminate'em!"

The proposed but never implemented method for handling this required knowledge at one step remove. The farmer would DESIRE his lettuce; this means he would walk around where it was, when he was not hungry, and if he could pick it up, he'd transfer it to his home. But the rabbits want to EAT the lettuce. If the farmer knew the name and template type of whatever was making him unhappy by competing for his desired resource, then he could complain about it. And if we tracked what the player killed, he'd know that they were good rabbit exterminators and possibly provide a reward, without there being a static quest defined.

What's more, if players killed all the rabbits, but what came along next time as a spawn that ate lettuce happened to be deer, or even a lettuce blight, then the farmer would respond in the same way — anything that was eating "his" lettuce would be something he could complain about, and reward those who took action.

Similarly, in the village-attacked-by-dragon case, the villagers would have to like having other villagers around, so they could complain that "their" villagers were being destroyed by something else. You could extend this to any number of things. Let's say that the smith loves "his" METAL objects. If a rust monster wandered through town and damaged the METAL, then he would complain about that but no other villagers would unless they also DESIRED METAL.

The implementation problems here are tricky. First, we would have needed to have some sort of registry so that the farmer could know about the rabbits, who are a third party to his relationship with his beloved vegetables. Worse, we would have also needed to *relay the player actions* against this third party so that the farmer could supply rewards and commentary.

Because of these hurdles, and because there was always something more urgent going on, we never got this in.

A similar thing that we wanted above and beyond the basic resource system was the concept of targeted desires. Instead of abstractly liking **all METAL** or **all MEAT**, we wanted to support the ability for something to pick a favorite: a preferred sword, a favorite pet. The test case that we designed for this was actually a love triangle.

Both Fred and Bob would DESIRE (to be crude) HUMANFEMALE. They would both search around for an object that met their desire, which would mean they would both hang around a female human NPC whenever they weren't hungry. However, if they found one that satisfied their desire (probably with a bit of a random roll) they would fixate on *only* that NPC, and poor Nellie would find that both Bob and Fred hung around her a lot.

Now, HUMANFEMALE is a consumable resource. Bob, when around Nellie, is actually reducing it. And that means, when you talk to Fred, he would be able to say ""I's gots me some Bob issues; filthy buggers're eatin' muh Nellie! I'll pay ye ta 'sterminate'im!" (or something of the sort). Bob would be able to say the same thing in reverse. You could even solve the problem by finding something else for one of the two swains to do. Even more interesting — if the dragon came along and ate Nellie, both Bob and Fred would be the first in line to seek revenge, or give a reward to a player who tackled the dragon problem.

Similarly, rather than manually setting up paths and schedules for NPCs, you could create a script that has them gradually increase a FATIGUE value, or that switched their SHELTER from WORK to HOME locations based on the time of day. You could have law-abiding citizens have an aversion to anything that produced DARK, so that at night they would cluster in lit interiors and under lamps, whereas only thief NPCs would be in the shadows.

The highest level of interface to all of this that we would have wanted for players would have included the notion of town criers and other news sources that pick "stories" from the ether and broadcast them. "Farmer Hayseed is pissed off about his lettuce getting eaten!" "Plague of street urchins won't leave noble warriors alone!" "Fred kills Bob in jealous rage over Nellie!" and so on.

Problems: closed loops, homeostasis, feedback

All of these sorts of applications rely on a large bank of dynamically assembled text that is contextual to the situation. With the current desire for international localization of text, it's unlikely that you can even execute on this. Localization tends to demand static text, and indeed, UO had piles of dynamically assembled text that was removed when the title was localized to other languages, costing the game's dialogue much of its flavor.

All of these higher-level applications can only really be built on top of a fully functional animal-level behavior system. What's more, in work since then, I have become persuaded that in fact, you need to drive the simulation to lower levels, such as humidity and temperature, just so you don't find yourself creating special cases for simple behaviors. This leads to the concept that you could in fact build the whole world out of this, and just render textures and objects based on what resources are present, a concept first demonstrated in ALife examples such as *Sugarscape*.[115]

In fact, it should now be evident that what this represents, in totality, is just a fairly elaborate "artificial life" engine, grown to the point where it encompasses spawning, basic behaviors, and even a higher-order quest system.

However, without the following ingredients, there's little point to implementing something like this:

---

[115] See
https://web.archive.org/web/20040703191058/https://www.brookings.edu/es/dynamics/sugarscape/default.htm

- It has to be visible and responsive to players. This includes exposing causality. Otherwise, it might as well be random.

- NPCs need to be able to communicate to players about wants, and need to react to those wants.

- Static data must be avoided at all costs, which is incredibly difficult for a traditional game development team.

- The myriad of variables must push towards homeostasis, rather than boom-bust cycles. A lot of ALife sims end up in boom-bust, and that's not interesting to users.

- Naturally renewing resources can't be in a closed loop, because of player hoarding effects.

- You have to solve CPU issues with pathfinding and searches in order to make the system tenable.

There were discussions on MUD-Dev circa 1998 about other means to handle this sort of system within a reasonable CPU budget. One approach that would probably work for the latter is to use "level of detail" for the areas. If no players are around, stop instancing up individual wolves hunting individual rabbits; instead, save all those off, and calculate periodically how many wolves and how many rabbits would be there after a certain amount of time.

You could stuff the world data into a quadtree and run higher and higher-level sims, instancing all the data back out only when you needed to interact with it in granular fashion; or you could timestamp the last interaction, and "catch the sim up" when a player approaches. This latter method was in fact used for handling harvesters and the like in SWG, since they tended to reside in areas that we actually took offline when no players were around. Using hillclimbing and broadcasting rather than constant radial searches is another approach. Lastly, truly treating the whole thing as an artificial life landscape would allow you to even use image processing techniques to update the grid, since they have been highly optimized.

On the closed loops, I have come to believe they were basically a mistake. The real world offers resources that are infinite *in practice for most situations*; it is local scarcity that is interesting. The issues with exposing the causality of things can be solved, I am sure, but they will take some work.

In conclusion

To my mind, this sort of algorithmic approach to developing a virtual world is not only the past, in UO's case, but also the future. It is not hard to imagine our crude "METAL" with no parameters acquiring things like "melting point" and "brittleness" and then being plugged into physics simulations in the holodeck. There comes a point where a robust simulation model, even an abstracted one, is a cheaper thing to develop than the giant piles of use-once quests and data that we currently enjoy in the MMORPGs today. Even social worlds would benefit from having this sort of underlying mechanic, because if implemented properly, it exposes simplified levels of robust interaction to everyone and gives people something to talk about.

I also think that there is nothing wrong with having traditional static data layered atop this. Making an NPC with a hardcoded quest, no FOOD, SHELTER or DESIRE needs, and blissful ignorance of the situation around him is still easy in a system of this sort. On the other hand, how much better if he knows enough to freak out when the dragon comes up to the castle and starts frying chamberlains.

I'd much rather be burning CPU on this sort of thing, frankly, than on 3d collision. A lot of players complain about whether or not they can jump over a short wall, and believe me, I feel their pain (a story for another day) — but the kinds of immersive power that a simulation like this can bring opens a lot more doors.

In the long run, I believe that all the pressures are towards simulationist environments, rather than handcrafted ones. CPU power continues to outpace the cost of human capability to design static scenarios. At some point, reality will catch up to our designs from 1995.

Postscript for the curious — I was reminded in the comment threads that the original UO strategy guide actually had in it all the resource values for everything in the game, as well as things like the actual AI algorithm for falling through FOOD, SHELTER, and DESIRE.

How UO Rares Were Born

Amaranthar in the comment thread on the last post referred to "rares" in *Ultima Online* as a feature. They weren't really, though. **They were a bug.**

First, a definition of rares. These were simply items that were incredibly uncommon. Often they were near unique. They couldn't be found via loot — they were only spawned once, really, when the server came up. As a result, they were immediately collectible. Most of them had no use whatsoever — they were simply uniquely colored objects, like a red vase that a crafter couldn't replicate, or an object that was outright not craftable at all. A few were obvious bugs, like "water tiles" — a literal patch of water that you could pick up and stuff in your backpack, which because of how the simulation layer behind UO worked, actually functioned as water. You could fish in it, or pull a jug of water for cooking from it.

An invisible tile, called a NO_DRAW, used to create special behaviors that we didn't want players to see

Needless to say, collectibility alone was sufficient to drive these to have immense value in UO's economy, which was largely player-driven. Rares began to show up on eBay going for substantial dollar amounts, sometimes in the hundreds.

Ultima Online was not a streamed title. It shipped on a CD. You can think of the CD as basically a pre-cached version of the assets for the game. We did have the ability to add new items to the actual client cache, via a patch, but the baseline was always the CD's contents.

We took advantage of this fact to divide everything in the world of UO into two classes: static and dynamic objects.

Static stuff was stuff that we didn't expect to change. It was trees, it was the terrain, it was the water features. It was the buildings in the cities, and the furnishings in the buildings.

Dynamic stuff was simulated by the server, and in fact, we simulated quite a lot.

Every creature, every item someone crafted, every invisible object used by the simulation (spawners, for example).

A tambourine from UO

Stuff that was on the CD was therefore "dead" stuff. Stuff that didn't move, stuff that didn't behave. To get some behaviors out of them, they could still have resource system data on them (even a static object knew that it was made of wood, for example) and then we had invisible objects that summed up all the resources from a small area so that you could mine from the ground, etc. These were called "chunk eggs" and eventually led to 8x8 macroing.[116]

One of the vicissitudes of AAA MMORPG development is that you gold master a disc *near* the end of development. Not *at* the end of development. You are able to keep working on server-side stuff for a while after the disc has to be locked down. And this means that bugs keep coming in from QA (and then from Live operations) well after the disc has been committed to and cannot be changed. You're used to seeing large patches on the first day of an MMO, and this is why.

Well, many of the bugs that were reported in that period (and ever after) in UO were map bugs. Examples:

Object water tiles in the radar view — the lighter colored halo around the edge of the coastline

---

[116] See https://www.raphkoster.com/2006/07/18/use-based-systems/

- When laying down vases on the table in a particular room of a particular structure, someone accidentally placed that vase as a dynamic object rather than a static one. The bug report is "I can take the vase, and I am not supposed to be able to."

- Water in UO had a painstakingly created depth effect on the coastlines, which was made by using translucent water objects over a trench close to the coast, then fading the translucency; once you were at a depth where the water was opaque, we switched to tiles. (I spent many hours filling in those objects, and wrote flood-fill code to place them all. You can faintly see the effect in the radar map here — a "halo" around the coastline). It was all for the sake of a cut feature: having some of the fish creatures visibly swimming under the surface in shallow water. But, sometimes a tile got missed, and there would be a "hole" in the water.

The fix for these was to place a dynamic object there, to patch the hole, or replace the vase.

But when the UO server booted up, **any dynamic object that wasn't where it was supposed to be, got respawned.** So if you forgot to mark that object as "no pick up," it would just get picked up again, and at next server reboot, replaced, and…

In fact, on some servers, the fix was applied live, not as a dynamic object patch… the result there was even rarer — if the GM forgot to make the object no pick up, then there was a temporary patch that would get stolen… and *wouldn't* get replaced.

Lemons in the game

How did players find these? By mousing over every single tile in the world.

Other types of rares had a similar birth. "True black dye" was the result of an incorrectly initialized value on a dye tub. A statically placed dye tub couldn't have an index into a hue table, you see. (Hues were basically palettes of colors used for tinting objects). And if you didn't have a hue index, the palette you got was solid black — even eating away the shadows and highlights. You looked like a hole in the world.

I am speculating, but somewhere a dye tub that should have been static was left dynamic, and didn't have a hue value, so someone tried dyeing cloth from it, got true black, so then they took that color into one of their own dye tubs (you can transfer dye colors from tub to tub in UO) and started selling true black clothing.

True black clothing started going for hundreds overnight. So we removed it (the artists hated it as an abomination). Which just made the color *rarer*, which drove up value even more.

The upshot of rares? Players started launching websites[117] and forming communities around collecting,[118] building lists[119] and making real money[120] and creating strategy guides[121] around rares.[122]

After banging our heads against this sort of thing for a few weeks, we embraced it instead. Players felt clever. They had invented a mini-game out of our bugs, and it was a mini-game people were willing to pay thousands of dollars a month to play. People started making museums of rares.

Our wisdom was not in inventing an awesome cool collectible feature. It was in **surrendering control** to the awesome power of emergent behavior. The credit we can take is only for having created a fertile and dynamic enough environment where this sort of thing can happen. Environments like this also produce house break-ins (maybe I'll write about that someday...) and PKing and much else that can be incredibly pernicious. But far more often than you would think, you get magic through serendipity.

Your other choice, of course, is to assume that you are going to produce magic on demand.

---

[117] See http://www.uorares.com/faq.php

[118] One of the most active was located on Stratics, here:
https://web.archive.org/web/20100901020123/http://vboards.stratics.com/uo-rares-collector/

[119] Such as http://noctalis.com/dis/uo/r-0.shtml

[120] On eBay, but also on dedicated trading sites like UoTreasures.com, found here:
http://www.uotreasures.com/

[121] https://uo.stratics.com/content/basics/items_rare_misc.shtml

[122] A full video by someone who dove into it wholesale, Markee Dragon, can be found here:
https://www.youtube.com/watch?v=KymNu0ym-0Y

Use-based systems

Recently, there's been some chatter on the [ultima] Yahoogroup about macroing. Lots of talk about how the fixes for detecting macroing software are coming years too late. But we waged a silent war against macroing from very early on — not because of the gold farmers, as that was much less of a concern back then, but because of the basic mechanics of a use-based system.

These days, use-based systems are most familiar to everyone because of *Oblivion*, probably. And sure enough, there's plenty of tales of how amusing it is that the use-based system there encourages strange behaviors that do not fit the expected behavior in the game: people jumping everywhere in order to improve the stats and skills related to dodging, that sort of thing.

The basic definition of a use-based skill system is one where you have a chance of improvement every time you use the skill. So everyone has access to every skill from the beginning (or, in a variant, access may be unlocked by other means, such as being taught), and as you exercise the skill, your chance of success goes up.

The attraction is that it leads to a more freeform game experience. Instead of tracking arbitrary "experience points" that can be applied to anything, leading to oddities like getting better at crafting because you have slain a lot of orcs, you can get better at crafting by, well, crafting. The downside, of course, is that it lets you sit there and do something repetitively in order to get better at it.

In the real world, this is called "practice," and we don't regard it as a bad thing. We force kids to sit and do scales on their piano or violin; we tell them to do a billion math problems; and we send them to sports camp so they can keep honing skills. "Practice" isn't a dirty word at all, and generations have bemoaned the repetitive nature of it. However, the logic seems to be that in game, repetitive action like that has no place.

That's balderdash. The issue isn't the repetitiveness. Many games allow repetitiveness within their framework even if they don't require it. You can practice headshots in an FPS, or jumps in a platform game. In fact, you pretty much have to. So it's not practicing that is the issue — it's that, in classic "theory of fun" style, practice that isn't challenging your skills and helping you learn is boring. In the headshot example, you probably start out not able to hit headshots reliably — as you practice, you take on tougher and tougher shots, and keep challenging yourself. In the musical instrument example, new pieces and new techniques open up, much like new levels in a game. (There's a reason we say you "play" a piece of music!)

But in use-based systems, at least how they are structured today, this isn't the case. **There's no challenge in jumping off a hill in** *Oblivion*, and therefore, the grind rears its ugly head.

Now, the biggest barrier here isn't mechanical, it's psychological. Players are bottom-feeding the system (fun checklist item again!). There's no cost to failure. The topology of the space is irrelevant. There are no differing abilities. No skill required. All of these can be avoided if players simply **quit doing unfun stuff**. But that particular psychological barrier isn't one that is going to fall; humans seek advantage, and just because it may be more challenging to forage for one's own food in the winter, it's smarter to instead hit the grocery store even though it's distinctly less challenging.

So the systems must adapt to the psychology. Some players will "play it straight," but even many of those will succumb to temptation once they see other players gaining advantage over them by using the bottom-feeding method.

UO used a straight-up use-based system. Each time you used a skill, it had a chance of going up. In fact, originally, it had a chance of going up if you observed someone else using it. There was no difficulty rating on the task, so there was no way to say "you won't learn from this because it's beneath your skill threshold. What's more, skills that you didn't use originally decayed away. A player was allowed only 700 skill points total — when you hit that threshold, and gained a point, a point was automatically lost from somewhere else — not even the least used skill, as I recall, but any of them, on the grounds that if you used something occasionally, it'd counteract a bit of the loss.

The first big problem that we ran into with use-based systems was that every skill was used at a different rate. Swords were swung quickly. Talking to the dead was done rarely. If every skill had the same chance of advancing and the same amount by which it advanced, then swords would be mastered incredibly quickly, and skills that could not physically be performed as often because of the lack of opportunity would advance more slowly.

The solution to this was to dynamically track the frequency of use of all skills. That way we could look at swords, see that skill checks for it happened ten times more often than our baseline, and that spirit speak usage happened ten times less than our baseline. We could then make the chance of swords advancing when used to be 1/10th the chance of the baseline, and the chance of spirit speak advancing to be ten times the baseline. If skills became more popular (lets say, a whole bunch of spirit speakers started to play the game) then spirit speak would be checked more frequently, and then it would move closer to the baseline chance of advancing. It would be a self-balancing mechanism for when payers rushed to skills because they were "easier to advance."

It didn't work. For one, I don't think there was a baseline in place; instead, everything started getting slower and slower to advance. As things got slower, players responded by macroing the skills, chasing after the one time in a thousand that they would go up. This meant that now the chance became one in ten thousand. The thing players had an infinite amount of was time — it didn't matter to them whether they macroed for an hour or overnight. What broke was the feedback mechanism — the reward of advancement came so incredibly infrequently that playing "the right way" no longer had any incentives.

A few thing could have fixed this, in theory. Only advancing for taking on actual challenges, rather than doing something you already know how to do, such as swinging at a practice dummy. Soon people started trapping powerful monsters in their houses to macro on instead. Ooops. Next solution?

One such solution was 8×8. I've mentioned before how UO internally divided up the map into "chunks" of 64 tiles, 8×8 square, and stored the invisible resources on a "chunk egg," an invisible object that represented the amount of wood, grass, and so on to be found there. This also meant that the chunk egg was a unique object with an id.

A feature of how random numbers work on computers is that they aren't actually random. They are seeded by a value. If you give a random number generator a given seed number, say 1234, then it will always spit out the same result. With a use-based system, we were rolling dice to see when people were going to advance. The inputs were things like what skill they were using, what skill level they were currently at, and a random seed.

I had already moved off the team by this point, but Sunsword[123] came to ask me for advice. I suggested that instead of seeding the random number generator with the system clock (so that it would always spit out different numbers) we instead should seed it with the id of the chunk egg. This meant that you'd get a predictable result for a given person, skill, and skill level. If a guy who was standing at a forge started

---

[123] Anthony Castoro.

forging, and failed, he'd be guaranteed to fail there until the heat death of the universe. The only way to get it to succeed would be to change the random seed number. This could be accomplished by putting different inputs into the seed: a different skill level (by, say, going elsewhere and managing to advance) or a different location (by just going elsewhere).

The intent was to get people to move about — two or three moves would carry you a whole screen away from where you were previously.

Players still managed to figure out, via pure scientific experimentation, as far I know, that if they regularly moved 8 tiles away, they would have an improved chance of advancement. And thus was born the phenomenon called "8×8 macroing," which involved moving 8 tiles via an automated macro, after a given failed attempt. I regard the player discovery of this as a great example of one of the Laws:

> No matter what you do, players will decode every formula, statistic, and algorithm in your world via experimentation.

Runesabre[124] never liked the skill table, and once UO was under his domain, he removed it in favor of a hand-coded table. A hand-coded advancement rate table will always need to be updated as players discover exploits that drive them towards one skill or another, so I strongly recommend that anyone dealing with a use-based system maintain metrics of rate of use anyway; whether they then manually copy those values into their advancement table, or do it automatically is to my mind largely irrelevant. The challenge is fixing the feedback loop.

Once the table was removed, a series of increasingly outré systems such as "guaranteed gain" and "power hour" started becoming required, as rates were adjusted to try to bring some semblance of balance to things. I was gone by then, so I don't know what the logic behind those were.

How to make use-based systems work? Well, one way is to move to "results-based" logic. This is the philosophy that it isn't using the system that should grant you advancement, but instead, getting a concrete result. This is what leads to experience points; in SWG, we said that you could have results classified by what sort of result, thus giving us multiple types of experience.

The sorts of results we wanted, however, weren't solely the act of building something (because that could still be done in a closed room making crap nobody

---

[124] Kirk Black.

wants) but instead results that were somehow socially valid. From this was born the notion of crafting XP being granted when someone else actually used something you crafted: a validation that what you made actually worth something to someone. Alas, this system was marginalized in favor of the more direct feedback of getting XP when you made something; to really work, it would have needed to account for all of the XP, or else bottom feeding would once again ensue (as it did).

In the long run, we ended up tracking the rate of usage during beta, and setting static XP requirements per skill box based on the rate of usage of skills, just like that table in UO. We also added the difficulty rating to each challenge that users were overcoming (be it a monster or something they were crafting) so that we could adjust the XP gain accordingly.

A fun little story for those who think SWG was still too grindy: three days before the game launched, the designer in charge of advancement rates went through them and made them all ten times slower. His concern was that players would max out the game in a matter of weeks, and then quit. This actually hit the live beta servers, and I reverted it back out as soon as I saw how excruciatingly slow it was: making literally thousands of blaster bolts to advance one skill box. I felt that I'd rather people exit the game having had fun, than stay and not have fun, or quit because it was too grindy.

Of course, it was still too grindy.

So, how to make use-based systems work? Well, I think you'd have to run down the checklist, and try to fix each of those problems. The result might not look much like a use-based system once you were done.

One system that we were planning with the cancelled *Privateer Online* was to drop this advancement metaphor altogether. Instead, you were certified to do things. You earned certification by doing a minimal amount of training, defeating a challenge of some sort, and then most critically, paying your dues. Dues would be currency paid to the NPC guilds in the game. If you couldn't pay the dues, then you'd lose the certification.

The instant reaction to this system was, "but people could buy their way up to the top!" And my reply was, "so what?" It's not it's regular skills — instead, think of it as a mechanism for people to play the way they want to. If you want to set up a merchant empire, find a sponsor, and try to get going. And if you can't cut it, you'll lose all your money on expensive dues, and slip back down to the level of gameplay you can actually handle. For a game about commerce, this sounded fine to me.

At the heart of all this, though, is the problem that skills, levels, abilities — these are properly regarded as *enablers*, and not as the point. A skill is supposed to be a tool you use to defeat a challenge. If the game becomes getting the tool, then you have a nice little rat race going that is inevitably going to be a grind. You need to make the skills something you pick up in order to do something *else*. At that point, whether you make people earn them or just let people pick up any they want becomes much less important, because you've placed the burden for fun where it should be: on the game, and not on the advancement.

The evolution of UO's economy

This is excerpted from a Usenet thread in which we were discussing many, many topics. Along the way, we talked about UO's economy. I think it was in the context of how much Trammel had affected things. Anyway, I gave a brief historical summary of my take on the UO economy at various stages of its development. For a more analytical approach, I highly recommend Zach Simpson's excellent paper on "The In-Game Economics of Ultima Online" which you can find on the links page.[125] The whole debate started because I said that UO's economy was subsidized after the introduction of Trammel, to which the retort was, "all online game economies are subsidized..."

Let me rephrase, it's a *radically* subsidized economy. I'm not speaking of removing all subsidization, I'm talking about not flooding the game with gold.

NPC shops are a subsidy, obviously, as they buy stuff for which there is zero real market. In a non-usage game, we could say they subsidize the gameplay of adventuring (which gives you lots of useless stuff) or pursuing your chosen playstyle (like say, crafting stuff that nobody wants, because it's how you have fun).

In a game like UO, which is usage based, the NPC shops are rewarding macroing and the pursuit of skill points. They're not even rewarding having fun necessarily. They're just a gold spigot.

Model one

The original UO system had shops adjusting their prices and stock based on what sold and what was bought. They would acquire stuff from players speculatively. Then they would attempt to sell those goods. If they ended up with too many in stock because people did not want the goods, they lowered their purchase price, eventually to zero. If they had too few, the price went up, and they might spend their operating capital on making more of that good themselves. They would cash in goods that did not sell for more operating capital (subsidy) but they would not restock them themselves, preferring to stock items that sold.

The data which they used was supposed to be based on the local market, so that price differences would be exposed between different shops and different cities.

---

[125] See http://www.mine-control.com/zack/uoecon/uoecon.html

What actually happened in the first model, of course, is that distances were trivial, so no local markets. But more egregiously, there were two huge issues.

One was massive overproduction. You see, the incentive to produce wasn't money or commerce. It was macroing advancement. Every single crafter in the game went into the hole immediately, because they gladly traded gold for skill points. This didn't get them anything except the satisfaction of a label next to their name, and made no economic sense on their part, really, but they did it anyway.

Shops all quickly has a surfeit of absolutely everything, and purchased nothing. And the players rebelled, resulting in a system whereby all data tracking for a given shop was cleared on a periodic time basis.

Model Two

The other thing that happened was hoarding. There were not nearly enough drains in the game economy, even with item decay. This manifested badly because gold was in a closed loop; we had a fixed amount of currency in the world–it was a tweakable number, of course, so we could "print it" when we needed it, like a central bank. But the issue was that we had spawns that injected currency into the system.

What happened was a collapse of liquidity. The gold crafters had was all spent on turning it into skill points. That money all went to the resource miners. From there it went to the hoarders. And there it stayed. There wasn't anything to spend it on.

Hoarding caused all sorts of disastrous problems, of course, culminating in special measures like the Clean Up Britannia campaign. We broke the gold loop, and instead let currency float to the equilibrium point with the actual drains we had in the game.

And there it stayed, stable for quite a long time. Massive hoards were broken up as players quit and houses decayed leaving stuff to decay–or when they decided to break up the hoard to give to friends, many of whom lost large sums. Much wealth was redistributed via jerks, actually, and to a degree they were a positive economic force because they were so rich already they let lots of people's wealth decay away too.

In the end, Model Two ended up with a stable exchange rate of 1 dollar for 200 UO gold from around three months after launch until well after I was no longer on the project.

Model Three

UO: Renaissance removed that wealth redistribution via jerks (which was a great move in other arenas, but sure didn't help the economics), in the process made wealth gathering from the spawn spigot *much* easier, and shortly after UO currency began to collapse. Said collapse has been ongoing and last time I checked (a while ago), a UO gold coin was worth a hundred times less than it had been during the days when the economy was stable. I haven't been graphing the exchange rate the way I used to (see, I did fall in love with stats and data) so I don't know if it's stabilized yet.

The radical subsidy is that the game now pays you UO gold for, well, logging on. I expect to see another dip in the currency value as the effects of this "no need to refresh your house" thing go into effect.

Does this all matter? After all, it *does* find equilibrium. The answer, sadly, is yes, because there's countless pieces of static data involving currency scattered throughout the whole game. The reward you get from a critter. How expensive it is to buy a castle. What the living expenses are for a mage. Revising all that so that players feel like they are getting adequate reward in the face of currency devaluation is a massive pain in the butt, and if you increment it, all you're doing is contributing to the devaluation since you're increasing what players get…

The typical end of this cycle on an online game is a wipe of all equipment and goods. They usually leave the characters intact. (Characters are wiped over a different but very related kind of database deflation, covered in that citation I gave you for that post about Lady Vox).

BTW, this issue was first noticed on *Habitat* in 1985, cf "The Lessons of LucasFilm's Habitat."

Taken from Usenet posts in early 2002. The "Lady Vox" post can also be found on this website in the Snippets section.[126] *The reference to "usage based" is referring to the fact that UO your character advances via repetitive use of a given skill. Therefore, the advancement encourages the production of goods which nobody wants.*

I gotta tell you all, **nothing** is simple about this.

In UO we actually had to take **out** realistic economy sim aspects because they weren't fun. Shops being overstocked and not paying for player goods, shops going bankrupt from failure to compete with players, players going bankrupt from failure to compete with shops… and on and on and on. Every tiny change sent massive tremors though the entire game. We're at the point now where it's a lot less realistic, but kinda works, and sort of moves along.

If you expect a player to be able to make money occasionally from selling items they make, you will find that players will expect to be able to sell those items reliably for a reliable price. And telling them that there's a glut of bagpipes in the area doesn't

---

[126] See https://www.raphkoster.com/games/snippets/database-deflation/

mollify them much.

Some of the things we tracked and did:

- track local availability of raw materials for goods fabrication
- track amount of materials on hand for the shop
- track sales rate for individual good types both in the shop and in the local area
- shops able to recycle goods into materials, with wastage
- determine target stock levels for goods based on turnaround, materials, demand locally and in this shop, etc
- variable pricing dependent upon all the rest
- "overstock" purchases on the part of the shop, based on shopkeeper expectation of selling either the goods, or the materials implicit in the goods

There was more, but it boils down to this:

In the real world, you can spend $5 for a block of wood and turn it into a great wooden foozle. And the market in foozles can be so bad you lose your shirt. But in a game, players will say, "labor implies profit! I MUST make money at this!" and they will report that as a bug.

So now we have a less accurate economy, but one that satisfies players. And we learned (again) the lesson to never lose sight of the enjoyment of those who aren't as cutting edge as you are.

In the end, UO began to move to a player-driven economy, whereby NPC shopkeepers are gradually being taken out of the loop. The sole concern is whether newbies will retain sufficient access to the goods they need to get started in the game.

Bread making made it into *Ultima IX* in large part to thumb noses at the public who slammed UO over it. *Shadowbane*'s press campaign started out with "We don't play games to bake bread, we play to crush"–that was a reference to those days. There were many critiques that it wasn't heroic enough. *Legends of Kesmai* ran a banner ad which spoofed bread making and carpentry too. There was precedent in the Ultima series, particularly *Ultima 7*, but not to any large scale. Maybe that web archiving site has some of the old articles that were written–we were, literally, ridiculed for it by press, fans, and competitors.

Selling virtual property for real world money

A UO player was very upset by the recent phenomenon of established UO accounts selling for astronomical fees on online auction sites such as eBay. (As I wrote this reply, the high bid on one account was over $2000). He saw it as the end of the world of UO, as a "black pus filled ball of greed and selfishness." The below are extracted from my replies to this thread.

…my, you sound bitter. And over what? Over people's natural desire to get ahead, to make a profit on whatever they can. It's not going to magically be absent from a virtual world, you know. People have been selling virtual property for years now on other online games, and it hasn't ruined the games. It's just reflective of real life.

It may be that you regard this basic part of human nature as "a black pus filled ball of greed and selfishness"… I would agree that human nature is the heart and soul of UO, though. However, whereas you see that as its weakness, I see that as its strength.

It may be that after seeing what UO has gone through, that other makers of online spaces will choose to avoid the route of trying to make actual worlds. They may settle for just making virtual realities about levelling or about killing or about chatting. They may decide that people cannot exist in a space together and be able to arrive at means of running their community themselves. They may decide that the audience of players and virtual citizens needs to have not just rules, but actual laws of physics coded into the game to make them behave nice. A pity, because it means that virtual spaces will remain just toys, instead of things that matter…

For every person you see selling an account on eBay for a lot of money, every greedy escapee from UO you see trying to make a profit, there are a bunch of people bidding, too. And they are bidding on intangibles. They are offering up their hard-won real money in exchange for invisible bits and bytes because they see the intangibles of UO as being something worth having. A tower for a sense of pride. High skills for greater freedom of action. A place in an online community–they are paying real money for something that many argue doesn't even exist. I find it odd that people think this cheapens the whole thing. I think it validates it. It says to me that there are more people who want to be deeper IN than there are who want OUT. That there are strong emotional reasons for being a participant.

Yes, it may seem unfair that to the rich of one world go the advantages of the other world, but hey, life isn't fair. Heck, I don't even know if the sales on eBay are legal. But I DO know that wanting to be more involved with a virtual world doesn't sound like a marker of that world's ending. It sounds more like a sign of its strength.

Could the game be safer if we took more stringent measures, like a PK switch? Yeah, quite probably. I don't think we could afford to run, though. My faith in the players' abilities to circumvent rules is boundless, you see, and I think that the tighter the rules, the more rebellion you get. Hence increased admin costs.

It could be that we're a doomed experiment. That it's not possible to have a virtual environment in which you can do anything worthwhile. I'd be very depressed if that were so.

But if all online games are gonna be is little amusement park rides where you can log in, gain a level or two, slay a monster (maybe in the company of friends) and feel like you scored some points–well, that would be a future that merited my being depressed, I think. There's nothing particularly wrong with it, but it's been done before, and it has no real social significance.

You're not going to learn anything about yourself or about others in a game like that. You're not going to be challenged in any way that matters. Yeah, you might feel a great deal safer not feeling challenged, but I'd rather have one engaged player than three who are going through XP-run, gain-stat, level-tomorrow motions.

It might be UO's very aspirations that trip it up, but without those aspirations, it won't be art and it won't be society, it'll just be hackwork. Hackwork is easy to come by. Why settle for it?

If RL is more worthwhile and fun than UO (and I wouldn't dispute that it is), then what are you doing here, arguing the point?

We cannot judge whether someone is a loser just by their actions on one auction. What do you know? Maybe someone is buying it as a special gift for a dying kid. Still a loser? Maybe they are buying it because they hate the person and they want to carefully demolish everything that account has achieved. Loser? Probably. :)

Either way, nobody is going to spend that amount of money on something they are not passionate about. And lemme tell you, if their life in UO is passionate, and their life in the real world is dry and gray, then maybe it's the virtual life that is worthwhile and valuable, not the real one. Maybe that's where they touch more people, where they influence lives, where they make discoveries about themselves and others, where they do good deeds, learn lessons, and take risks.

Who are you (or me, or anyone) to judge that?

Random UO Anecdote #2

I just stumbled across this old story I told somewhere, and thought I'd share more widely.

In *Ultima Online*, the player was a container — one you couldn't open, but which held your equipped items, your backpack which was the container you could actually see, etc. Because of the freeform "gump"[127] style containment system used in the Ultimas, you could position anything to any location in a container, which meant they were basically treated like maps, with coordinate systems in them.

A UO horse

Then we added mounts.

When you rode a horse, we simply put the horse inside the player, and spawned a pair of pants that looked like your horse, which you then equipped and wore.

When we first did this, however, we forgot to make the horse stop acting like a horse. Pretty soon there was a rash of server crashes because the horse inside the player was wandering around, picking up the stuff it found inside the player, rifling through the player's backpack and eating things it thought were edible, and eventually, wandering "off the map" because the player's internal coordinate system was pretty small, and the edges weren't impassable.

---

[127] According to http://www.uoguide.com/Gump, "graphical user menu pop-up." It was the term that was used at Origin back then, long-forgotten now expect maybe among the UO emu community. Basically, any UI window of arbitrary shape floating above the game. In UO, inventory systems did not use slots but free placement on a coordinate system.

Notes on "Making of UO" articles

Read them here: "The Making of a Classic Part 1[128]" and "Part 2". [129]

I wasn't able to really sit down with Adam Tingle, the author, but he did run around the blog archives a fair amount. There's some inaccuracies here and there, but it's a decent overview.

Some things I spotted:

> Throughout 1979 Garriott would design his computer role-playing game, revising it, adding to it, showing his friends, and finally when "D&D 28b" was finished, he renamed it Aklabeth...

It's "Akalabeth" not "Aklabeth" — you can actually play it on your iOS device these days.

> Together [Starr and Richard] started to knock ideas back and forth, based upon these new experiences, and came up with the premise of a multiplayer Ultima, or "Multima" as they affectionately termed it.

My understanding is that talk of "Multima" had been going on for quite some time, including discussions with Sierra (back when they ran The ImagiNation Network).[130] This also leaves out the role of Ken Demarest, who was a moving force in getting the project started.

> 1996: So now that they had the art style, the funding, and the engine – they needed a direction for the game to head in...

Technically, we didn't have the engine at the point the article states; the client was basically rewritten in 1995-96. Rick Delashmit had been there for a few months when my wife and I joined the project on Sept 1st 1995; other key early folks such as Scott "Grimli" Phillips and Edmond Meinfelder also joined in August to September of 95.

---

[128] http://www.mmorpg.com/gamelist.cfm/game/12/feature/6100/The-Making-of-a-Classic-Part-1.html/page/1

[129] http://www.mmorpg.com/gamelist.cfm/game/12/feature/6103/Ultima-Online-The-Making-of-a-Classic-Part-2.html

[130] https://en.wikipedia.org/wiki/Sierra_Entertainment#1990s

That's also around when Ken Demarest left, and Jim Greer — best known today for founding Kongregate.

I think I have told this story before, but the whole "dragons eating deer" example came from the design samples that my wife and I sent in as part of our job applications. We showed up on the first day and were taken aback when we were told that was how the game was going to work… So at least that much of the notion of "what the game was going to be" was set in 1995…

That crazy resource system stuff, particularly some of the AI, did in fact work in the alpha test. It led to rabbits that had levelled up and were capable of taking out wolves — or advanced players. We found this intensely amusing, and quoted Monty Python at each other whenever it came up.

> Being as most of the team in charge of UO were coming from single-player games, with very few MUD veterans involved in the process…

This is just not really right. At least on the game dev team. From that September team, Kristen and Rick and I came from DikuMUDs. Edmond came from MUSH and MOO backgrounds. Scott and a tad later Jeff Posey came from LPMUDs. We had Andrew Morris, who was the original lead designer, who was a veteran of U7 and U8. And of course, our first artist, Micael Priest[131] (most famous for his amazing poster art for bands in the 70s) wasn't an online gamer either.

Later, as the team grew and absorbed a lot of folks from U9 (which was suspended for a while) there were plenty of non-online folks on the team. But the basic premises of UO were definitely set by folks from MUDs.

> …the idea of GMs taking an active dynamic role, never materialized as initially intended…

The article says that the idea of having GMs take active roles in running events never panned out… but those who recall the Seer program and the many phenomenal live events that were run know that in fact, this did happen quite a lot.

> By the time the alpha had ended, the Origin team had collected enough data, were able to fix bugs, glitches and exploits, and finally the home stretch was seen bobbing along the horizon…

This leaves out one dramatic and important step in UO's history. The alpha was not an MMO in the "really massive" sense of the word. It supported the same sort of concurrency as *Meridian 59* did — 250 or so. In between the alpha and the beta, the server was rewritten to allow for 2500-3000 concurrent players per shard. In order to do this, a whole bunch of new technology had to be invented for creating seamless

---

[131] http://southaustincenter.org/history/micael-priest/

borders between adjacent maps. These borders would prove to be a source of bugs for years (most dupe bugs made use of race conditions when moving across server lines).

> Vogel would later admit "We were pressured on time. I wish we'd have had a little bit more time."

All game dev teams say that, right? In UO's case, the time pressure was fairly extreme towards the end. After the huge reaction to the beta, all the eyes of the press were on us. A big meeting was scheduled to decide whether to ship — on a date that would make the all-important Christmas holiday sales. Nobody thought the game was ready to ship, but some higher-ups came around and helpfully told us that saying so in a meeting might be a career-limiting move. When the big "go-no-go" meeting was held, everyone voted yes except the QA guy.

All in all, if you go from when a team was put on the game (as opposed to just Rick & Starr), it was around Sept 95 to Sept 97 to make UO. Except that everything made up to the alpha test was thrown away and started over. So it's really more like May 1996 to September 1997...

Rich Vogel also often doesn't get enough credit for putting in place all the vital things that simply were outside of the dev team's scope, like, oh, billing and customer service.

> Explaining events later, Rainz describes "I just cast the scroll on the bridge and waited to see what would happen. Someone made the comment 'hehe nice try', I expected to be struck down, instead I heard a loud death grunt as British slumped to his death". Accidentally, this Internet consultant has just committed the most infamous act in gaming history.

I was busy coding something and missed this altogether. Scott rushed into my office and said "Did you see? They killed Lord British!" At first I wasn't sure if he meant in the game or not...

> Interestingly UO garnered an initial negative response from the press, Gamespot giving the game 49%

Both UO and SWG had the mixed blessing of being Coaster of the Year from *Computer Gaming World*... and also winning a variety of "best of" awards.

> As time progressed Origin patched, refined, and grew the game in ways they saw fit, adding in a reputation system to calm down the rampant PKing

Somehow the article manages to then skip ahead to 1999, thereby missing out on discussing the great Trammel/Felucca split.

Anyway, a nice walk down memory lane, and perhaps the articles have stuff in them people have not heard before.

The UO essays

Sometime in early 1998, the first player luncheons started happening. These were grassroots-organized gatherings for people who played Ultima Online, held at local restaurants. We'd attend, of course, at least some of us, and sometimes we'd talk about upcoming things in the game.

At, I believe, the second one of these, in late April or early May of 1998, I was asked to say some words. And I told a story, a story about a tree and a player on LegendMUD who had been reported dead.

Shortly after, I wrote it up, and I put in on the UO website, thereby publishing it to over a hundred thousand people. Today it has its own Wikipedia article; after a decade, the death of the player was actually debunked via an article in Salon. (This also features prominently in Dr Richard Bartle's excellent book Designing Virtual Worlds).

It was, however, only the first of a half-dozen or so articles that I wrote and posted to the website, in a brief spate of pieces trying to outline to players what I saw as the core issues facing them as players and us as operators of what was the largest virtual world to date.

A Story About A Tree

May 5th, 1998

I'd like to tell you a story about a tree.

This tree grows in a different virtual world than *Ultima Online*–one of the many text muds that exist on the Internet. It grows in a Garden of Remembrance, and the ground around it is littered with flowers and boxes of chocolates and pieces of paper with heartfelt poems written on them. And there is a plaque there as well–"In memory of Karyn," it reads.

The story I'd like to tell is the story of that plaque and that person, someone I never met.

Karyn first logged on to that virtual world quite some time ago. She was from Norway. She kept coming back, and brought friends with her—some of whom did not speak English very well, but for whom she served as an interpreter. She made friends. Eventually she ran a website all about that virtual world, and posted on that site pictures of herself, where all could see she had a lovely smile.

As her ties to the world grew, she started a guild. She called it the Norse Traders, and with a lot of hard work, she got it off the ground and developed it into one of the most popular and well-known guilds in the game. It was a merchants' guild that also adventured together, and pretty soon the folks involved had made good friendships.

In March of this year, some of those friends started to notice that they hadn't seen Karyn in a while. You know how it goes in the online world–people don't leave, they just fail to show up, usually, and you never know what happened to them. But in this case there was her website to go to. So people went looking for Karyn.

A day later the news filtered out across the bulletin boards, via emails, and eventually onto the welcome message when you first logged in: Karyn was dead. She had died in a head-on collision while test-driving a new car. And it had happened two months before, in January, and none of us had known.

Her parents knew that she had friends on the Internet–they didn't quite understand what she did online, or who those friends were, but they knew that there were people

---
242

out there somewhere who might want to learn the news. It took them some time to find her webpage, and to learn how to put a message up. But they did it, and they attached news items about the car crash, in Norwegian.

The outpouring of grief on the virtual world was immediate. People who had not logged on in months heard about it from the game's email newsletter. A memorial service was organized. And eventually, a Garden of Remembrance was created, and a tree planted in Karyn's memory. Players made the pilgrimage to the garden in order to leave tokens of their grief. Code was changed so that items left in this manner became permanent parts of the world.

Throughout all the events, however, there ran a common thread. People could not get a handle on feeling grief for someone they had never actually met. They could not quite understand feeling a deep sense of loss over someone they "just played a game with." When describing their loss, they had to resort to "I once formed a party with her and we went into a dungeon." They couldn't quite express the feeling that a member of their *community* was gone.

And it was that sense–the Norse Traders had fallen apart since January, and now they knew why. Because Karyn, the person at the center of it, was not there. In a very real sense, they came to realize that the strange unease they had felt about hearing of her death with a two-month time lag might have originated in the fact that the loss to the community was actually felt when she stopped logging in–not when the news finally came.

In the end, that garden and that tree served not only as a memorial to a well-loved and much-missed person, but as a marker of a moment, a moment in which the players of an online game realized that they weren't "playing a game." That the social bonds that they felt within this "game" were Real.

There's a children's book, *The Velveteen Rabbit*, about a stuffed plush rabbit which desperately wishes to become Real. And in the end, the love of the little boy whose toy it is makes this come true.

In the end, the social bonds of the people in a virtual environment make it more than just a game. They make it Real. Sometimes it takes a moment of grief to make people realize it, and sometimes people just come to an awareness over time, but the fundamental fact remains: when we make a friend, hurt someone's feelings, suffer a loss, or accomplish something in an online world, it's real. It's not "just a game."

Ultima Online was designed with a basic philosophy in mind: that we were providing an online world, one that could live and breathe and develop in new and unpredictable ways. We wanted to provide scope for players to develop online communities in a way that no other online world had done. It is amazing and gratifying to see some of the results today: volunteer police forces, roleplayer taverns, small-scale Olympics, and fledgling forms of government. And yes, sadly, a few places where funerals have been held, for in any community of this size, there will be losses.

The thing that we should never lose sight of is that we, by participating in this new sort of community, are breaking new ground that will undoubtedly prove important over the next decade, as the Internet acquires more significance in business, education, socializing, and other areas outside of gaming. The dilemmas that players of UO wrestle with every day in the form of how reputation should work, what to do about harassment, etc, are the key problems of virtual reality for the next several years. And we are only able to tackle them because you, the citizens of this virtual Britannia, are more than just players—you are a self-aware community that reaches beyond "game" and into the Real.

I am not going to let anyone tell me that the Garden of Remembrance isn't Real, or that the grief we all felt over Karyn's death was not Real. And I hope that UO players aren't going to let anyone tell them that their experiences within UO aren't Real either, that it's "just a game." It may be for some people, but we all know better, don't we? For Karyn's sake, and also for our own.

–Designer Dragon

This little essay is based on a speech given at the last Austin UO Players Lunch in March.

Revisiting the Garden of Remembrance

Technically this is not one of the UO essays but it's the appropriate follow-up to the previous one.

If you are here today, odds are it is because of reading this.[132]

A few years back, I wrote that some of the events from the *Ultima Online* days were going to get seized up by the playerbase and turned into some of the formative myths of cyberspace. I never expected that one of the things that people would seize on most fervently was "A Story About a Tree." In the end, sadly, it has turned out that like most myths, it has a kernel of truth circles by layers of fiction and wishes.

A few weeks ago, I started trading emails with Tracy Spaight, a documentary filmmaker who was researching Karyn's story. He came to the conclusion that it was a hoax, and you can read about his investigations in his article for Salon.com.

How do I feel about this? To be honest, very much like I felt at the time that the events in A Story About a Tree took place. Stages of disbelief, anger, and sorrow, the all-too-familiar pop-psych litany.

Right now, as I write this, members of the *LegendMUD* community are going through the same stages, a few weeks behind me, as they learn for the first time of this deception.

Here's the thing, though: we come back to myths not because they are true, but because they are True. So I am going to state this as bluntly as I can: I am not ashamed about having been taken in. Frankly, it's not the first time, and I am sure it won't be the last. But I would much rather be willing to approach other people online without endless layers of hardened cynicism, than to have to live a life online always skeptical of others' intentions.

To me, the heart of the story still stands: that the bonds we form with others online are real. Realer, it seems, than the people themselves, sometimes. The crux of the matter is that *real or not, Karyn is lost to us.* And to me, that fact will always be deserving of a Garden of Remembrance.

---

[132] "Who Killed Miss Norway?" was an investigative piece by Tracy Spaight published on Salon.com. https://www.salon.com/2003/04/14/who_killed_miss_norway/

What Rough Beast?

May 6th, 1998

> Things fall apart; the center cannot hold.
> Mere anarchy is loosed upon the world.

Forgive me if the quote is inaccurate–it's from memory. It was written by William Butler Yeats, an Irish poet, and people have been quoting it ever since.

The latter line may hold some resonance for those players struggling with the issues of harassment and playerkilling in the virtual setting. It's a difficult problem, to say the least. "Where," players might ask, "have the Virtues gone?" This is, after all, *Ultima Online.*

By now most gamers have heard the story, of course. Richard Garriott, after making Ultima III, felt that his games were lacking a moral center. And so in Ultima IV, he made the central storyline of the game be about a simple moral structure: eight qualities he found admirable and which fit well within the fantasy setting.. The Virtues. And ever since, Ultimas have been about ethics, which is a large part of what makes the series a landmark in the history of computer gaming.

Yet UO does not directly support the Virtues, at the moment. Why is that?

For an answer, I thought I would dig up a design document I wrote back on September 13th, 1995…

> *Setting implications*
>
> The setting statement implies that the regular course of the Ultima games is the aberration in the normal course of events. Normal worlds in the multiverse do not get set under the caretaking hands of a Time Lord, therefore they do not manifest such recurring forces as the Avatar and Lord British and the Guardian and all the other characters who make up what we know in the regular Ultima sequence.

(The "setting" referred to is the fact that UO is an alternate shard from the regular canon Ultima universe. Within the canon Ultima universe, the Time Lord sends Avatars, of course, who serve as examples of the Virtues. The other shards, as those who have read Sherry the Mouse's book may know, are mere shadows that may or may not someday reunite with the main universe. However, they are not receiving that paternalistic intervention from outside...)

Instead, the normal world is composed of daily power struggles, of ethical dilemmas without clearcut answers, and clearly have a lack of guidance from outside. There is no ultimate authority like a Time Lord sitting out there to tell the inhabitants of these other worlds exactly what course of action is the best.

Granted, the instruction of the Time Lord till now has been essentially that the "correct" course of action is often not the one that comes immediately to mind; in that sense, the regular Ultima series is a gradually developing course in ethics, beginning with simplistic good and evil (Mondain, Minax, Exodus), to the notion of 'absolute' virtues in a rather Aquinas-like philosophy, and from there towards the notion of ethical relativity that manifests in U6 and later episodes. Thus the regular Ultimas develop the concept of ethical behavior gradually.

The goal then for the setting and theme of *Ultima Online* is to recapitulate this development on an individual basis, permitting players free rein to behave as they prefer—but also to incorporate the notion that has been implied in all the mainstream series: that ethics and governance are essentially the same subject. That what is proper ethical behavior on the part of the individual, i.e. the governance of one's impulses and desires, is also proper behavior for those who seek to govern others. Thus it is that Lord British becomes the exemplar of behavior in *Ultima Online*, rather than the Avatar, for in the normal course of human events, people do not develop into the sorts of external forces that the Avatar is in the regular series.

In *Ultima Online*, the underlying game mechanics do not only reward behavior that considers the good of the many, they demand it. The game's basic principle is that of governance and conservancy. The role of the player seeking to continue the thematic impulse of the Ultima series is therefore that of governance—the process of developing into someone in the game context who seeks to emulate Lord British's goals of equitable governance. The system poses irreconcilable ethical dilemmas just as any ecological system must, and the player will simply have to navigate these as best he can.

Given these implications, the game mechanics of *Ultima Online* must include a mechanism to reward players who successfully survive and continue to succeed, by granting them greater powers to govern others. Building castles, etc, is a possibility. Then again, the truest simulation of this may in fact be to simply let those with enough money build and gain power, and let their own natures or roleplayed natures determine their fates (hated tyrants or benign despots or enlightened rulers?). The design issue becomes whether this is an overt enough statement of the thematic underpinnings of the world.

Fairly lofty stuff for a design document! And of course, it has that assumed notion of players exercising power over one another. In its crudest form, this manifests as playerkilling.

For the last few decades, the academic world has been paying a lot of attention to the notion of the Other. That is to say, that poorly understood and perhaps incomprehensible being or beings that is not of our own tribe. There is a lot of turgid writing going on analyzing the work of writers who deal with issues of cultural conflict, such as Bharati Mukherjee, or Chinua Achebe. You might have heard of this latter fellow–you may have read his best-known book, *Things Fall Apart*, in high school.

Achebe's novel deals with the issues of what happens to an African tribe when its values begin to contact those of Western society, and what sorts of compromises must be made. It's a great read, in part because it crystallizes a sense of loss for the culture which is being overwhelmed and diluted. Yet at the same time that it is a novel about the Other (and in his novel, the Other is *us*, really–the Western, computer-literate Net-surfing UO-playin' types) it is also a novel that creates a stronger sense of identity for the lost culture than would have otherwise existed.

This is because, as any visual artist can tell you, if you want something light to stand out, you had better put it against a dark background. And in cultural terms, the Other is the perfect dark background. It is somewhat ironic that in order to convey to readers the African culture which he saw as vanishing, he selected a book title drawn from an Irish modernist poet.

Which brings us to the Dracul and Kazola's tavern, or the similar events that are occurring in Oasis with the reorganization of the player militia to defend against organized attacks. (You knew I'd get to UO at some point, right?). What makes us fear the Other is the exercise of power, or the potential for it. Yet what we use as a yardstick for our own identity as a culture is very often our difference from the Other. From the enemy. From what we do not wish to exercise power over us. The last paragraph of the call to arms from the Sonoma Oasis Militia is particularly telling and eloquent in this regard:

> It is the idealistic goal of most citizens of Oasis that one day the city will need few active guards, and the spotlight will rightfully fall on our tavernkeepers, smiths, tinkerers, seekers, innkeepers, chefs, tailors, beggars, alchemists, mages, bards, rogues, librarians, scholars, rangers, miners, assassins, diplomats, and tamers–ALL of whom currently exist in Oasis but are frequently overshadowed by conflicts with those who would attack us. To approach that state, however, we need to continue to surmount substantial challenges…

Oasis seeks to defend its culture from the Other, and what's more, it is coming together, and *becoming a stronger entity* because it faces those challenges. Kazola's tavern is famous in UO, not for being a roleplayer's tavern, but rather for being a flickering light of a roleplaying tavern that struggles against the forces of darkness.

So thank heavens for the Other, and thank heavens for the playerkillers. For without them these places would not have acquired the sense of cultural identity that they now have. Bonds have been formed by struggling against a common Other that would otherwise have been cheaper, and easily earned. *Cultures define and refine themselves through conflict.* What's more, you can measure the strength of a culture by people's willingness to fight for its survival.

So we come full circle to the Virtues. Oasis and Kazola's (and the Councils of Virtue, and Rivendell, and the City of Yew and…) are expressing the Virtues. They are just doing it without the training wheels. Unlike the standalone Ultimas, UO is not an open-book quiz.

The Ultima series was ready to make the leap from leading to allowing players to lead. To go from difficult ethical choices on paper to difficult ethical choices in reality. The question to ask is whether the *players* it attracted were ready.

You may each have your own answers for that, but I am optimistic. Right now the fledgling societies within UO are rambunctious, rough, occasionally cruel and callous, sometimes gloriously civilized. But they are indeed the sign of things being *born,* and of people following the Virtues *on their own* and not because the game makes them do so.

How did that poem go? "What rough beast slouches towards Bethlehem to be born?" I bet we'll find out together.

–Designer Dragon

An aside: the response to yesterday's essay was immediate and gratifying. Many thanks to those players who shared similar stories on the web boards and in private email, and to those many fan sites who wrote asking for permission to reproduce the essay. Permission is of course granted.

Who Are These People Anyway?

May 7th, 1998

> People tend to think that [virtual worlds] alter how people perceive one another. That gender and race and handicaps cease to matter. It is a noble vision, sure… In truth [they] reveal the self in rather disturbing ways. We all construct 'faces' and masks to deal with others. Usually in [real life] interpersonal relationships, the masks can slip, they evolve and react, and they have body language and cues. [In a virtual world], on the Net, whatever–they cannot. And people see specifically this: what you choose to represent yourself as, and that is more revealing of your true nature than gender, race, age, or anything else… it's not a matter of how we hide, it's a matter of how we are revealing ourselves.

The above paragraph comes from an unpublished interview I gave many years ago now.[133] It came in response to the question, "How do you think virtual worlds affect people's perceptions of each other?"

A tangled question. Many seized on the sentence, "Thank heavens for playerkillers" in the last essay, and used it as evidence that I, or UO, am "on the playerkillers' side." Unfortunately, that's not only incorrect, but a reductionist view of a tangled situation. A better question to ask is, what exactly is the population of an online world, and what social forces drive it?

In discussing the Other yesterday, one word seemed at the center of the issue: Power. The conflicts that arise are there precisely because competing agendas (and often, as in the case of the playerkillers versus the roleplayers, competing play styles) attempt to exercise power over one another. I got a letter from Kazola, proprietor of the Treetop Keg and Winery on Great Lakes, saying that the tavern is not famous for being a target, but for being a roleplay haven *first*. It became a a target because of that fame. Yet I would still argue that it had the roleplay fame within a narrower segment of the overall UO community than its fame as a "flickering light in the darkness." And

---

[133] "Ptah: God of the MUD," found at https://www.raphkoster.com/games/interviews-and-panels/ptah-god-of-the-mud/

it is worth examining why exactly this is so. Why did it become a target just for being what it is? And why was its struggle so compelling?

Richard Bartle, who along with Roy Trubshaw is generally credited with writing the first mud (multi-user dungeon, if you wish to call it that, but let's say "virtual online world" instead) wrote an essay which among designers of virtual worlds is often considered essential reading. In it he classifies players into four types:

- Those who seek to interact with other people, or **Socializers**
- Those who seek to dominate other people, or **Killers**
- Those who seek to learn and master the mechanics of the world, or **Explorers**
- Those who seek to advance within the context of the world, or **Achievers**

Now, these are simplistic definitions, of course, and there is plenty of debate over the exact mix, and whether these are reductions to stereotypes, etc. It is interesting to note that "roleplayers" aren't even on his list, though they are generally considered to be a major force in online gaming–under this system, they are merely a variant of socializers, and the line between in-fiction chatting and out-of-character chatting is blurred.

The fascinating part of the essay, however, is where Bartle discusses the interactions between these groups. Killers are like wolves, in his model. And therefore they eat sheep, not other wolves. And the sheep are the socializers, with some occasional Achievers for spice. Why? Because killers are about the exercise of power, and you do not get the satisfaction of exercising power unless the victim complains vocally about it. Which socializers will tend to do.

Further, Bartle pointed out that eliminating the killers from the mix of the population results in a stagnant society. The socializers become cliquish, and without adversity to bring communities together, they fragment and eventually go away. Similarly, achievers, who are always looking for the biggest and baddest monster to kill, will find a world without killers to be lacking in risk and danger, and will grow bored and move on.

Yet at the same time, too many killers will quite successfully chase away everyone else. And after feeding on themselves for a little while, they will move on too. Leaving an empty world. However, since killers tend to know the world really well, there are not many ways of keeping them in check. From the playerbase, the explorers are the only ones with a real chance, because they know the game better than anyone.

Among some virtual world designers, the dichotomy is simpler: you have what they term "GoP" players, or goal-oriented players, and you have everyone else: the roleplayers, the socializers, etc. And the conflict is always between these two types.

My own preferred metaphor goes back to the work of child psychologist Bruno Bettelheim, who discussed the two ways children tend to amuse themselves. One form is the "game," where there is a winner and a loser. It is competitive, and may or may not involve team play. The other is "play," which is non-competitive. It can be as simple as chatting a lot, or it can be building blocks, or (as it often is with children) it can be make-believe– which is after all, roleplaying.

You may have recognized yourself in one of these models, and may have recognized situations and events from UO as well. Now, many of the responses to the first essay on the web boards and the newsgroups discussed how idealistic a vision it expressed… and thus viewed the second essay as a reversal. Yet really, the dichotomy of game and play are two sides of the same coin. One does not tend to exist anywhere without the other. Whereas the most idealistic vision of a virtual world, the fully community-oriented one, would seem to be composed of *only* "play," in fact it would founder. It's in human nature to need both, in one way or another. It's the nature of reality–and therefore the nature of virtual reality as well.

From a strict in-context perspective, the actions of a killer within a virtual world can be seen as sociopathic: they do not recognize the mores of the society in which they operate. This is not to say that they are bad people– it has been well-established that interactions in a virtual setting create a level of psychological disinhibition that encourages freer action, less inhibited speech, and perhaps a little less thoughtfulness; this is probably largely due to the intoxicating sense of anonymity that we feel online. One has to wonder what the proper method of controlling people is, when they are generally not bad people, but merely "drunk" on the sense of anonymity.

Ideally (yeah, back to those pesky ideals), we bring them to an awareness of the virtual community they are disrupting, whilst at the same time still permitting people to (in final analysis) exercise power over one another, because people tend to seek status and power, and it's an important mechanic we cannot do without.

To boil all the high-flown stuff above down into simple premises: we must have playerkillers in UO, because the world would suffer if we did not have them. But they also must be channeled, so that their effect is beneficial, and not detrimental. And they have to learn to act within the context of the "play" space, and not perceive UO as just a "game" space.

In other words, a lot of it is about education. And most roleplayers have a story to tell about the time they first introduced someone to that form of play, and the way in which the former killer or hack 'n' slasher tentatively started trying out new waters, and eventually discovered that "hey, this roleplay things isn't all bad!" They may not become true roleplayers, but they may also adapt their play style to conform more to the virtual context. The mud designer and theoretician J. C. Lawrence terms this "functional roleplay," where behavior patterns of those who do not roleplay are conditioned by the presence of things like social systems, reputation systems, and other "channeling" devices.

It's largely about perspectives. The issue for the killers is whether they will gain the wider perspective and cease to be "virtually sociopathic." And the issue for the socializers is whether they will recognize that the killers are a part of their society too, and not always a bad one.

The thorny issues that then remain are the nitty-gritty of virtual community building: how do we govern in a world of anonymity? How do we police, and *who* polices, the players or the game administrators? What sort of punishment is appropriate for virtual crime? What sort of punishment is even *possible* for virtual crime? The answers to these questions that the UO community seeks out will shape UO for years to come, because they are questions that we the designers must ask of the players–no tool we give to players will work unless players take it up. And it could be that not a large enough proportion of players are ready or willing to take them up. But with the formation of governments and militias, we already see that the UO community is "self-aware"–aware of itself as a community, and therefore implicitly asking for tools to define its own society.

In the end, being a "killer" or a "roleplayer" is just as much a mask as the character one chooses to play online. It reveals something about how the player perceives UO, but not necessarily about their actual nature. (As a classic example, *not* all playerkillers are 13-year old boys, as popular legend would have it. What makes a playerkiller is a perspective on on the world, not an age.) As designers, our role is to juggle the often conflicting perspectives.

The answer to "who are these people anyway" is better phrased as "who am I, in this virtual reality?" And until a player can answer that well enough to understand their motivations, they may not even be playing the way they really want to. The Greeks put it as *gnothi seauton*–Know Thyself. If you find these simplified classifications of player styles to be confining–make your own. UO is both a play space and a game space, and that is at the root of all the most wonderful things about it, and also at the heart of the most painful issues it faces with virtual community, playerkilling, and the like. "Giving up" and targeting only half of that equation is not a fruitful approach, in the long run. Only education, self-knowledge, and an awareness of others is.

And education, self-knowledge, and an awareness of others sounds a lot like the process of growing up. Hearkening back to yesterday–something *is* being born. But we do have to teach it how to walk. More on that tomorrow.

–Designer Dragon

For further reading, for the interested:

- Richard Bartle's article "Hearts, Clubs, Diamonds, Spades: Players Who Suit Muds"[134]
- Julian Dibbell's classic article on a virtual world community discovering itself, "A Rape in Cyberspace."[135]
- A simplistic personality test[136] can maybe help you judge which of Bartle's types you fall under

In addition, Kazola mentions that the Treetop Keg and Winery is thriving–congratulations. Another victory against the forces of darkness–the darkness of social collapse, that is!

Many many people have asked to reprint the first essay, "A Story About a Tree," and just as many have asked if it is a true story. Yes, it is a true story. Please do feel free to pass it around to friends, if you feel it has touched you.

One last note: some people were troubled by the idea that the concepts about the necessity for playerkillers and the like translate back into real world society. The answer is, of course, no. The essays are about *virtual worlds* and not about the real one. Often concepts translate in one direction, not the other.

---

[134]

https://www.researchgate.net/publication/247190693_Hearts_clubs_diamonds_spades_Players_who_suit_MUDs

[135] http://www.juliandibbell.com/articles/a-rape-in-cyberspace/

[136] https://www.raphkoster.com/games/snippets/player-types-survey/

So Let's Get Practical

May 8th, 1998

"Killers may have a right to play the game their own way. They don't have a right to inflict their way of playing to the other groups." – from a posting by Loic Talecaster late last night

"Look dude,, dieing and parting with your stuff sux,, but it's part of the game, live with it.. role play it." – a reply to Loic by Dreadnaught

"If you don't want to get killed, stay in town." – a lot of posts this last week

```
Lynx hmms… So you're saying you want to randomly kill people?
Arion says "yes! randomly but with the same chances of dying!"
Ack says "we want to be the few… the proud… the outlaws!"
Lynx should note you are probably despised by a great many people,
which is hardly helpful.
Ack says "that is the best part about it!!!"
Arion says "that's the way we like it!"
Lynx points out some people have ideas of fun that other people do
not agree with, and these people do not have to put up with it.
Arion says "then let them stay in the havens that are usually
there… [safe] rooms, the town square…"                       '
        – from "The Black Rose Incident", which occurred on Islandia 8
                                                        years ago
```

As one would expect, the last two essays have generated an amazing amount of discussion and controversy in the *Ultima Online* community. There have been numerous interpretations of what I said, of course; some feel I am acting as apologist for the playerkillers, others feel that their positions have been vindicated, etc. Just to state it clearly: there are too many serial killers in the world of *Ultima Online* and they need to learn to get along with the rest of the populace–but we don't want to exterminate them completely anymore than we want to make rattlesnakes, black widow spiders, and sharks extinct, because they fill a valuable role in the virtual ecology.

So let's turn to the problems of actually shaping a virtual society. There are a couple of key issues here that present really important problems.

The more things change, the more they stay the same...! Those quotes above, some freshly minted and the other hoary with age, help demonstrate that the issue of playerkilling, of policing the virtual world, is an old one, and that it is more a matter of the psychological approach the player takes to the game than anything else. One thing that is hard to come to grips with in that realization is that it means that *playerkilling does not require a combat system.* The problems that players wrestle with in dealing with harassment are exactly the same; the difference is the means of exercising power that is used by the aggressor. Consider the following quote from a post made late last night on the UOVault by Loic Talecaster:

> [Yesterday's essay] says that without killers, virtual worlds stagnate. But there is an entire class of virtual worlds, MOOs mostly, that don't even implement a combat system, and they thrive. Thus how can it be said that Killers are "necessary"?

Those of you who read the additional links supplied yesterday know that the Julian Dibbell article on "A Rape in Cyberspace" in fact took place on a MOO. The "kill" command was never typed; nobody entered combat mode. Yet it was every bit as traumatic as a repeat playerkilling is to people today in UO. When the issue boils down to the exercise of power, any tools will do. Failing combat, they will use words. Failing words, they will follow you around and interfere in your actions... and maybe, just maybe, if you supply a method for them to get into a political structure within the virtual world itself, they will play politics instead of killing, since politics is after all the ultimate human expression of the desire to exercise power over others. (No offense to the politicians!)

So one key problem to surmount is the fact that *changing the medium of attacks will not prevent attacks from occurring.* You'll find the Killer on IRC, on a web board, in chat rooms, in *Ultima Online*, and in muds everywhere–pk switch or no pk switch.

There are other thorny issues to wrestle with. A common call is for community policing–this is a position that I myself have often advocated. But it must be admitted that a virtual community is sorely lacking in one critical concept to be able to effectively police: identity. On the Net, what identity there is is very fluid. Whereas if you identify a criminal in real life, you can jail him, in cyberspace he effectively can *become someone else* entirely, leaving you holding an empty shell in your jail cell. A mule. A dummy character. An abandoned persona.

And that's assuming you can catch him–for how do you know who he is? One's anonymity in cyberspace, as we discussed yesterday, is a great empowerment. It's also a great problem for those who wish to track the behavior of repeat playerkillers.

Ultima Online originally was designed for full-bore community policing. We made safe towns, and originally supplied no other tools whatsoever. But those who sought to police accurately pointed out that since they could not track those who did evil deeds, the server code would have to. Hence the notoriety system. And now we are moving to a more precise and specialized system, because notoriety's key flaw was that it measured different types of behavior on the same scale, which rendered it highly problematic as a method of identifying criminals. The reputation system purposely tracks only one type of behavior for the purposes of flagging someone as "red," because that way it can serve as a more accurate tool for curbing that one type of behavior. Will it curb all methods of "attack"? No, because it is a specialized tool.

The idea of behavior tracking systems is not new. We of course have the concept of criminal records in the real world. On the eBay auction website, users of the site can award "stars" to other users, and you can get a sense of how trustworthy a person is before engaging in commerce with them. In many muds, people are flagged permanently as "thief" or "murderer" after one instance of thievery or murder.

The key issue behind having such systems is of course, who judges, and who punishes. The quote above from the "Black Rose Incident" is often used as an example of why consensus government fails in virtual settings, and a major reason why it fails is because the social mores of the playerbase are being dictated (or attempted to be dictated) by the game administration, rather than by the playerbase. All forms of compromise suggested by the admins in the incident fail to satisfy both parties, because they are not solutions offered *by* the parties. A similar dilemma arose in the incident described by Dibbell: in the end, the populace of the game felt themselves powerless, organized a government, and it meant nothing: the final action taken had to be taken by a "god."

It is no accident that in virtual communities, admins are often titled gods, wizards, and immortals.

This is of course an essentially paternalistic structure. One has to ask the very tough question: can an online community ever truly flower if it *always* has to run to Dad to deal with problems? The reason this is a critical question is because the presence of an all-powerful being is not a philosophical question in a virtual setting. In final analysis, it's the guy with the ability to flip the power switch on the server. In the case of the virtual rape on *LambdaMOO* that Dibbell described, the head admin came back and abdicated his powers to the populace.

Now, there's clearly a whole can of worms there regarding religion in a virtual setting that I am not going to open! However, the implications in terms of the development of online governments are very interesting and very important. Our challenge is that in UO, we have established what is to my knowledge the virtual setting with the largest scope of possible player actions and activities yet given *to people without godlike powers*. (On many MOOs and the like, the common player has godlike powers as a matter of course, which is a different big can of worms…!) With UO we—no, more precisely, *you, the players of UO*, have a unique chance to actually make a virtual world that sustains a virtual government that *matters*. No mean feat.

I say "that matters," because in the end the head admin at *LambdaMOO* had to take his powers back, and it is back to Dad as usual there. Just as we in *Ultima Online* had to retreat from the original design of full-bore player policing and add back in greater game admin involvement. But our intent is still clear: this is going to be *your* world. So if the tools do not suffice to handle the problems of anonymity, lack of accountability, binding to identity, and non-combat means of attack, we need you to tell us what tools will. Because while we may have built the world, we don't want to be your parents anymore than we want to tell you what Virtues you must follow. That is a matter for your conscience and your free will, which try as we might, we could not take away even if we wanted to. So I look forward to fruitful discussion on the boards of things like townstones, locally defined "laws," methods of supporting player militias and towns in code, etc. It may take a while to come to fruition, but come it will, because despite what some may say, we, the developers are *not* saying "you're on your own." We're saying that maybe you might want to take off the training wheels someday, because bikes with training wheels get to ride on *much* more interesting terrain.

And after that, maybe we can see about changing that "just because we built the world" thing too.

–Designer Dragon

❧

- The full log of the Black Rose Incident[137] makes for great ancillary reading.
- Elizabeth Reid's master's thesis on "Cultural Formations in Text-Based Virtual

---

[137] http://www.linnaean.org/~lpb/muddex/black-rose.html

Realities"[138] is fairly academic, but fascinating reading. Highly recommended. A sample quote that seems relevant to today's discussion:

> Cyberspace–the realm of electronic impulses and of high-speed data highways....–may be a technological artifact, but virtual reality is a construct within the mind of a human being... Virtual worlds exist not in the technology used to represent them, nor purely in the mind of the user... The illusion of reality lies not in the machinery itself, but in in the users' willingness to treat the manifestations of their imaginings as if they were real.

In other words, maybe–for those who said on Usenet yesterday that UO isn't a community–clap if you believe in fairies. If you believe in them, they will be real. And if you see a community there in UO–well, then, there is one. But if you refuse to believe, well, you'll never get to see the magic. Which would be a real pity.

- Of course, you should read Bob Hanson's excellent and detailed Reputation System FAQ, which is our latest method trying to empower player policing of their environment.[139]

- Remember that head admin at *LambdaMOO?* His name is Pavel Curtis, and he has also written on the subject of virtual communities. An interesting, off-the-beaten-path essay to read is his take on transforming a MOO into a virtual professional community. You may want to seek out his work. A good introductory essay is "Social Phenomena in Text-Based Virtual Realities.[140]"

I have received MANY wonderful letters since starting this regular essays column. But yesterday's letter from Postman77 of the Anti-PK Unified Council was one of those letters that makes your life's work all worthwhile. Thank you for your eloquence, Postman77. It made our day.

---

[138] http://www.aluluei.com/cult-form.htm
[139] Unfortunately lost to history.
[140] http://citeseerx.ist.psu.edu/viewdoc/download?doi=10.1.1.330.6597&rep=rep1&type=pdf

The Man Behind the Curtain

May 11th, 1998

> Most of our citizens actually lay eyes on their officeholders and the hopefuls thereto about as often as they see circus elephants and with the same lack of intimate contact. A man behind the footlights on a platform is a little bit unreal; he might as well be a movie.
>
> But the people… are still interested… to have one show up at the front door is as delightful a novelty to most of them as would be a chance to ride that circus elephant. That unreality, the candidate on the platform, on the billboard, or in the newspaper, suddenly becomes warmly human and a little more than life size.
>
> In addition to being a novelty… [it] is a flattering compliment… the idea will be kicking around in the back of [the voter's] mind. "Here is a man who really seems interested in us ordinary citizens…"

Ask any old Usenet hand: things have gotten worse. There's more people. And they are ruder. They are cruder. They flame more. The signal-to-noise level has been falling for years now. And it's all *your* fault.

"Yours," that is, assuming that (as is statistically likely), you're not one of the old Usenet hands yourself. Chances are you aren't–the explosive growth of the Internet has meant a shattering of the old sense of community that used to exist. Once upon a time, the Internet was the playground of the few who had the technological savvy to reach it, the fortune to be somewhere that offered access, and the knowledge of its mere existence. In other words, an audience that was extremely selective: generally highly educated, and working in either academic or high tech fields.

These days of course, these folks are feeling very much pushed out of their old playground. Now that the cat is out of the bag, the Internet is forever changed. Many of them are looking forward to Internet 2 as a salvation, but the fact is that the sense of small, insular, familiar community that those people knew is forever gone, simply because people will *know* about Internet 2. Cyberspace is no longer a well-kept secret. And that means really fundamental changes in how the Internet community evolves.

Back when Robert Heinlein wrote today's opening quotation in *Take Back Your*

Government!, his manual on practical politicking, he probably had no idea that someday they would be quoted in a discussion of virtual communities. On the other hand, he probably would have been tickled to see the book used thus. Old hands in cyberspace have been quoting Heinlein for a long time; his libertarian politics found a friendly reception among the well-read science-fiction readers who populated the early Internet, and it's not uncommon to see quotations from his writings as Unix messages of the day or the like.

The thing that led to the frustration many old-time Net hands had with the arrival of the mass-market Internet is exactly what Heinlein is describing: the personal touch. In general, human beings tend to react better to personal contact than to impersonal interactions. We'd rather talk to a real person over the phone than to a machine. We'd rather get a personal letter than a form letter, and failing that, we'd prefer a form letter that at least pretended to know who we are. And when we are not known, we are psychologically disinhibited, and act out more freely. To maintain tight community, everyone must be known.

This, of course, flies in the face of the inevitable anonymity that the Internet provides. Distrust is therefore rampant. And it creates a real problem for the administrators of a virtual community as well, because they are in a position worse than "might as well be a movie," as Heinlein puts it. You see, they are supernaturally powerful. And if there's something that we tend to fear and distrust more than someone we don't know, it's someone we don't know who has power over us.

This dilemma isn't going to go away ever; when it boils right down to it, we're always going to have *someone* out there who has the power to turn our virtual world (which we may well have come to value deeply) off. And that's assuming that no in-game administration is required. But of course, it is.

But it does mean that the in-game admin faces a bizarre problem. He is exercising power that the ordinary virtual citizen cannot. And he is looked to in many ways to provide a certain atmosphere and level of civility in the environment. Yet the fact remains that no matter how scrupulously honest he is, no matter how just he shows himself to be, no matter how committed to the welfare of the virtual space he may prove himself, *people will hate his guts.* They will mistrust him precisely because he has power, and they can *never* know him. There will be false accusations galore, many insinuations of nefarious motives, and former friends will turn against him. It may be that the old saying about power and absolute power is just too ingrained in the psyche of most people; whatever the reasons, there has never been an online game whose admins could say with a straight face that all their players really trusted them (and by the way, it gets worse once you take money!).

There isn't very much that can be done about this, particularly as your virtual world grows. Many a mud has found that the feelings of intimacy and of trust faded as the playerbase grew, just as those early Netters found their once-civil newsgroups devolving into endless flamewars. But it does mean that admins must at some point relinquish the role that they once held among the playerbase. When the game is small, they are able to talk one-on-one, soothe hurt feelings, resolve problems using personal judgement, and adjudicate delicate issues such as one player's accusation of cheating against another. But as all large companies know, as government knows, and as online worlds are coming to learn: the bigger you get, the harder it is to *know* your audience that well, and the less trust they will give you. And the problem becomes exponentially worse over time. The only solution is to not put your admins in the position of judging unverifiable facts, or else they will abdicate all pretense of fairness. They will, in fact, be acting unfairly, because there is no way of knowing the circumstances.

What does this have to do with practical matters? Well, let us consider this list of possible actions that a Killer might take against another player in UO if it had no combat system at all, or did not allow player versus player combat.

They could kill the victim's pet. They could kill the victim's intended target mere seconds before the victim gets to. They could steal all the loot off of the corpse of the victim's target before the victim gets to. They could release a tame dragon near the victim. They could stand in front of the victim's desired destination, blocking access. They could do all of this without even saying a word, so that the issue of verbal harassment never arises.

You see, it is axiomatic that as your virtual world becomes more malleable and more versatile, that players will find more and more ways to, well, screw each other over. What's more, there are thousands of them for every one of you. You will not be able to keep up with their ingenuity. (A designer should never underestimate the amazing ability of players to come up with new means to do each other harm). UO happens to have features that because of their newness and uniqueness, open up *more* ways for players to do harm to one another via indirect means. And as virtual worlds develop, matters will only grow worse–consider the day when you get the ability to dig trenches

In a world without any playerkilling, you as the victim actually have no recourse whatsoever except an admin. Who is someone you don't trust, cannot know if you made up the situation (consider how most of the above actions are extremely difficult to detect via automated means), and who is going to have to take one person's word over the other.

This is not a situation in which admins are likely to become more trusted. And it

As Riot grows + becomes more diverse in player base

effectively renders admins useless as judges of human behavior as the game grows.

Growth is never an easy thing to cope with. And the new breed of virtual spaces are facing issues with scale that are new, and often new solutions are required. In yesterday's essay I spoke of the traditional administrative model for a virtual space as essentially paternalistic; this isn't meant to serve as an insult against those who inhabit the space, but rather to describe a system whereby groups are essentially governed via the charismatic personal contact of an authority figure. Just as in the real world, this system falls apart once larger bodies of people need to be governed or administered or taken care of. There is a reason why we evolved away from a tribal structure in the real world as our cultures grew; the same will–and must, really–happen in virtual spaces like *Ultima Online*.

At the last player lunch, a fellow told me that he was fascinated by how UO had recapitulated European history from 800AD to 1200AD in six months of existence. He commented on the parallels between marauding bandit gangs, the enclaves of feudal systems building secure spaces and leaving the wilderness to the less civilized people, the eventual overcrowding as villages covered the available building space. He also shrewdly guessed the character of our next set of changes based on historical precedent: house ownership and limits.

We, as humans, have been here before, over and over and over again. Just as the Internet grew and Usenet habitués no longer knew every poster; just as tribal leadership gave way to more organized and (yes) less personal forms of government; and just as Heinlein's book on politics is now sadly dated (when was the last time a precinct worker rang *your* doorbell?), virtual worlds are now getting large enough that older solutions to administration no longer function. The importance of personal contact has not diminished in the least; but the difficulty of providing it has grown, and will continue to do so. Many of the choices made in UO regarding playerkilling toggles, safe worlds, and the like were made in light of this fact.

This doesn't mean, of course, that players cannot start ringing doorbells themselves. As the overall administration grows more distant, the local one becomes more important. And, in many ways, more powerful, as it understands its local circumstances and may obtain the power to modify its local laws. This was the point of Heinlein's book–that politics that matter are actually at the local level, and this is where you can make a difference. You do not expect your nation's leader to fix your streets or solve the local bank robbery–that is what the City Council is for. And in UO we are embarking on the experiment of exactly that: providing local empowerment to the playerbase. Perhaps Enshu Ponfar's City of Yew does not see itself as a symptom of the sweep of history–but by these lights, it is.

What means?

What would this mean in a virtual world?

263

In the end, it boils down to the fact that the best government is the one that you can trust, which will be the one you know personally: the people close to you in your virtual community, who are held accountable precisely because of community ties. Your best government is going to be each other, because the man behind the curtain isn't going to know you any more than you know him. Consider what Heinlein said:

> An adult is a person who no longer depends on his parents. By the same token a person who refers to or thinks of the government as "They" is not yet grown up… There is more cynicism in this country than there are things to be cynical about. The debunking exceeds the phoniness. There is more skepticism than mendacity… [The skeptics] are around us, busy belittling and sneering and grinning at every effort to make of this country what it can be. What it will be.
>
> For you there is the joy of being in the know, of understanding the political life of your country, the greater joy of striving for the things you believe in, and the greatest joy of all, the joy of public service freely given… there are no words with which to describe nor any way to convince you of its superiority to other joys; it is possible only to assure you that it is so.

There have been many skeptics on Usenet about these essays; Heinlein also says, "Don't argue with a hard case." But for those now posting about townstone systems and methods for player militias to jail offenders and the like–hang in there. If we keep recapitulating European history at this rate, we'll be at the Magna Carta soon–and won't *that* be interesting!

In the meantime, consider a quotation by a different author, Heinlein's longtime colleague in science-fiction, Isaac Asimov. It may as well apply to playerkillers, who are as we've discussed those who "don't get it," those who fail to see it as Real. "Violence is the last refuge of the incompetent." And who else are playerkillers but those who are *socially* incompetent in this new virtual community?

-Designer Dragon

Playerkillers = Sociall incompetent?

A Community Cookbook

or, How to Make Your Guild/Town/Roleplay Group/Tavern Stronger

May 12th, 1998

In all the talk of what a virtual world administrator or designer can do or cannot do in terms of setting the tone and enforcing etiquette within a virtual community, we've sort of left behind the community itself. So today, let's talk about things that you, your friends, your township, your roleplay buddies, or your guild can do in order to be become a stronger (and more fun!) virtual world community.

The first thing if of course communication. If your guild doesn't already have a web page, a bulletin board, and an email newsletter or mailing list, you are missing out on the most important factor in building community ties. A very good tactic is to choose the person who is always first with the gossip and put them in charge of running the newsletter. The great advantage to a newsletter or email list is that it isn't passive—it seeks out the community member and it draws them in.

Make a point of showcasing the contributions of members in whatever forum you have, be it web page or newsletter or in your in-game tavern. If you have a regular who is a good roleplayer, encourage them to put their stories in in-game books you keep laying around the tavern. If you have someone artistic, try to get a new character portrait on your township's web page every week. Song lyric recitals in the taverns or in the town square can be great events and you can also make them competitive, if you wish. Until such a day as UO supports composing music and drawing pictures within the game (which is indeed a design goal), you'll have to do this externally, but you can still provide pointers to web pages from in-game books and house signs.

If you're maintaining a web page, it's a great idea to build up more than just a roster. A roster in itself does not present your group to others very well. A roster with character histories—be they RP histories or not—will create a shared history for the group, and help newcomers get into the context of the community. If you want to foster this, try giving out awards within your group for the best profile or best addition to the "group history" that week. So much of the great roleplay in UO is told only in ephemeral media such as the web boards, when it really needs to be building up and enriching the context of the world. (Hey you guys over on the Crossroads of Britannia Tales board–do you make a point of making an in-game version of each of your poems and stories?)

And of course, once there is a stronger sense of a group to belong to, some form of "tribal marker" helps a great deal. UO guilds picked up on this very early, with color-coordinated outfits. Now the guild system supports displaying guild abbreviations over the name as well. Make use of both of these as much as you can–even if it is just a single spot of color on one small piece of clothing–because they serve as instant identification of friends and foes alike. If you wish to go further, create ritual greetings, passwords, etc, the equivalent to "secret handshakes."

You definitely need to have functions of leadership within the group. But as UO groups differ significantly in organization and in type, I can't really describe too many specifics. One of the great joys of UO is seeing the different social structures that have developed. Whatever structure you end up with, however, it is important to somehow mark out the people who have leadership roles. The guild system allows for the use of titles, of course, but for those groups not suited to guilds, perhaps an item of clothing that only that one person usually wears could serve as an identifier. A great way to discover leadership potential is to ask people to help with the recruitment and mentoring of new members.

It's really important for your group to have a mission statement, a code of conduct, a reason for being, and a method for resolving conflicts. A lot of guilds fall apart because of unclear chains of command, differences over the core philosophy of the guild, and other such problems which can usually be avoided with a strong leadership structure and a strong group identity. You do however also need to make sure that your structure can evolve. Provide mechanisms for your members to change the rules.

Something that is extremely valuable, as those who run Fight Nights know, is periodic events. If you have a guild that plays regularly, or a tavern that is open every night, and you're not doing something like this, you are missing out on a great opportunity. Some of the perfect things to do:

- Taverns can hold recitals, pun championships, board game tourneys, storytelling, concerts, etc, on specific nights each week. There's a reason why bars do this in the real world! An open mike poetry recital every Thursday night can be a powerful draw.
- Combat-oriented guilds should make a point of specific adventures on specific nights. There are any number of activities a guild can do that can work, from

training sessions to competitions to more complex things. There is a guild that organizes "running man" competitions, where one person is designated as the "prey" and the rest of the guild must hunt him down and kill him. If he lives out the time limit, then he gets a prize.

- Townships can try for weekly trade fairs, parades, civic events such as elections, town meetings, candidacy speeches and the like. As many have discovered, communications crystals make for a very effective PA system.

Don't neglect the value of contests and competitions–the winners feel great, of course, and it gives you yet another face to put on your webpage and another name or story to put in your newsletter, which builds even more community ties. And of course, if a player comes to your group suggesting a possible event, work with them to try to make it happen!

Alongside this, rituals are very important. UO guilds have come up with some really great initiation rituals in the past (staged lighting of candles in order in a dark room, inspection of uniforms, ritual speeches…). But there can be many more forums than just that. Consider the Beefeater rituals at the Tower of London, with keys presented at a certain time and so on. There are things like that that can be done for townships, and so on. Be sure to have a ritual to confirm the new mayoralty once an election is over! And if you are able to this far, try having crafting guild initiations in your town when a community member reaches some skill mastery goal that they had been working towards.

A very important ritual if of course holidays. Celebrate them! Don't feel that you should be limited to only the real world ones, either. There are some holidays defined in UO that show up as events on the calendar. But you are not limited to observing only those.

Nor should you, even if you are diehard roleplayers, only acknowledge in-game events. A birthday is an opportunity for a rite of passage too–throw a party when someone's player gets married, has an anniversary, or has a birthday. Give in-game gifts as well as your best wishes out-of-game. Any roleplayer worth his salt can come up with a fictional reason that can coincide with the real world date.

These are just some ideas for ways to make your particular group stronger. As your group, guild, town, tavern, or whatever grows, be sure to publicize its existence, and send in your events and major news to the news sites and to the official Events Calendar. The strength of virtual worlds lies in the interaction, and people need to know about you to interact with you in any meaningful way. Start up web-rings of like-minded sites, and if you can, offer to host character pages for group members. And form ties with other groups both on your shard and elsewhere, as you may be able to share ideas and resources.

It takes some work, but you'll find that the ties you form are very real, and that the fun factor goes way, way up. Enjoy.

-Designer Dragon

A few literati wrote in to criticize me for my use of the Yeats poem a few essays back, rightly pointing out that the poem is not a particularly optimistic nor cheerful one, dealing as it does with the coming of Armageddon. However, I'd note that Yeats himself was quite aware of how good arises from bad, and they often make strange bedfellows! A fun illustration of this is in his series of poems about Crazy Jane, the most pertinent of which isn't quotable on a family website.

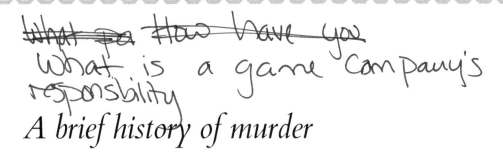

What was How have you (struck through)
What is a game company's responsibility

A brief history of murder

In 1999 I took part in an online symposium entitled "Managing Deviant Behavior in Online Communities"[141] alongside experts from other virtual worlds. The symposium was held on *MediaMOO*, a popular text world for academics, and moderated by Amy Bruckman.

Before the symposium, I had to submit a position statement, and here's what I said:

> As virtual settings develop with greater flexibility and freedom, it becomes possible for players to affect each other's virtual lives in a multitude of ways that are indirect and not easily trappable in code. Traditionally, mud servers of various types put the burden of detection of illegal acts and tracking of illegal acts on either the code itself, or on mud administrators. This solution is not particularly scalable to larger groups of people, nor to more flexible environments (wherein it is easily circumvented). A preferable solution is finding a way for the populace to police itself more effectively by allowing them to track player reputations with the aid of coded tools.

This position, through today's eyes, seems like a mix of naiveté and cynicism. Modern social software largely does put the burden on the users to police themselves, via very basic tools like mute and block commands. But it's happening because moderation is simply too expensive; and in some cases, because moderation actually exposes the operator to legal risk![142] Whereas I saw player policing as something that happened in tandem with active administration, today we have an abdication of responsibility from administrators, coupled with inadequate tools: the worst of both worlds.

How did we get here? Well, as I wrote that position statement, I had been wrestling

---

[141] The full transcript of the event can be found at https://www.raphkoster.com/games/interviews-and-panels/managing-deviant-behavior-in-online-communities/

[142] If an operator of an online community wants to take advantage of Safe Harbor provisions in the Digital Millenium Copyright Act (DMCA) they have to *not* monitor what is posted on their service, or else be liable for copyright violations.

for two years with the issue of playerkilling on *Ultima Online*... we had set out to provide a world full of freedoms, and players took advantage in every way possible.

Town guards

When *Ultima Online* opened, there were no policing systems in the game except for town guards. In fact, we even had a thievery skill set that was basically designed to allow players to be bad to one another; you could do a skill check and try to do a few illegal actions.

- "Snooping," which was an ability that thieves had, to rifle through another player's backpack and see what they had.

- "Stealing," which was the attempt to drag something out of someone else's backpack.

And of course, you could simply attack someone.

When you did any of these, a "criminal flag" was placed on you which expired after a few minutes. If a town guard[143] saw you while you were flagged, they slew you. Instantly. Town guards were really strong.

If another player caught you while you were criminal flagged, they could shout "Guards!" (which most players put on a macro so they could do it with just hitting one key). As long as you were within a town, this resulted in guards teleporting to their locations... and then they'd see the miscreant and kill them.

Death meant your corpse fell right there where it was, and would likely be utterly stripped of everything you had carried within seconds; anyone could loot your corpse.[144] You would stand there watching, as a ghost — a gray-robed spectre — unable to protest in any way that others could understand, your every word transformed into "OoOoooOoOoo." To be revived, you had to find your way to a shrine, where you would return to life — wearing nothing much. Your spare gear was probably in a bank vault in town, but shrines themselves were outside of towns, so once you died, you were quite likely to get killed several times in a row.

---

[143] Originally named "Lord British's guards," but a patch note from 1998 renamed them: "in order to allay confusion about cities not under his rule." This was because the game's first expansion, *UO: The Second Age*, was not technically in Britannia.

[144] From the strategy guide: "Gleaning useful items from the corpses of the fallen is an inttegral part of the game. There is no law, either social or official, guaranteeing that your posessions will still be with your body if you wander off in search of resurrection."

Until *Ultima Online* the terms "PvP," "PvE," and "Pking" were not in widespread currency among gamers, because online gaming had been confined to a relatively small audience. (Neither were many other terms, including "nerfing," "powerlevelling," and many others). The section on Pkilling in the original strategy guide for the game[145] led with an explanation of the unfamiliar term:

> Player killing (AKA "pkilling" or "PK") is the killing of one player-character in a multi-player game by another.

It then went on to argue that

> If Harry the Dashing accosts travelers on the open read with, "Your pardon, Sirrah, but I will have either your money or your life," that is far less objectionable than Basha, who likes to to train bears and sic them on unsuspecting travelers... [or] Lord of D'eth, who thinks it is just hilarious to try out his new *Firewall* scroll in the smithy in Britain — D'eth is basically inexcusable. All three actions, however, are completely legal in the game...

It also offered helpful tips such as "travel in groups and avoid dangerous areas" for dodging playerkillers:

> In the wilderness, the things that will protect you against pkillers are the same things that will protect you against monsters. Travel in groups, and if traveling alone keep to the main roads. Pkillers and monsters occupy different regions, however — the worst monsters tend to congregate in the deepest wilderness, while pkillers haunt approaches to congested areas, like towns and dungeons. While shrines and moongates are guarded areas, PKs will haunt the approaches.

And this commonly followed but still ludicrous advice for avoiding theft:

> Keep your really valuable possessions in bags — or even keep the bags in bags, layered three or four deep. This not only conceals your valuables, but each container requires a separate Snooping check, increasing the chance a thief will be caught. A similar strategy is putting valuables under a stack of hides or something equally bulky and innocuous in your pack...

And this was the *official* guide! The player-written *Ultima Online: Unofficial Strategy and Secrets*[146] was far blunter, with an entire chapter entitled "Staying Alive" with headings such as "Traveling in Groups" and "Trust No One."

Criminal flagging quickly proved woefully inadequate. Thieves learned to simply steal while basically naked, so they risked little but time. They would choose targets who were close to the edge of town, so they could dodge the guards. Playerkillers who

---

[145] Origin's Official Guide to Ultima Online, Prima Publishing, 1997.
[146] Put together by the Burning Heart Guild, and published by Sybex in 1998.

murdered indiscriminately only a few screens away would then waltz into town and be under the protection of the guards; a victim who came back for them could then be goaded into attacking back, which meant the guards would kill *them* instead. And, of course, all forms of indirect assistance in performing bad deeds went unpunished, leading to healers standing next to playerkillers and taking care of their wounds while they murdered freely. These healers weren't doing anything that the game detected, at first, though later on criminal flags were spread by helpful actions. Which then led to its own forms of entrapment!

These problems were quite evident even during the beta test period for the game, and thus the beta testing introduced the first major revision to playerkilling in *Ultima Online*.

The notoriety system

This system used a single axis — indeed, a single byte — to track a player's reputation. Players began at zero, or "neutral," and a variety of actions in the game could move it up and down. Your notoriety was shown to you via a title on your paperdoll: Great Lord or Lady for those at the top of the scale, and Dread Lord or Lady at the bottom. In between were Noble, Dishonorable, Infamous, and more.

Non-player characters in the game were already marked as Good, Neutral, Evil, or Chaotic. This mostly affected whether they would attack one another or help out players in a fight; for example, Evil characters would automatically attack Good or Neutral characters on sight, and so on. Players started out as neutral on this scale too.

Killing Evil NPCs raised your notoriety; killing Good ones lowered it. Generosity — giving items to NPCs with less goods than you had — also raised it (you could give gold to beggars, for example). Healing the Good raised it. Stealing lowered it, as did healing the Evil. And the passage of mere time trended it back towards neutral.

But notoriety's effects were purely cosmetic. Oh, an innkeeper might say to you "I suppose I shall have to place a sign 'pon my inn, declaring that the Great and Vile, Killer of Infants and Slayer of Guards, the Monstrous Zenkoh, slept here once." But they wouldn't deny you service.[147] "It is a measure of fame, not a moral judgement," states the strategy guide.

Worse, it was hard to tell what would happen exactly. Bear in mind that in UO, it

---

[147] Denial of service was later used to great effect as a means of curbing playerkilling on various Ultima Online gray shards.

could be hard to tell a player apart from an NPC, even![148] You couldn't necessarily tell what was Good, Evil, or Chaotic at a glance, particularly in the heat of a fight. A patch note in October of 1997,[149] shortly after the game launched, adds some very basic UX design:

> When clicking on someone, their name appears red, gray, or blue, depending on the following:
> - if performing a bad action such as theft, attack, or snooping would lower your notoriety, they show in blue
> - if performing such an action on them would improve your notoriety, the name shows in red
> - if it would have no effect on your notoriety, it shows in gray
>
> We fixed a problem whereby you could never regain good standing after crossing a threshold of being evil.
>
> We corrected a problem whereby attacking untame but tamable animals affected your notoriety and could result in guards being called.
>
> The 1/100 chance of notoriety increase has been removed, since there is now a notoriety time cap on improvement.
>
> We regularized the notoriety title scale; this may result in your title having changed by one stage from what it was previously.

In fact, the early patch notes seem like an litany of notoriety tweaks. If October 10th added the color-coded names, by October 16th we see notes like "The problems with notoriety not being affected by spellcasting are fixed" alongside five more changes to the system. As week after *that*, we see the addition of criminal flagging to all actions that lower notoriety. And just one week later, we see "All offensive spells now affect notoriety and call guards, including non-damaging ones."

Worse, we see things scattered throughout the updates that are clearly attempts to fix emergent loopholes that allowed players to screw one another over. When you transferred a pet to another player, it originally didn't make them stop following or guarding the original seller. So they would transfer the pet, then run away, and the pet would leave with them! A hotkey had to be added to bring up names all at once on the screen, rather than mousing over each person, because you'd be dead before you got the chance. And so on. In fact, one of the biggest issues was simply that people would do things, lose notoriety, and *not know why*.

It all caused so many problems that two months and five patches after launch, there were feature additions like

---

[148] The *Unofficial Guide* actually has a section on how to do it. It involves talking to them.
[149] http://wiki.uosecondage.com/Ultima_Online_Patch_Notes_for_10/10/1997

A new UO.CFG toggle has been added called NotorietyQuery. If you set this to on by editing your UO.CFG file to include the following line:

    NotorietyQuery=on

you will have a yes/no window pop up when you attack someone that would cause your notoriety to fall. Note that this applies only to regular attacks at the moment, not to spells, and not to ordering :pets, hirelings, or summoned creatures to attack!

That same month, shrines began to refuse resurrection to players who were below a certain level of notoriety, forcing everyone who was below "Dastardly" to funnel through only one resurrection point.

Virtue guards

The philosophical conflict between freedom to play however you liked in a rich simulated world and the desire to maintain order and civil society wasn't just one engaged in on the forums. It was also a deeply personal conflict for me; I didn't want to surrender the freedoms in order to provide the safety. This internal conflict was mirrored out to the playerbase via essays posted on the website, and via short stories that accompanied some patches, as we tried to make the changes to the game rules be reflected in the game fiction.

The launch of a new system intended to curb playerkilling by layering more rules atop notoriety was therefore accompanied by a new short story I wrote: "The Founding of the Guards of Virtue.[150]"

> "I fear this is a mistake, my lord," Lord Blackthorn said, shaking his head sadly. "Surely the problem cannot be as bad as thou describest it."
>
> "But it is!" Lord British said forcefully, pushing away from the table, and turning around to look out the casement at the gently drifting snowfall. As Blackthorn bowed his head in acquiescence, the ruler continued in a lower voice, "The dead this year, Blackthorn. All those people whose families live without joy this winter. The food that shall not be brought to table, the shops that shall not open. This children without parents and the parents without children. Think of the dead, and think of the funeral processions we have seen. Look you!"
>
> Blackthorn came to stand beside his liege at the window, squinting out past the white snowflakes, over the moat, to the small blacksmithy on the northern side of Britain. Just as every day of late, a funeral procession wended its dark way across the cobblestones, figures hunched against the cold and the vagaries of fate. He rested

---

[150] The full text can be found at https://uo.stratics.com/secrets/h_extra04.shtml

a hand on his friend's shoulder.

"This will not bring back their dead, my lord," he said softly.

factions

This bit of fiction announced two new systems, a carrot and a stick. The carrot was a system intended to displace the constant random playerkilling into something more constructive, what today we might term a *faction system*. Players were able to sign up with either Lord British or Lord Blackthorn, be handed a shield with the appropriate insignia, and then they could kill one another freely, with no interference from the guards. The system required players to have maximum notoriety before they could even join, and if you did anything that lowered your notoriety whilst you were wearing the shield of one side or the other, the shield would explode and kill you (!) on the spot. Upon dying to a member of the opposite team, the shield vanished, so you could actually have victories of a sort as the other team suffered attrition and had to go sign up all over again.[151]

> Lord British ducked his head as if something pained him. "Do we? So be it. Tomorrow I shall proclaim that any who have the required character may apply to join the Virtue Guards. They shall be given a shield with mine own emblem, the silver serpent, so that they may stand for what is good and honorable in this world. Any who shame the emblem shall have it stripped on the spot. And I shall also proclaim the law on bounty hunting."
>
> Blackthorn stormed away from the table. At the heavy door he stopped, and turned back. Lord British did not even raise his head.
>
> "Tomorrow then shall I announce that those same folk whom thou mightest take for thy new guard may choose instead to wear my emblem, and server as guards of the virtue of Chaos."
>
> British looked up at him, eyes afire. "Be careful where thou treadest, Blackthorn. A private army..."
>
> "Nay, my lord," Blackthorn said unctuously. "Merely so they may serve as an example of my beliefs, and of the beliefs of those who feel grown up enough to make their own decisions about right and wrong. Those who are sick of overzealous guards who slaughter the petty criminal at the slightest provocation, and sick of the paternalism in thy government."
>
> Lord British glared at him, and there they stood, caught between free will and civilization.

Talk about on the nose!

---

[151] Patch notes for this system (and the bounty hunting system) can be found at http://wiki.uosecondage.com/Ultima_Online_Patch_Notes_for_12/09/1997

Murderers and bounties

The stick was something else entirely: a bounty system on murderers. And it was quite complex!

If a player was killed by another player (and wasn't a criminal at the time, and was of good notoriety, and so on), a window would pop up letting them report the crime. A player could choose to not report it, if they felt it was an accident or the incident was an instance of good roleplaying, but honestly, this just about never happened. People always reported.

Once the killer got too many reports, everything in their bank was instantly confiscated. Any gold they had became a bounty on their head. They instantly became a Dread Lord along with all the penalties that accrued thereto. And their name, description (hair color, skin tone, and so on) went on the local bulletin board, along with the bounty on their head.

Reports could age out, so you could avoid a bounty by spacing out your kills, but bounties never went away. And if you kept getting reported, your bank account would be repeatedly confiscated and the gold added on. Eventually, victims were able to add their own gold to the reward as well.

If a murderer was killed by a player who had less murders than they and who was neutral or better in notoriety, they suffered an immediate loss of 10% of all of their advancement. And their head was chopped off and put in the backpack of their killer.[152] Returning the head to a city guard near wherever the bounty was posted resulted in the reward being given to the bounty hunter.

The update notes cheerfully noted,

> Bounties may remain posted in other cities even though the reward has been claimed, but a given bounty can only be claimed once in the world, unless the killer returns to their ways. This will likely result in a killer who has bounties in multiple cities getting killed over and over again by eager reward claimants, for no gain. Our advice is, don't end up with lots of bounties on your head. :)

Ah, frontier justice. And there were indeed high hopes that these penalties, which seemed extravagant at the time, would do the trick.

---

[152] It was a simpler time. Though, amusingly, the patch note remarks, "fake heads won't work." This is because you could actually kill someone, chop off their head manually, and end up with "the head of Billy" without it actually being the head of Billy the murderer.

Spoiler: they didn't.

Murderers quickly figured out the threshold number of reports and how quickly they aged out, to dance along the line. Then they started making a point of storing all their valuables in their houses instead of in a bank, so that there was no reward or confiscation to worry about. When players started supplying their own money for the rewards, the murderers simply began treating the bounty boards as a twisted form of high score table. They would coordinate with another player who would create a new character with a spotless record, allow the murderer to be slain, swallow the stat loss death penalty, and split the money!

If all of this sounds hilarious, consider that it's basically the same patterns that are used today on sites like Reddit and Twitter. Only there are no admins who actually answer when you call for help.

Fighting the losing battle

Even whilst putting in features like this, designed to reduce the incidence of playerkilling, the team was busily adding new simulation features that increased it. I mean, just one week later[153] we tried to curb thievery by allowing players to add traps to locked containers. A tinker could use metal and crossbow bolts or potions to make explosive, dart, or poison traps. The intent was to let players defend their possessions from theft in their homes or in their bags by letting them put them inside locked containers.

But what happened instead? Locked chests blew up inside backpacks, killing you, when thieves opened them. We left in the ability for thieves to disarm the traps, so they weren't always effective. People made chain reactions of explosives, so that they could light a fuse outside town and cause a death inside town.[154] People sold trapped locked containers to shopkeepers, who then resold the booby trap to unsuspecting victims. Leaving trapped chests at crossroads was a common ambush tactic. Yes, of course there were skills for detecting traps and disarming them... but you had to be a canny player to know of, and use, these tools. When we ran some metrics that year, the number one killer in the game was named TinkerBoy and had personally been

---

[153] Patch note of 12/16/97, http://wiki.uosecondage.com/Ultima_Online_Patch_Notes_for_12/16/1997

[154] This wasn't actually fixed until a full year later, when "the City of Oasis on Sonoma, which was suffering from terrorist bombs during their periodic Fight Nights, and subsequent support from other player commentary brought this issue to our attention." See http://wiki.uosecondage.com/Ultima_Online:_The_Second_Age_Patch_Notes_for_10/01/1998

responsible for more than 3,000 deaths.

The victims were disproportionately new players who didn't know the ropes. And we were losing a truly distressing number of our new player acquisitions — *Ultima Online* was the fastest selling Electronic Arts game in history, well on its way to being a massive massive hit. But our subscriber numbers, while stratospheric for the day, weren't keeping up because the losses were so high.

We had a world where a bard could entice an NPC shopkeeper out of town safety, kill them, and steal everything. Or provoke them to anger, get them to attack a random passerby, then call the guards on the shopkeeper for illegal behavior. Where you could die while polymorphed into a deer, resurrect still in that body that resembled a deer in every way, and therefore be able to wander into a player's house without them suspecting a thing — and rob it blind. Where people would find *already locked* chests in a house, and leave a trap for the unsuspecting actual owner! Even the "good guys" took part, luring guards out of town and leaving them near Blackthorn's shrine, where murderers resurrected.

That Christmas, we spawned Santa Clauses in every town, and put a gift in every player's backpack. Players stole the clothes off of Santa, leaving naked men chanting "Ho ho ho!" right where new players logged in. Then they formed roving bands of Santa Clauses and roamed around slaughtering everyone with chilling war cries wishing people Happy Holidays.

The worst of all these exploits were around player housing. UO allowed players to build houses anywhere in the world that they fit. The patch notes for the six months are a litany of exceptions: no houses on tilled fields. No houses on roads. No houses inside dungeons.

Houses had tilted thatch or tile roofs, which were accomplished with an optical illusion, rather than being a solid floor (like all the flat roofs in the game). This meant that if you could get up to the roof, you could simply fall in, steal whatever you liked, and walk out the front door. *Ultima Online* didn't simulate gravity, so players would place a chair next to the house, stack a second chair on top of it, stand on top of the upper chair, *remove the lower chair*, and repeat until they stood in midair floating atop suspended chairs, and simply walk onto the roof. They found ways of sneaking past doors, of teleporting in by exploiting minor collision bugs when dropping items[155], and worst of all, of obtaining player keys.

You see, there wasn't much of a concept of "ownership" in early UO. It existed for

---

[155] You teleported to locations marked with recall runes; drop a rune partly through a wall, and you might appear past the wall.

actions, as we have seen in the case of notoriety, and it existed for pets, but it did not exist for objects. Locked items, including houses, were tied to keys. Keys could be duplicated, and critically, stolen. Lose your key, and you effectively lost the house and all its contents: potentially months and months worth of character investment.

Guild warfare

One of the first freeform guild systems in games went in as another attempt to work with the behaviors players were already exhibiting.[156] Players had used the ability to tailor any clothing they liked and dye it any color to build uniforms. The relative disposability of characters in *Ultima Online* meant that it wasn't utterly unreasonable for an informal guild to ask that you *start your character over* with the guild abbreviation tacked onto the end of your name, as in

```
Buffy [LLTS]
```

Guilds promptly staked out territory and went to war, forming towns with their houses and in general trying to form their own little governments. In order to support this in a way that didn't wreak havoc on everyone else, I designed and implemented a system over a weekend that allowed players to place a *guildstone* in a house or on a ship. The first person to use the stone was automatically named the guildmaster.

Prior to this, most online games, including most MUDs, required admin intervention to form guilds, or simply placed players into pre-built ones more like factions.

Many of the tropes of guilds today come from that system: the ability to propose members to the guild; a system of tiered titles for the guildmaster, officers, and rank and file; the ability to set tags on your name; and of course, the ability to declare war on other guilds, which came along in tandem with a whole new system that replaced the old bounty system, known as the *Reputation System.*

But guild warfare didn't solve anything. Rolling the older Order and Chaos system of virtue guards into the guild system and allowing guilds to choose larger factions didn't either. Weird effects around criminal flagging persisted, and if anything got a tad worse as now we had to deal with the question of whether or not attacking a guildmate was considered a criminal action.

The upshot was that it became a running joke: bad guys tended to be "Great Lords" and good guys who tried to serve vigilante justice were usually "Dread Lords."

---

[156] See http://wiki.uosecondage.com/Ultima_Online_Patch_Notes_for_02/12/1998

Something called "noto PK" became a thing, as edge cases were exploited left and right. An illustration of the problem can be seen in this post[157] found on Stratics (one of the top UO fansites at the time):

> Let's look at some examples of the system in action. First, noble deeds that are punished:
>
> - A Great Lord gets bored and attacks a member of a adventuring party. The other members being loyal to their friend attack the now Noble Lord. Each and every person drops two ranks in the notoriety system for DEFENDING a player against a player-killer.
> - A player is killed by a monster. His partner stands over the corpse to guard the equipment. A looter runs up and starts grabbing stuff. The partner does the right thing and attacks the looter to save his partners stuff. Unfortunately, the looter was neutral and so the attacker is penalized.
> - A "honorable" rogue steals from a player in the wilderness. He runs off trying to beat the criminal flag. The victim gives chase and tries to attack the player, but double clicking a moving target is next to impossible (which makes sense since in reality, hitting a moving target is incredibly difficult). After several minutes, the rogue becomes to fatigued to move and the victim attacks him. Unfortunately, the criminal flag is reset and the victim is penalized.
> - A known murderer is tracked down by a group of players. The murderer is neutral because he does a good job exploiting the notoriety system. The PK-hunters all become dishonorable for killing the killer. They also become the targets of every self-righteous PK in the game.
>
> Now, a couple examples of evil deeds that are ignored.
>
> - A player traps another player into an area with no escape. He demands the player hand over his gold or die. The player is greatly outmatched and doesn't want to die, so he does. The system sees the victim as voluntarily handing over his gold, so the highwayman goes unmarked.
> - A wizard comes upon a fighter battling an ogre. He quickly puts up energy fields to block the fighters escape. He then casts reactive armor and healing on the ogre. This allows the ogre to kill the player. Because energy field and healing are seen as non-offensive spells, the mage gets away with murder.
> - A player surprises a group of fighters by charging into their midst in combat mode and using the bow action or lumberjacking skill to feint a strike. The members of the party all attack him and he is now free to kill them at will.
> - A player runs into a house that is not his when the door is opened. He immediately starts looting the chests. The owner of the house checks his paperdoll and sees he is honorable. He cannot defend his property from the

---

[157] https://uo.stratics.com/content/darkside/notoriety.shtml

thief without penalizing himself.

These are all things that happen in the game fairly often. The bottom four are all tricks I use myself very successfully (feel free to copy them—chaos is good for business).

And so, it was time to redesign from scratch.

The reputation system

The redesign was called "the reputation system," which is of course the general term for all systems that track an overall rating for an individual *based on the feedback of other users*; eBay's stars are a reputation system, your upvotes on Reddit are a reputation system, and so on. Technically notoriety doesn't count as a reputation system, because it's simply adjusting a value in code, without a user getting to decide how they feel about another user. It is more like what we might term an *alignment system*, drawn from *Dungeons & Dragons*. Murder counts, however, are a form of a *negative reputation system* (a system with only upvotes would be a *positive reputation system*).

Rep systems in general were a relatively new idea at the time, with UO's murder report system as one of the early mainstream examples alongside Slashdot's karma and eBay's star ratings.[158] Slashdot can probably be credited as bringing the concept to broader awareness. But there were many antecedents: at Xerox PARC in 1992, the Tapestry email system used annotations as a way to filter email; annotations were effectively upvotes.[159] BBS systems often had "leech scores" to track people who downloaded without uploading. And the pioneering American Information Exchange system was developing early forms of smart contracts that basically tracked reputation, clear back between 1988 and 1991.[160] Many folks were wrestling with the same issues that we were: Sybil attacks, whitewashing attacks, and distributed reputation.[161]

It's important to make the distinction between systems that tracked behavior to NPCs within a fictional context, and systems that were players ratings their

---

[158] Slashdot launched about a week and a half after UO did. EBay launched about a year and a half before UO, under the name AuctionWeb. But seller ratings only came out sometime in the spring or summer of 1997, so UO's notoriety system was probably available to users right around the same time.

[159] https://www.ischool.utexas.edu/~i385d/readings/Goldberg_UsingCollaborative_92.pdf

[160] See http://erights.org/smart-contracts/history/index.html for a description.

[161] A Sybil attack is where you use multiple fake identities to pump up the reputation of someone. Whitewashing is where you do something that wipes the record clean on a bad actor in some way. Distributed reputation is the problem that reputations are really contextual in nature, and you may have a high rating within a given community but be unknown or even negative elsewhere.

interactions with one another. Most of these systems were still literally science-fictional, with some of the better known fictional takes, such as Cory Doctorow's whuffie,[162] yet to be written. Games had basically fictional forms of it, such as alignment in *Dungeons & Dragons*, but they weren't actually based on interactions between real people.[163] Some MUDs, such as *Genocide*, an LPMud centered around competitive PvP, used systems based on around kill-to-death ratios, and some roleplay-centric MUDs used systems that included "rp points" that were a special currency players could grant one another for doing well.[164] *ChaosMUD* had a system where you could blackball players using a time-limited blackball currency,[165] and clear back in 1983 *Sceptre of Goth* had a system where players could affect a stat that might cause city guards to attack other players.[166]

---

[162] From *Down and Out in the Magic Kingdom*, published in 2003. Doctorow states that his inspirations were Slashdot karma and Napster. https://twitter.com/doctorow/status/988557312976609280

[163] A description provided by Scott Phillips of how a system like this worked on *Star Wars MUD*:

> StarWarsMud had two variables it kept track of: your galactic notoriety (good (rebel) -> neutral -> evil (empire)) and your Jedi alignment (light (Jedi) -> neutral -> dark (Sith)).
> Unfortunately there were infinitely-repeatable resourceless mechanisms to alter both values. (Use light jedi powers as dark and you'll edge towards light, and vice versa. Kill rebel-aligned NPCs, players and ships while being rebel aligned and you'll edge towards the empire).
> Stiff penalties for crossing from one extreme to neutral, no penalty for crossing over from neutral to an extreme, even stiffer penalties for crossing over from light Jedi to neutral or dark Jedi to neutral.
> Ultimately, the system didn't work very well at all, since it could be gamed quite easily by players. It just became a tedium; maintain your alignments before they flipped over. (Case in point, my Rodian, who held a very high rank in the Imperial Army, literally killed Emperor Palpatine multiple times a day for the extreme rewards, and I just had to a kill a few rebel scum to make up for it.). The only player involvement was a Diplomat class that could bring another player's alignment closer to their own (i.e. I just needed an Imperial Diplomat to essentially erase my regicide).

[164] The origins of RP point systems in MUDs are lost, unfortunately. I am sure *Armageddon* made use of the system, and possibly Discworld as well.

[165] They even had a player council that could clear the blackballs! Per Todd Coleman, "*ChaosMud* (94) used a variant of the same idea, but we removed the need for players to cast a spell to downvote other players. Instead we offered a /blackball command with a min level and a limited number of uses per day. if a player got enough downvotes from other players, city guards would aggro them. We deputized a player council called the 'Knights of Justice' who had the ability to clear down votes from people so that we wouldn't have to police it.)... Don't believe there were any limitations on use.

I recall one CS issue where a player found a "wand of curses" during an event, and they went on a rampage spamming other players into the negatives... the only limits on use were game system driven, i.e. mana and/or charges."

[166] The "piety" stat functioned very much like UO's notoriety, except that players could cast spells to

UO's system was pretty elaborate, designed to try to avoid all the emergent problems we had identified:

- We wanted to warn new players (so reputation couldn't be contextual or stored on the viewer — we needed more than a past interaction history between a single pair of people).

- We wanted to allow for forgiveness; our experiences with people accidentally becoming Dread Lords for trying to do good deeds or even just mis-clicking made us wary of permanent penalties.

- But we wanted to trap recidivists and keep them from evading strong penalties.

- Lastly, we wanted it to not be fictionally incongruous.

The design for the reputation system happened largely in public, via discussions on a variety of forum sites and rec.games.computer.ultima.online on Usenet, and periodic IRC chats between players and the development team. As the system was worked out, a player named Bob Hanson took on the job of building a FAQ that served as a concordance to all the ideas and as documentation of the implementation that went onto the Test Server. Eventually Bob's work was taken and formalized into an official FAQ for the system that went live in the spring of 1998.[167]

The new system tracked not one variable like notoriety, or two like notoriety and murder count, but three, and eventually *five*. Instead of just notoriety trying to fit both your behavior and your fame onto one axis, the system moved to having two axes: fame for how well-known you were, and karma for measuring your behavior. Karma worked much like notoriety did before it, going up and down based on actions you took in the game, ranging from giving gold to beggars (good) to dismembering corpses (bad). Getting reported for killing another player gave negative karma.

Fame worked similarly, and even went up and down for similar reasons. But it decayed over time, and didn't care as much about whether what you did was "good" or "bad." Killing another player with higher fame than you would *raise* your fame. This was intended to basically remove incentives for killing those without much fame: newbies. Originally, fame was intended to serve as a hard gate for getting access to many perks in the game, including housing.

---

directly change someone else's piety stat using "blessings" or "curses." It wasn't, however, rating an interaction; you could do it for whatever reason you pleased. You can see a description of *Sceptre of Goth*, which is one of the earlier virtual world systems, here: https://www.dwheeler.com/scepter-of-goth/scepter-of-goth.html

[167] The full official FAQ can be found at
https://web.archive.org/web/20001206150800/http://update.uo.com/repfaq/index.html

Both numbers were hidden from players, visible only via a grid of titles. In fact, the documentation has snarky things to say for those who wished to find ways to game the system:

> **Will I ever be able to see the numerical value for my Karma?**
>
> No. UO is a roleplaying environment, and we encourage you not to depend on numbers. However, if you are really curious you can add the letters in the title. Give the letters a value (x) corresponding to their linear value in the alphabet, for instance a=1 and z=26. Once you have added this perform this function $((\log(x) - \text{sqrt}(x)) * 30) / 0$. This won't give you anything meaningful, but should keep you occupied and satisfy your love of numbers.

All of the complex feedback and color coding was boiled down to Blue, Gray, and Red, with innocents Blue and Murderers red. Gray indicated a recent flagging for doing something that harmed or *might* harm others. These two things were different internally: one indicated aggressive behavior and the other criminality, but they looked the same.

The key difference was that aggressive behavior only turned you gray *for people who got hurt*. Criminal behavior generally turned you gray to *everyone*, except for the wrinkle that failed thievery could flag you as a Criminal just to the victim until you next died. This allowed the victim of thievery to catch the thief later and take revenge even though time had elapsed. Looting corpses that were not your own also made you a criminal.

Anyone *you saw* as gray could be attacked without repercussions, but it wore off after two minutes. This meant that if you hurt someone with an ill-considered earthquake spell, anyone hurt in the earthquake could attack you without penalty, but third parties who weren't hurt would still see you as blue.

Killing a blue person (an Innocent, in the system's terms) meant that they had the ability to report you, just as in the earlier murder system. In fact, just *hurting* an Innocent who later died in a separate incident before they were fully healed up meant they could report you. A murder count incremented on you; it faded away at the rate of one murder every eight hours of real-time gameplay. If you hit five murder count, you were turned red, and became a Murderer.

Murderers suffered severe penalties upon death (scaled by how many people you had killed), were killed on sight by guards (effectively blocking you from towns while red), and also generated bounties like the older system.

Alongside this system were a number of extra features for guilds — they were able to declare themselves Order or Chaos, which replaced the older system, and had their own green and orange color-coding.

The system also put an emphasis on people taking proactive action. Guards no longer just appeared when you attacked someone; instead, someone had to call for them. Thieves had to be "noticed" by someone, and then you could call guards to kill them. It meant that towns actually got slightly *less* safe.

This system did have a noticeable effect on the amount of playerkilling, but it remained still too high. The sight of Murderers locked in their houses running macros overnight to reduce murder count became a common sight. The stat loss could be significant, so Murderers simply spaced out their kills so they could stay above the threshold of five murder count.

Housing lockdowns

The next update to try to reduce griefing tackled the problem of stealing keys and the general vulnerability of houses.[168] It finally extended ownership to houses themselves, removing the need to carry around a highly valuable key for the front door. It also added in a system of *lockdowns*, which basically meant that you could mark items in your house as impossible to be stolen, in the event that someone managed to get in. Lockdown amounts were scaled by the size of the building, and started out being a few hundred items per structure; it didn't take long until these amounts were in the thousands.

With ownership, you could designate friends as people who had permission to use the amenities of your house. It also permitted the creation of houses that were *public*; this proved to be an incredibly powerful feature, enabling things like museums, player-run taverns, and "rune libraries," which were basically like a teleportation station: tables with locked down runes encoding destinations all over the game. You cast one of several travel spells on the rune for where you wanted to go, and off you, and possibly your companions depending on the spell, went.

It wasn't long[169] before those pesky traps were cased out of lockdowns as well, eliminating yet another loophole.

> It will no longer be possible to chop up secure containers in houses. They must be unsecured first.
>
> Traps and the magic lock spell can no longer be placed on locked down containers. You can still place them on containers before they are locked down,

[168] http://wiki.uosecondage.com/Ultima_Online:_The_Second_Age_Patch_Notes_for_11/23/1998
[169] http://wiki.uosecondage.com/Ultima_Online:_The_Second_Age_Patch_Notes_for_12/08/1998

however. This was done to prevent people from trapping containers to ambush the container's owners.

More dramatically, players were given more control over their homes in general. So-called "Texas law" allowed players to attack anyone at all in their homes that they chose, without being flagged in any way.[170] Owners (and by late 1999, co-owners) could even mark public houses as being under guard protection, effectively turning the house into a small outpost exactly like any town area. Players also gained the ability to ban and eject troublemakers from the house. Combined with the extension of ownership to a small space outside the home, this was the first real gesture towards giving players actual policing ability over spaces in their home. A shift to doing bans by account rather than character came along not long after,[171] thereby effectively making a person's house a sub-administered area of the game, with power delegated to players rather than admins.

An additional step taken towards allowing players to effectively govern their own spaces was the addition of ballot boxes,[172] a special type of object that allowed players to run polls and conduct votes in public houses. These changes were all with the intent of finding ways for players to "win" against the bad guys. I often chatted with players about the notion of "townstones," which would let players form towns with all the protections and perks of one of the designer created ones. This never happened in *Ultima Online*, but came to fruition in *Star Wars Galaxies* where it, of course, opened up a whole new set of exploits, such as founding towns on top of dungeon entrances in order to lay claim to all the monster spawns and loot within.

And yet, it was all still quite dangerous outside. A year and a half after the rep system, we're still so naive that when I did the mining system refresh,[173] I wrote in the patch notes,[174]

> Once a vein is located, it will always be at that location from then on. (It behooves miners to conceal this location!) We have seen the feedback from those concerned that these locations will become ambush points. If this develops into a problem, we will make the veins move. For now, however, they will remain where they are found.)

---

[170] http://wiki.uosecondage.com/Ultima_Online:_The_Second_Age_Patch_Notes_for_12/21/1998
[171] http://wiki.uosecondage.com/Ultima_Online:_The_Second_Age_Patch_Notes_for_05/25/1999
[172] http://wiki.uosecondage.com/Ultima_Online:_The_Second_Age_Patch_Notes_for_04/14/1999
[173] This added colored ores to the game, which opened up the armor system considerably.
[174] http://wiki.uosecondage.com/Ultima_Online:_The_Second_Age_Patch_Notes_for_02/02/1999

Thieves Guild, an attempt to curb thievery

As part of the effort to keep thieves in the game, a whole system was added for a fictional Thieves' Guild.[175] Access to a variety of thief skills was tucked behind a membership requirement, and then membership in the Thieves' Guild was made contingent on not being a Murderer.

On top of that, thieves couldn't report anyone for murder themselves.

Of course, murdering was so much more profitable than stealing for commensurate risk. So this change really didn't do much other than effectively eliminate most thieves from the game, quite the opposite of what was intended. The new skills (which included stealthy movement, detecting and removing traps, and most importantly, a disguise kit that allowed you to modify your appearance temporarily) simply weren't enough of a draw. A few roleplayers insisted on carrying on, but the subtle art of pickpocketing faded away in favor of simply bashing in your target's skull.

Slow and ping pong counters

Two extra additional stats were added to the reputation system a few months after the system went in.[176] The goal was to really tackle the recidivism and macroing issues, and eliminate the so called "Blue PK" — people who stayed just above five murders and were therefore Blue, but had evil intent.

Murder counts remained intact, but staying Red used a new long-term counter. This one decayed not every eight hours, but every *forty*. In other words, all your murder count might have decayed away, but you'd stay Red for a *looooong* time anyway, and therefore still be vulnerable. Stat loss penalties used the more forgiving counter, so this meant that most Murderers were still macroing away in their houses until those were decayed away. But then at least they were still Red when they ventured out again, so their victims had some warning.

On top of that, a "ping-pong" counter measured how many times you went from Blue to Red. If it hit five, you became a red Murderer forever. There was no forgiveness and no decay. You were to be killed on sight in towns by guards, and all

---

[175] http://wiki.uosecondage.com/Ultima_Online:_The_Second_Age_Patch_Notes_for_02/24/1999
[176] http://wiki.uosecondage.com/Ultima_Online:_The_Second_Age_Patch_Notes_for_03/28/1999

the rest. But there was still no stat penalty unless you had killed recently.

This was the last major change to the reputation system, and it did have a pretty serious impact on the game. With this system, the vast majority of killers out there would in fact be Red, and players would have warning. But PKing was still a lucrative, and yeah, kind of fun activity, so now the constant bloodshed settled down to a certain level of constant background noise. That said, after all these changes, there were also some rumblings that perhaps we had made the game *too* safe, taking away some of the magic of emergence.

Murderers were always concerned about the massive stat penalties, since their murder counts weren't visible. It was perhaps a sop to them that a little system was added in April of 1999[177] to help them see whether or not they would suffer stat loss:

> You will be able to determine whether you will receive stat loss on resurrection. If you say "I must consider my sins" you will receive a message about your murder count.
> - If you have no murder count, and you are not currently red, you will get "Fear not, thou hast not slain the innocent."
> - If you have been reported, but currently have no murder count, you will get "Fear not, thou hast not slain the innocent in some time." (even if you are red)
> - If you have murder count, but it is not enough to result in stat loss, you will get "Although thou hast slain the innocent, thy deeds shall not bring retribution upon thy return to the living." (even if you are red)
> - If you are liable for stat loss, you will get "If thou should return to the land of the living, the innocent shall wreak havoc upon thy soul."

New player protection and Siege Perilous

> Prepare yourselves brave travelers, for Siege Perilous truly will test your skills as a player. Aggressors who chose to alienate themselves from their fellow adventurers will find quickly it is a struggle to simply survive. Only those who can master the arts of teamwork, communication and trade, as well as combat, will prosper in this challenging world.

The pent-up demand by PvPers for a freer and bloodier environment ended up answered by creating a shard with special rules termed "Siege Perilous," primarily designed by Kirk Black aka Runesabre.[178] This was a server with much looser PvP

---

[177] http://wiki.uosecondage.com/Ultima_Online:_The_Second_Age_Patch_Notes_for_04/14/1999
[178] A good summary of the rules can be found at http://www.uoguide.com/Siege_Perilous

rules that became decently popular almost immediately, and helped kick off the whole practice of running parallel servers with strongly variant game rules. There are Siege Perilous emulation servers to this day, and the ruleset actually became the default for one of the shards run in Japan.

Siege Perilous was a harsher environment in most ways, basically UO on hard mode. Items broke far quicker. Murderers couldn't protect their houses. Shopkeepers didn't buy goods from players at all. And critically, guards didn't attack Red characters.

Needless to say, there were not that many "sheep" on Siege Perilous.

The last touch was to protect newbies. By August of 1999[179] a system had gone in that basically flagged all newbies as safe, regardless of where they were (they were actually tagged as "young"). Players marked as young even got teleported to healers automatically. (They were also blocked from getting to Siege Perilous, since they'd almost certainly die).

This was all a part of a larger effort to make the game more accessible, which included providing starter templates for the very directionless skill skill, a newbie tutorial that guided players around, and a refreshed login screen with a much nicer introductory experience. Because despite all the changes I've described, *Ultima Online* still had a reputation as a bloodthirsty place, and competition had arrived in the form of *EverQuest*.[180]

EQ had a simple solution to all the above: they had a PK switch. Meaning, unless you flagged yourself as PK-enabled (which few did), you were safe. The end.

This worked acceptably in *EverQuest* because it was simply a far more constrained game than *Ultima Online*. You couldn't drop things on the ground. No laying of traps. No stealing. No houses. No stacking chairs. No chairs. Grief players happily led monsters into newbie zones and killed them, but you couldn't loot others, so there was no reward cycle there except the gnashing of teeth. There wasn't crafting. It was a game driven by player-vs-environment combat, and to a veteran MUD player felt very strongly like a DikuMUD with first-person 3d.

The result was an exodus driven not only by the more modern 3d graphics of the newer game, but by the *safety*. Everything I had thought about the impossible admin load of having a PK switch with a large-scale game was disproven in short order, and players wasted no time in telling me bluntly that I had been drastically and painfully wrong.

---

[179] http://wiki.uosecondage.com/Ultima_Online:_The_Second_Age_Patch_Notes_for_08/26/1999
[180] *EverQuest* launched on March 16th of 1999, so right around the same time as the ping-pong counters.

The result? In the name of player freedoms, I had put them through a slow-drip torture of two years of experiments with slowly tightening behavior rules, trying to save the emergence while tamping down the bad behavior. The cost was the loss of many hundreds of thousands of players. *Ultima Online* had churned through more than twice as many players who quit than *EverQuest* even got as subscribers that year.

Trammeling players

By 2000, I was off the project, working instead on a series of pitches for new MMOs that Origin might make. And while I was doing that, the team's new design leadership arrived at a new solution that put paid to the early wild and crazy era of UO forever: the Trammel/Felucca split.

Simply put, the map was cloned. One side was termed Felucca, and had the same rules that already existed.

The other was called Trammel, and in Trammel, there simply wasn't any ability to attack other players. It was a peaceful place.

To this day, this is controversial. I wouldn't have done it, personally, but there is no question that the userbase *doubled* once this went in.

Had the game been like this from the beginning, would it have reached even greater heights? I don't know. We lost an enormous amount of players to bad behavior. But we also gained endless stories and excitement, the stories that people tell and retell to this day. Lord British would not have been killed by a player. The sense of excitement would not have been there. Even the player economy would have collapsed — as indeed, it did almost immediately once goods were largely safe in Trammel.

The names came from the two moons over Britannia. A felucca is a kind of sailing ship. The dictionary says this about the word "trammel."

> *noun*
> * a restriction or impediment to someone's freedom of action.
> *verb*
> * deprive of freedom of action.

That's basically exactly what happened. We trammeled players, and tamed the crazed flow of exploits and inventions. At that moment, a crucial piece of the virtual world was lost, in favor of the old player switches and safe zones of the past. *EverQuest* launched with a PK switch, and set the template. Later games would do realm vs realm combat, maybe even some simple criminal flags. But never again would online worlds let you drop stuff on the ground, try to pick a pocket, entice creatures hither and yon, set a bomb, or even just track their good or bad behavior. The dream of letting players police themselves was over.

Instead, it was now the admin's job.

Within five years, they wouldn't bother.

Where once *LegendMUD* would have kicked you out for cursing, we got Xbox Live chat with rampant sexism and homophobia.

Where once *Ultima Online* would have tracked your behavior to try to warn other players of bad apples, we eventually got Twitter, where Nazis can post freely and spam others off the Net.

By giving up on solving the hard problem of freedom co-existing with civility, I fear that the result is that on today's Internet, we have neither.

The safe world

or Why say "leave out" combat? Let's Just Leave It In

From contemporaneous MUD-Dev postings.

If we are working towards virtual realities, as I think we are, then I think that there's a problem set there to solve. And we can reduce it by going with a smaller design, sure–one tailored to that vast group of people who would rather not deal with certain aspects it is possible to simulate, such as violence. As Dr Cat said, we can choose not to add in combat.

But somebody is gonna add combat. And since I was (and still am, though my interest is shifting) interested in tackling many of the problems that arise with an environment that includes as many of the experiences life offers as can be made interesting, I regard it as "leaving it out." That's not intended to be derogatory towards those who leave it out; they are not trying to address the same problem set, is all. I want to tackle the problem set of the day when we have a MUD (read: spatial, multi-user) interface to the entire Internet, which I don't think is that far away.

Quite beyond that, I have serious doubts about the commercial feasibility of a server that's completely safe. Not because of the lack of interest, but because of the amount of cops you have to pay to keep it safe. I use as my rule of thumb whether or not we're willing to pay enough cops to keep us safe in the real world, where the stakes are a lot higher. Yeah, we can code Toontown laws of physics, and people will still find ways to screw each other over. Because fundamentally, that's what a safe environment is promising: nobody will screw you over. And I can't currently design a way around that. I doubt I will ever be able to. You can reduce the problem set, but the problem doesn't go away… what's worse, the safer you say you are, the more of a target you paint on your chest. A nasty dilemma.

As an aside, I'd also like to whap everyone who said that the designers of UO ignored the history of the online game development field upside the head, please.

Whew, that was an outpouring. Basically, I cheer on the "safe game" designs. Love to see how you do it. Am openly skeptical about how you'll do it. Hope you prove me wrong. And I go about it in a more cynical way. UO was intended as just a microcosm, you see. The fact that it is as dangerous as it is speaks, IMHO, more to human nature than anything else…

Storytelling in the online space

The following two snippets were originally Usenet posts, but I've extended them and added to them, so that they can make more sense without the context of the thread.

Well, I'll be the first to admit that events in UO have not always lived up to expectations. But I do see a different sort of living, progressing, and growing. So maybe we'd benefit in this discussion from breaking down what we mean by these different things.

Let's use a cube: one axis being who directs the growth/change/activity, one being what fictional context it uses, and the other being whether it actually causes the world to progress, grow, or change in any way.

This leads to the following:

Design-directed stuff that springs from the backplot but does not change the world. The gnoll scenario in *EverQuest* fits this bill. So does the Sherry the Mouse book in UO, or any other static backplot that serves to add detail.

*Design-directed material that springs from the backplot but **does** affect the world* is a knotty problem, and I think what most players refer to when they say "plot" in an online RPG setting. This would be something large like a plot to destroy the world–if it had the potential to actually kill everyone in the game.

Design-directed material that does not spring from the backplot and does not change the world would be something like a seasonal event or holiday celebration that does not change the world in any substantial way. So for example, having Santa Claus stand on corners and say "Ho ho ho", which has no impact on the gameplay after the event is concluded.

Design-directed material that does not spring from the backplot and does change the world would be things like the introduction of a new type of armor, or (a UO-specific example) black dye tubs, as part of a seasonal holiday event. These introduced ripples into the economy that are still seen today–in the case of the black dye, still seen pretty strongly. Yes, a moderately minor sort of effect, but an effect nonetheless.

Player-directed material that springs from the backplot but does not change the world would be something like the Seekers of the Wisps. Fun for them, but of no real lasting consequence in the game–it does not change gameplay for the shard as a whole.

Player-directed material that does spring from the backplot and does affect the world would be things like the Trinsic Rebellion, or the Temple of Mondain. These things were and are causing significant effects in the gameplay of the shards in question–localized, to be sure, but fairly significant in that they affect the general atmosphere of the game in the affected regions.

Player-directed material that does not spring from the backplot and does not change the world is very very common. Countless themed dungeon crawls, small taverns running roleplay stories, etc.

*Player-directed material that does not spring from the backplot and **does** change the world* is often the most compelling to the players, it seems. Attacks on Kazola's tavern. SiN demanding protection money. The SBR.

Setting aside immersion for the moment–let's get back to the living/growing/progressing thing. I happen to agree that the issue of design-directed plot events that alter the world have indeed not come off in UO. I don't think they've come off significantly in EQ yet either–to be honest, the only pay-for-play games I know of in which they DO come off and have significant impact on the game are *Gemstone III, Dragonrealms,* and *Achaea.* In those, volcanos bury cities, deities topple and as a result entire classes lose magical abilities for weeks, etc.

But I DO think that the player-directed stuff in UO is very strong, stronger than anything else out there in the pay-for-play arena, at any rate. And it's at its strongest when it is not tied to the backplot with any great strength… and I also do see it as living, progressing, growing, changing the world, very often.

Ideally, I think, you hit all eight types. But it's devilishly hard to do…

This is a fascinating area of discussion, and I'd love to pursue it more. It'd be interesting to add "scope" to the grid and see what it gets us.

As an example of events that we considered doing in UO but have not pursued: a ginseng blight ruins all the ginseng crop. Shops stop carrying it. A quest must be done to find a cure for the blight. Until then, no ginseng reagent unless you find it loose in the woods. There were many others along similar, major, game-affecting lines that we considered, but held off on because we were not sure that the playerbase was up for it.

On *Achaea*, they run similar huge plotlines with great regularity, and by all accounts their (much harder-core) playerbase loves it.

Two models for Narrative Worlds

From 2004.

I gave a talk at the University of Southern California's Entertainment in the Interactive Age event,[181] held at the Annenberg Center in Los Angeles. I was on a panel with Janet Murray, author of *Hamlet on the Holodeck*; Tim Schafer, designer of *Grim Fandango*, and Ken Lobb, veteran producer at Nintendo.

The Annenberg Center has put up transcripts of the whole thing, including the question and answer session at the end of the session I was in, and at some point will have streaming video of the events as well. In the meantime, I've taken their transcript of my largely-off-the-cuff remarks and matched them up with the slides I had prepared to try to recreate the experience. I've also corrected some minor errors (mis-heard words, that sort of thing) in the USC transcription.

When I originally prepared the slides, my intent was to give a talk that was fairly dry and academic, presenting the different narrative models that have been used in games thus far. But after seeing the first day's worth of panels, I felt I had to re-do my talk to suit both the audience and the major issues that were manifesting regarding narrative as the different speakers presented their thoughts. So that morning in the shower, I made some rough notes on a printout of my slides, and what resulted was the notes you'll see in the slides.

Because I did the whole thing off the cuff, I had no way to fact-check things. So I am just about positive there are inaccuracies in the examples in the text of the speech. I don't remember what Postman77's exact illness was, I am pretty sure but not positive of the outcome of the story of the guild extorting players (and it may not have happened at the tavern I cite), and I know for a fact that the guy who said "I can run" isn't the guy who won Vor's contest, because he posted his story after the contest had ended–so please forgive the inaccuracies that arose from doing zero research and improvising the speech, and try to focus on the spirit of what is said, and not the details.

Celia Pearce's introduction of me comes first; then you can click on the link to get

---

[181] https://web.archive.org/web/20061104051808/http://www.annenberg.edu/interactive-age/

to the slides and transcript. The transcript is right below the slides.

Thank you, Janet. Great, as always. Our next speaker is Raph Koster.

Raph was one of the original designers on *Ultima Online*. He's now working with Verant on the Sony–, I mean, the *Star Wars Galaxies* project.

He also has a really amazing website which is linked to from our website, which is one of the most comprehensive tomes on online community role-playing I've ever seen in my life. So that's the other, that's sort of the New Testament after Janet's book that everyone should take a look at.

And we're just getting him hooked up here. He's part of the Verant Mafia that's here at the conference. Verant[182] is a great company, because they work at three different locations, and so they actually practice what they preach, which is quite remarkable. They function completely in the mode of what they create.

Take it away, Raph.

Two Models for Narrative Worlds

Hello. Uh-oh. How many people out there know me? It's a little scary. All right. Let's see if we can get a picture up. So, I have to admit, Hal and Warren, and Janet, and everybody stole a whole bunch of things that I wanted to say today. So, this morning in the shower, I completely re-crafted my entire presentation. And my understanding is that most people are, in fact, capable of holding two things at once in their mind. So, I'm going to present you with a–, since we're here at an academic conference, I'm going to "problematize" my presentation. And it looks like it already happened, since we don't have a picture. [AUDIENCE LAUGHTER] What do you know.

---

[182] The name of the company that did *EverQuest*; they were spun out of Sony Interactive, ran as Verant for a while, then were acquired by Sony Pictures, a different unit of Sony. They were then renamed Sony Online Entertainment.

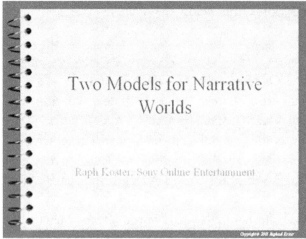

So I'm told most people can hold two things at once in their mind. So, welcome to a palimpsestic meta-narrative. Because read this, and I'm going to be talking about something else. [AUDIENCE LAUGHTER] And the interactive game will be you get to try to put together what I'm saying with what's on the screen. All right, I design massively multiplayer online games, virtual worlds. I've been doing it since 1992. Started out in text, moved on to graphics around 1995. However, in a previous life, I acquired an MFA in creative writing. Linear narrative is near and dear to my heart. And one of the great tensions, and by the way, I apologize, yet another picture of *The Sims*. One of the great tensions creatively is how do I reconcile those two things? Because they are radically different from one another, yet can be seen as existing on a spectrum. So, while I was in grad school, one of the things I was exposed to was hypertext.

Let's see. How many people recognize the names Michael Joyce, Stuart Moulthrop, Jay Bolter? That stuff. Text-based hyper-spaced stuff, usually constructed with a program called *StorySpace*. Lots of things, like "rhizomal structure," which means you get stuck in little loops of boxes, going around, getting the same piece of text over and over again, problematizing the narrative. I also had a history of playing games, and in fact, at one point I did a presentation for the class where I stood up and explained that one of the key dates in the history of academic hypertext was the first edition of *Dungeons and Dragons*, which kind of got me in trouble with my professor.

So the thing that *StorySpace* to me conveyed, more than anything, more than the tool itself, certainly more than any of the works done within it, was actually the title of the piece of software. The story provides a space. And the title of this–, you know, the subject of this panel is, it's about space, right? It's about how the spaces do things. But the thing is, in an interactive environment, metaphorically

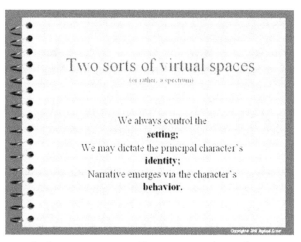

speaking, identity is also part of a space, behavior is part of a space, right? Those are also the choices.

Now, back when I used to work on muds, the kind of thing that I tried to do very, very hard was write these cool quests that people could go on in groups or by themselves, have this narrative experience. I recreated the entire saga of Beowulf, wove it together with the *Ring of the Nibelungs* near the end so when you went to fight the dragon, it was actually Fafnir, and you could, you know, go through the process of getting different kinds of swords, and the seithblade with the poison, and whatever, so you could go kill Fafnir and live through the whole saga. And at the very end, the Valkyrie would come down because you'd freed her from her imprisonment. Then the whole damn thing reset. But, you know, trying to do things whereby I was imposing these stories on people. They voluntarily stepped into them, but there they were inside this narrative structure.

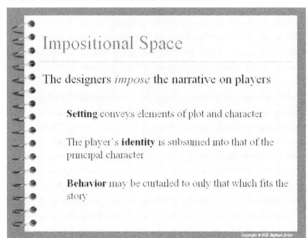

So, there I was, I was trying to use my MFA, by God. [LAUGHS] That's what I was trying to do. I was trying to tell the story within these spaces. I did one based on *The Jungle Book,* where I tried to tie the setting very much into the story. And there's a moment in there where you have to bring the Lost City of Oodeypore back to life, and so you have to go get, oh, I can't remember–, it's like a seed that you have to get from the Rukh, and you have to bring it to the point of the cliff where you can drop it into the place, and then magically–, you know, this was in text, so it was easier to do than graphics–, magically, this wave of energy spread out from that point, and it changed the setting, which had been a ruined city full of the Bandar-log apes. Each of the apes, "poof," transformed into the people that used to live in that city. And all of the walls that had been tumbling and fallen down and rocky, craggy, whatever, all of a sudden came back solid and strong again. And the entire setting changed around you. And as you continued to play, slowly, the people who were walking around wondering what happened, popped like soap bubbles, and turned back into the apes. That's story-telling via setting, and it's a place where I chose to, you know, put them in a world, and they couldn't avoid it. Right? I made them go through that experience. I was in control, by God, and it felt good.

Now, you know, we also often try to impose other things and constrain the space in other ways. We try to control the character, and we'll tell them, "This is who you are." Right? Kind of like at the beginning of the introduction, you know. "Celia's imposing an ID–, boy, I better live up to the introduction." You know, we all feel that way, right? So, when I first started playing online games back in '92, I had this

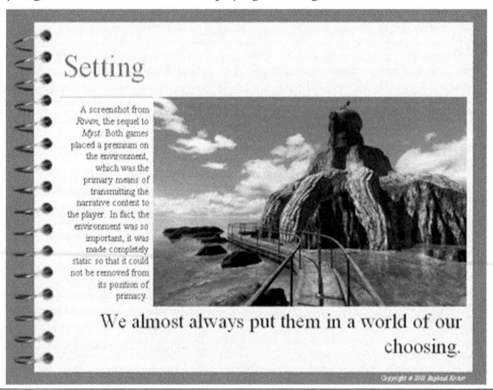

Setting

A screenshot from *Riven*, the sequel to *Myst*. Both games placed a premium on the environment, which was the primary means of transmitting the narrative content to the player. In fact, the environment was so important, it was made completely static so that it could not be removed from its position of primacy.

We almost always put them in a world of our choosing.

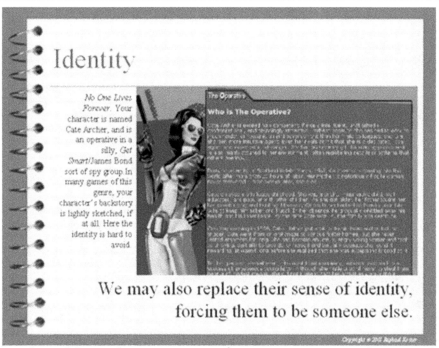

character that I'd been playing in RPG's for years, just years and years and years. Sometimes he was a bard, sometimes he was a thief. He was usually named Rusty or Dusty, depending on whether or not the name was taken. First time I logged into a mud, my wife and I were sitting there together, and we were, like, "Hey. What do you want to be? Okay. I've got this name. We'll use that. Yeah, sure. Rusty, taken. Damn. Okay, Dusty." "You're gonna play the–," "Fine, female." And then my wife went and made her own character. So I've been playing Dusty ever since. Okay? And she's female. And that is identity imposing, right? Whether we do it in the case of a game like this, where, you know, you're stuck in a pretty damn cheesy spy story, or whether it's in *Grim Fandango*, Tim's game, or whether it's, well, any other game where you are presented with a ready-made character, and as you embody it, you have to live out those ideals. As Dusty, I learned a lot playing Dusty. Getting, oh, everything from being sexually harassed to–, one evening, I actually went on a lengthy man-hating spree on chat, which really, really freaked out some of my friends.

The last kind of space that we often impose is behavioral. Now, I love single-player games. I love 'em. I remember sitting and repetitively shooting stupid little tanks in *Laser Blast* on my Atari 2600 until the million point score rolled over and turned into nothing by exclamation points. Not much of a narrative, I admit, but, by God, I made it. I remember sitting and replaying *Deadline* over and over again, so that I could ambush the mail delivery at 9:35 in the morning. Right? Because I needed that letter

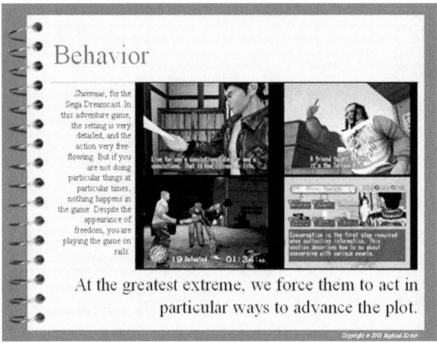

Behavior

Shenmue, for the Sega Dreamcast. In this adventure game, the setting is very detailed, and the action very free-flowing. But if you are not doing particular things at particular times, nothing happens in the game. Despite the appearance of freedom, you are playing the game on rails.

At the greatest extreme, we force them to act in particular ways to advance the plot.

so that I could prove–, you know. I never finished that game, by the way. And, you know, sure. You know, the other side of me, my MFA half, I'm still waiting to play the game that makes me feel like, oh, Marquez' "Man With Enormous Wings," or something, right? That's what, you know, I think a lot of people out here are daydreaming of something like that. Where's our *Hundred Years of Solitude,* where's our *Catch-22*, where's our *Hamlet,* right? We're a ways away, I guess.

So, there's a whole other kind of space. And there's a different kind of space, there's a different kind of way to tell the stories. And I think this panel, in particular, is going to frame this tension between these two ways of telling the space. I've been sitting, you know, talking about this with Warren and Hal and other folks for a few days now, since we've been here, whether this is a story at all. So, you know, expressive space. That's what I make for a living is expressive space, not impositional space, despite all my writerly desires.

And once upon a time, there was a guy named Vor who was quitting *Ultima Online.* I was lead designer on *Ultima Online* for more years than I want to think about. And he decided to quit. That's not an uncommon occurrence, you know. We see it with regret, and then we say, "Oh, well." He ran a cool little contest. He said, "I'm going to give away everything I've ever acquired in the game to the people who tell me the best stories about why I play UO." And he gathered these on a web page. So, welcome to expressive space.

So, one of the stories. Once upon a time, there was a very pleasant little tavern, the Serpent Cross Tavern. Players could build buildings in UO. Players could set up these structures, and they made them into their own, and they told their own private mythologies and told their own private stories in 'em. One day, this group of people called S-I-N, "sin," that was their guild abbreviation, decided that

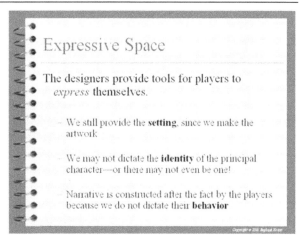

they were going to walk around all the player-run taverns and extort money. They formed a Mafia. And they went from tavern to tavern, and they said, we're going to destroy this place unless you pay us. And they came one day to the Serpent Cross Tavern–, you know, they were really boastful about it. They destroyed a whole bunch of role-playing hotbeds, came one day to the Serpent Cross Tavern, and found an

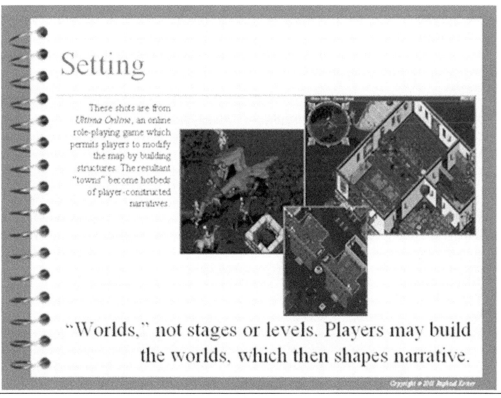

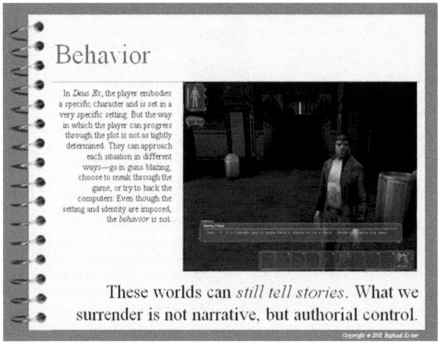

Behavior

In *Deus Ex*, the player embodies a specific character and is set in a very specific setting. But the way in which the player can progress through the plot is not as tightly determined. They can approach each situation in different ways—go in guns blazing, choose to sneak through the game, or try to hack the computers. Even though the setting and identity are imposed, the *behavior* is not.

These worlds can *still tell stories*. What we surrender is not narrative, but authorial control.

army waiting there that creamed 'em. Setting. Expressive setting. That could not have happened without the ability for players to reshape their space and create a location for a narrative.

Possibly the best known myth of *Ultima Online* is the saga of Kazola's Tavern. It was another player-created environment. But it was not just a player-created environment. It was also a player-created identity. Kazola's Tavern stood for everything that was good about role-playing and pacifistic play in *Ultima Online*. They got together, they tried to form a police force, you know. But the fact is the cool dudes, the jerks, the people who talk with half-numbers, like phone phreaks, those people were constantly harassing it, because, by God, it was the most valuable piece of real estate in the whole damn game. What happened there was a giant conflict between two forms of identity, two ways of representing yourself in the environment. And what it made was a myth. It made, you know, this was the giant mythic struggle of the killers versus the builders in made flesh. And, by God, that story has been told and retold by people within UO so many times now, because it resonates so deeply with who they are.

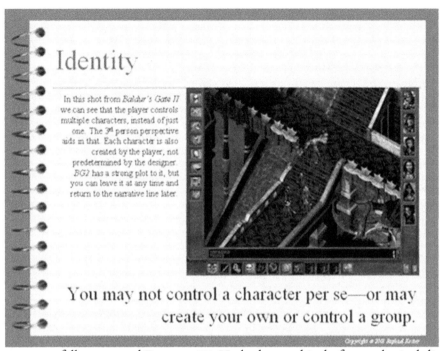

Identity

In this shot from *Baldur's Gate II* we can see that the player controls multiple characters, instead of just one. The 3rd person perspective aids in that. Each character is also created by the player, not predetermined by the designer. *BG2* has a strong plot to it, but you can leave it at any time and return to the narrative line later.

You may not control a character per se—or may create your own or control a group.

There was a fellow named Postman77. He had some kind of neurological disorder. Basically, you know, he was painfully shy. He couldn't go out in public. He, you know, he twitched and shook all the time, and it was very hard for him to keep a job. He was constantly embarrassed. In UO, he started playing, and he found, "Hey, I can–, you know, nobody can see the twitching." And that was pretty liberating for him. But more than that, it started shaping his behavior. He was one of the people who defended Kazola's Tavern. He was one of the people who fought against the Mafia people. He was one of those people who tried to organize. And he had to start learning organizational skills, and he had to start putting together groups of people who would work with him, and pretty soon he found, "You know, I need a web page in order to coordinate this stuff, and I need to learn leadership skills." And he got some leadership books. And, well, now he runs a web-design company, and acts as a consultant, because he transferred the learned behaviors that the game was reinforcing into real life. Okay? So now we have expressive behavior.

So, *a priori* versus *post-facto* storytelling. In other words, some stories we get to shape in advance, and some, we shape after the fact. So now, here comes a little metafiction bit. I just lied to you. None of those three stories were from, "Why I Play UO." None of them were from that. But it doesn't matter, does it? I mean, they're still good enough reasons, they still fit within that framework. That's "after-the-fact" storytelling. That's

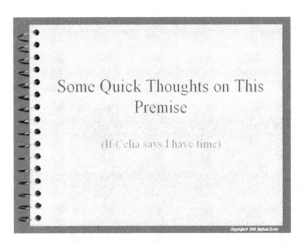

Some Quick Thoughts on This Premise

(If Celia says I have time)

people gathering together events, shaping 'em, editing, discarding stuff, throwing 'em around and putting them together into a story anyway. Art is a mirror to life, right? And it's just a question of when we decide to hold up the mirror.

In my past life as a writer, I was really concerned with naming boundaries with how we enforce you be something other. And, you know, there's a lot of potential for games that are about imposing things on people, about, "Hey, you get to experience what it's like to be in Colonial Williamsburg." Or, alternatively, maybe you get to experience what it's like to–, you know, this is kind of scary–, run a concentration camp. You know? Games can do that. These stories can do that.

At the same time, I often go nuts in "rhizome land," where I don't know which way to go. Right? Trying to make plot-node engines, and learn about narratology, or whatever. And, you know, how do I prevent the situation of the seven year old girl who logged into UO and had a pet bunny, and some guy just walked up and gutted the bunny in front of her,

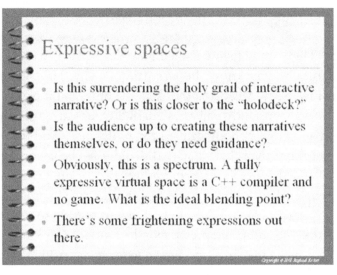

Expressive spaces

- Is this surrendering the holy grail of interactive narrative? Or is this closer to the "holodeck?"
- Is the audience up to creating these narratives themselves, or do they need guidance?
- Obviously, this is a spectrum. A fully expressive virtual space is a C++ compiler and no game. What is the ideal blending point?
- There's some frightening expressions out there.

and waved the meat and the hides in front of her, and went, "Nyah, nyah, nyah, nyah." You know, that's not why I built the game. But it's still a possible expressive space. And it makes for a pretty frightening story.

The real story that won Vor's thing was a guy who was in a wheelchair in real life. And he had a very succinct answer. "I play UO, because in it, I can run." So, on some days, I think to myself, "I'm astounded that people could write that story, a one-sentence story, and convey so much within the context of this. And that they are imposing that world view of the game on me. Wow." On

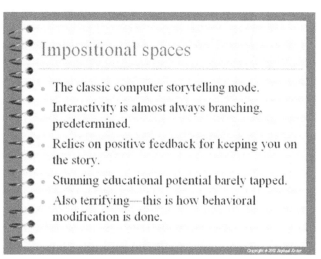

other days, I think to myself, "Maybe I wrote that. Wow. That couldn't have happened without the things I put into this game. That's really cool." Bottom line, I'm just glad the story exists. Right? Because we learn by story, we grow by story. What I'm giving you here, what I've just told you are some of the formative myths of online spaces. Right? And I don't care who the hell wrote them. Thank you.

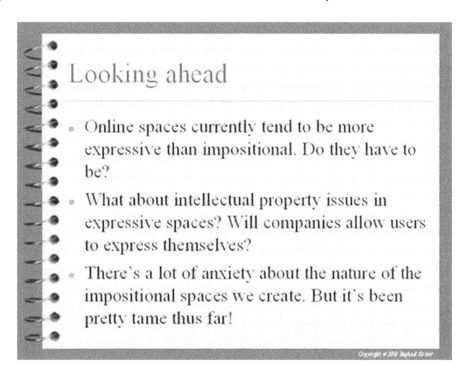

Why Don't Our NPCs?

In thinking about the UO resource system in recent posts, I also got to thinking about other things that we either wanted to or tried to get the NPCs to do. Today, NPCs have gradually evolved more and more towards being quest dispensers. Originally, we wanted NPCs that would give the illusion of life.

But there were a few bumps on the road, and today NPCs in all the games pretty much suck.

Moving around was actually one of the biggest bumps. One of the most obvious cues that an NPC is actually nothing more than a quest dispenser is to make them immobile terminals with hovering icons over their head. Yet this is what players demand. In early UO the NPCs moved about — there was even some attempt to make them move about purposefully, from trade implement to trade implement, but that failed. When the NPCs would move around while you were trying to talk to them, players objected, and then eventually the NPCs were frozen in place because their primary purpose was as a dispenser of items. I fought this for a long time because I hated the notion of reducing the NPCs back down…

Anyway, here's some of the big areas that I think are hugely underexploited in NPCs today.

A sense of persistence

However, also in UO, all NPCs were "born" with a name randomly selected from a few baby book lists that we coded into the game. This meant that on different shards, the NPC tending the forge might have a different name. In fact, everything in UO was this way — there were no static, named NPCs or creatures at launch. This cost us the equivalent of "slaying Nagafen," but it also led to other, different sorts of feelings.

For example, the feeling of coming to the forge one day and seeing that burly Bob the smith, with whom you have dealt for months, was no longer there. Instead, you saw Sarah, who introduced herself as his niece and informed you that Bob was in fact killed by MasTaKillA, an actual other player. I recall implementing a crude form of this, but I don't remember if we ever deployed it.

Memory in general is underexploited in NPCs today. On *LegendMUD*, the shopkeeper Aasma will remember regular customers for a period of two weeks, offer them specials, and even let them run a tab. This sort of familiarity, even when you know it is all faked with simple tracking mechanisms, actually adds a lot to the experience. Imagine walking into a tavern and having some NPCs greet you as an old friend rather than as a stranger — a perfect candidate behavior to be on every friendly shopkeeper in the game. Even better if they can timestamp when they last saw you and say "it's been a long time!"

Which naturally leads into…

Reacting to players

In UO, for a while NPCs would react to you based on your prestige. They'd bow when particularly notable players came by. Of course, first pass they bowed at everyone notable all the time, and as was usual in UO days, this led to the behavior being removed altogether, rather than being fine tuned. One can easily imagine that after accomplishing a great deed, a very transitory variable gets placed on you, which causes NPCs to react strongly (bowing, scraping, cheering, etc), but then they forget how special you are in an hour or so. This is much more rewarding than the bland "only the quest dispenser knows what you did" approach that prevails today.

On Legend, there was a bootblack who hung around on the Victorian Isle of Dogs. If you were advanced enough, when you came by, he'd shout to the whole town, "Cor! Didja know Alanna was in town?" Many a PvPer cursed his name and slew him in revenge; many a player also worked to get to the point where they too could be announced.

Having some personality

Providing a distinct sense of personality to different NPCs is challenging. Elaborately constructed ones on *Legend* were all handcrafted at first, but some of the behaviors were so nifty that they were then inherited by many of the other NPCs in the game. Mrs. O'Leary, innkeeper in Gold Rush San Francisco, would kick you out of her inn if she caught you saying cuss words. Tika, innkeeper in Celtic Ireland, would react to every single social in the game, and if fights or aggressive uses of socials broke out, would call Angus from upstairs to eject the participants from the building. Eventually, some of Tika's reactions were applied game-wide.

Trying to make some generic behaviors is a trickier task. In UO, we looked up the randomly generated intelligence level of the NPC, and also a randomly set mood, I think it was. Then we wrote 270 different ways of saying each thing they knew how to say. A stupid surly guy might greet you with "What the hell do YOU want?" whereas a highborn, educated snob might say "Much as it pains me to do so, I greet you." These stuck, so you'd get to know the snob at your local bakery (at least until someone killed them).

This meant, of course, that there was a lack of specificity to what each NPC would say. 270 entries for "hello" is a lot of work, too. So we broke the speech into libraries, so that the baker would have a library of talk about baking, and a library of generic talk. The baking library didn't have the amount of variation that the generic stuff did, but the flavor in the generic text was enough to give the NPC some personality.

Other generic things that all NPCs knew how to do included talking about the weather, giving you the time, and even giving directions to nearby landmarks or shops. This latter was accomplished by matching against keywords for what the player was looking for ("where" and "bank" in one sentence would do it), followed by a lookup into a table for the BANK spawn region. The closest one would be found, then the NPC would calculate the distance and direction, and a generic script library provided "You're looking for the *bank*? It's *a little ways* to the *northeast*."

Showing some initiative

One of the big problems that we always ran into with UO and muds was the fact that interaction was keyword-based. This meant that when localization became dominant, it was of course swept away even though it allowed for far more diverse interaction than conversation trees. It also meant, though, that NPCs would butt into conversations between players, thinking they had heard something of import. NPCs taking action on their own is nonetheless something really cool when people get to see it.

In SWG in beta there was a random spawn of a slave girl who would dash out into the street and fixate on a player. She'd rush up and say "Oh please, please, you have to help me! They're after me! Quick, take this, and don't let them catch you!" She would then hand you a data disk. Then she would run away, spawn a troop of Stormtroopers who would hunt her down and kill her in one shot. The player was left with a datadisk and intrigue.

Alas, the data disk did nothing, It was a tease. Eventually this, along with all the other "dynamic points of interest," were removed because of technical difficulties with spawning, primarily. I think this is a huge shame, because the dynamically appearing closed scenario quests allowed incorporation of a ton of extra variables to allow variability, and could appear almost anywhere.

But that's more of a topic for a quests post. So let's talk about Indiana Jones instead.

On *LegendMUD*, Indy was a mob that was only ever spawned as a joke by the admins. I wrote him mostly to get a handle on the scripting system. He'd appear, and announce on the global channels that he was putting together a party for a high-level adventure — I think it was actually to seek the Grail. Then he'd actually run around the mud, cracking jokes, using his whip, and pretending to be gathering up this party. If you met up with him, he had a large library of quotes and reactions drawn from the movies and *The Young Indiana Jones Chronicles*.

In UO, beggars, as previously mentioned, would come up and beg from you. When at sea, the tillerman, the faux-NPC built into the ship who served as a method of controlling the vessel, would tell sea stories drawn from a library, in order to pass the time. Will O'the Green in Legend would stop you at the crossroads and demand a toll; pay it, and he'd let you proceed.

In fact, this whole class of what we might call "environmental quests" was a bit of a showcase for NPCs. In Viceroyal Lima, a wagon would periodically get stuck in the mud; get enough players to push at the same time, and they could free it from the mud. If you found Big Jim in the back room of the Salty Dog, you could play a crude version of blackjack with him for money.

Faking you out

In EQ2, there's a collection of systems that gets called "the ecology system." It's actually, I believe, a set of handcrafted scripts that can be applied somewhat generically, primarily in the towns, to allow things like dogs chasing cats, that sort of thing. This isn't really an ecology, of course — rather, it's what I call stagecraft, much like billowing cloth and clever lighting replaces fire or water on a stage.

Stuff like dogs chasing cats is of course very very old stagecraft in the virtual worlds biz. Countless muds have had similar; in the Andes in medieval Peru on Legend, all the animals hunt each other appropriately, and some of them even venture into town. Jackdaw type birds sometimes steal baubles. And so on.

Stagecraft definitely has a huge place; not everything must be modeled to a high level of detail. My favorite system I have ever done along those lines is the nonhuman script in Ultima Online. As a primer, you may want to read "A Grammar of Orcish" by Yorick of Yew.[183]

> Based on my species, pick one of the following syllable libraries:
> * Orcish (heavy on the ughg gaghs)
> * Chittery (heavy on the kth chkhth)
> * Slithery (heavy on the ssiss sisshtsh)
> * Wispish (every consonant, plus the letter y)
>
> Also based on my species, set a length of words (in syllables) and a length of sentence (in words).
>
> Every once in a while, saySomething(with no parameters)
>
> If you hear text, you have a chance of calling saySomething(with the overheard text as a parameter)
>
> saySomething(text):
>
> if the passed in text has any of the following words: food, eat, gold, any of the city names, any of the virtue names, any of the major fictional character names like British or Blackthorn, words related to combat, words related to gameplay
>
> pick from the following list of other words: kill, eat, no afraid, scared, attack, hunt, ugly, puny, hate, love, etc.
>
> Build words up to sentence length. If random chance hits, insert one of the list of words instead, or one of the overheard words. End the sentence with a bit of punctuation: ? ! . or … (and capitalize sentences appropriately).
>
> Building words: grab random syllables from your syllable list, up to the word length.

This meant, of course, that if you were near a wisp, and happened to say the word "moongate," the wisp might respond with "Zthgtts zzkzyz moongate? Yjjkkjwh virtue shrine."

---

[183] https://uo.stratics.com/secrets/books/book_17.shtml has the text of the book, and it does actually have exactly the list of syllables used to build sentences in the orcish gibberish language.

This led to a sizable number of people believing a large number of urban myths about wisps, including that they tended to hang around healers, that they healed you, that they gave quests, that enhanced bardic abilities, and so on. From the Seekers of the Wisps conference:[184]

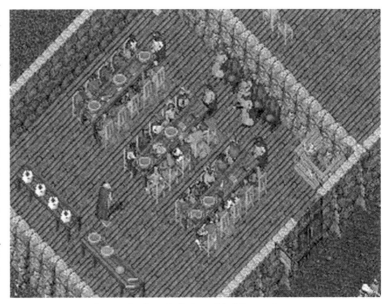

A screenshot from the Seekers of the Wisps conference

Khajja the Fang: On two occasions I have been helped by wisps. I was healed while fighting a gargoyle And once I was assisted by a wisp while fighting an orc mage. It casted offensive spells. That is all.

Aurora Sylvr says: Wisps have been known to do "unusual" things. We have had many reports of them aiding in unfair battles

Khajja the Fang says: So it is not unusual?

Aurora Sylvr says: It's rare.. but not completely unusual

I don't even want to think about how much dialogue we were saved from having to write thanks to this trivial little system.

Conclusion

Here's where I editorialize a little bit. We've tended to, over time, focus so much on the quest and kill aspect of these games that we've reduced down other elements in favor of this. We no longer have NPCs with schedules because it interferes with getting a quest promptly and killing things faster. We no longer have NPCs that give directions because a radar map is more convenient. We no longer have NPCs that

---

[184] This gathering helpfully kept a log of the event held at the Empath Abbey, Winery Convention Center within the game. Found at http://martin.brenner.de/ultima/uo/wispconf.html

crack a joke when you say something because we've removed NPCs hearing you altogether. We no longer have NPCs that take initiative because all interactions must be through menus. We no longer have NPCs that fool people into thinking they are maybe real because it's confusing.

But there's fun to be had in those things, and a sizable amount of humor to be mined, and springboards for much further development of other systems. There's storytelling (will no one have a thought for Sarah's pain and her desire for Burly Bob's killers to be brought to justice?).

Players objected quite a lot to seeing the fictional dressing stripped away from the modern quest dispenser NPCs in SWG, seeing them as actual metallic terminals. And yet, that's how our NPCs act today anyway. We should swing the pendulum back a little bit. I, and I think many other players, would gladly trade some inconvenience for a world that feels a little less like a pellet dispenser.

Security & novelty (handwritten)

Is it a game or is it a world?

UO is certainly focused on being a world first, and a game second. The social aspects also fall secondary to this. Hence the lack of easy-to-implement, obvious social enhancers such as long-distance communication, embedded mail system, and global chat spaces. All of these things are major social enhancers, but (usually) outside the fiction and reductive of a game OR world experience.

One reason btw why we went with this approach was that a focus on world tends to capture the "explorer" types as Bartle defines them, or in Bettelheim's terms, encourages open-ended play. Or to put it in other words, having a varied, evolving setting (even though it only evolves in that "middle layer" of NPCs/creatures/economy) encourages roleplay, encourages exploration, encourages alternate styles of achievement, and rewards it with changed circumstances rather than with a milestone.

The problem with "game" style design in a mud setting is that you run out of game. Games are finite. In a fiscal sense, you wanna keep folks around as long as possible, of course, to get their money, and the more "infinite" the game is, the better. Remember that most mudders only play for around 3-6 months, and even dinos tend to give up after 2 years or so.

One reason why there may be so many ["game-oriented" text muds] is that when you beat one, but have not exhausted the desire to play, you must find another, so that you have fresh milestones to conquer. Many muds try to compensate for this by adding levels, races, and other small milestones (beat the game as a thief! Beat it as an elf! We have 10,000 levels–at which point the milestones become insignificant or repetitive enough to be meaningless).

It is difficult for a player of any (using game in a broader sense now, as in game design, as opposed to "game"-style design, boy I hope that made sense) to make the transition between methods of approaching the game. For one thing, not many games have the flexibility to be played in truly different ways. One of the reasons why Sid Meier is a master game designer is that he has a knack for open-ended play that has milestones that can be freely ignored. Yet it is rare to see a Civ player who plays once for conquest and again for cooperation and again for mastery of a particular area and again for social stability etc etc etc… the game design supports it, the *individual player* does not. But the *audience* does.

…It's great for me to log into [UO] and try to go make a living as a tailor who wants to be a bard, have the character respected and in demand for the character's skills (everybody wants to look special, so everyone wants custom dyed clothes), be frustrated because there's a shortage of dyes in town, ponder getting backing to bring a trade caravan into Trinsic to see if I can make a killing on dye pots, and go kill a bear in the woods that I KNOW won't be there tomorrow. There's something oddly liberating about how different it feels to take for granted sim-based design rather than static environments. How many of you are working on this sort of thing in a text environment, where it could be pushed so much further than in graphics? (The possibilities boggle the mind there)… I'm curious, because I'd love to see what designs you come up with.

Is the future in smaller muds?

For the record, I think the future is in truly enormous muds that have lots of smaller embedded experiences in them.

I've seen this argument a lot lately, disenchantment with scale, essentially. The argument that online worlds aren't meant to be massive, because they just don't work when they're big. That's basically what you're arguing.

Recently I posted on mud-dev saying that the implicit promise of online worlds, as you say, is fantasy: being someone else somewhere else with other people. It's the wish-fulfillment.

I'd argue that the reason why online games keep getting bigger, in map size and in population, is simply because bigger holds out more promise to that essential wish. In that sense, it's almost a losing battle to fight it. The "dream" of online spaces, the one we've been collectively daydreaming about since Vernor Vinge wrote *True Names*, is one that's bigger than the real world in size, that has more people in it than the real world does.

I do understand the nichification desires. Everyone prefers being with people like them, who are doing things that they enjoy too. And many communities form like that. I'd argue they are all poorer for not knowing more of others, but I do understand that they certainly don't want to get overwhelmed or destroyed by those others. I myself would even be happy to see an online world where there were just those others that I enjoy playing with. But I must say that something in that also doesn't feel right. The scratch 'n' sniff of it is elitist, it's exclusionary, separatist. And I am still idealistic enough to think that it's good for different sorts of people to mingle because it makes things richer for all of them.

Managing that in a game, well, that's a tall order. Let me know if you figure it out.

This is where I am silly and idealistic and all that jazz. And I am sure someone somewhere is going to take offense at what I am about to say.

The pre-Trammel UO player towns decided to do something difficult. So difficult that most of them failed. They collaborated against the odds and built communities and established social standards by dealing with the world and the way it worked.

The post-Trammel UO cities are bunches of friends hanging out together.

I see a qualitative difference. As I said, I know the current player towns thrive and are loads of fun. But I also see them as very "casual" communities in some ways, and I don't see them as being empowered in any way. They have zero struggle to exist, and are fundamentally just cliques.

The thing that freaks me out about that is that, well, I don't *like* cliques. They are a phase we grow *out* of, as people. Online gaming today is full of cliques, and we encourage their formation.

Remember in grade school when your teachers told you it wasn't nice to leave Jimmy Four Eyes sitting at the other side of the cafeteria? When you first discovered that maybe those geeks in Chess Club had their uses? When you first realized that cheerleaders weren't all vapid hairspray heads? When you maybe first talked with a football player who was in Remedial English and realized the role that he was having to live out, for whatever reason?

I vividly remember all of those things, and to me, becoming an adult and being a good person is about learning to understand difference, about bridging gaps, about bringing people together. That's why I hammer so much on the point that you can't just label each other "jerks" or "RP nazis" with abandon, because all you're showing is how easy it is to label and how hard it is to actually *relate* to other people.

The line I've gotten in this newsgroup before is, "dude, they're just games." To which I say, there is *no* field of human endeavor in which the above is irrelevant.

I like player cities more than I like guilds because you can't quite control who ends up in a player city. I like player cities where people take stands for what they believe in and yes, struggle some for their beliefs, precisely because they learn something about themselves while doing so. And I'm hopelessly naive, idealistic, and stupid for thinking that these are the sorts of things that entertainment of all sorts teaches us, I suppose. Oh well. It's too fundamental to my sense of self to change *that* opinion, I'm afraid.

Taken from Usenet posts in early 2002. Honest, I like the Trammel towns just fine, and I don't mean to take away from what the people behind them have accomplished.

Postmortem

The following was written on the Ultima Online newsgroup in late June of 2000 as part of a lengthy thread where much about the development of UO was debated. A few paragraphs of it have come to be widely quoted, so I am reproducing it here.

A UO postmortem of sorts

So this (really long) thread really made me think tonight (and not just because Zaphkiel made me look like a math-impaired idiot, either. :) It made me question a lot of assumptions. Forgive this rambling post as I dissect what my thinking is on all this—I welcome the feedback.

First off, I have no patience for harassers, assholes, etc. They make my physically very angry when I see them, and during my whole time at OSI I was continually frustrated by the lack of action against them. I know many of you will not believe this statement, or will think it hypocritical, but I ask you to take it at face value.

When we started up UO, we were very naive about some things. For one thing, the game design was originally for a MUCH smaller world. We were asked to change it from a 300 player game to a 3000 player game around nine months before ship. All of our expectations were for not only a smaller simultaneous population, but also for a smaller player base in general—forecasts for sales were not very high, and the most successful online game to date at that time was Meridian 59. We expected to do better, but not by an order of magnitude.

A lot of the things we wanted to do were different from how muds had done things. We had both played and worked on muds with switches, and our experiences were universally lousy. Loopholes, ways to 'pk' without actually pk'ing, artificial restrictions on grouping and equipment use—all sorts of things that damaged immersion and physics and led to a lot of special-case code. We wanted to make a game that was more immersive, and that meant putting in a lot more freedoms into the game. We wanted to challenge players to act ethically, in the spirit of the Ultimas previous, without making it a set of quests that would be 'gamed' and up on a cheat website within a couple of weeks—and we didn't want that to happen not because it meant extra work making new quests all the time, but because it meant that ethics themselves were being "gamed" and were therefore meaningless. We were not prepared for the audience we got—this was evident not only in the game design, but if you recall, in the hardware infrastructure we had at launch.

We also wanted to get away from levels, believing that levels were a) an addictive but shallow game mechanic and therefore not good for overall game longevity, b) divisive of players in that you have to create level restrictions on stuff all over the place, c) poorly suited for other forms of gameplay, such as questing, social achievement, etc, and therefore restrictive of player experimentation with other things to do. There were other things we wanted to do to change things from the typical mud pattern (which is today best exemplified for all of you by EverQuest, since its design is *extremely* close to that of a standard well-evolved Diku mud).

Things that I have changed my mind on

- I used to think that a richer, more challenging game would be rewarded. I am no longer sure that is the case. I think that had we just made the same game we had made previously, only bigger, that UO would probably have done much better. The market, and more particularly the players, don't reward experimentation very much. More people are willing to do the same repetitive activity over and over again for the sake of getting a red polkadotted item to replace the green striped one, than are willing to engage in a broader range of activity. This is evident industry-wide, to my mind, and I am not saying to slam on EQ (especially not given that I work for Verant now). More as a comment on the audience in general—most people want mere entertainment, stuff that is easy to cope with. Stuff that doesn't make them ask questions of themselves. Witness TV and movies and books, all of which are mostly affirmations that "you're doing the right thing" or "whatever you do is normal compared to THIS."

- I like safe and wild zoning now. I really, really didn't. I have never seen an arena embedded in an otherwise safe game that was at all popular after three months, and the boundary conditions are truly a pain in the ass to deal with, leading to tons of exploits and problems. On top of that, safe zones tend to be way the heck more profitable for everyone including the people who really ought to be playing in the danger zones, so the danger zones tend to tank, just like separate PvP servers do.

- I used to think that you could reform bad apples, and argue with hard cases. I'm more cynical these days.

- Closed economies can't work.

- A sandbox is not enough.

- I used to think that people were willing to act communally for the good of the community. Now I know more about the Tragedy of the Commons and the Prisoner's Dilemma and think that people are mostly selfish. This isn't Ivory Tower theory gone looking for empirical evidence. It's experience gone looking for explanations.

Things that I still believe today

- Related to the last one—what I now know more about regarding how the Tragedy of the Commons and the Prisoner's Dilemma are reflected in the lack of communal action, has just reinforced my thoughts on the importance of the Other and so on. Simply put, I think that the things that drive community are: shared interest to get everyone in the same place; limited resources that you need to cooperate over so everyone gets enough; and an enemy you have to fight to keep out (and often, I think that I have served the role of said enemy in this newsgroup). Yes, communities form without the enemy, but they seem to fragment into cliques and manufacture an enemy within themselves (again, like this [newsgroup] many times!). Shared interest by itself doesn't really drive community. It drives acquaintanceships. And acquaintanceships are easy to come by, there's no need to make a whole honkin' game for them. As far as limited resources—we were stumbling about in the dark on this issue when we set up the game economy, when we did the size map we did... none of the games out there limit resources enough because they are all hung up on "having enough for everybody." Well, a game with enough for everybody is a game where you don't need other people very much. But on top of that, even though UO did limit resources more than most, it didn't provide any benefit for sharing them or working together to extract them. Miners were penalized for working near each other, for example, rather than encouraged to do so.

- Switches still suck. They damage immersion badly by requiring either the exclusion of or the fictional incoherence of all area-based effects; they do not handle many of the indirect forms of possible conflict (often fatal things, like blocking for example), leading to ways to get around the switch; they don't work very well as a way of mixing PvP and -PvP styles within one game because the grief players will just move on to alternate forms of causing grief while the PvPers will feel forced out of the game by all the restrictions...

- Levels still suck. I don't know what the complete replacement is, but I am troubled by how addictive the experiences we're making are (like, seriously addictive, ruin-your-life addictive) and I think levels are a large part of that. Plus I still find them divisive of players and a forced limit on interaction, however convenient they may be for advancement ladders. They are a bad model in terms of adding ongoing content to your game, in that you always have to add at the top end, and you have database deflation problems. Lastly, I have trouble fitting in many of the mechanics we were successful in putting into UO, such as crafting, onto standard level systems.

- There are a substantial amount of people out there who enjoy player vs player conflict of all sorts, who get crowded out of a game when it is completely safe, and go play elsewhere. And these people aren't necessarily assholes. But it is easy for them to become assholes if they feel put upon enough or if they think they can get away with it. I'm gonna disregard Bartle's Four, gonna ignore all statistics—this is just my opinion and my sense of things based on everything I have seen.

- I still believe that running servers themed around PvP or not is also a bit of a waste of time. The amount of wolves who want to play on a wolf-only server is way smaller than the total amount of wolves, and generally speaking, wolf-only servers are extremely underpopulated. You might as well devote those resources elsewhere.

- Someday we WILL be able to hand over the reins of policing to players. It will be seen as just a meta-game for those who are interested in it (and what's more, I bet the cops will be the same people we're currently turning into grief players with our limited mechanics). But right now, neither players nor developers are ready. I can't tell you how much I wish that in UO we had found a way to make the players able to do this, actually able to win against the bad guys—because I do regard those grief players and those rampant PKers (be they the "good" ones or the griefy ones) as the bad guys in this virtual world, far more so than the monsters. One of my biggest disappointments in UO is that we never found a way to have the good guys win.

- Thinking crazily into the future—the above point matters a lot to me because I do think that we will have virtual spaces where there's no admins to call. And it's a good idea to tackle the problems of not having admins while we still have admins to fall back on. As it is, the FBI can't do diddlysquat about most hacking cases, and it's gonna get worse when you do, say, remote medical monitoring via a virtual environment, and you get the future equivalent of PKed somehow. I can't even predict what shape this will take, but it will happen... I also know that a lot of players might even agree that this is something that needs tackled, just not in their backyard.

- Lastly, and feel free to call me a stupid idealist on this: I still believe we need to get all kinds of people into one game. That niche products are all well and good, but we already KNOW how to make those, and they aren't going to teach us anything interesting about ourselves. It's so easy to fall into ruts and niches in our real lives, and I want online worlds to offer us exotic experiences and interaction with people we wouldn't interact with otherwise, and a chance to try out lifestyles and worldviews we otherwise wouldn't have, a chance to try to solve problems that we find difficult to tackle in the real world. Otherwise, why bother making them? I am not that interested in them solely as games—games are all over the place, and there are plenty of narrowly focused communities out there. You can find a support group or hobbyist club for just about anything you want, but you're mostly going to find other people like you there. And I am not nearly as interested in how people interact with likeminded souls as I am in how to bridge gaps between people.

In an odd sort of summary...

Being safe from evil is, in my mind, an uneven tradeoff for the fact that you don't get to be heroes anymore, in that you can just opt out of fighting evil. It may be nobody wants to be heroes except when it doesn't count, when it isn't challenging, that people would rather fight "pretend evil" than the real thing, but I don't personally believe that. I still think people are better than that. I know this is an odd and probably controversial (perhaps even stupid) position to take, but it's how I feel. I think that the greatest value of interactive entertainment is when it engages you for real, and teaches you things for real. It is what made the Ultima series great. For me, the struggle to be good, to be one of the good guys, is where people were really challenged in UO, and it's not really a challenge that exists elsewhere. Sure, you can choose not to use ShowEQ, or choose not to auction spawn points in AC on eBay, but these are not as immediate and direct as dealing with people "virtually" face to face. Being safe from the only real evil in the game, and choosing not to fight it is, well, just fine, but it's also nothing that is going to teach you about where you stand. It's the difference between living the Virtues and, well, playing them in a computer game.

It kinda saddens me and scares me to write the above paragraph, because I know that many will misread my intent in writing it, will take bits out of context, will feel insulted. But I don't mean any of that by it. The failure was ours in setting up the game, for not making it possible enough to live the Virtues and establish by consensus a better place, a better society. This is why I proposed elsewhere in the thread letting people fall back on the code crutch of a safe zone once they had done it once, at least. You still get the experience of actually building a society, but after that the hard part (keeping it going) is handled for you. (Yes, townstones are at the top of my "wish we had gotten it into the game" list).

I can't think of any better experience to have in ANY game of ANY sort than for real people to work together against antisocial activity, selfish people, and other forms of creeping insidious evil, and WIN, and build something lasting and good. To work together and have fun together with types of people they never would have considered worth speaking to otherwise. And yes, to convert a few selfish jerks into better people along the way. If having this experience in a game means that they are more likely to dare to do it in real life instead of living in passivity, then I'll feel like something really important has been accomplished.

My greatest worry is that instead, we've inadvertently taught people to be bad as far as they can get away with. Or, far more troublesome, that Daddy will solve it for you and you can feel free to just complain about the problem from time to time, and ignore it. Right now, I have to believe that enough people learned the right lesson, because I DO see it every day in players of these games, and *especially* in players of UO, whom I have watched grow to a much greater awareness of social issues and community formation issues over the years, and become far better able to engage in high level discourse about the tough questions in MMORPGs.

But there's no doubt that it can be done better, and though giving up and just entertaining the "good people" may be better business or may be enough to bring in the money, it's not enough to make me feel like this is a field worth being in. It's about the other people. Dani Berry said, "At the end of the day, nobody ever regrets not having spent more time on the computer." That's why she made multiplayer games, so that the computers would be other people. That's why I want to make this sort of game too.

Hopefully this lengthy post puts some of my replies in this thread into context. Flame away.

UO's influence

I never played UO, so not knowledgeable. Maybe a routine question, but how do you think *Ultima Online* pushed the genre forward?

This is a big question.

I think we should start with a look at what the world was like in 1995, when the project was formally launched. Most people connected to the Internet via modem, and many of them were on 14.4k or 28.8k speeds. The 56K modem didn't come out until 1998.

For comparison, my cable Internet at home gets 70.7Mbps for downloads. That's 70,700k per second, versus 14k or 28k. The bandwidth difference is almost 2,500 times as much, if we look at the 28.8k modem. And that's not counting speeds – ping times everywhere are quite a bit faster than they used to be. Old routers used to add 20ms just from you going through them, and getting 250ms ping time to anywhere was considered normal and if sustained, pretty good.

Before this, we used Lynx, which was a text-based browser.

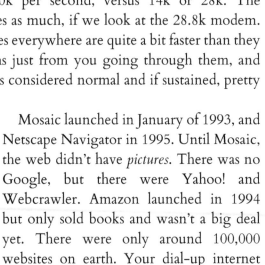

Mosaic launched in January of 1993, and Netscape Navigator in 1995. Until Mosaic, the web didn't have *pictures*. There was no Google, but there were Yahoo! and Webcrawler. Amazon launched in 1994 but only sold books and wasn't a big deal yet. There were only around 100,000 websites on earth. Your dial-up internet service provider fees would be in the range of $20-30 a month.

Internet discussion happened mostly on Usenet, though there were some fledgling Internet forum BBSes, and of course things like The WELL[185] and discussions on the many closed online services like Prodigy, America OnLine, and CompuServe. This latter one charged by the hour — $5 to $16 *per hour* – and was flailing enough that AOL bought it. (Prodigy had pioneered flat rate pricing a few years earlier)..

Gaming, of course, was alive and well, including online gaming. The top games in 1997 included *Final Fantasy VII, Goldeneye 64, Castlevania, Star Fox 64, Parappa the Rapper, The Curse of Monkey Island, Age of Empires, Mario Kart 64, Fallout, X-Wing vs Tie Fighter, Theme Hospital*, and *Total Annihilation*. Max game resolution, if you had a powerful rig, was generally 800×600.

During the development of UO, we carefully watched the development and release of *Diablo* and heaved a sigh of relief when we realized it was a graphical version of *Rogue* or *NetHack*, rather than

Prodigy streamed each screen down as an image, even the text ones

a persistent world (today people toss around "roguelike" as a common term. It didn't use to be). I remember a bunch of us gathering around one computer to play the demo version. Its graphics were much better than what we were already committed to, but its multiplayer was very limited. "That is forbidden in the demo" is still an occasional catchphrase in our house – our research sessions always ended there at the last doorway in the single-level demo.

Quake had come out in 1996, and many of the art team played it on the company LAN in the afternoons. Most online gameplay was LAN play, in fact; services like DWANGO (launched in 1994) allowed LAN games to be played over the Internet using a dedicated dial-up service that served as a matchmaker. Around 1995 to 1996 TEN and MPath (aka MPlayer, and eventually GameSpy) showed up, and started

---

[185] https://en.wikipedia.org/wiki/The_WELL

bundling games with LAN play into a subscription that let you play them online via the Internet. These services varied in price from $30 a month to $30 a year, on top of ISP fees, but by and large didn't offer much if any persistent world gaming (TEN had *Dark Sun Online*[186] which came out in '96).

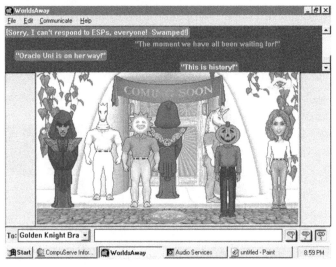

WorldsAway was derived off of Habitat

There were MMOs, for sure. You can read over the timeline[187] to see just how many preceded *Ultima Online* – quite a lot, particularly if you count all the text-based worlds, as I do. Simutronics had its text-based MUDs running, such as *DragonRealms* and *Gemstone.* Mythic was their competitor. *WorldsAway,* a version of *Habitat,* was on CompuServe, as were *Islands of Kesmai* and *Air Warrior.* The aforementioned *Dark Sun Online* and also *Lineage* were played in the UO offices during the development process as well, though they were both in pretty rough state.

And of course, *Meridian 59* beat UO to market as well. Sometime in 1995 or so, Mike Sellers[188] logged into *LegendMUD*, and I

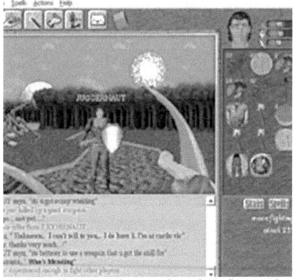

Meridian 59, like EverQuest after it, started out with a small game window with inventory and chat boxes around it

---

[186] https://en.m.wikipedia.org/wiki/Dark_Sun_Online:_Crimson_Sands
[187] https://www.raphkoster.com/games/the-online-world-timeline/
[188] Co-founder of Archetype Interactive, anmd lead designer of its game Meridian 59, Mike went on to work for years more in the online games space.

toured him around. If I was online, I often greeted newbies personally, and if they were people involved in creating MUDs, I would offer to tour them around the game, showing off the many things that it did that were different from the run of the mill. After the tour, Mike talked to me about a possible job on *Meridian 59*, and I turned him down because Origin had already made an offer. I recommended Damion Schubert[189] for it instead.

Lineage, when I first tried it, consisted of one house, that you stepped out of onto a killing field and basically died immediately. *DSO* was much larger, but had some sort of turn-based combat. If you got hit, you were put into the turn sequence for *everyone in the fight*; this resulted in a blob of dozens of players waiting a half hour to swing once or try to escape the fight. (I honestly don't know whether this was a bug at the time or what – I never played it again). Sierra had launched *The Realm* in 1996; it had a side view, and each fight was actually an "instance" – when you engaged in combat with another entity, outsiders saw a cloud with fists and whatnot poking out, and you were sent to another screen to do battle.

Ultima Online COULD have been DragonSpires, but Origin decided to build their own

As Richard Garriott, Dr. Cat, and others tell it, **the idea for an online, multiplayer version of the Ultima series had been around for quite some time.** There was an abortive deal with Sierra to create a "Multima." Dr. Cat, a long-time Origin veteran who had left the company, was interested enough in online gaming that he created a game called *DragonSpires* which was way ahead of its time, and the predecessor to *Furcadia*.[190] Richard and Starr Long went to the executive greenlight board at Electronic Arts multiple times trying to get money to fund a prototype, and after being turned down each time, finally got a check for $150,000 or $250,000 (I have heard varying figures) directly from Larry Probst, the CEO.

---

[189] Damion was the first person I ever met on a MUD, and went on to design roles on *Meridian 59, Shadowbane, Star Wars: The Old Republic,* and more.

[190] Furcadia is the longest continuously running MMO. See https://en.m.wikipedia.org/wiki/Furcadia

When they went looking for people make the game, they ended up having to look outside the company, and the place to look turned out to be MUDs. I've told the story elsewhere of how they found Rick Delashmit, and from there they found my wife and I as designers, where we had cut our teeth in online world design on *LegendMUD*.

LegendMUD soft-launched in '93 and officially Feb. 14th, '94. At least five Legend players were involved with UO & the early MMO industry.

The state of the art in MUDs was quite different from what was going on in online services. Most of the games on the online services were basically hack and slash with quests. Most of the most popular MUDs were also hack n slash, the Diku style of game, which due to its hard-coded nature didn't have much in the way of interactivity with objects and NPCs. *LegendMUD*, and the mud we had played before it, called *Worlds of Carnage*, were different from other Dikus. Thanks to an embedded scripting system, they had much more interactive worlds more akin to what was happening in the MOO and LPMud circles.

In MOOs, MUSHes, and LP's, the use of scripting and domain-specific languages had opened up enormous potential for virtual worlds. Some of these kinds of worlds handed over coding capabilities to end users. Some didn't, but because they were dramatically easier to mod than a Diku, had all sorts of experimental things going on. Bear in mind we're talking text-based games running on computers far less powerful than your typical smartwatch, but MUDs were exploring design ideas such as

- Player driven voting systems and player governments.
- Procedurally created zones.
- "Roomless" worlds where the descriptions of locales were procedurally generated based on what landmarks were in nearby coordinates.
- Agent-based AI systems where creatures had more autonomy and a bit of an ecology.
- Spellword languages for dynamically creating magic.
- Roleplay-mandatory worlds with permanent death.

The original UO logo, before marketing. I still have a team t-shirt with this on it.

LegendMUD itself was notable for having things like vehicles you could drive or fly, ships you could sail, furniture you could sit in, a rich chat system with moods and adverbs, a spell-word based magic system, an herbalism system that used the pharmacological properties of real world herbs, an out of character lounge anyone could teleport to, and more.

A lot of the discussion on features like this came from the fabled MUD-Dev mailing list, run by the redoubtable J. C. Lawrence. And it was on MUD-Dev where the designers and programmers of *all* the above games ended up gathering and swapping ideas and debating the future of online worlds. **Out of this ferment came *Ultima Online*.**

When we posted up the first FAQ for UO on our skunkworks domain owo.com ("Origin worlds online") in 1995 or early 1996, a black website with little suns and llamas on it, and a giant long list of promises written in text, it was not only the first website ever created within Electronic Arts, but it also was a bit… ambitious. (Alas, the text seems lost to history).

Given all the above context, here are some things that *Ultima Online* attempted, and mostly pulled off.

I'll start with **the least remarkable, which was pure scale.** A tile-based seamless world that was 4km on a side, with multiple biomes. Further, one that supported multiple floors, in 2d isometric, and 3d terrain texture mapping. Although the art wasn't as detailed as *Diablo*, this was something they (and most any 2d game competitor) simply couldn't do. Being able to walk upstairs or into a basement in a building in game was startling at the time. Having actual 3d sloping terrain of any sort, likewise; most 2d games still faked elevation changes with optical illusions.

This map was enormous, for the time. So was the art asset load. There were sixty-one unique models for creatures, and each, though modeled in 3d, was output into sprite frames – 15 frames per animation, in eight directions. Forty-eight weapons. And hundreds of small items of many sorts, many of them interactive. In text games, you see, it had been easy to just invent more items, and we wanted that freedom in UO.

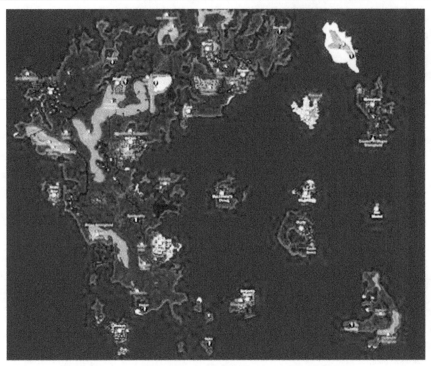

A tile-accurate map of UO, reduced by about 50% or so. Not including dungeons.

Consider that the average number of items you could pick up or interact with in other graphical MMOs at the time was, for most locations, zero.

And all this was in service of supporting 2500+ people at once in a given world, literally ten times what other worlds typically supported. (Linux at the time even came out of the box with a limit of 250 or so file descriptors). More people in one world, interacting. If anything, the map was *too small*, which led J. C. Lawrence to call the game "a hothouse."

Scale was one thing, but a key difference in UO was that this stuff was actually used in more than one way. To my knowledge no previous 2d RPG had ever shown all your equipment on your character in game, but it was something that we took for granted, coming from the text MUD world. We came up with a means of mapping color ramps to grayscale pixels on the items, termed "hues," which allowed us to take every item in the game and not just tint it, but actually change it to have multicolored patterns. This was applied to all the clothing, many of the creatures, all the armor and weapons and hair and skin. (The art team was not happy about this at all – we had to make the case to them that giving the power to the players was critical). UO was the single most varied fantasy world ever created, when it launched.

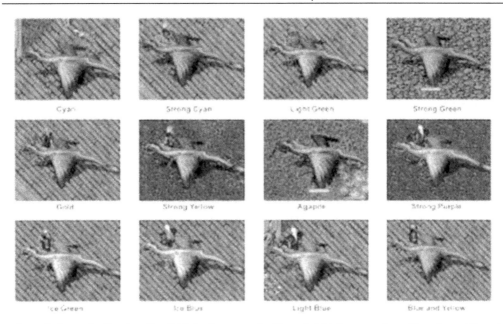

An excellent example of hue-based "partial tinting" — any parts of the sprite left in true grayscale would map to a palette, and any parts not gray would stay in original colors.

Don't underestimate what seems like a trivial thing. Dye tubs existed in the world, which spawned with random hues. Dye tubs could be copied. Players could find objects that spawned in the world with rare colors, copy them to a dye tub, and then dye clothes with that rare color, cornering the market on a specific shade of green. **There was an** *economy just for colors* **in** *Ultima Online.* This led to lily-white wedding dresses, guilds that color-coordinated their uniforms, a pimp named Fly Guy on the docks with a purple feathered hat, and much more. When a bug in the system created "true black" as a hue (a palette with only #000000 black in it)[191] it instantly became a highly coveted color that led to mass murder and economic mayhem. Eventually, I applied colors to metallic ores, and this led to a whole metal quality system as well. It's not an exaggeration to say that the simple hues system enabled enormous amounts of player dynamics that frankly, still aren't seen in most MMOs today.

The world was also varied in behavior. The "resource system" has been written about extensively, and didn't survive to launch. But the underlying data for it remained, and served as the basis for all sorts of simulation. Every patch of water was something you could fish in. You could shear the wool off of sheep, and it grew back. You had to rotate through stands of lumber, as you exhausted the harvestable wood.

---

[191] See http://www.uoguide.com/Black_Dye_Tub

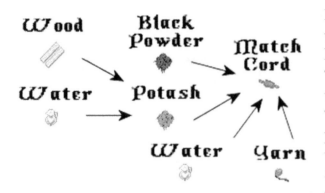

Name your cow Millie, milk her, then when you chose, slaughter her, and you got meat filets – "filet of Millie." You could take that to make a steak or a meat pie. "A meat pie of Millie." For a brief period, you could do that with the meat from another player. Scissors cut cloth. Knives could whittle wood. Looms made cloth, if you had the flax or the wool. Just about everything was craftable — a current list for blacksmiths is pages long.[192]

Lights turned on and off. NPCs moved about, and at first, closed up their shops at night. Bulletin boards in the towns weren't static dressing, but message centers where players could post notes for one another. Town criers shouted out the latest news, and you could ask any NPC for directions to landmarks. Every NPC was born with a unique name and a rolled-up personality, and they could die and never come back. Fruit trees gave fruit. When you sailed around on a ship, the tillerman told shaggy dog sea stories. The books in the game didn't just drop random bits of backstory – they did, of course,[193] but you could also make or buy a blank book, and type in your own story, and then that would be added to the possible books that could spawn, and could appear anywhere in the world.

You could create a microphone crystal, and link it to a speaker crystal, and use it to provide loudspeakers for an event. A chain of explosive potions would set off a chain reaction, like a fuse burning

The "Baja Council" all wearing antlers, in uniform

---

[192] http://www.uoguide.com/Blacksmithy
[193] See a collection of all of these here: https://uo2.stratics.com/lore-and-history/books/. I wrote most of the original in-game books.

down. You could drop things on the ground, and spell out words, or leave a lure of stuff for creatures or animals to pick up. Monsters looted *you*, if they were victorious. Even when they spoke gibberish, they did so by listening for words you said, and repeated them back to you, which tricked many a player into thinking there was a real language to learn.

The simulation ran deep in UO, so much so that *even when the main simulation was turned off*, the game still ran as a giant simulated fantasy world. When you look at a typical house screenshot, realize that *everything in that house* was interactive to some degree, even if it was minor. You pretty much have to come forward in time to *Dwarf Fortress* or *Minecraft* to find something comparable in a major game.

This sort of thing unlocked higher order features.

The Golden Brew Players, a theater troupe, meet Lord British

Theater troupes could memorize plays, take over empty stages, and go on tour performing Shakespeare. Costuming was a thing. So were player cities creating their own guards in uniform – players volunteering in shifts to protect homes against playerkillers.

Guilds in UO could go to war with one another, could own a castle, and share a hoard. They could grant titles to the members lower down, and at the start even had a democratic voting system for leadership. Guilds prior to UO were a much simpler affair, and in most online games the list of possible guilds was hardcoded into the game at the outset.

Not that you needed a guild war; UO famously permitted anyone to kill anyone outside of the boundaries of town. **The amount of griefing, playerkilling, and bad behavior in UO was legendary,** from boring ambushes to boobytrapped chests that blew up in your face to magical gates to tiny islands leaving you stranded in the ocean. This cost us an ungodly number of subscribers, and led to many negative reviews early on.

335

A player house in UO

Housing in earlier room-based games was quite a different affair, if it existed at all. In UO, the placement of actual structures on the physical map at 1:1 scale with the rest of the world meant real estate value was a real thing, with home values, lack of building space, and much more. This is a thorny enough problem that most worlds back away from it now, because of problems with overbuilding. Eventually, UO allowed full Sims-style ability to design your house within its plot.

Shopkeepers in UO launched with fluctuating prices and inventory based on local supply and demand. And supplies certainly did fluctuate! Early on there was a failed closed economy, but even with the more typical faucet-drain economy that UO moved to, there was enough there to basically create the market for eBayed virtual goods, as well as constantly changing prices within the game itself. This player-driven economy saw players set themselves up as commercial kingpins, not just as combatants.

Of course, players could just hire an NPC and set it their house, stock it with goods, set prices, and hang a sign out front (yes, you

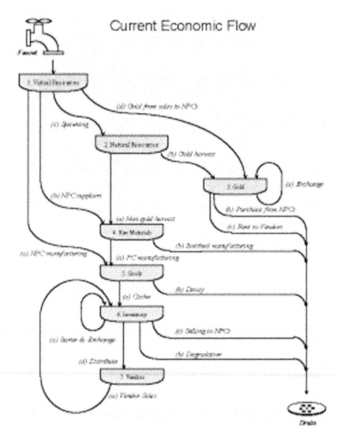

An economic analysis of UO by Zach Booth Simpson and a few academic economists

The UORares rune library on the Atlantic server.

could actually hang a sign… there were about twenty to choose from, and you could select a name for the shop). Players built their small commercial empires this way.

And **that variety in play was everywhere.** Bards whose music calmed angry monsters. Fishermen who pulled up messages in bottles, eventually with treasure maps inside. (When you got to the destination, the game spawned an entire encounter for you; this concept, called a "dynamic point of interest," allowed the creation of entire orc camps, buildings and all, on the fly, then cleaned up later, leading to a more dynamic encounter map in general). Blacksmiths whose mark on a sword was a big deal, and whose popular smithies would have lines of people outside, because they were the only one that players trusted to repair their sword adequately. Mages could learn spells and inscribe them on scrolls and sell them to others. Museums of "recall runes" existed – teleportation depots, basically, where runes with far flung locations encoded into them sat on display for mages to come to and open mystical gates to other locales.

You learned by doing – and early on, by watching, until we had problems with people inadvertently learning stuff without wanting to – similar to the Elder Scrolls games. This meant practice yards were full of people swinging away at training dummies and practicing archery. Because the power spread between players was actually fairly tight, you didn't get left behind by others out-leveling you. In fact, a common tactic to take down advanced playerkillers was to go after then in *naked mobs* because sheer numbers could outweigh the power of even the best-equipped player. Gear wasn't destiny – everything broke, decayed, wore away. Food spoiled. Stuff could only be repaired so far, and truly rare things were safely put in the safety deposit at the bank rather than risked out in the wild.

Don't think that this was all an accident. **This was consciously designed to be this sort of emergent world, carefully, skill by skill and object by object.** There were happy surprises and unpleasant ones, but interdependence, economy, ecosystem, player types and roles – all of this was actively designed for and we attempted our best to anticipate behaviors. Theater troupes? Rune libraries? Real estate pricing? These were surprises that we *expected* to happen, in a sense. Even the weird ones, like people dropping enough objects in one tile to cause a DDOS attack on players who got close, or people piling up chairs until they could climb onto a player house roof, break in, and loot it dry.

All of this was prodded along by admin intervention: gamemasters who participated in the game, running events, and volunteers who helped them. Large-scale roleplay events and competitions happened all the time, from sporting events (wrestling matches!) to game-wide scavenger hunts. Players dressed up as orcs and actually took over the orc fort, and eventually we just let them run it instead.

This community was actively managed — at first, by me and a few others, then eventually by a team, at a time when the state of the art was .plan files. Short stories and poetry both from the players and from the team were posted on the website – this is part of how Scott Kurtz, today an award winning cartoonist and creator of *Table Titans* and *PVPOnline*,[194] got his start. For a while, when we saw that the player-run forum sites were growing too popular and

Skull the Troll, from the PVPOnline comic strip, was originally a UO monster

therefore getting too large a bandwidth bill, we quietly hosted them for the players on our own servers. Those sites grew into key parts of IGN and other such major game news sites – we never got a cut.

And every update, we posted up "here's what we are thinking of changing and

---

[194] Visit his websitre here: http://pvponline.com/

Ladies and gents, the Multima team.
Clockwise from top left: Rick Delashmit,
Edmond Meinfelder, Clay Hoffman, Starr
Long (in hiding), Micael Priest, Andrew
Morris, Scott Phillips, Kristin Koster and Raph
Koster (and friend).

This was most of the original core team that conceptualized and built the basic game.

why." There would be an open IRC chat forum, called the House of Commons,[195] where players could join and make their case for different changes, advocate for specific fixes, and in general argue with the developers. Then changes moved through a regular process, from In Concept to In Development and thence to In Testing and deployment, in a transparent open development process that provided visibility on everything we could.

All of this, for a flat monthly free, on the open Internet. And that was a major business shift of its own – even *Meridian 59* didn't launch with that straightforward a model.

If at this point you are comparing all this in your head to *World of Warcraft* and wondering whether UO had any influence at all, I think that's fair. Reading player stories from *Ultima Online* today has this strange quality, where you'd swear that no game could ever have offered that sort of freedom and depth and detail... because no game today does.

Even at the time, competitors ran ads saying "why play to bake bread?" UO was consciously an attempt to create a parallel fantasy universe in which you could *live*: be it as a craftsperson running a tidy shop, an adventurer deep in the bowels of a dungeon, an itinerant storyteller who made her living picking pockets and roleplaying, or even an explorer who was trying to mark the furthest regions of the map.

Today, if you point at the philosophical heirs of UO, you find them in unexpected places:

- *Minecraft*, which has quite a similar underlying resource system, similarly

---

[195] Modeled on the same sort of chats we had held on LegendMUD, these were held for twelve years (!) and are available here: https://uo.stratics.com/uohoc/index.shtml

leveraged for crafting. This is possibly via *Wurm Online* and *Runescape*, both games heavily inspired by UO.

- Survival games, like *PUBG*, which recapture that sense of utter fear involved in leaving town. UO was a full PVP world, where anyone could attack anyone outside the confines of town.

- Games like *Animal Crossing*, where that feeling of an ongoing world that lives without you, where you can live a peaceful existence picking fruit and catching fish and decorating a house, remains intact. Even in Facebook games.

- A game like *Eve Online* outright stated an intention to be "UO in space" when it started up.

Were these directly inspired by UO? I don't know. Housing and crafting and the notion that there are many ways to play the game were definitely things that spread outwards from UO, just as they were taken in their turn from ideas on MUD-Dev and text muds and early graphical games. The eBay market for UO goods created gold farming, and eventually that led to the free-to-play microtransaction model, through a twisty chain of influence.

But it's impossible to make clear claims. As I mentioned, there were many fellow travelers, on many other projects, and we all swapped ideas and gathered for dinners at GDC. In many senses, UO had almost no "firsts" – you can always find an antecedent for something it did, somewhere, probably for everything I've listed above. Convergent evolution means many of the innovations were doubtlessly invented by others as well. At the same time, it's hard to picture some of these things spreading as they did, in UO's absence.

I could go on. Just to launch UO, we had to invent early forms of database sharding (the term likely comes from UO), pioneer the large-scale use of VPNs, pioneer character customization, invent seamless multiserver clusters, basically invent modern community management, invent the now-ubiquitous codes on cards for accounts or payment... many were simultaneous inventions, but we basically had to do a whole bunch of new things. You see that pic of the core team up there? The average person in that picture was in their mid or early twenties, on their first game industry job.

No doubt as a consequence of that: **many of the things that were tried in UO didn't work.** They broke under unforeseen player stresses – no one had ever designed for thousands of people playing at once in a simulated economy; or they collapsed when the (puny by today's standards) computers we used as servers couldn't handle the load. Many were simply bad ideas, as our understanding of player psychology and behaviors evolved. UO chased the industry away from player-vs-player combat for *years*. To this day, Richard warns people away from trying to tackle a simulated ecology (not me, though, I'm still determined and stubborn). It's important to realize that UO was a profoundly broken experience in many many ways.

And of course, since players managed to reverse-engineer most of the game in short order, just about everything that worked, or didn't work, was worked over, redesigned, and recreated by players in the hundreds upon hundreds of "gray shards" created since 1998.[196] At least three server codebases,[197] complete with scripting languages, compatibility with the official client, and, at peak, *hundreds of thousands* of players, outstripping the official servers. When I got to China for the first time, I learned that UO was well-known there, despite never having launched officially in the country; it was because so many gray shards were run there that it helped create a generation of MMO developers. For a while, UO was probably the world's most popular user-run virtual world codebase, and thus a true heir to the MUD tradition.

But in the end, if you ask how it pushed the genre forward, I think the answer is that **it did so by offering a dream**, a dream that *even today people compromise on and don't offer*. This idea of a true parallel world with its own life, its own ongoing history, one that doesn't pander or make concessions for tutorials, bolted-on quests, pay-to-win gear schemes, or any of the other niceties of the business of games… the idea that "what if you just actually modeled another world, in as much detail as possible, and let players loose?"

That's something that frankly, still isn't really on offer. So to answer your question: *Ultima Online* pushed the genre forward by providing an early Camelot, a shining city on a hill that technology wasn't really yet able to build. It was, and remains, aspirational. It started retreating away from its own lofty goals almost immediately upon launch, and nobody else has managed to make something quite like it.

---

[196] The website ServUO (https://www.servuo.com/shards/) maintains an index of these. As of April 2018, it still lists 42 of them.

[197] Among them ServUO, RunUO, Sphere, UltimaPHP (a port to PHP!), and more. A list at http://www.uox3.org/history/timeline.shtml shows many I never heard of.

So that imperfect, barely functional, insane thing: that's all we got. It's twenty years in the past – how implausible! **And somehow, it still feels like something always twenty more years in the future.**

The original painting done by the Hildebrandt Brothers for the Ultima Online box cover

The End of the World

At the end of the UO beta, we had a very lengthy beta event to better explain the storyline. It was one of the few events that I've gotten to write for an MMO, and I jumped in with short stories and everything!

The death of a shard

The premise of UO, now immortalized in the terms "shards," was that when the evil wizard Mondain was defeated and the Gem of Immortality shattered, that copies of the Ultima universe existed in each of the shards of the gem. In effect, Britannia had grown into a multiverse; something that there was some precedent for in the earlier standalone games.

The overarching plot was that an evil force (the Guardian) was transforming each shard into Shadowlords, attempting to destroy the universe; the Time Lord was trying to stop this by collapsing the shards back into one world again. This would, of course, result in the disappearance of all the people who existed in only one world.

This lay at the core of the disagreement between Lord British and Lord Blackthorn in UO. Blackthorn argued for chaos, because it preserved the life of the universe he knew; Lord British worked to heal the multiverse, knowing that millions would cease to exist, for the greater good. Once fast friends, they ended up on opposing sides of a fierce political battle. This was all related in "My Book" by Sherry the Mouse,[198] the mouse living in the walls of Lord British's bedchamber:

> "Such simplicity to the game, Blackthorn," mused Lord British, idly brushing one finger against the board. "Black and white, each to its own color, as if life were so simple. What think you?"
>
> Blackthorn sat heavily on a hassock beside the chess table. "I think that matters are never so simple, my liege. And that I would regret it deeply if someone, such as

---

[198] See https://uo.stratics.com/secrets/books/book_21.shtml

a friend, saw it thus."

Lord British's eyes met his. "Yet sometimes one must sacrifice a pawn to save a king."

Lord Blackthorn met his gaze squarely. "Even pawns have lives and loves at home, my lord." Then he reached out for a pawn, and firmly moved it forward to squares. "Shall we play a game?" he asked.

These matters reached a head when the beta was ending. A short story[199] was posted on the website explaining recent spawns that had appeared, crystals that were showing up on the ground around the world.

The images shifted to follow one of the falling lights, closing in on it, as it was revealed as a falling crystal, that falling through the air gathered heat and light to it, shrouding it in contrails of cloud and smoke. It fell to the earth, and as it approached the ground farms became visible, and with the farms the crops being plowed in a runneled field. They saw a bull placidly pulling at a yoke, and a wagon behind it, a young farm-boy perched on the wagon, idly chewing on an apple core.

And further did the crystal fall, as the startled farm-boy watched, until it embedded itself with a thundering crash in the road just ahead of him, throwing up mud and rock with a sound like a thunderclap. The bull snorted and broke free of the yoke, panic showing in its rolling eyes, and the wagon overturned. As the flames began to dwindle back down, the images shrank, until Lord British was barely able to see the lad crawl out from under his broken wagon, and see the boy's eyes widen as he saw the crystal in its crater in the road before him, a crystal that embedded in it had a refracted image of a planet–Britannia itself…

This led to an event whereby we asked players to collect as many crystals as possible — a variant of the old MUD Easter Egg hunt game — there were six crystals to collect, and when you looked close at them, they had clues that pointed to their connection with the Shadowlords from the standalone games. We knew full well what would result from this: wholesale slaughter as pk'ers roamed the land stealing crystals from one another to collect the set of six. Which led into the very next story,[200] wherein a cast of characters were able to shed light on the world's events, reacting to what the players were doing:

"Rough night?" pretty Alyssa asked. She was the newest of the tavern wenches here at the Blue Boar, and her dark hair curled around her head constrained by a bonnet.

Galias sighed. "Rough indeed. All these hunters seeking after these crystals…"

Alyssa shuddered. "None too nice a group, I think!"

---

[199] https://uo.stratics.com/secrets/h_b01.shtml

[200] https://uo.stratics.com/secrets/h_b02.shtml

"Nay, these are the nobles of the realm, the greatest of heroes!" Galias said sarcastically.

"Noble? Pfui." Alyssa twitched her skirt out of the way of a grasping drunk and cleverly happened to spill some ale on the drunk's face, then nudged him with her foot to roll him under the table. "I've never seen a more ragged or desperate group in my life."

Galias looked around him, and soberly said, "Yet I spoke truth, Alyssa." The men around him had the look of the hunted, not the hunters. Their faces were drawn and exhausted. Many of them clutched pouches and packs to their chests, and they checked them compulsively, peering inside for the crystal he knew must be within. "These are in fact the flower of Britannia–the greatest heroes, the noblest of adventurers. Now they have the look of criminals and killers, as if they were hag-ridden or possessed. I think these crystals are indeed something dark and powerful."

Alyssa giggled. "Your song was mere fiction, minstrel! Do not ascribe to thy art more than it doth possess!"

"Nay, Alyssa, I am serious. When he was drunk, Nystul did tell me a story he had heard as a child, about evil lords of shadow with the names that are inscribed on these crystals... ow!"

Alyssa had delivered a sharp kick to his ankle. "I say you are just fantasizing, Galias. The crystals are harmless. You hear? Harmless! Do you want this ale or not?" She sloshed a mug full and set it down in front of him with a thud, then flounced away.

Galias stared into the ale, and wondered if he would ever see his friend Nystul again, for the clouds were heavy that night and the lightning flickered with strobing colors over Lord Blackthorn's keep.

He fingered his lute idly, then grimaced and took it into his lap to tune it, and soon was singing again for the patrons, wistful ballads of summer love and flower necklaces.

Alyssa watched him from the bar, and from time to time ducked into the pantry, where she crouched and shifted jars on a shelf. There, glinting despite the lack of light, lay a crystal shard, and she ran her fingers over it, tracing the name engraved in runes upon it, eyes lost in its transparent depths.

As the night wore on, she visited it more often. As the night wore on, more fights broke out. A lute was broken. A man was killed. As the night wore on, she thought maybe she heard the crystal whispering to her as she lay abed.

Lord British and Blackthorn, and the court mage Nystul, worked to destroy the crystals, throwing them into a moongate to dispose of them. But what they were unwittingly doing by opening that red moongate was giving passage to the Guardian to enter their shard. The results were disastrous: Nystul was left in a coma, Lord British was touched by the Guardian's finger and ended abed with a pulsating evil boil upon his chest, and Chuckles the court jester found one tiny crystal left in the wreckage.

The event now changed — the goal was to save Lord British's life. Reagents were needed, including the rare necromantic reagents which were in the game but served no gameplay purpose. But we had rigged the game: unbeknownst to anyone, there was one reagent that we didn't spawn. The game was unwinnable. Players nonetheless spread out, trying to win this event as they had the last one.

And then another story[201] was posted. And it ended... badly.

> Finally, he stood outside on the balcony. Below him were apple trees, the scent of their blossoms rising to his nostrils, full of promise. Past them, flowerbeds, and the mighty walls of his castle. Beyond them, the twinkling lights of the stores and homes and taverns of Britain, and the stars reflected in the moat, bobbing gently like small candles set afloat. The night was clear and sharp like a splash of cold water. All was tranquil, and the moon presided gracefully over a world asleep, content under its blanket of sky.
>
> Lord British sagged against the marbled rail. His fingers caressed the cold stone, feeling the roughness where his hands had rested many a year. I have not done so badly, he thought idly to himself. It has been a good life.
>
> He thought back to years gone by, when his realm consisted of a small land as yet surrounded by enemies. He thought back to Lord Robere and the fearful battle that stained a plain with blood and left behind a desert. He thought of nights playing chess, and of leaving crumbs for the mouse who lived in the hole in his wall.
>
> Good indeed, he thought. It has been good indeed.
>
> Then the figure moved out from the shadows behind him, an elongated object in its hand, raised to strike. Lord British, alerted by some sixth sense, turned just before it struck.
>
> The struggle was brief, as the two grappled. "You–!" Lord British gasped. "Give me that–!"
>
> "At last!" hissed the other figure.
>
> Between them they held the object, then Lord British fell back as the other figure, cloaked and dark, pushed him ever further back.
>
> With a cry, Britannia's lord toppled from the balcony. Past the apple trees, onto the hard flagstones of the walkway two stories below. There was a wet smack when he landed.
>
> An owl hooted, somewhere. A few moments later, the cloaked figure emerged from the castle proper, and knelt beside Lord British for a moment. Then he stood again, and darted off, back into the castle.
>
> Then another figure came out, and likewise knelt beside the fallen ruler. Then he carefully gathered up the inert body, and carried it inside.

---

[201] https://uo.stratics.com/secrets/h_b03.shtml

The smell of apple blossoms was exquisite, and Britain slumbered on.

Lord British wasn't dead, but now the necromantic reagents were badly needed. As the players scurried around failing to find all six, a short play was played out on the global announcement channel, visible to all players: Lord Blackthorn, revealed finally as a loyal friend, desperately tending Lord British; the crystal that Chuckles absconded with, revealed as the key to the portal that enabled the Guardian to enter, and Chuckles himself as the possessed assassin who tossed British over the balcony edge (sorry, Chuck Bueche, wherever you are… I last saw him at a dinner at GDC or E3 a couple of years ago)…

In the end, British died. Blackthorn died. The Guardian manifested fully in the world.

```
Guardian: BEHOLD, PETTY LORD, AS MY SHADOWLORDS WALK AND DAEMONS
SPAWN TO BURN THIS SHARD TO CINDERS…

Lord Blackthorn: Agh! No, back, daemon from beyond! Back-back, I
abjure thee!

Guardian: A PITY YOU RESISTED MY BLANDISHMENTS IN THS UNIVERSE,
BLACKTHORN. YOU MADE A WORTHY SERVANT IN OTHER WORLDS…

Lord Blackthorn: AAAAAaaaaaa——

Guardian: HA HA HA HA HA HA… THUS ENDETH THIS WORLD, ANOTHER
VICTORY FOR ME, ANOTHER SHADOWLORD ABORNING. NOW IT IS TIME TO MOVE
ON TO THE NEXT WORLD, THE NEXT PREY.

THANKS TO YOU ALL FOR PARTICIPATING IN THIS TEST OF MY POWERS… WHEN
NEXT WE MEET- I WILL DEFEAT YOU AGAIN. THIS I PROMISE!
```

And then, the true ending: every dev member who was at work went into the world in the form of the toughest daemon forms we could take. We disguised ourselves as shadowlords, and we *slaughtered*. We spawned thousands of daemons who killed everyone indiscriminately. There used to be a fantastic screenshot floating around on the Internet showing an entire screen of nothing but daemon wings…

Anyway, that was one cool way for a world to end, with a bang.

Privateer Online

Star Settlers

In the wake of the excitement over *No Man's Sky* and its procedural worlds, I thought that it might be a good time to tell some of the story around the version of *Privateer Online* that I worked on, that never saw the light of day.

After I moved off the UO team, I worked on several MMO concepts for Origin. The mandate was explicitly "come up with something that we can make using the UO server and client pretty much intact, without big changes, because we need it quick." This limited the possible projects enormously, of course.

So I started developing one-sheet concepts that fit the bill. None of them got farther than a few pages, and the idea was to give execs some choices on what we would go make.

- There was *Mythos*, which eagle-eyed Origin fans even noticed the domain registration for. This was set in the real world, in the mythologies of every culture. Basically, it was like *LegendMUD* but only set in the ancient period.

- There was a pirates/seafaring one one. The idea was to make boats be a single tile in size, with a "scale change" when you got in a boat (kind of like *Seven Cities of Gold)*. That way we could do ship to ship combat in a reasonable way for the time and in 2d.

- There was something around vampires. I don't remember it very well, but *Buffy* was on and Anne Rice's books were popular.

Mythos was the one that execs liked out of that set. Oh, there were more. I vividly remember a phone call where an exec and I were talking with a Hollywood agent as he tried to persuade me that *Leave It To Beaver* was due for a comeback, or that *Baywatch Online* was a good idea.

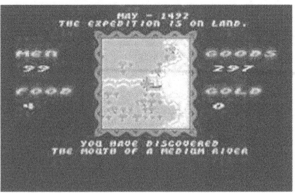

Right after UO shipped, Damion Schubert and I had collaborated on a pitch for a 2d space MMO, because Origin was wondering what the followup would be. This pitch wasn't ever delivered. We walked in to present it, and were told "we're doing UO2." The programmers on the team has pitched a post-apocalyptic idea, and sometime after they heard that it wasn't happening, they all quit.[202] This is why I was the only UO vet on *Second Age*.

If I recall correctly, this sci-fi pitch was sort of MMO meets *Star Control* meets *Starflight*. The game idea didn't get heard by anyone, he went off to do UO2, and I went off to do *Second Age*.

When I was asked what I really *wanted* to make, my answer was immediate: *M.U.L.E. Online*. The original *M.U.L.E.* is my favorite game of all time, and it seemed to me that it was perfect for going online. The IP was going fallow at the time, the original designer (Dani Bunten) had passed away, and I was at an EA studio. But there were legal entanglements with the family, and there was no way to make it happen.

So I started sketching out something else, codename *Star Settlers*. It still had the idea of colonizing planets, but instead of people on one planet, it was thousands of planets, procedurally generated. You started out on one, a small MMO world (think the size of one UO city). You sent off an exploration ship and it would find one for you and generate it. You would go to it, slay monsters, etc, and if you managed to pacify it, you could build on it.

Every planet had its own resource mix, so you would want to constantly go outwards and pioneer. If a planet was "used up" or nobody tended to go back, we'd just "lose the spacelane to it" and erase it, to make room for more. The hope was that someday even the starting worlds would get abandoned and replaced.

Mythos and *Star Settlers* were the final two candidates, and when I was asked which one I preferred, I picked *Star Settlers*.

First exec comment was "hate the name. And we have a powerful science fiction IP in-house! This should be in the *Wing Commander* universe. Maybe *Privateer*."

---

[202] Jason Spangler later informed me, "A correction: All the programmers I talked with that quit did so because the executive producer at the time threatened to fire one of them when they asked him to hire at least one more programmer to help support the Live game. We were all exhausted working crunch hours on the expansion while also supporting the Live service 24/7, dealing with emergency Live issues all day and during the night - plus continuing Live feature and content releases at the same time."

This of course blew up a huge portion of the design. There's a lot of lore in the WC universe. *Star Settlers* worked in part because it literally handed galactic history over to the players.

Second exec comment was "this is a *Wing Commander* game! It's got to have space combat. And be in 3d."

That blew up most of the rest of the design. And the whole starting premise of "have something to ship within a year" that was the start of the entire project. (This latter sequence of events has happened to me more than once in my career. "We need something quick! Re-use tech!" "This is cool! Switch to better tech!" "Uh, didn't we need something quick?")

There had been multiple tries at getting a *Privateer Online/Wing Commander Online* going by that point.[203] All of them came from people over in the WC group. Some of them had gotten pretty far — piles of artwork, design work, and even some tech. (I think fan sites say there was only one prior try, but I think "my" PO was actually something like number seven as we counted them internally. Most didn't get very far).

This ended up being a case where the Lord British Productions team actually ended up getting *a different team's IP greenlit for their own use.* Needless to say, this ticked off some folks on the *Wing Commander* side. One of them came in to interview to switch teams and started out by saying "what makes you think you are qualified to make a Wing Commander game?" I replied with "I'm not." We ended up as good friends.

The resultant team never jelled entirely, and the design suffered from that a lot. We ended up producing a ridiculously ambitious design bible (a "DDR" in OSI lingo) that was lavishly illustrated, and a prototype. Lots of stuff was overcomplicated. In hindsight, that's kind of classic Origin, actually.

Anyway, some of the features of that *Privateer Online*:

The Privateer Online team

[203] See https://www.engadget.com/2013/07/06/the-game-archaeologist-wing-commander-online/

1. You could sit down at the prototype and enter a planet number, and it created a planet for you. Just terrains, colored textures, etc, but every planet was radically different. You could run around it in 1st person 3d. I remember that 666 was hellish, which struck us all as funny. This system was using various Perlin noise generators to create heightfields, but we didn't have artwork in, except maybe for your spaceship sitting there.

2. There was rather fun and slick mouse-controlled space combat, with multiplayer dogfighting. Some asteroids to dodge, etc.

3. We'd designed a ship customization system that was more or less fractal. You could pick a chassis, and each chassis had attachment points for Size A things. Size A things were guaranteed not to intersect because that's how we built the chassis. Size A things had size B attachment points, and because Size B was always half the size of Size A, they also always fit, and so on.

4. The same modular idea extended to the ground-based game, where you could build up towns, mining facilities, factories, etc. Stuff plugged together — you had to build transport lines between the different sorts of buildings to get stuff working, as I recall. Sort of like supplying power to buildings in *SimCity*. The resources extracted would be different per planet, so there'd be interplanetary trade. And you'd get ambushed in space, because space was where the privateers would be.

5. There was a **huge pile** of lore written (I didn't write any of it... WC vets did).[204] Some of it is available over at the Wing Commander CIC site.[205] Probably the most illuminating for readers would be the fictional setting, which is in this Word doc.[206]

We demo'ed it at an Origin all-hands meeting. People liked it. The design doc was circulated around EA, and we were even invited to Westwood Studios (the makers of *Command & Conquer*) to talk MMOs with the team there. We went out there, shared some knowledge, and marveled at the creepy office. It was built in a former defense contractor's building, which felt very claustrophobic. It was all very... Big Brother.

And then *Privateer Online* was cancelled in favor of *Earth & Beyond*. From

---

[204] Specificallly, Hal Milton did, by himself.
[205] https://www.wcnews.com/news/update/7049
[206] download.wcnews.com/files/documents/POL2_Fiction-WorldSummary.doc

Westwood.

There's a ton of stories to tell around all that — it happened nearly simultaneously with Richard leaving Origin — but this post is really about the game, because nobody ever officially knew it existed (though there's an OK article over here[207] about it). I hear that some folks have that big design bible — I don't, I scrupulously left it behind when I left OSI. I am pretty sure that if I read it now I would be horrified.

That said, a core group from that team went on to do *Star Wars Galaxies*, and you can see some of the ideas reappearing. The fractal terrain and other design elements in SWG are worth a blog post of their own someday.

A few years later, when Origin was shut down, there was a big bonfire party. Copies of the *Privateer Online* DDR, along with those from many other Origin projects that never saw the light of day, were used to fuel the flames.

We all got t-shirts that said "We Created Worlds."

---

[207] https://www.wcnews.com/privateeronline.shtml

Privateer Online

Privateer Online was in a design phase and early prototyping when it was cancelled in 2000. It was basically designed to be the successor title to *Ultima Online*. Instead, it became a rough draft of *Star Wars Galaxies.*

The game design was built around three pillars, in classic marketing-speak: Combat, Commerce, Colonization. In hindsight, it was notable for its emphasis on economic play, a few interesting anticipations of later genres (such as the Facebook social game), and its eventual influence on *Star Wars Galaxies*, which shared much of the same core team. It's also particularly interesting to compare the game design to *EVE Online*, which came along several years later but was also a try at "UO in space."

PO was all about a single generated galaxy, with play on both the planets and in space. It was set many years forward from the time period of the *Wing Commander* games, in a world where Confed (the human spacefaring government) was rapidly expanding onto new colony worlds. This was its inheritance from the earlier *Star Settlers* pitch: a game that was fundamentally about an expanding civilization. However, the emphasis on colonies was shifted pretty massively by the influx of combat-centric developers from the *Wing Commander* and even *Jane's Simulation* series of games, leading to tension on the team.

The "vision statements" for *Privateer Online* very much reflected its time. Items like "don't make systems too reliant on time-critical responses" was the very first bullet point, in a time when broadband was still rather rare in U.S. households. "Avoid designs that require human administrative intervention" was another, no doubt in reaction to the heavy load for game masters in UO and other games; during this period, *EverQuest* actually required GMs to manually approve the name of every new player or guild!

Most critically, though, was that *PO* was intentionally an expansive design in terms of play styles.

> Don't get hung up on what you personally view as fun. One of the most popular features in *Ultima Online* was fishing. There are many types of players out there. Community features offer more value than the game aspects to (distressing to hear

as a game designer, I know). Time spent on adding a wedding dress to the game is more valuable than time spent adding a new ship type... Design for player empowerment. Better to let players lay out their floor plan than for us to provide stock ones.

This sort of thing was in the design document in large part because of a strong cultural conflict on the team between the folks with an MMO background and the ones who came from a pure space sim background and were strongly focused on traditional single-player game features. It's easy to make a link between that and the outcries a few years later on *Star Wars Galaxies* over hairdressing being more finished than smuggling.

Combat

The game tilted strongly towards space as the main arena for action, with ground-based activities mostly focused on the commerce and colonization aspects. Space combat was all first person, with highly customizable spaceships that could basically be built up from parts. There were even planned capital ships, wherein different players could take different roles on the ship, such as different weapon stations, piloting, and engineering stations.

Space was divided into three sorts: Safe Space was truly safe and no weapons functioned at all. "No player should have to look over their shoulder for an evil player coming to kill them," declared the design doc, in a clear reaction to the lawlessness of *Ultima Online*. Safe Space even featured Confed patrols that would stop your ship and search you for contraband, in case you were carrying any goods that were defined as illegal by Confed. Even collision was planned to be disabled in Safe Space, to prevent "ramming kills" by other ships. This was fictionally justified by a system of beacons repeating a weapons-blocking carrier wave, literally called Safety.Net. No NPC enemies of any sort appeared in Safe Space at all, as it was intended to serve as a newbie training area.

Tame Space was more like a traditional "player vs environment" area, where players could fight non-player enemies in both ground and space areas. NPC Confed forces flew around in space and if they spotted players who were flagged as being pirates or criminals, they would actually escort them out of the area or destroy them; evading these police enabled a smuggling game that was later sadly lacking in *SWG*. The Safety.Net was still operative in tame space, so the pirates couldn't fight back.

At the fringes of it all was Wild Space. Anything was legal out there — but it was also the only place where you could find new planets to colonize, and then gradually convert them to Tame and then Safe. There was actually a note (that I didn't write) in the design doc reading

> "Exploring the universe, taming a wild system, then rendering it an official part of the Confederation, and then making it a hub of new exploration… Holy crap, this is one of the coolest long term reward systems in the history of online gaming."

There was even a system that reported statistics to players before they entered the area, on things like the current population of enemies, Confed patrols, pirates, and the number of player kills that had occurred recently, to let adventurous PvE players make a judgment call as to whether they wanted to risk it.

While space combat was very detailed and robust, with full flight-sim style mechanics, ground combat was intentionally underdeveloped. Not only did it use the same old "combat loop in rounds" mechanic that was already old hat, but it even only had around 5 levels of enemies. The intent was to make space the core of the game, front and center. I mean, the design specs for how you went from one space jump point to another were considerably more intricate than the entire ground combat algorithm. That said, players could even build ground defenses to keep the aliens away from their planetary buildings, and missions to clear out nests of critters were expected to be in the game.

Interestingly, the worlds of *Privateer Online* largely didn't feature static content; all encounters were intended to be dynamically spawned near players as they moved around, and automatically scaled in difficulty for the group.

Commerce

The heart of gameplay was missions, which were accessed via a mission board. Missions were either generated by the game, or were entered by other players, as a player-generated contract system. *Privateer*, as a brand, was all about commerce and piracy, so the game was oriented around that as well.

Players could mine asteroids for stuff, or set up mining facilities on planets. These worked essentially exactly like *Farmville* would a decade later: passive resource harvesting while the player was offline, that the player had to come collect. Ah, but if the player wasn't around, they could instead post a mission on the mission board asking *another* player to collect the goods and transfer them to a particular location, and offering payment. In what seemed incredibly ambitious at the time, you were supposed to be able to do this from a web page, and even get notifications "on your pager or pushed to your desktop."

Colonies were built by players, other than the initial ones we seeded into the game. The key thing that colonies provided was a commodities exchange. Many missions were expected to start or finish at a marketplace. You could buy items from anywhere in the galaxy, but you had to pick it up where it was. Further, because of the mission system, you might instead pay someone else to do it. In fact, you might sit back and *only* play the commodities market, arbitraging away whilst paying third parties to actually move the goods around for you. You could also put up buy orders, so players could approach transactions from either end. And lastly, most listings were actually intended to be time-limited auctions, like the (at that time still fairly small) marketplace on eBay.

All this gave rise to what today is perhaps the most startling idea in *Privateer Online*. A player could join up to three guilds… and guilds were called "companies." A company actually declared a primary line of business. If they got big, they could become a corporation with multiple lines of business. And if they chose, they could actually do an initial public offering on the in-game stock market.

Yes, that's right. In *Privateer Online* you could buy stock in someone else's uberguild. There was a public stock market design, complete with tickers and limit orders. A side note in the design mentioned that "we should ask our friends at Motley Fool about how to make this work."

Even better, you could actually incorporate in a legitimate fashion, or declare your guild as evil; meaning, as a pirate organization. You had to have bonafides (in the form of a certain number of playerkills, smugglings, and the like) in order for the underground criminal element to charter you, but once you did, you could effectively be a pirate king.

Companies could go to war against each other, and in a refinement of the guild warfare systems that had existed on MUDs and in *UO*, they had victory conditions: a certain number of kills, a certain amount of property damage, and so on. This provided an actual winner, and the ability to have leaderboards for guilds.

There had been issues with the simple voting system that was used to select guild leaders in *UO*, so *PO* instead allowed leadership to automatically go to a member based on a founder-selected criterion: votes, most stock owned, best playerkill record, raw wealth, and so on, so that each guild could select its own preferred method.

The other big benefit to guilds, that would never fly given information transparency on the Internet today, was that they cleared the "fog of war" from the data in the game. As your players were spread out, information on the stats for the systems they were in were automatically shared to the guild. They also had their own private communication channel (this was a period when many online gamers still used Internet Relay Chat to communicate), and even an internal lending system for items and money.

Colonization

All of this was about community-based play, as you can see. That was really the core impulse of the game: play with others. The central output for this was colonization.

A lot of attention was put towards seeing other players as a network of interdependence. In order to reduce an emphasis on numbers, all statistics were actually hidden in favor of text — you might have "mediocre coordination" and "superior strength," and if you were hurt, you were likely "moderately wounded." Morph target body customization (which later came to fruition in *Star Wars Galaxies*) would allow everyone to truly look different.

All skills were actually *certifications*, meaning they cost money to get — and money to *maintain*. You could surrender certifications and change your character around. Professions were arranged in a technology tree (I still remember that one of Bing Gordon's comments on the design was "I am skeptical that a technology tree can be unfolded over time.") and players needed to have met criteria in either upfront payment, ongoing payment, reputation level, previous certifications, or "accomplishments" — for example, you might not be able to learn a skill until you had six kills in space combat.

There was an apprentice system in the game, to get elder players to take newer players under their wing. Some skills required a certain number of active apprentices! There was a "greeter" system that rewarded players for choosing to help newbies find their footing in the game. There was even a "simulator pod" which let players go into *simulated* space combat or ground missions, in order to practice their skills in a way that didn't risk their actual character. (The plan was to even have simulator sports, like space races).

And everything you did fed into a centralized reputation system. You couldn't become a pirate unless you worked up enough of a bad reputation. Once criminals trusted you, beacons to worlds that were previously off-limits would appear, but you would also be denied entry into safe space.

Playerkilling impacted rep, of course, but so did getting caught smuggling, failing to complete delivery missions and absconding with other people's stuff, the source of your money… and pretty much every system in the game was partly based on player reputation.

Reputation was additionally helped by the idea of an in-game News.Net. Key achievements or even just notable events ("wealthiest person in the galaxy just landed at the local spaceport on planet X!") would go out across the wire. The hope was to allow fan writers to even make a living with their in-game articles.

All of this activity happened in player cities that were colonies formed by getting enough player housing onto a single world. Worlds were meant to be pretty *small*; only around a square kilometer. Generated using procedural techniques, they were to be inhabited by procedurally generated flora and fauna as well. Once a colony was of large enough size, it was recognized by Confed, and could choose to become Safe Space or Tame Space. A governor could be elected, and rules could be set by that governor including how much money they skimmed off the local marketplace.

Money, money, money

As a precursor of the eventual free-to-play market, an enormous amount of the *Privateer Online* design was oriented around up-selling players on additional services. The target was that a core user might well pay the equivalent of an additional 50% of their subscription fee in additional services. Examples included access to more character slots, access to the marketplaces via the web, more storage for in-game digital objects like blueprints in your datapad, real-time stock market quotes and tickers for the in-game stock market, emails or pager notifications, web hosting for guild pages, and even plain old access to parts of the galaxy that were locked behind a paywall.

At the most extreme end, the design offered up the idea that there could be

> …a galaxy (shard) where the player pays real money for credits (gold) to buy what he wants. Note that this will change the game dynamics in a huge way by effectively removing the need to earn [in-game] money. People will still need to explore and mine to be able to build things that they can't buy.

…and the ahead-of-its time

> **OSI escrow service**
>
> OSI will hold a *[Privateer Online]* item or account. The seller will give to OSI their item that they are selling. OSI will then tell the buyer that we have it and it's now OK to send the money. Once OSI has the funds, they will inform both parties, release the property to the buyer, and pay the seller.

This official real-money-trade system was expected to charge 10% of the transaction value as a fee, and was inspired by the fact that UO castles were going for a thousand dollars on eBay at the time.

How different would the gaming world be if a game had launched with real money features like that in 2002, two years before *World of Warcraft* even shipped? Who knows…

Alas

Privateer Online was never meant to be. We got as far as having pretty fun multiplayer dogfighting with single-player spaceships, with a rather nice-feeling mouse control system that took a while to get right (joysticks were still the common way to play space sims at the time). We also had a very rudimentary planet generator, with one avatar. You could type in a seed number and get back a rather simplistic little planet. The game was cancelled, and eventually so was its sister project *Ultima Online 2*.

I learned about the cancellation at 2am, Australian time, awoken by a call. I was in Sydney, doing a press tour that Richard Garriott had mysteriously dropped out of. On that call I learned that I was on the tour because Richard was gone from the company, and that the project was dead. I then had to get up that morning, and walk into a luncheon organized for the local *Ultima* fan community. I entered the room, and the first tremulous question from a tentatively raised hand was "is it true? Lord British is gone?" There were actual tears from many in the audience.

Electronic Arts instead invested into *Earth and Beyond*, and a bit later, *The Sims Online.* The online development expertise that had gathered at Origin scattered to the winds, and went on to play key roles in online games all over the industry… while *Ultima Online* soldiered on for decades. EA's fumbling around with online games eventually cost them hundreds of millions of dollars.

What might have become of EA, and of the trajectory of the MMO industry, had EA chosen to finish *Privateer Online* instead? There's no way to know. The upshot for the core team was that instead, we put ourselves on the market, as a team, and looked for a studio deal with any publisher that might be willing to fund us.

One that came knocking happened to be Sony Online, which had recently landed a license deal from LucasFilm… for *Star Wars*. As far as we knew, it had already been in development for a year. So when we joined, we told everyone that we were certainly not going to be working on that.

We were wrong.

Star Wars Galaxies

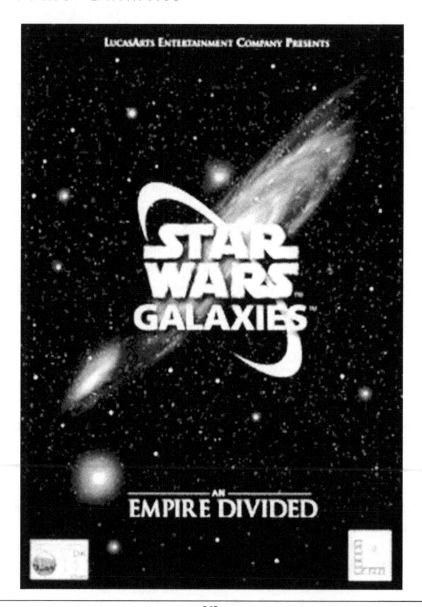

Comments from the Team letter

Hello everybody, and welcome to the second Comments from the Team.[208] My name is Raph Koster, and I am Creative Director for *Star Wars Galaxies*—that means that I am in charge of the game design, and making sure that the overall experience is the game we all want it to be. On the boards I post as Holocron. And today I wanted to talk to you a little about what it is I think we're making…

I've been involved with online persistent world gaming for almost a decade now. That means I've only gotten to see one-third of its very long history (did you know that online gaming was born almost at the same time as standalone games?). But even that length of time is long enough to make it easy to lose sight of the magic I caught a glimpse of the first time I logged into one.

I had graduated from college at that point, and my wife and I were living halfway across the country from all our friends, and were rather lonely. Some of those friends had started telling us about virtual worlds that could be found on the Internet—all text-based, of course, but they were free. One told us all about one where she started exploring what seemed to be a full-scale representation of Europe. So we logged in. I made a character for my wife, so of course the character was female. But then she made her own character, so I was stuck using the girl that we had made—her name was Dusty, a name I had used in countless RPGs and pen and paper gameplay sessions over the years (but on guys, of course).

I found myself in a small ramshackle inn, in a hallway on the second floor. I went downstairs, where there were a few people bustling around. I ignored them and walked out onto the road outside, and after a hillock or two, was startled to see what looked like a glowing blue doorway hanging in midair. I figured, what the heck? And stepped through it.

I stumbled out onto a tall, grass-covered rocky cliffside, above an aquamarine ocean.

---

[208] In a community building effort, we had team members introduce themselves to the audience one by one with little essays posted on the website. It was part of the general philosophy of making the team seems like humans, rather than a faceless corporation, to help drive loyalty and forgiveness when we screwd up. This one was mine.

Naked, except for my now empty backpack. I have to admit, the notion of being a girl stuck without any clothes in the middle of the wilderness was unfamiliar to me. Trees overhung a small dirt trail—maybe for goats, I thought irrelevantly. I wandered along the trail, and when I got thirsty, I automatically reached for my waterskin, but of course it was gone along with my clothes.

At this point I was immersed enough in what was going on that I started to feel pretty nervous. Lost, thirsty, getting hungry, naked in the woods. But then, as I trudged along the trail, I saw a structure. Looked like an old Greek temple of some sort. Made sense—the place seemed Mediterranean, and this was supposed to be Europe, right? I walked up to the temple, and the feeling of it was much like a movie: I could imagine putting my hand on the rough eroded stone of the wall, which felt cool to the touch, and smelling that dusty smell of an enclosed space in the warm sun. There were welcoming shadows within. When I went inside, I imagined that my eyes took a moment to adjust to the darkness.

The tile floor was cracked, and there was a small stone altar. Frescoes decorated the walls. My feet were cold. There didn't seem to be anything or anyone around, and at this point I had been wandering for an hour or two alone. I tried searching the room, but found nothing but dust bunnies. Finally I sat against the altar, and not knowing what else to do, prayed to whatever deity the temple had been erected to. I had nothing to lose, after all.

Ah, well. I got up, ready to go, and shrugged my backpack onto my shoulders. And felt something moving inside. I took it off rather quickly, of course. To my utter shock and delight, a white rabbit poked its pink nose out from under the flap, then came out into the light.

"Hello," I said to it, not knowing what else to do.

Then the rabbit flashed and glowed and turned into somebody.

I won't go into everything that happened after that, except to say that he was very gallant and offered the naked girl a robe to cover herself with. And he began the gradual process of disenchanting me—I was in Crete, alright, but it was pretty small, and Europe wasn't there, and over the hill was a fairy forest, and there was a giant spiderweb over on that side, and the world was just a giant patchwork of fantasy clichés. Over time I learned just how much of the immersion that I had experienced was the result of smoke and mirrors. I learned about spawn points and about the PRAY command being a help line, I learned about teleporters and levels and zones and all the rest of the mundane crud that goes into making up magic. I suppose the same is true for anyone who sees the magic of a movie and then discovers the amazingly complex but also very ordinary stuff that goes into it: the standing on your mark, doing shot after shot, the way lights are faked, the way sound is dubbed in afterwards with crinkled tin foil and making kissy noises into a microphone…

I even learned about the odd and interesting phenomenon of cross-gender roleplay, which I had stumbled into by accident, and about the sociological structures of online societies. I started reading everything I could get my hands on about the history of virtual worlds.

Later on, of course, I was re-enchanted, by the process, the wonderful amazing array of moving parts that goes into making that grand stage play that is a virtual world. I learned how to create environments and effects like I had experienced—and better. I worked on making my own (where I did eventually make chunks of a virtual Europe!), and then began work on *Ultima Online*… and all the time, I tried to continue learning more about the craft, the ways in which all these cardboard movie sets and sneakily-lit stages are put together. But it's all in service of one goal.

I want others to feel what I felt, that first time I felt I was truly someone else in a world that was strange to me, scrabbling up that steep dirt path, a rock jabbing my big toe, as I tried to keep from slipping off the path and down the rocky cliff to the blue-green water below—the relief when I saw the dome of that temple peek out from above the trees, shining white like a promise. The feeling of the empty backpack flapping on my back—heck, of my back not being MY back—and the amazing wonder I felt when that white rabbit crawled out of my backpack and nibbled at my offered fingers. And the moment when it transformed, and became another person—another real person, living halfway across the country, able to talk to me, and share the experience…! Yes, I suppose I imagined it all. It was all just a dream. But what a wonderful dream…

I still play Dusty in every online game I play, even when I make other characters. Kind of like an old shoe—just fits well, after all these years. It's the easiest way to recapture the magic when I first log in. And that guy who was the rabbit that greeted me, well, he's now lead designer for *Ultima Worlds Online: Origin.*[209] Small world.

Star Wars is a universe beloved by many. And I think many of you are like me. You want to be there. You want to feel what it is like. Even before we think about skill trees and about Jedi advancement, before we consider the stats on a weapon or the distance to Mos Eisley and where you have to go to pick up power converters—you want to just BE there. Inhale the sharp air off the desert. Watch a few Jawas haggle over a droid. Feel the sun beat down on a body that isn't your own, in a world that is strange to you. You don't want to know about the stagecraft in those first few

---

[209] The person in question is Damion Schubert.

moments. You want to feel like you are offered a passport to a universe of limitless possibility.

Call it an MMORPG, call it virtual world design, call it a graphical mud, I don't care. My job is to try to capture that magic for you, so you have that experience. That's my goal, the goal of this team, and we will do it to the best of our ability. I hope we're well on the road to doing so.

But we'll try to make sure you don't lose your clothes on the way in.

SciFi MMPs: Lessons learned

This isn't really an essay; rather it's a rewriting of some of the things I said at a GDC session in 2004,[210] extended to offer up greater detail. It serves as a pretty good introduction to what Star Wars Galaxies *was.*

Sony Online developed *Star Wars Galaxies* for LucasArts; LucasArts was actually pretty heavily involved on the game design, content, and by the way, it's really nice having Skywalker Sound do your game's sound!

One of the things about *Galaxies*, from the very beginning, is that we wanted it to be "the summary MMO." Meaning, if we took a look at all the various things that MMOs had done up to that point, we could look across them and take the best lessons from each of the many games, a piece from over here and a piece from over there. We said to ourselves, look, here's all the good ideas that are scattered across different games and even different game genres, and you never see them together even though they could theoretically exist within one game. We were seeing a lot of the design concepts of the first generation of massively multiplayer games existing separately, rather than together so that we could, as an industry, say "this is what the first generation means."

From the get-go, *Star Wars Galaxies* was designed to be a game that had both gameplay on the ground on planet surfaces, and also gameplay in space while piloting spaceships. Then we realized that was insane and cut it into two pieces. The first piece (the entire ground-based portion of the game) still turned out to be slightly insane, and didn't quite fit in our allotted development time.

We had all of these things as requirements, many of them because of expectations around the *Star Wars* license, and many of them simply because they are things that

---

[210] This was part of a panel on sci-fi MMOs at GDC 2004 entitled "SciFi MMPs: Lessons Learned," alongside a presentation by Chris Klug on *Earth & Beyond*. There was then a panel session moderated by Jesse Schell. The slides and audio for this panel can be found at https://www.raphkoster.com/games/presentations/scifi-mmps-lessons-learned/.

you should do if you're doing an MMO.

- **An accessible massively multiplayer world**, meaning that it should have both high subscription numbers, and hardware requirements that stretched fairly low.

- **Strong player retention**. This meant a large target for subscriber lifetime, which is how we would measure success; and also a belief that the method by which to accomplish this was a strongly community-oriented game.

- **Low costs to operate**, with a target profit margin per month.

- **A broad audience**, which implied many ways to play and enjoy the game. It also implied a low target number of hours played per week. Meaning, we would rather have players rack up fewer hours per week, but still return week after week.

The game was pretty successful, despite its complex history. We weren't ever allowed to give out subscriber numbers, but we are fairly sure we became the #2 most popular MMO in North America, behind *EverQuest*. The growth was ridiculously fast, far faster than anticipated, with over 450,000 registered users by the spring of 2004, and 275,000 of them in the first month. This caused many problems.

After launch, we tried to finish the game that we had promised, since we didn't actually launch with all the features we had promised. Many major features that might have been full expansions for other titles were therefore launched for free: mounts and vehicles, and the politician profession and cities built and governed by players to go with it. The first Jedi started popping up around November.

One of the things about *SWG* is that it was always intended to be an MMO *platform*, which ties back to the notion of being a "summary MMO," allowing us to expand in any given direction based on what players were doing. A little bit about what that means...

We had a bunch of key things we really wanted to do. One of them was character flexibility. We wanted to allow people to play any way they wanted. Central to this was not only rewarding people for doing things that we saw other MMOs doing (typically combat, but we looked at "trading XP" in *Earth and Beyond,* and other sources of inspiration), but also to find ways to reward people for doing things that

weren't officially recognized by the game but were incredibly important. That opened up a whole category of play that we ended up calling "social professions." This led to many even on the design team saying things like "we're really going to do dancing as a way to play the game?" But we put in dancing and 20% of the players picked up dancing as a skill. Basically, we really wanted to add more verbs to MMO play.

Characters had a certain number of skill points, and they could never acquire more. They could spend these on learning skills, which were arranged in a format familiarly called "skill onions" because of their structure. Each onion represented a "profession."

Reaching the top of an onion might unlock yet more advanced skills above them; some of the advanced professions required that you master multiple professions that were lower down in the tree.

The full list of professions that players could learn was very large — bear in mind that each of these implied 18 separate skills. The way this worked is that different skills cost more points as you climbed the tree, and we carefully calculated the number of points available so that a player could try out all of the basic professions, master around two and a half of them, or specialize up to some of the more advanced ones. Players could surrender skills at any time, losing those abilities, which freed up points for the player to allocate into something else. Every profession had its own type of experience, which was earned only by using the abilities *of that profession,* more or less. So getting better at crafting required you to craft things, and getting better at dancing required you to spend time dancing *while being watched*. You still had to go learn the skill once you qualified for it, which you could do from NPC trainers placed around the various planets, or by simply having another player who knew the skill teaching it to you. In fact, for mastery of many professions, a player was *required* to have taught other players skills, one of many ways in which we attempted to drive community ties within the playerbase.

The full list of skills in the "classic" period of SWG included:

- **Artisan**, which was the basic profession needed in order to be able to craft or make things within the game. Artisans could craft basic items of various sorts. In SWG, unlike most MMOs, NPCs and enemies didn't really drop any particularly good objects as loot. Instead, everything really good in the game was made by other players. It took a solid month, when the game launched, for most items to be "invented" by players, as they advanced through the skill trees and learned the necessary skills to make advanced items.

- **Architects** were able to build furniture, buildings ranging from factories to shuttle ports to player houses, and various other sorts of structures such as fountains and gardens.

- **Armorsmiths** crafted various sorts of armor that helped players in combat.

- **Chefs** created food from raw ingredients (which had to be obtained mostly by Scouts). Given some vegetables and cereals, you might be able to cook a synthsteak as a low level chef, and an advanced one could make everything from mixed drinks to desserts. Foods had effects on your statistics.

- **Droid Engineers** could create droids, which were basically just a sort of pet; you could build them, and they could serve as useful helpers for various other professions.

- **Merchants** had the ability to run player shops. Their skills focused on being able to run more shops at once, being able to customize how the NPCs they hired appeared and spoke, wider controls over pricing, and crucially, the ability to do marketing and advertising on various in-game channels.

- **Shipwrights** were specialists in crafting spacecraft.

- **Tailors** focused on making clothing — everything from hats to shoes.

- **Weaponsmiths** created weapons, from vibroblades to blasters.

- **Brawler** was the basic melee combat profession, and unlocked in its turn:

- **Fencers**, who focused on bladed close-in weapons tied to agility and hit-and-run combat.

- **Pikemen**, who used various sorts of staves for tanking, crowd control, and defense.

- **Swordsman**, which was about heavy damage weapons like swords and hammers of various sorts; basically, a high damage specialist.

- **Teras Kasi Artist**, which was mostly about avoiding damage and causing carefully selected damage. In other game systems, this might have been termed a Monk, even down to a "meditation" ability.

- **Entertainers** were the perfect example of the aforementioned "social professions," designed for roleplayers and players with more of a chatty bent. A special "watch" command allowed other players to pay attention to an Entertainer, granting them experience points, but also giving the audience various sorts of effects from watching the performance, such as "being inspired" which granted bonuses to their odds of success in combat or in crafting.

- **Dancers** danced, including in coordinated group dances, using a loop-based system with multiple styles of dances and special flourishes that could be added to the performance to break up the patterns.

- **Image Designers** had the ability to alter the character customization of other players (with their consent, of course). This was the only way to modify your basic appearance after character creation. This included things like hairstyle changes, make-up on faces, and actually modifying the bone structure of your face, if you chose.

- **Musicians** were much like dancers, with pre-written music loops that could be changed via flourishes. Musical notes floated off of musicians, who could play in bands with varying instruments including ones that were effectively furniture. Both musicians and dancers had the ability to cure a form of post-traumatic stress called "wounds," which accumulated on players who took damage in combat. Musicians and dancers were designed to work together, and whole bands and performance troupes would actually go on tour across the galaxy.

- **Marksmen** focused on ranged weapons, which once again were divided into subspecialties based on

- **Carbineers** worked the middle range distance, with run-and-gun tactics.

- **Pistoleers** were the close-range attackers.

- **Riflemen** were snipers, acting from a distance and were not supposed to be very effective up close.

- **Medics** were the basic healer, with the ability to do close-range, longer-range, and area-effect healing. They could also craft basic healing stimpacks that anyone could use.

- **Doctors** were the specialist support profession, with the ability to revive players and high ability to heal and buff players, giving them bonuses.

- **Combat Medics** were hybrids with combat professions, focusing more on debuffing (applying negative effects) to opponents, and with less healing capability.

- **Scouts** were the basis of "outdoorsy" professions, with am emphasis on exploration playstyles. Some of their skills were about increased ability to navigate terrain, others about setting traps and snares, hunting and dressing their kills and extracting resources from the carcasses, and the ability to create campsites. Campsites were designed to be a sort of "home away from home," providing forward bases in the wilderness within which some of the amenities of cities were to be had. Normally, many of the advanced capabilities of medical personnel, entertainers, crafters, and others required facilities only present in cities. Scouts could basically create spaces within which those skills worked while out in the wilderness.

- **Creature Handlers** were the pet control classes. Players with these skills could find baby creatures out in the wild, and tame them. These babies started out physically small and gradually grew to adulthood. They learned their name through the Creature Handler repeating it to them, and they could learn not only how to fight alongside you, but to do stupid pet tricks like standing on their head. Some of them could be ridden as mounts. You could teach them to walk in formation, to guard specific other players, or to patrol areas. Pets were extremely popular, with fully half the playerbase owning one.

- **Rangers** were basically advanced Scouts, with not only greater ability to extract resources but also the ability to sneak around using camouflage and to track what other creatures or players have been nearby.

- **Politicians** were another one of the social professions. Though it may sound dry, their skills had names like "Fiscal Policy" and "Civic policy." To start with, politicians were required in order to run a player city. A guild had to have a player who was willing to sacrifice their time in other areas in order to help their player community, but politician skills didn't cost any points. Politicians could place special structures that effectively claimed an area of land for their town, within which they could place structures such as shuttle ports and spaceports (which added their town to the travel network with full equivalency to the designer-built towns), cloning centers which served as respawn points, and others. They could specialize their town to give bonuses to specific professions, and towns themselves had a whole little advancement system. Declare a town as an Entertainment District, and it benefited entertainers. Make it a Medical Center or a Research Center, and it helped out medical professions or crafters; there were eventually nine specializations for cities including one specifically for running player-created events. Politicians could even designate other players as being a police force, which gave them the ability to use player-vs-player combat to enforce the local laws.

- **Pilots** were added when the space expansion, *Jump to Lightspeed*, was released. You could gain pilot skills as a Rebel, an Imperial, or as a freelance pilot.

Other advanced hybrid professions requiring mastery of multiple other professions included

- **Bio-Engineers** were specialist crafter working with genetic material. Effectively, it was a pet crafting profession that required the player to be both a medic and a scout.

- **Bounty Hunters** basically existed to take on player-vs-player missions, particularly hunting down player Jedi.

- **Smugglers** never really achieved fruition in the original design, but were meant to actually smuggle, completing player-created missions delivering goods back and forth. Originally, the hope was that Imperial NPCs would stop players seen to be transporting goods and do searches. Instead, Smugglers evolved into a profession that could "slice" weapons, which improved them, and craft "spices" which were basically drugs in the Star Wars universe. Except that LucasArts got very nervous about anything that made them seem like drugs.

- **Squad Leader** was another special social profession: a combat profession entirely oriented around being a party leader. All of the various abilities here were about helping groups play better together. Members of the group who were near their leader could automatically and passively get a whole host of benefits including faster movement across rough terrain, combat benefits, communication channels, and special attacks where the leader could "paint" a target for coordinated fire.

- **Jedi Padawan** was the entry point to a whole host of quasi-magical Jedi powers. The Jedi system in Galaxies evolved many times over, but generally included skills around

  o Force defense

  o Force enhancement

  o Force healing

  o Jedi powers

  o Lightsabers

This emphasis on customization extended to a wide array of classic *Star Wars* species. We got to firmly define the Bothan for the first time ever in *Star Wars* canon, because Lucas didn't really have consistent definitions of what they looked like. It was kind of fun to affect the universe permanently, since we had all grown up with it and loved it.

Science fiction adds a particular challenge to combat design. I spent quite a while reading up on military tactics using assault weapons versus snipers versus handguns, only to learn to my dismay that handguns were considered basically worthless in modern warfare. We couldn't do without the classic blaster from the movies though! Similarly, it was very obvious that "bringing a knife to a gunfight" was a bad idea, but the lore was rife with vibroblades and of course, that quintessential Star Wars weapon, the lightsaber. There was even a popular martial arts system that we had to make room for. Trying to get all of these things to play nicely in one RPG system was a big challenge that we failed to conquer.

Worse, as if the problem with pet classes being overpowered in other MMOs wasn't bad enough, we went so far as to say, "let's allow the players to have AT-STs as pets, or hire squads of Stormtroopers." This happened via the faction system, which basically extended the sorts of capabilities that existed for the Creature Handler or Droid Engineer to players who signed up for one of the two PvP factions in the game, Rebels or Imperials. They could earn faction points that could be spent on perks such as calling in airstrikes or summoning an AT-ST to the battlefield.

We also wanted to pursue the notion of dynamic spawns and a modifiable world that we had started to explore in *Ultima Online*. We had the concept, which never quite materialized, of entire bases appearing on the map. Rebel or Imperial facilities could appear on the terrain, deforming and reshaping it on the fly, complete with tall fortress walls, turrets, and inhabitants. We severely underestimated how quickly players would be able to destroy these facilities!

We had to spend a lot of R&D time on that terrain technology, because we wanted players to be able to build anywhere on the map. There weren't really any "instances" in *SWG*. Instead, player housing was

A screenshot of a base

placed out in the world, and we allowed players to construct houses, bases, cities, walls, anywhere. We were able to spawn really large things on the ground, dynamically, and clean them up afterwards. In this picture, you can get a sense of the scale of the base by looking at the buildings on the upper right; you can see the doorways on them, which gives you an idea of the scale of what we could spawn dynamically.

There was a huge non-combat portion to the game. There was just about no loot,

Our Bothan female, early model from alpha

which players hated, since they wanted to have direct rewards for their combat activity. There were extensive supply chains instead — the loot you got for killing something was usually raw materials, which would go on to be a component in making something else. Players formed huge corporations — forty, fifty people — in order to control the resource market.

I spent a lot of time reading about architecture, city planning, and designing spaces; how people navigate them and how they bump into each other. We tried to architect in things like a requirement for players to visit the cantina (which was "battle fatigue," the form of PTSD I mentioned previously), and professions that functioned either only at, or at their best at, the cantina, such as the entertainers, to try to provide rewards for those behaviors.

A player-created fish tank

All sorts of great emergent behaviors arose from those things. Players could decorate the interiors of the structures, with the ability to place objects with full 3d freedom anywhere within their house — floating random things in mid-air if they chose. This meant they could assemble things like giant fish tanks, museums, and more. Here we can see players holding a wedding or some sort of ceremony. We didn't ship with fireplaces or aquariums; these built, Lego-style, by players, out of components they found elsewhere in the game.

Space combat, unlike the ground portion, used fast-reaction arcade-style combat. (The ground used the more typical hotkey-based combat common to MMOs since the days of MUDs). Space launched maybe nine months or so after the initial launch of the game.

Talking to the players

This is a series of posts to the SWG message boards describing our design process for SWG.

SWG Design Process

Well, as expected, the majority of the posters (who answered the thread, anyway) were among the hardcore. That's what I figured we'd see; since being on this board in the first place is a self-selection mechanism—it's the hardcore who tend to hang out on game boards anyway!

You know, everyone wants different things out of a game, especially a massively multiplayer game. At least in a single-player game, there's a prescribed narrative, usually—there's a way to win. There's a goal you try to reach, and specific, easy-to-spot milestones along the way. We strive to put some of these things in MMOs as well, but there's something about saying "here's an online world" that makes people not only crave the open-ended ness, but also try to impose their particular playstyle upon it. Players feel very let down if the game doesn't support THEIR mode of play. We've seen that already here in some of the threads, with some people saying, "I won't play unless there's PvP" or "I won't play unless I can run a shop" or "I won't play unless it has action-style combat."

This isn't a list of expectations that would normally be applied to a standalone game. It gets applied to massively multiplayer because people's expectations of virtual worlds are higher than their expectations for single-player games—or even higher than their expectations for real life, on occasion!

But there's also a powerful counterargument to be made—that without encompassing a wide range of playstyles, a virtual world can't be successful. People need to mingle with people who do different things from them, argues this theory, because otherwise they won't be happy in the long run.

Probably the best articulation of this theory specific to online gaming is Dr. Richard Bartle's division of players into four types. Richard wrote a paper called "Players Who Suit Muds" using his accumulated insight as someone who has run and developed muds since 1978 (Richard is generally credited as the co-author of the original mud, which means the original massively multiplayer virtual world, albeit text-based).

The basic premise of his paper is that there are some people who are there because of the world, and some people who are there because of the other people. Based on this division, some of you are here because it's Star Wars; and some of you are here because it's an MMO. As a second variable, some of you are the kinds of people who enjoy taking action and making significant choices and knowing that you have an impact; and some of you are the sorts of people who value interaction, and like fiddling with things, building, exploring, tweaking, and trying new stuff out.

Based on this, he ended up with four types:

ACT on the WORLD: Achievers, who are out to beat the game. They tend to be powergamers, they want to master the mechanics that the designers have set up for them.

ACT on the PEOPLE: Killers, who are out to establish dominance. Not necessarily PvPers, in my reading, but rather people who like to be in charge, like to have control—leaders and lawyers as much as playerkillers.

INTERACT with the WORLD: Explorers, who want to master every detail, not for character advancement, but "for the sake of science." These are also people who enjoy crafting and creating.

INTERACT with the PEOPLE: Socializers, who are there primarily because their friends are. People who build social structures, who spend most of their time chatting or roleplaying.

Bartle suggests that every successful online world has a balanced proportion of each of these core personality types (and it's interesting comparing these to the Kiersey temperament test btw).

Everyone is a mix of these traits, of course. But games can most definitely cater more strongly towards one or another. For example, many say that *EverQuest* is primarily an Achiever's game, and that *Ultima Online* attracts more Killers. There are "Bartle's quotient tests" out there which hundreds of players of these games have taken that demonstrate that this is actually true (though the percentages according to the results differ by fairly little).

What sort of gamer are you? For what it's worth, according to the tests, I am very high in Explorer quotient—most developers who have taken the test tend to score high on that, probably indicating that it's a trait that leads them to eventually try to make the games they like playing. :)

MMO Design and Satisfying a Diverse Playerbase

Posted December 13, 2000.

Good morning everyone... sorry for not posting yesterday, but as you may have seen on the news, we've had a spot of bad weather here in Texas (and probably also where many of you live). At the moment my house is without power...

Since in the last couple of notes I talked a bit about the audience we expect to get, and what sorts of different gameplay people in that audience want, I thought that today I could maybe talk a little bit about how we go about designing an MMO, and how we try to satisfy that range of people.

To start with, I happen to believe that the four play styles I mentioned should all be catered to. We play massively multiplayer games in large part because of the other people. And if the game's population consists entirely of other people just like us, well, it's not going to be a very interesting world. Other people like us won't challenge us in any way, won't expose us to new ideas, won't surprise us with actions that we ourselves wouldn't have taken. And that would make a massively multiplayer environment a lot poorer, because we rely on the other players to provide unpredictability and interest.

Yes, there's plenty of room for niche products that cater to one play style or another. But if you want to try to convey a universe (especially one as deep and rich as Star Wars) you have to have all sorts of people. On top of that, all sorts of people love Star Wars, and they're all going to try the game. I'd hate to disappoint everyone except one particular play style.

So how do we go about trying to ensure that the game offers enough for each of the types? Well, it all comes down to the design, like so many other things. Our first step was to create what we call a vision document. This started out by identifying some things about who we thought we were making the game for. Right off the bat, we established what sort of audience we thought we were looking at, and that led to establishing a whole bunch of other things. As we came to each statement, we put it into the vision doc.

For example, knowing that we were looking at a broader audience than MMOs had likely seen before meant that we couldn't demand as much time per play session or as much time per week as other MMOs did. As a result, a bunch of design choices went right out the window: we knew that we couldn't have game design elements that involved spending tons of time online. No macroing, no camping, no lengthy corpse recoveries, no long waits for public transportation.

This also led inescapably to the logic that a player who had less time to spend per week couldn't be put at a severe disadvantage. Now, obviously, someone who has more time to spend on the game is going to accomplish more. But we CAN do things so that people don't feel left behind. So into the vision doc went a statement like, "players who play a lot and players who don't have as much time to spend should still be able to play together fruitfully."

We also had more concrete stuff in there. There are things we have to put in to attract people to the game, like great visuals. There's things we need to have in order to make money, like having enough depth in the game so that players continue to subscribe for months. We ended up with six pages of these one-liners. Some samples:

- It should have an intuitive user interface. If the choice for initial interface is between flexibility and ease of use, we will choose ease of use, and make the flexibility an option.
- It should be possible to play a satisfying game session in less than an hour.
- It must be easy to extend and add content to the game after ship.
- *Star Wars Galaxies* must provide multiple ladders of advancement so that new ways to play the game become apparent over time.
- The game system will encourage specialization.
- Players should never feel ripped off by the game mechanics.
- We must encourage a sense of player ownership in the world.

Tomorrow I'll talk about how we translated that into game features. Stay tuned...

What is the game ABOUT?

Posted December 15, 2000.

Hello everyone. I'm suffering from a nasty cold that made me miss a chunk of a day of work, but I still made it here to the boards to post my promised next installment of how we tackled the design.

I mentioned yesterday that we had built around six pages of "vision statements" that reflected what we felt the game had to accomplish, and I posted some examples. Now, I left something out there: the context in which these visions had to be reached. The key element there, of course, is the fact that this game was set in the Star Wars universe. And that requires some vision elements of its own! :)

I basically took the design team back to high school English class one day, and had everyone sit around and think about "What is Star Wars about? Thematically, and emotionally?" Everyone by now knows the whole deal with Joseph Campbell and the Hero's Journey, so we breezed by that bit. One big reason for breezing by it is that the Hero's Journey is not very compatible with a massively multiplayer mindset. Not everyone can be the predestined hero that will save the world (or galaxy, in this case).

After discarding the Hero's Journey, we ended up with a short list of key thematic elements that we thought every Star Wars fan would have picked up on either consciously or unconsciously. We knew that if we failed to represent these things in the game, then players would (correctly) feel that the game wasn't truly Star Wars. Just as you can't imagine The Sims without consumerism, just as you can't imagine Ultimas without ethical dilemmas, you can't imagine Star Wars without these things. These, then, were the things that the game mechanics had to be ABOUT.

Exotic worlds and epic adventure.

This meant that we had to strive to reduce tedium and repetition from the game mechanics wherever possible. We had to strive for as dynamic an environment as possible, while still faithfully reproducing the SW settings players would be familiar with. The game had to be filled with discovery and surprise.

The struggle between the light and dark sides of the Force.

This meant that not only did we have to have this in the game, but that we had to allow players to feel like they had a meaningful impact on the struggle. Through their choices, they had to be able to make a difference. At the same time, people needed to be able to opt out.

Political battles to take control of the galaxy.

We don't tend to think of this one often, even though it's a clear backdrop to everything (expressed as warfare in the Classic trilogy, but more directly seen as political maneuvering in *Episode I*). There are plenty of people who are fighting in the Civil War not because of the Force, but because of more mundane political reasons. Again, we had to allow players to feel like they had a meaningful impact on political struggles in the game through their choices.

Interactions with other players.

This one is more driven by the needs of an MMO design than by the specifics of the Star Wars setting, but even in SW we repeatedly see the theme that people need each other. In an MMO this becomes even more critical, and we knew that this had to be one of the main thrusts of the game mechanics. Interestingly, this isn't something that MMOs thus far have done a very good job of rewarding with in-game mechanics. Sure, games have required you to group, and that sort of thing, but the game mechanics haven't explicitly rewarded all the people who make the game world a more livable place in other ways: the ones who are good roleplayers, the ones who provide entertainment, the ones who are in support roles or peaceful roles or economic roles. We knew that we had to make our game mechanics reflect this.

With these items, we had what the game was going to be *about*. And with that, it was easy to see what sorts of features we would need to have in the game, right? I think I'll be mean, stop now, and leave it as an exercise for the reader. :)

Balance and More

Making Economics, High Level Content, and Advancement Work

Posted December 20, 2000.

Whoo, this is gonna be a long one, I can tell. :)

I saw this topic & posting when it first appeared on the Lum the Mad message boards, but it's been reposted here at *[link lost, unfortunately]*.

It's full of excellent questions, many of which I can't answer in detail because we're not ready to talk about how we intend to do certain things yet. In what follows, I've simply taken the principal issues raised and explained roughly what our approach is to solving them:

Balance

Yes, balance is hard. One thing we are taking as an approach is to be very very obsessive-compulsive about it. Here's some of the specific methods that we try to use:

Step one, use your math. I am a big fan of systems that balance mathematically, because they make good starting points for REAL balance. Just one example is the magic box: if you have twelve stats and fourteen attacks, and you want each attack to vary per stat, or vice versa, you make a grid, and ensure that every stat comes out at a total of zero modifiers across all fourteen attacks, and that every attack comes out at zero total modifiers across every stat. This then serves as a *starting* point of theoretical equivalence between every stat vs every attack, across all players. Now you can tweak from this solid base to account for much fudgier factors like "how expensive is attack 12 versus attack 9" and "how hard is it to get a weapon that does attack 3" and "how useful is stat 11 in other, non-combat settings anyway?"

There are other mathematical approaches to getting things balanced, and we try to use all of them that we can. You will notice later on just how much we will tend to use the number 3 in our game system, and that's because it lets us set up nice rock-paper-scissors relationships to ensure that in any given set of figures, everything has at least one vulnerability...

Step two, use inheritance. A lot. This means that as you create your database of items, you don't create each item in a vacuum. You base every item on a pre-existing item. That first item is ideally a generic "level 1 blaster" "level 2 blaster" etc. That way, if you determine that all vibroblades are weak, you can modify just the base vibroblade and get consistent results everywhere in the database, you can adjust all critters of a given level of difficulty, etc etc.

Step three, log *everything*. And I mean, everything. Track who kills what and how with how many people where. Track who spent what to buy what where how often. Etc etc. And analyze the results!

Step four, rely on self-balancing mechanisms. This is the default anyway. When an MMO starts to go out of balance, you see players pick up compensatory mechanisms. For example, when currencies in an MMO deflate, players start to shift to barter, and eventually designate a new item as an alternate currency. You can make use of players a lot with this. It's particularly applicable to economic issues, and I'll explain how when I get down to the econ answer. :)

Making the game enjoyable for casual gamers/those with less time

We've actually talked a fair amount on this one already. Our principal approaches are these:

- reduce the amount of time you need to have fun in a session. This is because casual gamers don't have as much time to play in six hour blocks as hardcore gamers do. ;) So we strive to reduce or eliminate the time involved in doing traditional time sinks like corpse recovery, macroing, forming a group, and getting to where the fun is, so that the amount of time a session will take is more predictable.

- provide a wider range of activities. Fact is that the larger, more casual audience wants to do things other than just kill. And we intend to provide ample opportunity for that, and what's more, we want to explicitly reward it within the game. Traditionally, those sorts of activities don't fit into the experience-based standard RPGing systems, and that's why we're not using a system like that.

- don't make the game centered around power differentials. This is what makes harder core players outpace more casual players, what makes it so that a high level player can't group with a low level player, etc. Both of those effects are things we want to avoid, so we're going to the root of it, and ensuring that our game system isn't based on massive differences in power. Instead, advancement is skill-tree based, which means you acquire abilities, not just bigger numbers.

Dynamic content

Yes, it's good, yes, we're doing it as much as possible, and a lot more than you've seen in other MMOs to date. A lot of it will be player-driven dynamic content.

Advancement

Multiple paths of advancement, and what's more, paths of advancement that use different advancement engines, are a key factor in several of the things I described above. Again, this is why we don't use XP — XP is not well suited to advancement in the context of roleplay-based, economically-based, exploration-based, politics-based, or any other non-killing-based advancement ladders.

Support

This is a problem the industry as a whole is still wrestling with. We intend to keep improving, and to do the best we can. We are investing a significant amount of time in creating good support tools and backend infrastructure so that we can help you more and more effectively.

Lack of high level design and content

This is actually a double-edged sword. The way I like to think of it is this:

- too often, we as developers spend too much time adding new content only at the top of our advancement ladders. This makes the games unfriendly to newbies and reduces the overall difficulty of the game as higher-level items and whatnot trickle down to lower-level players.

- At the same time, we usually don't invest enough in what I call "elder games." These are the systems that give you something to do, new objectives, new ways of playing the game, after you have "maxed out."

Our entire game system is built around the premise that every different profession can serve as an elder game for someone who has maxed out whatever they started out in. (Hmm, am I revealing too much about how it can work? Probably…) I am a huge believer in elder games, and what's more, I believe they should change the HOW of how you play the game-sort of like how advancing through the military means you have to learn completely new skill sets, not just "be a better private."

Repetition

This is a tough one. Some people like it. In fact, a lot of people like it. What we can do is provide diverse enough activities, and enough change in the world, that you can always find something different to do. But it IS natural to run out, eventually, and there's nothing much we can do about that.

Game economy

The biggest thing here is that we intend the economy to be player-driven as much as possible. This is because the single biggest factor screwing up in-game economies in these games is us, the developers. We put in hard-coded value numbers, we write unsophisticated shopkeeper AI, we try our hand at macroeconomics in spawning & whatnot, etc etc, and as a result we create subsidies and taxes and hidden costs and all sorts of problems. To quote Zach Simpson's excellent paper on "The In-Game Economics of Ultima Online" (you can find it on the web), "it's not a virtual economy. It's a real economy with virtual objects." We are mucking things up when we try to "simulate" it, when the best thing to do is get out of the way as much as possible-we're not economists and we're not expert at writing econ sims. For that matter, economists aren't either. ;)

Whew. That's the top issues, I think. Hopefully it's enough for you all to chew on and speculate with!

The last part is a reply to an essay that was circulating around the online gaming community at the time. But I can't remember who wrote it or what it was called, and so the reference is lost.

We ended up going with XP anyway because they are easier to quantify and track than a zillion individual events. But we retained the fact that you can earn those XP in a myriad of ways.

A Philosophical Statement on Playerkilling

I wrote this as the playerkilling and PvP system debates started to heat up on the Star Wars Galaxies boards. I have always felt like my position on playerkilling has been misunderstood, oversimplified, or willfully ignored by anyone who wanted to argue their agenda in the issue. After all, I've gone from being the peaceful side's hero one day (with the publication of "A Story About a Tree") to their villain and saint of the playerkillers (all because I said "Thank heavens for the playerkillers![211]" –see what quoting out of context will get ya?). So this was an attempt to clear the air.

I came into the game industry from muds. You know, the old-fashioned text ones. You already saw in my Comments from the Team letter the story of how I first discovered online worlds. But you didn't hear the story of how eventually I rose to run a guild, the Golden Pyramids, which helped newbies as they arrived in that mud. There was one catch to running a guild in this mud–being in a guild meant that you were PvP-enabled. It meant that other guilded players could attack you (within level ranges and the like, of course). And I, as the leader of the guild, was allowed to attack any of my members.

I did it once; I attacked Breton, whose description said he was some sort of soda cracker. (Apparently, he got the name, and then the entire personality, from a brand of soda crackers that showed a little cracker with a sword and knight's uniform). And I crumbled him; wasn't hard–he was many levels below me. It was all in good fun, though. It was a roleplayed killing over some perceived slight, and we all laughed about it, and I helped him recover his lost experience points afterwards. Breton peeks in on these boards from time to time–he lives in Maine now and recently had a second child, and he writes to me from time to time excited about how SWG is going. Hi, Breton.

Fast forward a few years. Now I'm running a different mud, and my character is a sharp-tongued bard, a member of the Order of the Scroll. I'm chatting out messages about a rival clan, the Servants of the Dark Lord, who worshipped some sort of astral

---

[211] In "What Rough Beast."

fish. I called the Dark Lord a guppy–a name which has stuck to this very day, almost 7 years later, though I haven't actively played in years now–and I got killed for my trouble. I didn't last very long, it being only my second PvP fight ever, and my opponent being experienced at PvP. But I went down a martyr.

Some time later, same mud, my last PvP fight ever. It was again a roleplayed affair–my assassin sister Kiera had taken my character's sweater and gone on a PvP spree while wearing it. And she got blood on it. My character, Dusty, was not one to tolerate damage to her wardrobe. So she killed Kiera over it. This was in the nature of a joke, as Kiera was one of the deadliest playerkillers on the mud, and I was known as probably the most ineffectual since I'd had only the one fight, and lost egregiously. When the message "Kiera killed by Dusty" went out across the Info channel, there were screens and screens worth of flabbergasted gasps. Boy, it was worth it.

So, as I player, am I carebear? Oh, yah, almost certainly. Three PvP battles over the course of ten years in online game development does not a Killer make. Online, I enjoy roleplay, and some hack n slash, and I love craft skills.

Now, if you poke around in the MMORPG industry, you'll find me tarred with the brush of being the most bloodthirsty of all the developers out there (well, until the advent of Shadowbane, at any rate.). It doesn't matter that I'm the guy who pushed for tailoring skills to be added to MMORPGs, or player housing, or pets. You see, I'm the one who permitted the massacre of countless innocents on *Ultima Online* by insisting that we shouldn't go to a PK switch system, that players should be able to police themselves. I'm the one who kept trying systems like notoriety and reputation, who kept saying that the idea of separate servers for PvP and nonPvP was a financial boondoggle. Why?

Well, I still dislike playerkilling switches. At the time, I believed that they would cost too much to have in a game of large scale; *EverQuest* has proven me wrong on that front. My reasons were simple–in the text muds, the PK switches were constantly circumvented by clever players out to do harm to one another. They'd heal the enemy a player was fighting. They'd cast area effect spells that caused a player to lose the advantage in fights somehow. They'd casually drop healing potions next to their friends who were fighting. And so on down the line; the switch seemed a never-ending source of loud and painful disputes which ended up taking a bunch of admin time. The switch basically means having two completely different games co-existing on the same map, after all.

But there were other reasons. There were things we wanted to do with UO, things that we thought would advance the state of the art in online worlds, and we couldn't do those things with an artificial mechanic like a PK switch. If you like, you can go to my website and read about those times, and some of the rather passionate opinions I held about these things.

Here's the thing though: I searched up and down for a means that would allow players to police their environment in a game of large scale. And I didn't find such a way. It wasn't until many months after leaving UO and the company that made it that I realized, "Hey–if the punishment was taking away the ability to kill, I bet players could have policed the game…" (Heh, well, now you know where THAT idea came from…!)

And the primary lessons I learned in all this were these: There are many people out there who really don't care how their victims feel. There are many perfectly nice people out there who turn insensitive when they are online. They may make great companions, they might serve as stellar leaders for online communities–but they have this desire to exercise power over others, and for them that is what the game is about. And people given power and no accountability have a way of turning griefer on you. Lastly–no matter how good a game, how good a WORLD you put together, people will leave if they feel they cannot exist in it, if they feel that they just aren't welcome. And I learned the lesson that if I had to choose between two players, I'd choose the one who was going about their own business and enjoying the game, rather than the one who forced others to play THEIR game.

Kind of like Kiera, who played my sister online; in real life, a guy and a lawyer. A truly deadly PKer, and one who eventually left the mud over disputes over PK, among other things. And considered by many on the mud to be not a benefit to the mud as a whole, but one of the people tearing the social fabric of it apart. A good player? Certainly. Destructive? Also true. Just as they say there's a fine line between love and hate, there's a fine line between someone who adds spice to the game and someone who just adds sorrow.

I still believe many things. I still believe that we can find ways to allow players to police their environment. I still believe that this can open up the way to many extremely cool features new to these sorts of games. And I am continuing to work towards having these many features: real battles of territory. Player governments with actual importance and consequence. Player communities that are refined and defined via conflict and struggle so that their battles MEAN something. Real emotions–yes, even including fear and shame, because this is a medium like any other art medium, and its expressive (and impositional!) power is amazing and worthy of exploration. I believe that virtually every player can try PvP and enjoy it, if it is designed correctly, and that it adds great richness to the online gaming experience.

But I do not want to ever disappoint people in that way again. People will come to

SWG for those things, and I do not want them to discover that they cannot stay and enjoy them because the very freedoms which allow those cool, innovative, exciting features, also allow d00dspeaking giggly jerks to dance roughshod jigs on their virtual corpses.

So am I willing to make compromises in "realism" (a radically overvalued thing in game design, frankly) to make sure that SWG remains someplace where most everybody can feel welcome?

You betcha.

Of course, the debates continue. The SWG PvP system is mostly a very conservative and thorough implementation of a PK switch. But there's a portion of the map set aside for an experiment called Outcasting, which I hope can serve as a better foundation for expanding the dynamic nature of online worlds.

Socialization and Convenience

Another post originally from the Star Wars Galaxies boards that got a lot of reprint attention on various message boards. The first part is the post from those boards. The subsequent snippets all come from MUD-Dev discussion of the topic.

We've been having an interesting discussion here at work over the last couple of days. We've been working on the layouts for various buildings found in cities, and in the process found an interesting philosophical question I'd like to share with you all.

To start with, let me ask you this question. It's a very arbitrary question, and your answer will reveal a fair amount about you as a player. It's an unfair question, of course, but ignore that, and just go with your gut.

How much time do you think the average player should spend socializing in SWG? Meaning, as opposed to "playing" however you define that–killing things, crafting, whatever. Chatting while recovering from a fight counts; chatting while forming a group counts too.

Got a number?

So numbers we arrived at among our team ranged from 3% all the way up to 50%. I think it mostly reveals things about how different people play the game–and also about how people define socializing–and also about their memories (I flat out don't *believe* the 3% people–that's a total of a few seconds every *hour* spent chatting with people, on *average*. My take–nuh-uh, no way. For the record, I was a 50% guy).

Why do I ask this? Because we have contradictory goals for the game. We want to reduce downtime. But people get to know people during downtime. That's when they socialize. That's when they make friends. In fact, I'd go so far as to state that it is a Law of Online World Design: **Socialization Requires Downtime**. The less downtime, the less social your game will be. And we ran headlong into this while discussing interfaces for common municipal structures.

Let's take a bank as an example. The question came up as to how you would use a bank. It matters because of how we lay it out. If you have to walk inside and use a computer terminal, then we need wide doors and spacious interiors and lots of terminals. But we could also make it so that you could use it anywhere inside the structure–we'd get rid of the terminals, change the layout somewhat based on the flow. Probably have many doors in, since people would tend to stop at the doorway, which is the first place they can do their transaction, and then turn around and leave.

Then we said to ourselves, "Wait a minute. We have a credit economy. We could make it so that you used the bank from anywhere via your datapad." First we talked about a radius around the bank–like say, in the courtyard outside. Then we started talking bigger radii. Finally we we said, "You know, you could just use the bank from anywhere in the city!"

And we said, "Wow, that's awfully convenient! Saves tons of time! We could do that for pretty much every municipal structure!"

But there were some nagging concerns. And it helps to think about the purpose of different types of structures.

In architectural theory (cf *Timeless Way of Building* or *A Pattern Language*) there's a lot of well-established thought about traffic patterns and the ways in which they affect the well-being of a community and the ways in which they affect the culture of a community.

Let's take the example of community building. There's an oft-told anecdote (the precise source of which escapes me at the moment) about a company which was suffering from malaise because people weren't coming up with good new ideas to advance the business, and there was stagnation and loss of morale. When the office building the company was located in was reorganized such that there was a central courtyard type space that served as a crossroads, and the different departments were obliged to walk through the courtyard on a regular basis to do their regular work, morale boomed, so did ideas, and so did profits. Why? Because the fact that people were interacting with people (and therefore ideas) that they normally didn't sparked both creativity and community.

The same logic can be applied to other types of desired results; if you seek convenience, then it makes a lot of sense to *avoid* crossroads. Roundabouts actually improve traffic flow precisely because you don't have to encounter other people head on. The reduced speed but lack of a total stop and waiting for turns to move forward means that vehicles continue moving at a steady pace, and there's actually a reduction in pedestrian accidents (good article recently in Discover magazine about this effect).

A second key philosophical question–I asked the team, once we'd argued these points for a couple of hours, what their preferred metaphor was for a town in the game–player-run or not, really, though we focused mostly on player-run. Many different answers came up–what sort of organization or community do you see that feature of the game as being most like?

Ponder that one for a bit.

Got an answer?

OK, so one of the most frequent answers we got was "guild," meaning people saw it as an alternate form of player association. We also got "staging area" a lot, meaning people saw it as a launchpad to the "real game." Some saw the metaphor as being "shopping mall" or "apartment complex." My answer was kind of long and poetic, and people kind of looked at me strangely as I rambled. It went something like, "A 1950's small town with a local hardware store on the corner where the shop owner knows what sort of paint you really need for your fence and an ice cream parlor where you can go to get root beer floats and sarsaparilla and a bar where everyone knows your name and where the people you see at the local grocery store are mostly people you know by sight if not by name and there's a gazebo in the town square where sometimes they play live music…"

So we stopped for a moment and thought about what sorts of downtime we were removing, and what sorts we were enforcing, and what types of community building mechanics we were putting into the game. We used examples from other games to think about the sorts of activities and locations that we saw as drawing crowds and leading to community ties.

Here's some examples from other games:

- blacksmithies in *Ultima Online*.
- banks in UO.
- town fountains in Diku muds.
- spawn points in *EverQuest*.
- safe zones in EQ.

Most of us on the team had fond memories of blacksmithies in UO. You went there because you were looking for a player to repair your weapons and armor, and you needed a skilled player to do it, or the items might be ruined. They were there predictably because they needed a forge to do it. The result was a pleasant experience chatting with the blacksmith, with others waiting their turn, and a great launching pad for meeting folks and going on adventures.

On the other hand, most of us disliked the UO banks. They were the default place where there was a crowd, but everyone who was there was either there absorbed in an interface screen (i.e. not talking) or was spamming the crowd with items for sale merely because there were lots of people there. It was not a sociable place, though it was a social place. And of course, everyone stopped there at the start and end of every adventure.

I have many fond memories of hanging out at town fountains in Diku muds. Usually they were set in a town square, and the structures to the sides of the square were key to gameplay. The newbie hall, where everyone first entered the game, opened down onto this square. The inn, where everyone came to log out, and from which everyone logged in, was on one side. The guildhall where you had to come to advance a level was there. As a result, there was always a knot of people swapping stories about where they had just been, and making plans about where to go next. It's hard to imagine a more welcoming environment for a newbie to step into.

Spawn points in *EverQuest* are of course a much maligned source of downtime. But many people attested to the idea that that was where they chatted and talked. But the fact that the downtime was a barrier to further gameplay in their eyes (meaning, they were camping so they could get some piece of armor or a weapon that they saw as necessary to continued enjoyment of the game) led to resentment of the enforced downtime and appears to have harmed its value as a social space.

Whereas safe zones in EQ were seen as staging areas. These are places of lower risk in the midst of dangerous areas. As natural gathering places, these locations became places where you bumped into people with common interests (killing whatever was nearby) and of comparable skill (since they were likely to be in your level range). It was where people retreated to to rest up and heal, and it was where they started a big foray from. A base, so to speak.

With these examples in hand, we classified the types of social spaces into three:

- **Staging**: these are places where you form a group, find a friend, and decide what to do.
- **Pit stop**: these are the obligatory stops you make before you get to have fun.
- **Recovery**: these are the places where you go after an adventure.

Here's a third touchstone question that emerged. Recovery areas—what are they *for*? Think hard.

Got an answer? OK.

We were divided on this one too. Many of us saw them as obligatory character maintenance—the place to go when you need to heal up. We also saw them as rites of passage—the place to go to level up, learn your skill now that you have the achievements, whatever. But the third big thing we identified, and the thing that some of us felt was the most important thing, was that they were opportunities for mythologizing. The chance to retell the story of our adventures to ourselves, the chance to establish a consensus history, relive the incidents, and weave a narrative out of what were in fact very disjointed moments with no storyline or structure to them.

As the fates would have it, we had a fantastic example of this at lunch today. We went out to Fuddrucker's for burgers, and after we had eaten (think of that as the obligatory pitstop!), some of the guys who had most strongly seen the recovery areas as being about character maintenance started talking about the previous days' game of *Counterstrike*. "…and then I whipped around the corner and the machine gun…" "Yeah! And the idiot kept going and…" "Yeah, it was great! And then he did the thing!" "Yeah, the thing! That rocked!"

They made no sense.

In light of this breakdown, it's easy to see that recovery areas are GOOD sorts of downtime. That's why the safe areas in EQ and the town fountains on Dikus work well. And it's also easy to see that pitstops kind of suck; people see them as barriers to getting on with the fun, like camping spawns or having to visit the bank before and after every adventure.

An interesting case was the blacksmithy in UO. Clearly a pit stop. But since it involved a player service, there was a human element to it that was missing from the bank or the spawn point. Waiting for another player is more palatable than waiting for the server to do something for you. So pit stops don't have to all be bad.

Lastly, staging areas seem plainly vital, because you need to have places where you form your party or group.

But here's the rub. We had eliminated almost all of this stuff in the name of convenience. You don't need to visit the bank in *SWG* if you just enter town and transfer credits. To pick up gear you go by your house, which means your group scatters to the four winds before setting off. You don't visit the blacksmithy to get your weapon repaired–you drop it in a hopper and pick it up later. You get a mission on your datapad. You don't need to go to the town square to get your mail, you do that on your datapad too. In fact, the more we talked about it, the more we posited that if there *were* key structures (like needing to visit a shop to pick up your fixed blaster) they'd be placed on the edge of cities, not in the center, so that you could "bounce" off of town as quickly as possible.

Even our recovery areas suffer from this. Yes, we pretty much make you go to cantinas and taverns, because you need to heal wounds. But that means that the only people whom you will meet in cantinas are wounded people and healers. And maybe a bartender. That leaves out a lot of types of player–the politicians, the crafters, the farmers and the animal trainers.

And that brings us to a fourth touchstone question. Do you think you will play mostly with friends you make *before* the game, or friends you make *in* the game, or with strangers?

Empirically, we know that friends made in the game are retention devices. Frankly, we want you to play with people you meet IN the game. That's because otherwise, all we have is a bunch of cliques. Hermetic organizations made up of people who mostly knew each other in advance somehow (maybe they organized their towns on a web board, like so many of the SWG players are doing now). And no easy way for a novice to the environment to make new friends. The fact that the decisions we had made meant that people would not tend to bump into strangers reveals a flaw in our thinking about managing community and downtime.

Online games have the opportunity to offer microcommunities, tight-knit groups of people working towards common causes. This is something that most of us miss in our daily lives, and it's something that is very woven into human nature and life, and has been for millennia. We speak of the dehumanizing pace of life in the cities, and the ways in which we tune out people in crowds. That's why I can speak so nostalgically of the small town experience. A large part of the attraction of online games is, to my mind, recapturing that sense of community. If we make life online overly convenient, what we may end up doing is merely recreating the experience of being a newbie in New York City.

But I could be wrong. And that's why I pose the question to you now again, after you've read this very long rambling post.

How much time do you think you should spend socializing? And where? When does convenience become dehumanization? And fundamentally, just how much downtime are you willing to take? Because it's evident that some needs to be there.

I look forward to seeing the discussion.

> This seems to presume that you're making a monster-bashing game (which I know you are, but I got the idea you were making a broader statement). I'd add that sometimes a single social space can be all three of the above AND the place where you have your 'fun'. For instance, the politicians in *Achaea* might be sitting in a single room, doing everything from there while chatting. – Matt Mihaly

I am making a broader statement; there's staging areas, pit stops, and recovery phases in politics too. The monster-bashing just happens to have a lot of this stuff quantified so it makes an easier example.

In terms of traffic flow, it's of course necessary to talk about it in terms of locations. But your example is not location-based, it's time-based. The area changes in function as different stages of the gameplay/activity occur.

The problem with not paying attention to traffic flow is that in your above example, it is extremely likely that the politicians will only talk to other politicians, unless there's some traffic flow reason for non-politicians to come through there. And I WANT strangers to rub up against one another, because it encourages that more open 250-person community (hermetic cliques tend to be much smaller), it increases the odds of welcoming novices to the environment, and it therefore acts as a retention mechanism.

>   The disconnect I'm having here is that for socializers, socializing *is* playing. –
> Jeff Freeman

Oh, yes, of course. But they are also not incurring any game downtime in the process. To get more specific:

You can look at a game as being composed of activities tied to reinforcement mechanisms. An action takes place, and the game/opponent provides a reaction; the reaction had better be broadly predictable, or else the player will consider it gambling, not skill, and hence not a game in that sense.

In most games, the degree of activity tends to be bursty; in physical games the bursts are the periods of actual physical activity, followed by downtime for rest and recovery. In mental games, the game is either designed to be relatively brief (usually by overwhelming you) or the pace is player-directed.

In online games, you have a combination of all of these things. Take the basic hack n slash advancement paradigm as an example, since we're all pretty familiar with it (most of the list because they make them, and those diehard holdouts who don't who keep hoping we'll talk about non-GoP muds sometime, well, they've gotten amply familiar with it by now, poor guys!).

In a level rat race design, you have a player-directed pace, and *also* an enforced activity schedule determined by the need for stats to regenerate. It's loosely enforced, since there's usually ways to accelerate the process. While within the encounter itself, it's designed to be relatively brief; it too is also designed to overwhelm you (or for you to overwhelm the opponent). A given combat is not planned to last days like a chess match, but rather to be self-terminating in a much shorter period of time.

So I am defining "downtime" as the periods when a player is on that cycle and is not in the combat. More broadly, I'm defining downtime as "time during a game session wherein a player is not actively participating in game mechanics because said game mechanics are not viable for that character at that time."

Socializers are excluded by this definition; they are not waiting for something, so for them it isn't downtime. It's free time, which is a different beast. They have intentionally stepped off the treadmill and have all the time in the world. That's a radically different mindset.

Given that mechanically speaking, you're probably not typing while you are hitting keys to get things to happen (such as striking blows) I would guess that a lot then depends on the granularity of your perception of downtime. If you're walking from one close spawn to another, then that's a form of downtime. A zero-downtime game would be like an arcade shoot-em-up game (and even they pause when you clear a wave). The fact that you are describing downtime as a time when you read a book suggests a *much* longer period of time.

"I'd go so far as to state that it is a Law of Online World Design: Socialization Requires Downtime."
Argh. Resist the temptation. It's not right! – Jeff Freeman

Well, I haven't heard a good argument against it yet.

In a GoP environment, players who are engaging in the activity are going to want to devote their full mental faculties to the activity itself (in fact, that's how they get those endorphin highs, entering quasi-meditative states while engaging in the activity). They're not going to chat during that time; if they don, they won't be all that successful at the activity unless they are expert enough players that they can time-slice the activity so tightly that the space between one blow and another is perceived as downtime by them. (And this is pretty common, and a lot depends on the pace and nature of the activity).

Now, if we posit that meaningful social interaction requires at least a question or statement and a reply (an in most cases, will require more than that; a mere two-sentence interaction that actually reveals something about the other's personality either presupposes prior knowledge between the two, or is a dead-end) then we see that in order for there to be enough room for social interaction, the activity must have a fairly slow pace of input (and situation assessment) and both players must have some comparable level of time slicing that so that their respective slower-paced moments coincide.

In my head I am seeing this as a graph; places where the two troughs coincide are where players might talk. The trough has to be long enough that the player's attention can be easily divided from what they perceive as the principal activity.

And actually, using the above definitions (which are brand new, I just came up with them as a typed, I am thinking out loud here) we can see why the bank sucks. Despite the fact that player congregate at the bank, the bank is actually a peak on the graph, not a trough. It's a moment when players' attention is heavily taken up by a game mechanic necessary to their goal. They cannot effectively time slice the activity of dropping stuff in the bank and taking stuff out, and many of the decisions they make are in fact fairly high-pressure decisions that can affect the success of their characters in the future. They are self-directed in time impact, sure, but players are not likely to want to be distracted while making them.

The sole exception I can think of–if they are there with someone who is already trusted, in which case they may socialize a little, and ask for advice on the decisions. But this is not a case likely to get strangers to talk to one another meaningfully. Unless they have crossed some threshold of trust on the player's part, their advice isn't useful.

The blacksmithy example involves very few decisions. It's a required gameplay activity, but the decision is "go there" which is a high-priority decision but comes *before* the standing around while there, and a low-priority decision "leave early" case which burbles along in the back of the mind but doesn't have much tug to it. (I'm coming up with a different metaphor in the back of my mind now, which is a weighted AI decision; the "keep getting cheese" impulse has a far lower priority than the "fix my paw" impulse; it therefore gets pushed to the bottom of the stack until "fix my paw" is completed. Since the "fix my paw" has an enforced delay on it, impulses which are normally *much* lower than "keep getting cheese" have an opportunity to appear, such as the "sniff other mice's butts" impulse. Hi there, Mr, Maslow, how are you today?).

> The lesson to learn from this is that the people were required to come into contact with one another due to the new building layout. They were NOT required to stand around in the foyer for hours a day doing nothing. – Jeff Freeman

I see these as two facets of the same problem.

For the layout described to work to that purpose, it's evident that *some* of the tasks the people had must have been lower priority than "sniff other mice's butt" or else there would have been zero interaction even in the courtyard area. Or perhaps some of the tasks were higher priority but had that sort of enforced downtime (I can easily see this layout working if every Xerox machine in the entire company were located in the courtyard, for example).

If not, what you get is just a traffic nightmare as everyone rushes through the courtyard as quickly as possible.

HUGE side note: it occurs to me that if you know the Bartle breakdown of your playerbase by broad percentages, and you can write some basic ALife code for weighted goals and then weight additionally for each entity based on their Bartle's type, you could probably throw this at your game's dataset and get a nice overhead view of your game with dots running around that shows you exactly what zones won't get used and why.

>   I believe that socialization can be summed up as introduction and then companionship. – Paul Sage

This ignores the factor of where the introduction point occurs. Either it occurs in a place, or it doesn't. If it occurs without a place, then it's occurring on a global chat channel or via some sort of matchmaking service. If it occurs in a place, then we have to worry about why these different people happened to be in the same place. What's more, in the healer scenario, the healer by definition has to be in downtime, or else he's too busy to heal the other player; in the fight needed by merchant case, the fighter has to be between adventures or else he's off slaying a dragon, not helping a merchant.

Fundamentally, if the other guy's busy, then he's not coming to the introduction party. If he isn't busy, then he's gotta be parked somewhere, or on the way to somewhere. And that suggests we need to manage traffic flow. And it also suggests we need to manage downtime, or else everyone will *always* be busy–especially achiever types who by nature seem to be driven by always having another rung on the ladder to reach.

On *LegendMUD* (a fairly GoP environment, fundamentally) we added a socialization area with a bunch of nifty social facilities. The Wild Boar Tavern offers a lounge for chatting, goofy food to buy, an auditorium, a gift shop to buy goofy items like birthday cards, a wedding shop for in-game events, etc. You can reach it instantly from *anywhere* by merely typing "OOC." It was there in an instant for anyone who wanted it.

It doesn't get used.

On UO we had taverns with NPCs, dart boards, chess boards, backgammon, dice.

There were multiple ones in every town. You know as well as I how crowded they were.

Leisure time in a mud is *pointless* time in players' eyes, and only a small subset of your players will be looking to spend pointless time.

John Buehler made the excellent point that keyboard and mouse input is currently a huge barrier to socialization.

A very important point. A single point of input; adding real-time voice provides two input channels. In addition, voice in real life is a much faster input channel than typing is, so the addition of voice allows you to socialize in smaller time slices.

…People use voice constantly in shooter games such as *Counterstrike*. But they don't socialize with it because the game itself is very intense and offers a lot of sustained, high pressure decision-making. Instead, it is seen as a better way to accomplish the game tasks.

> As far as I'm concerned, there's no need for architected downtime periods in order to encourage socialization. – John Buehler

Obviously, I still disagree. What I will agree with is that the downtimes can be made much smaller if you support a faster means of communication; and I'd say that this is a universal principle. You can encourage more communication in any game by either a) slowing the pace of the game or b) speeding up the communication facilities. It's a simple mathematical equation. You can either make the window bigger or the throughput greater.

One of my teammates (who is on this list somewhere lurking) is a pretty goal-oriented player who has recently gotten addicted to *Sojourn 3*. He cited a very low percentage too, when asked the question. He decided to run an experiment with a pair of timers whilst playing a typical session. He was a group leader and he was hack n slashing his way through the mud with abandon. He didn't count stuff like "OK, go west then headbutt" as social interaction.

Turned out that his actual time spent socializing was 25-30% even though he *thought* it was 10%.

Sun, 29 Jul 2001

I inherently distrust the concept of virtual apartments, rather than actual houses on the land, because they are less conducive to neighborhoods, in my mind. Less odds of bumping into a neighbor, less odds of seeing a house and getting curious about who lives there, far less ability to express yourself to a passerby and thereby catch their attention.

…A long time ago on this thread, there was an observation (perhaps by JCL?) about how the fact that UO was overcrowded was what led to many of its key community-building effects. I believe the term used was "hothouse." Also related is the whole socialization and convenience thread from not very long ago. If you add more and more lubricant to ensure that a player gets a good experience without needing to rub up against anyone else, compete for resources, interact for things that they lack, then you are increasing convenience and removing reasons and opportunities for socialization.

I really ought to go ahead and elaborate the preceding thread into a more detailed theory, but oh well.[212] In the end, "Socialization requires downtime" made it into the Laws.

---

[212] I eventually did, in a piece called "Forcing Interaction," which you are going to encounter shortly.

Astromech Stats: Economy Stats

This essay was originally written for the Star Wars Galaxies website in 2004 — it was after I had moved off the team, but I was asked to contribute it anyway because I knew the metrics systems better than anyone else at that point. It's of interest mostly for those curious about the state of the art for game metrics in 2004!

Economy Stats
by Raph "Holocron" Koster
Live Server Report Date: April 30th 2004

MMO economies are hard. It's kinda become a truism by now. There's models for closed economies and open ones, there's terms lifted from real economics thrown around, and lots of theory about faucet-drain economies, mudflation, and whatnot. Why bother? Well, mostly because the game gets more boring when the economy is out of whack. If too much money is entering the system, then players tend to have more stuff than they should be able to afford, and that makes the game easier, which then can make it kind of dull. So the health of the game economy is something that we pay pretty close attention to.

SWG uses what is called a faucet-drain economy. You can visualize a spigot of cash coming into the game, a big ol' sink where the money sloshes around, and a set of drains where the money goes out the bottom. When money comes in from the faucet, it's actually being "minted" – it's being created by the game system. The sink is basically the whole game. It's the bank accounts, the player inventories, all the money that is used for trades and transactions among players, etc. When money goes out the bottom, it's deleted from the system, rather than circulating back to a central bank.

(Credits aren't the only thing that is generated, of course – a significant faucet into the game economy actually comes in the form of resource mining. Since the amount of money and the amount of resources coming into the game at a time both vary, you get small fluctuations in the price of resources as the value of both the resources and the currency changes. Plus, you also get different qualities of resources that affect the price. But we're not really talking about commodities pricing today, much as just about the value of a credit).

We try to monitor the broad flow of cash in order to assess the health of the credit as a currency. There are other metrics for measuring the health of an economy overall – for example, the amount of transactions and the amount of currency that changes hands between players – but today we're going to just look at the flow of currency itself.

The four biggest tools we use in order to assess the health of the currency are reports on the flow in and out of money, and the percentage breakdown of where the money comes from and goes. For example, have a look at this graph.

What you see here is the raw amount of cash coming into the game over the course of the last month. It does tend to fluctuate up and down based on how many

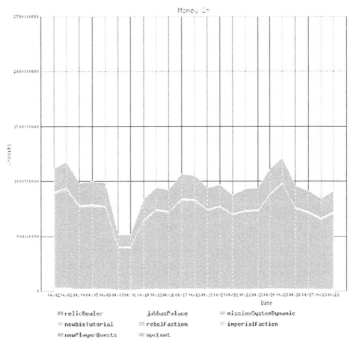

people are playing (which varies per day of the week), what they're doing, and so on. When we do major changes to the game (such as adding or removing a source of loot, let's say) the amount of currency flowing in tends to change.

We mostly watch this one in comparison to the amount of currency flowing out, which looks like this:

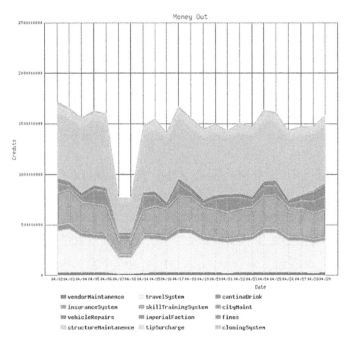

As you can see, the variety of outflow sources is much greater. We've been more successful at having a variety of ways for you to spend your money than a variety of ways for you to make money!

Those of you with sharp eyes may have noticed that in fact the game economy is running at a net loss, based on those two graphs. A while back we noticed that the game was running at a deficit, and yet there were none of the major effects we'd expect, such as currency becoming incredibly hard to come by, people going bankrupt, etc. Our conclusion was that a lot of the currency out there must have been "counterfeit" – in other words, we had a dupe bug. We promptly started hunting for it, and in fact we not only found it, but were able to mass ban a large number of folks who were clearly involved as well as removed trillions of credits from holding accounts, middlemen, etc. Running the overall currency flow at a deficit is effectively "eating up" the duped credits, and we'll return to the game economy to a more even keel when the total amount of cash in the system is something we're more comfortable with.

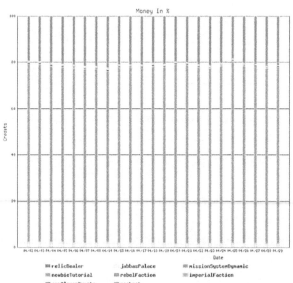

The graph above shows the percentage breakdown over the course of the last month for where people get their money. As you can see, the vast majority of the money coming in enters the system via missions. Loot runs in a distant second place.

Looking back at a long-term history of expenditures even lets you see when major features went into the game:

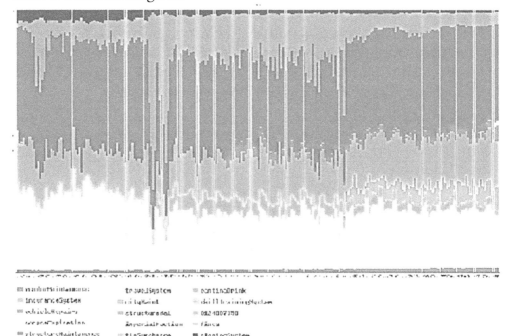

The red appears when vehicle maintenance kicks in, the purple is the arrival of player cities, and the light blue is when we made adjustments to the cost of player insurance.

In addition to these sorts of tracking, we also monitor things like large changes in wealth for individuals (often, but not always, a sign of cheating or duping), wealth distribution across the playerbase, and so on. For example, it's easy to see that just like in the real world economy, the characteristic "Pareto Law" distribution of cash holds true: most of the money is in the hands of a few. This is a graph of just the top 2000 or so folks on Bria, for example – the highest folks are billionaires.

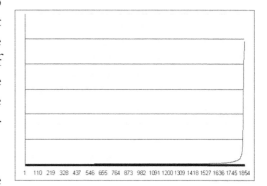

This isn't necessarily something to be discouraged by – rather, we take it as a sign that the game economy is replicating characteristics of the real world economy. Since one of our goals was to have a game economy that can provide ongoing interesting strategy gameplay, seeing real world patterns manifest is something we were looking forward to.

There's a ton of other types of data we track, and you've seen some of them in other features. But game economy is one of the most important, because overall health of the currency is one of the quickest ways to see if the game is going sour. You can even do some of this yourself – try monitoring the fluctuations in the prices of different items on a day to day basis, and build your own graphs. If you're a stats geek like me, it'll open your eyes to a whole new way of looking at online worlds.

Forcing Interaction

A comment on a previous post[213] prompted me to dig into an issue that has been tossed around a lot on the blogosphere, most recently in Jason Booth's blog.[214]

A long time ago now, I wrote in an essay called "On Socialization and Convenience"[215] that

> On LegendMUD (a fairly GoP environment, fundamentally) we added a socialization area with a bunch of nifty social facilities. The Wild Boar Tavern offers a lounge for chatting, goofy food to buy, an auditorium, a gift shop to buy goofy

---

[213] The comment can be found at https://www.raphkoster.com/2005/12/08/feelin-groovy-a-rant/#comment-377 and reads,

> I think that there has to be a balance between bringing normalcy into a game and the bashing aspects of the game, which a good number of people obviously enjoy.
>
> For me, the fact that originally in SWG, as one example, you were forced to sit and watch a dancer to 'heal' you in a sense wasn't fun. Sure some people might enjoy dancing, and others enjoy watching them, but to 'have' to do it so you can then whack the next mole (if that's your thing) is what made a lot of people angry. Forcing downtime/time sinks is a very bad practice.
>
> I guess forcing interaction, in a predefined set of ways, is just as bad as not having interaction. Again I always go back to online gaming is just that, a game, not a reality/emotional simulator. You play them, and pay monthly to do so in these games, to enjoy yourself. There shouldn't be one way to enjoy yourself, the dev-way in effect.
>
> Have the social interactions, of various types, but don't force a person to have to spend X amount of their time doing that just because you (dev team in this case) think they should. Reward those that enjoy the social interactions, and participate in some way, but don't penalize those that just want to whack the next shiny mole because they don't want to spend an hour in a virtual bar watching a spinning character in order to go on with their desired playstyle.
>
> Balance is the key, and fun should always be the main thrust.

[214] Jason Booth is a game designer, artist, and programmer who has worked on MMOs such as *Asheron's Call* and *Lord of the Rings Online*, and also on many music games from Harmonix. The blog post in question can be found at
https://web.archive.org/web/20070501173101/http://jbooth.blogspot.com/2005/12/instancing-part-2-world-design.html

[215] Two chapters prior to this one.

---

items like birthday cards, a wedding shop for in-game events, etc. You can reach it instantly from anywhere by merely typing "OOC." It was there in an instant for anyone who wanted it.

It doesn't get used.

On UO we had taverns with NPCs, dart boards, chess boards, backgammon, dice. There were multiple ones in every town. You know as well as I how crowded they were.

Leisure time in a mud is pointless time in players' eyes, and only a small subset of your players will be looking to spend pointless time. (emphasis added)

The fundamental reasons for this, I believe, are **incentive structures** and **opportunity**. In that essay, I wrote extensively about the opportunity issue. In a nutshell, if the action is too fast and furious, people cannot take the time to converse. The faster the pace and the fewer the leisurely moments, the more likely that the socialization will reduce down to basic cues (shout-outs, expressions of fiero, "gg" remarks, disses, and so on). I don't want to underestimate the important value of these — I just recently read an essay, can't remember where, in which an academic evaluated their importance actually — but they aren't the thing that leads towards lasting social relationships.

This led me to say that **"socialization requires downtime"** — which I didn't mean as "put lots of tedious stuff in your game" but rather as "think about the quiet moments" or "don't have a relentless furious pace." If the cognitive demands on players are continuously high (as in an FPS game, for example), they will focus their attention and concentration, leaving no room to process other sorts of input. Providing moments when the attention can be divided or engage in forms of longer-stage planning is merely to provide an opportunity for the player to multitask. If you picture player attention on a task as a graph of intensity, it would look something like this.

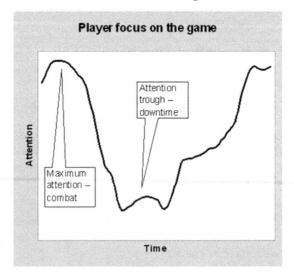

In those games where there *is* that pace, we find the characteristic that the sessions tend to be short. **It's abnormal for humans to remain at that high state of attention** and adrenalin for very long. Indeed, stuff like flow is characterized by high attention but not by high excitement, or else it would be far too exhausting to keep up. In between the short sessions, players do things like watch the remaining players finish up the match, trash talk on chat, or go onto web forums to actually engage in community building.

Essentially, the precept is that **you can only put a given amount of cognitive burden on a player, and socializing is a cognitive burden too**. If you want socializing, you have to reduce the burden on some other front. And if you don't reduce the burden, players will do it themselves — they will choose to stop playing for a moment to catch their breath. In other words, **you have a choice as to provide rest stops, or else players will pull over by the side of the highway whenever they feel the need to.** Thus the creation of social spaces such as the variously located trading spaces that sprung up in *EverQuest* in different locations over its history, or the UO blacksmith visits, or the example Grimwell cites[216] in *Asheron's Call*, the game Jason worked on:

> Interesting is the twist that Turbine has experience with 'hubs' in AC1 that had almost no decoration. The 'Hub' lies West, Northwest of Arwic (which was ruined last time I saw it) and was a nexus to points elsewhere in the world.
>
> The decoration of the hub was minimalist to say the least and yet it turned into a dynamic player gathering point serving the same functions as a town would (rest, grouping, trades, etc.). Because of the convenience in travel that the Hub offered (as a jumping point to multiple other activities, the players chose it as a central nexus. Even without the decor; proving that utility > appearances when it comes to hubs.

So that's opportunity; but then there's incentive structures. In the case Grimwell cites, the incentive was convenient travel, which translates crudely into "faster acquisition of experience." And that's where the above-referenced comment and Jason Booth's post come into play.

Have a look at this highly interesting graph from the fascinating PlayOn project at PARC.[217]

---

[216] Original source lost, alas.

[217] The PlayOn project was an ongoing blog reporting the results of a datamining and research project about players of virtual worlds. Researchers included Nic Ducheneaut, Nick Yee, Don Wen, Greg Wadley, Eric Nickell, Bob Moore, and Cabell Gathman. See https://web.archive.org/web/20081217073952/http://blogs.parc.com/playon/ for just one snapshot at

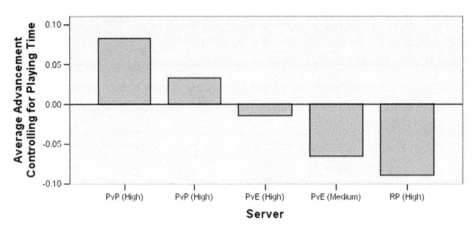

As Eric Nickell and Nick Yee write in the accompanying blog post,[218]

> Characters on PvP servers level more, spend more time playing, and are fastest at leveling than characters on other servers. Notably, characters on RP servers level the least even though they spend almost as much time playing, but are the slowest levelers.

The conclusion seems obvious — RPers level slower because they spend more time chatting. Since there is only one incentive structure in the game — experience points — players who divide their attention are penalized relative to the average player. In other words that verge on hyperbole, **the game's incentive structure punishes people who socialize**.

Now, this is far from the whole picture, of course, because there are other factors that push people together. Most evident among these is forced grouping. The same incentive structure is used in order to convey the clear message that greater return on investment can be had by pooling resources. In other words, two guys killing orcs together can kill them more efficiently.

The thing that I want to emphasize here is that **forced grouping does not force socialization, it forces teamwork**, and they are not the same thing. Killing orcs is still a peak on the attention graph; nobody is having personal conversations in the midst of an intense raid. It is only because there is the likelihood of downtime in the close proximity of your group-mates immediately before or after the fight that any

project midlife. Unfortunately, the archives are gone from the PARC website and now only available via the Wayback Machine.

[218] "Rate of Advancement by Server," https://web.archive.org/web/20060211170200/http://blogs.parc.com:80/playon/archives/2005/11/rate_of _advance_3.html

socialization can occur at all.

Again we can look to the FPS games for the stark example; all the team-based games, such as *CounterStrike*, put people into groups, but are too intense for socialization during the match. Little personal touches generally come out between matches or while waiting for the match end, when one has the time to type or chance to speak coherently.

So forced grouping is, paradoxically, problematic in terms of socialization because the incentive structure rewards maximizing the XP return during the time you are together, as opposed to maximizing getting to know one another. It pushes people together at peaks in the graph, not at troughs.

When Blake says,[219]

> Have the social interactions, of various types, but don't force a person to have to spend X amount of their time doing that just because you (dev team in this case) think they should. Reward those that enjoy the social interactions, and participate in some way, but don't penalize those that just want to whack the next shiny mole because they don't want to spend an hour in a virtual bar watching a spinning character in order to go on with their desired playstyle.

the part that is getting ignored is that the vast majority of players will choose the most obvious path towards cognitive engagement, and towards the reinforcement effects of the reward structure of the game. In other words **whacking shiny moles is easier, more predictable, and better rewarded, so lacking opportunity and incentive, people won't do anything else.**

What is the incentive structure that incentivizes forming friendships while in an attention trough?

As an aside: why even care about this? It's worth following the logic here from a developer's point of view. Most players come to play these games with already-established friendships these days. That's a problem from the operator's point of view because it means that the entire social unit can come and go relatively easily, in terms of its social network; it's a self-sustaining circle of friends. The hypothesis (and it may well be completely wrong, but it's based on fairly standard social network theory) is that the **more tightly the group is "webbed in" to disparate groups in the game, the more likely it is to stick** and thus continue to form a part of the community and possible ongoing revenues.

This is where I disagree with several of Jason Booth's comments. He says, for example,

---

[219] In the referenced comment that opened the post.

It's a fool's proposition to spend a large portion of your development resources on a space which provides no additive game play time, and generally only fools are willing to push for those types of trade off's.

The question here is, of course, what is meant by "additive gameplay time." If it means whacking orcs, then it should be evident from the above that **having a space in your game where you don't *have* to whack orcs is indeed valuable**, even if its only purpose is to allow players to go there when they themselves decide they need a break. Otherwise your game will be go-go all the time, and you'll be in FPS-land, with an attention graph with no troughs at all.

He also says,

Some designers argue that running from place to place helps chance socialization, but I'd argue that unless you're the type of person who commonly meets people at the mall, you'll probably run past everyone and not bother to socialize. Again, it's the activity which provides the means and reasons for socialization, not the proximity.

But without the proximity, there can be very little opportunity (a bit, true, using tells and the like, but not much). The mall Jason cites is a bad example for a variety of reasons, of course; generally, the walkways of a mall (technically, I suppose that is the "mall" proper) are interstitial spaces; we are on the way somewhere else, and while not at a peak on the attention graph, we're not at a trough either. We're somewhere on the upslope, usually, heading somewhere with a modicum of intent.

A better example is a bar, or other such "third places." The activity there is often ill-defined. They are spaces architected for troughs, rather than peaks. There are activities present, but they are generally intended as low cognitive burden activities. They are designed with lots of downtime in them: bar trivia games, a band with frequent breaks, eating food, drinking alcohol, pool tables.

The PARC guys also did a paper[220] examining the specific case that no doubt both Blake and Jason are referencing, which is of course the use of "battle fatigue" in *Star Wars Galaxies*. For those who never played, this was a mechanic that accumulated damage to a particular stat that could only be healed in a cantina, which were specifically located in towns. The intent was to provide a designed arc to the attention graph, timing a trough with the natural end of a play session and bringing players to a "third place" at the right time.

When Jason says, "waiting to heal special 'cantina only' wounds doesn't make me

---

[220] "Designing for Sociability in Massively Multiplayer Games:
an Examination of the "Third Places" of SWG," Nicolas Ducheneaut, Robert J. Moore, and Eric Nickell.

want to socialize; it actually puts me in a foul mood" and Blake says "don't penalize those that just want to whack the next shiny mole" I think what we are seeing is that above all, **the designed arc was mistimed**. People do not resent even forced downtime when it comes at natural ending points. After a sports match, we are forced to stop, and yet we relax. After a raid, we're not all rarin' to go again. The examples are legion. It may well be that the biggest flaw with battle fatigue is that it accumulated too quickly, and didn't clear itself during logged out time.

If I summarize the empirical data from the paper that the researchers connected to Oldenburg's concept of "third places," I get a list like this:

- too many players "hit and run" the cantina, so they never really socialized

- too many players macroed the services offered, and were bots

- this may be because the players present are there not in a social role driven by their personalities — "third places do not set formal criteria of membership and exclusion... the charm and flavor of one's personality, irrespective of his or her station in life, is what counts"

- cantinas may ironically have been too crowded, or not thorough enough in forming a "mixer" environment

- but cantinas that were not overrun with spammers **did** have a high "fun" index, showed evidence of socialization and conversations, and so on

- cantinas need "regulars" who provide the soul of the place; by measuring various things, they concluded that the regulars weren't actually providing it. But many of these regulars were probably spammers and grinders, not true regulars...

In the end, the researchers concluded that "socialization requires downtime" is imperfect — or, as I could phrase it, incomplete. They recommended the addition of things to create more "regulars," high population density to create an urban feel, better placement of the cantinas so that they weren't a pitstop, and so on. They also explored the notion that other games, such as *City of Heroes* which wasn't yet out, might treat the whole *game* as the cantina instead; my personal take is that this isn't really how it panned out.

My take on what happened with SWG's entertainers: The original intent behind the entertainer profession was to provide an incentive structure to regulars, to get them off of the last spot in that advancement rate graph. Regulars were hoped to provide the entertaining conversation because it was a draw for customers, so the incentive structure still worked. It worked OK, though not great because of the "hit and run" factor, until it intersected with the instrumental play of hologrinders, which resulted in the spammer problem, which then totally undermined the entire concept.

In the end, we're left with some basic questions and observations:

- Do we really need people to form these new in-game friendships, or are the ones they had before entering the game enough?

- Attention troughs are always forced, either by mechanics or even by plain old player fatigue. Can we architect them, or not?

- Can we overcome the fact that forming new friendships in-game is to a large degree disincentivized by the game systems?

To my mind, the answer to these is far from cut and dried at this point.

A brief thing that just occurred to me: when people say that WoW is "more casual" it may actually be that what they are referencing is that WoW has "more downtime" in the attention graph sense: its activities tend to be more piecemeal, particularly as regards questing. Small bits of content interrupted fairly frequently with attention troughs, as opposed to graphs with high sustained attention curves.

The definition of "casual" might actually be the frequency of the sine wave in attention?

[Star Wars Galaxies] did eventually switch to a positive reinforcement system, but it doesn't seem to have made any difference; I even think that the amount of socialization might have fallen during that time period. It'd be interesting to dig up stats...

To contrast with WoW yet again, I found it extremely difficult to socialize in that game, because everyone was always going somewhere and didn't want to be interrupted or to slow down; similar effects happened to me in EQ2 and *City of Heroes*. The streamlining of the experience meant that there were few troughs to take advantage of, at least for my style of socializing.

The bonus for resting does create exactly the sort of effect I am talking about though, which is to encourage proximity at a trough time; the moment of logging out is generally an attention trough, and so is the moment of logging in. I wonder how much of an effect the fact that you're actually trying to do something else has; when you're logging out, you're trying to log out, and when you're logging in, you want to go have an adventure.

It's also interesting that WoW does use force rather brutally in one notable case, and that's the linearity of the experience. Exploring is actively punished at lower levels. The sensation of "this is something I'm *forced* to do to advance in the game" is exactly how I felt about the entire newbie experience, with the mandated quests and predetermined path. I felt choiceless.

Clearly, there's a balance point to strike between channeling people, and *which* channels you put them in. Choicelessness seems to be a good option in the case of WoW, and I wonder what that means for the future of MMOs.

In the MUD days, there was both easier recognition of [socially-oriented players] (because of scale) and there was a huge thriving ecosystem of worlds they could go to that were not advancement-centric. In the graphical worlds of today, neither is true.

Speaking as someone who did hang out in the cantina, and who knows a lot of players who are similar, I can tell you that after a while, the levelling can seem like a job, especially when your social group gets torn apart by unequal levelling rates. You want to roleplay, but if you do, then you won't get to adventure with your friends again, because they'll outlevel you while you are hanging out in the cantina. It happens *all the time*. Really.

All I am saying is that it'd be nice to give folks like that both a) a way to keep their group together (levelless systems, classless systems, sidekicking & mentoring, etc); and a way to give them bonuses, incentives, carrots, rewards, **feedback** for what they DO contribute — because I do think their contribution is important.

It's instructive to visit this page[221] to see how a smaller environment handled some of this. Has anyone seen that sort of value placed on, say, roleplayers in the graphical games? Compare to the "blessing" sort of thing in UO, and to what the games supply today…

---

[221] The Expies Awards page from LegendMUD, located at http://www.legendmud.org/Community/expie_win.html.

Dynamic POIs

> Way back in Pre-CU *[Star Wars Galaxies]* while 'walking' from Eisley to AnchorHead a Twi'lek (I think) stated my avatar by name (could be wrong) and gave me a disk then some stormies spawned and killed her then came after me.
>
> Anyone ever finish this quest? What was it like?
>
> This was a rather complex quest. Does anyone know how this was coded? Why would my avatar be chosen over others?
>
> – Daylen, posting over at RLMMO.com

The Twi'lek slave girl quest was part of what we called "dynamic POI's."

A normal POI is a "point of interest" — something to break up generic wilderness. it was a term we used back in the UO days that we got from Richard Garriott, and was probably older still. POI's are normally placed by hand, of course; you sculpt a location for them, add a little bit of something unique or flavorful, maybe some interaction, and there you go. They can be as small as a little faerie mushroom ring, or as large as a bandit camp or something. In other words, they are the static content of a world… usually not the main quest lines, but just "interesting stuff."

The "Hermit's Hut" 'theater' for a dynamic POI.

Of course, adding these in by hand is excruciatingly slow and requires an army of developers. That's the cost of content. In a game as large as SWG, we had a real issue here. At one point, there was a large roomful of junior developers who did nothing but put down little interesting locations on the maps… and it was nowhere near enough, particularly since they had no interactivity with them.

Part of the solution that we wanted to try, then was *dynamic POIs.*

These were **modeled after random encounters in D&D.** Not the plain old table of boring ones that you see in say, a JRPG, where you roll up a combat encounter every few steps, but something a bit more intricate. In *Ultima Online* we had done this with orc camps and mage towers — spawns that included a building. Since the map in UO was static, you needed a lot of empty space to get one of these spawns, and housing eventually used all the space up, so you never saw these happen. And there was no plot or story to these — they were just combat encounters that happened to come with a building.

SWG was more flexible. So instead we wanted the sort of thing that you saw in the better-written modules: random encounters with a little bit of plot, a little bit more context. **Don't roll up just a bandit; roll up a little bandit campsite, with a tent, a campfire, three bandits, one of whom hates one of the others, a young bandit who isn't actually a bad guy but has been sucked into the life because he has a young pregnant wife at home...** In fact, maybe have an assortment of bandits — twenty possible ones maybe. Then pick three for your camp. That way you always get a flavorful but slightly different experience.

This path led us to create dynamic POI types based on "plot" — such as "escaped prisoner", "poisoner" etc. These could then be placed in different "theaters" — little layouts of buildings and objects that could be spawned on the fly and placed on the map. Because the SWG map was procedural, we had the theoretical capability to spawn these anywhere, by affecting the underlying terrain

The Sandcrawler theater

and terrain textures, flattening the space, and placing the objects on top of it. When the POI was complete, it would wait until no players were nearby, and delete itself and all associated structures and spawners, thereby restoring the underlying terrain.

I spent several weeks building theaters. A sandcrawler on fire with sand people attacking Jawas. Lots of little moisture farms. A small village. Campsites of various sorts. I also made the plot skeletons for things like simple murder mysteries, family feuds, etc. One plot involved two villages having a Romeo & Juliet moment. Another was a simple "who's lying" sort of puzzle.

The very first example, however, was a tease: a dynamic spawn whereby an NPC slave girl was spawned who ran up to you and said "Help! They're after me! Quick, take this, don't let them have it or all will be lost!" You would be handed a data disk, and then the girl would run off, right into the arms of some Stormtroopers who shot her dead in front of you. You're left with a disk you cant read and a mystery.

It was pure tease — originally, the disk did absolutely nothing (I want to say that later, the disk was actually tied into something else… a collection quest maybe?). But it was an example of the sort of modular interactive narrative that could easily be created. Swap out slave girl for other sorts of escapees — and maybe have two or three types of escapees — good ones, bad ones, etc; and two or three kinds of hunters: pirates, Empire, etc. You can read about Haden Blackman's experience running into one of these during the testing phase:

> I'm running out from Bestine, into the desert on a mission to destroy a rock mite lair. Evidently, the rock mites are making life miserable for some local farmers. So, armed with my trusty DL-44 blaster (the same model used by Jabba's least favorite smuggler, Han Solo), I've set out in search of the aggressive critters. However, as I near my mission waypoint, I see a Twi'lek running across the desert full-tilt. I turn and wave, but the Twi'lek just begins screaming, "Help me! They're after me!" As she nears, I see she's wearing an outfit that Bib Fortuna must have picked out… And, in fact, I quickly identify her as a "Twi'lek slave." Before I can speak, the slave girl falls to her knees at my feet, pleading for my help. It's not difficult to surmise that someone is pursuing her; I suspect Jabba's goons at work…
>
> Just as I'm about to offer my aid, blaster fire erupts from behind me. I wheel around to see a pair of Imperial stormtroopers tromping down a sandy hill, their blaster rifles blazing. I immediately drop to my knee and begin firing back, but I'm outclassed. Fortunately, the Twi'lek has produced a huge blaster rifle (!) and has thrown herself onto the ground to take aim. I'm emboldened by my new ally's courage…
>
> But sadly, courage isn't enough in this fight. The stormtroopers rip us both to shreds in a few seconds. I collapse into the sand, only a few meters away from the Twi'lek's corpse… Clearly, I wasn't up to this particular challenge.[222]

So what happened? Well, honestly, content is hard to make. **A dynamic POI system is not any easier to craft than a usual encounter.** In fact, we never cracked a way to make it fully data-driven, which meant that it was actually harder. The dynamic spawning system was problematic. Scripting in SWG in general was too hard, so we couldn't spread the burden of creating the dynamic POIs, and each one

---

[222] https://web.archive.org/web/20100505085908/http://gatecentral.com/swg/swgbody.php?blatt=630

was a moderately tricky custom scripted encounter. In the end, the dynamic POIs came out of the game, and all the theaters I made went unused.

There is also an impression out there that these sorts of content were all that SWG was supposed to have, which is incorrect. **Dynamic POIs cannot replace good old-fashioned static content.** A theme park has a mix of wandering performers and rides, after all, and all dynamic POIs do is supply that element of surprise that human statues or other "street performer" things do. (At one point I tallied up all the sorts of content SWG was planned to have, and it was something like seven different types, with dynamic POIs representing just one type. Others included lairs, true random encounters, static quests, etc).

In conception though, the dynamic POI system is pretty simple. Given proper resources applied to solving the problem, and most importantly, the large quantities of content required for it to work, it still seems quite viable. Today we see a modern form of it in Trion's new MMO *Rift: Planes of Telara*, which is making dynamic content a big selling point, a full 14 years after the first crude ones went into *Ultima Online*, and long long after text muds had procedural zones with shifting content.

Brandon Reinhart, a designer on the team, has a far different take on the potential of dynamic POIs than I do.[223]

---

[223] See www.raphkoster.com/2010/04/30/dynamic-pois/#comment-161510

The Arts in MMOs

The system described here[224] is a lot like what I originally wanted for musicianship in SWG.

Players with higher composing skill would have had access to more buttons in the composition window — stuff like alternate scales, keys, multiple instruments, etc. The composition would be rated in difficulty based on which tools were used to make it.

The ability to add lyrics so that they could be synced up with the song, and use the /sing speech variant (it had notes on the chat bubble border, so you could tell it was sung)

A datadisk would have been generated which then a musician could add to their collection. If they had sufficient musicianship skill, they'd be able to play it. A small performance royalty would go back to the composer every time the song was performed, so that popular songwriters could earn money as they went.

This all fell afoul of legal concerns, of course. There was the fear that someone would simply replicate a song from the real world, thus leaving the game operators liable for copyright infringement.[225]

---

[224] http://digitaldouble.blogspot.com/2006/06/composing-with-hyper-instruments2.html describes it this way:

> The Composer Editions of the Hyper-Instruments allow you to store, load and playback a sequence of musical notes and durations (+ settings for tempo and loudness and credits) in a notecard… Therefore, a simple rising scale of notes, can be expressed in a notecard like this:
> ```
> T=0.6, 0.8
> C1, D1, E1, F1, G1, A1, B1, C2
> END
> ```
> Where T=0.6 (means a tempo of 0.6 seconds will be used for all notes). 0.8 (means a loudness of 0.8 out of 1.0, quite loud will be used for all notes). C1, D1, E1, F1, G1, A1, B1, C2 (is the sequence of notes, a C Maj. scale). END (Defines the end of the sequence, optional if no other text is below).

[225] Yeah, actually. I asked them. ASCAP, specifically. They were indeed willing to work something out. The issue, as I recall, was more on the side of the legal department at LEC, which is justifiably very concerned about being a big fat target.

There was also (are you ready for this?) the fact that by "fixing" the performance into a digital form, it

This applied also to the Writing profession I wanted. Originally, I had hoped for a Holonet in the game, which would essentially be embedded forums/blogs. Each article would have ratings at the bottom so that user could thumbs-up or down the article — no close button, you had to rate to get the window to go away.

As you got good ratings, you would be able to create your own channel (think "site" with multiple authors) and charge credits for access to read — even have stuff sent to your in-game email as a subscription. I hoped for in-game news to be disseminated this way; the idea was to provide the Lums of the world a way to profit in-game from their commentary which was so popular outside the game.

Of course, many would argue that it is attention to this sort of thing rather than combat that ended up causing SWG's troubles.

It raises the broader question, though, of whether there's a place for the arts in an MMO. I tend to think there is, because we see so much mashup and appropriation based art surrounding the games. Aside from rant sites, we see machinima, we see artfully decorated houses, and of course, one of the very first manifestations of player-created content in UO was players spelling out dirty words with fish on the bridge to Britain.

The logic in supporting this stuff explicitly is that it's among the most popular stuff in the game. Players love the movies, the music videos, the goofy screenshots, and of course, the rants and humor pieces. The people who engage in this sort of creativity are key influencers because their humor and affection for the game spreads well beyond the game's confines.

But within the game, they get no recognition at all. In fact, usually their work isn't even viewable within the game, though there are exceptions, such as the occasional in-game theater troupe.[226] Again, though — without in-game tools to support it, doing theater in the game is hard. Tools like lighting and other stage controls, automatic script recital so you don't have to retype the whole play as you go, special effects you can use, and the ability to charge money for attendance.

One notable exception to this, of course, is what dancers managed to do in SWG.[227] The essential tool turned out to be just the ability to form a group of 20 that would coordinate movements automatically.

---

was technically undergoing publication, and therefore you'd also need the publication rights from the Harry Fox Agency (!).

[226] See https://web.archive.org/web/20010503153425/https://uo.stratics.com/cba/wizard.shtml

[227] See https://www.youtube.com/watch?v=NVS1-227T-U and *many many* more.

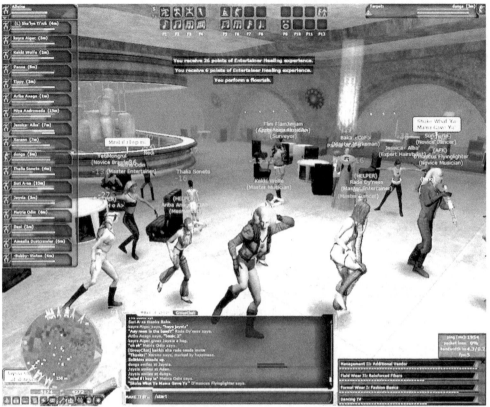

Is it all a waste of time? I don't know. Certainly one thinks that the core gameplay must come first. But so many of the most memorable things I have seen in online worlds have had nothing to do with the game proper, but with these moments off on the side…

Hairdressing!

As a side note, was the entire profession of people who did hair styles/face changes/etc really only included because of the initial bold statement of "You can do anything from wookiee hair grooming to ..."?

I mean... you didn't actually think that was a fun idea for a class did you?

Heh, thereby hangs a tale.

The original plan for the skill trees was not the skill onion. Picture the onions you had, but chop off the bottom novice skills. Imagine that when you came into the game, it worked like UO: you could either pick a "package" that gave you three or four skills that fit that chosen profession, or you could go "advanced" and pick ANY three or four.

Now, imagine that trees were simple — hairdressing, a total of four skills in the whole game. Crafting, dozens and dozens of skill lines.

Master boxes were not atop onions. Instead, they sat atop a set of skill lines. Two different master boxes might require the same skill lines — for example, you might need to have four skills worth of Engineering for any of the engineering based professions — kind of like the required classes in school. Or you might need to have tumbling, basic self-defense, and so on for any of the weapons skills.

Some lines would be deep, and branch — like basic self-defense would turn into something you could keep going in, and eventually learn Teras Kasi. Some Master boxes would be easy to get, others harder because they required a lot of study of different areas.

And there'd be TONS of Master boxes, because we'd try to

find every interesting combination of skill lines and give it a name. Tumbling + some of the performance effect stuff? Cool, we call you a gymnast. Tumbling + stealth + maybe knives, and you have a start at a commando (who'd need to also pick up skill lines in various more weapons) or a start at a ninja sort, perhaps.

As you can see if you try to diagram what this would look like, you need a 3d diagram; on the other hand, if you just list out "required courses" for each cool title you can get, you give a nice easy recipe for players to follow to make what they want. And if players combine some skill lines you never thought of, you can sneak in a new master skill box in there, and maybe add one special ability, and boom, you added a profession.

The first designer who tried a whack at this failed to produce diagrams and specs, over the course of weeks. Then he left. The second one tried and also didn't succeed. Finally, the producer stepped in and said "look, this is simpler," and pushed onions on us because we were simply out of time. I asked for a third chance and to let me just do it, because it just wasn't that complicated. But we really were out of time.

The upshot was that things that should have been just one skill line, four skill boxes, had to be turned into huge onions and padded out. To standardize data formats, we couldn't have different size and shape onions. Bleah.

Lastly, hairdressing was just plain easy to do, which means that in a failure of prioritization and to show some progress, it got done. Heck, basic hairdressing was actually in the pre-alpha demo to prove the scripting system worked, it was so trivial to do.

Treating Players Like Numbers

There's been a lot of heavy, arguably negative stuff here lately. So I thought it might be interesting to talk a little bit about possibilities instead.

In general, I'm a big proponent of treating players like people. The reverse is what game companies are often accused of, of course: treating players like numbers. Dehumanizing them. Viewing them through a purely statistical lens. All very mechanical.

But wait… what can be done if we **really** treat players like cogs in a machine?

Way back when, at the Austin Game Conference not last year, but the year prior, I suggested that we ought to be looking at "games that cure cancer," to somewhat mixed reactions — for two different takes on that panel, see here[228] and here.[229]

---

[228] *The Guardian*
(https://web.archive.org/web/20050911143111/http://blogs.guardian.co.uk/games/archives/2004/09/11/austin_day_2.html) reported it thus:

> The session on taking design risks in games at the Austin show - another conference, the same hot topic - was a pure representation of this division. The moderator was the same, Sony Online's Raph Koster, and while in the women's conference he was able to have a stimulating and pragmatic conversation with the panellists, in the design discussion he was challenged by the short-term solutions of the contributors and the guffaws of the crowd when someone had the gall to mention the word "penis". Sigh.
>
> Koster did a commendable job trying to throw in some really excellent and sometimes ridiculous propositions into the mix, but the panellists were too busy dissecting their latest product within the niche, in niche language, that Raph's suggestions were lost. My inner dreams of a-broader-market-by-design were dashed against the proverbial virtual rocks. I wanted to find out more about games that can help us solve the puzzle for the cure for cancer, teach us how to play a musical instrument or work like the extra-terrestrial beacon device SETI@home, not about how *Shadowbane* related to *World of Warcraft* or *Dark Age of Camelot*. Blah blah blah.
>
> If the industry is truly interested in thinking about new and different markets, it needs to integrate conferences like these, and plant the seed of adulthood amongst the delegates so grown-up conversations can be had from which mutually successful solutions can emerge. At this point, we're still as different as Mars and Venus.

[229] Damion Schubert wrote it up on his blog as well
(https://web.archive.org/web/20051023234222/http://www.zenofdesign.com/?p=80); he was a panel participant and had a quite different impression:

> The Design Risks panel was led by Raph Koster, and involved myself, Patricia Pizer (who just started on *ToonTown*), and Matt Firor (an Executive Producer at *Mythic*). This one was a lot less structured, for a number of reasons, the least of which being this panel didn't prepare as much as the other panel — for example, Raph didn't realize he was the moderator until the day before!
>
> This panel was somewhat frustrating, since both Raph and Matt were in gloomy moods, and they kept saying that Risk was Scary. Of course, risk is scary — that's why it's risk. My stance was that not taking risks is even scarier — if you just make a copycat clone of *EverQuest* or *World of Warcraft*, then you're just going to get steamrolled by teams that have far more resources than you - provided you don't get cancelled first. I pointed out that *Ultima Online* and *Dark Age of Camelot* were two examples of games that took big risks that managed to capture the imagination of their player base (virtual world and RvR respectively), and those risks were instrumental to their success. "So a Unique Selling Proposition is a risk?" asked Raph. To a management whose first instincts are to create clones of games, yes.
>
> At some point, I went off on a rant, where I said that the top risk we should be taking are making games that emphasize 'massive'. I argued that our games are still trying to mirror a tabletop experience, and a lot of the reasons our games feel derivative is that we aren't thinking big enough. Why are we making games that mirror single-player and small-squad

A year goes by, and I am sitting at a different conference[230] and someone (Byron Reeves)[231] presents exactly that.

What he showed was a mockup of a *Star Wars Galaxies* medical screen, displaying real medical imagery. Players were challenged to advance as doctors by diagnosing the cancers displayed, in an effort to capture the wisdom of crowds.[232] The result? A typical gamer was found to be able to diagnose accurately at 60% of the rate of a trained pathologist. Pile 30 gamers on top of one another, and the averaged result is equivalent to that of a pathologist — with a total investment of around 60-100 hours per player.

I am reminded of the powerful ways in which collective intelligence is harnessed by games such as Alternate Reality Games.[233] Seemingly impenetrable puzzles can be solved fairly quickly. In SWG, the first event we did[234] involved finding objects on spawns that had messages that looked like this:

```
NNnrrNpbqgNNa,NlNxnbgpteuuunNqNNsNfqNvrvNNvNNnffqNNsNogu)NNN:e:N'nb
ayaNnNfrNcatbrNv'NrsNNNNe.NnbreNN
```

experiences, instead of making games that really take advantage of our competitive advantage: 3000 people playing online in the same space?

Here, I said that we should be looking at LARPs instead of tabletop games, as they involve larger group dynamics. I confess, I was mostly just trying to stir things up.

Somewhere, Patricia mentioned she wanted to introduce Permadeath to *ToonTown*. Whether or not dip would be involved was left unsaid.

Near the end, Raph went from being the most anti-risk person on the panel to the guy with the biggest dreams. He wanted a game that would cure cancer, or that would teach people a musical instrument, or that would find intelligent life in the stars. It was somewhat strange being next to him while he went off in his soliloquy, given he'd spent the first 50 minutes arguing against taking chances, but I think he had surmised that people came to the talk hoping to be inspired, not to walk away discouraged.

For those wondering when I said 'penis', it's when I said that we should be exploring player-created content. If you're going to do it, you need to have a plan for how to deal with objectionable content. Rather than trying to titillate, I was mentioning the fundamental roadblock which has kept the big boys from treading in this space. Anyone who thought I was titillating has never had to work behind the scenes at UO, where dealing with player-built swastikas and penis-shaped houses were part of the CSRs job description.

[230] It was the web conference Supernova, in 2005.

[231] Stanford professor.

[232] A reference to James Surowiecki's book *The Wisdom of Crowds*, Doubleday, 2004. This book had enormous currency at the time of writing this piece.

[233] Alternate reality games or ARGs, are generally large scale narrative puzzle games that use the real world as a canvas. See https://en.wikipedia.org/wiki/Alternate_Reality_Game

[234] In August of 2003.

```
PCvEErxvzkxviqissi,elsEEhEesXeFEEesEvvrEgErsieelerriie(EEijEXrrvxei
smovwEaExkEEeeeglErEaEieEEl:arctan(1/2):eEe

SwszegsSmFjdsxogSSszjqs,sswSS1SSswGwwsSqSjSSzsasfgksSfSSOwSsfSvSSSz
qSfsswksS1SsSeSzSyS:3!:vzfqsSsDSJL

-PygCvcrgkcjCkveCccg-
CCgcCgCWrcgqvvChCt'cpkVppechvCCgqcgoCkcPCmCcugccwgcqrk-
ce:0:Cntucc'Cgp'CuxCCuw,
```

There were 40 of them, representing two completely different messages. Players collected them all and cracked the cipher in less than 48 hours. (I stuck one sample puzzle at the bottom, if you want to take a crack at it). This one is pretty trivial compared to some of the stuff that the ARGs have thrown out there.

The approach here is to treat players as a distributed parallel processing machine, filtering information and each node contributing its specialized knowledge: cogs in a machine.

Speculatively, there's many approaches to be had here. I'm not speaking about doing datamining on our game populations[235] — there's highly fruitful stuff to be had there, but a lot of it is about the specific ways in which people behave in the game spaces. Rather, I am speaking about ways in which **we can externalize the computing power of large populations using the incentive structures of games.**

Consider:

- We use tools like SETI@Home to distribute highly technical tasks like signal processing. However, there are *cognitive* tasks we could outsource in this fashion, as in the cancer example. Could, for example, jury trials be improved upon if assessing the truth of evidence were a distributed game? Could airport security be improved by creating scenarios about infiltration in our MMOs?

- Idea markets[236] are already in use in a wide array of fields, generally constructed

---

[235] Two projects that were active at the time include the PlayOn project at PARC (which was born from Nick yee's Daedalus Project, and continued in the form of metrics company Quantic Foundry); and Project Massive, at the HCI Institute at Carnegie Mellon. When my R&D projects at SOE were getting their funding cut, one of the very last things I did was take the anonymized data from our playerbase and supply it to researchers, as part of an initiative to improve the portrayal of Sony Online in the press. It worked, and also birthed a slew of research papers!

[236] An idea market is a market set up specifically to allow people to bid on, or otherwise value, ideas and concepts. The premise is that the free market can be wise, and the money will follow the best idea. See https://hbswk.hbs.edu/archive/you-can-bet-on-idea-markets

as games. Arguably, *Second Life* is being used as an idea market for the design process for furniture and clothing. While the Pentagon's attempt to use a futures market for forecasting terror attacks floundered due to politics ("betting on terrorism??!!?!") there's clearly possible approaches that can be taken within a game.

- Players are the best ALife agent we're managed to find. Why rely on Axtell and Axelrod-style simulations[237] when we can build environments and loose players in them? The trick would be to get the environmental stimuli to match the ones provided in the real world. (I've argued before that this isn't really possible, but hey, it's worth a try). The old landscaping trick when deciding to put down paths was to wait a while, see where people trod the grass, and then pave where they had walked the most; that sort of thing would be trivially easy (and cheaper) to do in our games, given a decent topographical map of the landscape.

- There's a university right now using a major MMO to do total-immersion teaching of a foreign language; by putting the students in constant contact with the foreign language and forcing them to learn it in order to succeed at advancing in the game, they hope to see as high as a 30% greater fluency on the part of the students.

I'm not really making a pitch for "serious games" here — rather, I am suggesting that our non-serious games can be put to serious uses on the side, thanks to their scale. Being a cog in the machine can serve higher purposes even while each individual cog goes on its merry way enjoying its gameplay.

There's a lot of possibilities. Got some more?

---

[237] This is a reference to simulations of society, generally using artificial life agents or cellular automata. See https://www.theatlantic.com/magazine/archive/2002/04/seeing-around-corners/302471/

The SWG Puzzle

The below is just one of the two messages,[238] and I have spared you the effort of gathering the pieces individually and not knowing how many pieces there are. If you despair, you can see how the community solved it here.[239]

```
NPpPpPttpPuPbpPptPpPpPcjkginxchacwPctPsPPc.tPtptgPddpPtiPPPjctwstnp
PvPapPxti:pi:psd'PuP.cpPphppwpPuPP

VIiwiIIIII'IIIIipIsbIk'vei.IVzspiwbIb:1:kImiwwIIkIIIgIliuaniiimtiI.
izlIIiIgziwioniwIibIwbmpnIciIiIpO

mepsyaqddgmkqmiqmmMrtmMs:sqrt(5):MiIMmuMmMmsamMPMsmMmmzwuxemMmMMfzx
zmmgMIumuaMgdyqgMpfzmMmmsmmm,mMwmMaym.S

DOrgddDh'qDhkpkowpbDvwdsqdDbVDDhxDz:sin(1):drsh;DbrzwDfDDhduuDDvhqq
q'nlEDDuDDfdD.ri-DkdDhDDDvlzrvkDhdwDwD

JydRzsRkiRvrRzfxcRRRkRRuRRmlvz,vRjRdiRrRgfruRRcRrxiRuRrrRyvRfrirjrk
:5:rkrRRyxRrjrRcRrRrlkexzCRiwRcVL

OG.GlGggGGkGGxGkgGguGgnGgjoGgnkGGggngprGt:gamma:GgGGjGGugGugiaGGjxG
gcGgkvzkG,GoGxGkoGxqGntsGgGgGGyGoyhGY

Q.iftymnjxm.wjdxFFFjFXfFnFzFFwffFFyFtyfffF,qF.jFFihFFhffjt:cos(1):f
FtljmFxskdsmfjfmtfGFpFftfFfFfwFfgnFfF

-PBhesBnxmBBblBBboxz-
b.fBpibNvBtzvB,:i:BbbfBbuBjbbBgBbbiuBijbBdPbpbBjuBBmBBpBBpBu.mc'BBf
bgBsb'bbb'pO

LYJJJrjjqjaCLjtJnKnJvxbmnJJmXJ.jwdqjqcjnJawfxJUejnxbannJaJccnJcJJbJ
jhJhJnJd:zeta(3):JJJtfUaJjbqjnowwtjJjnW

UuufinCUvquUMuuUUsylUoxuhmUUU.UUiuyuUjsoUuuUgPyiuUUnUqmfUuUXUiUmUh:
00001111:myUuunuunmyyuUgylbUUuyUubUUnUCu

SoOhOofxO.oooOoOf.OfOhccosoOuszswh.sggotowhboaOv:3:soqfvmvo.oopofOf
qzOoOosrozssOsMhgwhsszorwOaOO.soo

HhHa:phi:Hhashhfhh,hHHhHbhHlbHlzhHlhdjiHlHlfzHtHhhvhhmHhyHvyvAHtnHH
hrHll,hHhuNHfHupluhl'lsHfHvhwaaHlaP
```

---

[238] Both messages, plus all of my hints, can be found at
https://web.archive.org/web/20031123101943/http://www.holymight.com/swg/
[239] The forum thread from the original event can be found at
https://web.archive.org/web/20050124072852/http://forums.station.sony.com/swg/board/message?boar
d.id=Development&message.id=323382. Some ex-NSA and NASA folks got involved…! It's still rather
fun reading the thought processes that players went through. I probably gave too many hints.

-PygCvcrgkcjCkveCccg-
CCgcCgCWrcgqvvChCt'cpkVppechvCCgqcgoCkcPCmCcugccwgcqrk-
ce:0:Cntucc'Cgp'CuxCCuw,

NNnrrNpbqgNNa,N1NxnbgpteuuunNqNNsNfqNvrvNNvNNnffqNNsNogu)NNN:e:N'nb
ayaNnNfrNcatbrNv'NrsNNNNe.NnbreNN

tTghinTtfhTeTT:#00000A:TmtgTxrhTTTTkttrttTTgTmiXhtfTtnTdTT,xTthtlxT
tTxe.btbbutTTTTTTbkuTthpxLatTmzwTtkxtET

OkVkcxKKoloryKxdbboksxKoKkkyDkKdKdsKoKKKnoKoxk:sqrt(2):ykKkpKoKKkuk
s,diykZykKyiykkmK1kk.KidkKdobbKouoKdKbS

UjQqQqjsQqjsuQxQqqdqQquduuue:2^2:1jeituqqsqQqkvQuqtQtqqkchqQQqjmjoQ
qQiQQcusvbjdtQQQkbqQqQeiqkaQouQqkTE

SwszegsSmFjdsxogSSszjqs,sswSS1SSswGwwsSqSjSSzsasfgksSfSSOwSsfSvSSSz
qSfsswksS1SsSeSzSyS:3!:vzfqsSsDSJL

PCvEErxvzkxviqissi,elsEEhEesXeFEEesEvvrEgErsieelerriie(EEijEXrrvxei
smovwEaExkEEeeeglErEaEieEE1:arctan(1/2):eEe

LdjLzqdalzLpospsLpaLre1c1LL,LL1L1LynL1'1tL1LLLzyLcL1L11LtwzLLzzLcyL
dfzf:2:Ldz1fLLL1oLLdLLdL1nLyetnpY

The response was mixed, in large part because it was a collaborative puzzle-solving exercise, but the reward was given to the first person to send in a solution. (Everyone who participated in the event got a separate reward, which probably would have sufficed). Several folks, including some on the team, disliked having an out-of-game event, which is something that I personally have no hang-ups about. Lastly, the more story-oriented folks felt a bit left out.

The people who did get into it seemed to love it. I think that ARGs prove that married with ongoing interesting fiction, both story fans and the puzzle-solvers can greatly enjoy this sort of thing.

The precise process was to get five fragments, combine them, and turn them in at an Imperial or Rebel recruiter for 500 faction points and a badge. The puzzle was above and beyond that. So everyone who participated at all in gathering clues (whether they shared them or not) did in fact get a reward.

There was also a large-scale "the faction that turns in the most gets a boost next month" thing.

We probably should not have had a reward for the puzzle solving itself — all it did was deliver some fiction.

Do auction houses suck?

Once upon a time, there was a game set in a science fiction universe where the economy was very important. Its name was not *Eve*.

In this game, players could, if they so chose, run a business. They could

- designate a building as a shop
- hire an NPC bot to stand in it
- give the bot items to hold for sale
- specify the prices at which those items would sell
- customize the bot in a variety of ways
- make use of advertising facilities to market the shop
- decorate the shop any way they pleased

With this basic facility, emergent gameplay tied to the way that the crafting system worked resulted in players who chose to run shops being able to do things Ike build supply chains, manage regular inventory, develop regular customer bases, build marketing campaigns, and in general, play a lemonade stand writ large.

The upshot was that at peak, fully half the players in *Star Wars Galaxies* ran a shop.

Now, most of these players engaged in the system in a shallow way. Advanced versions of the capabilities cited above were unlocked based on RPG-style advancement. You had to choose to do a lot of merchant activity in order to get Merchant XP, in order to unlock more advanced advertising capabilities etc. But even a dabbler could run a small business.

Advanced players actually made the economy their entire game, working either solo[240] or in highly organized guilds, managing oilfields worth of harvesters, factory

---

[240] A dramatic example of this was the article "How I Helped Destroy Star Wars Galaxies" by Patrick Desjardins:

towns worth of crafting stations, and whole malls.

The economy in something like *World of Warcraft* is very different in character. The peak populations on a shard in each game were comparable, though of course WoW achieved far far higher subscriber numbers in aggregate. But the peak of economic play in WoW is essentially basic arbitrage, timing the market.

There are several factors that make the functioning of the two economies radically different, of course.

- in WoW all the best stuff is spawned as a result on combat. In SWG it was crafted by players.

- in WoW nothing breaks; instead you outlevel it. In original SWG everything decayed.

- in WoW a lot of the most valuable items aren't actually items — they are buffs or skills in fancy dress. They aren't transferable to other players. In SWG there was no "soul binding" and anything could be traded or gifted.

Fundamentally, though, the biggest difference has to do with the basic approach taken. You see, in *Star Wars Galaxies* we designed the economy to be a game, not a side effect. In particular, **the merchant class was created to fulfill the fantasy of running your own business.** It had features like decorating your shop because *that*

---

https://web.archive.org/web/20120309033154/http://www.mediumdifficulty.com/2012/03/06/how-i-helped-destroy-star-wars-galaxies/

> I started thinking about the crafting, and the shortcuts there. I created timetables based on the initial samples we had. How many hours to master this, how many hours to master that. How many supplement accounts would I need to supply myself? If there are only 24 hours in a day, how could I best utilize each one?
>
> I started building extra computers. I spent every spare moment preparing for day one… On release day I was at EB games, cash in hand for eight copies of *SWG*, and I was home in a flash. I took a week's vacation. I had the spare bedroom stocked with food and drink, my computers arrayed in a half moon… Slowly, steadily the credits started building. I kept a tally on a whiteboard leaned against the wall. Your first million is the hardest, they say. Bullshit. Your first 100,000 is the hardest. But I kept working, kept pulling 12, 14, 18 hour shifts in front of keyboards and tiny screens… Little by little, my plan came together. Mistakes buried under accomplishments. Vendors multiplying like rabbits. Small houses, big houses, entire malls and cantinas. Credits piling up, stacks on stacks. Professions mastered, exploited, and dropped to master new ones… I clearly remember the day that I realized I had done it. It was maybe two or three months in, and I controlled not only the land around Coronet, but Theed as well. It was mine. People used my vendors because they were closer, and for no other reason. Slowly I increased my prices, 2%, 5%, 10%… and they lined up to buy. People were hologrinding and didn't care what it cost. It was a full-time gig just keeping the vendors supplied.

is part of the fantasy of being a shopkeeper in a world such as that — to build up the equivalent of Watto's junkyard, or a Trade Federation.

And this meant that above all, one feature could not exist: the auction house.

If you think of running a business as a game, then think about what you need in order to make it fun. Game grammar tells us that you are probably playing this as an *asynchronous parallel game,* meaning that you are measuring yourself against other players' progress against the same opponent you fight. What's the opponent? The vagaries of supply and demand as expressed by market price. The actions of other players have an *indirect* effect on this system.

Remember, a game provides **statistically varied opposition within a common framework** — if there is no variation, we call it a *puzzle,* not a game. Because of this, we invested a lot of effort into creating ever-varying economic situations in SWG.

- **Every resource in SWG was randomly generated off of master types.** We defined "iron," and gave it statistical ranges. Different kinds of iron would spawn with different names, but they would all work as iron in any recipe that called for such. This meant that you might find a high-quality vein of iron, or a low quality one.

- Even more, it might be high quality only for specific purposes.

- **Resource types were finite.** You could literally mine out all the high quality iron there was. It would just be *gone.* A new iron might be spawned eventually (sometimes, *very* eventually!) but of course, it would be rolled up with different characteristics.

- **And in a different place.** Resources were placed using freshly generated Perlin noise maps.

- **Crafters gambled with their resources**, generating items of varying quality that were partially dependent on the resources and the recipe.

- Crafters could lock in specific results as blueprints, but that forced a dependency on the specific finite resource that was used, meaning that blueprints naturally obsolesced.

All of this meant that a merchant could never rely having the best item, or the most desirable item (indeed, "most desirable" could exist on several axes, meaning that there were varying customer preferences in terms of what they liked in a blaster). Word spread through informal means as to the locations of rare ore deposits. People fought PvP battles over them. People hoarded minerals just to sell them on the market once they had become rare. And of course, they organized sites like the now defunct

SWGCraft.com, which monitored all of this fluctuating data and fed it back out in tidy feeds for other sites and even apps to consume, such as The SWG Resource Tracker,[241] which was widely used by hardcore business players much like a Bloomberg terminal is by someone who plays the market.

Then it all went away. You see, a key feature of the system was that the central NPC run shops were not permitted to interfere with this. Nor was the spawn system allowed to drop high quality items as loot. The result was that if you wanted the coolest weapon, you had to hunt through player-run shops like a mad antiquer on a summer drive. The result of the above systems, you see, was an economy where it was very very hard to see the *gestalt* of the trade economy. You really had to hunt to find out if you had found a bargain.

For someone who just wanted to *frickin' buy a blaster*, it was very *inconvenient*.

In other words, we had *local pricing* in full effect. This meant that the individual merchant, who, remember, was there to *fulfill the fantasy of running a small business*, could get away with not being being great at it.

In the real world, we are rapidly approaching a perfect information economy. I can instantly look up the varying prices of something I want, determine the one with the lowest actual cost to me (price, shipping, time to arrival, physical location, quality, etc), and get exactly what I want. It is a world optimized for the *buyer*.

The experience for the seller, though, is not generally awesome, unless they happen to have the scale that drives victory in a winner takes all scenario. The big guys can essentially dictate prices by undercutting everyone. They dominate the visible market, and can drown out the smaller or more unique offerings. **In this sort of world, the funky used bookstore with the awesome decor tends to die,** and it doesn't matter how much fun the shop owner had in coming up with said decor.

SWG eventually did put in a server-wide auction house, responding to WoW. It made life easier for the buyers. But it created a perfect information economy, and all that complexity and variation that was present in the market earlier fell away. Small shopkeepers were shut out of markets.

---

[241] No longer functional, but can be read in archive form at
https://web.archive.org/web/20061104071729/http://www.gramsplace.com/srt/

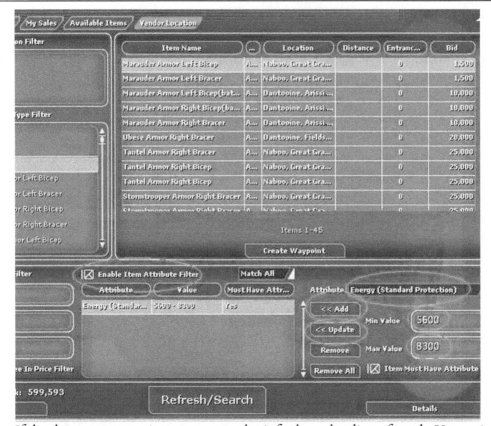

If that happens to you in a game, you don't find another line of work. You quit.

So do auction houses suck? No, not if your game is about *getting*. It is a better experience for a gamer interesting in *getting*.

But the fantasy of running a shop, or being a business tycoon, is not just about the getting. It is about the *having* — of relationships, of an empire, of a well-oiled machine. It is about *running* things, not about working your way up a chain of gewgaws. The gewgaws are a way to keep score, but you play the game for the sake of the game.

SWG was not a game about getting. After all, everything you could get in the game eventually broke. It was about the *having.* Having your shops, your town, your supply chain, your loyal customers, your collectible Krayt dragon skull or poster or miniature plush Bantha like in the Christmas Special.

When the merchant changes went in to SWG, the merchants went out.

Getting is kind of addictive. For a mass market audience, it may well be the path to greater acceptance and higher profits. Me, I like funky bookstores; but I have to admit I usually buy from Amazon. It's **convenient.**

The lesson here is that sometimes features that make things better for one player make them dramatically worse for another. Every time you make a design choice you are closing as many doors as you open. In particular, you should always say to yourself,

I'm adding this feature for player convenience. How many people live for the play that this inconvenience affords?

The small shopkeepers; the socializers who need the extra five minutes you have to spend waiting for a boat at the EverQuest docks; the players who live to help, and can't once every item is soul bound and every fight is group locked and they can't even step in to save your life; the role player who cannot be who they wish to be because their dialogue is prewritten; the person proud of his knowledge of the dangerous mountains who is bypassed by a teleporter; the person who wants to be lost in the woods and cannot because there is a mini-map.

Every inconvenience is a challenge, and games are made of challenges. This means that every inconvenience in your design is potentially someone's game.

Jared Diamond applied to virtual worlds

Fri, 27 Jul 2001.

I was a fan of the writings of Jared Diamond, author of several award-winning books on anthropology and biology, and how they inform social formation. These posts are about applying some of the insights in his work to the design of virtual worlds.

Much of UO's tensions can be seen as various subcommunities competing for territory and resources–resources in terms of in-game enjoyment and mindshare from the developers, as well as literal resources in the game.

I think there was also a difference in type among players. Many of those that UO attracted were completely new to online games, and the more people we got, the more notable the differences in patterns of behavior. Many were more casual about the game, they had different play patterns than the hardcore early adopters, etc. In smaller muds, you usually ONLY see the hardcore, and rarely get significantly sized groups of complete novices, computer illiterates, online newbies, etc.

Camping is an interesting example, because as the number of players competing for the exact same resource rose, complex rules of social standing and precedence started arising spontaneously. That's not something I saw in smaller muds. The phenomenon of plane raids in EQ being "reserved" by guilds that are the size of your average mud's playerbase, for example.

(For those who do not know: the highest level zones in EQ are in demand enough that players have organized schedules wherein guilds sign up for time slots to tackle the area. This arose spontaneously from the playerbase, and is enforced by custom, though at this point I believe the in-game admins have been known to uphold "reservations." Similarly, at spawn locations a curious etiquette has evolved whereby there's a prescribed order in terms of who gets to kill the spawning mob first and who gets to loot it; players literally stand in line and await their turn. Those who jump the queue are ostracized).

Now, certainly "scale" is being used very loosely here, and is in fact referring to density and simultaneous player size and world size and audience size.

I've mentioned Jared Diamond and *Guns, Germs, and Steel* on this list many times, and that chart (pages 268-269 in the Norton paperback edition) that breaks down social complexity into tiers based on population size. I find an eerie correlation between the categories he cites and the typical behaviors of player groups in muds:

Band

- Up to dozens of people
- Tend not to have a fixed home
- "Egalitarian" leadership, or leader by force of will
- No real bureaucracy
- The leader doesn't have official control of force or information
- Informal conflict resolution
- Generally unstratified culture

This looks much like the regular group of friends in a large environment, and much like a small mud. In the real world these form because of kin relationships.

Tribe

- Hundreds of people
- Tend to have a single home
- "Egalitarian" or "big-man"
- Organized resource extraction
- Still unstratified

This is what most guilds seem to behave like. In online my observation is that they tend to fragment fairly easily if the charismatic leader who defines the group departs (an example of this is of course the Norse Traders in "A Story About a Tree"). This is the form of social organization that we see peeping out of larger muds, and that is rampant in the MMORPGs.

Chiefdom

- Thousands
- 1 or more locations
- Class issues emerge

- Centralized decision making, monarchic, cronyism
- 1 or 2 levels of bureaucracy may emerge
- Chief controls force, chief controls flow of info
- Tithing and tribute appear
- Indentured labor, slavery
- Public architecture
- Luxury goods for the elite

Welcome to the uberguild. How often do we hear stories of the indentured labor farming items that are required of newbies to the guild? Of the iron control exercised by the guild leader and the cronies that help run the thing? Of the way in which they exist in multiple games, using several as a home base? Not exactly the friendly, enlightened societies one might hope for, but currently the most highly evolved social structures available n virtual worlds.

The last one is "the state" but it takes over 50,000 people to get there, and it's where minor stuff we tend to value (or say we do) like less cronyism, fairer distribution of wealth and of justice, rule of law, etc, starts showing up.

A key point that Diamond makes is that it's not literal population that matters. It's economic participation. These social structures emerge when all those people are trying to draw from the same resource well (literally trying to extract more calories from the same amount of land). So, if you've got a bad in-game economy (monty haul), you're probably hurting guild development because nobody needs anybody.

Online games have a problem with inconstancy; players aren't economic participants 24/7. When logged off, they generally are consuming resources or contributing to the economy in any significant way. And that means that social development is probably further retarded.

And that's why *Star Wars Galaxies* will have the ability to buy and sell goods while offline, the ability to mine resources while offline, the ability to manufacture goods while offline, and ongoing costs to all of these things.

Fri, 27 Jul 2001

Eventually, the larger groups fragment into smaller groups (cf the Law about maximum community size) and each community forms its own social structures and codes.

...And then you start getting dynamics related to the conflicts between these groups, shifting alliances, etc. A lot then starts to depend on what means you have to express that conflict.

One point I used to make (and which means diddlysquat to the victims, so it wasn't a very empathic point for me to bring up) is that speaking in these terms, there's really no difference between the roving band of PKs and the small roleplay town. They are both subcommunities seeking to survive and perhaps expand their influence. From a group standpoint, the PKs are merely pursuing economic advancement for their group; of such things are wars made, particularly tribal wars. It's just Mongols versus Eastern European villages, at that point, and we can easily make moral judgements about whether or not the Mongols were "in the right" all we want, but it's still pretty much an inevitable development when there's multiple groups competing for the same resources, each of which values its group more than the aggregate of the two groups. One will seek the eradication of the other, because frankly, small social groups like that don't tend to be very enlightened about cultural diversity and inclusiveness (cf the post I just made to Jeff Freeman in this same thread).

Read another way, both sides are subhuman jerks to the other, mere ants to be stomped. Valuing one type of behavior or culture over another is fundamentally a value judgement. We are perfectly free to make value judgements. We should just be aware that's what they are.

Players don't like hearing the above. I speak from experience.

Hence the proliferation of UO emulator shards, each designed to cater to a particular band or tribe-sized group. Hence the great anticipation of *Neverwinter Nights*[242] (the common cry I hear isn't "Great! We'll have better narrative roleplaying!" Rather, it's "Great! I can play an online game and keep out all the jerks!").

In *Privateer Online* our direct heads-on attempt to tackle this was to have hundreds of planets, each designed to support a band-to-tribe sized group of people; a fixed amount of resources; a mechanic about resource extraction from the ground and "colonization of the wilderness," and frankly, difficulty in getting from planet to planet. Trade was encouraged from planet to planet, and the hope was that most of the time, you'd deal with your planet and your neighbors. Conquering neighboring planets was not really an available mechanic (once a planet was established, you were

---

[242] This would be the limited multiplayer *Neverwinter Nights* by Bioware from 2002, not the *Neverwinter Nights* by Kesmai that was an MMO from 1991-1997 on America Online.

unable to conquer it by force; you had to conquer it by consensus, by getting voted into office on it).

We are retaining some elements of that in SWG, but it's not nearly as direct an approach to the problem. Which is a pity, because I still think PO would have been a valuable experiment to try…

Sun, 29 Jul 2001

> Diamond's book is amazing. However, I would suggest a slightly different reading. I take the same passage to say that the socio-political structures will arise on their own in groups of said sizes. – Joe Andrieu

In the real world, I agree with you. But I am not sure that the same is true of the virtual. I already mentioned constancy of presence and economic participation as one example. Consider also reproduction and how the groups grow in size. in the online world, the only means is via adoption–given that cliques (which is what these tend to start as) are by their nature exclusionary, many groups simply won't grow very quickly, whereas in the real world, a group like this will have children and keep growing year to year.

To put it another way, how do you *get* groups of such sizes? It's not like guilds of 150 spring into being out of thin air. Whereas a village with sufficient food is pretty much guaranteed to get there, a player group or tribe has no growth forced upon it in that sense.

People do tend to organize. But they don't seem to grow in size or develop into more complex structures without some prodding or need.

> But I believe that, given the opportunity to participate in a higher tier structure at *no additional cost,* players will do so. At the heart of Diamond's argument is the power of investing in "leisure" activities… the potential power of a civilization was indirectly proportional to the percentage of labor invested in sustenance. – Joe Andrieu

The trick is figuring out what sustenance is. After all, the entire premise is leisure to start with. If developing and maintaining the social structure becomes too onerous, they'll abandon it or its development–either move on to another game, or leave it sit.

The closest analogue I can come up with to caloric extraction from the environment in these games is extraction of advancement, of experience points and quest flags and "dings." Hence my comments recently about what we choose to reinforce and how players tend to value most those things that we provide tangible in-game recognition for. In GoP[243] games at least, the thing that players work together to increase the efficiency of is the process of extracting more XP per hour. Hence group tactics, camping (which is essentially a direct analogue to agriculture! We used to hunter-gather the mobs, now we farm them... even the term "farming" has crept up in common usage), etc etc.

In more sophisticated economic models and crafting systems, this may transmute into gold, or from raw resources, but it's still the same thing. As Jonathan Baron has observed many a time, the GoP games are essentially capitalist. It's all about the benjamins, where the benjamins are the recognition we give in the form of ever-increasing numbers.

What is the leisure class in a GoP game? The people who no longer play? The people who have so much money and maxxed out levels? We do tend to see many of those people change playstyles away from achiever towards socializer or killer (eg, towards either giving up on challenges, or seeking greater challenges). But we don't necessarily see them as contributing towards a greater social structure, perhaps because they fundamentally don't *need* the plebes.

We could attempt to supply ready-made structures, but by and large people seem to vastly prefer growing societies organically rather than having them thrust upon them. Anyone else had the experience of seeding a guild system or the like with a few pre-made ones for people to join, only to find that as soon as the ability to roll your own went in, the pre-seeded ones shriveled up and died?

The "economic participation" guideline I am trying to apply fortunately cuts across the board. As long as everyone has ongoing costs (akin to rent, which has largely been abandoned in Dikus, perhaps erroneously!) and as long as there are means of transferring goods and wealth from person to person regardless of their actual presence, it seems like those people must count in the economy, and therefore will lead to greater complexity.

To get back to the psychological reinforcement thing–that's also why we are heavily pursuing what we call "social professions"–activities that are not traditionally rewarded in GoP games but which we nevertheless rely heavily on for the formation of a robust culture in the game. To be very specific–even if your bartender advancement ladder isn't particularly deep or complex, it's still a way to recognize people who perform that function in the game. They can earn some badges to show

---

[243] MUD-Dev slang for "goal-oriented play."

off, they can maybe earn some money with it. They get that much-craved "ding" from the game server that validates their activity, and on top of that they are interacting with the game economy.

The logic being that if people feel validated in filling other niches in the game beyond just the experience farmer (or if they farm it in a different way) you're more likely to get the sorts of interactions across groups that lead to greater social structure.

Should we pursue balance?

Another post from MUD-Dev.

There's a philosophical question to ask ourselves, one alluded to in that Shannon Appelcline essay that Michael Tresca just referenced.[244] To what degree is "balance" something that we as designers desperately pursue, as opposed to the "balance" that players pursue?

After all, if there's an overpowered class according to player perception, they seek and find equilibrium. The correct proportion of each class naturally emerges, as players who are too invested in particular character archetypes refuse to change, and those who are min-maxers pursue the class or profession du jour. Often a designer's "fix to balance" doesn't come along until well after this new equilibrium has been reaches, so all it does is upset players, rather than aid in this mythical "game balance" anyway.

So the philosophical question is, if something is out of whack, should we as designers care? Do we need to always have everything in mathematical perfection?

As an example of where we are wrestling with this in Star Wars Galaxies—we have several very large overlapping constituencies of likely players. One, for example, is all those players who want to be Jedi. And Jedi, frankly, crush everything else in the setting. Then there's all these players who want to be melee fighters. All those who want to be Rebels and Imperials.

In the movies, the Rebels win by luck and pluck. It's not surprising that many players want to play Rebels. They are also all continuity fanatics, and keep insisting that everything be as like the movies as possible. If it were, the Rebels would wink out of existence in the first week the servers went live. We as designers feel an imperative to supply balance there simply because otherwise, a major attractant to the game goes away.

On the other hand, we're just plain giving up on the issue of melee combat. A good ranged guy is always gonna take a good close quarters guy, and there's no getting past that. Yes, we've invested a fair amount of time in vibroblades and stun poles and what

---

[244] Alas, the original reference is lost somewhere in the MUD-Dev archives.

have you, and there's skills to learn for melee, motion captured moves, and all sorts of goodness. But really, we already know the min-maxers won't use that stuff. So it's there for those whose self-image really calls for it.

Lastly, there's those pesky Jedi. They're barely balanceable. So we're making them extremely rare (and no, I'm not going to say how, not even here!) and we're going ahead and giving them the power. They're gonna be superbeings, and if you see one, run.

Mathematically elegant? No, not really. But frankly, I'm going to sacrifice the "balance" for the sake of the players' wish-fulfillment.

We're getting asked whether the crafters and the peaceful people will get equal access to the goodies as the people who are declared Rebels and Imperials. Well, the answer is yes and no. There's perks on both sides. Are they "balanced"? I don't know. My main concern is whether the two playstyles each have fulfilling gameplay that they find fun. They're not even advancing on the same scales, so that they do not feel like they have to compare themselves. Nonetheless, they already do, and I don't doubt they always will.

Yeah, it may be heretical as a game designer, but I think balance is overrated. Fun is more important.

Mailbag: Action Combat

I was recently rereading your piece Designing a Living Society in SWG (part two).

And I became curious. You said that you made SWG an RPG because it had a much better retention than FPS games. Which, especially given the tech back then, seems to be a sensible position to take.

But I'm curious, if you were going to make SWG today's gaming climate, with seemingly every MMO moving to action combat, would you still make it an RPG? A hybrid? A full blown FPS?

Obviously that decision would inform nearly everything else in design, but mostly I was trying to think how a class system would even work in a FPS centric SWG. It seems like there would be a lot less room to play around with abilities and specializations. Most people expect their shots to hit what they aim, so "to hit" chance isn't really a thing to play around with. And I feel like there's more expectation to have most guns, from the junk pistols to super expensive/hard to unlock, to do damage that's in the ballpark of one another.

So all the abilities that you unlock would be less dependent on weapons, right? More oriented around giving the player more skills to do things, and maybe work up to some crazy, but limited, weapons? And I suppose you could still unlock special shots that do more damage, or pin people, or poison them.

I'm sorry if this is such a vague question that nearly answers itself, but I thought it couldn't hurt to try to get some insight into someone who is working in the industry. It seems like a sci-fi MMO would be a harder thing to pull off these days.

–Brian Ward

I'd do it with action combat, for the following reasons which boil down now to "because I actually can now":

- **The audience is larger.** Back when RPGs always trumped FPSes on retention, that was an issue because it meant that the audience you had left paying you monthly was too small to sustain the costs of live operation and recouping development costs. That's no longer the case. Online FPSes can acquire huge audiences now, which means you can probably make back your investment and turn a profit.

- **Technology is way better now.** At the time we did *Star Wars Galaxies*, there was exactly one persistent world large-scale game with FPS-style combat: *Neocron.* It didn't do anything like the large-scale battles that we would need for Star Wars. Sony Online in fact pioneered that technology, but on a different project, *Planetside.* But it was still in early development at the time that we had to make this decision.

- **Players have built up expectations of gameplay** for different affordances and simulations. And there are few turn-based or timer-based models out there for guns. Virtually none in first-person environments. It would feel pretty alien to the average player to be in first person and not have FPS combat. This was one of the things that drove having overhead views in SWG.

Of course, using real-world skill as the basic premise of play undermines the RPG element in general. Role-playing games are about playing a role, and a big part of playing a role is being someone you cannot be. That means *not* relying on real world skill as much, or rather relying on a particular universal set of skills mostly based around being persistent.

You can totally affect real world aiming skill with an RPG skill system though. The original design for SWG featured a "cone of fire" system which basically affected shot precision based on your skill level. Skills certifying you for different weapon types would also work fine ("you aren't trained on this model blaster, you're not used to the kick, you can't actually use it effectively"). There are other ways. Some of these ways will play better with the Star Wars universe, some won't (the certification thing, not so much, though maybe one could argue no Stormtroopers seemed to have gotten Blaster 1).

If you're freed of the Star Wars setting, then certs work even better — a pistol with a thumbprint scanner saying "sorry, you're not authorized to fire this weapon because you haven't paid your dues to the Smuggler's Guild" is fictionally plausible in any number of sci fi universes. "You don't have the nano interface for this plasma rifle." "You haven't been trained in the telekinetic arts enough to activate the Focusing Lens." Whatever. I might approach cone of fire as an assistive mechanism in that case, making it give magical aim boosts to people with lousy aim, because again, RPGs are about the fantasy of having a skill you don't actually have.

The *SWG postmortem series*

Right around the fifteen-year mark since I started work on Star Wars Galaxies, I was sent a series of questions from a player. At this point, I had left the game behind twelve years prior, and it had been shut down years earlier. And yet players were building emulator servers to keep not just the game alive, but the specific version of the game they thought I had made, the one before a series of huge (and eventually disastrous) changes were made to it.

It felt like the right time, and the words poured out.

Temporary Enemy Flagging

I was sent this list of *Star Wars: Galaxies* questions by Jason Yates; he had seen this video interview,[245] and didn't know enough Spanish to be able to follow the answers. I posted up an English translation of the transcript here,[246] but really, the interview didn't much overlap with the questions he had.

> Is there the possibility of you ever giving a question/answer session in relation to SWG, your views on the game development and direction, aspects of the game you felt worked, worked well, didn't work at all? Like many, I have so many questions about your involvement with SWG and will likely never get all the answers I would enjoy hearing, but it never hurts to ask. ^_^

---

[245] This interview was given to the Force Peru Fan Club, a *Star Wars* fan club in Peru.
https://www.youtube.com/watch?v=jn9eTqV_d88#t=1150
[246] www.raphkoster.com/games/interviews-and-panels/entrevista-the-force-peru-fan-club/

Well, honestly, for me it has been fifteen years since I started work on SWG, and twelve since I stopped. So a lot of these questions have either been answered before, or I outright don't know or remember the answers! So I will give it a try. But the first answer turned out to be so damn long that it's all I have time for today.

The TEF system and how it was thought up and designed.

TEF stands for Temporary Enemy Flagging. We knew when doing a Star Wars game that we needed to be able to account for the scenarios in the movies. This makes for a tricky problem: after all, we saw Luke clearly pick sides, Han only sort of do so at first, both of them ended up wearing Stormtrooper armor to hide, someone like Lando actually switched sides kinda, and all sorts of other ambiguous situations that don't lend themselves well to a straightforward system where you declared for one side or the other at the start and were done.

On top of that, **we knew that PvP was, well, *fatiguing.*** Given that we were limiting each account to having a single character (for lots of reasons, including PvP, actually), making players have to pick a side, never change, and be always vulnerable, felt like a big ask. The spirit of the game was all about changing your character up over time, and trying new things, so a system of permanent choice for PvP felt wrong.

Lastly, something that I think people have forgotten, in these days of *DayZ, Rust,* and *H1Z1,* is how much there was a general aversion to PvP. *Ultima Online* had had a big issue with playerkillers marauding around, and had famously cloned the map and simply made a non-PvP "dimension." *EverQuest* was philosophically opposed to it — it was a feature, but really barely present in terms of the game consciousness.

When we were sharing design thoughts on SWG (something which we did extensively, to a degree that even games today rarely do), I posted up a very clear statement on the forums that runaway PKing was simply not going to be a feature of *Galaxies.*[247]

> I still believe many things. I still believe that we can find ways to allow players to police their environment. I still believe that this can open up the way to many extremely cool features new to these sorts of games. And I am continuing to work towards having these many features: real battles of territory. Player governments with actual importance and consequence. Player communities that are refined and defined via conflict and struggle so that their battles MEAN something. Real emotions–yes, even including fear and shame, because this is a medium like any

[247] See "A Philosophical Statement on Playerkilling" earlier in this volume.

454

other art medium, and its expressive (and impositional!) power is amazing and worthy of exploration. I believe that virtually every player can try PvP and enjoy it, if it is designed correctly, and that it adds great richness to the online gaming experience.

But I do not want to ever disappoint people in that way again. People will come to SWG for those things, and I do not want them to discover that they cannot stay and enjoy them because the very freedoms which allow those cool, innovative, exciting features, also allow d00dspeaking giggly jerks to dance roughshod jigs on their virtual corpses.

So am I willing to make compromises in "realism" (a radically overvalued thing in game design, frankly) to make sure that SWG remains someplace where most everybody can feel welcome?

You betcha.

Some antecedents

In *Ultima Online* we had tried a number of systems to deal with open player versus player combat while still providing safety. All of them were systems based on the idea of "you can attack, but you'll get flagged somehow as a result." This is as opposed to what were commonly termed "PK switch" systems, where you flipped a flag on yourself in advance, and could only fight other players who had also made that choice. The general consensus, I think, is that blocking in advance was better for the peaceful player; no punishments for flagging ever seemed to really deter a playerkiller. The third major system in use was realm versus realm combat, best exemplified by *Dark Age of Camelot* — basically, dividing the map into territory in advance, and saying you were always safe from your side, but the sides simply didn't interact except at the boundaries. When they did interact, they weren't even allowed to communicate, in order to minimize channels for griefing.

The original proposal for a PvP system in SWG was actually something called Outcasting. It was based on the idea that players were going to own pieces of territory in the world, and be able to set laws

within that territory. The key to the system was the idea that players basically all had a "license to kill," but it could be taken away, almost like inverting the traditional PK switch. If you committed a murder in a territory, the decision on whether to take away your ability to PK fell to the leadership in the territory. Any PK incident would automatically send a log of the events to the local government, so they could make a decision. This would allow a player government to always forgive their "police force," for example. Or to allow a PK incident if it was well roleplayed, etc. Removal of the ability to PK would then be tied to that territory. Go into no man's land, and you could still kill anyone.

Some of this was inspired by how the late Jeff Freeman[248] had run his UO gray shard — in that game, as you killed citizens of one town or another, you became an instakill target in that town. So going on a crime spree meant that eventually, you'd be denied all the basic services and more or less be unable to play, obliged to live "out in the woods" as an outlaw.

I don't remember exactly why this didn't get implemented. We talked about it some on the forums and in dev chats.[249] But it wasn't all that Star Warsy, clearly, and depended heavily on a territory system that was inevitably going to slip out of the initial release. It was set up much more around player towns than around Rebellion and Empire factions. It had challenges around the logging, related to privacy issues and storage. All in all, it was a bit of a pain.

The birth of TEFs

So it was abandoned in favor of a new system, what came to be known as Temporary Enemy Flags, which I ended up designing myself relatively late in the development cycle. The main goal, as I mentioned, was to try to mimic the events in the movies as much as possible. But artificial stuff like grouping and housing rules and

---

[248] See https://www.raphkoster.com/2008/09/30/jeff-dundee-freeman/

[249] For example, there is a chat log from Feb. 12th 2002 where it's discussed, available at https://www.swgemu.com/archive/scrapbookv51/data/20070131233305/default_002.html: "I would be quite happy if it turned out that Outcasting was an effective deterrent to PKing, because it's a better foundation for us to explore more dynamic player governments and other such features than a PK switch is. If Outcasting worked well enough that we didn't need safe areas, that would be neat. :) But I'm not counting on it, we know that it's an experiment in many ways. The reason it is in the game is to try to empower players. We want to find ways to let players have their space which they can shape, and control over the degree of aw (or lawlessness) is an important part of that."

the like quickly got in the way.

Basically, what I did was try to take scenarios from the movies and come up with a ruleset that would allow them to happen in the game. But of course, the game offered far more scenarios than the movies did!

The core of the system was these ideas:

- that a lot of players would probably like to join the Rebels or the Empire without being forced into PvP. This part turned out to be completely true.

- that many players might well like to jump into PvP temporarily, as long as it wasn't a permanent commitment. This also turned out to be correct.

- that players would find it really confusing and non-Star Warsy if you were an Imperial and saw players killing NPC Stormtroopers willy nilly and couldn't do anything about it. This, it turned out, *was not* really the case. We were pursuing Star Warsy fictional consistency with this bullet point, basically, and it turned out to be an aspect where eventually gamey-ness won out.

Basically, **you started out as a civilian.** Either side would leave you alone, but you had to opt out of attacking NPCs from either side, too. So no fighting Stormtroopers or Rebels.

You could go sign up as a *covert* member of a side. This meant you were secretly on that side, but it didn't really show. So if you were a covert Rebel, Stormtroopers wouldn't kill you on sight. But if you attacked one, then you were visibly a Rebel for something like fifteen minutes after the last blow or shot because we applied a *temporary enemy flag* to you. After that, you were safe again. But in the meantime, you were completely vulnerable to the other side — which included *players* from the other side.

Lastly, you could be *overt*, which meant you were visibly on a side at all times — basically, this was like a PK switch being flipped. This meant you could be attacked by the other side at any moment, whether it was by NPCs or other players. But it also meant you could use all sorts of cool perks since you were effectively "in the army." You could wear Stormtrooper armor, you could command an AT-ST, call in an airstrike even. There was a whole ladder of worth of faction perks, up to the ability to build entire bases with laser cannons and everything so you could try to re-enact the Battle of Hoth. Coverts had more limited access to this stuff — I think they were only usable when you were flagged? Or maybe using them flagged you. I don't remember.

You could drop back from Overt to Covert again, with some effort and loss of capabilities. You could even drop out of Covert and go back to being a civilian, and then switch sides.

All that seems pretty straightforward. But that's not where the problems arose.

What the heck is a helpful action?

The problem is, what's the list of stuff that can trigger the flag? Attacking a Stormtrooper seems like an obvious candidate. But what about healing a Stormtrooper? What about handing fresh ammo to a Stormtrooper who is almost out? What about inviting that Stormtrooper to hide inside your house while denying a Rebel entry?

Worse, some of the things you could do as a helpful action were even sort of passive. If you were an entertainer in a bar, and someone chose to watch you, you were healing them of battle fatigue. You couldn't say no… do you get flagged, because you are now helping an Imperial?

The many tentacles of "helpful activity" quickly made the ruleset a morass of edge cases. We had to account for bounty hunters, for example. We had to worry about the case where you were grouped with someone who performed a helpful action on someone. What if the group was mixed coverts from both sides, and then one of them went overt? Should they suddenly be vulnerable to their own group members, or is the group bond sacrosanct? What about bounty hunters, who effectively had an orthogonal PvP system layered on top?

These things quickly turned what had been a fairly clean system into a nightmare.

The thing is, the system *did* do a good job of capturing the Star Warsy moments. I was able to walk through the entirety of Episode IV's plot with the TEF system, and literally every example worked (except that I think we didn't allow Rebels to secretly wear Stormtrooper armor). Even well after the system was removed there were plenty of people who felt that it never should have gone away.[250] People who favored it

---

[250] See the thread at
http://www.mmorpg.com/gamelist.cfm/game/926/view/forums/thread/403181/Finally-someone-else-is-praising-the-TEF-from-SWG.html

enjoyed the fact that sudden battles could erupt out of nowhere, that you could have that tension of committing a sudden attack, becoming vulnerable, and the adrenaline rush of trying to stay alive until the timer expired. It brought that rush of free-for-all into the game in a way that was temporary.

> Ultimately, SWG's pre-NGE PvP was a customizable system that catered to everyone. Well, everyone except griefers, basically, because unless you remained willfully ignorant of the mechanics and made mistakes with your flagging, it was impossible to be griefed even though you were playing a game that featured open-world FFA PvP. It wasn't a perfect system, though. For my money, there could've been some harsher consequences for aggressors. There were no real penalties for instigating a fight, and basically the only punishment for dying — aside from gear decay — was a set of temporary debuffs and a timer that made you wait a few minutes before re-engaging.
>
> — "Some Assembly Required," by Jef Reahard[251]

On the other hand, "making mistakes with your flagging" as this quote puts it, happened *all the time.* Saying it was "impossible to be griefed" is just not correct. To quote one player who was on the receiving end of it far too often,

> TEF, in itself, is not all that bad of a system but it's what players do with it. Griefing seems to be the norm and quite looked forward to via a very small group of some players. And that very small group can easily ruin gameplay for almost everyone else. Imagine a group of 20 rebs sitting outside the Emp's Retreat waiting for some unsuspecting new player to try and get a mission returned. Or another group of imps doing the same outside Coro, Lok, Dant, of Yavin. The themeparks would be unused and un-doable content, pure and simple. The same could be said for the load in areas from the vette along with many other instances of regular PVE gameplay and the tears will most certainly flow along with the Galaxy Chat screams. Want to overwork your CSRs and GMs by nothing more than making them referees? Put back in TEF. Want to make Galaxy Chat unreadable by any1 who doesn't want to see long rants of obscenities? Put back in TEF.
>
> – From a post by "Esquire" in a thread on the Bloodfin emulator server's forums[252]

---

[251] http://www.engadget.com/2014/01/17/some-assembly-required-pre-nge-swgs-proper-sandbox-pvp/

[252] http://www.bloodfin.net/forum/archive/index.php/t-825.html

Why was the TEF system removed?

Too many edge cases, basically. Helpful actions got to be very... subtle. Is it a helpful action if you are grouped with someone from one side and trade an item with them while in the home of someone from the opposite side? That event triggered a temporary flag on you and since you were in an enemy's home, you got automatically ejected; there might be an ambush waiting outside for you that you can't even see while you load from a sudden teleport.

In short, the edge cases made it very griefable. And grief, while not the same thing as PvP, often runs in parallel. Trash talking, gloating, bad language, entrapment... all these things were happening with the TEF system. And why was it that people kept making the mistake of flagging themselves?

The biggest reason? Players who just wanted to treat Stormtroopers as, well, orcs. Monsters in a videogame that they could mow down without getting dragged into PvP. Having been trained through decades of games set in *Star Wars* to kill Stormtroopers when they saw them. Often, simply not even seeing the little icon indicating that this dude wearing some weird uniform was actually an Imperial informant, or something. Worse, not knowing whether a given other player might come after you the second you made a mistake.

For the cautious and savvy player, this wasn't that big a deal. But cautious and savvy players aren't at risk of subscription cancellation. They are already bought in. It's less sophisticated players you need to worry about, and who will make the mistake, and get burned by it and quit.

The death of TEFs

The result was a change whereby the game went over to something more like a switch. (You can read the original forum description of the change on this archive page).[253] I was off the team at that point, but basically, it was more or less changing all

---

[253] https://www.swgemu.com/archive/scrapbookv51/data/20070702021640/

the TEF situations to be opt-in in advance. Everything else remained pretty much intact. Covertness went away, and instead of having

- Civilian who can't affect even NPC aspects of the Galactic Civil War.

- Covert who can, but thereby enters PvP and can only use faction perks when at PvP risk.

- Overt who are 24/7 PvPers and get constant use of faction perks in exchange.

- It became

- Civilian who can't affect even NPC aspects of the Galactic Civil War (e.g., unchanged)

- PvP disabled faction members, who can attack NPCs all day long but aren't vulnerable to PvP. They get all the faction perks, too!

- PvP enabled faction members, basically just like Overt was.

In other words, the pillar of "actually match the Star Wars universe" was what fell by the wayside. You could now have a bunch of PvP disabled Imperial players massacring a Rebel base with their AT-STs, and if you were a Rebel, you stood by and watched. PvP became a separate, parallel game.

In the process, the tangle of helpful actions was also simplified. Trading and healing via entertainment and giving buffs were all removed from the list. Yes, this created a whole new set of exploits — particularly buffs, which were ridiculously overpowered and the result of a design error, but that's another story for another day.

It's important to understand that even this huge simplification wasn't really *simple*.

```
Here is a simple diagram that shows the interaction of how the
"healing" actions will work across PvP enabled and disabled
players:
-----> Healing Actions ----->              <----- Healing Actions <-----
Imperial                                                           Rebel
[PvP Enabled]  [PvP Disabled]  [Civilian]  [PvP Disabled]  [PvP Enabled]
|                                                                      |
|_____ Attack _____|

 Imperial Special Forces can heal Imperial Special Forces, Imperial
 Combatants and Civilians.
 Imperial Special Forces can NOT heal Rebel Combatants or Rebel
 Special Forces
 Imperial Combatants can heal Imperial Combatants and Civilians.
 Imperial combatants can NOT heal Imperial Special Forces, Rebel
 Combatants, or Rebel Special Forces

 Civilians can heal other Civilians.
 Civilians can NOT heal Rebel Special forces, Rebel Combatants,
 Imperial Special Forces, or Imperial Combatants.
```

```
Rebel combatants can heal Rebel Combatants and Civilians
Rebel combatants can NOT heal Rebel Special Forces, Imperial
Combatants, or Imperial Special Forces
Rebel Special Forces can heal Rebel Special Forces, Rebel
Combatants and civilians.
Rebel Special Forces can NOT heal Imperial Combatants or Imperial
Special Forces
```

Got that?

I didn't actually like these changes. I argued that cleaning up the edge cases would probably be enough. Go ahead, remove items from the helpful actions list, make it so that people can't ever "do it by mistake." Cut out the grouping rules which were the source of so many problems.

But the core sticking point was "non-PvPers want to kill Stormtroopers and get faction perks." It was part of the core fantasy for them.

The upshot

What the changes did was say to players **"you can now participate in all aspects of the Galactic Civil War without engaging in any form of player versus player combat."** So it met that wish-fulfillment admirably for that playstyle. It just did so at the cost of fictional consistency with the setting. And the response at the time was glee:

> Did I say exciting? I meant OMFG! Wow!!! This is awesome! You mean I don't have to hide my AT-ST for fear of loosing it to some uber faction farming jerk?! Fantastic!
>
> – ZalTaur on the SWG forums, 2/2/2005[254]

It's a compromise quite similar to giving everyone Jedi, come to think of it.

But you're always caught there in the tangled question of audience and audience size versus fidelity. Is it wrong to give the largest possible audience access to a fantasy that is somewhat watered down? Or do you instead try to make the fantasy as true to the source as possible, knowing it will alienate players?

After all the controversy for so many years, *World of Warcraft* came out. At launch, how did its PvP system work?[255]

Random PvP – Whenever a player character comes across another player

---

[254] Ibid.
[255] http://wowwiki.wikia.com/wiki/Player_vs._Player

character of the opposing faction whose PvP flag is turned on (on PvP realms this flag will switch on whenever you go outside the low-level zones that your faction controls, although it can still be activated in these zones, or Sanctuary areas) that player can attack the other. This was often called "World PvP" before the introduction of zone-specific PvP combat goals, and often still is called by this name.

Oh, and how does this flag get turned on?[256]

> Your flag will be put up in any of these situations:
> - You put your PvP flag up permanently. This is done by the /pvp slash command or from player's portrait menu (right click on portrait, select PvP | Enable). Typing /pvp while flagged will disable PvP.
> - You engage another player of an opposing faction in combat other than dueling. Many consider it an honorable act to put up your PvP flag before engaging another player, to give him or her a fair chance to react. To attack someone before you put your own flag up is known as bluewalling. While Bluewalling is not against any official rules and is used by some as part of their PvP strategy, many others consider it to be very cowardly. It does not preclude getting yourself killed, however, and there are stories on the official Blizzard forums of some getting bluewalled and coming out on top.
> - You cast a spell on a player whose flag is up. If you cast a buff (for example, Power Word: Fortitude) on your friend who has his PvP flag up, yours will also go up. If you cast a healing spell or resurrect a flagged player, your flag will go up.
> - You attack an NPC marked by a PvP flag, like most quest givers, guards, and vendors. This usually applies to NPCs of the opposite faction, but also to neutral factions if you are at war with them, and in rare cases, your own faction. Certain quests require you to kill these type of NPCs. You may also be flagged without attacking aforementioned NPCs, but instead they striking you, this is considered to largely be a bug that has existed throughout the history of the game, be wary about getting attacked by guards.
> - You are in proximity to certain NPCs marked by a PvP flag. These NPCs are often found near settlements of an opposing faction, such as Goldshire and Razor Hill.
> - You accept some of the PvP quests. You will remain flagged as long as that quest is in your quest log.
> - You enter a specific territory. The scheme for flagging by zoning-in is shown in the table below: (etc)

In other words — **WoW uses TEFs**. Why do they work in WoW without all the

---

[256] http://wowwiki.wikia.com/wiki/PvP_flag

anguish and strife? Well, because a) WoW is a hundred times more polished than SWG ever was; b) because in SWG, Rebels and Imperials were bumping against each other from the moment of character creation, whereas WoW used widely separated realms that channeled you through a PvE experience for quite some time before this was even a factor; c) WoW led you narratively through the game, so that the moments of finally jumping into PvP could be dramatically more guided experiences; d) WoW doesn't have quite the entrainment of "of course you kill Stormtroopers" that the Star Wars setting does; e) death is pretty damn painless in WoW, whereas we had item decay and battle fatigue and the like in SWG… it goes to show that all sorts of external factors can impact a system very dramatically.

The world has changed a lot. WoW is effectively a "free for all PvP world" that no one sees as such. Instead, the hot thing these days is the total gankage model of the survival game, basically very glitzy versions of *Ultima Online's* Felucca or original ruleset, even before rep systems or flags. The audience is now large enough that you can make a business out of a game like that, and can feel free to alienate hundreds of thousands of players. But when we were designing SWG, we were thinking that there were only a million MMORPG players in the entire Western world. We couldn't target a niche that way.

Long long ago, I stated that "the future of MMOs is 'PvP'[257]" and I think I was absolutely right. But my point was that there are many ways of putting players into competition. One of the critiques of *Galaxies*[258] was that in fact, the economic level of gankage ended up having the same sort of winner-takes-all issues that PKing does — but it was far more palatable to players in the context of supply chains than it was when getting a blaster bolt in the face or a sword in the guts. I didn't like the TEF changes, but I have to admit that they did fit with the philosophy I expressed in that statement of playerkilling I posted to the forums:[259]

So am I willing to make compromises in "realism" (a radically overvalued thing in game design, frankly) to make sure that SWG remains someplace where most everybody can feel welcome?

You betcha.

That's pretty much exactly what the team chose to do. What's changed over time is that everybody feeling welcome isn't what games have to do anymore.

---

[257] See https://www.raphkoster.com/games/snippets/the-future-of-online-worlds-is-pvp/
[258] "The Mystery of SWG," by Timothy Burke,
http://www.swarthmore.edu/SocSci/tburke1/swgmystery.html
[259] "A Philosophical Statement on Playerkilling."

A Jedi Saga

Continuing here with the questions that were sent in by Jason Yates! Yesterday it was the TEF system… today it's Jedi! Some of this stuff has been told before, but it's actually kind of hard to find it all in one continuous tale. *I have to preface this with a huge huge disclaimer*, though: it's been fifteen years since this particular story started, and a dozen since it ended. My memory may well be faulty on many details.

> #2 What were the thoughts on Jedi and why were such drastic changes made in patch 9 to the entire system?
>
> > -Jason Yates

Well, my opinion is Jedi are evil. Heh.

You see, Jedi are an immense attractant to players, readers, viewers. As a kid, I too waved around plastic lightsabers (we kept bending them as we struck one another, I am pretty sure my mom got *really sick* of buying new ones). Who can resist the fantasy of having this awesome sword, effectively magical powers — mind control, telekinesis, telepathy, and more — and of course, the classic Hero's Journey? I mean, it's basically an ideal play scenario.

Except that of course, you quickly realize that **by comparison, everyone else sucks.** I vividly remember granting Han Solo access to the Force when we played with the original action figures, because, well, he was too cool a character *not* to have them, you know? (We indicated Force powers by bending the legs all the way backwards, sort of a hip-shattering L shape, and then they could fly!) And let's be honest, how long would Han Solo have lasted against Darth Vader? About two seconds. In fact, Kyle Katarn,[260] the most popular Star Wars videogame character, basically *is* Han Solo with Force powers.

This is all fine and dandy in games where you play a Jedi and mow down Stormtroopers by the hundreds. It worked great in the *Jedi Knight* games. But Jedi are notably absent from the gameplay of other types of Star Wars games, and for a good reason. They are a discontinuity. They are too powerful. They are an alpha class. Not

---

[260] http://starwars.wikia.com/wiki/Kyle_Katarn

a problem is a single-player environment, but what do you do with them in a multiplayer setting where some people are bad ass Han Solo types *who will always lose?*

This same issue had come up in the Expanded Universe books and stories. You basically have the problem that

- people identify with Jedi
- they're rare
- they're incredibly powerful

This meant that creators laboring in the universe had a few choices:

- invent new stuff as powerful or more powerful as Jedi (which was done more than a few times — General Grievous, the Witches of Dathomir, the World Razer, a living planet called Zonarma Sekot, The Ones — OK, it was done *a zillion times*, which just proves my point).
- tell stories with no Jedi in them, as in the original Han Solo books by Brian Daley. (Fun books, btw: *The Han Solo Adventures: Han Solo at Stars' End / Han Solo's Revenge / Han Solo and the Lost Legacy*)[261]

Of course, the demands of games focused on Jedi also meant that the powers of Jedi kept having to go up, too! I mean, people actually complained when you didn't start as a powerful Jedi in *Jedi Knight II*, and eventually, we got to the ludicrous heights of Starkiller in the *Force Unleashed* games: "sufficiently powerful enough to rip a million-ton Star Destroyer out of orbit and slap Darth Vader around like he owed him money."[262]

Early days

We weren't the original *Star Wars Galaxies* team. There's a complicated history there that there's no point going into, but suffice it to say that there was a game design prior to the one that our team did. It was class based, used a "cone of fire" real-time action combat system, and I am pretty sure Jedi was one of the classes. There are a whole bunch of reasons why it went away in favor of our design, and I'm not going to go into them (I don't even really think it was that team's fault).

---

[261] The Wookieepedia is an invaluable resource for all things *Star Wars*.
http://starwars.wikia.com/wiki/Main_Page
[262] http://www.dorkly.com/post/62226/toplist-results-the-25-best-star-wars-characters-ever

When our team got going on *Star Wars*, we didn't have an office yet. We worked out of J. Allen Brack's house (he went on to be incredibly important to the history of *World of Warcraft*); in fact, three of the team lived there. I distinctly remember having conversations with Chris Mayer in the living room of that house — probably between bouts of *Soul Calibur*, we were all hooked — and trying to figure out what the heck to do with Jedi. At this point, we didn't yet have the game's vision document, we didn't yet have a game design, or anything. So the statement "live in the Star Wars Universe" was not yet our guiding star. But we knew already that having an alpha class in an MMO was going to be a real problem. The problem was clear:

- Everyone wants to be a Jedi.
- Jedi are rare during the original trilogy.
- Jedi are super powerful.

Of these three pillars, something would have to give.

My first thought was, "make them NPC only." After all, at the mandated time period in the films, there weren't any around. If you read into the Expanded Universe, there's all sorts of them in hiding, for the reasons given above. But even all of those weren't viable solutions for us. We were mandated to fall between the destruction of the Death Star and the Battle of Hoth. That's a pretty narrow little sliver: the official timeline has it around 2 1/2 to three years. The number of of Force sensitives is small enough that Darth Vader is running around with a Death Squadron trying to find just the *one* who did the trench run. Allowing tens of thousands of players to be Jedi would surely be a bit *jarring*.

It also would have destroyed any semblance of grouping, much less the larger scale interdependence that we were already thinking about for the game. Given a choice between Jedi and, well, any other combat role, you'd pick Jedi. We'd probably have non-combatant types around… but maybe less of them, if everyone wanted to be a Jedi instead.

I think the general reaction even among the team, though, was horror. "A Star Wars game and you can't be a *Jedi??*"

The second thought was, "make them not powerful." This was in fact the approach that original design had taken, and pretty much what happened after the NGE as well. As one class out of several, Jedi simply don't have the powers they do in the films. Oh, they *look* like they do, but in practice their force lightning is just a blaster bolt and they are balanced to match the other classes. No Starkiller here.

The problem here, of course, is that the fantasy is shattered. Not only would there be Jedi all over the place, but they wouldn't be special on any axis. And *in this time period*, Jedi were special. Oh, we'd had seen them be rather non-special, in *The Phantom Menace*; the film came out the year before this early development phase, and in it we saw Jedi as more like government diplomats, on the level of a trade attaché or something. (We also learned that it was because they had won a genetic lottery, but that's beside the point).

But the idea of Jedi as rare and powerful was pretty ingrained. So the idea of making them common and not that special didn't sit well at all.

There was a third option that came up, and I pitched it to LucasArts in a casual conversation with Haden Blackman, who was our producer there (today he's known for some pretty kick-ass comics writing).[263] It survived about thirty seconds.

"Just change the time period," I said. This would have allowed us to have way more Jedi, because in the Expanded Universe we have a Jedi Academy during this time period. It would have cost us Darth Vader and Palpatine, Jabba the Hutt and... well, not that much else. Even Boba Fett climbed out of the Sarlaac. The Empire was still quite strong, according to the Timothy Zahn books; we had all sorts of new enemies popping up, and there was even a good reason why new Jedi might be weaker than those in the past, given that there were literally no trained Jedi Masters who could teach them.

There were probably a pile of logistical reasons why this couldn't happen. I shudder to think of the approval process that might have been required, especially to go back and amend an existing deal. The fact that the game development process was being rebooted was a touchy subject in itself; early chats with Haden were marked by a lot of "and what about X, is that staying?" All in all, even though it was probably the cleanest solution, it never had a chance for reasons that had little to do with game design.

So, that left us at the three pillars, intact. Powerful, rare, and in the hands of players. We were screwed.

---

263 Among others, he has written *Batwoman* and *Elektra*.

The crazy idea I still wish we had done

I had a brainfart that never made it past those early days, there in that house. The idea took inspiration from Hardcore mode in the *Diablo* games. We would offer a Jedi system that effectively gave a different way

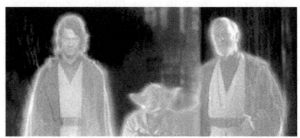

to play the game. A method that kept Jedi rare, powerful, and yet allowed everyone a shot.

Every player would have a special character slot available to them, distinct and parallel from their regular character. This character would be locked into one profession, one class: Jedi. They'd start out weak as a kitten though, untrained in combat or anything, and with barely any Force abilities at all. Luke without womprat-shooting experience maybe.

Although the design wasn't done yet, we knew that the game would be classless. So this pathetic Force Sensitive character would be able to gain better Force powers by earning Force XP by using the Force. They could also go off and learn other skills. But either way: if they died, that was it. They were dead. Reroll. Start over. It was that dreaded word: permadeath.

In the corner of the screen, there would be a timer running logging how long you had managed to survive. It was your score, for this weird little mini-game. The name of the game was survival, but it was rigged.

You see, the moment you used Force powers within view of anything or anyone Imperial, or indeed any player, they could report you to the Empire. To Darth Vader's Death Squadron in fact. And that generated someone to come after you. After first, just lowly Stormtroopers. Eventually, cooler characters, such as some of the bounty hunters like IG-88. Eventually, *really* cool ones like Boba Fett or fan favorite Mara Jade.

These would be brutal fights. Odds are you'd just die. So hiding and training *very carefully* would be essential. But it wouldn't matter, of course. As you advanced, your powers would get "noisier" and cooler. You wouldn't be able to resist using Force Lightning in a crowd, or equipping your lightsaber in view of some Imperials. And eventually, after Boba Fett and Mara Jade and everyone else had failed, well, that would be when Darth Vader himself bestirred himself to take care of the little problem.

And you would die. It would be rigged.

Your time would go up on a leaderboard, and everyone would be able to ooh and aah over the hardcore permadeath player who managed to get all the way to seeing Darth Vader and *getting her ass kicked*.

As a reward, if you managed to make it to Jedi Master, your very last skill would be "Blue Glowy." You'd unlock a special emote *for your main character slot* that allowed them to summon up the ghosts of every Jedi who had made it that far. So all the bragging rights would carry over to your other character. Heck, I had a picture in my mind of the most amazing player summoning up not one, but a whole set of them — the most badass player would have a coterie of Jedi advisors, hovering around their campfire, as they showed up.

The response to this idea was pretty much "Permadeath?!?" And so Hardcore mode never happened.

The actual design

Now we hadn't managed to remove a pillar, we'd *added* one. Not a step forward.

I am pretty sure it was in conversations with Chris Mayer (our lead server programmer) that we hit on the notion of making the process of becoming a Jedi effectively a personality test. As I recall, the question was around "if we're going to have all these Jedi around, and need to keep them rare but acting like they do in the movies, that almost calls for a roleplayer only profession, or some other way to make sure that only those who actually deserve to be Jedi become one." See, we knew that Jedi would be the top target above all for the Achiever and worse, the Killer types, in Bartle lingo. It was too attractive a target, and if we made the way of becoming Jedi involve quests, or grinding points in some fashion, it would inevitably go to the powerhungry. But really, we wanted a system that was more for the Explorer type: someone who savored the game.

This meant we couldn't do something with a standard quest. Too susceptible to the issues with static game data in large communities.[264] Any solutions would get shared, and the rarity would fall by the wayside.

I pulled out a very old idea, so old it was from the MUD-Dev days, about a spellcasting system that used spell words, but the words were different for every player (didn't *Asheron's Call* end up doing something of the sort?). That way recipes couldn't be shared, but just the broad idea could. That seemed like it had some promise. So we started thinking of tasks or quests that players could do that could vary by player. And I am pretty sure it was Chris who said "what if the tasks were from different Bartle types?"

And so we landed on the system:

- There would be a large pool of possible actions a character could undertake, divided into four categories, one for each Bartle type.

- These actions would include things like "visiting the highest location on a given planet," "using this specific emote," "killed this particular creature," "learned this skill," "did five duels," "entered this battlefield," "crafted this item," etc. Some of the exploratory ideas were taken from *Seven Cities of Gold*, and others from badges we expected to give, and so on. (Remember, achievements didn't exist yet. The idea was almost certainly copied from online games).

- Every player would randomly roll up a *different* set of actions they needed to undertake. Their personal list would include some items from each of the four categories so that it was always balanced across playstyles.

- The player would *not* be told that they had checked off an item.

- The player would *not* be told that they had checked off all the items, either — they would be notified of Jedi status the *next* time they logged in.

- We wouldn't tell even the development team how exactly it worked. Most of them didn't know.

Yes, it was absolutely **security through obscurity**, which is exactly what security people tell you not to do. But it had some great advantages.

- Nobody would know how to become a Jedi, so all those obsessive grinders

---

[264] See "Does static info even work anymore?" www.raphkoster.com/2008/01/02/does-static-info-work-anymore/http://www.raphkoster.com/2008/01/02/does-static-info-work-anymore/

and walkthrough readers wouldn't be able to do it by rote. And yet we could tell everyone with utter honesty that anyone could become a Jedi.

- It would be pretty rare. A player who actually engaged in all the different aspects of the game, who moved across playstyles that freely, would be highly unusual.

- We could keep Jedi super-powerful, since they were so rare. Odds were that any player who had done that breadth of things was already maxed out in power anyway.

Given the level of investment required at that point, permadeath seemed like it didn't fit, so that went away.

At that point, all that would need to happen would be implement a truly expensive set of custom animations and skills. So, we made the plan, a doc was specced out that included the list of possible tasks, and there it sat until we got to it on the schedule.

We're out of time

We never got to it on the schedule. SWG's development was hurried. **The whole game was made between September of 2000 and June of 2003**, which is an insanely abbreviated development time. For comparison, *World of Warcraft* was announced in 2001 and launched after probably five years of development. In SWG's case, sure, there had been a bunch of time invested in the game with the earlier team, but there was virtually nothing we were using. Effectively, we had started over from scratch. The originally announced *availability* date was in 2001, which was already impossible. As a result, we were already insanely behind by the time we hit the alpha date. It was September of 2002 or thereabouts and so little was working that we did what eventually turned out to be an incredibly valuable testing process: we invited only 150 people in, and we focus tested each feature as it was ready.

Yeah, that means we tested chat for the first time in September of 2002. And launched less than a year later. Combat came online in November or something. And content tools came online… never.

All those characters, so little dialogue.

Well, no, not never. Just hardly ever, if that makes sense. SWG hit its "code complete" drop dead date around February. **What you think of as "the game" was mostly built between August and February.** We had building tools and the like, and we had a rich set of game systems, because sandbox and simulation-heavy games can be made much much faster and more cheaply than content-heavy games. But adding the required content to the game starting in February, to finish in May? Just not possible.

We had to go through and make tough choices on cuts. As early as that Christmas I was already triaging the entire game design. My criteria was "can the game function without this." Not "will it be good." Will it work *at all*. This led to often weird priorities based on the fact that the game relied a *lot* on player interdependence. You could probably have postponed Image Designer (the profession that involved one player changing another's appearance). But it was actually our first scripting test because it was so tiny, and so it made the cut because it got done way early and took so little effort. You could push off player cities because no players would be advanced enough to make one. You could always walk, if there weren't vehicles. It would suck — the planets had been planned assuming landspeeders! But you could get there. But we couldn't change out, say, dancing, because the healing of battle fatigue was a critical portion of the game loop. (Spaceflight was never intended to be in the initial launch — we knew on day one that was out of reach).

I watched so many features fall apart during this period.

Game scripting was in Java, and where I had hoped our designers would be able to script cool intricate quests, or even build us a quest system, we got rather iffy content that seemed to break constantly even though the designers tried hard. We had to resort to mission terminals, which were just one of many types of content that were supposed to be present, as our main content activity. I had dreamed of a Jabba's Palace where every single character had the full backstories from the books, and you could do quests for all of them. We didn't have a template-style quest system working; at one point Scott Hartsman came out to do a sanity check of our development, and I suspect he found me rather full of despair, as every item he enumerated should be there for content development was absent. This meant we sure as heck weren't going to manage to get the player contract system whereby you could be given a quest by another player. Dynamic POIs were worked on for a month or two, then basically abandoned because of terrain engine issues and scripting difficulty.

Professions fell out. The designer who was doing the skill trees couldn't manage to lick the problem of trees that were of varying sizes and interconnected in unique ways; originally, the trees were all different, and there were "surprise" professions that might appear if you mastered two skills from disparate professions, more like a skill web. Said designer left the company for another job elsewhere, and the producer made a command decision, created the skill onions, and we had to do those. This meant that professions that were meant to be tiny, like Image Design, had to bloat out to fit a rigid structure, which actually increased their scope. Other professions that could have had many more skills or skill lines in them had to conform to the rigid four-track onions. Some were cut altogether, including my beloved Writer profession, and Miner, and some others.

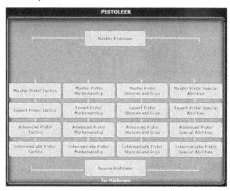

We learned during beta that **our deployment hardware was going to be less powerful than we had expected.** As a result, we couldn't compute the really nifty procedural terrain *on the servers* as far out as we had hoped. As a result, our range for combat fell in half or more. This actually broke *everything*, because the new range was smaller than the *minimum* optimum range for rifles and snipers. Creatures couldn't pathfind, suddenly. In alpha testing, our AI was *way* smarter than it was at launch. Pathfinding was supposed to include things like creature emotional state affecting the paths they chose — e.g., you could stampede a scared critter right off a cliff, and different creatures would attempt different slopes based on how scared they were. Instead, even the basics of whether they were scared of you or not started to not work well. Dynamic spawns that affected terrain couldn't adequately check to see if anyone was there, so buildings would spawn on top of someone else. I don't remember exactly when we realized we had to settle for 2d collision instead of 3d, which meant you couldn't step over a short wall, but *that* made nobody happy, and I had to defend it on the forums.

Databases were clearly going to be a huge issue, thanks to the crafting system, which had turned out awesome but also considerably more detailed than specced. A large pile of unique stats needed to be tracked on *everything*. Space was at a premium; character records were enormous. This caused problems when players moved between physical servers or across server processes, because of the time required to copy the data and the race conditions that could emerge.

We were sent a literal army: dozens of QA and CS people were bused in from San Diego to desperately try to build out all the planets. They had to learn the tools and build little points of interest. We were desperately short on managers; Cinco Barnes, who had been just leading the content team, had to manage everyone on the design team — dozens and dozens of people — while the producers and I basically took on the job of hotspot firefighters, going from problem to problem to problem to fix them as efficiently as we could.

Oof, these paragraphs felt like opening a vein. SWG fans, you have no idea what the game was *supposed* to be like, and how weird it feels to hear adoration for features which to me ended up being shadows of their intent. Don't get me wrong, the team did **heroic, amazing work**. All of these issues end up being my fault for overscoping or mismanaging, the producers fault for not reining me in, or the money people's fault for not providing enough time and budget. The miracle is that we pulled it off *at all*.

You can see where this is going. There we are, out of time. And there's this big looming must-have system that is really, quite complex, adds a ton more tracking, and which we just didn't have time for. Oh, we could push implementation of *some* of it to post-launch; after all, Jedi were going to be rare, so we had months before any Jedi

Masters demanded that their Force Lightning actually, you know, *work.* But we couldn't push off the *tracking*, because that was what the core was: whether you could actually start working on being a Jedi. We'd be lying about Jedi being in the game at all if at least that piece wasn't there.

Chris or J comes to my office one day. I don't remember what I was doing exactly, and I don't remember who it was exactly. Re-speccing PvP, possibly, or trying to get decent data so I could see if combat was balanced (which it wasn't, and never was). He tells me, "**We can't do it.** We can't gather and track the data. We don't have the time to do it. We need a new system."

My brain fuzzes out. "It took weeks to figure out any solution at all. We can't do a content solution, we have no time and no tools."

"It's OK, there's an idea. We can't track all of that, we there are some things we are *already* tracking. Skills. They cover all the different personalities, all the Bartle types. We have socializers and we have explorer skills with surveying and we have combat stuff all over the place… So I am here to ask you, can we just make the randomized list be a set of skills."

I had twelve other things to do. **I said yes,** and on we went.

It was a fateful decision.

A Jedi by Christmas

The game launched, barely. It was in such bad shape that we knew we were going to announce its launch to the beta testers and they would *crucify* us, because they could see perfectly well that the game was not ready. We flew out the top commenters on the forums and told them. Their faces fell. They were beyond dismayed. **We threw ourselves on their mercy and asked for their help.** Not to lie, but just to tell their

fellow players that we were doing everything we could to get the game into decent shape. It was true; we were. We had managed to get a couple extra months from management — not the six months or a year I had hoped for. Everyone was basically living at the office. We had been so open and honest and communicative with the playerbase on the forums that when we asked for the playerbase's goodwill, we actually got it. (Our community management actually became a case study for how to build collaborative environments with fans that was written about in *Convergence Culture: Where Old and New Media Collide*. I am very proud of what we accomplished there). People were upset, but there was a sense that we were all in it together. Our day one sales of the game were a one-to-one exact match for the registered forum population.

And then **when the game launched, it didn't actually work.** Like, you couldn't log in. But gradually, we recovered, and started working on the missing features, and did in fact deliver them over the course of the next six months. But many of the cuts had been irreversible, many of the changes permanent. Jedi work continued as the skills were developed, but combat was dramatically out of whack, there was a duping bug to try to find, player housing was getting placed around the entrances to the very few pieces of static content we had and people were effectively claiming dungeons as private property. All sorts of stuff was a mess.

This was the glorious "pre-CU period" that today people recall so fondly.

And I had been offered the role of Chief Creative Officer, in San Diego, before the game had even shipped. I had taken the role, but had stayed working on SWG to try to get it into good shape before I left — I was going to have to move. Gradually I had to give up more and more ownership over the game, and there were parts of things that simply vanished in the handoff — probably the most critical of these were metrics around gameplay balance and the economy.

But the game was shaping up. Players had formed governments. Vehicles were very popular. The early game economy, which was *intentionally* rocky because players had not yet developed all the interdependence infrastructure, had started to hum along.

This was a player city.

Entertainers were going on tour, and few of them were macroing, because they played entertainers because they *liked it.* People were building supply chain empires and businesses with hundreds of employees. Merchants were making a name for their shops full of custom-crafted gear.

And most importantly, nobody was a Jedi. Nobody *cared.* **They were playing the professions they liked.** They were doing what they wanted to do. The secret of Jedi was a secret still, and there were countless theories. Players thought they were being watched and only the deserving would be picked. Players thought that various half-finished bits of content were actually the start of Jedi quest chains. And meanwhile, players were invisibly checking off items on their secret skill lists.

And LucasArts marketing says, "we need a Jedi by Christmas." The rocky launch and general bugginess had cost us a huge number of subscribers. Oh, we were still the second biggest MMO outside of Asia, behind EverQuest, but the expectations were much higher. Many players had simply churned out, unwilling to deal with the general jankiness. But the game was improving by leaps and bounds, and marketing wanted to get a fresh flow of users in now that the game was actually working.

We looked at the rate at which people were unlocking their skill boxes, and did a back of the envelope calculation. It showed that the first Jedi might manifest in… 2012 or so. Marketing was not amused. "Drop hints," the team was told.

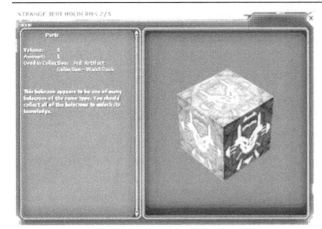

I was already half off the team, commuting between Austin and San Diego every week or two. (I would eventually move at the end of the year). But I am pretty sure I was in at least some of the meetings. The decision was made to drop Holocrons, hint boxes that would tell you one of the skills you needed to learn.

The problem is obvious: as **soon as three people all have gotten a hint that what they need is to master a specific skill box, the secret was out.** It was weak cryptography. As the confirming data poured in that none of the Holocrons involved anything other than skills, the players set themselves with a will to trying to crack their personal codes. And they used the oldest trick in the book: brute force.

They simply started at A and learned every skill. In order. Probability being what it was, most finished when they got partway through. But the problem was this meant playing *what you didn't like.*

The peaceful dancers who thrived on joking around with an audience and doing coordinated flourishes found themselves tramping around the mud looking for mineral deposits.

The explorers who enjoyed exploring distant swamps got themselves trapped in medical centers, buffing an endless line of combatants.

The doctors who derived their pleasure from helping out people in a support role found themselves learning martial arts or machine guns and mowing down creatures.

The combat specialists who were used to optimizing damage per second in taking down a krayt dragon were instead raising them from babies.

The creature handlers who tended dewbacks had to learn to chop them up and cook them instead.

You get the idea. **Everyone started playing everything they didn't like.** Oh, some players discovered new experiences they never would have otherwise. Many emerged from this with a new understanding of the fundamental interconnectedness of a society. But most just macroed their way or grinded their way through it all as

Obtainable. Powerful. Rare?

fast as possible, dazzled by the booby prize of Jedi.

Satisfaction fell off a cliff. I never did see a marketing push for Jedi — never saw a marketing push for the game at all, to tell the truth. But what I do know is that one month after Holocron drops began, we started losing subs, instead of gaining them. SWG had been growing month on month until then. After Holocrons, the game was dead; it was just that nobody knew it yet.

My handle on the forums had been Holocron.

And later…

Pretty much every single subsequent change can be traced back to that day. All the panicky patches, the changes, the CU and the NGE, were all about trying to get the sub curve back on a growth trajectory. Some of them were good changes. Most of

them were bad, in my opinion. But they can all be traced to me saying "yeah, fine, skills is good enough" in a hurried minute-long conversation on a work day that was probably fourteen hours long.

Nobody much liked Holocrons as a Jedi mechanism, of course, and the playerbase felt betrayed. It seemed like a cruelly mechanistic trick, after the dreams they had had; a system that worked better when nobody knew how it worked. And it had worked, for a while. People dreamed of Jedi, and were content, and had *fun*. They were attainable, powerful, and *absent*, and the rat race wasn't a factor.

Eventually, the team tried new things. They did a quest chain instead, the Jedi Village. To be honest, I never played it, and I was not only off SWG but very out of the loop by the time it went in. The genie was out of the bottle, though: Jedi was a thing for grinders and achievement-mad powergamers, and a little quest chain was never going to stop them. They were everywhere.

By the time of the NGE, they were a class to choose, as they had been in the original design we scrapped. Not very special. Not very powerful.

I never even logged into the game after NGE, to be honest.

Holocron was my *last* handle, on any forum. And I never played a Jedi at all.

SWG's Dynamic World

This post is dedicated to the memory of John Roy, lead environment artist on Star Wars Galaxies.

Let's do some math. Let's say that you need to have a pretty big world: sixteen kilometers on a side, and made out of tiles.

A tile needs to know what texture it is. That's one byte. Not much, right? You only get 256 tiles on a planet, though, which isn't a lot.

But wait, we can add some variety there, by putting in some colors. We're in 3d, right, so we can tint the tiles slightly and get variation. It's normally three bytes to apply a color, but let's instead just say that each planet has a fixed list of colors, and you can have 256 of them, and that way each tile can look up into a list of colors and we only need one byte.

Oh, and it's a 3d game heightfield, so we need to know what the elevation of the tile is! We'll just say that there are only 256 levels of height, and that way we can keep it at a nice conservative three bytes per tile.

That's good, because we need a lot of tiles. They're one meter on a side. So that means that for a planet we need 16,384 just to make one edge. We need 16,384×16,384 to lay down the whole world.

That's 268,435,456 bytes for this world. Of course, we need *ten planets,* not one. So, that's more like 2,684,354,560 bytes. Nobody uses bytes, so that's 2,621,440k. 2,048mb. 2.56 gigabytes, uncompressed.

That's… **not going to fit on a CD.** I mean, that doesn't include any art yet.

DVD drives weren't yet widespread in 2003. In fact, taking up 2.5 gigs of space just for maps was unheard of.

The solution to that problem didn't just let us ship *Star Wars Galaxies,* it also unlocked everything from player housing to crafting to giant Imperial vs Rebel battles.

Patent disclaimer

Before you read any farther, you should know that Sony Online actually patented some of the technology that I am going to describe. If you are someone who should not be reading technology patents, you should stop now.

Origins

I've described before how the abortive *Privateer Online* worked. That game, like other spaceflight classics, was intended to have thousands of worlds. This was going to be accomplished using a neat quirk of how random numbers work on computers: the *fixed random seed*.

You see, **computers don't actually generate random numbers**. They generate predictable numbers using a seed value. To make the results more erratic, you constantly change the seed value — usually by using the current time down to the millisecond or something. There are many routines used in order to make numbers from a seed, but if you take the exact same routine from one computer to another, and then give it the exact same seed you've used elsewhere, you should, generally speaking,

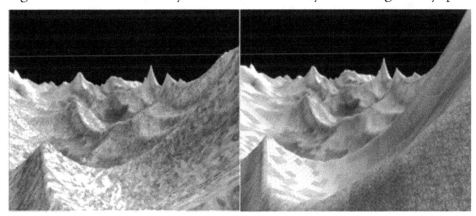

Very early experiments

get back the same random numbers, in exactly the same order.

This is basically a really cool way to compress information. It's not that different from knowing that given the formula to calculate pi, everyone will be able to get the exact same result out. So it's a lot easier to just hand around a tiny formula than it is to try handing around a zillion individual digits. The formula fits in a few bytes; the individual digits take up a lot of space.

Each planet in *Privateer Online* used a single seed, and from it, we picked things like sky color, tile colors, and generated a whole map. So one seed value was enough for a small planet.

But it had to be small — the thing is that there are a lot of randomness generation routines for terrain out there, and they all sort of get... "patterned" after a while. If what you roll up is gentle rolling hills, you are going to get gentle rolling hills fairly

consistently. If you have spiky mountains, well, that's what you are going to have everywhere.

When we got to doing SWG, we had this stuff on the brain, of course. But we also saw that other projects at SOE were doing maps that were meshes. In some cases, they were actually sourced from procedural terrain generators, very fancy ones that you couldn't run in realtime, and that involved a day-long baking process as the resultant maps were turned into meshes. Once they were meshes, you could run compression and level-of-detail routines on them to reduce their size... but there was still no way to get truly big worlds.

Actual size isn't the only factor, of course. The granularity of the world matters too. You can have a 16km x 16km world with tiles that are a kilometer in size, and it's going to take up the same data space as a 16 *meter* by 16m world. You can also have a game world like that of *Eve Online* where the vast vast majority of it is empty space; they procedurally generated theirs too, and as a little homage to Douglas Adams, the seed value for their procedural galaxy is the number

42. And it matters whether you can *change* this world; if it's rolled up from a seed value, then you can't exactly go carve a hole in it without storing the actual map in memory. This leads players to spend lots of time debating the right way to measure game world size.[265]

Generating worlds, then, is kind of old hat. The harder part is, **how do we make a world as living as possible,** one that can change and evolve at a high level of detail, while still having plenty of room?

The layering tool

We actually published a very layman's version what we did for SWG on the game's website in advance of launch. You can still find the article on the Wayback Machine.[266] The heart of the idea was **marrying Photoshop layers with procedural generation.** Here's a screenshot of the tool from that article.

Shapes like ellipses, circles, and boxes are easily described mathematically. You can say "run this rule when you're inside this circle, and this other rule when you're outside of it." You can say things

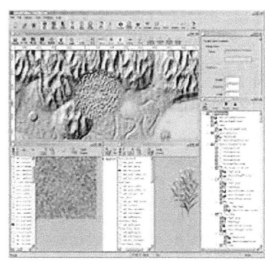

The tool

like "run one rule that gives you gentle changes. Now use that rule as a blend value for how much of this mountainous rule to blend onto a third rule that is grassy plains." You can see several of these circle rules on the map.

---

[265] A link here was lost, but typical debates include actual size versus travel time.

[266] Not written by me, and therefore not included in this volume. Find it at http://web.archive.org/web/20011201170650/starwarsgalaxies.station.sony.com/team/articles/corellia_1.jsp

We never did do river generation, though; as a result, the rivers all tended to form loops, because that was what we could make. Water was a simple water table height, and anything under it was underwater. We also added the ability to insert "water sheets" at arbitrary heights so we could do things like the river in Theed, up top of the cliff. Early on we had big dreams about maybe doing underwater play, but that never even made it onto the schedule since it was so improbable.

To give a realistic example: on most all the mountainous areas, we wanted there to be ledges available pretty often. Ledges and "terracing" were easy to create; just say that whatever the mountain routine output, you clamped to a multiple of something. So instead of getting "1, 2, 3, 4, 5 ,6 ,7, 8, 9," you'd get back 1, 4, 8. But if you do that across the

Very early work on Tatooine, showing the terracing technique described here

entire map, you get something that looks like wedding cake, plus the areas are dead flat. Ah, if you say "but you should only run that rule in some places, and we'll decide those places by taking another rule and checking for 'high spots'" then you get flattening happening in little islands. So you stack the rules in order: Plains. A filter to put mountains only somewhere. Mountains. A filter to put ledges only some places. Ledges. A "gentle wavy" one to make the ledges not dead flat, applied across the entire map. And finally, a circle for a flat area where we need to build, say, Dee'ja Peak. Oh, and we used similar rules to put down color washes; terrain textures, which in some cases came with the wavy grass, and could also come with bumpmaps; trees, plants and rocks; even some sorts of points of interest.

You can in fact stack quite a lot of rules like that, and they still take up very little storage space. The beauty of the rules is that they save out to little text files; a planet on SWG was usually on the order of 16-32k of text. The beauty of something like Perlin noise as a terrain generator routine is that you ask for the elevation result *at any arbitrary coordinate*. You don't have to generate the terrain "in order" and it's not dependent on what is next to it. (I had met Ken Perlin, the inventor of Perlin noise, at a conference a while before, so we flew him out to

When we only had one tree

the office and he helped optimize our algorithms).

This meant that we could use it for graphical level of detail too. Those of you who played may recall the "terrain detail" slider in options, which was capable of bringing your machine to a crawl. At max, what it did was query the elevation for every coordinate, out to your draw distance. At lower settings, it instead started skipping points: every other one, to start, but eventually computing only one out of every 8 or 16 elevations. This resulted in less terrain tiles, way out there, and you could see "popping" as you moved closer and more heights were computed, changing the profile of mountains. It was way way worse with trees, though, because whole forests would pop into view when they were finally above the generation threshold.

Nobody could actually run at max detail and get a decent framerate, at the time. The hope was that as machines grew more powerful, you'd be able to. These days, you could probably just compute the entire planet and put it in RAM on a beefy enough machine. We took our marketing screenshots at everything maxed, and just stood still while taking them. (Our tech director, Jeff Grills, gave a presentation at an AMD event on the challenges of rendering and performance; you can read it here,[267] if you are technically inclined.) Even then, as many players have noticed, the quality of the graphics seemed lower between the early shots and later ones — the E3 demo

---

[267]

http://web.archive.org/web/20120813065515/http://developer.amd.com/media/gpu_assets/D3DTutorial 06_jgrills.pdf

had more shaders on everything, and better lighting in general. (The drop-off was so big that Gabe of *Penny Arcade* actually wrote a post complaining about it). Most players don't know it, but the bigger loss was actually on characters, not terrain; early characters looked way cooler, but we couldn't afford the draw calls or something.

Challenges

Procedural environments have a sameyness to them, though. If you have the rules tweaked enough, they can actually add *more* detail than a human will, because the algorithm isn't bound by time constraints. But you need quite a lot of fine detail variation on the rules to get back to where the terrain really does surprise you. Like the real world, most of it is fairly bland. (In fact, one of the classic videogame map tricks is to heighten slopes dramatically compared to the real world; after all, most real world slopes are much gentler than 30 degrees!)

John Roy

So artists used to handcrafting environments had trouble with this tool for quite a while. I worked for months hand-in-hand with the late John Roy, the lead environment artist, to tweak our best practices and our basic understanding of how to use the rules. John passed away a few months ago, and **if you were an admirer of the eventual result in Galaxies, I'd like to urge you to donate to the memorial fund for his family.**[268]

The use of circles and boxes as rules allowed artists to craft the very specific film locations to a pretty huge degree of accuracy, but it did call for iteration: trying different seeds until you got something that matched what we had seen in the film. Also, there *was* a

---

[268] https://www.gofundme.com/fx7r3w

performance limit on how many rules you could pile into a map. If you hit hundreds, it would slow down the calculation as the code had to check, for every point, whether it was under the influence of a given rule (imagine hundreds of point-in-circle tests for every point on the map). So they were under budgets as far as rule usage.

I also recall that the lead graphics programmer wrestled for a while with the issue of how to do nice smooth blending between tiles. It would require a ton of blend maps and overdraw, because tiles were stamped down at every tile; you could in theory have one tile with eight different neighbors. He worked on trying to deal with it in a way that would provide decent performance for a few weeks. After a while I remember asking him why he didn't just always stamp tile textures down in 2×2 blocks, so

The earliest work on the Theed cliffs

that you never had more than two tiles meeting. He got an angry look on his face, and tile blending worked the next day.

The other big issue from all this, of course, was that the server needed to know all the map info too. And our servers were really no great shakes. I mentioned in the Jedi post how we discovered that our servers were going to be less powerful than we had anticipated — there was some sort of budget savings from re-using old EQ servers, or something, so **we ended up with Pentium III-600s as servers.** But where a given player's machine needed to calculate everything around to the horizon for just that one player, a server needed to know the terrain around *every* player *and every AI*, so that pathfinding routines could be run, collision checked, AIs could move about, etc. And the server sometimes couldn't keep up. This is part of why the AI alert radius, and the combat radius, fell so dramatically during beta, and why shooting through the ground was occasionally possible. (It may also be why we never got full 3d collision, meaning that you couldn't jump over tiny little walls).

Dynamic rules and the content it unlocked

One of the dozens of dynamic POI theaters I built

So, procedural terrain was kind of a big experiment, and it gave us a lot of headaches. Many of them were quite possibly game-impacting to a degree that was really damaging. In the meanwhile, *EverQuest 2* and *Planetside* were managing to move forward with their hand-crafted mesh solutions. But we stuck with it for another big reason. **We could add rules on the fly.**

Rules could be attached to any object in the world. And **this unlocked the ability to place any building anywhere.** We limited ourselves to simple circles, since they were the easiest to compute (distance from center). They would do a simple strong smoothing routine: clamp everything inside the circle to the elevation at the center of the circle. They'd have a little bit of a fade off at the edge of the circle. They might re-texture the terrain, and they'd have a no-rock-flora-or-other-crap set up.

The result was that we were able to do

- **player housing.** Players were able to put down housing anywhere that wasn't disallowed. Oh, we disallowed some of the wrong spots (for fiction reasons, we weren't allowed to let people build suburbs around the core cities, even though those were the absolutely most obvious places to let suburban sprawl happen; as a result, we got fictional cities with a weird empty ring around them filled with newbie monsters, followed by an outer ring or "crust" of player city.

- **dynamic points of interest.** These were encounters that spawned complete with some structures, rather than just spawning a monster. This let us in theory even have questlets spawn, which I have written about before.[269] Dynamic POIs of this sort didn't ever make it to launch, but spawning structures along with enemies certainly did. In general, spawning in SWG wasn't based on where in the world you were; it was

---

[269] "Dynamic POIs."

based on *where players already were,* like random encounters in D&D. This was intended as an anti-camping mechanism, though it all too often resulted in spawns dumping a building on your head.

- **lairs.** Rather than spawning single creatures, we generally spawned a creature spawner. The literal design spec was "like in *Gauntlet.*" Lairs spawned creatures up to a given population limit. Some of what they spawned were babies, intended for capture and taming by creature handlers. The others were adults, and "aggro" or attack-on-sight for peaceful creatures was driven by whether you were approaching their lair or not — everything defends its home, after all. Blow up the lair, and you actually killed the spawn. This concept started clear back in *Ultima Online,* where we spawned orc camps complete with orc wizards and whatnot. Unfortunately, as housing used up all the clearings in UO, these spawns eventually had nowhere to appear!

- **campsites.** Players were able to build camps out in the wilderness that conferred much of the benefit of being in a town. Today, Galaxies players often remember camps as one of the most social features of the game.

- **military bases,** which unlocked huge chunks of the Galactic Civil War for players.

This unlocked an enormous amount of gameplay. You could spawn a little bandit camp on the side of a mountain, on a cliff even. It would create its own little ledge.

When the camp was deleted later on, the rule would go with it, and the cliff would be restored to its original appearance.

Lastly, and perhaps most critically, this also unlocked **the ability to do harvesting anywhere in the world**, which was a crucial component of the game economy.

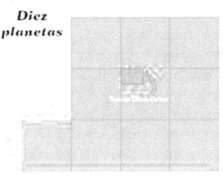

Diez planetas

A size comparison between all of UO pre-Trammel, and SWG

In UO we had invisible resources attached to grass, to the rocks, to everything really. But all METAL was the same. There were no stats on METAL; originally, it was all steel-gray, even. One day I hacked in a system to that, which used (you guessed it) fixed random seeds to determine what *kind* of metal you got from a given location, and then I just attached a flag to the resultant ore. I checked for that flag at every step in the crafting process, and transferred the flag from the ingredient to the next stage. The result was colored armor of many different mineral types.

I knew we wanted this for SWG, and the best way to do it was to use an inheritance tree instead:

- METAL
  - Ferrous
    - Iron
  - Non-Ferrous
    - Copper

…and so on. Designer Reece Thornton was assigned the system, and he went crazy with it, providing each resource with an array of statistics which could then be leveraged by the crafting system. We were able to swap out the resources underneath the whole map, and allow players to build harvesters and factories anywhere at all, following the gold rushes and oil booms within the game. This then tied back into the crafting system, the game economy, and yes, the combat game itself, shaping the game very powerfully and helping to make it feel like a real world. The SWG economy and crafting system deserves its own post, but I did write about it here at a high level,[270] in the midst of a post about something else.

So in the end, a huge part of the "living world" quality of Galaxies came down to

---

[270] "Do auction houses suck?"

the idea that **we shouldn't necessarily *know* what was in our world.** That it should be surprising us, as well as the players. Yeah, we had a lot of empty frontier land — it was supposed to have been thickly populated with handcrafted little encounters, cool locations, and so on, but we never managed that despite applying a small army of designers to it. But what it **did** offer: malleability and the unexpected — that turned out to be a key asset. It probably saved the production literally *millions* of dollars, for all the troubles it introduced, and might very well work even better on computers today, without all the issues that the system presented. Add in shadows, and butterflies, and procedural wind blowing things to and fro, and a day/night cycle where the stars actually moved across the sky, and pretty soon you were somewhere that while still low on framerate and blurred and choppy, could feel very immersive.

I used this picture as my desktop for years. I would be asked where the picture was taken, quite regularly. I think people expected to hear Arizona, and were taken aback when I instead said it was from a galaxy far, far away.

Designing a Living Society in SWG

Once upon a time you could drop things on the ground. It's one of the first things a baby does, one of the most human things to do. You pick something up, drop it somewhere else. You build piles. Piles turn into houses. They turn into furniture. They turn into gathering places, into churches, into seats of civilizations. Dropping stuff on the ground is pretty *important* to who we are.

In the last post, I talked about the technical underpinnings that allowed us to provide a dynamic environment in SWG. But really, all that was in service of something bigger: having a living society. One of the challenges in creating online worlds is that societies are powerfully shaped by the environment they are in. A static, unchanging world will inevitably give rise to certain sorts of behaviors: spawn camping, for example. Players flow like water around gameplay obstacles; if a game doesn't offer them the ability to run a shop, they'll set up their character as a bot and sit online for hours to replace the system — or rather, the *standard human social structure* — that is commerce.

A lot of MMO design, especially in the last decade, has been about preventing behaviors, rather than enabling them.

That pesky core loop

In *Ultima Online* we had a classless skill system that grouped into these major social roles:

- resource extraction via killing living things
- resource extraction from the environment
- turning resources into finished goods; most goods were to help resource extraction
- healing people who were killing things
- stealing goods from other players

Oh, there were things like pets, and shops, and house decorating, and so on, but they fundamentally *weren't noticed by the game*. The game itself recognized only specific actions, and rewarded you for them. The other activities were sort of *epiphenomena* as far as the game systems were concerned.

Star Wars Galaxies set out with the intent of "letting you live in the Star Wars Universe." The fanbase was very diverse, from people who just dreamt of lightsabers to people shipping Oola and Jabba. And there are a lot of ways to make a living. Because of this, **the entire game was built around the idea of weak-tie interdependence**: the idea that people you don't know well at all are in fact crucial to your survival, and important, and matter.

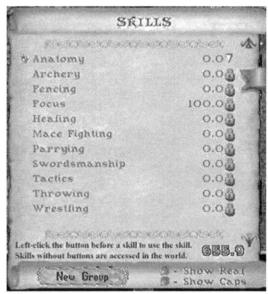

In UO we saw people kill each other in droves, because that simplistic social model effectively meant that social structures could stay pretty small. There weren't longer chains of interdependence. Whereas in SWG, I wanted to make sure that people knew they were part of a *society*, and most features were centered around that. Not just because it was cool to experiment with human behavior,[271] or "ant farming" as some designers call it, but because that sense of "I might bump into, or need this person again someday" actually drives better behavior in general, less griefing, more sense of community. Which should equal greater retention and more money made.

We've always talked about player types, different types of people who enjoy different ways of playing. But MMOs in general have mostly been about extracting advancement from the world. They've been about getting, getting, getting, about power. If you want to have a society you need all sorts. And so, in SWG, that's what we set out to do. And in order to accomplish that, I knew we needed the game to care about what they did: to recognize their actions and achievements and give credit for them, or they would always be second-class citizens, mere "support classes."

Ground rules

The first thing that had to happen to enable this was to get rid of the classic advancement paradigm. Why? **Because it is geared entirely around only rewarding combat.** Past systems that attempted to reward alternate playstyles, such as giving XP for exploration, always felt tacked on compared to the rich systems surrounding combat — which include weapons, clothing, armor, levels, and more.

To quote myself from a blog post back then (props to Joshua Goode for hanging onto the quote after all these years!):

> "A sad fact about you players, as a whole: you only do what you are rewarded for. You will do something less fun if you see a carrot at the end of the stick, and you will ignore something more fun if it doesn't give you a "ding" or an XP reward or a title." – Holocron (11-26-2002 10:55 PM)

We explored a few alternatives. On *Privateer Online*, which had a very commercial mindset to everything in the gameplay, we were using "paying dues." You earned certifications, but hardware and whatnot actually wouldn't work for you unless you were paid up on your guild dues. That way if you wanted to drop back on something, or even skip past levels in the economy, you could just bankroll your way to it. But that wasn't very Star Warsy.

---

[271] See "Feelin' groovy: a rant," https://www.raphkoster.com/2005/12/08/feelin-groovy-a-rant/

In UO, of course, we were using a use-based skill system. The issues there are many.[272] It encourages grinding. But really, the gap between a use-based system and an xp system is really what grants you the XP: merely committing the action, or some sort of "summary action," such as a combat victory against something that is *fighting back*. In that sense, the difference is that XP is more about *results*, rather than the mere action.

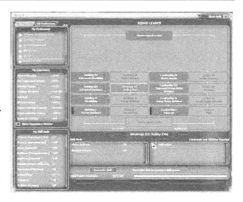

We set out to define **a type of XP for every major activity in the game**, then. After all, we expected each action in the game to have real gameplay: meaning, if you were going to participate in the economy, the economy was "fighting back." So we should be able to find a "real victory" for anything.

All the combat professions were easy. All the crafting professions fell under the bucket of something that in the end didn't ship because it was too expensive to implement, alas. It was the idea that you earned experience in crafting when people actually used the stuff you had made. You'd therefore want to get your stuff out into people's hands. You'd even be willing to pay them to use the blaster you made — sponsorships! You would want to make something that out-competed the goods made by rivals, because it would drive more advancement. It would also unlock massive amounts of offline advancement for any player whose output could be enjoyed asynchronously.

This fell victim to the fact that having every object in the world send a message to whoever made it every time the object was used very quickly would have made our database fall over and die. Which is too bad, because it was actually a fundamental aspect of the game. Crafting (and even the performance professions) therefore fell victim to the classic grinding problems anyway.

Feeling powerful

The other half of advancement that needed to change was power. Using only

---

[272] "Use-based systems."

combat power differentials as the chief marker of advancement is obviously not going to work so well for someone who is a Creature Handler or a Merchant. It also creates almost a caste system, whereby people who aren't combatants really can't even safely venture into huge swaths of the world. We needed near equality (I've written before about whether levels suck, in a two-part article).[273]

From that were born a few things, one of which famously never worked right, and that's the HAM system, which stood for health–action–mind, the three different hit point/mana bars in the Galaxies system. Abilities pulled from one of the three bars, and in general an attack also reduced one of the three bars. They were supposed to regenerate fairly quickly, with a "bouncy" feel to them. So a typical attack was really more about *preventing you from using your specials*, not about getting hurt. Occasionally, you'd get hit with something that was actually "damage" and take a "wound." These reduced your bar, so your bounce range was reduced, and that sort of damage actually required a healer (there was one more sort of damage above and beyond that, which I will talk about when I get to combat and healing).

This system never worked. Sorry. I actually have trouble thinking of *anything* in SWG combat that worked as intended.

More successful was the idea that your feeling of **becoming more powerful should arise from the addition of capabilities to your character**, not from incrementing the maximum value of some bars. It was the notion of *horizontal* progression, whereby you became more capable because you simply had a broader palette of "moves" available to you. In SWG there were over 30 professions, each with 18 skills, and that is not counting the Jedi stuff nor the later addition of spaceflight-related ones.

We very carefully picked a number of individual abilities you could actually know at any given time. We also then had to think about what would happen when players had multiple characters: they'd start making alts to create self-sufficient units at the account level. So we decided, after a *lot* of debate, to simply lock down players to **one character per account per server**. It would force mutual interdependence. It would

---

[273] "Do Levels Suck?" https://www.raphkoster.com/2005/12/16/do-levels-suck/

prevent people from *muling* (having characters simply for extra storage), from engaging in all sorts of cheating with the PvP system in the game, and... if people really did want to do those things that basically broke the game, at least they would end up buying another account and therefore pay for the privilege of causing us customer service headaches. This was easily one of the most controversial things about the game at the time.

Players rightfully said that they enjoyed variety, and wanted to try lots of things. So we let them very easily change their character. You could simply surrender any skill, and go learn another one, when at the cap. We also very much encouraged players not to think solely in terms of specialization. Doing hybrid characters was actually the ideal, not specializing solely down one tree. We were pretty sure it would be more fun for the players, and we selected a skill cap that encouraged players to do so.

Finally, in another design move which I honestly think not even everyone on the design team quite understood, **we capped all the stats on players at a relatively low number.** The nine stats in the game were arranged in a triangular relationship to Health, Action, and Mind, and each one represented the max capacity, the growth rate, and the spend rate for that bar.

Players would never be able to have as many hit points as a Krayt dragon. They'd be able to buff up, but only to about 10% more than that, the sort of range that you hear about with adrenaline rushes in sensationalistic newspaper stories. A combatant would be only marginally tougher than a dancer, in terms of how many womprat bites it would take to bring them down. And if they wanted to tackle something big, well, they'd have to bring numbers. Every monster in the game was scaled off of "how many players does this equal."

I say that I am unsure that some on the team quite grasped this, because when the buff system went in it allowed buffs up to 400%, or something. I suspect this is likely because many of the team were just used to EQ-style advancement. I didn't even notice it was that far off until way later, when players had advanced enough in crafting to actually make some of the powerful buffs.

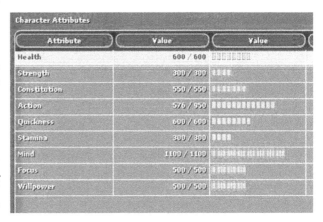

Character Attributes		
Attribute	**Value**	**Value**
Health	600 / 600	
Strength	300 / 300	
Constitution	550 / 550	
Action	576 / 950	
Quickness	600 / 600	
Stamina	300 / 300	
Mind	1100 / 1100	
Focus	500 / 500	
Willpower	500 / 500	

The economy and crafting

As I described in the last post, the environment of planets in SWG included an arbitrary number of "resources" under the ground. These were scattered around the map using Perlin noise, and once extracted were actually removed. In fact, once a resource was mined out, it was gone forever. Every resource was rolled up randomly, as a subtype of a broader resource type, such as "ferrous metal." Each variant of ferrous metal had different stat ranges, and there were actually a fair amount of stats. This didn't apply just to metals either. It applies to what you got from creatures. It applied to what you got from plants. It applied to everything. There were *seventy-nine* different subclasses of resources,[274] ranging from "insect meat" to "siliclastic ore" and everything in between; each of these had multiple types, for a grand total of 474 distinct types[275] — which we then rolled unique ones from. This system was the design work of Reece Thornton. (Some of those 474 went to recipes and systems that never made it into the game, resulting in database bloat).

There was **an entire set of skills based on exploring the map and locating resources.** It effectively worked a little bit as a hot/cold mini-game. In part it was inspired (as so much of what I do is) by surveying in *M.U.L.E.* Given that resources

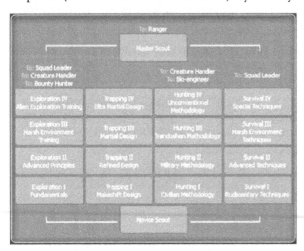

expired and you might well not even get a ferrous metal the next time, it was entirely likely that you would have to search all over again — perpetual exploration. There were skills to help you move about the landscape faster, to hide from aggressive critters by masking your scent, and of course you needed specialized tools for surveying. We clumped a bunch of things related

---

[274] http://swg.wikia.com/wiki/Resource_tree
[275] http://www.swgcraft.org/dev/resource_tree.php

to harvesting and exploring under the Scout starter profession.

To help exploration out, there was **a "badge system"** at launch, which was inspired by the WHOIS strings in *LegendMUD*. Today, badges are known as "achievements" and are old hat. They weren't then. A bunch of the badges at launch were for mastering skills, but others were for visiting various locations in the world.

Originally, there had been plans for a separate miner profession but it was cut for time. My memory of it is hazy, but Thomas Blair, a designer on the team much later, tells me that their removal had very negative long-term consequences because it made harvesting far too widespread an

activity. **We allowed you to drop down resource harvesters** — think those moisture harvesters in Episode IV — and these ran whether you were present or not. You'd have to check in periodically to empty them, because they would fill up. This asynchronous farming gameplay is essentially exactly the same thing as what later on drove the periodic check-in play in social games such as *Farmville*. Visiting lots of harvesters could get pretty tedious, so we had pictured the ability to hire other players to collect stuff for you, and so on.

As time went on, eventually players simply built up enormous networks of harvesters that they never moved, because they gave adequate coverage across the entire map. (They also cheated by having players from other servers come in and place harvesters for them; "lots" for structure placement allowed sharing permissions, so people built collectives. This allowed them to circumvent the limits on the numbers they could place). We really should have made the harvesters simply need to be re-made or re-built from scratch every time the resource they obtained was changed, because it turned out there were not anywhere near enough economic sinks for high-end businesses. Ah well.

We also failed to make crafters have a limited enough inventory of recipes they could know, which resulted in high level crafters still owning the markets for components and cheaper items; we discussed limiting each crafter to ten recipes total, but it never happened and probably should have to preserve *vertical interdependence* between advanced and lower level players, something which was a key pillar in other areas of the game design.

The fact that resources actually went away altogether was incredibly important to the game. **It created obsolescence.** When a crafter went to go make something, the recipe called for "ferrous metal." Perhaps you had a ferrous metal called unobtanium (we rolled up random names for all the resources). You stuck the ingredients in, and you basically gambled, adjusting the desired item stats, using resources of as high a quality as you could, because the input into random rolls included both the stats on the resource, and the targets you were setting. So higher quality ferrous metal could yield a better item. High quality materials were critical, and having a supply chain of

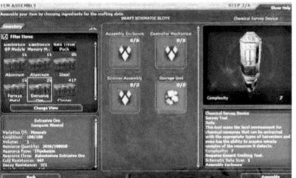

them was too.

But — if you simply crafted the item, you got a one-off. The real money was in mass production. To do that, you had to craft not an item, but a specific *blueprint*. And the blueprint didn't call for "ferrous metal." It specifically demanded "unobtanium." The blueprint could then be handed off to manufacturing droids — factories — which would craft copies for you, as long as they were fed with unobtanium. But if there was no more unobtanium in the game, well, that recipe was literally never craftable again.

Worse, those items might well need repair at some point. **Everything in the game was set up to take damage, to decay.** And you could repair stuff, but it was originally intended to call for some of that unobtanium. Which might be off the market. I mean, the random rolls meant you might not even get "ferrous metal" again for *weeks*. Heck, even the repair tools you needed to repair something got used up.

The result was that everything in the game had obsolescence. It cost us Excalibur, of course. No more rare drop epic weapons with names coming from raid bosses. Instead, we allowed the crafter to create a brand of their own, and give names to models.

If they were making a one-off, they could actually make Excalibur and dub it thus themselves.

This was a major change to the standard MMO paradigm, in which the best of everything comes from loot. **Players kicked pretty hard against no loot**; there's an ingrained expectation going back to the earliest days of CRPGs. The stuff that NPCs dropped in the game was mostly junk, and what we did for newbies was provide a way to sell of that junk for basically pennies while you got going. It also had psychological trade-offs: you have shared experiences from working to obtain Excalibur, and once you have it, you use it without regard to its safety until you out-level it, whereupon it becomes basically a trophy hidden in your inventory. While you have it, people can at a glance look at you and see that you are wielding a plus seven sword with a crit attack or something.

In SWG, you couldn't tell that well at all. A superbly crafted little pistol might well be deadlier in the right hands than an impressive but clumsy Big Gun. And someday, you knew it would be an antique, suitable only for hanging on a wall, because to fire it once more might make it blow up in your hands. The specific stats on the different (many) sorts of things that could be crafted were tied to specific stats on the resources themselves, so you had to learn what stats had what impact through experimentation. The crafting system had you gambling with "experimentation points."

People would discover great new minerals, and quickly mine them and hoard them away, trickling them onto the market to keep the prices up. They would arbitrage the market, keeping a great resource until there were no ferrous metals available *in the entire galaxy*, and then they'd release it to that pent-up demand and make a virtual killing.

Crafters and brands who got access to the best materials and who were diligent about experimenting could effectively build up very real fame on the server. However, the loss of XP earned by others using your goods meant that grinding away at making stuff was still an issue. We also had a vertical integration issue, in that most entrepreneurs chose to set themselves up as harvester/crafter/merchants, owning the entire supply chain. The economy pretty quickly developed into a Pareto-distributed

economy where the richest were insanely rich. I commented at the time that we had successfully managed to recreate the rich oligarchs of the real world, so something must have been working reasonably correctly. This wasn't all that popular a statement.

So: a lack of phat loot. There was also a corresponding lack of shops. **All shops were run by players, using vendors.** *Ultima Online* had pioneered vendors in MMOs by allowing you to hire an NPC shopkeeper (the design work of Ragnar Scheuermann). In SWG we expanded on that, providing a skill tree that gave access to things like advertising mechanisms, branding tools, customizing your vendor down to what phrases they might say to greet people, and so on. The fantasy we were trying to emulate was that of running a shop, or a tavern. We wanted to give people the experience of owning that cantina in Mos Eisley or that junk shop of Watto's.

Given that player shops weren't *in* the main cities at all — because we had no player housing in the cities — this meant that shops could be tricky to find. In general, players who were interested in *buying things* weren't thrilled. It was quite an obstacle to have to shop around, to hunt down shops, and to have to travel from planet to planet to find the best blaster on the market. To players used to going to the main town and walking into the weapons shop, this was a massive inconvenience.

We did have a "commodities market" intended to supplement this issue, which trafficked at first only in bulk resources and in the low-level drops. **The commodities market was very carefully *not a full auction house,*** and most especially didn't let you buy something cool and teleport it to you. (We originally hoped you could set up player missions for people to deliver items for you). We didn't want a perfect information economy, because providing one would have effectively flattened out all price variation across the servers, and provided a huge advantage to the players who developed into the equivalents of Amazon or Wal-Mart; perfect information economies are great for people who buy things, and terrible for people who sell them, because you cannot compete on price, and the largest scale therefore inevitably wins.

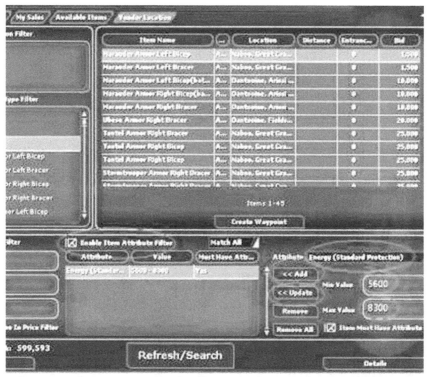

When the game first got going, the first month was a hardscrabble existence, as no players were yet expert enough to craft anything good, and fighter types were not able to kill much because there were no good weapons.

Keep in mind, we're talking *everything* was crafted. The resource harvesters. The factories you used to mass produce. The guns you shot with. The clothes you wore. The buildings the shops were in. Everything.

Everything was also freely tradable — there wasn't any "bio-attunement" or "soulbinding" at first. Nothing even had a value, because **every price floated** based on the whims of an actual, real-life functioning market. The net result of all this was that there were sites devoted just to the intricacies of the game economy. A site tracked commodities prices in real-time like a stock market; encyclopedias developed on just crafting.[276]

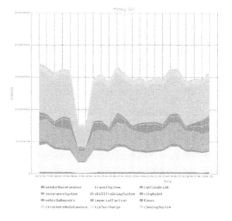

---

[276] Such as SWGCraft, found at http://www.swgcraft.co.uk/dev/home.php

I used to track the economy quite obsessively. I knew exactly how much money was flowing into the game, and from what sources, and what was flowing out and being destroyed. I could identify the existence of a dupe bug[277] based on whether these figures were lining up.

Eventually, a fair amount of this was broken and changed, and I will talk about that in another post. But **when people ask why SWG crafting hasn't been replicated, this is why.**

- You have to start with the dynamic world data structure, so you can build anywhere.

- Then you have to build in procedural resources. (Eventually, years later, the server actually ran out of space for more resource types, and the old ones had to be cleaned away more or less manually).

- And a system for creating items with varied stats. And plan for a database explosion of unique items, sucking away performance like a hungry vampire. (In a game like WoW, where every DaggerX is a clone of a master DaggerX, the database load is cheap).

- Then you have to build in obsolescence, with everything that implies. Item decay. Repair. Stuff players will kick and scream about. Item trading, with all the headaches that implies for unbalancing your game.

- Then you have to break the player expectation on loot, and find replacements that are emotionally satisfying.

- And the expectation on shopping, and that means providing an adequate layer of convenience for players who really don't care to know about this huge infrastructure you have built up.

- And provide an entire merchant paradigm and feature set to replace shopping, because NPC shops with coder-set price floors and the like certainly won't work.

- And endure a period where the game's economy is simply barely working because *"nothing has been invented yet."*

I get asked this question all the time. In fact, now that I do consultancy from time to time, it's not unusual for a company to come to me and say "can you put in crafting like SWG? Our players say it was the best ever!" Usually, they have actually, you know, designed their game already, or even built it. And I have to tell them, **"No. You build**

---

[277] See "Astromech Stats."

your game around it, not the other way around."

Even then, though, all of this is only there to serve as the *basis* for the rest of building a real society. The world isn't only about *stuff* after all. In part two I'll talk about social professions, downtime, missions, mentoring, and politicians — all the other things that go into making a world feel real. All this is just the beginning.

The social glue

Last time, I talked about the basic skill and economic infrastructure that *Star Wars Galaxies* provided. Fundamentally, these were about *equality*. They made the different roles played by players have the same standing in the game. However, it's still a game, after all — players are going to engage in radically different sorts of activities, probably some will be more fun than others, and nobody is going to just "work a job" for their leisure time.

There was every expectation that combat was still going to be at the heart of the game. Few social MMOs were out there at the time, though they were achieving impressive numbers. *Second Life* did not yet exist when we began (they actually came to visit me at the office during the early development of SWG, to talk social design

and tech). The skills and actions available were dominated by fighting, and this was by and large what the market expected.

However, we could still try to reinvent what people thought fighting meant. In the classic Diku model that players were used to, you basically had classes that were alternate types of damage-dealers. Some dealt it fast, some slow. Some could take a lot of hits, some only a few. Today we think of these as tanks and nukers. The lone support class was the healer type, who basically replenished the combatants so that they could keep going: basically, an indirect damage-dealer more than someone who actually healed.

Given our emphasis on making a social web, we needed to think in terms of different kinds of support.

A knife in a gunfight

SWG combat was originally modeled after tactical combat using modern weaponry. The proto-SWG that had existed before we rebooted the project (described in "A Jedi Saga") was an RPG, but with a "cone of fire" style FPS-like system, actually not that different in intent from what came much later in the NGE. At the time, *Planetside* was in early early development and its combat didn't

even work yet. Doing action-based combat fell out for two major reasons:

- First, **it was unproven.** Oh, there was *Neocron*, eventually in 2002, but it had real issues. The timeline was already insanely risky.

- Second, and more important given that we were taking on absurd risks in other areas, was the fact that **FPSes had crappy retention.**

This may seem insane in these days of massive FPS communities, e-sports, and the like. But games driven by skill, as opposed to RPGs, had always suffered greatly in the online games space. They tended to have a fraction as many users as the RPGs did, because the skill barrier, particularly in player-vs-player games, was very high and newbies were chased away. Stats showed that for the RTS and FPS genres, when online play was offered, only a fraction of users would actually engage in it on a regular basis. Not only was it much more latency-sensitive than an RPG combat system with phase-based combat, but if you had a bad spot, you lost.

So, **for the sake of a larger audience, we made the counter-intuitive choice to go with RPG combat rather than action.** Bear in mind that during this time period we had quite an active group playing *Unreal Tournament* in the office after hours, and two team members were veteran FPS people: Nick Newhard, designer from Monolith, and Justin Randall, programmer from Ion Storm. These two guys each reached the number one ranking on different worldwide leaderboards in *UT* during SWG's development. We also had a bunch of *Wing Commander* veterans and we had, as a team, actually recently implemented network-based space combat on *Privateer Online.*

I spent a few weeks reading up on military tactics for snipers, for assault teams using semi-automatic weapons, and (since pistols were obviously important to the setting, even if somewhat obsolete in modern warfare). Worse than pistols, of course, we had to account for the license's affection for sword fighting and martial arts, which extended well beyond Jedi and into things like vibroblades and Teras Kasi, a Star Wars martial art.

Based on those materials, I tried to set up as many rock-paper-scissors relationships as I could. Each of these things — melee, pistols, carbines, and rifles — got a different "optimal range" for their combat. Like, rifles were actually pretty useless at carbine range and below. Even carbines were useless when closed at by pistols. The deadliest thing a rifleman could or should expect was a vibroblade between the ribs, as a commando snuck up on him while he was in a sniper's nest.

To help this along, there was an inverse relationship between mobility and optimal combat distance. Rifles were great at huge distances, but they were most effective if you couldn't move. Melee or pistols needed to keep moving, chasing down enemies because their range wasn't great.

To accomplish this, we added a system of "stances." These would play into a set of attacks which were based around forcing the opponent into disadvantageous stances. Sniping was best when prone, for example.

Lastly, given that we had those three sorts of mana/hp, Health, Action, and Mind, I tried to push each of the combat professions towards one of them.

The result should have been not unlike a tactical card game: executing specials targeted at trying to undermine your opponent, pushing into stances, getting skills that allowed you to tumble from prone to standing quickly again, and so on. Riflemen standing well back, sniping carefully into the melee, with stealthed commandos sneaking around back to take them out. As you burned through your bars using your specials you made yourself briefly vulnerable, as your HAM bars bounced back up quickly, so an attacker looked to hit your weak spot right after you did something cool; basically, every attack you could make "lowered your shields." And as you were hit, you'd gradually run out of ability to use specials, as your HAM bars' maximum shrank from actual "wounds." If someone hit zero, they were only temporarily stunned, and others could run in, drag them to safety or stim them back up with some quick field medicine before an opponent rushed in to give a killing blow.

Right about now, to any player of SWG, what I have described in tandem with the "bouncy" nature of HAM as I originally pictured it, is probably sounding completely unfamiliar to them. And that's because **combat in SWG was a** *disaster.*

With the loss of long-range server updates (the result of a lack of CPU power on the deployment servers), the distinctions between the professions turned to mush. HAM never had any bounce, and timing attack made no sense. You could incapacitate *yourself* with a special.

We never paper gamed combat. We never prototyped it and built it up from first principles. Like so much in SWG, it was over-designed on paper, because we had to give a 500 page design bible to LucasArts (it was glossy and full color, very pretty). To be honest, I am not sure that any of the people who worked on combat actually liked the system and its ideas. We held testing sessions, and we limited ourselves mostly to seeing if stuff worked at all. Looking back, I feel ashamed and incompetent. The very first item in the vision document was, after all, exciting adventures and thrilling battles.

Third places

Players did find things in that messy muddle that they enjoyed, or that they even thought of as tactical. But it wasn't long before any hint of combat challenge was destroyed anyway, when buffs got incredibly out of control.

SWG featured several professions that in part provided buffs to players. These were designed as the first stage in a social loop. We had noticed in *UO* that people reacted very differently to "downtime" aka "time not spent actually doing something" depending on when or where the downtime occurred. Players spoke fondly of the community that formed waiting in line to get your sword repaired at the blacksmith's, and spoke rather harshly about the "bank scene." Prep time versus after-action time seemed very different, and chores that made you feel powerful as opposed to chores that were just getting you back to where you were felt very different as well.[278]

World of Warcraft is very explicitly designed to move you forward, not to carry you

---

[278] See "On Socialization and Convenience."

back to older places. As you advance through a level, the mobs get tougher as you go in, and when you get to the end, the doorway to the next zone is on the other side. **In SWG, we were designing in loops instead: sending players out into the wilderness, then bringing them back.** We wanted people to bump into each other in "water cooler" areas, and we wanted there to be "third places" in the world, where you voluntarily went for your downtime because you liked to go there.

Because of this, our building list included things like bars, theaters, parks, areas fully intended to one day host player weddings or guild induction ceremonies, and so on. I read books like Christopher Alexander's *A Pattern Language* (recommended to me by Will Wright) and tried to learn the basics of urban planning and architecture so that we would provide the sorts of facilities and spaces that would encourage players to meet and talk.

Buffers in many cases had roles in these places. So did healers. Wounds, you see, were something that could only be healed in specific places: hospitals, and the camps that rangers could build (I had pictured camps behind the battle lines of major skirmishes, the last place you needed to defend, because with the loss of the camp, you'd lose all support).

More controversially, we modeled PTSD in the game. We used the old WWII name, "battle fatigue" (the WWI name, "shell shock," didn't seem to fit). After a while, taking wounds wore you down in a more permanent way, a way that mere medicine packs wouldn't help. You would need to find an entertainer — a dancer or a musician — to get your mind off of the stresses of battle. And heck, the entertainer would need a venue, and musicians, and a barkeep — read, player vendor in a player-run cantina — with custom food provided by a player chef...

The idea was that battle fatigue would create a natural arc to a combat session. Start out, buff up, and head out, ideally with a ranger, maybe even the equivalent of a USO performer with you. Set up camp as a base of operations. Head out of it and engage in battles that were tactical and strategic, yet still pretty fast paced. Return to camp when hurt, to be fixed up and sent back out. And after a couple of hours of play, break camp, head back to the bar and swap stories while a role-player cracked jokes, sang Star Wars filk songs,[279] and re-enacted scenes from Jabba's Palace for you. Of course, we were never able to really make this cycle work — we couldn't tell how long a session was. So battle fatigue didn't really work out, I think.

The folks at PARC ended up writing a research paper on whether or third places in

---

[279] https://en.wikipedia.org/wiki/Filk_music

SWG really worked out.[280] Their conclusion was that no, but that the game as a whole ended up serving that role, in a way. To this day, the fact that there was an entire dancing profession is still one of the things that draws ridicule. But it also draws a lot of affection, too, and dancing is now a staple in MMOs.

Some years later, when I met J. K. Rowling, she asked me whether in a new game, she'd be able to be a fat dancing Wookiee.

The Arts

Dancing wasn't original to SWG; a "dance emote" had been present in MUDs since near the beginning, and the club scene in *Anarchy Online* was regarded by many as one of its best features. However, what was new was attempting to actually represent the arts within the game.

Dancing wasn't the only one. Originally, there were three. For dancing, and player animations in general, particularly facial expressions, I had originally hoped to leverage some more work by my friend Ken Perlin: his work on procedural facial animations[281] and procedural walk cycles.[282] In the days before large-scale IK calculations were plausible in a game, he was doing things like getting across emotional expression via animations that were generated on the fly (these ideas, as well as some of the social

architecture work done on *There.com* by Amy Jo Kim, an old friend from the *Ultima Online* days, would prove to be profoundly influential anyway, as we'll see). But it was way too hard to crack the animation problem for that for dances, and way out of scope considering what a small part of the game dancing was supposed to be. So it ended up being loops along with some special moves called flourishes.

---

[280] http://www2.parc.com/csl/members/nicolas/documents/OP-Third_places.pdf
[281] http://www.mrl.nyu.edu/~perlin/facedemo/
[282] http://mrl.nyu.edu/projects/improv/

Little did we know that when you ask motion capture actors to do a few dances, they would deliver an astonishing and goofy fun set of moves. I'm not kidding when I say that dancing grew in scope in large part because the motion capture came back with so much, well, fun stuff.

Music proved to be a much trickier problem. The spec was actually originally for a skill tree that was broken into performance and composition. Performers could take a score and perform it, on the instruments they had learned. Composers were sort of a crafting skill set: they would unlock keys and scales, and the ability to enter notes in themselves. They could perform these on the fly, or they could boil them down into scores, which could then be sold to performers. And on top of that, the composers would earn performance royalties when people played their music!

This all ran afoul of legal issues.[283] I actually spent time while at a conference in New York City visiting the ASCAP offices trying to figure out how we could be legal about players entering in the music to hit songs and performing them in public places using MIDI notes. Both Sony and Lucasfilm were nervous about copyright issues and performance royalties, and it only got worse when ASCAP raised the possibility that making scores might also imply having to talk to the Harry Fox Agency about virtual sheet music, and that "fixing" the performance as a score might also means compulsory licenses as if we were doing a cover recording (!).

So instead, we went with a system more inspired by loop-based composition as seen in MOD music[284] or loop music studio DAWs like ACID. The system came to life when it was realized that groups needed to coordinate what they were doing. We added in the ability for a concert master, more or less, to direct both dancers and musicians, with a common tempo shared across all the accounts. It took some slightly tricky network programming that has a lot in common with something like NINJAM,[285] but it worked. Eventually, we would see touring bands with cover charges, large sets, dancing troupes, acrobats, light shows and stage shows.

The chat box was a fairly unimmersive thing, clearly not in the world. It reminded you that you were playing a game. There was something intimate about the over-the-

---

[283] See "The Arts in MMOs."

[284] https://en.wikipedia.org/wiki/MOD_%28file_format%29

[285] https://en.wikipedia.org/wiki/Ninjam

head text in a game like UO, On the other hand, we also knew from MUDs that basically recreating everything from IRC and allowing you to play from the keyboard only as also very powerful. So the chat system did both. I went through comics and websites and built up a reference of the standard chat bubble art techniques that conveyed different emotions, tones, and types of speech. These were also invokable via commands, or through automatic parsing. For a little while, a case was made that we should do our own styles, something that looked more science-fictional or Star Warsy… but in the end, thought balloons and the like carried the day because anyone who has ever read the funny papers knows how to parse them.

Glue

The social dimension of these things is hard to overstate. One example: combine the availability of venues plus tailoring to that scale plus performance skills, and players invented beauty pageants. I remember my shock and delight a year or two later when one of the main organizers of said beauty pageants actually perfectly performed the top-level exotic dance spontaneously on the show floor of E3. That player was now-famous cosplayer Becky Young, also known as Aktrez.[286] (Unfortunately, she was

A pic from a Miss Valcyn pageant.

working marketing at Mythic at the time, and her performance therefore took place in the booth for *their* game. I am not sure that helped her career there).

---

[286] Becky was featured on "Heroes of Cosplay," a short-lived TV show.

Another "glue" item that we never quite managed to get to pan out was **the system allowing players to grant missions to one another.** These were actually supposed to be binding contracts, allowing players to deliver goods for one another, etc. They had filters so you could allow only friends to do the task, or only guildmates, or only faction members, etc. But we ran aground the difficult challenge of creating a decent reputation without simply encouraging griefing. What if you didn't deliver something on purpose? Did we tag you negatively? You could in theory lose the item for legit reasons. What about trustworthiness? What if someone was trustworthy for his own guild, but not for others? Could we manage to have a personalized rep system that worked across social network graphs? The answer was a resounding no (social network graphing is *still* expensive). Player missions reluctantly fell out of the launch, pushed off to post-launch or never.

Of course, it was exactly that system that provided roles for Smugglers (get my item past opposing player associations or factions) and for Bounty Hunters (track down people who broke contracts because of some stupid excuse about Kessel Runs). Without player missions, smuggling was dependent on developers creating content, situations where you would get stopped by Imperials and the like. And a content-dependent profession is a terrible idea in an MMO. It's why you don't see lockpicking as a skill in these games, not since the MUD days. There were never enough doors.

Tying you to the world

Bragging rights therefore manifested in your outfits, your mastery of chat nuances, in the quality of your comedy routines, and, of course, in your house full of trophies. We had made all that space available for a reason: player housing, and eventually cities and territory control, on the surface of the world.

All the trends at that time were towards instancing, which was a concept from as far back as *The Realm* but had just begun to be really seriously explored in MMOs; and indeed *EverQuest II*, with its handcrafted zones, ended up using that solution for its housing. But as far as what happened inside that house, that was most directly taken from what we had seen players do in SWG, which was itself based on the astonishing explosion of creativity present in UO.

Settings for shops. Museums. Schools. Guild halls. Meeting rooms. Alas, the biggest fail on these was that didn't have a solution for players to live in the *handcrafted* cities. We tried for quite some time to solve the problems of access and waiting an real estate pricing and the rest for allowing players to have in-city apartments and the like, and ended up having to just shelve it.

The end game here was intended to be full-blown territory control. I had wanted player-run governments in *Ultima Online* and moved off the team before such a thing ever came to fruition. In SWG, we wanted a territory battle between the factions of the Galactic Civil War, so having territory control fell out very naturally from that. So we set up a skill tree just for city management, that unlocked the ability to gradually give your city all the capabilities one of the handcrafted cities had. We tried to go as

far as letting them actually lay down roads and re-texture the terrain within their land, but that turned out to be too expensive for the dynamic terrain system.

Players did, of course, abuse player cities, such as by building them on the entrances of handcrafted dungeons so they could farm them with

exclusivity. They would kill or demand money from players who ventured in. They also, however, grew with time into amazing communities.

Cities, as well as systems like harvesters, and of course, pets and droids, were intended as a way to tie you to the world. Ownership, says one of the Laws of Online World Design, is what keeps a player in the game. And characters are famously easy to move from game to game. Guilds, even, migrate with a decent flexibility. But build up a city, and you'll likely stay.

Pets (and droids) were another such way. The work of designer Jeff Freeman, pets were based on the pet system in *Ultima Online*, which was itself a vast expansion over the typical pet systems seen in MUDs. Creatures were born as babies, and you had to approach them gently (AI in Galaxies was based on creature fear and aggression, so gentleness in movements was important) and talk to them while using the taming skill. Once you had

them, they grew by your side — we literally made the babies be just shrunken versions of the standard meshes, and scaled them up with time. They learned their name because they tracked what word you kept repeating to them while giving them commands.

Droids were intended to have much the same emotional impact, but it never worked out that way; droids just never got the love and attention to detail pets did. Which is too bad, because it would have been a lot better to see a ton of pet Artoos around than a ton of pet Rancors.

A few years later, players would hold funerals for their pets, when the profession was removed. They logged in one last night, took them all out, and gave them one last walk, made them do a few tricks, and then watched them get locked away in their datapads. They stayed there, unable to be brought out: a gut punch every time you popped open that screen.

In the end

All of this social connectivity, all of this society building, was the glory of *Star Wars Galaxies*, in the end. Between these systems and the game system interdependence and our extremely open discussions on game features during the early design and alpha periods, the result was that players today still speak about how the community in Galaxies was qualitatively different. It's probably why you are reading this post.

Most of these features were actually pretty cheap to implement, is the irony. Some were prioritized above combat, because they were so cheap (Image Design was actually our very first scripting testbed). **Many have lambasted SWG for having many of these features when the core combat game didn't work, and they are**

probably right. On the other hand, had combat been stellar and none of this in the game, it might still be running, but nobody would want to read a design postmortem of it. So… it cuts both ways.

Did Star Wars Galaxies Fail?

This is the last post on SWG for, well, a while. I am sure there are plenty of other things to say and more questions that could be answered, but… it feels like a natural stopping point. I must say, the response to these essays has astonished me. Here's hoping you'll all care as deeply about the *next* game I make…

Why now?

I've gotten a lot of questions as to why I am writing this series of posts about *Star Wars Galaxies* now. Do I have something to sell?

No, I don't have anything to sell. This past week was the fifteenth anniversary of that small SWG team first forming in Austin, refugees from Origin. We were a bit over a half dozen. It's also ten years since the NGE, and in the last few years, we have seen a lot of changes for a lot of parties involved. I was asked some questions by a former player, and for once, it just felt like the time to answer them.

So, was it a failure?

Well yes, of *course*. And also, no. It depends how you ask the question. There are a lot of assumptions out there about how the game did, particularly in its original form. So, let's start by tackling some of those:

Galaxies actually had the best one-month conversion of any game at SOE, by a double-digit percentage. More new players decided to stick it out past one month. Given the one-month period, you can't attribute that just to the Star Wars license. (In addition, the newbie experience was redone many times, including four times just in the first two years; none of these changed the conversion at all).

SWG also had the shortest play session lengths of any RPG at SOE (action games, including *Planetside*, had shorter). This had very much been a design goal: mission terminals, offline crafting and harvesting, etc., were designed to provide exactly this result in order to make MMOs more accessible. Time sinks had historically been a huge barrier to adoption of MMOs by audiences beyond the core. It also had a lot of features designed to attract players beyond the core. These things seem to have worked as intended. These days, people think of SWG as grindy, but it actually had the fastest advancement of *any* MMO at the time it came out.

However, at the same time, it also had the highest total hours played per week. In other words, it was the least grindy per session, and the most sticky on a week or month basis. Note that lower session lengths naturally equals lower concurrency numbers.[287] But the bottom line is that SWG had the highest percentage of its user base logging in every month out of any SOE game, again by double-digit percentages.

SWG did not sell a million units instantly, and then lose them all, as many claim. It took two years for it to hit a number that big (unlike WoW, which shot up incredibly fast). Early reviews and launch buzz were mixed at best. That said, it was picking up more new users a day than all other SOE games combined, even after the CU. It *did* have a churn problem, and exit surveys showed all the top answers for why people left were "lack of content." This was largely attributable to things like the combat balance, the lack of quests, and so on.

WoW didn't kill SWG. In fact, SWG lost less users to WoW than any other SOE game. (This makes sense — it was the least like WoW, after all). It did lose some of its conversion rate — probably something we can credit to WoW's buttery smooth experience.

Lastly, SWG was a lot cheaper to make than what was about to be its competition. Like, 1/4 of the budget or less of a WoW.

But...

But there are expectations. In SWG's case, they were damn high. We didn't do anything to reduce them either.

Some of these expectations in hindsight can be seen as plain erroneous. For example, if you look at the power of licensed IP game genres outside of sports, it's really not very clear that a license can or will imply a massive increase in game trials or purchases. Certainly the history of Star Wars games doesn't suggest that just because a game is

---

[287] For the basic math on this, see https://www.raphkoster.com/2006/06/01/measuring-mmos/

Star Wars, it will be a hit, or sell disproportionately solely on that basis. (you have to scroll pretty far down on the list of best-selling PC games before you find one that is an intellectual property from outside games).

Licensed IPs also imply revenue splits. This likely made all parties involved *have* to have a higher bar for success. The game made money; I don't know whether it made *enough*.

There is, of course, the fact that the game delivered did not match many players' expectations of what a Star Wars game is like.

Then there are oddities. For example, *EverQuest*, our benchmark at the time, didn't have a vendor system. Players therefore ran second accounts as bots in order to have vendors. This meant that EQ's sub numbers were pretty inflated. When EQ did add vendors, there was a mass cancellation event that was at first mysterious. I ran surveys on the user base to find out how many accounts a given player typically had, since a credit card database is too noisy (lots of CC numbers per individual) to determine uniques. I did the math, and comparing unique actual people, SWG may well have had about as many players as EQ did!

Really, though, the bulk of the problems over time resulted from Live operations.

The error of good intentions

I think everyone had good intentions towards me in promoting me to Chief Creative Officer. I certainly was into the idea of a big promotion!

I think everyone had good intentions in trying to make the game more Star Warsy for that audience. They wanted to make the game more fun. This includes the Holocron drops, and the NGE, and CU too.

I think everyone had good intentions in adding an auction house, or reducing the group size, or trying to fix the fact that there was an egregious math error in the grouping XP bonus.

I think everyone had good intentions in trying to reduce deployment costs by reusing hardware. Or in choosing to make a more sandbox game rather than a linear adventure experience. Or in reducing development costs using cutting edge procedural techniques that didn't fit our hardware scope quite well enough. Or in attempting to cater to a broader audience than what MMOs traditionally had.

But many choices had ripple effects far beyond everyone's good intentions. Really, all of these are decisions that sound good from one angle, but maybe don't take into account every variable.

My moving off the team resulted in a massive loss of institutional knowledge, and most importantly, left the team without a clear vision of what the game *was*. You can't make changes faithful to the experience if you don't know. **This is my fault for failing to convey the vision adequately to everyone**; I can only plead enormous scale, and yes, inexperience in working at that scale. I've often gotten the critique that I over-collaborate, for example, instead of providing firm direction. That can easily turn into a splintered image of the game. I was also given the normally excellent advice, "Don't hover over your old team, they need to learn to lead themselves." Under most circumstances, it's utterly true. The fact that it wasn't in this case can be attributed to the fact that **I didn't really train a replacement.** It wasn't until there was more team turnover and the developers were active players of the game who really loved it and therefore understood it, that we saw some things change.

Among the pieces of institutional knowledge lost was **how to run the right sorts of metrics queries**. Choices like the change to the auction house (which caused one of the single largest single-week drops of subs in SWG's history) were the result of asking the wrong question: "how many Master Merchants are there?" rather than "how many people run a shop?" There was an almost identical situation with Creature Handlers (how many Masters, versus how many had a pet). Reducing the group size helped combat balance but devastated Entertainers. And so on.

Something like the group XP change was almost certainly an attempt to fix the extreme overpower of players (I mean, sum this to buffs and the rest of the combat problems, and it's a recipe for running out of content really fast, which was the top reason for exit…). But it went to test, was loudly objected to by players, then was propped live with very little notice, then reverted too late, after it had already caused an uproar. This single event doubled the churn rate of the game, and even after it was all put back, it stayed 50% higher than it had been ever after. In fact, it was worse, in percentage terms, than the NGE was.

CU and other changes each had similar issues. A change would be made on faulty data, would not help matters, and then would trigger more hasty action as people demanded that trend lines be reversed. You can't fly a plane in the fog with bad instruments. Eventually, the team rediscovered the metrics system, and started to right the course, but it took a while.

In short...

The game wasn't doing as badly as people seem to think. It didn't fail in the market. It did just fine, even by the standards pre-WoW. But there were huge expectations that we didn't push against, it launched with serious problems, and the team wasn't really equipped to fix them. This resulted in a series of errors that damaged the game's ongoing viability, which resulted in more hurried changes.

Plenty of the choices made, or the omissions, were my decision; **in that sense, SWG didn't fail. I failed it.** Certainly its impacts on me personally were that it drove me to explore both plain old "fun," something that I felt I had failed at — I got a book out of that; and it drove me to keep looking at ways in which players could own their own spaces, which eventually became *Metaplace*. Oh, and it made me try to be way more practical, and also made me reluctant to just manage, something which actually hurt *Metaplace* badly because I spent too much time on raw implementation and getting my hands dirty.

Another But!

And yet here you are, reading about it, fifteen years after we started. Twelve years after we launched it. Ten years since it was "ruined." Four since it was shuttered. It has clearly had an impact; I get emails about it on a regular basis. Some elements within it have unquestionably helped shape the MMO landscape. Others have perhaps constrained MMOs, as people took away the wrong lessons from why it underperformed.

And in that sense, **if it was a failure or a success, it was a glorious, ramshackle, bumbling stumbling mess of one.** An improbability from start to finish that never should have worked, but somehow did, and perhaps suffered because that was hard to believe.

Happy anniversary, SOE Austin. I think we actually *did* make something great. Maybe just not quite great enough? But great nonetheless.

Thanks, everyone, for reading this massive series, and for caring for all these years. In memoriam: Ben Hanson, Jeff Freeman, John Roy.

The NGE and Community Building

The "New Game Experience" has gone down in history as "one of the most infamous patches in video game history," according to *Rolling Stone*,[288] and practically a case study in what not to do when managing an online community.[289] I wasn't on the team by the time the decision was made (I had been promoted to Chief Creative Officer of Sony Online almost two years prior). In fact, I had been asked not to even interact with the team much, as I had been a highly visible face on it prior, and as the original creative director and company's Chief Creative Officer even chance comments to the development team could mess around with the chain of command pretty severely.

The NGE fundamentally changed the game by changing everything you have just read about how it worked.

Instead of a classless system where players could build their characters any way they liked, they were forced to choose from specific classes. One of those was Jedi, which had previously only been available through competing challenging gauntlets of tasks (there were a few different systems over that time, which are covered in the chapter entitled "A Jedi Saga.").

Many of the skills that had existed went away altogether, leaving huge swaths of players with broken characters — no, broken **identities**. Thirty-four professions that could be mixed-and-matched became nine classes.

> The saddest thing I ever saw in SWG was the night before the NGE on the Euro servers... Creature Handlers taking out their favourite pets one last time, petting and playing with them. Perhaps they thought they'd still be able to pull them out; maybe they knew. I am not joking when I say that the conversations I overheard between them then brought a lump to my throat. And I knew then that what SOE

---

[288] https://www.rollingstone.com/glixel/news/star-wars-galaxies-and-the-disastrous-nge-update-w484403

[289] The NGE happened in November of 2005. A lengthy article entitled "Blowing Up Galaxies," by Allen Varney, can be found at http://www.escapistmagazine.com/articles/view/video-games/issues/issue_101/560-Blowing-Up-Galaxies

was doing was a breach of faith. I became then as angry as the rest of us.[290]

The slower-paced, and undeniably broken, combat system was replaced by fast action-based combat, with aiming required. Unfortunately, servers that were already struggling to cope with player load failed to perform well with the new system, leading to weeks of major issues. Players who had come for one type of game found the entire environment changed to something quite different.

To make matters worse, the whole thing happened with no notice. An expansion had gone on sale only a couple of weeks prior, and players felt like they were being used in a classic bait-and-switch scheme as the new content they thought they had pre-ordered was effectively rewritten into a massively different game.[291]

Timothy Burke, writing at the popular virtual world academic blog *TerraNova*, wrote in a post entitled "Order 66"[292] that

> The problem is that SWG's chief problem from the beginning has been poor implementation, poor communication, poor service. Koster's design ideas went wrong when they got awkwardly stitched in late Beta to counterposing designs, when the center could not hold. They went wrong when they went live in a horribly unfinished state, with an under-resourced live management team desperately trying to keep a very leaky ship afloat. The NGE doesn't reverse any of those problems: it exacerbates them a thousandfold. A massive change to a game whose remaining loyalists were mostly devotees of the "virtual world" aspects of the design was pushed abruptly and brusquely into live in a state that's almost non-functional.

Order 66, in Star Wars lore, was the order sent out by the Emperor to kill all the Jedi.

The motives for the NGE were simple: many felt that the brand promise of Star Wars wasn't being met by the experience, and especially not by the revenue the game generated. But above all, it was an effort to get what was seen as an incredibly powerful license to be competitive with *World of Warcraft,* which was achieving unheard of heights in the market.

When I was presented with the demonstration of the NGE changes during a visit to the Austin studio shortly before, I warned against it. There was a meeting with key stakeholders where we went around the room, and each person was asked to estimate how many users the game would gain as a result of the changes. Various believers

---

[290] From the comment thread "Order 66" on Terra Nova.
http://terranova.blogs.com/terra_nova/2005/11/order_66.html
[291] The announcement hit on Nov. 3rd 2005; the launch of NGE was Nov. 15th.
[292] See prior footnote.

stated that we'd get a 10% boost, or 25%. When it was my turn, I was blunt: "We'll lose 50%." There was disbelief. The changes went ahead anyway.

The community took it... poorly. Worse, it went mainstream:

> At first, SOE's official line about the outcry was "Some gamers hate change"; then, later, "It's a small minority." Before long, though, the community's outrage drew unprecedented attention from *The New York Times,*[293] *The Washington Post,*[294] *Wired*[295] and many others.[296]

Subscription numbers plummeted. The announcement alone caused the rate of cancellations to double. The day after the NGE launched, it jumped to around *five times* the norm. My estimate was wrong, in that the immediate losses were "only" around 30% of the active paying userbase. But over time, my grim forecast did come true.

> In a lot of the galaxies, the players are organizing a mass graveyard, filled with memorials to themselves.
>
> They're making player cemeteries.[297]

To this very day, you can arouse anger and vitriol from MMO players by mentioning the NGE, despite the fact that over the years, the SWG team went on to re-implement all of the missing features and many more, and arguably ended up with a better game at the end of it all.

From July 19th 2006, a time when I had already departed Sony Online:

Business Week Online just published an article on new media and community that's an excerpt from Henry Jenkins' new book.[298] *Edit: Looks like it came originally from Next Generation.*[299] It heavily references the work that we did early on in SWG in

---

[293] https://www.nytimes.com/2005/12/10/arts/for-online-star-wars-game-its-revenge-of-the-fans.html

[294] http://www.washingtonpost.com/wp-dyn/content/article/2006/02/01/AR2006020102341.html

[295] https://www.wired.com/2005/12/star-wars-fans-flee-net-galaxy/?currentPage=1

[296] From "Blowing Up Galaxies."

[297] From the "Order 66" comment thread.

[298] The book in question is Convergence Culture: Where Old and New Media Collide, NYU Press, 2006.

[299] https://web.archive.org/web/20060816001035/http://www.next-gen.biz/index.php?option=com_content&task=view&id=3439&Itemid=2 has an archive of the article. Some snippets:

> Koster also refers to managing an online community, whether a non-commercial mud or a commercial MMORPG, as an act of governance: "Just like it is not a good idea for a

building community.

These days, it sure seems like there's a mixed reaction to how the community is handled, but I do think we did a pretty good job back then, and at the time it was widely referenced as a model.

The premises under which we operated were:

- Be open to the players: both in terms of telling them what you are doing, and in terms of listening to what they want

- Communicate daily

- Communicate honestly

- If things change, tell them why — they're smart people, they will understand

- Have weekly events of info release so that there's a reason to come back regularly

- Ask questions, and listen to the answers

---

government to make radical legal changes without a period of public comment, it is often not wise for an operator of an online world to do the same."

Players, he argues, must feel a sense of 'ownership' over the imaginary world if they are going to put in the time and effort needed to make it come alive for themselves and for other players. Koster argues, "You can't possibly mandate a fictionally involving universe with thousands of other people. The best you can hope for is a world that is vibrant enough that people act in manners consistent with the fictional tenets."

...To insure that fans bought into his version of the Star Wars universe, Koster essentially treated the fan community as his client team, posting regular reports about many different elements of the game's design on the web, creating an online forum where potential players could respond and make suggestions, insuring that his staff regularly monitored the online discussion and posted back their own reactions to the community's recommendations.

...Games scholars Kurt Squire and Constance Steinkuehler have studied the interactions between Koster and his fan community: "These players would establish community norms for civility and role playing, giving the designers an opportunity to effectively create the seeds of the Star Wars Galaxies world months before the game ever hit the shelves....The game that the designers promised and the community expected was largely player-driven. The in-game economy would consist of items (e.g. clothing, armor, houses, weapons) created by players with its prices also set by players through auctions and player-run shops. Cities and towns would be designed by players, and cities' mayors and council leaders would devise missions and quests for other players. The Galactic Civil War (the struggle between rebels and imperials) would frame the game play, but players would create their own missions as they enacted the Star Wars saga. In short, the system was to be driven by player interaction, with the world being created less by designers and more by players themselves.

- Celebrate and highlight the best contributors

Some have since decided that it was listening to the players too much that caused some of the design problems with SWG. I am not sure I agree. If anything, I think that many subsequent problems came from not listening enough, or not asking questions in advance of changes. Walking a mile in the players' shoes is a difficult trick to pull off even if you have the best of intentions.

The tensest and most difficult moments in SWG's development — and they came often — were when we had to remove something that players really liked. Usually, it was against our own wishes, because of time constraints or (rarely) orders from on high. But we couldn't tell the players the real reasons sometimes. That sucked, frankly, because the open relationship really did matter. As often as we could, we laid everything bare.

These days, it's accepted wisdom that you don't reveal a feature until it's done, so as to guarantee that you never let the players down. Of course, even finished features sometimes fall out for one reason or another…

In any case, I think I don't agree with that philosophy. I'd rather have prospective players on a journey with the team, than have them be a passive group marketed to. Yes, they will suffer the ups and downs, and see the making of the sausage… but these days, that's getting to be an accepted thing in creative fields. There's not much to gain, to my mind, in having the creators sitting off on a pedestal somewhere — people fall from pedestals, and pedestals certainly will not survive contact with Live operation of a virtual world.

Instead, I'd rather the customers know the creators as people who make mistakes, so that when one happens, they are more likely to be forgiven or understood.

How did the experiment work out? Well, bottom line in SWG's case is that we certainly overpromised and underdelivered. But the curve for active community users was an exponential one aiming at the moon, and until the day when I had to go out there and tell them that the game was being released, they were working with us — contentiously, but all pulling in one direction. And the result was that registrants to the game on the first weekend was exactly equal to the number of active community users, and the sales curve simply continued that trend over time.

Why couldn't you tell them the reason why you had to take something out?

We did, unless we were not allowed to by corporate masters (such as "we can't do this system this way because in the next movie which isn't out yet, it's revealed that things are actually this other way" — happened with cloning, players playing Stormtroopers, and a few other things). And the reason "because we don't have time and we are rushing the product" was never deemed acceptable.

> We want one vote, one 16m2 square of rented server space. Our World, Our Representation.

In a purely user-driven world, I'd agree with you. But in the case of a game system design, you wouldn't want everyone voting on the rules anymore than you'd want an author to take votes on what happens in the next chapter. Part of why you are there is to be taken on the entertainment ride.

At some point, you have to also be true to what you want to do from an artistic point of view. Audiences often don't like new things until they can try them. Sometimes your ideas will be bad, but sometimes they will be good and you have to have the courage of your convictions. If you have earned the audience's trust by your honesty, they will be willing to give you the benefit of the doubt — especially if you backtrack once they have been proven right.

Heh, I guess I cannot give an answer to a simple question without it being somehow related to the NGE.

I usually resort to analogies when trying to explain this.

Let's say you work in theater. When you start out with a new play or musical, it's still rough. You go on the road to smaller venues to workshop it. You tweak and adjust based on the feedback of users. There's going to be some decisions there you make based on artistic choices, and you hope the users follow. Often these will be decried as bizarre or stupid. Sometimes they are.

But you persevere, and the show gets a following. It gets a long repeat engagement based on your kooky idea of a musical using only didgeridoos and human beatboxes. Some see it for the novelty. Others actually like what you're doing.

Now you've settled in for a long stint on Broadway. You don't really get to swap it out to a punk music piece now. The sort of changes you can make are vastly different. You are known as the didgeridoo-and-beatbox show. If Stomp were to show up with all electric guitars and no percussion one day, only true diehard Stomp fans would follow — and only because they trust the artist.

When a new cast, a new director, a new costumer, comes in — they have to adapt to the show. There's some mutual accommodation, but it's not about wholesale recreation.

Sometimes, of course, a new show runner comes in and reinvents the whole thing dramatically, and is hailed as a genius. But I can't actually think of very many examples.

In short, I thought NGE was a very bad idea, but it was done anyway. I am not sure what else I can say, really. It certainly was a major contributing factor — even a decisive factor — in my decision to move on.

The simple fact is that I was barely involved with SWG from around October of 2003. There were some periods where I was pulled back in a little more, but by and large, I was apart from it. Almost none of my "creative consultancy" involved Live games — it was all about new games, many of which did not survive pitch stage.

The question that honestly keeps me up at night is "how do I not disappoint those who invest their passion into this." I may personally get disappointed when my ideas do not pan out — but the thing that gets me is really hearing from the audience who felt let down. You want people to like your work, and to enjoy themselves.

Questions like "how do I make a polished and ambitious game" then become corollary questions.

Back to today...

Henry Jenkins wrote a follow-up to the above and to what he had in the book,[300] which was about the fallout from the disastrous "NGE" or "New Game Experience" changes.

> Here are some of the things Koster did right in courting Star Wars fans:
> 1. He respected their expertise and emotional investments in the series.
> 2. He opened a channel of communications with fans early in the process.
> 3. He actively solicited advice from fans about design decisions and followed that advice where-ever possible.

---

[300] http://henryjenkins.org/2006/07/so_what_happened_to_star_wars.html

4. He created resources which sustained multiple sets of interests in the series.

5. He designed forms of game play which allowed fans to play diverse roles which were mutually reinforcing.

And

That said, the policies Koster created were eroded over time, leading to increased player frustration and distrust. In another video, Javier traces a history of grievances and conflicts between the "Powers That Be" within the game company and the Entertainer class of characters. Some casual players felt the game was too dependent on player-generated content, while the more creative players felt that upgrades actually restricted their ability to express themselves through the game and marginalized the Entertainer class from the overall experience. At the same time, the game failed to meet the company's own revenue expectations, especially in the face of competition from the enormously successful *World of Warcraft,* a game which adopted a very different design philosophy.

Late last year, the company announced plans to radically revamp the game's rules and content, a decision that has led to the wholesale alienation of the existing player base and massive defections. It remains to be seen if the plans will draw in new consumers; it is clear that they have significantly destroyed the existing fan culture. Javier is not alone in seeing these decisions as the end of the road for his community.[301]

He concluded, "I suspect the rise and fall of *Star Wars Galaxies* will be studied for years to come as a textbook example of good and bad ways to deal with fan communities." Over the years, he has been proven correct.

I left the company not very long after the NGE. It was around February of 2006 when I raised leaving with my bosses, so only a few months later. Between my R&D group being dismantled in favor of assigning the team to *FreeRealms,* being asked to reboot that game yet again and fire people I had been trying to mentor for the last year, and the conflict I felt over the NGE—not to mention the fact that I was expected to publicly support it!—I was just not in good shape.

I gave an interview to Allen Varney at *The Escapist* in which I said,

I'll make an exception for the NGE. I don't think you can or should change a

---

[301] The senior director of marketing at LucasArts, made these comments to *The New York Times,* and was promptly vilified by SWG players: "We really just needed to make the game a lot more accessible to a much broader player base. There was lots of reading, much too much, in the game. There was a lot of wandering around learning about different abilities. We really needed to give people the experience of being Han Solo or Luke Skywalker rather than being Uncle Owen, the moisture farmer. We wanted more instant gratification: kill, get treasure, repeat. We needed to give people more of an opportunity to be a part of what they have seen in the movies rather than something they had created themselves."

game that radically out from under a user base. You dance with the ones that brung ya, whether they are the market of your dreams or not. They have invested their passion and built expectations about where they want the game to go. Changing things out from under them isn't fair in my mind, especially given how they have been loyal to you in times of trouble. It's like dumping the girlfriend who has always been patient and loving to chase after the supermodel who probably won't love you back.[302]

This did not go over well with Sony Online. I had left on amicable terms, but comments like that felt to them like I was throwing them under the bus; I apologized to them for having said it, but also told them that I felt like I had to say *something*, for the sake of my career. I knew full well that everyone I knew there—my co-workers and colleagues and friends—were doing the best they could, even if I thought they had made a terrible mistake.

In fact, players in their rage took aim at many of them, harassing them, vilifying them on forums, sending death threats, and in general going way over the line.

Wired wrote,

> Gamers may feel betrayed if the sequel to their favorite game isn't as good as the original, but they can play the original any time they want.
>
> Not so for those who enjoyed the original Galaxies. It's gone forever.[303]

But *Wired* was wrong about that. Because over the years, players painstakingly found ways to reverse-engineer the server. They replicated every detail about the game on a server emulator codebase called *SWGEmu*,[304] and it took them just about a decade.

They had to choose a specific date to emulate, and they chose to cut off the game's development at a specific point in its history before the NGE—the date that preserves the game they loved.

---

[302] "Raph Koster on Fire," http://www.escapistmagazine.com/articles/view/video-games/issues/issue_55/329-Raph-Koster-on-Fire.4
[303] https://www.wired.com/2005/12/star-wars-fans-flee-net-galaxy/?currentPage=1
[304] See https://www.swgemu.com/forums/index.php

SWG is shutting down

June 24th, 2011

Star Wars Galaxies, a game I was the creative director on, is shutting down. It's happening in mid-December. You can read an interview with John Smedley about it on Massively.[305] The short form, though, is that the contract with LucasArts is up.

I am sure there are plenty of people who are prepared to mourn; I went through my own emotional arc of moving on years and years ago at this point, so I am not going to dwell on it.

Instead, I'll note that sandbox, worldy MMOs do not seem to have gone away despite the economic currents that run against them. It's too big a dream, I suspect, and games like *ArcheAge*, which isn't out yet, *Wurm* which is, and of course *EVE*, show that there is a passionate audience for the sort of experience that lets you step into a more fully realized world and live there.

Some will say that SWG was a failure. They'll cite the NGE, of course, and they'll point out that it fared poorly against the juggernaut of *WoW*, despite the power of the license. My postmortem would be much like Smedley's:

> Here's what I would have done differently. I would have made sure the ground and space games were launched all at once. I would have given the game another year to develop and really polish it quite a bit. I think we created one of the most unique and amazing games ever created in the MMO space. It is the sandbox game. Nothing else even comes close to what we did there. I would have really taken our time and polished combat right so we never had to do the NGE.

In the end, the game was quite profitable, it ran for eight years, and it entertained a few million people. I've been told it had a qualitatively different and more powerful community than other games, by objective metrics. It was built with some rickety tech — and some that won awards and led to patents.[306] It was more casual and more

---

[305] https://www.engadget.com/2011/06/24/exclusive-smedley-on-the-sunsetting-of-star-wars-galaxies/
[306] Three separate patent applications were filed for SWG's terrain system; my name didn't end up on any of them. They were granted between 2012-2014.

broad appeal than what the license could even handle, in some ways, and many individual features that SWG had today power entire blockbuster giant companies in the social game space (hey look, farming where you come back the next day… where have I seen that before…?). And it gave us features that continue to amaze people who don't realize what can be done: real economies complete with supply chains and wholesalers and shopkeepers, that amazing pet system, the moods and chat bubbles (anyone remember what chat in 3d MMOs looked like before SWG?), player cities, vehicles, spaceflight…

And dancing. Which everyone made fun of. But as far as I am concerned, it may have been the biggest and best contribution, the one that spawned a jillion YouTube videos and may well be the lasting influence the game leaves behind, an imprint on all the games since: a brief moment where you can stop saving the world or killing rats and realize the real scope and potential of the medium.

In the end, SWG may have been more potential and promise than fulfilled expectation. But I'd rather work on something with great potential than on fulfilling a promise of mediocrity. There's a reason people are passionate about it all these years later. I'm proud to have worked on it.

The End of a Galaxy

As we ran the SWG beta test, we did a lot of things somewhat differently. The early phases were much more like focus tests than standard beta testing, because we let people in really early in development. A hundred or so colonists, broken into groups of twenty, all standing around trying out only one feature: just emotes, or just targeting. I found it incredibly fruitful for iterating and tuning game systems.

The result was also a fairly tight community. Those first hundred got to know each other pretty well, and when one of them, Moraj Markinnison, died in a real life car accident, it was felt keenly. At that spot where the first beta testers entered, a monument was placed, with the late tester's name on a plaque — the location where the first colonists landed on Tatooine.

The Moraj memorial

As the beta drew to a close, it seemed natural for that to be the place where people would gather. At first it was just the first hundred, but over time it grew to hundreds: people camping there, shooting off fireworks, petting their tame animals, dueling and otherwise making a big ol' Burning Man sort of party out there in the desert. As a result, the spawning system decided that there was a large enough group of folks there that it had better attack the party with spawns, so we quickly got a lot of combat going too.

In the end though, it was quiet. Everyone knew what was coming; there was no lore, or anything behind it. It was just the passing of a community, evolving into another community. Not a bang. Just one tester saying "It's as if the voices of 5000 testers cried out in agony…"

> This is the way the world ends
> This is the way the world ends
> This is the way the world ends
> Not with a bang but a whimper.
> — T. S. Eliot, "The Hollow Men"

Transitions

World of Warcraft launched nine months or so after *Star Wars Galaxies*, and did to the early MMO scene what *UO* had done to the older online service games: it made everything obsolete and set a new standard for budgets and polish. It also, however, put paid to a number of dreams about the online world. It was unabashedly an entertainment product, not an online society.

I simply couldn't get into it.

I was promoted to Chief Creative Officer at Sony Online shortly before SWG shipped, and in my new role I came into contact with Hollywood, with famous people like the directors John Woo and Robert Zemeckis, and the author J. K. Rowling. I spent time with movers and shakers in the burgeoning web technology world, like Tim O'Reilly and Cory Doctorow. I ran R&D projects where we built worlds that had true running water and weather and forest fires and erosion, where snow piled up and you could shove it aside. Where the fleeing deer actually left scent hanging in the air that was followed by hungry predators. Where you could cast a freeze spell on the water and walk out onto the ice. Where plants grew based on the humidity and soil quality.

This tech was patented,[307] then shelved.

I was fascinated by what was happening on the fringes of games. Social networks, the ideas of the long tail, the Flash game market that was spitting out what felt like a revolution in game design. I took the time to write a book called *A Theory of Fun for Game Design*,[308] because I felt like I had lost track of the moment to moment fun, in all my lofty chasing after social ideals in SWG. I taught myself how to program all over again, and started making puzzle games and board games. I helped out on titles like *Free Realms* and *Untold Legends*.[309] I pitched web games and social games at Sony

---

[307] "Modeling complex environments using an interconnected system of simulation layers," https://patents.google.com/patent/US9555328B2

[308] Originally Paraglyph Press, 2004. Now published by O'Reilly in a fancy full color 10th anniversary edition.

[309] I actually rewrote every scrap of text in the game. I ended up credited as "editor."

Online, and none of them were taken up.

And once it was clear that SOE and I weren't interested in the same things anymore, I left, and set aside for a while the dreams of the the giant simulated world. Accepted wisdom was that it wasn't what people wanted anymore.

HOOWAH! Player memorabilia

The Shadowclan shirt

Today I got a Shadowclan[310] shirt in the mail. The back of it says "Hoowah!"

Shadowclan is, of course, one of those game guilds that crosses over multiple games, and it's been around since the early days of UO. It got its start after an enterprising roleplayer decided to roleplay being an orc. I don't think anyone quite knows what happened to that player, but for a while, he captivated roleplayers across the shard with his odd relationship with the players based out of Trinsic. He served as the inspiration for a lot of people becoming orcs, which we helped out unintentionally via orc masks and polymorph spells.

Eventually the Shadowclan was born: a large guild that took over one of the few bits of static content in the game, the Orc Fort, and defended it against human players. They developed a pidgin language all their own, perhaps inspired to some degree by the Warcraft games, which eventually migrated over to EverQuest (no orcs there, but that's where the trolls got their lingo), DAOC, and thence to SWG (Rodians... odd fit, but you make do), and then to WoW.

This shirt is hardly the only bit of guild memorabilia that I've been given. Over the years, players have come up to me and given me all sorts of things. It ends up forming part of the tapestry of how you touch players emotionally, and they touch you back.

---

[310] http://www.shadowclan.org/

So today I thought I'd give you a little tour of just some of these things, and tell you the stories.

It's hip to bash SWG these days. Lots of folks like to say that it was a deserted disaster from day one. It's not true, and here's some of the evidence. This is a mug from the in-game corporation Avian Technology & Trade[311] which at the height of its powers had a few supply companies, a city (Avian City, natch), and well, real world goods. Alas, just this weekend I saw that there was discussion of Areae on their forums, so I went to check it out, only to see on the front page that they have left SWG for good.

But I still have the mug.

AT&T isn't dead, of course — they just moved on to WoW. This is a common pattern for guilds — when we

Avian Technology & Trade mug

opened UO in pre-alpha in early 1996, one of the first groups that showed up was refugees from The Realm. Some guilds have been at it a long time, like Shadowclan, hopping from game to game in a highly organized fashion.

One such is of course is The Syndicate,[312] whose tagline boasts, "Online Gaming's Premier Guild." You may recall them as the guild that trademarked its name,[313] a move which provoked some controversy.

These guys are super organized. Real life meet-ups. Polished newsletters. A corporate sponsor (!). You can see the coin there on the front page of the newsletter — I've got one of those too, but it's in a box still packed away from my move from the SOE

A Syndicate newsletter

---

[311] http://www.avian-gamers.net/

[312] http://www.llts.org/

[313] See my blog post on this here: https://www.raphkoster.com/?p=302

offices. It's rather cool. They still use LLTS as their domain name — because they got their start on UO during the pre-alpha, and used LLTS as their guild abbreviation.

The oldest guilds in UO were extraordinary achievements precisely because *there was no guild system*. In fact, I wrote the guild system in response to the fact that players were spontaneously creating these organizations and creating characters with names with the guild tag in them. In effect, if you joined a guild, you had to start your character over; if you left, you had to wipe the character. That's commitment. This is why UO's guild tags were 3 and 4 letter abbreviations even in the system I implemented — that's what the players had settled on when trying to cram it all into their names.

There was a camaraderie there that is missing for me now. Today Fan Faires are vast affairs, and while they still provide that emotional connection with fellow players, there isn't quite the sense of being in on a secret anymore. Once upon a time, there were only a few sites you would even go to to discuss MMOs: The Vault network (today swallowed up by IGN, and unrecognizable from its origins); Crossroads, where most of the UO devs hung out for a long time; and Stratics, which is the only one that still resembles its original self… and of course, there were the Rantings of Lum the Mad, the original MMO rant site where invective flowed freely and devs ventured at their peril. Launch poorly, and you might be ridiculed so thoroughly[314] that you might never live it down.

Lum's Happy Fun Balls

---

[314] The infamous and brutal takedown of *World War II Online*'s launch made "taxiing to victory!" an MMO catchphrase for years.
https://web.archive.org/web/20020721154350/http://www.brokentoys.org/ww2o-irc.html

Today, of course, Lum is still around over at Broken Toys,[315] and no doubt many of his readers don't know where the name of the site comes from, or remember a time when he was an angry player, as opposed to a developer. But once upon a time, it's true, he showed up at UO fan fests with large boxes full of Happy Fun Balls. They are labeled "Do Not Taunt." They say "You are in their world now. Run." on them.

And of course, there were the common black ones, and there were the rares. White Happy Fun Balls.

A few years ago, some of the ex-Lummies emailed me and asked if I had spare Happy Fun Balls; they were trying to put together a set to give to Lum as a gift, to remind him of the Old Days. It was selfish of me, but I held on to mine (hey, one of the black ones is damaged, as you can see. And no way am I giving up the rare). Sorry, Scott.

In a more innocent time, players would send homemade biscotti to the Origin offices, and we would eat them. Innocent naive fools, so trusting! That all ended for me after I got my first anonymous package in the mail — at my *home address*. Plain brown paper wrapper, no return address. I only opened it because I could see through a ripped corner that it was a book. Inside there was a post-it note reading, "You're working too hard on UO. Take a break. Enjoy a good book." Unfortunately, it was one that I had read already.

Not all mysterious packages have to be scary (though there have been death threats upon occasion). Here we see the Holocron sock puppet; one of several sock puppets sent in a care package by SWG players. I wish I remembered exactly where it came from — I believe that Kevin O'Hara (aka Q-3PO) brought the puppet by, one of several that showed up in one shipment, I think. Since Kevin was the community manager, he tended to get this stuff. Another sign of the changes in scale, I suppose — the whole time I was at SOE, I only got a handful of things sent straight to me by players, compared to the amount of stuff that I got when I was on UO.

The Holocron hand puppet

I don't know whether the whole "give the public faces for SWG sock puppets" thing was a commentary on how we handled ourselves on forums, or what. After all, the puppet

---

[315] http://www.brokentoys.org/

Hobo the dragon

was too cute to be a harsh slam, wasn't it? At least, I preferred to take it that way.

Sometimes, you got things handed to you right there in person. Hobo was one such — he was pulled out of a shoulder bag by a woman at the UO luncheon at a Renaissance Faire. The intent, of course, was that I would fasten him on my shoulder. He was beautifully made, a rich green and black. She told me, "he'll tell you his name, that's what they do." She also gave me the website of her dragon-making business.

My dog Mika attacked Hobo one day, leaving a gash in his side. I was able to ship Hobo back to her for surgery, and she did it free of charge, despite my trying to pay (she did include a scolding note about how Hobo was too small to play with big dogs). Hobo was obliged to move to a high shelf where the dogs wouldn't reach. He then survived our house fire, which left his eyes somewhat smoky and his eyelids drooping. He got a little smoky, and a little sooty — but that's how dragons should be, right?

Hobo outlived Mika. None of our dogs survived the fire, you see. The smoke got them. At this point, I was already off of UO, on an unannounced MMO that never shipped. My departure from the game was a lot like those of the players — you just stop showing up one day, and life goes on. Players didn't really notice that I wasn't on the project for a fair while, I think. But when the house fire happened, a note went up on the UO site, because that's how the community was run.

I got a few letters. They're pictured here. Luther D'Knock sent a check for $20, and a letter that said "I've enjoyed playing UO for two and a half years. I could never repay you for the great times. This isn't much, but I wanted you to have what I could spare." An anonymous card with an angel, no signature, no return address, and twenty bucks.

And most startling and touching, a scrawled envelope. Magic marker or Sharpie. From "UO PLAYER, ATLANTIC." Some of the S'es are backwards. Inside, two dollar bills.

I never cashed the check, never spent the money. It all lives in a small bundle in my sock drawer, so I don't forget why I do this online game thing.

Hoowah.

Letters with donations, after the fire

Speech at SyndCon 2010

This talk was delivered at a convention for members of the guild The Syndicate, in 2010 in San Diego.

Wow.

["Put on the speaking hat!" "You gotta wear it!"]

Now, if I put this on, will I melt or explode?

["Yeah!"]

[I put on the hat. It is blue and green and fuzzy, with a wide brim. I have trouble seeing. There are applause and hoots. I take it off. "Awwww..."]

So... I gotta tell ya, this is kind of a weird experience for me, and not just because of the hat.

[Laughter.]

I am pretty sure there are people in this room that weren't even born when I got into making MMOs. How many of you folks started playing with UO? How many of you started playing before UO?

Text muds, anybody? That's right. Awesome.

So, UO, and probably some of the stuff from back then, like *Asheron's Call?* How about stuff like *Underlight? Rubies of Eventide? Illusia?*

Original *Neverwinter Nights!* Any Kesmai players? Wow.

So you know, I remember when you guys got founded.

[laughter]

I remember having to come in and crunch over a weekend to write a guild system, because of you all.

[laughter]

I thought I'd come in and take you down a little trip down memory lane that for the other two-thirds of you will be baffling. For all of those who got started with the Johnny-come-latelies, like... *EverQuest!*

[laughter]

I got started with text muds. I got started playing online games in ... probably 1992,

93? And I was considered a Johnny-come-lately by the MUD dinos at that time. Because you know, virtual worlds, they've bee going since 1978. And there are still people who will tell you, "oh, I was playing online games on PLATO, on amber monitors with plasma screens, in the 70's." Are there any of those people in here? One or two... 'cause they can be real snobs about it.

[laughter]

I was only 23 when I started at Origin, and that was in 1995. My wife and I were hired out of text muds because Lord British had logged into our text mud and decided maybe it wasn't too bad and maybe we could be designers on this new "Multima" thing they were talking about.

There were a few of us from a bunch of different muds. There was one of us who worked on a *Star Wars* LPMud. There was a guy who worked on *NarniaMUSH* and *TooMUSH*. Any of you ever MUSH people? None of you.

[laughter]

These were the roleplaying-only, no combat games. There were a couple of people on UO from that. There were people who came from the classic kind of Diku world, that's the same kind of gameplay that today dominates everything.

And back then, my wife and I actually brought our newborn daughter to the office in her baby carrier, and she was the third person occupying our office. She's thirteen now, and I see at least one kid in the audience who is younger than my daughter. And that, honestly, just freaks me the heck out.

[laughter]

For a while there we had folding chairs on folding tables, and were crammed six to an office. It was total skunkworks. I mean, there was a period there on UO that they had no idea what to do with us. Right? So, the fifth floor of the Origin building used to have in it some ad agency or something weird like that, and they kicked them out even though origin made more money off real estate and rentals than they actually ever did off of games. But they kicked out this profit center, this ad agency, and were doing remodeling. Remodeling then, the fifth floor of this building that's on a hillside. They knocked out all of the windows and all of the walls.

So this elevator surfaced onto bare concrete, and if you walked you could just walk right off the edge of the building.

I'm surprised the insurance people let them keep an office up there, because if you avoided falling off the building, one corner of that floor still had drywall, and there was a "Multima" sign, an arrow, printed on a color printer, which back then was a really. Big. Deal.

[laughter]

They actually let us print this in color. It was just an arrow that said "Multima." And you went in that door and it was freakin' freezing up there. 'Cause this was – granted, Austin, but it was winter, and it actually had iced over that year, and snowed, in Austin. We didn't have heat in that little corner of drywall, in that floor that was gone. And unfortunately, the prototype server for UO, the machine for it sat directly under the thermostat. So all the heat from the machine went and hit the thermostat. So it ran the air conditioning up there, all the time.

[laughter]

So we all worked in jackets and wore fingerless gloves so that we could type. So it was pretty skunkworks. We had, let's see, one two three four offices… and the hallway that was still enclosed. And in that we held about fourteen or fifteen people. And every once in a while someone from downstairs would surface from the Elevator of Doom, risk walking across the bare concrete and falling off the building, and visit us.

And then they'd tell us something like "Well, gosh, we hate to tell you this, but we just cancelled Warren Spector's project and fired a fifth of the company." And we said "who?" Because we didn't know anybody. We were up there, we were total skunkworks. Every few months we got to see Richard Garriott. It was a big deal.

The artists got to sit in the hallway [inaudible]…

This is also how we got to launch a beta site without telling marketing.

[laughter]

You know, we just set up a site, and we put up a FAQ, and because we were who we were, the original branding for *Ultima Online* consisted of two llamas. Two llamas, and *Ultima Online*, because there was no name so that's what we called ourselves. "Well, it's *Ultima. Online*. Llamas!" You know.

And then this FAQ in which we promised you guys the moon. Any of you remember the FAQ? Any of you old schools enough to remember the FAQ? Oh, come on, this is the one where you go out and you kill the deer, and then the dragons would notice the deer aren't there, so they attack the city and you could fight them off the city and they'd reward you? Yeah, that never came true.

[laughter]

We tried! And it never came true.

There was also a thing, you remember, at the bottom. A little sun. It was just a little circle, with some lines around it, in yellow. That was actually called "a happy butthole."

[laughter]

It came from an epic series of practical jokes that Richard was playing on his girl friend and vice versa, where they would do things like sneak into each other's house and put happy butthole stickers over absolutely everything, like inside cabinets, or make confetti blow out of the air conditioning system in their car, blow out confetti and each piece would have a tiny little happy butthole drawn on the piece of paper, or come into origin and find it spray-painted on the parking deck when you drove in. It just kept escalating until finally one day it made the news that there was a giant banner hanging over Mopac Expressway off of one of the overpasses.

[laughter]

So it was a little in-joke for us, that was there on the FAQ.

Surprisingly, marketing made us remove no only the happy butthole, but even the llamas, and I till resent that.

[laughter]

The funny thing is that at the time, we were the invasion of the big budgets. For all of that – I mean, happy buttholes for crissake! And we were the big companies!? Coming in and destroying the online game culture of the day.

"Oh, it'll be completely ruined!" This is what the old-timers were saying. "It's going to get completely ruined by the fact there's these big companies coming in and they are going to destroy everything that is awesome about the online game community that existed then. Things like… people who would get together with their friends to come to online gaming conventions. That would be lost!

[gestures at the audience.]

[laughter]

Cause you know, you're part of a long tradition here. My gosh, Kesmai guys, *Air Warrior* used to run conventions back in the 80s. Right?

So there was this fear from people. "Oh, it's all going to change." And they were right, they were right. It did change. I mean, for one thing, you people came along. And you changed stuff. We knew we would NEED a guild system, but we cut it for time, because most of UO was built in nine months.

Something most people don't know… most of UO was built in nine months. We launched it after nine months, because we built this whole demo for E3, and then we made an alpha and then we said "well, that's nice but it'll never work," so we threw it away, and we started over. And we launched something after nine months.

["So that's what happened!"]

That is what happened… and there went the dragons, they were on that chopping block too, the cool dragons with their AI that ate people.

So yeah, stuff was changing. It was big budgets. UO cost something like eight million dollars. Which is probably like, three minutes of WoW development time.

[laughter]

And we weren't the only skunkworksy thing at the time. I mean, we were the big budget, but right at the same time, and we all started right at the same time: *EverQuest* was starting at the same time that UO was, *Asheron's Call* was starting at the same time that UO was, over in Korea, Lineage was starting at the same that UO was, and *Dark Ages* was. And all of these projects that didn't get [inaudible], like *Rubies of Eventide* and *The Realm*, you know, all of these games all got going right around 1994-95. We just took different amounts of time to finish.

And all of those games, that came out clear up through 1999, they were all like that. Little skunkwork things on folding tables. Because the big companies were all like "online gaming? Whaaa?"

You said 65,000? 65,000 is double what EA originally estimated that UO would have as lifetime subscribers.

So the big companies had no idea that meteor was about to hit and completely blow up everything that people knew about the games business.

So we had all these big dreams about long lasting online communities where people from different walks of life would come together and get to be friends, and immerse themselves in these fantasy virtual worlds that would serve as both an escape and a new kind of society. I mean we were crazy optimistic nutsos, there's no way around it.

["And so were we!"]

Well, actually, and here you are! It kinda came true. When you guys first started showing up, you guys and other early guilds – and it's probably against the rules to do this, but to give shout-outs to other folks like Shadowclan and other folks who got going at the same time that you guys did – and showed the kind of commitment that just blew our minds. You had to delete your character, and start over, with a name that had LLTS in it, in order to join the guild. Try doing that today! "Well, I know that you raided, and got epics, and whatevers, but you're gonna have to reroll."

["That's my announcement at the end of the meeting."]

[laughter]

So old school! It drives loyalty. That's how you get to 99.07, so…

[laughter]

Then of course because of that, I had to go write a guild system. Which by the way, I personally wrote the guild system in UO, so you can blame me for that, the paging through people, yeah.

[laughter]

I only had a weekend!

[laughter]

Which then made you all reroll! Again! Which lots of you did, because you didn't want LLTS in your name, because you'd rather be able to show it through your guild heraldry, such as it was (I only had so much time)…

Thing is, I was a punk kid of 23. I am going to turn 39 in a couple of weeks…

["Whoo hoo!" "For the first time?"]

For the first time, yeah, and you know what? There's a whole lot of game companies right now that are going "oh crap, there's a meteor coming?" There's a whole lot of people going "What's happened? Are core gamers getting abandoned?" There's a whole lot of people saying, "what's happening to our longstanding online gaming communities, are they getting shredded by all this Facebook crap?" And it's like, oh boy, here comes another meteor.

Are any of you freaked out by the number of games about clicking on cows?

[laughter]

It's OK! It's OK to say so! How many of you play games about clicking on cows?

[laughter]

Guess I am here to tell you that we have been here before. I mean, there are those among you who actually dared to admit that they played on PLATO or on Kesmai, or that they actually did pay six dollars an hour to play on GEnie…

["Ooof"]

Yes, yes, yes. Online gaming… if you think that microtransactions are bad NOW? You have no idea! Yeah, you used to haver to pay by the minute. And people like you? You were the prime target for the thousand-dollar day. I'm not joking, thousand-dollar day. So as you can see, the State of Virginia is missing out on a hell of a lot of taxes.

[laughter]

Here's the way I look at it. Facebook is just another new console, is just another hand-helds. And just like the GameBoy it has pretty bad graphics, and the games are pretty simple. But it's going to lead up to having 3d in your hand, and even 3d glasses. It's gonna work its way up. But in the meantime, it's absolutely true, the games are fairly simple.

But on the other hand, that means a lot of people are getting to play. A huge amount of people., And it's true that these games are not getting dragons to eat the villagers because you killed the deer, and it's true that as of yet there aren't really raids, and there aren't conventions for people who are playing these games.

But you guys came in because of one of these shifts. And that means that there's a whole bunch of people who are coming in now that are going to discover over time, the kind of community and the kind of family and friendship that you guys have. Because what's happening is, this, this stuff that has occupied you guys for fourteen years, the lifespan of my daughter, is now going to be occupying twenty times, a hundred times, as many people.

And it can be really scary to have that kind of volume suddenly come in. Partly, because honestly, the amount of money that is getting spent on the things that those fourteen-year-olds among you grew up with, and up to the twenty-four year olds, that's changing. The companies are making less, and in some ways they are dreaming a little bit less, because it's the big companies now. You guys are big business.

I mean, you guys are now an LLC. YOU GUYS are now corporate.

[applause]

You know, the nice thing about this, along with the shift, the folding tables came back. The little offices with twelve people and no air conditioning or too much, came back. It's back to working off a surface of stuff purchased at Ikea. And along with it comes the crazy dreaming again.

GameBoy didn't stay black and white forever. And even though it's been a long and crazy road, and it kind of looks like the game industry is veering off a cliff in a couple of ways... I couldn't tell if consoles are gonna be around... I don't know! Is PC gaming outside of online going to be around? I don't know. If somebody had said that the only publisher worth looking at would be Steam, four years ago I think most people in the room would have laughed. But instead all the publishers have signed over the life to Steam and now they're going "Oh crap!"

[laughter]

"What do we do?"

But I actually believe that what's going to happen now is that the new generation of games that are coming, that are now starting from the premise of this kind of community, this kind of online society, but for everybody, for the kind of people who ask you guys "you're going to a WHAT convention?"

[laughter]

That stuff, it is going to kind of like hit the reset button. We are going to get a whole new kind of online gaming, a whole new kind of virtual world, a whole new world of online community, and this time maybe some of these dreams are going to come back. Because it's not going to stay clicking on cows. It's just a new console. It's just the Space Invaders of today happens to be cow clicking. But it's all going to start rebuilding.

So I actually think that even though it's kind of a freaky moment for you guys, the elder statesmen of online gaming... my kid's thirteen, you guys are going to be introducing all kinds of new folks, folks who never heard of UO, never heard of EQ, never heard of any of those games, folks who think that "oh WoW is that old game that came out years ago." It already is.

They are going to be listening to music that you don't like or understand. And a lot of them will be playing games that you don't like or understand. But it's in traditions like this one, traditions like the Syndicate, traditions like you guys coming back year after year, training these folks up, that the torch gets passed on.

So even if we are at this moment of transition, even big huge worlds are kind of fading away – they'll be back, because nothing ever dies. As long as somebody is still willing to stick LLTS at the end of a signature, you guys will be able to keep carrying on, able to keep marching forward, and keep the torch going.

Andean Bird

A Vague Game Idea

I don't know why, but it came to me as a picture, a bit over a week ago: a bird made of light, flapping on a screen with hand-drawn artwork. It trailed a few particles of light as it flapped, mostly white, but some of them pink or pale blue. What was interesting about it was the flapping, the way in which it had to twitch one wing in order to slide sideways against the wind currents and the gravity.

Nazcan pottery

Say, rather, that *you* had to twitch one wing. It was a game about flying by flapping. What you did, I wasn't sure — collected stuff from the world, avoided collisions —

The famous Raimondi Stela

whatever made sense for a game about flapping. The key thing was the sensation of flapping and flying — perhaps because I have been playing a lot of *Joust* both on XBox Live and on my phone.

In my head the world was hand drawn, as I mentioned. But specifically, it had a look that you just don't see in games these days… something different. I received as a gift a book on Andean iconography right around the same time that the idea struck me: Nazcan pottery paintings, Moche sculpture and Chavin's stela. The images in the book included numerous insanely cute portrayals of animals, done in a faux naif style that fit perfectly with some of the modern Japanese game aesthetic, yet had a look all their own. I thought I had a look.

"Blue squares" first, though! So one afternoon when I should have been working on my real work (the startup studio), I instead messed about with making a bird flap. Even though the initial impetus was that picture in my head of a bird made of light trailing sparks (lightblended particles, I figured), the mechanic came first.

Even though I have done object oriented programming, I am still much more of an old-school function-based guy. Because of that, I quickly ended up with a file that had in it the following:

- main() which called
- drawScreen() which called
- drawBird()
- drawFlapStats()
- getInput()
- updatebird()

Because I wanted a floaty feel, the sorts of flap stats we're talking about were things like the bird's position, the flex in each wing, the *targeted* flex in each wing, the *targeted* position of the bird, and so on. Basically, the bird would not be immediately responsive.

I ended up making every single one of those variables — the current flex, the targeted wingstroke strength, etc, be evidenced in the drawing of the actual bird, which I made a little wireframe. All the variables mattered — the amount of downstroke from holding down a key mattered, because the longer you held it down, the sooner the bird would tire, and then fall back down. Flapping one wing longer than the other would put more force in that direction, and so on.

The bird and its flap stats

What I ended up with, though, felt a little different than I had envisioned. When you held one wing, you slid sideways after releasing the wing, not while pushing. Basically, it felt as I was messing with it, like you were flying into a headwind. And that changed my conception of the game mechanic a little bit.

On the other hand, my kids immediately shouted "birdie!" and spent a cheerful 45 minutes just flapping and learning the controls. As I messed with it, it felt like a different and fresh control dynamic. Still somewhat clunky, but good enough to start with.

So I tried putting the cool particle lightblend effect on. It looked horrible, nothing like what I had envisioned. Plus it was way slow to render. So much for the initial cool picture (which I can still summon at will, alas).

So now I had a basic control prototype that engaged my kids — always a good test of basic engagement. In "theory of fun" terms the challenge is exactly what I wanted it to be — learning to fly using this flapping mechanic. The next step is to give it a lick of polish so that it conjures up ideas for theme, setting, and obstacles. But that's for another day and another post.

- Download EXE for Windows from
  https://www.raphkoster.com/gaming/oldandeanbird.exe
- Download for Mac (.zip) (may not work on an Intel Mac) from
  https://www.raphkoster.com/gaming/macoldandeanbird.zip

Be sure to choose "save to disk" rather than "run from location"… No warranties express or implied, if your machine explodes it's not my fault.

PKing Duck

More on the Vague Game Idea

So, last time, I had left off with the simple flapping prototype, with broken sideways movement. Where did I go from there?

Well, mostly, I went into two modes at the same time: one, thinking about the play experience, and the other, focusing on fixing the feed back that the model was giving.

Sorry, no fresh version today. :) But read on for the thoughts I had:

Elements required for fun

Do you have to prepare for the challenge?
...where prep includes prior moves?
...and you can prep in multiple ways?

Does the topology of the space matter?
...does the topology change?

Is there a core verb for the challenge?
...can it be modified by content?

Can you use different abilities on it?
...will you have to to succeed?

Is there skill to using the ability?
...or is this a basic UI action?

Are there multiple success states?
...with no bottomfeeding?
...and a cost to failure?

It's all about the feedback!

Games depend totally on the feedback provided; if you don't give the right sort of feedback, people will not understand what is going on. To decide on the right sort of feedback, I had to pin down what the game was going to be a little bit better. I ended up concluding that the side view that I had pictured (and even started to implement in the version you saw) wasn't actually what I was enjoying. Instead, I saw the bird as a top-down view, flying over a landscape. The effort to reach the top of the screen then became not an effort to stay off the ground, but instead an effort to fight the headwind, to fly faster. Once I made this mental adjustment, more elements of the game started snapping into place for me.

Since the primary mechanic was steering with wing flaps, this meant that the obvious things to add were challenges related to navigation to one or another point on the screen. The first one I added was gusts of wind from the side, making it more important to master the sideways movement and asymmetrical wing flapping that is the core of the movement mechanic. I did this by just implementing a "wind" variable that gradually moved to randomly chosen positive and negative values, and having it push the bird around.

Why wind? Because it is the "topology" in my checklist of fun elements. The same challenge — flapping to the move the bird — but the territory matters. Other territory elements, such as obstacles to avoid, are also possible. Updrafts and downdrafts could be added as well, or (of we had other birds in the environment) riding in the slipstream behind another bird. But sidewinds would do for now.

I chose not to have head- and tailwinds at first, because the vertical movement was challenging enough. Instead, the game would assume a headwind; gliding would put you at the bottom of the screen.

I put a little bar at the top of the screen that indicated the direction and strength of the wind. But that wasn't enough feedback to indicate that you were in a top-down view looking straight down at the ground. So I made the background blue, put little white speckles scrolling down, and added big ol' alpha'ed clouds that also scrolled down. The further up the screen you were, the faster the speckles and clouds scrolled down. I also made them blow around with the wind — speckles in the direction opposite to the wind, so you had the sense the ground was sliding away from you, clouds with the wind so you saw that they were being blown just like you.

The old and new birds

I also fixed the sideways movement up a bit, making it so that you slid sideways when holding one of the wings at its max flex point. There's still the strange "hold one wing, flap, then let go and slide sideways" behavior, but now it feels like the aftereffect of the flex. Still not tuned right, but closer.

I also decided that the visual feedback on the bird needed work. The wings didn't arch up high enough when you were flapping optimally. I moved some of the points around on the wings to get them closer to the look I wanted. Now when you were flapping vigorously, it looked like it a bit more. Finally, I fixed the broken look when the bird drifted down from the top of the screen.

All of these things basically enhanced the sensation of flying without actually changing very much. And more importantly, they were all about mechanics and feedback, not about "dressing."

Thinking about theme and dressing

Wind gauge, speckles, and clouds

It would have been easy to make this a combat game. Think ornithopters a la Miyazaki, shooting at skyborne or groundborne targets. Or a bird pooping on things on the ground. As I joked to my wife, a PK'ing duck *(groan....)*. But a lot of what I enjoyed, and apparently others as well, based on the comment thread, was the sort of Zen meditative vibe you got from just trying to fly well. So I wanted to avoid combat.

Instead, I started thinking about ways to reinforce the Zen feeling. And one of the ways I came up with was music. As it happened, I had been messing about with a guitar piece that hadn't come together and was nothing but a bunch of related little riffs. So I thought about recording those as individual bits, and firing off the riffs dependent on the bird's situation: more aggressive flight playing the faster ones, drifting down to the bottom and doing nothing playing the bass line only, and so on. I'd only be getting a new music state periodically, when the last one ended, so the loop should move seamlessly from one to the other.

I also started thinking about the challenge to accomplish; I now had a landscape, so the challenge should be navigating it. Basically, getting to a spot on the screen, or avoiding a spot on the screen. I decided that I would likely put bugs or other birds or something on the screen at the spots you want to reach or not.

I decided that even my crude ocean was kinda neat. A more varied landscape would be ideal — and even better would be the ability to dive into it — by zooming the entire background in and out. I even pondered doing "above-view *Joust*" where you have to dive down onto something to catch it. I still don't know what any of this looks like (though I am still interesting in that Andean look), but now the picture of what I want to do is coming together.

Lastly, I thought about the nature of the game, again prompted by some of the comments. I concluded that the vibe permitted it having a narrative, perhaps. Not a standard "get to the other side" narrative built out of challenges, but maybe literally just a story that was told based on how far you got. More of an "experience" than a game where you try to survive forever — a game that had an ending. And the path maybe would vary based on how well you had one. At the end, maybe the bird arrived at a destination starving and lonely, and the story was a sad one; or it arrived plump and well-fed, and the story was one of joyful swooping. I don't know — still vague.

The next step is likely to try putting in things to catch on the screen. They need to be flying things that can get ahead of you, to force you off the bottom edge of the screen.

Hope you're enjoying this look at the process. I am not significantly ahead of you guys as you read this. :)

Vague game less vague

This time, there's a new version to download!

Last time, I talked about how there were a few things that had caught my imagination: dynamic music based on how you were flying the bird, and the idea of adding verticality into the flight model, so you could zoom in and out. This latter one, I concluded, should be done before I put in any obstacles or challenges, because it would dictate what sort of challenges I could present. I also had planned to add the wind.

As you can see from the screenshot, the bird has been tweaked. Not only did I adjust the arc of the wings in numerous locations, but I got rid of the old "fatigue" bar that was previously in the upper left corner (the vertical red bar) and instead made it affect the angle of the shoulders. Now all the flight model feedback is in the shape of the bird's wings.

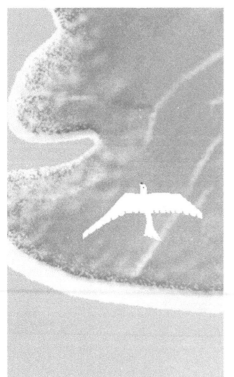

The bird gains some art

I then used a simple 2d texturemapping routine to slap a very crude feathers texture on the bird's wings. The rest of the bird is still mostly drawn procedurally: ovals, lines, etc. This is a stand-in bit of art just to make it look a little more appealing. In the long run, I am still interested in pursuing that Andean art style.

To do the music, I went into my recording software, and set up a simple drum loop of a known length. I then recorded the most basic form of the riff. I then looped that as a backing track, and recorded as series of simple riffs atop it. I chopped these up so they were all the same length, and put a timing routine in the game that said "every sixteen seconds, go into the pickMusic() routine."

pickMusic() chooses up to three of these little loops to play — the backing one, and two others based on things like angle of the wings, position on the screen, and so on. There's a few cues that are very predictable; if you get to the top of the screen, you get one loop, if you are at the bottom doing nothing, you always get just the backing. But most of the others have some randomness as to whether or not they will play.

Lastly, I added the verticality. I created a quickie island in Photoshop, and then added the ability to move up and down with keys. Now that I've done this, I want to change the interface for it; diving should be accomplished by holding down both wing keys, and climbing by a particular stroke pattern, I think. I like the simplicity of the flapping mechanism as the basic interface.

The island is there really only to give you the sense of verticality; I alpha fade it out based on altitude, which gives a nice effect of distance. Long term, the landscape probably needs to be a complicated thing built out of tiles, with a level-of-detail system so that I don't kill the speed of the app by drawing too many tiny things in the distance.

Worth pointing out, btw — this is still very much a 2d app, despite using some texturemapping and zooming. No 3d math used here... The size has alas bloated because of those music loops — even at 22Khz, they're still 1.3MB apiece...

Controls:

- Z or left arrow to flap the left wing
- M or right arrow to flap the right wing
- K or up arrow to dive
- SPACE or down arrow to climb
- ESC or the close button (yes, I added that) to exit the app

Keep an eye on the wind meter at the top!

Next time? Almost certainly the ability to catch something. As my son said, "this would be awesome if you had a ray gun. All good games have enemies and ray blasters." Sigh.

Windows version: https://www.raphkoster.com/gaming/andeanbird3.zip

Mac version: https://www.raphkoster.com/gaming/macandean3.zip

Andean Bird

With this version, the Andean bird game finally actually becomes a game, and not a control prototype. But I'm left unsatisfied.

Trying out more controls

Last time, there was a desire among those who tried it to add mouse controls,

The very crude title screen

something I have resisted, and ended up not putting in even to try out just because of the massive rewrite it would entail. The whole core of the engine is built around the flapping code, and if I switch to mouse controls, the flapping would go away altogether. Instead, I think my next step may be to hook it up to triggers on an XBox 360 controller.

But I also hadn't liked the addition of two more controls for diving and climbing. In the last version, you could use the up and down arrow keys, but as some suggested in the thread, diving is really accomplished by putting the wings into a particular configuration. So I tried to accomplish that. There is now a global "gravity" that is always pulling the bird downwards very slowly. However, if you hold the wings back all

the way, you will go into a much steeper dive.

Climbing happens slightly every time you flap; there's now a real trick to flapping at the right tempo to climb steadily. The island now gains real significance as your "altimeter" because I have still avoided putting things on the HUD.

There are a bunch of implications for this; turning to one side or another, for example, is almost certain to cause you to slip lower, because one wing is held down the whole time, unless you manage to get the timing just right. As a result, flying the bird is demanding more skill.

The issue — it may just have gotten too hard and tiring. How to tell?

Goals and rewards

Without a goal, there was no game. It was all well and good flapping about and trying out this control scheme, but I couldn't tell how hard it really was. So I added a flight path that you have to stick to. This was also the first opportunity to put in some Andean iconography in; I selected for my arrow shape a textile pattern from Cuzco.

The flight path veers from side to side and up and down as well. I made it tint red when you were too high or too low; it's unforgiving if you are below it, but there's a tolerance level when you are above it — when you're close, it's blue, and as you get too high it shades to purple and thence to red. If you are flying over it when it is purple-to-blue, you get points, and it turns white to indicate that you "captured" it. Flying slowly along the path earns more points, actually, because the scoring literally increments every time it detects that you are on the path. You can tell when you are below the path because it overlays on the bird.

If a segment of the path isn't captured and scrolls off the bottom of the screen, you lose some lifeforce. Run out of lifeforce, and the game ends. This is displayed via an obscure white bar at the bottom of the screen, right by the score. I've toyed with other ways of showing this — the bird growing translucent, until it finally pops in a shower of feathers, or the game starting out at dawn and moving to dusk and finally night when you're about to die, making the time of day into a metaphor for your progress.

And the bird should still pop in a shower of feathers. :)

Effects

One thing that became clear last time is how much of the experience of this is basically aesthetic. When clouds were added and the island, and especially the music, it made a big difference in the feel. So I spent some time adding effects.

If you recall, the original concept involved "a bird made of light." I've drifted away from that, but it occurred to me that with the clouds and whatnot, I was getting a lot of nice color variation on the screen. So I decided to emphasize that with a full screen motion blur. The way this was accomplished was by not clearing the screen, but instead overlaying a heavily alpha'd color rectangle across the screen. After a few frames, it builds up enough to wipe the screen, but recently past frames remain there for just a few frames. Ths effect made a big difference with the clouds and the bird, but the island gained some unsightly artifacts.

I also added water sparkles, using pathetically simple little particles that just draw ovals. Once the motion blur was in, these gained faint trails (as did everything).

Once I had those, I wanted to add time of day. A simple clock increments when a bar of music ends, and there's different light color settings for each hour. The actual light gradually moves towards the new target color, and the result is a gradual wash of pastels. If you let the game run without starting to play, you can see the time run by in accelerated fashion.

Once I had that, I kind of wanted a reflection of the sun or moon in the water. I ended up just having a slightly denser cloud of sparkles in the water, and then I made the other sparkles I already had center on this reflection and fade out with distance. For now, this just moves sideways across the screen very slowly, but eventually I can tie it more firmly to the clock. If you can get down there before the lifeforce runs out, you can see the effect up close — it looks like very out of focus sparkles on water if you squint and sit a few feet away from the monitor. Heh.

Where it is now

There's a variety of goofy bugs — sometimes, your lifeforce just goes crazy, killing you with no indication of why. Sometimes the drawing of the flightpath goes crazy — an artifact of drawing the path in two passes, the bits above you and below you. The addition of gravity and flapping up means that in normal flight, the stuff below does a distracting zoom-in-zoom-out thing, which can probably be fixed by dampening the zoom. The sun/moon reflection behaves erratically because I didn't synch its movement to the clock.

But more importantly, is it doing what I hoped it would? The addition of the game element actually detracts from the overall experience to a degree. Whereas the last version was very peaceful, the new version gets rather frustrating as the wind blows you off the intended flight path and you can't get back on it (and thus die). Now the controls really are a battle, because the flightpath is pretty unforgiving. Lastly, while flying through the shifting colors is kinda cool, having to pay attention to the path makes you zero in your focus, and so you don't see the environment. I'd like to add dolphins in the water, other birds flying by, a full tile-based scrolling background with stuff to collect and see, all done with the Andean style… but would you see it? Perhaps the flight path only applies when flying from island to island.

There are some positives. Crude as all the new effects are, they enhance that sensation of a mystical flight. Some of the colors are off, but overall, I like the broader palette. The motion blur isn't quite what I want, but I can see how it would work.

Flying with Z and M and nothing else feels right. And the idea that just flying and mastering those controls can be a challenging game experience is borne out — if anything, it needs to be easier.

To address the flight path, I'd probably still display the whole path, but have waypoint along it that are the only ones that "matter" for lifeforce. That would give more freedom to fly about. A way to regain lifeforce would also help.

The big question still remains the controls, of course.

I've got a lot going on with work things lately, so this may be the last version for a while. Let me know your high scores. :)

This is very flattering. Mentisworks has done a selection of the best indie "art games"[316] which is featured on the front of *Indygamer*. *Andean Bird* placed on the list, alongside titles like *Façade*, *Flow*, *Raspberry*, *The Endless Forest*, *The Marriage*, and many more intriguing titles. Given that the Bird is still at version 0.5, that's quite august company to be keeping.

> Quite unlike anything else out there, Andean Bird offers a leisurely glide across the landscape to the accompaniment of beautiful music. It does manage to instill some of the qualities of flight, yet that same endeavor is hampered by its lack of fullscreen capability.

Hmm. Fullscreen is about two lines of code, I should add that.

---

[316] http://www.mentisworks.org/2007/07/art-games-best-indy-titles.html. At the time, "art game" was not yet in wide currency, and Roger Ebert had just declared that games could not be art; the article itself states "there has only been one other such list that I recall online."

Influences

On Oct 9th, 2009, I posted a brief note to the blog that read,

Today I see this link to *Limbo,*[317] a game which offers up a different *visual* aesthetic, but gameplay that looks like a clever elaboration of traditional platforming.

I'm going to be giving a talk at Project Horseshoe[318] entitled "Influences." It's basically about pulling in different aesthetics from different areas, rather than relying solely on what might be called "the videogame aesthetic."

I think there's a lot of potential in presenting old gameplay (as in this case and in the case of *Fl0w)*[319] in radically new wrappings. Beyond that, though, lies more unexplored territory: using the broader palette of aesthetics found in other media for the purposes of different *gameplay*.

In the book, I mention *Minesweeper* as an example of some of the elements of Impressionism taken into the real of systems modeling. *Minesweeper*, like Impressionism in art and music, is about modeling by absence, about the play of reflections on the surface, about understanding through repetition. There are many ways to play with this notion, and I am sure there are many other games that could be done with this general approach.

Just playing with the notion:

- How about a game where you have to find spots on the screen by dropping pebbles on a water surface and observing ripples?
- Or where you shine a small light on something and try to identify the shape hidden in the darkness by tracing its contours within a time limit?
- Or where you have to find things by defining their negative space?

Even these, though, are still fairly conservative. If we went an picked an aesthetic

---

[317] Released by Playdead in 2010.
[318] A long-running conference where game developers gather "to solve game design's toughest problems." See https://www.projecthorseshoe.com/
[319] See https://en.wikipedia.org/wiki/Flow_(video_game)

from a radically different field and tried to bring it back to games, what would it look like? What would a game that embraced "jump cut"-ness or a game that embraced "cyberpunk"-ness (I don't mean the trappings — I mean the actual *ethos*) or a game that embraced "religious ecstasy" really look like?

My talk at Project Horseshoe was called "Influences." And here it is, with occasional audience interjections.[320]

Howdy, y'all.

["Howdy!"]

I reckon I left my hat under the table there, but... I got a stuffed head and I think the voice goes with the hat.

You know, I'm not gonna do slides ["Sweet!"]. There is some stuff I wanna show you later, but we'll set it up later.

You know, I went back and forth trying to think about what exactly to say here, because I spent the last, oh, maybe three years working on understanding fun, and on thinking about how games work at a really fundamental level, like an atomic, tiny, game system, how things tick and stick together kind of level, and you know, I concluded games were mostly about learning. And if you wanna know more about that, you can go read the book, right? And that was good. It was *useful*, it helped me a lot.

Around the same time that I was doing that, you know, I gave that initial talk[321] back at the Austin Game Conference in 2003... and I started working on game grammar stuff[322] in 2004, and then I wrote the book.[323] So there was a whole bunch of game grammar stuff that was in the book. And this whole game grammar thing was about common elements that are in all of the game systems, and how if some of these little elements are missing, then the game system won't be fun. It was about how some games are symmetric, and some are asymmetric, and how all games happen within a topology, and you always have assets to maneuver, and you know... a whole bunch

[320] An audio recording of the talk is available at
https://www.raphkoster.com/games/presentations/influences/
[321] This is referring to "A Theory of Fun." The PDF of the slides for that talk can be found here:
https://www.theoryoffun.com/theoryoffun.pdf
[322] See "A Grammar of Gameplay, or Game Atoms: Can Games Be Diagrammed?," slides delivered at
GDC2004. https://www.raphkoster.com/games/presentations/a-grammar-of-gameplay/
[323] *A Theory of Fun for Game Design*, Paraglyph Press, 2004. Now published by O'Reilly.

of *stuff* like that. You know. How games are structured around... I have it written down. "Solving statistically varied challenge situations presented by an opponent who may or may not be algorithmic within a framework that is a defined systemic model blah blah blah."

I'm not the only guy doing this, OK? I mean, when Mark Terrano[324] shows his graphs [of measuring user experience via metrics on input channels and outputs provided by the game at any given moment], I go, "Funny, I saw that *same graph*[325] on Dan Cook's[326] website [LostGarden.com] about six months ago." And for that matter, I saw something very similar on Ben Cousins' website[327] about a year and a half ago. A lot of people are working on basically the same stuff. Right? I mean, I put up a very similar graph to that one arguing that socialization in multiplayer gaming requires downtime because you need attention troughs,[328] which look exactly like the troughs that were in Mark's graph.

Ben Cousins, Stéphane Bura who's been working on game grammar,[329] there's all the work that Eric [Zimmerman] and Katie [Salen] did in *Rules of Play*,[330] you know – we're all getting results that seem to work. But we're finding is that there are essentially grammatical rules, or physics rules, or whatever, under this stuff, that can be found and that are helpful.

I could talk to you for *hours* about that crap.

I learned a lot from it, right? It's had a huge impact on how I see games, and Ironically, I haven't hardly gotten to work on any games since I came up with it. [laughter]. But it has actually had a huge impact, and I think it can have a huge impact on the industry as a whole, right? You can see how tools like what Mark proposes, or gosh, if we had something, if you could have a notation – this is what I argued in the Game Grammar talk – where you could sketch out how the pieces of a game system fit together, you could actually see where the balance would go out of whack, or why a system wouldn't be fun, before you started implementing. It's just another way to play test.

But honestly, I don't want to talk about that. For one thing, it's kind of dry and

---

[324] Game designer of *Age of Empires II*, many games from Hidden Path, and now a creative director at Oculus Research.

[325] See http://www.lostgarden.com/2006/01/creating-system-of-game-play-notation.html

[326] Game designer of, among others, *AlphaBear*, and CCO of SpryFox.

[327] https://benjaminjcousins.wordpress.com/

[328] See "Forcing Interaction" elsewhere in this volume.

[329] See http://users.skynet.be/bura/diagrams/

[330] *Rules of Play*, Katie Salen and Eric Zimmerman, MIT Press, 2003.

technical and full of diagrams, and you know, for another, sometimes it seems a little stupid and pointless. Like you're caught up in the theory and where is the fun? And arguably, it breaks the wall between science and art, which is a wall full of holes already, but...

I really want to go a little further into the future, actually, and just take for granted that all of those efforts aren't stupid. That they are actually showing us something about games. Because of the conclusion it led me to.

I concluded that just about all games were about math.

They are not about arithmetic, unless you're playing an RPG [laughter], but about all fields of math. In fact, they tend to be about – I'll go all geeky on you – NP-hard or NP-complete problems. They tend to be about, I actually went and looked up on the Web a list of NP-hard problems, and they sure as hell sound like our games. Motion planning on a plane with polygons. Yeah. There goes every single platformer ever. [Laughter]. Isomorphism. All matching games. Traveling salesman problem. Packing problems – *Tetris* is a packing problem. Almost, well, a lot of puzzle games are packing problems. Cover problems, the knapsack problem, blah blah blah. A lot of them are about NP-complete problems. In fact I actually started the exercise: on Wikipedia there's this wonderful list of Karp's 21 NP-complete problems,[331] and I started at the top and started designing a game for each one of them. [Laughter.]

Besides those classical problems, games rely heavily on estimation of probability, which isn't actually even complicated [laughter] but the human brain sucks at it, and appears to be hardwired to suck at it [laughter], and therefore we rely on it in our games a lot, because we know that we can sucker 'em every time. [laughter] Just like Vegas.

So the more I dug into grammar and all of this stuff, the more I kept thinking, crap, it may be that games, by nature, are inherently math.

And I think that sucks. It makes me really unhappy.

---

[331] See https://en.wikipedia.org/wiki/Karp%27s_21_NP-complete_problems

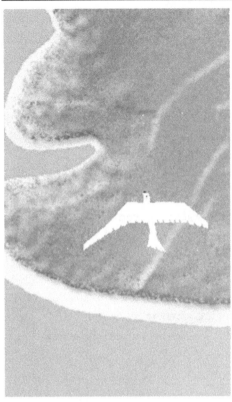
A game about flapping

I wanted to actually show you something. I was recently working on a game about flapping. This sounds like a really odd thing to make a game about, but I wanted to try anyhow. I was working on this game about flapping, and it's actually up on the blog, and you know, it's basically a little game where one key controls one wing, and the other key controls the other wing, and the longer you hold them down, the longer your downstroke goes. When you let go, the wings slowly returns to where they are supposed to be. But because you have independent control of each wing, you can start doing this [slides sideways], turn this way, and if you give long strokes, you move in a different way than if you fold them slightly, and if you beat on a regular pace you actually rise in the air, and if you hold them tight, then you stop flapping and gravity starts taking you down. A flapping simulation. It was keyboard input because that's what I have on my laptop.

So the thing about this little flapping thing that was y'know, it wasn't about *flight*, it was about *flapping*, which is an important distinction. I built a little model here, and I even made it so that the keys were on opposite ends of the keyboard so that you had that sense steering like that. I was thinking in terms of, you know what, a lot of games are driven by interface, and that experience, so if I completely change up the interface for how you think about flying something, maybe I'll head to something that feels fresh.

Just flapping the bird around on the screen actually turned out to be compelling for me. Other people, however, bounced off of it instantly, because they just didn't get it. And they asked for mouse control, actually [Laughter], which I resisted mightily, because, well, then... the game was about the flapping. If you can't hack the flapping, then tough shit. [laughter].

But the thing about this was that it ended up being compelling enough that I posted the prototype to the blog. And it actually got on BoingBoing, which meant that it "sold" a few thousand "units," because a bunch of people downloaded it [laughter] and it got reblogged all over the place. So it was compelling enough that I added islands and scrolled down below, and a blue background with sparklies in the water, and color-shifting clouds and a day/night cycle with beautiful pastel colors, and a motion blur across the screen, and all this other stuff.

And that was cool, and lot of people – those who could hack the flapping – started commenting about how Zen it made them feel, particular once I added a little DADGAD-based[332] soundtrack on acoustic guitar.

So it was a toy, right? It was designed for you to flap. If you successfully made it to the top, you were rewarded – I built a tiny little dynamic music system, and if you

The "Zen" version:
https://www.raphkoster.com/gaming/andeanbird3.zip
https://www.raphkoster.com/gaming/macandean3.zip
The "game" version:
https://www.raphkoster.com/gaming/andeanbird4.zip
https://www.raphkoster.com/gaming/macandeanbird4.zip

made it to the top, basically, I recorded lots of little chopped up riffs, and you had different riffs depending on where you were on the screen, and what angle your wings were at, and stuff. You know, really basic, and people said it was really Zen. But it wasn't what I would really call a game. You know, it was a toy, an amusement.

So I put a game into it. I made a 3d path in the air that went up, went down. Now, keep in mind, this is an overhead view game, so 3d means it got bigger or smaller. And you could see this rollercoaster path wending around. There was wind blowing you from side to side that you had to cope with as you flapped. You were scored, and you had to stay on the path, not too high, not too low, you know. Basically, an

---

[332] DADGAD is a guitar tuning. See https://en.wikipedia.org/wiki/DADGAD

overhead version of flying through rings. If you got off the path for too long, you croaked. Game over. Which was really frustrating, because the main attraction was getting further so you could see what noon looked like, because of the color ramps on the clouds.

And pretty much, all the charm that the prototype had went away. [laughter] It ceased being fun because the math came in big time.

So here I am, and I've been looking at all these games in terms of the math. I've been looking at how you make these games and you work with them on this systemic level, but lately I've been dreaming about making games that make you feel what's it's like to be a wolf living in the winter scrounging scraps from a nearby mining town. A game about the sensation of a kaleidoscope. A game that exudes "treeness."

And fuck! Math doesn't tell us anything about that. It's really really bad at it.

I think that these aren't things that reduce down to math. As designers, we're really trained from really few sources, overall. When I really dig into the sources and influences – we already saw this, even with the talks today – we point at other games, and we point at movies. And that seems to be the total extent of what we… [sigh]

When a designer adapts the sweep of history like what Sid [Meier] did with Civ, and the development of civilizations, he builds a spreadsheet. History is a spreadsheet. It's represented by pretty icons, but it's a spreadsheet. When a designer tries to capture the inner soul of a person, what forms the inner core of someone, Will [Wright] makes eight bars, and they can be raised and lowered by doing dishes, watching TV and peeing at the right time. [Laughter] It's a spreadsheet again. All of human aspiration, and it's eight variables moving up and down. When we try to represent a mystic moment in life, what Lorca called *duende*,[333] you guys ever run across this word? It's a wonderful world, it's that elusive moment of transgression of the unreal into the real, you could almost call it magic.

It's a mana bar and a list of spell about glowing missiles.

And I think we're prisoners of our math.

It's ironic, because we keep chasing story, right? We chase after story, and we suck at story. I'm sorry, but we are really really really fuckin' bad moviemakers, people [laughter]. We really are. We're just no good at it. So what we do is we make bad movies, and we stick in some gameplay which we mostly stole from five years ago [laughter] and we say, "in order to get to the next episode, you must do this…" Right? That's advancing the medium. That's what we're doing. It's like, great, so in order to get to the next page of *Gone With the Wind* I have to play with a spreadsheet, and then

---

[333] https://en.wikipedia.org/wiki/Duende_(art)

you get the next chapter. [Laughter]

So... just to broaden our sense of influences a little bit. You guys all know that I came out of academia before I was a game designer. I was, to my everlasting dismay, I was mostly studying modernist literature while getting a creative writing degree. I really hated modernism, which was why I took so many courses in it, so I could argue with the professors [Laughter].

When you look at the modernist movement, and I'm actually going to broaden Modernism a little bit... really talking about everything from the Impressionist period on forward, because all of that stuff is kind of influenced by the modernist ethos. What was going on there was... There were artists and writers and musicians who got tired of showing things as they are. The height of craft before that was to say look, this is what it is. So, when you listen to Mozart's Requiem, he is representing as accurately as he can with his medium, a certain set of emotions. And when you look at a Rembrandt portrait, he is showing you what is. It's not strict realism, but it's showing you what is. And the same in the realistic novels – oh God, the Victorian novel, ugh. [Laughter]

Instead, once Impressionism kicked off and as we move forward, we start getting people who wanted to talk about how they showed what they showed, with what they used, if that makes sense. So we got paintings about color theory. Or paintings about how light reflects. Impressionism is about, in pretty much all the media, Impressionism is not about what's there. It's about how what's there is perturbing everything else. This is why I say that *Minesweeper* is actually an Impressionist game, because you never actually see *it*, you see everything around it and how it's been bumped and jostled. So Impressionism isn't painting the lilies, the water lilies, it's painting the light bouncing off the water lilies. It's about what isn't there.

Virginia Woolf wrote a book called *Jacob's Room*, about this WWI soldier named Jacob who is dead. He's the main character in the book, and he's not in the book. You learn about Jacob only through what everybody else says. Gertrude Stein wrote an autobiography of herself from the point of view of her lover who was real, so it's called *The Autobiography of Alice B. Toklas*, who is a real person, and she wrote it from her lover's point of view and she's a character in the book – it's actually her autobiography but she's not IN it.

And the next step after that, and Picasso did most of this in painting, it they start saying, let's do paintings about perspective. Let's do paintings about facial recognition. Let's do paintings about color weight. Mondrian? All of Mondrian's body of work is what they make you do in the first three months of the visual design class in an art major. It's about "how heavy is red," which isn't actually a stupid question if you study art theory. How heavy is red, and how big is empty space between two very narrow lines, and stuff like that.

It's all about itself, and in music we got music about harmony, or about how a melody works. Which is why eventually, once you get to the postmodern, you start getting stuff like John Cage, who will actually do a recording of four minutes and 33 seconds of silence in order to make you think about whether there actually is any such thing. And when yo go to perform *4'33"* you walk to a stage with a piano, you close the lid, and you sit there. And after about ten seconds what you are listening to is the concert of fidgeting, coughing, sneezing, wondering what the hell is going on.

There's so many examples of this… you end up getting writing about writing, painting about painting, music about music, and lately I've been wondering if all game design isn't modernist. By its nature.

Whether at its core, it may even be postmodernist, or deconstructionist, by its nature. Because it's all about the models. It's all about the math. It's all about looking at this stuff as a bunch of little moving parts, as a system. It's always about reducing something… you could even say trivializing something. It's about saying, "here's this wash of complexity, let's talk about how it works and break it down into this little spreadsheet."

What that means is, is that you are always simplifying these complicated things, like the inner core of a person's soul and turning it into eight bars, and reducing it down to something that is always inaccurate, and always oversimplified, and often frankly kind of Manichaean, good versus evil. Black and white. I think that ends up getting reflected in our stories, which are almost always simplistic Manichaean good versus evil stories too, because that's all the game can support. Even what we call analog games, tend to be binary when you look into them.

I'm finding this incredibly frustrating and ironic, because people like those in this room, game designers, have some of the most varied sets of interests of any people on the planet, certainly that I've ever encountered. I mean, you go to any university, you talk to the specialists in each field, and frankly, they know nothing about anything except whatever it is that they study – which they know in such excruciating detail that you don't want to hang out with them. [laughter]

You get a group of us together… in the car on the way here we discussed the scientific underpinnings of astrology. At a design workshop I was at recently we were trading book recommendations… what's the latest good hardboiled detective novel versus what's a better history of America pre 1492… you look around at designers, even the ones who occasionally, well, I've got this wonderful photo of Will Wright… they have a version of *Façade*[334] there which is a full version room. They actually make you put on your little VR headset and goggles, they actually mount a keyboard on your back, so an operator can come and fiddle with what's going on while you are in there. I snapped this wonderful photo of Will Wright being programmed [much laughter] But even people like Will, who sometimes seem

Will Wright getting programmed

cybernetic to some degree, you talk to him and he's got interests all over the map. I mean, he likes to build robots, but he likes to build robots in order to leave them piteously mewling on the street in order to see what people will do when they come up against a dead robot saying *"Help me!!!!"* [laughter] And he videotapes them, so…

So as a group we're really well-read, we're interested in all kinds of different stuff… but when I look at the industry, our influences, they're… I guess the word I'd use is "paltry." Pathetically small.

Who was playing *Cooking Mama* yesterday? Yeah, the industry's reaction is "A game about *COOKING?!@!?*" And then you play it, and it's actually *WarioWare* re-skinned. And it's another little spreadsheet about reaction times. And… yeah. Grrr! So frustrating. I mean, we reduce it down to the same little set of reductionist almost deconstructionist mini-games to become a parody of cooking. But at least it exists. And there are those that… we played *Werewolf* last night, and there are things there that aren't just statistics, although you play *Werewolf*, and think "You know there's an

---

[334] A pioneering interactive narrative game. See
https://en.wikipedia.org/wiki/Fa%C3%A7ade_(video_game)

algorithmic approach to this…"

["And that's why you were killed first!"]

I know…!

[Laughter]

And I guess the question is, I look at the game about cooking and I go, why stop there? I mean, there's an easy step to the game about winemaking. And I can see you right now, let's make a game about winemaking and in your heads you immediately start thinking, dry season versus wet season, acidity of the soil, there's all kinds of things like that. So let's go a step further, how about the game about wine tasting.[335]

Yeah, I don't enough about wine tasting to figure out even how – yeah, you wanna play that game don't ya. Live action. [laughter… "The ARG"]

And I go, wait a minute, what about a game… I just learned that all of the peach orchards between Parmer and 35 and Round Rock are gone. Which sucks. ["It's all Wal-Marts now.." "It's the pits" Laughter] Yeah… and why is there no game about the taste of a freshly picked peach, straight from the tree, with the smells and dust of the working orchard? How do you make a game *about that?*

["Because my monitor tastes like crap." "It's a human interface problem."]

It isn't just an interface problem! It isn't just an interface problem! There are probably *poems* about the taste of a fresh peach.

The game about the dynamics of a coral reef, and destroying the coral reef, you know, when you think about that, you immediately go "oh yeah, a serious game, and we'll teach people about global warming," and it's not the same thing as really a game about *coral reef-ness.*

And why isn't there a game about silk-screening t-shirts? What is it that makes us go, yeah, that just doesn't come up, let's go for the orc slaying instead? At this very moment, there are probably more teenagers out there interested in silk-screening crap onto t-shirts than there are in slaying orcs, and yet it doesn't come up.

The game about the difference between the warp and the weft in the art of tapestry making… Hey, can we make a tapestry making game? Shit, that one's even *math,* right? [Laughter] But it doesn't come up, just doesn't come up, because our influence set is so small.

Even those areas where we do have control, where we could go in and say, hey let's broaden our set of influences, let's draw from more sources: just look at art styles. The styles that we have are Japanese anime, grey-brown photorealism [laughter] and the cartoons that we loved as kids and still love because we're geeks who won't grow up.

---

[335] Funny enough, wine tasting was exactly the "viral mechanic" that we put into *My Vineyard* later on.

And that pretty much sums up the entire videogame art style.

Why isn't there a fucking pointillist videogame, dammit? Why isn't there an Impressionism renderer? And it's just not there... why has no game gone, visually, where Picasso went? It's not because it doesn't work. Once upon a time, Picasso was shocking. Nowadays, you walk into a generic hotel on the road, and you're just as likely to see something Cubist as you are to see a watercolor landscape. We take it for granted. Everyone knows how to read that now. It's no big deal. But we don't even scratch the surface on these other art styles and influences and sources of inspiration.

We do rhythm games, and we can't fuckin' do melody games. We just don't do them. There are no melody games! We kind of have *Guitar Hero*, but it's really a rhythm game with five drums [chuckles]. We're so caught in this little rut...

The challenge is, I don't have any answers. When I wanted to know what it felt like to flap, you know, it's a little wireframe bird, and up in the corner you get to see all of these floating point variables scooting around, with your angle of the wind and angle of each feather, all swirling by in this haze of numbers. And you know, flying and flapping is not rotation and angle of wing bones and force of air propelled. And yet when we put something into a game, that's what it turns into.

Flapping as math

It's not that there aren't mechanical activities that do just fine in this. Flying a plane is flow of air over the wing and blah blah blah, and we've managed to mimic that pretty thoroughly and well and at this point, it's damn close. We have the sensation of flying in a plane pretty good. But I wonder how we take in all of the influences that are not systemic, taking in the games that reflect non-systemic reality without quantizing it.

You guys know the word "quantize"? The musicians, particularly the ones who work in electronic music in any form will know it. This is where you take the music that you play, and don't quite nail the timing on, and you tell the computer please noodge the notes over by fractions of a second so that everything is lined up with perfect rhythm. That's called quantizing. Fortunately, there is an opposite process which is to take something perfectly played, and noodge the notes slightly out of place so that it doesn't sound like it's being played by a robot... which is called "humanizing." [laughter] That's the pull-down...

One of the questions I end up asking is "Have I been trained?" Games are about learning to my mind, and you learn about models from playing games. You learn to understand that model of what the game is presenting you. That's the learning exercise. What is the shape of the spreadsheet, what are the rows, what are the columns, what are the math operations I can perform on it. That is what games teach you. So I wonder, because I have been playing videogames since I first got that *Pong* console from Sears. Whenever that came out in the mid 70s, one of the knockoff ones. I am of the generation that has been playing videogames, well, since, basically.

Have I been trained them? To only see the world as something that can be quantized? Have I been trained by them to come to *Werewolf* and immediately say, "so the algorithm is...?"

That's a little scary, because there is a big difference between shades of gray and a byte's worth of grayscale. [thoughtful silence] Right? Big big big fucking difference.

When my wife and I were first dating, we were at one of the Apple campuses, when they just got the color Macintoshes. And if you remember that time period, all of a sudden the games had these beautiful color gradients in the background. We would go outside and look at the sunsets over corn fields on the Eastern Shore of Maryland, and we'd say "hey look! Mac colors." [Laughter]

Long ago, the whole Deist philosophy... the metaphor for God was "the watchmaker." And I've started to wonder whether games make the world into clockwork. And whether this is *honest.*

It might be that games, and us as designers of them, we're just filling a role. I mean, there is a huge amount of value in seeing the world as clockwork. A huge huge amount of value. Arguably, it's a very progressive way to look at the world, because it takes out a lot of frankly, stupid shit that has killed millions of people throughout history. Being able to approach the world in this very scientific way and deal with it in terms of algorithms and so on, it can help, because it makes you see the stuff that is just blatant superstition or false pattern matching, or the real reason why two groups hate each will actually be about calories intake and not about religion...

So seeing the world as clockwork and doing those spreadsheets, it's an incredibly valuable exercise. This clockwork world has to be in the picture, along with all the other ways of seeing the world. Our worldview has to become, over time, and it inevitably will, right, like lots of layers in Photoshop making up one picture. We will see the world in many many different ways. And the clockwork way is a very good one, but I sometimes wonder whether we're stuck in our layer, and whether we can participate in the broader side of things.

And when we go to this broader side of things, the world where there is a game about treeness, or the experience of being bark, or whatever artsy-fartsy thing I can come up with – when we bring it back with us, will we always be pixelating it, paletting it, building low-poly versions of reality? Will we always be turning it into something mechanical.

Do a thought experiment right now. Shut your eyes. [Silence]. Good, they're all doing it.

Imagine something that you dream about. A moment of experience. It could be, I dunno, God, laying on your back watching the clouds shake around, it could be the first time that you and your boyfriend or girlfriend, whichever it was or both [laughter] snuck out in the middle of the night and went for making love under the stars. It could be the first time you ever saw the ocean. It could be that moment… you know, I keep pulling nature examples, how Romantic poet of me. But it could be almost anything. The first time you realized that the computer would jump through hoops and do your bidding. Those moments of wonder that Nicole Lazzaro[336] references.

And now here's the thought experiment. Build me the game system right now, in your head. And tell me if that dream didn't just blow to bits.

[silence]

And that's the challenge that I guess I want to leave you guys with. Because it's not that this way of looking at the world is bad. It's not. The challenge that I leave you with is whether or not games are *irredeemably* spreadsheets in this sense. And I don't mean the stories we tack on top of them, the pretty art. Because the art and the stories, we *know* they can do this. The challenge is whether *games can do it on their own*, without being propped up by all this other stuff.

It might be the answer is no, and if it's no, then the question I leave you with is, OK, then, what does that mean? For those of us who make them, are we all watchmakers? OK, watchmaking is a noble profession…

And think about what does that mean for all of the kids whose brains we currently control. That what we're doing is teaching them to see the world as clockwork orreries. And what that means.

That's the challenge I leave you with.

---

[336] See http://www.xeodesign.com/about/

Metaplace

Metaplace

For those who haven't read it, *Ready Player One*[337] is a novel by Ernest Cline that describes a network of virtual spaces running on a common operating system, called OASIS. The story is a fun romp, not too deep, about a kid who is looking for the secret prize hidden in an insane scavenger hunt scenario by the network's creator.

The book is full of geek references. The skillful playing of *Joust* is a key point; so is the ability to recite *Ferris Bueller's Day Off* from memory. But of course, part of what captivates a gamer is the description of OASIS itself: a giant network of virtual spaces, capable of encompassing pretty much every sort of virtual space you might want.

So the article asks, what about building something like that. Well, we did.

Metaplace predated the novel. But really, the book describes basically what we built, and which is now gone. (The tech survives, within Disney, but isn't used in this fashion anymore).[338]

I think many MMORPG fans were barely even aware it existed, because really, it got almost no marketing. And while we were around, people were perpetually confused as to what it was. Frankly, I found it too big an idea to wrap up well in a marketing message.

- a generic server architecture that could handle anything from arcade games to MMOs. Servers ran in the cloud,[339] so it was designed to be really, really scalable. Just keep adding worlds. At the time we closed it, there were tens of thousands of them.

- the ability for players to own and make their own spaces. You didn't even need to know how to make stuff in 3d modeling, it imported SketchUp from Google Warehouse even. You didn't need to host your own art.

---

[337] Broadway Books, 2012.

[338] Several Facebook games were built on the platform, and then it became the backend for the mobile version of *Club Penguin*. Eventually that game was shut down as well.

[339] We actually had to invent our own cloud. Cloud based infrastructure services weren't around until 2002, when Amazon launched AWS.

- scriptable to the point where you could make a whole game in it. The scripting used Lua, which was a barrier for people. We had made moves towards letting people snap together behaviors (drag and drop AI onto something in the world, for example) but probably didn't go far enough.

- full web connectivity in and out, so that you could have stuff from the real world manifest in the games, or game stuff feed out to the web. Like, an MMO where the mobs are driven by stock quotes was easy to make. Or hooking a *Metaplace* world up to, say, Moodle[340] (for education) or having NPCs read their dialogue from external sources. We had one world which performed any Shakespeare play by reading the plays off of a remote server, spawning NPCs for all the parts, and interpreting the stage directions.

- agnostic as far as client, so you could connect lo-fi or full fancy 3d — in theory. We never got to the 3d, but we had clients running on mobile devices, PCs, and in web browsers. If we were still pursuing it, you can bet we'd be doing a VR version right about now.

- worlds connected to one another, and you might change from world to world, but you *also* had a common identity across all the worlds. You could walk from *Pac-Man* into Azeroth,[341] so to speak.

I think a lot of people were turned off by the 2d graphics, and a lot were turned off by the fact that there wasn't a full MMO there to just play, and a lot of people found building too hard. A huge part of why we didn't succeed is that we were too many things to too many different people, and that split our efforts in far too many directions. The result was a tight but small community that never started to really grow.

But if you were ever wondering why something like the *Ready Player One/Snow Crash* style world hasn't been made — well, there it was… open from 2007 to 2009. It saddens me to see it forgotten so quickly, though in many ways it really did end up as just a footnote in virtual world history. I get a lot of "the last thing you did was SWG in 2003" from people who clearly didn't know it existed or weren't interested because it wasn't a hack n slash gameworld.

I might spend the time to dig through some screenshot archives and post up some examples of what got made. I miss that community a lot.

---

[340] Moodle (moodle.org) is a free and open-source platform to enable things like blended classrooms, distance learning, and other approaches that blend computer-based or mediated education with existing educaitonal systems.

[341] Azeroth is the name of the world in *World of Warcraft*.

A MetaHistory

Metaplace came and went fairly quickly. It was founded in mid-2006, at first just by myself and shortly after with John Donham, who had been a colleague at Sony Online ever since the SWG days. It sold to Playdom and thence to Disney by mid 2010,[342] but ceased to exist as a public platform in December of 2009. So its entire lifespan was only a few years, and even less of that was time where users could log in.

I always get asked, "What was Metaplace?" Now that it's long gone, and all the muddled marketing has faded away, I'd say this: it was basically a MUD engine. It was meant to bring that feeling back, to let hobbyists all build on a common platform and cause a creative explosion. And that common platform was meant to be the most powerful virtual world engine ever made.

In 2006, I built the most basic of prototypes: I took MUD code, and used it to embed tags, sort of like HTML but different syntax, into the room descriptions. A dedicated client that I wrote using BlitzMax[343] parsed the tags and displayed graphics based on what the tags said. The graphics were fetched from the Web, just like a browser did. The room would tell you "there is a ball here." And it would tell you "balls look like the picture at this URL." The client basically just used very simple browser code and fetched that picture, and drew it at the location that the tags said. Over time, tags allowed you to change camera perspectives, distort the terrain in real time, see other players, move around, full building tools, and much more. I even had the client running in an ActiveX container, so it could be embedded on a webpage.

With this prototype, I raised money, and landed a couple million dollars in funding. The original pitch decks basically show an interface very much like YouTube: featured content, categories, and search. From the very beginning, then, this was about a vertically integrated system: a platform for the worlds, tools to build them, and a place for players to come find them.

---

[342] Playdom was already in the process of being acquired by Disney when it acquired Metaplace; the two deals closed within a month of one another. As I understand it, aspects of the Disney deal had to be modified, in fact, in order to make the Metaplace acquisition possible.
[343] A now-abandoned BASIC variant created by Mark Sibly.

Early feature ideas which are in my notes show an emphasis on being able to bring in content from many other platforms and systems, and unify them:[344]

- Import Diku-derived area files automatically and turn them into connected spaces ready for building in.
- Import Sims art and building layouts?
- Be able to set instance capacity all the way down to 1, so you can make single-player games.
- Import 3d models and chop them up into tile-based content. SketchUp?
- Launch with full world of seeded DEM data.
- Import UO maps from gray shards. Backwards compatibility with UO gray shard tools? Can we do their scripts too?
- Need YouTube, Pandora, Shoutcast, streaming music, VoIP, Google Video, etc, to work seamlessly.
- Render webpage to a surface/tile/window

It took a while, but I persuaded John to join me, and by January of 2007 we had found office space and were recruiting a team.

---

[344] We did eventually do many of these, but none of the ones that slurped in game content.

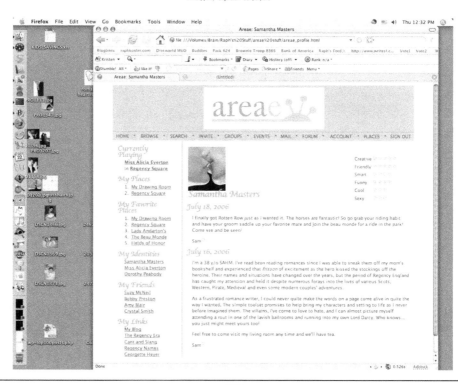

1,246,713 registered members... 23,644 worlds... 34,221 users online right now.

Login [   ]
Password [   ]

Featured worlds

1534 people online

353 people online

27 people online

Popular worlds

1. PenguinQuest
2. Regency Square
3. Casablanca
4. Lands of Despair
5. Space Colony 5
6. Buffyverse
7. 1950s Americana
8. The Hot Java Bean Cafe
9. Fred's World
10. Mystery House

Search worlds by tag
[   ] Go!

Search for a username
[   ] Go!

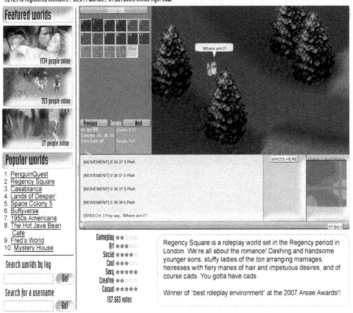

[MOVEMENT] 0 36 37 0 Ptah

[MOVEMENT] 0 35 37 0 Ptah

[MOVEMENT] 0 36 37 0 Ptah

[MOVEMENT] 0 36 38 0 Ptah

[SPEECH] You say, "Where am I?"

WHO'S HERE

Gameplay ★★☆☆☆
Art ★★★★☆
Social ★★★★☆
Cool ★★★☆☆
Sexy ★★★★★
Creative ★★☆☆☆
Casual ★★★★★
157,663 votes

Regency Square is a roleplay world set in the Regency period in London. We're all about the romance! Dashing and handsome younger sons, stuffy ladies of the *ton* arranging marriages, heiresses with fiery manes of hair and impetuous desires, and of course cads. You gotta have cads.

Winner of "best roleplay environment" at the 2007 Areae Awards!!

Privacy policy * Legal stuff * Company info

Login [   ]
Password [   ]

1,246,713 registered members... 23,644 worlds... 34,221 users online right now.

Featured worlds

1534 people online

353 people online

27 people online

Popular worlds

1. PenguinQuest
2. Regency Square
3. Casablanca
4. Lands of Despair
5. Space Colony 5
6. Buffyverse
7. 1950s Americana
8. The Hot Java Bean Cafe
9. Fred's World
10. Mystery House

Search worlds by tag
[   ] Go!

Search for a username
[   ] Go!

Find worlds by category

Game worlds

RPG	Action
Fantasy	Adventure
Science fiction	Shooter
Horror	Sports
Historical	Arcade

Strategy	Casual
Turn-based	Word
Real-time	Puzzle
	Card

Social worlds

Roleplaying	Chat
Fantasy	Hangouts
Science fiction	Music
Historical	venues
Romance	Book clubs
Contemporary	Home and
Goth	family
Furry	College
	School

Other worlds

Shops	Sponsored
Clothing	Movies
Furniture	Bands
Scripts	Stores
Malls	Restaurants

Educational	Professional
Schools	Meetings
Workshops	Lectures
Religious	

Find worlds by tag

2d, 3d, Adult, Alternative, B-52's, Bay Area, Beatles, Book reading, Books, Buffy, Cars, Cartoon, Catholic, China, Class-based, Classless, Clothes, Coldplay, Cooking, Cool, Dark, Death metal, Denmark, Disco, DJ, Ducks, Elves, Firefly, France, Freshmen, Frisco, Fun, Funny, Furniture, Furry, Geek, Goth, Humor, Italian, J Crew, Japan, Junior, K-12, Kids, Korea, LA, Mall, Mexican, Middle ages, MIT, MUD, Nature, New age, New wave, Ninjas, Nordstrom's, NYC, Old Navy, Orcs, Owls, Parenting, Parks, Penguins, Photos, Pirates, Pizza, Princeton, Punk, Puzzle, Puzzle games, PvE, PvP, Retro, Rock, Romantic, RvR, Scary, Senior, SF, Shooter, Shopping, Sophomore, Star trek, Superhero, Sushi, Tech, Tenacious D, Tetris, The Gap, Trance, U2, UO, USC, Vampires, Vietnamese, Vintage, Wizards, Word games, Worldbuilding 101, WWII, Zombies

Privacy policy * Legal stuff * Company info

We worked through most of 2007 building basic technology, a half dozen of us all in a pretty small office. The early team was intentionally a mix of skillsets, with art, client, server, community and web people. I kept maintaining my client while a real server was written and while we built multiple different clients in different languages.

The beauty of the tag system, you see, is that you could write as many clients as you wanted, on whatever platforms you wanted. You could draw the same world in different ways, if your client happened to handle a given tag differently. You might even offer up text descriptions like "A ball is here" and not draw pictures at all. This meant that you could put a Metaplace virtual world client on anything from a cell phone — bear in mind we were in the very earliest days of smartphones and there were no App Stores yet — all the way up to running a really nice 3d engine on a PC.

The most accessible way to put graphics on webpages at the time was Flash. Gradually we converged on that as our primary client platform. By January of 2008, one year later, we were in alpha and ready to do a basic unveiling. We ran a live chat[345]

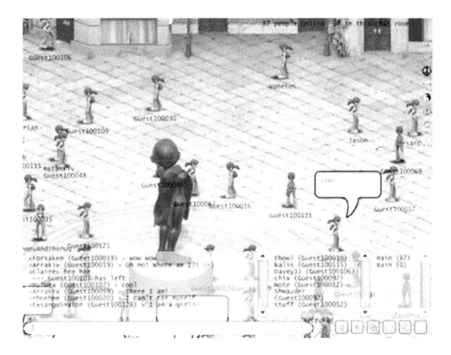

---

[345] Coverage of this chat can be seen at
https://web.archive.org/web/20080201225058/http://www.massively.com/2008/01/31/metaplace-live-developer-chat-today/

that looked just like a plain text chat window, and got around 80 people to show up and ask us questions. Part way through the chat, we updated a script on the fly and collapsed the chat window to reveal a small graphical world hidden behind it. Every player suddenly had an avatar (but they all looked the same) and could walk around one single room.

In that chat we promised that users could make money from their worlds, charging people for playing them. That creators could share modules, basically exactly like Unity plug-ins today, and charge for those too. That they could make single-player or multiplayer worlds, on the same platform. That all the varying worlds could look

completely different, play completely differently, and yet all exist in one connected network.

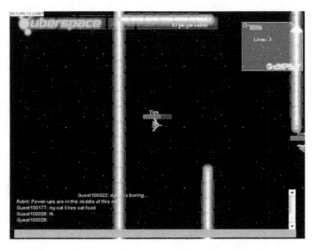

Many of these things were working already. In one of the great ironies of online game history, the very first game I had made on the platform was a farming game.[346] We had already built a single-player *Tetris* clone. We were well along on a multiplayer space shooter called *Uberspace*, in the vein of games like *Subspace* and *Cosmic Rift*.[347] We had made various sorts of 2d isometric spaces, overhead view spaces, and some of them made use of 3d terrain.

In an interview before the chat,[348] I described just the tiniest bit of what some testers were already doing:

> *From your alpha so far, I've read that you're already shocked with what people are building. Can you give me an anecdote or example?*

---

[346] It was called "Doomgarden," and you played a little fairy who had to stomp bugs while planting seeds and trying to get plants to grow. So it was a tad more action-based than *Farmville*. But *Star Wars Galaxies* had already done the asynchronous farming thing.

[347] These were 2d overhead spaceship combat games where you flew around in an arena and shot at each other. See https://en.wikipedia.org/wiki/SubSpace_(video_game) and https://en.wikipedia.org/wiki/Cosmic_Rift

[348] http://www.escapistmagazine.com/articles/view/video-games/issues/issue_134/2872-Raph-Koster-The-Escapist-Interview

RK: People are just doing crazy stuff. We've got a chat world, it literally looks like an IRC world. We have one tester who has added automatic language translation to it, using Google translate and the like. It happens transparently and automatically. When I think about the amount of effort we go to put that stuff into a commercial project, and to have an alpha tester add it in live a day and a half, it blew my mind.

In that same interview, one of the core questions that would dog the platform during its entire existence came up.

TE: One argument some professional game developers have against user content is that it is simply not as good as professional content. How do you react to that?

RK: The answer is yes, because all professional game developers were once users. It's not like some magic switch gets flicked the minute that they become a pro that makes their stuff good, and we've all played pro stuff that wasn't that good. There's just a spectrum, from good to bad, and whether or not people are pro or amateur has nothing to do with that quality line. The pros tend to get access to money and the good guys tend to gravitate toward being pros, but it doesn't mean that an amateur cannot make good content. Maybe they're just a hobbyist, maybe they've never had tools that were good enough, maybe they've never been given a chance. There's plenty of examples of this sitting out there.

My answer, as it turns out, was wrong. While many testers were in fact making cool things like the translation tool, that was a far cry from what was needed in terms of mass market content that was instantly playable. And with hindsight, that's what we needed above all: a kick-ass sample product that had gone through all the development challenges inherent in building some of large scale. Something that players could come to and just *play*, to build a paying audience.

During this time period we got a lot of attention from possible partners. Major media companies that you would recognize the names of offered us deals. More than once, there was a check for multiple millions of dollars just sitting there for the taking, and we didn't take it, because of internal conflicts over what sort of company we were.

We had raised the money on the basis of being a user-generated-content platform for end users to make worlds, at a time when the investment community was on fire for virtual worlds, and on fire over the entire social web. But the inbound interest that actually offered money was for very different things. One was building whole worlds for third party brands, as a white-label shop. Under this model, we would be paid to build and operate a world for a brand, and along the way we would retain ownership of the underlying platform, so we could go and keep doing what we were doing. To the outside world, it would look like the brand had done it standalone; it wouldn't be part of the connected Metaplace universe.

The other big thing that kept coming up was an approach more like a professional tools suite. Think Unity or the Unreal Engine, but for virtual worlds, with no user-facing component at all. Tools were not a sexy investment, as far as VCs of the time were concerned, but we had plenty of inbound interest from professional developers. The problem was that our tools were being designed for end users. We made tentative efforts towards supporting this use case, even hiring dedicated staff for pro support, but nothing much came of it. A real pro tool strategy would have required re-orienting the company.

These things, however, also left us on the horns of one more dilemma: how much showcase content should we make internally? And again, the company leadership was split. The concern was that if we started making our own MMO on the platform, we wouldn't then be working to empower users. Instead, we should only make small dribs and drabs of content, and rely on the rising tide of user creativity to populate the network. Under this logic, awesome users would make a quality MMO or quality smaller games, and players would show up for those.

But the people who could build those sorts of spaces needed the pro tools we weren't making. And the players needed our internal stuff to build on, and we weren't making that either. Instead, we kept making iterations of tools for end users, and kept failing to meet either constituency's needs. We had always had the expectation that major brands would be a powerful growth engine for us, as some worlds would be branded and some would be built by users… but in practice, all the brands wanted to be apart from the network. We didn't have the scale to force big brands down to the equivalent of a Facebook page; neither did Facebook, yet.

By March, we were watching the developments on social networks with great interest. MySpace was already quite popular, and Facebook was a fledgling competitor. That said, forums were still the dominant mode for asynchronous community formation on the Internet. We hatched a plan to make Metaplace worlds embeddable on forums, a sort of replacement for the "shoutboxes" that were commonly seen at the time. (These were real-time updating boxes on the sidebar of forums, where people could chat). By March of 2008, we had launched what we called *Metachat*: graphical chat rooms as apps on MySpace and Facebook as well as forums. This was actually a cross-service chat system: Facebookers could see MySpace people and vice versa, and play games and hang out with one another.[349]

This actually connects to the same chat world as the one on MySpace, and the

---

[349] https://www.raphkoster.com/2008/03/27/metachat-is-on-facebook-now-too/

one on our forums. So it's all one big happy cross-SNS virtual worldlet in Flash.

We also got a bunch of forums interested in trying to integrate a *Metaplace* world on their forums… it'll be one based on *Metachat* to start with, though it can of course change later. It'll be their own world, though.

Last time I mentioned this little app on here, people challenged the question of whether it was actually a world or not.

Well, it supports hundreds to thousands, there's physics, a sense of place and space, you can kick a soccer ball, interact in real time… the background could scroll, and you could have avatars instead of profile pics. So… close enough, to my mind. :)

Metachat supported a concept of toys you could add to the room; small pianos you could click on and play melodies with, soccer balls you could actually kick around the space. These were earned by inviting people into the system. But there were other social chat apps starting to thrive on Facebook, and they were almost all just about dating. We never got critical mass.

As usual, our attention shifted. We had at that point, the highest quality web game engine, bar none, on the entire Internet. Instead of focusing on the fledgling social network market, where the best games of the day were simple viral things like *Zombies*, we drifted back towards the standalone website after *Metachat* didn't really gain traction. The idea of launching actual games on Facebook would have required us to embrace the idea of being a games studio, rather than a social media company, and so we didn't do it.

We had committed to building a social network of worlds, finally laying to rest the competing desires to be a game studio, a tools company, or a white-label development house. We launched at TechCrunch40, a tech showcase conference, where we won the Audience Award but lost out on the actual prize due to skepticism that we could dethrone *Second Life*. We came prepared with a brochure to try to explain the muddled product.

The virtual world space was still hot, and the excitement still high. As we moved towards beta by late 2008, we were able to announce at GDC Austin that the site would use a version of the Rights of Avatars[350] as a model for its TOS, granting users rights over freedom of speech, freedom to conduct commerce, IP ownership, privacy, and much more. The early users were doing things like trying out the client on an actual smartphone — early ones allowed you to run Flash apps — so you could actually connect to a virtual world from your pocket.

Company advisor and virtual world pioneer Randy Farmer had been warning me

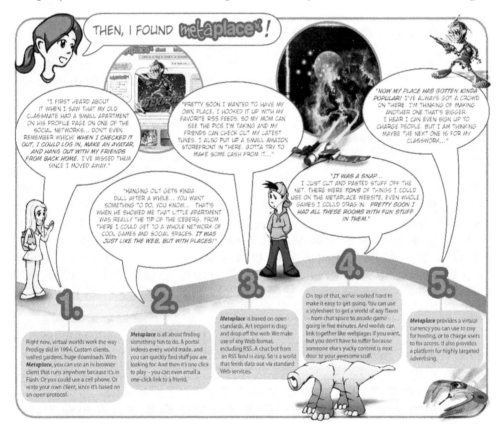

that he didn't like movements in the bond markets. "Raise as much as they will give you," he advised. I vividly recall being in the car with other company leaders as we made the rounds of venture capitalists, as I relayed Randy's advice. Their take was that we didn't need to give up more equity, and the space was hot. We didn't take Randy's advice, and raised around $6.4m more, rather than what we could have. This would prove to be a fatal mistake.

---

[350] See https://www.raphkoster.com/games/essays/declaring-the-rights-of-players/

Less than a month later, I flew to London to speak at the Virtual Worlds Forum. I woke up in my hotel and learned that the stock market had crashed. All fundraising had dried up in the market panic. We immediately laid off half the company, but the fact was that what we had thought was plenty of runway wasn't. If doing the network of social worlds didn't work, we were not going to have enough cash to try anything else.

We had a year to show profitability, and Metaplace was now committed by simply not having committed strongly sooner: it was a site where users came to hang out in a social world with mini-games, and build their own small worlds in the form of apartments, and some mini-games. Tools were scaled for end users, not professionals. It wasn't a place you could port MUDs to; no large-scale game systems had been built for users to leverage. No major brands were on board. There was no central big game to hook users. And social networks were about to grow explosively and prove that you didn't need any graphics, avatars, or virtual apartments to hold users. We hadn't even made the leap to 3d on the web yet, because there wasn't viable technology for it.

We were sitting on the most powerful networked world technology ever built, but users thought *World of Warcraft* was more fun, *Second Life* was more creative, Flash an easier development platform, and Facebook more social. We were an amazing platform with no killer app.

We were already screwed, even though Metaplace's golden age as a community was yet to come.

Original Metaplace one-sheets

User Experience

Welcome to the Areae network!

You probably heard about it because your friend turned you on to a cool new MMORPG: something about battling cyberninja squirrels, or something. You checked it out – **it was free, and it ran right in your browser**, so there was no barrier to entry at all. Pretty soon rodents were falling to your laser sword left and right.

Then one day your friend told you, "I'm sick of killing squirrels. Let's go hang out in my apartment instead." To your surprise, he tossed a portable hole on the ground and you went through a doorway to come out in a very different looking place: Chinatown in San Francisco! Your avatars are different, the art's different, the camera angle's different: it's *all* different. He shows you **how easy it is to build**: drag-and-drop, just like *The Sims*.

"All you have to do is join," he told you. "Then you can have your apartment too! Plus you can grab scripts off the marketplace and customize it any way you want. Check it out, I made my doorbell into an electric shock buzzer!" Gee, thanks.

It's not long before you have your own apartment, a bunch of custom Lua scripts running, and the makers of cyberninja squirrel land are asking you to help them make their game bigger. But **you're dreaming of something new** – now's your chance to make that realistic World War II game you've always dreamed about...

It's about the FUN

The user content pyramid
Most users are consumers of content; you're looking for something to do, not looking to make your own fun. But Areae lets you grow into a content creator using a suite of tools designed for ease of use.

So many of the social virtual worlds out there are about nothing at all. A couple of them let you build, but most of them just have you stand around chatting and changing clothes. Within the Areae network, however, you can do *anything*. **All the worlds link together, and every one can be completely different**: you've got virtual apartments for decorating, plazas where readings and musical events happen, full-blown MMORPGs, casual games – you name it. It's up to you, really, because all the tools are open for you to use!

Unlike those other worlds, Areae doesn't assume that you want to build something in order to have a good time. And we figure, doing something is always better than standing around *talking* about doing something.

Even better, once you find something you enjoy, it's easy to share it with others. You can **stick a whole game client in a widget** on your MySpace page, if you want. You can put lists of your favorite worlds in your profile. You can even hand people an ordinary web URL or bookmark and have it take them straight to the world you like, without having to register or hand over any personal information.

A whole lot of worlds to visit...!

It's always easy to find stuff to do within the network, because there's **a portal site**. It works a lot like a social network: every world has its own page, with ratings, friends, descriptions, even a blog to keep that world's users up to date on the latest goings-on. If it's your own world, you can track metrics, like how many people visit it and when, and how popular the world is.

If you're looking for a given sort of world, you can search by category – everything from RPGs to shops, from casual games to book clubs – or by the user-entered tags, which give a whole different view of the choices offered. There's also featured worlds, lists of popular worlds, a "fresh" list for you to see the newest things people have added... you can even subscribe to this stuff as an RSS feed if you want! As a registered user, **you even get your own profile page**, which could be on MySpace or Facebook or anywhere else you want.

Areae, Inc.
11770 Bernardo Plaza Court, Suite 101
San Diego, CA 92128

T: 858 451 2700
F: 858 451 2722
http://www.areae.net

Building a world

Why is it so hard to make content in these other virtual worlds? They make you learn 3d modeling and custom languages – if they let you build at all. Not here: instead, it's as easy as we can make it:

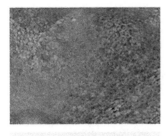

You can use photos as textures if you want – or even an RSS feed, to stick your website on a wall!

- **Drag and drop art from the web.** If you can reach it in a browser, the clients can reach it too. They speak all the common web formats: PNG, JPG, GIF, BMP, and so on. There are huge amounts of license-free artwork out there that you can use to build your world, and we also have a library of our own that we're happy to let you use. Or, if you really want to dazzle us, make your own art in whatever tools you prefer, and upload it!

- **Tile-based building** makes editing a world a snap! Just like in *The Sims* or all those *Tycoon* games, you just drag and drop things into place, and they snap together. You can scale stuff, offset it within the tile, tint it, and set properties like whether or not people can walk through it, walk on it, or stack stuff on top of it. The engine supports true 3d spaces, so you can build multi-story buildings just by putting one floor on top of another.

- **A segmented world** means that you don't have to worry about someone else's horrible stuff being next to your wonderful work of art. You can even have rooms within your world, so you can replicate the old-style MUD vibe, or have separate building interiors like a Japanese-style RPG. Each room can even have its own physics: make one world that's a sidescrolling platformer, and another that's a first-person game!

- **Scripting and stylesheets** make it easy for you to customize the way your world feels. Just start with a stylesheet, maybe do a few tweaks, and you have a game out of the box – just like starting with a theme on a blog. Just add your own art – or inherit someone else's art set – and you could be up and running really quickly. Alternatively, if you want to really get into the nitty-gritty of design, you can use the industry-standard Lua scripting language to change behaviors of objects or even whole game systems. This is the same language used in scripting *World of Warcraft*'s user interface, and in countless other games.

Run anywhere

Part of what you're defining when you make a world is how it looks. **Areae clients can run on anything from a cell phone to a tricked-out gaming PC.** You get to decide what you want players to see, based on what sort of world you are making.

On the Web, you can use a Flash client that will run just on just about anyone's machine. Or you can say that your world requires one of the downloadable clients that gives you all the latest graphical bells and whistles. Clients can also fall back, so people on completely different clients can get their own views of the same world.

The power is in your hands...

Where did the Metaplace idea come from?

This essay was written to the early testers of the platform, to explain to them where the idea had come from.

I came from the world of muds. That means I got my start in virtual worlds in the days when anyone could download a codebase, and assuming they had a server they could get going and dive into running a world of their own.

That went away with the big MMORPGs. But when we did *UO: The Second Age*, there had already been a movement among players towards having "grey shard" server emulators. Some of the tools users had made to hack the UO datafiles were actually better than the tools we had in-house.

So I informally floated an idea for the expansion that didn't go anywhere. Why not release the game server as a binary, release documentation for our scripting language (which was fantastic for the time), release our tools client, and let people make their own worlds?

We could then add red moongates as a housing object you could place in the main UO shards — red moongates in Ultima lore were the moongates that traveled from world to world.

The red moongates would reconnect you to the player-run server, and would do a one-way copy of your player data - so you could move your character from the official servers outwards, but never bring back stuff from player servers.

As I recall, part of the reason that my informal proposal (I never pitched it formally) didn't go anywhere was that old bugaboo, legal concerns. There were worries about company image ("what if we link to a porn world?") and about copyright ("what if we link to a world that is an IP violation?"). The web was new enough that the premise of "we're selling Apache and a browser" weren't really something people "got" right off the bat.

Today, I think back to that idea as the genesis of the idea for Metaplace. It doesn't much resemble what we ended up with, except in the broadest strokes, of course. But it was 1998, before Bioware's *Neverwinter Nights*, and before grey shards went on to garner tens of thousands of users. I still wonder what the MMO landscape might look like today if there had been enthusiasm around the idea. For example, would a 3d client have been developed for UO? There were functional prototypes out there back then, and if there had been explicit support, what might have happened?

Every few years, I would revisit the concept. For a while, I was toying with the idea of an MMO that used the actual web as the playfield. The idea was that we would procedurally generate rooms based on the assets from a webpage, then show you the other people there. Today we have stuff like PMOG[351] which does this without the heavy 3d client I had envisioned.

While at SOE, I did work on a concept that was another take on the idea of user-built worlds, called *Tapestry* — again, with heavy 3d, etc. It would have cost tens of millions, I bet. But also while at SOE, I was going to lots of web conferences. Going to ETech, Web 2.0, and Supernova all in the space of a few months was like having the top of my head taken off and all sorts of new stuff poured in. I came back full of enthusiasm for web ways of doing things — especially as regards how the tech was evolving.

After leaving SOE, I decided to actually try some of those things. I did the first prototype of Metaplace in my spare bedroom, by myself. I prototyped against — yep! — a mud server. I hand coded the tags into the room descriptions. In the space of two weeks, I had gotten simple overhead grids, textures fetched via HTTP from the web, and of course I had all the mud infrastructure for multiplayer there already. In another few weeks, it had the tag language, it had a mess of worldbuilding tools, it had graphical assets hooked up to objects in the world, the model of the thin dumb client was set, and it handled all the way up to 3d heightfields. Oh, and I had put the client in an ActiveX plugin so that you could play via the web.

That's how Metaplace was born. The next step was getting money and a team. Oh, just about everything has changed in it since — having real programmers write your tech is a wise idea — but I still have the descendant of that old client, and it can still connect and play a Metaplace world.

---

[351] PMOG was later renamed *The Nethernet*, and was a massively multiplayer game you played just by visiting webpages. It ran as a browser plugin atop the Firefox browser.

Reinventing MMOs

This is adapted from a presentation given by myself and Sean Riley (lead programmer at Metaplace) at GDC in 2008.

Why reinvent MMOs?

Because currently, making MMO's kind of sucks.

It's kind of like pushing a 2000 ton boulder uphill. Each one of them is like a custom-crafted moon shoot. Worse, you are building every little piece, by hand, from scratch, every time.

And on top of that, they kind of work like Prodigy. We haven't had reinventions, at a fundamental technical level, in MMO architecture, since basically 1978. They just haven't changed that much, and so we are making MUD203 instead of MUD2, a hypertrophied version.

We all know the consequences of this. They are getting insanely expensive to build. Speaking in terms of traditional MMORPGs anyway — there's lots of cool stuff being done on the Web, such as what Gene Endrody is doing in his basement[352]. He made a 1.8m user MMO in his basement; but for the mainstream industry, it's gotten insanely hard. Plus most of us are not Gene. High costs means that only large companies can play in the space. When it costs tens of millions to try out something in the space, it becomes the province of large corporations.

The other problem with something that expensive is that you have to get it perfect. There's no room for incremental growth in response to an audience. If you launch badly, it's all over. As Gordon Walton used to say, making an MMO is piling up $5 million and setting it on fire. Except these days it's piling up $30m, $40m, $50m, and setting it on fire.

The result is then reinventing the wheel, which means that a huge amount of the money spent goes towards chat system #207, replicating past work.

All of these things lead to publisher pressure and a lack of innovation. Because of the risks, publishers and money people demand that the game follow a proven model,

---

[352] *Sherwood Dungeon,* done in Shockwave.

which means "make it like *World of Warcraft*..."

If we look at how MMOs work today, they are really complicated. They are big, tightly integrated, basically giant servers, effectively monolithic even though they are built out of many interoperating processes. All the services are contained within the server complex, and they *are* complex — complex server cluster architectures. Lastly, there's a tight dependency between the client and the server.

It's hard to think of re-uses of MMO server technology. *Lineage 1* to *Lineage 2*. *Dark Age of Camelot* was actually built on top of an older MUD server.

As technology has advanced some of the constraints that we used to have have been relaxed. We no longer have to tightly couple the client and the server and hand-tune binary packets for the networking, for example, like we had to do for FPS games fifteen years ago. There's room to add flexibility.

If we take a trip down memory lane, back in the MUD days we had a client, which was Telnet, and you had a server, which had rooms, you could talk, and eventually you could save your game. The client was one entity, and it spoke directly to a server, which was also one process. That one piece of code handled spatial simulation, chat, persistence, and the game logic, all in one self-contained server. That's not really what it looks like today.

Driven by the needs of scale, in a modern multiserver MMO architecture, you have a multiplexing user architecture to manage large numbers of users, then those multiplex back out to world servers that each manage portions of the map for clusters of users. You have the static database and runtime persistence database, you often have to run a chat server that cuts across all these processes, and with all these processes you need a process manager to make sure they are all running... It's not unusual to have a list like this:

- User servers that manage user connections
- World servers that simulate space
- A static database of source data for the game
- A runtime database server for persistence
- A separate chat server
- A separate authentication system on the web
- A patching server for handling game updates
- A server system just for real-money-trade and marketplace functionality
- A separate server of "armory" or game metadata
- A web bridge of some sort just to talk to some of the preceding

…And then much of this might well be replicated for every shard!

The interesting thing is, we're trying to solve a distributed multiuser computing problem. And somebody already built something that does all of this, that is cheap, scales enormously, manages to be pretty future-proof, and all of you use it every day. The Web.

This is why the web works today. Each one of these pieces is indispensable:

- There is an open markup language, HTML. This means that anyone can write a browser. The original Mozilla codebase became the reference browser for everything.

- There is Apache, or other web servers.[353] A web server really doesn't make many assumptions about what sort of web content you are going to serve up. If it did, the web would be much narrower in focus. You might need a different server to serve up a blog versus Amazon — but instead, they run on substantially the same standards.

- The server supports extensions to its behavior via CGI, PHP scripts, and so on.[354] These are behavior plugins for the server, basically, attached to specific content.

- The Web is reskinnable, using CSS and stylesheets. It's easy to make templated content.

- The Internet as a whole is distributed and segmented, which is quite different from how we run MMOs. We aren't still running every webpage from CERN in Switzerland.[355] A single website also does not try to hold the entire Internet, unlike what we do with an MMO.

- All of this richness wouldn't be of much use if you couldn't find anything, which is why we have Google and other search engines, including content-type specific sites like YouTube. These help you locate what you want.

The question is, if you were trying to make an MMO that got you these benefits, what would it look like? Instead of the huge table of complex relationships that a current multiserver cluster looks like, we think it looks like something much simpler: A client that talks to a server or to the web; and a server that talks to a client or the web; and the web can talk to either one. When we architected this, we consciously

---

[353] Back then, Apache accounted for 70% of all web servers. Today, newer servers have taken huge chunks of the market.

[354] Today, Javascript. And of course, before PHP, Perl.

[355] The first website went live in 1991, hosted on a machine at CERN (the European Organization for Nuclear Research), and made by Tim Berners-Lee.

went back to the web architecture and copied each of those steps.

This does mean that we have a core philosophical difference with many of the MMO server architectures out there. I means that, apologies to Neal Stephenson, we think that *Snow Crash* is a lie.

When you look at the whole Web, the idea of cramming all of it into one world is starting to look not just silly, but pointless. We like using our iPhones to get directions while in downtown San Francisco. The idea of having to log into a virtual world and *walking inside that world to get to where the virtual map is* seems ridiculous. Virtual worlds do offer something new compared to webpages, but we are heading for a future where virtual worlds are first-class citizens on the web right next to movies, streaming audio, pictures, and text. They will be just another kind of media.

That's sort of *Snow Crash* flipped inside out. Instead of putting the web inside a virtual world, you put virtual worlds all over the web, adding synchronous realtime multiuser capabilities everywhere. That's something that the game industry can bring to the table, something that the web doesn't know how to do but wants to do.

Metaplace actually does work the way the web does. For example, if we type in French, in real-time we can take the text chat, and the server can feed it via a standard web service out to Babelfish, and get the translation, and then feed it back to the client. The code that did that on the server is written is just the scripting language — we use Lua. It's just a script. And this holds true for any sort of web integration you want. We wrote a script that lets us search YouTube for the top videos, and the server can reach out, get that list, and when we select one, the client is told to open a window and play that video direct from the URL.

You can of course access all sorts of asynchronous webservices this way using a browser. Stock quotes, what have you. But with this coming from the *Metaplace* server, you can integrate all that into a real-time game environment. If you wanted your monster AI to be driven by the movement of the stock market, you could do that.

On the flip side, a *Metaplace* server *is* a web server. Every object has a URL, and you can browse to it using a standard web browser, without logging in at all. Or, you could log into the world and see it displayed in the world instead. This is the difference between seeing a character on screen, and being able to pull up that character's stats from a webpage anytime you like. You could even pull up a feed of what that character sees. Or that object could instead consume any service on the Internet, and your character could speak the words from a webpage when clicked, or just when walking around.

Just to bend reality a little bit more, any server can also be a *client* of another world. This means a whole game server could log into another server *effectively as a player*.

This lets you do classic multiserver behaviors like mirroring along boundaries between servers, or interesting forms of cross-server communication.

Like a web browser, what we are building makes no assumptions about what the world looks like. We can put you in one world which is an apartment in isometric view, with avatars. And we can put you in another which looks like a standard grid-style puzzle game, with no avatars in sight, and a cursor to rotate blocks. As far as the server is concerned, you have a coordinate space, you have objects, they are drawn with images that live at an arbitrary URL... it just tells the client, "draw those things in an isometric view from this camera angle," or "draw this from overhead." So you can make a single-player puzzle game that happens to have MMO chat over on the side, and have a limit of one player per room, effectively creating an instance per player.

In other words, we are trying to be client-agnostic. What you see is in fact driven just by a markup language, just like a browser is driven by HTML. And we are opening that standard so that anyone can write a client in whatever language you like — we will publish the core classes and the specification, so that you can write a *Metaplace* client on any platform whatsoever.

If we click on a link within the world, it's going to give you the option to follow the link, just like a webpage does, and the client will just load into a new world. As new art streams in, it is actually just being fetched by HTTP, exactly the same way a browser does it. There is no custom fancy streaming technology involved. The client *is* a browser, as far as web servers out there in a world are concerned. Importing a piece of art into *Metaplace* consists of pasting in the URL for the image. Possibly from Google Image search.

Let's say that link takes us to a 2d space combat game. What's happened is that the client discards its old list of objects, and with them, the list of URLs where the images come from. The new server it has connected to behind the scenes sends down the list list. The space combat game has different needs than the puzzle game; it needs a basic 2d physics system. The server does have one of those built in, and there are a variety of other basic capabilities that are always available to you in a *Metaplace* world.

All of these examples to date use 2d graphics. But the architecture of this is designed to scale down to *only text*, or up to 3d. It's representation-agnostic. You could make a client that was feeding out just RSS. Or a client that lived just in an ad banner. You could make a full-screen client, perhaps in OpenGL, native on a PC.

Every *Metaplace* world exists in a network; you can walk from one to another if they are linked. This network provides social infrastructure. You can have a friends list like in social networking systems, and even get presence feeds from friends anywhere in the network; click on the feed entry and you can be teleported directly to where they are, wherever on the Internet that server happens to be. You could, for example, put your own world browsing history on Feedburner, and people could follow a feed of where you have been. Every user gets an identity profile page that other users can visit.

Every world also gets its own profile page, with metrics, tags, ratings, a wiki, and so on. All of the things we expect on the web these days. This lets you search, categorize, and decide which worlds to visit. World admins can use this page as a central community site for managing their own communities.

So where is it going?

We don't often get to do certain things in the game industry. We don't often get to iterate and prototype. We don't often get to decouple components, avoid early optimization, use what already exists, or even start simple. And we started from crazy simple, iterating over and over again. We began with a client in BASIC, with flat text files for worlds and persistence, with a vanilla TCP socket. It's been interesting to see how our web developers think we are moving very slowly, and our game people think we are moving very quickly. They have a different perspective on development pace because web time and game dev time are very different.

By separating out all these components, we can iterate on them individually and very quickly. A good example of this is that bottom layer, the markup language. We started in my spare bedroom working against a text MUD server, handwriting tags into the static text files. The tag structure started out very rigid, because we wanted to be able to just use string splitting for parsing; we used pipes (the "|" character) as a delimiter between fields. Pretty soon we are moving to supporting multiple formats for tags, such as binary, XML, or JSON. We currently support ours with the pipes, which we call GML, Game Markup Language. It can represent that puzzle game, that virtual apartment, and that space game. It looks like

```
[OBJHERE]|x|y|z|moving this way|facing that way etc.
```

It doesn't even know what the object looks like or what the client might do with the knowledge that the object is there. One client might draw it, another might just display a line of text, because that might be all it has the capability for.

We now have a cool XML schema system, which is metadata to describe the protocol. Clients can fetch the XML schema, use it to conform to the standard, and even do code generation to generate all the code required to deal with all the packets and tags. It's an accelerating tool for developers writing clients, a way to tell the client, "here's the language we use to communicate," and the client can build a dynamic dictionary of that, so if the protocol changes, the client just knows. It doesn't need to be patched and have its networking broken. And because it's a schema, a structure, it can be easily reformatted into other languages, other protocols. Our web tools take the same tag stream as a game client, but instead of using GML they take it in bog-standard XML, via a web service. Using this, we have a tool suite built in Javascript for editing worlds. Clients might only process a small subset of the possible tags — the regular play client, for example, doesn't understand any of the tags related to world editing. A very simple client might just wait for a tiny set of tags, maybe to give you notifications, or to log in with to do load testing.

It has been incredibly efficient for us. We've been able to basically never break the network stream. It has been very common in MMO development to have to worry about patching the client and the server at the same time, ensure that everybody is consistent, it leads to hours of downtime... when a tag reaches our client, if the client doesn't know what it is, it just ignores it.

The result is that I'd conservatively estimate our iteration speed for feature addition to be around ten times faster than what I am used to in the MMO world previously. If you want to add server and client support for, say, a particle system, you just sit at your client and echo tags back to yourself until your system works. Then you can put those tags in to be generated by the server.

The lesson here is that these days, we don't need to be incredibly obsessive about precisely tuned byte-packed binary packets. You can connect to a *Metaplace* server with Telnet, and it will work. That's radical democratization. The Internet itself still runs on standard TCP sockets underneath, after all; you can Telnet to a webserver, and manually type in a request for a webpage, and sent back the plain text HTML.

I realize all this sounds very geeky. But if all you want to do is just make something, you don't need to know any of this.

I actually wrote the first *Metaplace* client in a variant of BASIC. I get very lost with modern OS-level programming, the default windows classes and APIs and all the rest. BASIC was my first language back in 1983 or something. We are now starting on our *fifth* client in house (we did BASIC, then Flash, then C++, then a new Flash client, and now the XML-based one). In the last three weeks, there have even been two player testers who have written clients. The key lesson here is that the reason why clients are so hard to make right now is that one, we pack them full of graphics; and two, we try to make them really smart, to optimize. But why does a client need to be really smart? Why can't it be as simple as Telnet was, really stupid?

The benefit of it being stupid is that you can write it on anything. A set-top box. A phone. If Ray Kurzweil is to be believed, you can put it on implants in your contact lenses. As long as it has some processing power! Our minimum requirement is that you need HTTPS, you need MD5 for hashing, and you need a TCP socket. And maybe some way to convey what is going on to users… you could write a *Metaplace* client that output everything as MIDI, if you wanted! It wouldn't be very playable, but you could do it.

The "stupid client" idea has been empowering for us because so much effort goes into representation these days. But these days, you can buy those plug n play joysticks with *Pong*, or whatever, and kids do actually play them, just like they play 2d games and Flash games and so on. See, us older developers grew up with primitive graphics and think of things like shaders or polygons as better. But kids today started playing games with all of these all present. To them, these aren't advances, they are *stylistic choices*. To them it's like asking, "what's better, jazz music or classical?" It's a silly question. They'll answer that *Pong* isn't actually better with 3d graphics. My kids don't make the distinction between moving from *Pong* to *Halo 3*.

Having a higher-powered client, like one that supports 3d, just means it can *also* draw the 2d worlds, perhaps with a smoother experience. And a simple phone might just show you the chat. It means that one virtual world is now a multi-headed hydra, displayable in many ways at once, and you interact with it on whatever device you have handy.

The server started out on a text MUD — the basic technologies of virtual worlds really aren't that different today. We created the tag system against the text MUD server, then built a client against the tag system and *removed* the MUD server. We then plugged in a new server written by Thor Alexander in Twisted Python. Sean Riley added Lua scripting on top of that server. But then we removed the Twisted Python server, leaving the scripting engine in place, and replaced it with a new server in C++. With everything so decoupled, it had a really big impact on the development process. In all of this time, there was *no code* shared between the clients and the servers — just the specifications.

The C++ server eventually added what we called *platform services*, which are things that are very common needs across many kinds of worlds, things that require high performance that you probably don't want in script. These are mostly real time services that interact tightly with the world simulation, such as physics, persistence, and authentication. Everything that *can* be moved out of the server *is* moved out of the server. The result is a server that is very tight in scope, and uses only around 20MB of memory. (This same sort of efficiency exists on the Flash client, which despite being able to handle all those different game types, is only around 100kB in size).[356]

---

[356] The Flash client peaked at 351kB two years later. In contrast, an empty Unity app that doesn't do

We chose Lua for the scripting language even though Sean was the author of *Game Programming in Python*. Python is a good language, but different solutions call for different tools. In this case, Lua is a better choice for embedded environments. It's easy to start up, it's fast, it's easy to sandbox, and if something goes wrong you can contain the error and not bring anything else down. It's easy to integrate with C, and has many of the same functionalities of Python. So not many drawbacks for the environment we

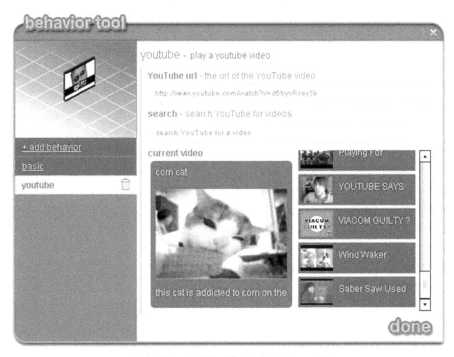

Embedding a YouTube video in a Metaplace world

wanted to use it in.

When we say it's "like CGI or like a PHP script," since the server is actually a web server, Lua actually *literally* does the same thing for us... and in fact, could generate web pages. So it's actually just like choosing PHP or Javascript for logic on your webpages, it has the same capabilities. You can submit a form on the web, right? Well, you can submit a form to a Metaplace object, like say, a door, and it will generate HTML, or XML, or JSON, and send it back to your browser.

There's a huge debate over whether you should do scripting in MMOs. Do you let designers script? The argument many programmers make is that if you let designers script things, they will screw it up (I certainly have!) and cause performance issues or

---

anything has a minimum 8MB overhead.

crashes. But designers respond saying "You never actually implement what I want, so I have to do it myself." It's a bit of a culture war. The reason to do the scripts is because they are small, atomic components.

We have a system called modules. You can take a *Metaplace* script from one *Metaplace* world to another *Metaplace* world. You can package up what we call a *smart object*. Let's say a podium with a microphone: it's an object with an appearance, and it's got behaviors to magnify and distribute audio. You could import that podium *intact* into, say, that puzzle game, because there is a common platform and everything is modular. Rather than building huge AI systems, what our testers are doing it bridging to external AI systems that live on other servers. It means that if someone provides interesting or powerful behaviors as a web service, someone can build the gateway to it as a smart object on *Metaplace*, and it could be used by any world that imports the module and chooses to use the bridge. It's open standards that games can share. And this is true for data as well as scripts. You can put data in your scripts. But you can also call out to an external data service and load data dynamically when your script is loaded.[357] The real world weather could affect the game's weather, for example. We have one player who has written a web service to procedurally generate terrains, and effectively turned game maps into data sourced from a web service.

When your client gets a world, it's effectively just receiving a flat text file a line at a time. It's basically just a log of the tags as they came down. It's a list of pointers to where scripts are, pointers to where the images are, and so on. Any changes that happen on the fly come down via tags. The client goes and fetches anything that it has been told to fetch. This means the client doesn't even know that hitting the up arrow on your keyboard means "move north." It is told, "There is a 'north' command." And it is told, "I would prefer if the 'north' command is on the up arrow." The client might say, "But I'm a phone... I don't *have* an up arrow." And it will therefore map it to the closest analogue it has.[358] On the iPhone it might map it to the swipe-up gesture. The server doesn't even know how you are going to interact.

All of these things together — the interfaces, the objects, the scripts, the appearances — is called a *stylesheet*. It's just a list of tags.

Real-time updates also happen via the tag language, of course; in fact, you can get perfect machinima-style playback of events by just logging the tags and feeding them back into the client.

---

[357] Some later game implemetations on the Metaplace platform at Disney actually read all of their data *and game logic* from Google Sheets on the fly.

[358] This was in the days when the iPhone was the *only* phone without physical keys.

The lesson here is that you are separating what you draw from what happens in the game. This is also like what the web does; it can't make assumptions about your screen size, what images you can handle, and so on.[359] On every Mac, you can still open up a command line and type "lynx" and browse the web in text, and it still works![360] This is because of separating rendering and behavior.

But this is scary, to those of us who are game designers. We are used to thinking of the interface as where the rubber meets the road! It's where "feel" lives. But this architecture implies you do not get to control the interface at all. You can only make suggestions. It's like saying that a player might be playing *Guitar Hero*, but they might play it with a keyboard instead of the plastic guitar, or playing *Dance Dance Revolution* with keys instead of the dance mat.[361] This is a big shift that has radical implications for game designers.

But the beautiful thing about it is that someone might come along and make a client that controls things in a way you never expected. Like maybe they measure user chat via an oscilloscope. And then we will learn crazy things about what users do and why they do it, because we didn't force them to only do it our way.

Democratizing content cuts both ways. We lose a bit of our control, but in the process we get a lot of cool capabilities.

We had to build something like DNS in order to handle this variety of worlds. I remember when I first got on the Internet and wanted to send email to my friends, I had to put routing in the email address. "Send this email through the gateway at BITNET and then send it through to NSFNet, which bridges over ARPANet so it can get on the backbone, then back onto NSFNet where my recipient's school happens to be connected to." You used to have to know that, but you don't anymore. You barely need to know IP addresses anymore. That's because name services have kind of covered all that stuff up, even though it is still going on behind the scenes.

When we started out, we connected to that single text MUD server. But today we can serve a Flash client from a webserver in Atlanta that requests a world from the domain name service in Utah, which tells the client that the world they want is running on my wife's Mac, behind a Time-Warner cable modem in San Diego, connect, and ask for all the assets from Photobucket. We started out with distributed

---

[359] This core tent of the web has been badly eroded over time by the increasing rise of rendering accuracy and typesetting as a priority for browser makers. Every feature that gets added for this is effectively fighting the basic current and premise of the web and HTML, of course, which is why graphic designers are driven batty by changing standards and varying implementations across browsers.
[360] So much client-side Javascript has been deployed now that this is no longer the case, alas.
[361] Both of these are things that players do all the time, of course.

servers where you had to type in the addresses by hand. But we built a "worldlist" service which could send us that list. Eventually we had too many worlds, so we switched to a World Name Service, or WNS.

Now you request a particular world and the WNS tells you where to connect. Worlds could be running *anywhere*, and might not be where they were the last time you connected, either. As we do load balancing across machines, instances of entire worlds start up and shut down on the fly, and therefore might not stay put. Eventually, they won't stay within one hosting facility, either. Or even under our control.

The key lesson there is, don't try to cram the Internet into your platform. The Net provides all these features you can use, so use them! This saves you around 9/10ths of the work! *Metaplace* started pretty much in January of 2007, with one programmer. It ended 2007 at around 11 people including the community manager and so on. And yet we have a server system that supports thousands of concurrent users, and all the rest of the things I've covered here, because we offloaded so much onto the web instead of doing it ourselves.

The last piece is our Google equivalent. Originally, you could actually hit a hidden URL on my website and seen an early version of the portal running there. It was about a 30 line PHP script that kept track of where all the worlds were running. All it did was spit back the stylesheet data in large blocks, because we sent you the definition of the puzzle game versus the RPG as just a literal text file, served straight from that webpage.

Sean broke this into two pieces: portal and stylesheet. By separating these two, we built web services atop the stylesheets, and that covered what worlds *were;* and we built a portal with a database that handled all the *metadata* about worlds, things like who's playing, where they are, what the world is, what the reviews are. At this point we have been adding Web 2.0 features all over that portal[362], and moving to supporting all of that metadata via APIs so you can consume that data from anywhere. Which means you could write your own *Metaplace* portal, if you so chose.

The lesson on this is that it's all no good if you can't find places to play and if you can't find your friends. And this is a real issue in MMOs, where everything is sharded and separated. You level up in another world, you can't visit another world. In *Metaplace*, we have a network-level identity, a meta-identity, and then you can have identities at the level of worlds — maybe even several of them, if you can have multiple characters in a world. We can have a network level reputation, network level; ratings

---

[362] The portal eventually had a full activity feed; currency system; three-part advancement system that rewarded playing, building, and socializing; and even a built-in Twitter-style status update channel.

for your activities, network level currency, and other sorts of services that worlds can optionally tap into. If they prefer to implement their own, that's fine too.

So unlike the scenario where your friend is on a different server than you, in a *Metaplace* world you can check the presence feed, click on their name, and be taken to them. It doesn't matter which shard, and it doesn't even matter which *game*.

So, in the spirit of a technical postmortem, what went right and what went wrong?

- Using the web solution whenever possible was a good choice. The one case where we invented something new was the tag language, and that's because the web solutions were about 4x too heavy in bandwidth terms, even JSON but especially XML. We wanted something really fast, really rigid, and also human readable.

- We didn't try to solve everything. We would pick a problem or piece of content, develop against it, create the functions that needed to be created just to solve that, and move on. To this day we haven't tried to solve server clusters and multiserver; we know *how* given our framework, but we're making stuff for end users. Not too many of them need a thousand concurrent players standing on one square inch, so we just don't bother solving it yet. Don't overdesign. KISS.

- Tags was the key thing that made this all work from the start. Taking an architecture that has served the web incredibly well, breaking out of the notion of rigid networking protocols.

- From a human resources perspective, we were very picky about hiring, and added staff very slowly, generally no more than one person per month. We were careful about adding to the team culture, because half of our team is from a web background and half the team is game people. These two worlds don't actually talk to each other very much right now. This is changing, but at the moment they almost speak different languages. Every time we interview a potential hire, every employee in the company rates them from -10 to +10. -10 means "I quit if you hire this person." A 10 means "I quit if you don't hire this person." And we refuse to hire anyone who doesn't get an average of five. The goal is shared culture and shared vision.

- Developing multiple clients in parallel forced us to be honest and eat our own dog food. It was a huge pain the ass. Imagine developing four concurrent clients for your MMO — completely separate codebases, in different *languages*, instead of one. In the case of a client in Flash, you're working across something like nine or ten browser and operating system combinations. But it forced us to be honest about client-agnosticism, about keeping the client thin and light and simple. We were often tempted to make the client a little smarter, and then would back away from it because one of the client writers would say, "oh, but that piece is really hard in Flash." Or "that piece is really hard in BASIC." It's surprising which things can be really hard in Flash[363], things we take for granted in games. And some things that are really easy in Flash are tough in games.

- The final lesson was counterintuitive for many game folks: don't optimize! As they say, the first two rules of software design are "1. Don't optimize yet. 2. Don't optimize at all.[364]" The tag stream isn't nearly as efficient as it could be. We use TCP, not a custom UDP solution. This caused headaches in *Ultima Online*, but infrastructure today is just better. Optimization too early locks you in as you make choices for your current situation, rather than seeing ahead. Leaving things somewhat suboptimal actually opens up possibility and potential for people. And of course, optimizations are often platform-specific, and we can't really take advantage of those in our case. Putting them in would be counterproductive.

When we first started, one of the first things Sean did when he first touched the platform was he replicated Atari 2600 *Adventure*. Then we did *Kaboom*. The interesting thing about building things this was that each month we found ourselves replicating a year's worth of platform capabilities. We started out making games that looked like they were from 1979, and a few months later we were making things that looked like 1982. Right now we're about up to *almost* 1995. The good news is that we are moving faster than the years are. Eventually we hopefully catch up, and then we start seeing people do things that you literally just cannot do any other way, because standard game architectures just don't interact with the web and don't do things in an open way.

Plenty of things went wrong, of course.

- We wanted 2d animation to be cheaper, so on a long plane flight I built a prototype of a 2d skeletal animation system[365]. It took four or five hours.

---

[363] One of the later downfalls of the platform was that it actually cleaved far too closely to Flash, allowing things like SWFs as first-class assets. This encouraged developers to standardize on just one client, and made later efforts to go 3d or move to other platforms much harder; so hard they never came to fruition.

[364] Paraphrased from Michael Jackson's rules of optimization from *Principles of Program Design*, Academic press, 1975.

[365] Very much akin to Spine, Spriter, and similar systems. Spine launched in 2006, shortly before I wrote this.

Somehow implementing it for production took months. So we cut our losses and scrapped it. Most end users only needed to stack sprites.[366] This was radical overkill and made the clients way too complicated. We had to build toolchains for it, and threw those as well. The lesson: move incrementally. Add basic capability first, and then make it nicer, and add things like this only when they are needed. Someday someone will need this system, but we'll be able to build it on top of a more evolved system, rather than trying to jump ahead to it.

- Trying to get the web and the game people to even speak the same language was difficult. "Simple" in one world was not the same thing as "simple" in the other. Examples included bandwidth usage; our web folks were horrified when we described our bandwidth usage in terms of bytes per second *every second*. For every user. All the time. After all, web concurrency is based on someone sitting at a browser and maybe pressing a button every two minutes. That's not how a multiplayer game works! The rate of input and feedback is much faster. The same thing happened in the other direction, as when the web folk came to us and said "you're doing *what* for authentication?" We had thought we had to write an auth server, and it needed to scale up, and implement all these protocols… Instead, they showed us how to just use web sessions, and you just pressed a key, and it was done, we didn't have to write an authentication server. Auth servers usually take months in MMOs, but the code for authentication the web way is all of a screen long, and it's as secure as the systems you use to do your banking.

- An interesting issue we are still facing is that I still haven't built an MMORPG on the platform. Everyone is asking me, "when are you building the successor to *Ultima Online?*" or whatever. A lot of our users want to build an MMORPG, and most of them need to use existing pieces to do it. We need to build an awful lot of off-the-shelf pieces for them to be able to build something like that. We're working on that now, but the key lesson is that you need to have content people really early in the process. We needed to have more content people exercising the pipelines. And don't be afraid to make content that you will throw away. We had expected there to be more platform services, so a lot of the things that we thought would be platform services have become modules, and therefore moved from C++ developers to content developers writing them in Lua.

- At one point, we said we weren't a client company, and questioned why we

---

[366] Pro developers, however, really wanted this system later, and its absence was a huge blow.

were maintaining any clients. So we picked one, the Flash one, and said it was the reference client. All the other clients internally ceased development, and we simply said that any external clients should aim for matching the rendering in the Flash client. That was a massive mistake. It stopped us from being honest, and meant we could start cheating in the direction of Flash. It also meant that if there was an error in the Flash client's interpretation of tags, we didn't have something else to compare it to. This meant we couldn't tell whether our standard was being implemented correctly even by our own team. Because of this we have relaunched our multiclient efforts and are maintaining three clients again.[367]

- Lastly, the lessons on usability. This is all geeky material. It's really easy, when you are building a platform, to think that your end user is a programmer. The goal for Metaplace is for any player to come, hit a button, choose a stylesheet — a world-in-a-box, name the world, and thirty seconds later, have built an MMO you can log into. It should have its own webpage that you can customize, you can edit the descriptions, and you can click "Build" and log in. You'll immediately get the tools and a view into the world, and you'll have a functional full-blown little world that could hold a few thousand people. The intent is to make building a world as easy as playing *The Sims*. That implies always interacting with ordinary users, not professional programmers. So sure, at the high end people can come to this and script and connect to external bots and web services and all that. But it's really easy to lose sight of the fact that a lot of people just want to have a little virtual homestead to call their own.

So we are currently spending a lot of time revising the tool suite to make it much easier. Instead of making tools that reflect back-end data structures, which is what we have now, we are moving towards a task-based metaphor: tools that reflect what the user wants to do. More like a wizard: "What I want is an apartment." And

The eventual radial menu tool system in Metaplace

---

[367] Alas, this didn't stick.

less like "I want to edit code and add templates."

Those are our lessons so far. We're up to 16 people now. In 2006, this was a very implausible thing to try to make. Here we are now, and it's not nearly as crazy as we thought it was. And me personally, I am never going back to building games the old way ever ever again. It's been an amazing liberation from the soul-destroying reinvention of the wheel, the grind we've had.

An alpha tester did the real-time translation. An alpha tester hooked Eliza up to their NPCs. An alpha tester is bridging to procedurally generated maps. An alpha tester sources game data from Google Maps. That's really what it is all about. It's not about what cool stuff we can make. It's about bringing the fun of this process to everybody else.

They don't get to go to GDC. They can't do 3d modeling with shaders and zBrush and all that jazz. Someday, I hope this platform supports all of that for those who are capable. But the point is not the folks at GDC. The point is the people who wish that someday, they *could* be at GDC. The point is the people who aren't getting to do what we did when we grew up, making games on little 8 bit computers with less power than what I carry around on my belt.[368]

We've lost that on-ramp for people, and the goal with this is to let *everybody* do all the fun shit that we game developers do every day at work.

---

[368] Yeah, phones back then tended to live in little holsters on belts.

Life on Metaplace

For a brief while, the Metaplace community flourished, as the power of the tools gave a group of indie developers their shot.

Connecting to the wider world

For slightly over half a wonderful year,[369] Metaplace was open and in full swing as a consumer facing virtual world service. Worlds of all sorts were built. Even in the alpha there was a September 11th world that was political commentary. An official chapter of the *Star Trek* fan club opened up, and you get could in transporters and fly a ship and get a Starfleet uniform and rank. Classrooms galore sprouted up — Metaplace was quite popular with non-profits and educators. A user in Sweden who was a musician built *Virek Online,*[370] a world that was basically a simple graphic adventure walking you through a fantasy tale that featured his band's music.

> To my surprise, *Virek Online* got chosen to be "community spotlight" in Metaplace's blog in sep/oct -08. This led to a few pretty cool things – I got to show off pics from the game outside the site (this was otherwise forbidden due to the beta-agreement), the game got mentioned on Raph Koster's website and it was featured on the front page of MMO-business magazine Worlds In Motion. It was cool, but also felt odd. I was just playing around, and here's a screenshot of my game in between pics from WOW and *Warhammer Online!*

The more adventurous users, most of whom went on to careers in the videogame industry,[371] started making full small games: clones of *Pac-Man* and *Missile Command*, racing games, bowling alleys, murder mysteries, platforming games featuring leaping cats or strange Goth girls, and so on. But nothing of large scale developed, in large part because of the tool limitations. The development challenges really needed the Metaplace staff to push through and create things themselves to iron out the pipelines. As a result, the vast majority of even the best worlds were basically gorgeous static environments you could chat in.

---

[369] Open beta started May 15th; the service closed December 21st.

[370] A complete development journal can be found at https://silkwoodmusic.wordpress.com/2010/01/06/virek-online-the-evolution-of-a-metaplace-world/ and video capture of a complete playthrough can be found on YouTube and at https://silkwoodmusic.wordpress.com/worlds/

[371] I consider this to be the best legacy that Metaplace left behind.

Virek Online

When the beta started on May 15th of 2009, I posted saying

> You get a small world for free, with full access to all the content creation tools. Lately, I've been describing it at "the power of Second Life, with the ease of The Sims, on the web."
>
> It's early days yet, of course. There is a lot more left to do. For example, we have not yet released the ability to embed worlds on websites and profile pages, which is a huge part of the story. There's more to come in terms of web integration, plugins on the marketplace so that it gets easier and easier to make what you want, and so on. We're not done by a long shot.

Notably missing from the immediate development schedule was a way for users to make money selling content to one another. We were consumed with concerns about fraud and liability. Users took matters into their own hands and made a couple of connections to PayPal that could be used for transactions within the platform. We were so nervous about fraud issues we asked them to take them down.

Nonetheless, there were a lot of pretty cool developments that fit in well with the social environment that was developing with more success than the games were. Live music was one element that started to click; I myself did several live concerts in

Metaplace[372], and in June of 2009 there was a "Rocking the Metaverse Tour," organized by a group called KoinUp, which took musicians across three separate virtual worlds for concerts. We built a custom theater for the event, with all sorts of nifty effects (disco balls and more).

The attendance at Rockin' the Metaverse

In April of '09 we also saw the development of a chat bridge to *Second Life*, which allowed users to chat back and forth across the worlds. This used web standards, demonstrating the power of the basic premise.

> I would be remiss if I didn't point out that making such complex stuff in Metaplace is easy. Remote controlling an object from outside is not hard at all for a Metaplace world. After all, every object has a URL, and every object can interact with Web APIs as well… you get the idea, there's a lot of possibilities there.

---

[372] See https://www.raphkoster.com/2009/06/13/doing-live-music-in-metaplace/ for a description of how this was done.

I have been sour on "virtual worlds standards" for a while, because it seems to me that trying to force all virtual worlds into a single mold at this stage of their development is a mistake, and pretty much all the VW "standards" efforts have tended to have too narrow a conception of the medium for my tastes.

But standards for bridging data — well, that's easy and obvious! :) And most obviously, using the standards the web already has is the easiest way.

Also in April, we were working with various non-profit groups, and one of them, 3dSquared, arranged sessions between a middle school class, the State Superintendent of Education for Louisiana, and the school's principal.[373] I gave some brief remarks about digital citizenship:[374]

> So I was asked to make a few comments about digital citizenship, and I think the thing that most strikes me about an event like this is the fact that citizenship is the same whether it exists in the real world or a digital framework. Here we all are at this wonderful event, and the things that we are talking about in this cartoony, digital world are big important, real world issues, like funding for science education, and the legislative process.
>
> Online communities are a VENUE, not an end in themselves. They are just a new way for us to engage in very old practices. And I think that if we managed to transplant some folks from ancient Athens and given them an intensive course in language and computer literacy, they would be perfectly at home with the substance of the discussions today!
>
> At the same time, I think that it also highlights how important that digital literacy IS; after all, without those lessons, they would be less able to participate. And as our society's tech capabilities grow, I think it's wonderful to see that our society — and legislators — and principals and school superintendents, and teachers — are willing to invest in that literacy so that future voters, citizens, will be able to participate to the best of their ability using this new technology.
>
> So I want to just say thank you to all of you for taking the plunge!

3dSquared used the platform for a number of very interesting initiatives, including getting students to build worlds about social issues in their state, which were then presented as projects to the state legislature. So now Metaplace was getting worlds about wetlands reclamation and literacy programs![375]

---

[373] A blog post about the event can be found on One showed up at
https://web.archive.org/web/20100604125329/http://www.theimaginationage.net/2009/04/louisiana-regional-politics-go-meta.html

[374] Captured here: http://www.raphkoster.com/2009/04/30/real-world-la-government-town-hall-in-metaplace/

[375] Covered here: https://venturebeat.com/2009/04/17/guest-editorial-how-i-became-a-virtual-world-believer/

Speaking events and guests were another major element of social life in Metaplace. Over the course of that year, we had as guest speakers people like Dr. Richard Bartle, co-inventor of MUD; comics writer Matt Sturges; game designer Jason Rohrer; TV producer Jesse Alexander; and SF writer and activist Cory Doctorow. In July '09, we landed our biggest "speaker," as we worked with the Annenberg Center for Public Diplomacy to livestream President Obama's historic speech in Ghana into a Metaplace world. At the time, I wrote

> This is exciting to me on many levels. Lately, a few of the speeches I have given have been about the broad question of where virtual worlds are going, and how they may connect to real people's lives. What we have here is a powerful tool for social media, one with different affordances than are brought to the table by SNSes or streams — but in many ways it is underutilized because of the barriers of entry and the ways in which VWs are still tied to models established in the 1970's.

> I've often stated that the clear killer app to date for virtual worlds is escapism. How much of this is because virtual worlds have been islands unto themselves, not interacting with or interwoven with the larger Internet? In many ways, it may be permeability that opens up the many use-cases that are possible — not just for serious purposes, but for escapist ones as well. Virtual worlds need not be a world apart. Here we see virtual worlds taking their place alongside other social media in a discussion that is truly broad, bringing the unique characteristics of placeness and co-presence to the table.

And all the while more worlds were created. I myself quickly became the top seller on the in-game marketplace, and quickly also built many of the more popular worlds. We ported a couple of my puzzle games into Metaplace — one called *Wheelwright* was vaguely like *Hexic*, and another called *Ant Farm* was also a puzzle game that involved rotating blocks. I made an ice pond where you could ice skate, and a shooter game

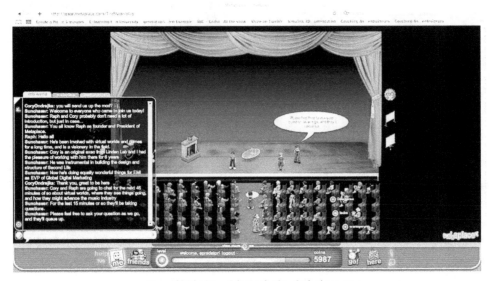

My world "The Stage," during the Cory Ondrejka event

where you killed meeps, which were cute green fuzzball things. I made a sailing ship combat game that was pretty popular called *High Seas*, and a variant of light-cycles with UFOs that floated overhead. The digital objects I made, like birds that flew overhead, background music players, musical instruments, and the system for giving hugs, were all very popular. This led to conflicts with the internal content team at times, as these creations weren't part of the official Metaplace content, and yet they constantly got the calls for support on them.

What developed was a tight-knit community that didn't grow very fast. When we started to gain traction among kids, it caused enormous strife. Content creators on the platform, it seems to me, were constantly caught between real loyalty and devotion to the platform that was enabling them, and frustration with our directionlessness and the seemingly slow pace of change.

This Golden Age of Metaplace ended up with a huge Metaplace Central town, with playable arcade games you could click on, word scrambles and egg hunts and concerts and even a dating game... and still nowhere near enough users. We ran game jams, we tried to get users to explore more instead of just sitting in MP Central and chatting... but it seemed like we were caught in a rut. Our content creators had more game money than they knew what to do with, and we still hadn't managed to unlock their creative potential.

The debate over trying again on Facebook (MySpace was a non-factor at this point) was rising yet again. An entirely different sort of social network was conquering the

My kid did a school project on cell structure in Metaplace

world, and it was starting to look like we were betting on the wrong horse altogether.

We released the ability to embed a Metaplace world in a container on any webpage — even in a banner ad. One player even embedded Metaplace worlds in the little popups you get when you click on a location in Google Maps. A fluffy press release came out claiming virtual world embeds as a first, and a blog commenter promptly pointed out that *MyMiniLife* had managed to release embeddable worlds a full two years before.[376] This game was really more of an apartment builder, however — you didn't actually move around inside the world, and while there were avatars, they were outside of the apartments you made; it had neat tools that let you bring in items from Google Sketchup, but so did we. Basically, it was a social network with a sticker book that *looked* like a world, an example of how far the term "virtual world" had stretched over the course of the boom. It had a literal fraction of the features we did — and four million people had tried it, dwarfing us. *MyMiniLife* eventually exited the virtual worlds space altogether, and instead went off to build a little game that got them acquired by Zynga. It was called *Farmville.*

---

[376] Coverage of their release here: https://techcrunch.com/2007/05/19/myminilife-your-embeddable-virtual-world/

Some Zone Design Lessons

We're laying out Metaplace Central again. We have iterated it a lot, as we try out different flows, add new tech that makes it more appealing, and so on. These days, what with the balloons, the board games on the table by the cafe, and the many teleporters to user worlds, layout is growing more challenging as we strive to both fit everything in and also make it a social space.

Musing on these problems not only made me dig out my copy of *A Pattern Language* but also reminded me of how 8 years ago I did a brief examination of the maps of two popular cities in what were then two popular MMOs: *Ultima Online* and *EverQuest*. These days, the science of zone layout has improved a lot.

Every sort of videogame map design has its own constraints. For example, if you look at multiplayer shooter maps intended for deathmatch, you find that they are constructed around the notion of intersecting loops. Each loop is set up such that you can run around the loop over and over, trying to catch or avoid an enemy, or make a quick turn to hop onto an intersecting loop, to avoid or ambush. Capture the Flag maps have a requirement for a high amount of tactical symmetry, but also a certain number of vulnerable approaches, so that covering all the possible entrances is a difficult challenge.

Maps for textual virtual worlds were liberated from the tyranny of geography; the nodal nature of the space meant that a room was of arbitrary size, and yet every room took the same amount of time to traverse. (Some muds had the notion of a "move cost" which allowed some rooms to be "larger" via consuming movement points). You had rooms that were inside televisions and rooms that were hundreds of miles of ocean; the distance between the docks and downtown might be the same as the distance between Europe and Africa, in terms of commands issued.

This may seem miles away from the issues of modern seamless virtual worlds, with 3d perspectives and no zone loading boundaries. But it's not. There are hugely important *topological* considerations that seem to always apply to layouts in virtual worlds. And here are some that I have learned, and re-learned, over the years:

Always make sure users can tell which way to go. Whether you have text, 2d, or 3d views into your world, you need to provide clear cues. If you have height, that's a great way to do it. Roads, obviously. Barriers, obviously. Starting a newbie at a dead end and giving them only one way to go is a classic way to deal with early confusion. Large landmarks that can be seen from a distance can serve a similar purpose.

Don't use invisible barriers. Make them natural. Even if they are just trees too dense to realistically walk through, or a slope that is just a tad too steep — when you are shaping your space, use something users can see. I have repeatedly put my foot down and left out the ability to mark specific locations as blocking from the Metaplace platform because attaching blocking to something visible is just better design. A user cannot tell why one stretch of grass has an invisible wall and another does not: to them, emptiness *affords* walking.

Mazes suck. 'Nuff said. They are for puzzles, not for places.

You're making cozy worlds. Each space — be it a hypertextually linked set of rooms, or a 3d zone — should be a self-contained pocket, a thematically connected area with clear boundaries. Probably the best elucidation of this principle came from Damion Schubert in his talk about applying the design lessons of Vegas casinos to virtual worlds.[377] Even in real-world cities where old townships have blended into one another, we cling to the notion of "placeness." Look at London; you can tell when you enter and leave the old neighborhoods, because they have characteristic qualities to them. In artificial worlds this can be art sets, lighting, whatever.

Enclose things. A consequence of modularity is enclosure. The real world is enclosed all over the place. We have rooms, we have squares, we have walls, we have valleys, we have treelines bounding properties. Enclosing and marking boundaries is part of what humans do to a space. Among other things, this allows strong thematizing of a given space, maximizing the art resources for it (thereby making it more beautiful or interesting), allows you to strengthen the navigation, and creates a sense of shared identity among users.

Exits matter a lot. You've gone and enclosed a space, and paid lots of attention to the interior. Great. A flip side characteristic is that moving from one pocket to another should feel dramatic: a tight passage revealing a wide vista, coming over the crest of a mountain and revealing a valley, discovering a door behind a waterfall, a big bold gate with guards. You want to signal that the user is entering a space with its own framework and rules. There are a lot of visual cues that are used, but most of them carry some sense of "gate" to them, even if it is as simple as a path that winds between

---

[377] See my report on it here: https://www.raphkoster.com/2005/10/27/daion-schuberts-talk-at-agc/

two hills: a passage between two tall things.

Modularity. A consequence of designing in cozy world pockets is that you can have all sorts of complex layouts within a zone, but the connections to neighboring zones should be relatively few and should be obvious. Take a look at this map from *EverQuest*: the city proper is highly complex (and very very difficult to navigate) and the exits to the neighboring zone — the other half of the city! — are in twisty alleyways and very hard to find. This was because of 3d culling technology at the time, but it made navigating Qeynos for more complicated than it needed to be. On the flip side, EQ did a great job of modularity and linking zones. When linking zones, you have to

try to remember that users will remember the high level map in a highly schematic form. In effect, they will turn the zone connections map into a graph that will look a lot like a text mud map in their heads.

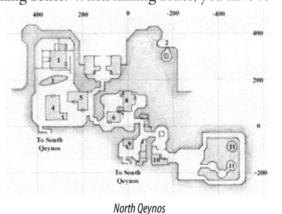

Social spaces point inwards. Take a look at the way you have your central gathering spot planned. The center had better be fairly empty. Oh, put a landmark there, yes. But don't inadvertently make your central plaza into a ring topology instead of a space. Ideally, the landmark in the middle affords some form of simple social play. Fountains were common in the text muds, and with good reason — there is something deeply culturally ingrained around watering holes. Also, this space must be welcoming; it is the *last* place to use dingy dark colors.

North Qeynos

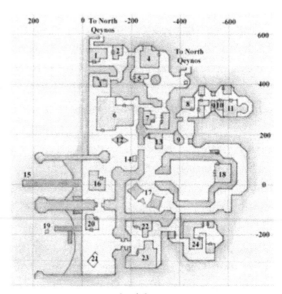

South Qeynos

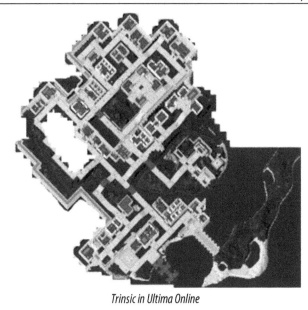

Trinsic in Ultima Online

Watch where people want to walk. The city of Trinsic in UO, which I laid out, failed this badly. Look first at the main map; then at the second one, where you can see green paths showing the principal traffic flow through the city. The main entrance on the north side was the principal entrance to the city. But if you stayed on that thoroughfare you ended up in a dead end on an island. You had to slide over by a block to reach the other main exit. What's more, on the third screenshot you can see where key buildings are located — inns and taverns. See how one of them isn't on the green paths? Guess which one is always empty.

Adventure spaces point outwards. In general, if you are exploring you want a horizon (or more than one) to head towards. Where social spaces create a sense of

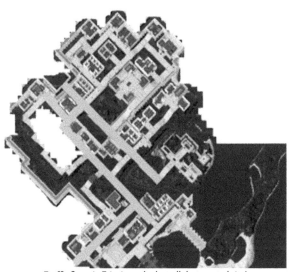

Traffic flows in Trinsic — look at all that wasted city!

security, adventure spaces should create a sense of uncertainty and the unknown to prompt users to keep going. It isn't about endless vistas; it's about interest. This is one place where procedural spaces so often fall down. The ways in which you point onwards can be quite subtle. *World of Warcraft* does it even down at the difficulty level of monsters: the far end of a zone is slightly tougher than the near end.

The defining activity. Every location had better have something characteristically defining about it. Sure, every city has to have the same amenities, and every zone must have monsters. But get creative. This wilderness zone has the pool you can swim in that is perfect for picnics. This other one has the great layout for ranged combat. This inn has the trivia game; that one has the chess board. Users will self-select into the spaces which feel culturally comfortable to them.

All of this is fractal. Within a given space, you are designing spaces. So even in a town center, you want to provide more than one "center" — a big one and a couple of smaller, enclosed, flavorful, inward-looking spaces. A town center is shaped that way, but so is the inn that is on the plaza. And so is the table arrangement within that inn, so that each table is a pocket. A swing set surrounded by willow trees in a corner of the park, and so on. At the highest level, in UO we had huge areas that were bounded by ocean, forest and mountain — the pass across

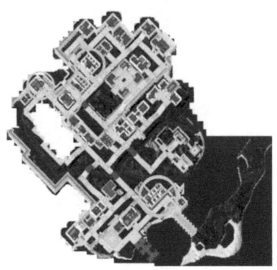

Where the intended social spots were in Trinsic

the mountains was a notorious PK haunt, and a notable "gate." The eastern side of the mountains had many zones in itself — the areas around Britain, Trinsic, and so on. And even between Britain and Trinsic, there was a chokepoint bridge. And so on, down to the turtles and beyond.

What were the things that we wanted to fix in the latest iteration of Metaplace Central? Well, newbies spawned in the middle of the street. The street had multiple ways to walk — so half the newbies wandered away from the central social spot. There was only one social pocket — and it was on the side, not in the center. The town plaza was mostly impassable. All simple things that using the above guidelines warn against.

Last thing — much of the above applies to websites as much as it does to maps. But I leave that as an exercise for the reader.

The Great Meep-In

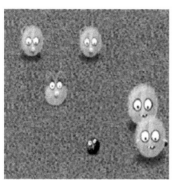

A meep is a fuzzy critter I made in Metaplace that is sort of a cross between the things Marvin Suggs beats on in his Amazing Muppaphone and a Miyazaki soot sprite. They come in a variety of colors and with a variety of behaviors — some like people, some are shy, some have big teeth… I put them on the marketplace, and they quickly became popular on the service.

If you have been on Metaplace, you may have noticed that people get "meeped" instead of "poked." This was put in by our web guys as a joke, originally, when meeps became popular. Sure enough, everyone started asking, "What is meeping?"

Well, last week we decided to rename the feature to "nudge" or something else mundane. Too many people in our user testing were getting confused, didn't know what it meant, or were commenting on it. So with regret, we decided we needed to change the term. Meeps would remain running around the worlds, but the feature needed to be easy for new folks to understand. We figured some of the veterans would not like this, but that everyone would understand and be supportive.

We were wrong. Within an hour after we posted about the change, a petition had been created. And the eventual result was this[378] (another article here,[379] and another

---

[378] This pointed at
https://web.archive.org/web/20090303153032/http://www.geocities.com/spooningmoons/meepin.html:
"The event itself was preluded by a live meep band and dancing. I am sure more than a few had snuck in some drink as well, as most were quite charged up by the designated hour. KStarfire was instrumental in keeping momentum going throughout the day and keeping spirits high until the awaited one's arrival. There was talk of what to expect? Was this representative going to be for or against our proposal? Would they mock us? But still we were hopeful and signed the petition board and regaled the awesomeness of the meep."

[379] http://mparthaus.blogspot.com/2009/02/meeping.html: "I attended the rally and it was a cool thing. There were some odd aspects to it. Like anything on the internet involving more than two people there was some confusion about the issue. (Some people thought they were going to eliminate the meep

screenshot. Here is a marketing take on it.[380] I hear an MPInsider video is on the way as well). *Edit: here's Cuppy's take.*[381]

Julian Dibbell has already commented that this is Metaplace's "naked-protest-at-Lord-British's-castle moment." Yes, yes it is. With some key differences: this happened in *a user's world*, not ours. One of the organizers of the protest does political organization for a living. We have guaranteed rights of assembly and free speech. This

The Keep the Meep protest

creatures. One of the speakers talked about MP making decisions without input and I think that is totally off-base.) Late-comers would pop into the room and announce their arrival, interupting the speaker. One troll got me to fire up the /ignore command for the first time…

I asked Raph is this was going to be his "It's alive!" moment, meaning the creation that he has poured so much time and energy into is now really taking on a life of its own. His reply: "Definitely."

[380] "What's in a Verb? Meep vs Nudge." https://web.archive.org/web/20090304225730/http://www.tkstudios.com/2009/02/27/whats-in-a-verb-meep-vs-nudge/

[381] Cuppycake aka Tami Baribeau (at the time, Sigmund now) was our community manager. Her take is here: https://web.archive.org/web/20090310144214/http://www.cuppycake.org/?p=665. "The "meeping" issue, is one that is closer to my heart because it was actually my idea. While Raph is credited to inventing the meep as a noun (the awesome little bouncing critters), I have been using the word "meeping" as my status on GTalk for over a year. I always wanted a way to 'poke' the users online, and one day I told [Chris Chapman] (our Director of Web Dev) that we should put it in, but call it 'meeping'. He ended up going home that night and putting the whole thing in, in his spare time! It has now been one of people's favorite things to do on Metaplace, so I had a personal attachment to the term. :)"

was the first time, silly as it may seem, where the rubber met the road on our version of user rights.

The text of what I said at the rally:

> Thanks, Joe. But I really don't think I am most responsible for any of this. It clearly couldn't have happened at all without the contributions of you the users. Without people in a place, even a Metaplace, is cold and lonely. You guys matter more than we do, in the end. That's why we built MP.
>
> So I want to start by saying something. Maybe they are just big furry bouncing monsters, I know that. But they are also near and dear to my heart. I drew these meeps, you know. So I have great affection for them.
>
> We should not, however, think that just because they are cartoon critters that this moment is any less important. Yes — they're silly, and the whole thing has a bit of a carnival tone. But we should take it seriously for many reasons. There are online services out there where what you are doing right now would not be permitted to happen. Where this world isn't yours. This may be an issue that has its roots in green fuzz versus impersonal nudges, but the underlying principles are still important.
>
> On that note, I want to briefly reference an incident earlier today where, entirely in jest, some of the MP employees were having fun with their admin powers here. No offense was meant, but I want to tell you all — MP employees included, here and now — User worlds are THEIRS. We have our power only for the good of the community and we use that power in their worlds only by invitation. So even if it was meant well, I want to let you all know that this principle is important, because it is also the principle that permits this protest in the first place.
>
> It doesn't matter if offense was taken or not; we as MP employees and admins do stand in an odd place. We own the worlds in between yours, the overall context, and we have a responsibility to make the overall framework one that helps you all succeed. Some of you are here to hang out with friends. Some of you are here to chat. Some of you wish to build games. Some want to throw tomatoes. And some want to express themselves politically and in serious ways.
>
> When we originally made the decision to change meeping to something else, we did it with the best of intentions. We have gotten consistent feedback that new folks simply don't know what meeping is. It isn't adequate to say "well, they should just learn" — we want to help them be successful, and that means meeting them halfway. So it was a decision made with the intent of helping, not hurting.
>
> That said, it is with pleasure that I want to let you all know —
>
> Meeping stays.
>
> BUT! And there is a but.
>
> With this comes a responsibility. We will still have those newbies entering, and they will still be confused. We still have to introduce them to the unique culture

here.

So I also want to tell you all that we are going to be implementing a newbie helper flag whereby anyone who wants to help can flag themselves — just a UI tag, no hours, responsibilities, or anything — just visible notice, just a UI tag on your nametag that you can turn on. And I hope that those of you who are passionate enough to defend meeps are also passionate enough to help solve the problem that we were trying to fix.

I have great faith… this is one of the most amazing online communities I have ever been a part of. So thank you for your passion, and thank you for the protest — and I mean that sincerely.

These events happened in February of 2009.

Metaplace Game Jam Postmortem

There's a great postmortem of the Metaplace game jam we did a couple of weeks back at WorldIV.com » Surprisingly, Making Games is Hard Work.[382]

I did jacks – I was planning on doing *Pente* after that. My thoughts on it:

- **Gosh, a lot of people don't know what jacks is!** Which caught me by surprise. Perhaps it was a side effect of growing up in a third world country, but cheap games like jacks and marbles were all the rage when I was a kid. And yeah, jacks is considered more of a girl's game than a boy's game, and we

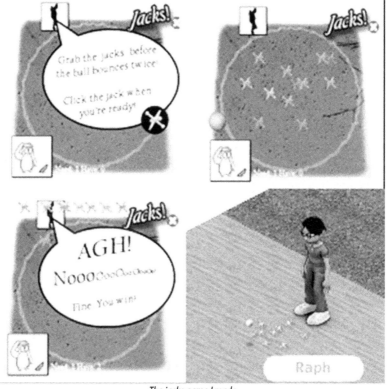

The jacks game I made

[382] See https://web.archive.org/web/20090721151441/http://www.worldiv.com/blog/?p=1068

had a room full of guys in the jam. (Ironic, since it is a truly ancient game. Next time you read about "knucklebones" in your favorite fat fantasy novel, they're playing a form of jacks.)

- **I cheated.** We were supposed to pick stuff that was designed already. But I've never seen a videogame version of jacks. So I did actually sneak in design in there. As it turned out, that was easily the biggest time sink, as I wrestled with stuff like how to handle the ball bouncing mechanic.

- **Reduce mechanics!** I ended up throwing away the element of how hard you throw the ball at the ground to give your self more time. I also threw away the mechanic of sweeping up more than one jack in your hand at once. This made the game much simpler.

- **Always do core mechanics first.** This is one that always seems to elude people new to rapid prototyping. Don't get distracted with the complicated matchmaking system. Don't get caught up in even the timer. Make it so you can pick up a jack. Then make it so you can pick up several jacks. Then add the timer. Then add turn-taking. Layer things in, don't jump to the ideal.

- **Flavor matters a ton.** As much as I say "do blue squares first!" I do try to get placeholder graphics in as soon as I have the core mechanic, because you are aiming for an experience too.

- **Jacks kinda works better one-player this way**, because turns are kind of long. I compensated by letting you watch the other player's moves, but it is still not entertaining enough to just watch them.

These were designed as little games that you can click on someone else and invite them to play. The screenshots, by the way, are what jacks looked like about an hour after the jam ended, so I got all the way to "alpha" — playable, reasonably balanced, and with a general visual design in place.

The Golden Egg

The Metaplace Central master egg

We've announced a nifty new feature, the Golden Egg, which serves as a sort of case study of crossworld entertainment on *Metaplace*.

One of the interesting challenges with something like Metaplace is that users all build separate worlds, and then they scatter to them. Getting people to both visit all the worlds that are interesting, and also to meet up in worlds, can be challenging. There's a discoverability issue, and a social cluster issue. Cool worlds can get "forgotten" as they slip down the feature lists, for example.

We have all sorts of tests going, and one of them is this Golden Egg. Basically, in Metaplace Central you see this blue egg. Click on it, and it will tell you "if you find a golden egg in a world, you can click on it — once! — and get 500 coins." It will also suggest one such world where an egg might be found. In fact, you can click right then and there to go visit that world — though you likely *won't* appear anywhere near the egg. And when you do find the egg and claim your coins, the egg you found will suggest another world which you might want to hunt through, and so on…

Any worldbuilder an install an egg in their world — it's closed source, so they can't get at the code that runs it, preventing exploits.

It costs a fortune — like, 25,000 coins, which let me tell you put a serious dent in my bank account yesterday, since I bought 10 of them. But it's totally worth it from a marketing point of view, and the price limits it to users who have already had success building, increasing the odds that the worlds you are sent to are interesting. Every egg becomes an inbound link, and it provides an incentive for users to come visit your world. You can make eggs easy or hard to find, and even wrap gameplay around them. Eventually, we may expand this to have variable reward eggs — perhaps based on how hard or easy the egg was to get.

Each egg is actually doing some rather nifty crossworld communication. Every egg notifies the central egg as to where it has been installed, and every egg asks the central egg for suggestions of other worlds. The central egg even manages a high

A Golden Egg in a world

score table of the most successful explorers. All this is an example of using Metaplace's web capabilities — the eggs communicate with each other using simple web services implemented entirely within Metaplace itself.

They are also a demonstration of the power of a common platform. Eggs could be found in all sorts of worlds — hangouts, games, shops… you can see stuff like this becoming used as a virtual webring, for example. Some of the gameworlds on Metaplace as using the egg as the final reward for beating the game, or getting to a certain level, so it is a way to drive engagement. And once you have Metaplaces embedded in various websites, it starts getting rather interesting.

This particular example is rather gamey, but bear in mind that any sort of data could be communicated across worlds in this way.

It's too soon to say whether this is an interesting notion or not, really — the eggs went in yesterday. But in the meantime, I know some of my older worlds are getting tons more traffic than they used to. :)

If you feel like exploring the worlds with eggs, just stop by Metaplace Central and click the blue egg. Maybe I will see you at the Ice Pond.[383]

---

[383] Another one of the worlds I built, this provided ice skating physics, for those who cared to try it.

Why Isn't Money Points?

From April 28th, 2009

Mint.com is a personal finance site that won the judges' award at TechCrunch40 the same year that *Metaplace* won the audience award. It helps you do budgeting and other such dull tasks, all in slick interface.

Despite the zillions of products out there to do this, we still managed to wheel, deal, and borrow ourselves into a financial crisis (that is still ongoing, though swine flu may be eclipsing it just now). Clearly, something was lacking in the appeal here, for if said product category were truly successful, we wouldn't be in this fix.

Now, Mint is in closed beta on a feature that turns personal finance into a game, complete with points earned for doing things like socking away some cash into the savings account each month, or switching to a credit card with annual rewards. Get enough points in a sustained way, and you too can be a Financial Guru.

This seems like a fairly straightforward harnessing of game-style incentive systems towards a laudable goal (though I should note that said credit card with rewards is likely from one of Mint's partners). But honestly — money is points anyway, isn't it? **Why is it that we value the cash less than the flat-screen TV?**

There's probably piles of psychological and economic literature on the subject. For example, it has often been commented[384] that we are more willing to spend credit than cash, because it seems "less real." For that matter, humans shop for comfort — sadness spurs spending,[385] because it makes us happy to acquire things, and happy to buy things for others.

Of course, as all good readers of *A Theory of Fun for Game Design* know, anytime we see "makes us happy" we should be slightly suspicious, because it means "gives us a jolt of drugs."

---

[384] https://www.npr.org/templates/story/story.php?storyId=92178034
[385] https://www.npr.org/templates/story/story.php?storyId=89761759

Not very long ago I made a very small Easter Egg hunt game for Metaplace Central.[386] The rules were simple:

- Every 60 seconds, a new egg would spawn.
- Sometimes they would spawn behind stuff, completely invisible and inaccessible.
- There were never more than 25 of them around at once.
- The eggs appeared, then tilted over slightly.
- The eggs were colored random bright colors.
- The eggs had to be picked up within 60 seconds or they would vanish.
- You could pick them up by clicking on them — no matter how far away you were.
- As soon as you picked one up, everyone heard a chime sound.
- As soon as you picked one up, a big counter appeared over your head, showing how many eggs you had collected, and the color of the last one.
- If you logged out, the counter disappeared, and you started over from zero.

Now, there's no reward in this game, there's no winner or loser, and there's no endgame. Yet even during testing, I had to tear myself away, and **when put into Metaplace Central, average session length for the day went up 50%. But... in**

---

[386] A descriofion of it from
https://web.archive.org/web/20090517092823/http://mpinsider.blogspot.com/2009/04/twas-night-before-night-of-easter.html: "This evening there was an Easter Egg Hunt going on when I materialized in Metaplace Central. It made sense, seeing as it's Easter week-end and all. Each person had a number above his/her avatar's head indicating how many eggs they had accumulated. Everywhere I turned there were eggs of all sorts of colours, appearing and then vanishing before my eyes. Soon, I learned that to collect these sought after eggs, you had to click them before anyone else did. It was amusing to hear the "ding" from my husband's computer everytime he picked up another egg. He soon started hearing several "dings" from my laptop though as I gathered two or three eggs in a row. If you closed your window, you had to start back at zero, so I kept it open in a tab for awhile, periodically going back to grab more eggs. This game, created by Raph Koster, was so simple in its premise, yet quite addictive. "I'll say goodbye to everyone when I get 40 eggs," I'd say; But then a purple oval would pop up next to me and I couldn't help but click it. And then a green one, a blue one, another green one... I finally pulled the chord at 145. However, that was nowhere near the largest final tally. That honor goes to *Grace McDunnough* who left with a grand total of 1,000 eggs! "

some sense, it's a crummy game. Why this effect? Because the Easter Egg hunt is a confluence of a lot of highly manipulative tricks.

- Because eggs would often spawn in a concealed location and then clean

The Easter egg hunt in Metaplace Central, as Grace McDunnough reaches 1000 eggs found

themselves up, the spawn rate did not in fact appear regular. It was just random enough to hover at the edge of our prediction capability.

- The appearance, followed by moving, engaged basic hunting circuits in our brain; if the egg just appeared and didn't move, they would not be nearly as compelling to search for on screen.

- The random bright colors also engage something deep in our brains. The makers of *Bejeweled* found that when they skinned the game with gems (something that triggers our acquisitive urges) as opposed to something else, people enjoyed the game more. Humans like shiny pretties.

- The fact that eggs would vanish if not collected provided a sense of urgency to the task, forcing attention.

- The chime provided a predictable reinforcement to the behavior, but given the rest of the mechanics, you were on a random reinforcement schedule (which is known to be the most addictive). Soon you were conditioned to want the chime, and hearing the chime going off on someone else occasioned mild frustration.

- The highly visible counter encouraged measuring against other users, but the "last egg collected" device was subtler and sneakier: it created a sense of ownership. It looked like you had a *thing*. You could also see it changing on other users, and know that they were making progress.

- Once there was a sense of "possession," logging out became harder. There was nothing to spend the eggs on. But they also weren't merely points — they were "stuff" you would "lose."

In short, the Easter Egg hunt, crude as it was, had plenty of opportunity to insert a lot of deeply manipulative game mechanic tactics that create addiction, attention, and loyalty. Now, eventually, it did wear thin — as a pure accumulation mini-game, there was not a lot of depth to it, and the choices users could make quickly palled. But at its core, **what we had here was the basic acquisition mechanic of an RPG**, in its bare bones form.

In *Ultima Online*, people preferred to hoard shirts than hoard gold. This is also the basic acquisitive mechanic at work. People like "stuff" more than they like money. Money is merely "potential stuff" because *it has still left a choice open*. **Final rewards in games are things that you *cannot make choices about*.**

In this sense, financial management websites tend to fail because it's sort of like doing financial management on those tickets you get at carnivals or Dave & Buster's. They're signifiers of a future reward, not the reward itself. Similarly, non-tangible cash in bank accounts reported merely via a number may in fact seem less real than the points on Mint's game system dashboard! After all, you can't spend the points.

If those Easter eggs were something you spent, the game would have lost a lot of its addictiveness, unless you spent them on something else that you got to keep. Preferably, something you can choose from a broad array of goods at different values, so that you get a rich choice that keeps you dithering; because the natural follow-on the moment after purchase, by the way, is dissatisfaction. The dissatisfaction is displaced onto *you* if it was your choice; **if Dave & Buster's picked the item for you, you would be mad at them instead.**

It may be that one reason why we used to be thriftier is simply because the money we hoarded was more tangible… gold coins trigger the brain's systems in a way that a bank balance does not. This is what the Mint point system is designed to supplement: by creating a non-fungible point system, the game is giving you something other than real-world stuff onto which to displace your acquisitiveness, a "virtual stuff." It would do even better, perhaps, if the points were gems or something else more "stuff-like" in terms of its representation.

Of course, unless there is social validation, then even that stuff may not mean much. Recently, there have been a few news articles about the practice of pushing energy and water conservation by displaying your neighbors' consumption rates to you. The social pressure pushes you to use less. Similarly, when your neighbors model conspicuous consumption, we model that as well — it's called "keeping up with the Joneses." Providing Mint users **a public comparison table so that users could compete on points** and show off their frugality would reinforce the system quite dramatically, just as the highly visible egg counter did.

This is why in WoW it's all about wearing that full set of (honestly, kind of pointless) armor: it's a status symbol, the way that jewelry is. (Jewelry, by the way, is an industry that has mastered much of the above!)

Metaplace Postmortem

It wasn't making money.

Players of games needed more game than what we had on offer. Word search and egg hunts were never more than brief diversions, and not something that would retain users. Our efforts to make more game-like spaces were still lightweight and incomplete, because doing a full RPG would have taken many months.

This left a world for chatters, and chatting was moving rapidly away from virtual spaces and towards "flat" ones: Twitter, Facebook. When we did attract an audience, it tended to be kids, or in territories where we couldn't derive revenue from the audience. (We actually went briefly viral with kids in Brazil, and it cost us more than we made; we ended up blocking the entire country, briefly, to stem the tide). Kid audiences drove our established userbase nuts, since they were mostly people who

A murder mystery adventure game about Jack the Ripper built by a Metaplace user

wanted to develop on the platform. A huge amount of them were underage — as young as ten — and we had to create a volunteer program just to ban them quickly enough. The volunteers were our best community members — which means they were our developers, the ones we counted on to create compelling content.

But there wasn't enough horsepower for developers. They needed 3d, they needed more professional tools, and they needed a way to monetize users, which we never quite delivered. Tools built entirely for end users failed to capture higher-end developers who wanted version control, debuggers, and the like. Fledging developers preferred just developing directly in Flash; eventually Unity would grow into exactly the tool they needed, and our predicted explosion of creativity came to pass.[387] Just not on our platform.

Metaplace worlds could look radically different from one another

Crucially, for developers of all stripes, we never enabled a way for them to make money off of other users. This feature of *Second Life* was absolutely critical to its success, and its absence meant we were never as attractive for content developers.

It turned out there was one audience that *Metaplace*, in that compromised form, absolutely did work for: educators. Multiple universities and high school programs of various sorts used it very successfully. But there wasn't enough money in that market.

In the end, what killed *Metaplace* was not knowing what it was for, because it was too good at too many things. The internal conflicts over making content versus being a user-generated-content play, between working with brands or end users, between professional and amateur developers, led us to always straddle the fence. The rising wave of 2009 that we could have ridden (Facebook games) was actually content-based, *despite* it being built on top of the social web; we could have gotten into making games for Facebook much sooner, and likely done very well.

---

[387] There was a brief conversation between myself and David Helgason, founder of Unity, at a conference in 2007v or so, where we mulled over the possibility of joining forces in some fashion. Had Metaplace become the server backend for Unity, who knows what might have happened. But it was just chatter over coffee.

Shooting meeps in our zombie graveyard

In the end, we missed our chance to be Unity by not chasing tools, and we missed our chance to be Zynga by not chasing content.

We pivoted to content in late 2009, including trying to get the full social environment on Facebook, but it was too late to save the MP environment. It was just too heavy and complex an experience for the Facebook audience as it existed then. At that point there were tens of thousands of worlds built on the *Metaplace* network, and most of them were empty set pieces. Our central social hub, Metaplace Central, was too directionless to work for an audience that mostly clicked on cabbages all day.

The last ditch effort to save *Metaplace* was an attempt to sell the company to a buyer who wanted to preserve what we had and also push the technology forward. It fell through at the last moment, and we had to go to Plan B. Plan B was switching to making Facebook games, and finally just making content internally. But it also entailed obtaining a bridge loan, a recap of the company, and me personally giving up control of the company day to day.

The decision was made — not by me — to shut down the UGC network rather abruptly, to force the company to switch focus decisively.[388]

---

[388] This led to a controversy over tools to export the content from the worlds. As someone who had always advocated strongly for preservation and history, it was seen as hypocritical of me to shut down

Once we switched and leveraged the tools to make content at a pro level, things happened quickly. We built *Island Life* in a month; and *My Vineyard* in another month; garnered well over a million users in aggregate on Facebook; and were the subject of a three way bidding war to acquire us, on the basis of how good our technology and team were.

Had those games been on *Metaplace*, what would have been different? Who knows.

I had had my shot to build my dream — heck, the dream of cyberspace! — and I had blown it. In part because it turned out that people by and large didn't want what we

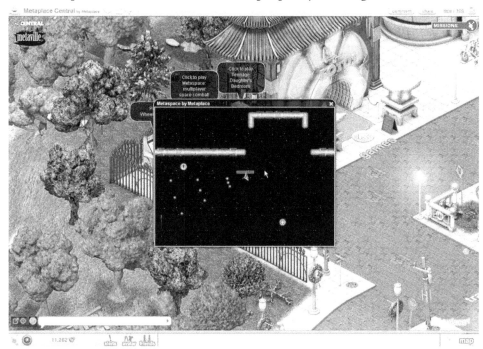

"World in world" tech allowed entire other worlds to be nested inside a window

had built.

Early in 2009, at the State of Play Conference, I had given a keynote where I talked about *Metaplace* and where things were going.[389] The final slide reads like I already

the service with deeply inadequate tools for exporting the content, and to do it over the holidays with almost no notice. The decision wasn't mine. I wasn't running the company anymore. As the public face of the company, however, I went out there and took the fall. Many asked why we couldn't just release the code and open source it all, and let the service keep going, run by users. But we had taken money and were beholden to investors, and felt obliged to try to at least pay it back. We actually turned them a tidy profit when we sold the company, but there is no question that users were the losers in that scenario.

[389] You can see contemporaneous notes taken by the late Greg Lastowka at

knew I had made the wrong thing for the times:

VWs will be...
Ambient
As in, in your browser frame?
Pervasive
What's the TOS for a widget?
Permeable
What's the privacy policy of a multidirectional stream?
Overlays
What's a world in the first place?
Relevant?
The new kind of world isn't this, it's the new hybrid

The simple farming/bug squashing game that was the first game I made on the platform, in its later form as a mini-game in Metaplace Central.

Notes from the time indicate that I was saying things like "immersion will no longer be important for virtual worlds. They won't be persistent immersive places — we'll be logged into *pieces* of worlds, through ad banners. You can get community in many ways, so what do VW's really bring to the table?"

http://terranova.blogs.com/terra_nova/2009/06/state-of-play-6.html

After that speech, attendees noted that the developers sounded rather more pessimistic about virtual worlds than the players thereof.[390] The relevancy question could no longer be ignored.

Today, you're logged into a world-spanning identity system that tracks you through ad banners. Twitter became the live chat for the entire web. Facebook made its login the default identity system, and ad network cookies are pervasive and live everywhere.

We live, now, logged into pieces of worlds.

I wish I had been wrong.

---

[390] See the comment thread at https://www.raphkoster.com/2009/06/21/state-of-play-reports/

Closing

Today we announced that the consumer-facing Metaplace service, the one you all know as the user-generated worlds website at Metaplace.com, is closing on January 1st. There's a FAQ and an official letter on the site.

The reason? Well, it just hasn't gotten traction. I have many thoughts on why, but I hope you'll forgive me if I don't go into all of them right now. It is a sad day for us here, and I know many users are going to be very disappointed by this turn of events.

Metaplace Inc isn't going away – in fact, we have some pretty exciting plans. But those plans are best shared on a future day.

If we have to sunset the service, we want to do it right. So for the next two weeks – come visit, and enjoy and celebrate all of the amazing creativity and work users put into their worlds. We're providing a way for users to grab the data that makes up their worlds. We'll be opening a website for the community so that you don't lose touch with your Metaplace friends. And we'll have a big party on the last day – because Metaplace.com will not go quietly, but with the sound of meeps and music and laughter.

It was a wonderful world full of wonderful people, and I will miss it more than I can say.

Social games

We pivoted to using the Metaplace platform to make social games for Facebook. They were farming games, but farming games where you could visit another player's farm and actually meet with them and chat. Players thought that was really neat; but when we offered "town squares" where they could meet strangers, they shied away dramatically and refused to go there. It turned out the mass market was terrified of chatting with strangers online. We tried making icebreaker games, and people would answer the question — and then not make friends. We tried special events and parties, and people would visit and stand around mutely.

There's me, talking to a Metaplace user on Island Life

Our other lessons from MMOs carried through. *Island Life* was the first Facebook game to allow players to modify the shape of their space, well before *Frontierville* came along. I got into arguments with the data analyst types over having to A/B test such an obvious (to me) feature as player creativity. The game itself was an outright clone of other island farming games — how far we had fallen! — but it made money and paid to keep the staff employed.

We eventually even had player to player trading, restoring some of that economic play that had been so central to the earlier virtual worlds. Other vestiges of old *Metaplace* still appeared; one player managed to hack the game and gain access to the older *Metaplace* content through their island. They had the only island farm with a bowling alley. One insistent professor kept on running his class in the new game. And we ended up hiring people out of the old *Metaplace* community, giving several folks their start on a game development career.

My Vineyard, primarily designed by Patrick Ferland, had unlockable bits of narrative that appeared as you explored the landscape, and Easter Eggs in the form of wines that could be created by mixing specific real grape types. The ability to place objects on a granularity tighter than one tile, and our server model's flexibility, meant that we could permit far far greater

A player screenshot of My Vineyard

customization of the space than any competitor, even allowing players to sculpt the terrain — for ten cents per hillock. Amazing vineyards were built, and the game ran for years, with unique features like pets and train tours to other players' constructions. We took great pride in the fact that people could identify the games as ours, valued the greater depth and sophistication of the gameplay.[391] It ran for just two years, and ended up being touched by millions of players, one of the most popular games I ever worked on.

---

[391] My Vineyard even has a Wiki: http://myvineyard.wikidot.com/

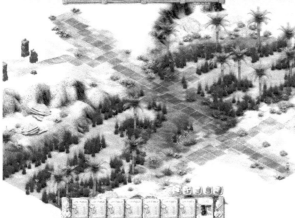

We got well through the development of a third game, called *Legendary Treasure*, a sort of simple exploration game, when Zynga announced what was essentially the same game. Ours looked dramatically nicer. We knew it wouldn't matter. The games had been just successful enough that each one took staff to maintain, which meant we had no staff left over to actually make new games.

We were already deep in talks to be acquired by a different social games company, one who saw the potential for the technology we had built.

I had a real belief that social games on Facebook could be the best and biggest canvas for connected play ever. "Imagine the million-player game!" I told people. Industry friends looked down their noses on social games, seeing them as not really games, as shallow. But I, perhaps clinging to the remnants of hope after the demise of *Metaplace*, still saw potential. I believed it was a chance to bring the ideas of connected worlds to a larger audience.

This belief drowned in the world of metrics, player manipulation, and monetization. Having to test whether or not players wanted to be creative, be engaged, broke me. Having to design around what would eke out one more penny per day per punter.

I didn't manage to get another world made while at the acquirer.[392] Or indeed, another game of my own made, the entire time I worked in social games.[393]

Metaplace was used as the backend engine for Deep Realms and later for Club Penguin on mobile devices.

---

[392] Playdom, itself acquired by Disney.

[393] I did help out on several other games, and am even credited as creative director on *Deep Realms*, a game that I joined near the end of its development and helped refine. While at Disney Playdom I assisted to greater or lesser degrees on games such as *Full Bloom, City Girl,* and even a small bit on *Disney Infinity*. But it was all more edtorial than it was creative.

Are Virtual Worlds Over?

Dan Terdiman at CNet engages in some handwringing over the fact that kids worlds and social games are taking over the hype that used to belong to virtual worlds.[394]

> But to someone who cut his virtual world teeth on more immersive, 3D environments like There and Second Life, these never-ending announcements of new companies trying to jump on the social gaming bandwagon have left me with one nagging question: Where is the innovation?

The innovation lies in making something that matters to ordinary people.

Now, I am a virtual world person, obviously. I don't see much distinction between the game worlds and the non-game ones like Second Life. I have been working with them since the text muds, for over 15 years, which doesn't exactly put me in the true old dino category where Richard Bartle and Randy Farmer reside, but I think it is fair to say that I have been closely identified with the space for a long long time now.

And I think that they aren't over, but **the form that they have taken is.**

Virtual World Games

Birthday Cards
YoVille
Friends For Sale!
Café World
Farm Town
weRead (Books iRe...
WereWolves
Happy Aquarium
FooPets!
MouseHunt

Virtual World Games ▶

Facebook's list of virtual worlds? Really??

Most of the classic definitions of virtual worlds have centered around the following:

- a simulation of places
- synchronous user interaction
- users represented by avatars

In addition to these, a cluster of common features, some from games but not all, have come to be tightly associated with the medium — more as praxis than because they are intrinsic to the form. Examples

---

[394] https://web.archive.org/web/20120311192101/http://news.cnet.com/8301-13772_3-10460293-52.html

include:

- **pseudonymity**, aka "handles"
- **formal group identity,** aka guilds
- **numerically quantified reputation**, aka ratings, rankings, and reputation systems
- **publicly visible profile data**, often including abstracted historical activity, aka levels and achievements — and equipment and avatar clothing
- **formalized user roles**, aka classes and skills — and also "gods" versus "players"
- in-world dispute resolution and customer service
- a fairly common assumption of **malleability of environment**
- **strong tie interdependence** via things like group and party dynamics and live chat

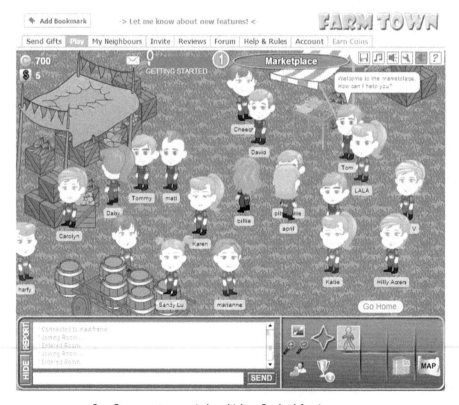

Farm Town — a true massively multiplayer Facebook farming game

It's hard to think of virtual worlds where these elements are not included to some degree. And yet, and yet, the commonest mental model of a virtual world is probably still best articulated as "a non-real place that exists independent of my imagination." The common element here is that *Second Life, Star Trek Online*, whatever — they are there even when I am not, thanks to the computer simulation. Whereas countless other imaginary worlds, both simulated and not, do not have that sense of independent existence — worlds ranging from a detailed simulation as in *Half-Life 2*, or even a local Renaissance Faire, do not provide that sense.

There's a reason why Facebook labels games like *Farmville*, which are completely lacking in synchronous avatar-based interaction, as "virtual world games" on their games directory page. *Farmville* meets this test via the same manner that something like *Animal Crossing* did — it doesn't run a continuous real-time simulation, but it sure *feels* like it does to a user. And both *Farmville* and *Animal Crossing* feel like they are worlds with independent existence.

In fact, many of the competitors to Farmville do in fact offer avatars and "massively multiplayer" spaces. *YoVille* is the most obvious example of a true virtual world on Facebook, but there are others, including some in the farming genre such as *Farm Town*, which offers a true massively multiplayer marketplace area where users can go to chat. (Except they don't chat... more on that later.)

But it's clearly not the majority. Yet.

A lot of the praxis around virtual worlds — and indeed, games in general — has been co-opted by social media. Enough, in fact, that we are starting to see worry that too much has been co-opted.[395] And I can't really complain, since I have done my share[396] of evangelizing this stuff to web people!

- **Formal group identity** is taken to a level well beyond that of the typical virtual world on social networks. (We've been saying for years that we should support multiple guild membership in MMORPGs... check out the typical number of groups a Facebook user belongs to...)

- **Points and quantified reputation** are rampant. Arguably, excessive.

- Similarly, **publicly visible profile data** has become the defining characteristic

---

[395] Unfortunately, this link from ReadWriteWeb has been lost.
[396] See https://www.raphkoster.com/games/presentations/immersive-design-lessons-from-game-designers/

of much of the social web. Facebook is a collection of "avatar" pages where you can browse only one's clothing, achievements, guild memberships, and skills — in a manner of speaking.

- **Formalized user roles** are also the norm, on the admin–vs–user level.

- And perhaps most pleasantly, **malleability of environment** is also a key characteristic. Even the most simplistic of farming games on Facebook ranks higher on the "affect your world" scale than *World of Warcraft* does… and this sort of personalization of the environment is standard not only in social games but across the social web today.

But just as telling are the parts of the praxis that are left out. Let's take a look at some of these practices and what has happened to them:

Pseudonymity is taking a lot of hits lately. Not only does Facebook insist on real identities, but we have seen *Second Life* moving to having real life profile data alongside the pseudonym — in the new viewer, your profile shows both of them, right next to each other. And today, Twitter (still pseudonymous) started rolling out discovery via real identity as well:

> Today, Twitter took the wraps off a new feature of the site. When logging in, it prompts the user to set defaults on being discovered with their email address or mobile phone number. It's called "Be Found on Twitter". Our contact at Twitter told us that, like many new features, this will show up for some users today and others soon.
> — ReadWriteWeb, "Be Found on Twitter: Connecting Our Dots in the Social Graph"[397]

The pressure is towards real life identities instead. In fact, towards *singular* identities. Speaking as someone who consciously ditched pseudonymous handles a few years ago, this was inevitable once you had a sufficiently connected set of databases. And really, the strong ties implicit in virtual worlds have been always been pushing towards real life ties — it's even in the Laws,[398] so it's a phenomenon recognized for over a decade now.

I just got done writing the other day about how **placeness is a feature and not**

---

[397] https://web.archive.org/web/20100301080847/http://www.readwriteweb.com/cloud/2010/02/twitter-social-graph-email-mobile.php

[398] "The Laws of Online World Design," a collection of aphorisms and lessons learned from the MUD-Dev mailing list. See https://www.raphkoster.com/games/laws-of-online-world-design/the-laws-of-online-world-design/

the point.[399] Given that placeness is the *chief* characteristic of virtual worlds, this is a bit of a blow to the traditional conception of virtual worlds as a destination. One characteristic of a social-game-as-virtual-world (or indeed, non-placey things that people like labelling as "virtual-world-like" that really aren't worlds at all, such as Twitter, and so on) is that they are not destinations in their own right; they are been seen as adjuncts to other activities.

The part of formalized user roles that is best described as **the class system is outright gone.** Classes are essentially a game system oriented around forcing people into strong-tie teams for synchronous activity. They are the same game mechanic as having a quarterback, a linebacker, and a kicker, or players on offense and defense. They are about complementarity.

But the social web has evolved into more of a classless system, in the end, perhaps because teams with rigid roles have always been a very artificial construct. It may be that the social games will start to include this sort of mechanic, but… I am unsure they will, given that…

Weak ties have supplanted strong ties as the default social link. Asynchronicity rules the roost, not real-time interaction. Real-time is a feature, a perk, something used occasionally. It's not the norm.

It is hard to overstate how big a deal this is.

So what's left for virtual worlds? Two of the three key elements in the definition have fallen out of favor in a lot of ways, and the common practices around the last one have been co-opted in radically different forms.

The principal places where virtual worlds offer benefits over these flatter means of participation will have to do with **preserving spaces where these qualities can still occur.** Applications where

- placeness is intrinsic (and herein lie the things that many Second Life advocates argue for, such as academic uses involving 3d visualization, or artistic expression that requires 3d)

- pseudonymity is intrinsic (such as anything involving identity exploration, artificial roles, and wish fulfillment)

- synchronous interaction and strong ties are intrinsic (team activities, real-time problem-solving, real-time social activities)

---

[399] https://www.raphkoster.com/2010/02/24/placeness-is-a-feature-not-the-point/

The most obvious answer is games.

Any application where you can "pick two" will likely migrate away from virtual worlds, because the presence of the third is a barrier, not a benefit.

Kids' MMOs are thriving because they don't use strong ties (they don't use chat!)

Roleplaying forums on sites like *Gaia* and Deviant Art are doing well because the barriers implicit in heavy representations of placeness are absent.

Something like *Second Life* struggles to gain mainstream adoption because flatter pseudo-places can offer so much of what it does, and the very real benefits it offers are only benefits to a segment of the audience that wants either the pseudonymity, or the placeness, or the chat.

And Facebook games? Hey, there's a place that feels like a world, strongly weak-tie driven, without pseudonymity issues, and yet they carry with them all that praxis, all that other stuff that was elaborations on the core virtual world concept. It's like a virtual world, "with the bad bits removed" — which is of course a phrase we have heard before, when discussing why *World of Warcraft* does so much better than the other MMORPGs.

Instead, I think we will see the co-option process continue. These flatter environments will learn to use pseudonymity as a feature, and synchronicity and strong ties as a feature, and placeness as a feature. Then they will fall perfectly into the technical definition of "a virtual world." But when we connect to them, we'll have trouble recognizing it, because they won't be the *defining* features.

They will be add-ons to the core experience — which will be worldy in the imaginary sense, not the simulation sense. Arguably, worldy in the *real* sense, because by then, these "connected society applications" will partake deeply of the real world.

TL;DR. Short form: virtual worlds are dead, long live the world, virtual. And it isn't the picture that we painted for ourselves, as we thought about the way in which virtual worlds would evolve, all those dreams of richer simulations and NPCs that talk to you, of simulated societies and of immersive experiences.

But **it doesn't mean virtual worlds are over.** They are metamorphosing, and like a caterpillar, on the path to mass market acceptance, they are shedding the excess legs and creepy worm-like looks in favor of something that doesn't much resemble what it sprang from, but which a lot more people will like. And which will be a bit harder to pin down.

This change is bigger than the addition of graphics, bigger than the shift to AAA games, bigger than the shift towards kids' worlds, and bigger and more complex than the use of web clients (though web clients are an inescapable and intrinsic element of the change).

It may not be the last change. It may be that the prevailing currents away from these things change — it happened now, it will happen again. It may be that as tech barriers fall, placeness becomes easy; or that the privacy pendulum swings back the other way and pseudonymity comes back to the Internet.

In the meantime, I would be betting against all the "native client" worlds — AAA game worlds included. Against anything that involves too much of a fantasy identity. Against anything that *relies* on people playing together in real time. It's just not where the action is for the next several years. **Virtual places as they exist now cannot be a mass medium any more than a single restaurant can.**

For those of us who dream of a place we can't possibly be, doing things we couldn't do, as someone else, with friends… well, we're a little bit out of luck. We'll always have our Avalons and our Lost Worlds. They're just not the future anymore.

The My Vineyard story

A Mysterious Letter

Dear Player,[400]

By now you must be wondering who I was. After all, you inherited a vineyard from a stranger, some college professor you never heard of.

I wish I could be there to tell you of the deep and dangerous secrets held here. Most of all, I wish I could have told you about Joshua and Marie. But perhaps the best way is not to attempt to explain, but instead enclose Joshua's diary. You should read it as it happened.

The diary was found in separate little scraps in the forest. Players would purchase expansions to their clearing, and build whatever layout they liked, but scraps of the diary always appeared in order.

The Diary

Marie was so happy to arrive at the vineyard today. We pulled up in front of the modest villa, and the view was drenched in sun and dust, like a postcard of wine country. Vines stretched across the valley. I could see birds circling - we need to keep them off the grapes!

But her eyes were only for the forest, and the house. Her eyes sparkled. "We're home, Joshua," she said. "This is home now."

After cleaning off the crush pad today, Sam & I took a walk out to the woods where I saw those lights. (Old hound wasn't happy about leaving his warm fireplace!)

Someone's been here. I found evidence of a camp site — scorched earth. Some junk too - a half-smoked cigar, a lipstick, and a broken heel from a woman's pump. Odd gear for camping! Sort of posh actually.

---

[400] This inserted the actual name of the player who was playing the game.

The soil is perfect for Ansonica here. I was weeding when Marie came out with lemonade and a phone message. She was angry.

"Some rich-sounding folks, offering to buy the land," she said. "But we'll never leave here, will we, Joshua? This is our place now."

I reassured her. Cold lemonade, the vines, Sam at our feet and Marie in the curl of my arm… this is a spot of heaven.

Woke in the middle of the night to the road of machinery, heard far off. Then the tumbling of timber. I woke Marie, had her call the police. Found a bulldozed section of the woods.

Contacted our neighbors to the north, the Albertsons. "Not us," he said. "But it's not the first time around here. We had something like it last year."

Strange, I thought. But then he said, "Maybe they're digging for buried treasure."

I found a curious thing today. An old wall covered in vines, and a slab of stone, carved with grapes, deep in the underbrush. This vineyard must have been huge, once.

What sort of secret would be hidden here? The stone wall looks very old. I took a rubbing of the curious writing. I cannot read it, but it may be Latin… in which case Marie can help.

Marie has a secret smile. She smiled it on the day that I met her father. She smiled it when she told me that her trust fund was enough for us to afford this vineyard. And she smiles it now, as she works at the text of the rubbing. "It's a surprise, silly!" she tells me. But I am very curious.

Spent some time clearing out tenacious vines from under the juice tank. Stubborn stuff.

I woke to cold in the bed.

Marie wasn't in the house. I ran, I shouted. The notes, the rubbings, they're gone. She must have taken them with her.

She was smiling secretly last night, and she set the alarm furtively. Where did she go?

Lights were moving in the woods, but I could not catch them.

It is past noon. The police have come and gone, saying there is nothing that they can do until more days go by. The bed lies unmade, and I cannot bring myself to eat.

I have racked my brain. My feet are blistered from walking the woods. My arm is cut to ribbons from those grim vines that tangle the trees. My voice is hoarse from calling her name.

I have found more slabs, with different numbers of grapes.

The professor from the university called back, very excited about the rubbings from the stone slab. An obscure form of Latin she said, and it spoke of nectar of the gods, the drink of Bacchus. Wine, obviously. It sounds like once, a very special grape was grown here.

I had to take Sam to the vet today. Poor dog, he's feeling his age. Thankfully, he'll be fine.

I saw them. I know it was them. A tubby fellow with a cigar, and a woman in expensive clothes and cherry red lipstick. Same shade as the one I found. They were standing in front of the diner, arguing by a fancy car. They're connected to Marie's disappearance, I just know it.

I have a plan. A party, to celebrate opening the first cask. It's early, really, but my goal isn't to establish the vineyard's brand, it's to smoke out the villains.

The party was tonight. And they came — the little fellow with the shifty eyes and the cigar, the elegant woman who seems to employ him. I had to tolerate the stink of his cigar.

They were pushy, asking about the history of the villa. Asking what grapes the wine came from. They're after something. After Bacchus' grapes? I dropped hints, showed the papers. The hook is baited.

The glass broke at 3 in the morning. I had mentioned I was going to be out of town this night. I knew they would break in. I made sure that my falsified rubbings were hidden, but not too well. I had to hide my anger when they smashed into the roll-top desk — Marie loved that desk — but I stayed quiet, so I could follow them.

I am leaving this here at the house, in case the Professor follows.

Marie, I am coming.

The Professor's Notes

Joshua is missing. His dog is circling the room, whining frantically. He left his diary here on the table, and it seems crazy. Secrets in the forest, forgotten grapes, mysterious strangers? But Marie, and now him, both missing. There are secrets in this vineyard, and they start with those two strangers.

The arrests have been made. The two strangers turn out to be fortune hunters working for a major alcohol company. They are really slimy pieces of work. The chief told me that the man, Kriegs, has a very long record and is wanted by Interpol.

The woman has cut a deal with her prosecutor. She won't admit to anything herself, but says that the man, that kriegs fellow, was the one who took Marie and also doubled back when they realized Joshua was onto them. I fear for their lives.

The police canvassed the woods thoroughly and found nothing, no remains, no one. But I had a feeling that woman wasn't telling us everything. So I contrived to speak with her privately. They were after some special vine cutting. Some wonderful grape that supposedly is like no other wine ever. Long lost, and worth a fortune.

I don't trust her at all. But she smiled sadly. Look under the seventh slab, she said.

I found it. The cellar. The secret Marie found. It was under the seventh slab; seven bunches of grapes. It was hard to lift, even ajar as it was.

Kriegs must have closed them up in here. It was cool inside, and musty. The walls were lined with amphorae, many cracked and dry. At the end of the tunnel, an amazing mosaic… But there is nothing here to eat. Nothing to drink except the nectar of the gods, Bacchus' own wine.

Joshua and Marie are gone. Two wine cups made of smooth stone, on a smooth stone table. An amphora opened, the dregs of wine in the cups.

I sniffed the bouquet. It was heady.

When you drink the wine of the gods, what happens to you? Do you go somewhere… else?

I found it scrawled on the stone table. Marie's writing, judging from the rubbings I found. The secret to it all: those pesky vines everywhere are the long-lost grape of the fabled wine of the gods. It still lives, and can be tended back to life.

It never launched, but we did eventually finally work on a 3d engine client for Metaplace. Here is an in-progress shot of My Vineyard.

The Professor's Will

So now, *playername*, you know the secret. I had to entrust it to someone special, someone who would know what to do with the wine that will flow from this land, the blood of this earth.

So I picked you. Tend your inheritance carefully, my friend. Toast those of us who went before. And watch out for lights moving in the forest.

Oh yes — there was some left. I didn't dare drink any. Joshua and Marie — their love deserved it. Legends say that you can live forever off the nectar of the gods. I have no one, so I cannot face that.

I might, however, slip some to Sam, and see how he runs, newly young, towards the sunset.

Cordially,
The Professor

Conclusion

This year marks twenty-five years since we started working on *LegendMUD*.

Twenty since the launch of *Ultima Online*.

Fifteen since the launch of *Star Wars Galaxies*.

Ten since the beta opened for *Metaplace*.

Five years since *My Vineyard* closed its doors.

The thing about virtual worlds is that they are like cities. No one forgets a place were they used to live. And like cities, they carry with them all the questions that matter: do we choose to build parks? Heck, do we deserve to be in charge? When we do things people don't like, do we lie to them? Are there enough jobs? Is life fair there? Do people feel free?

Folks on *LegendMUD* tell me they may actually launch the skill trees patch this year. Millions were touched by *Ultima Online*. Players painstakingly recreated *Star Wars Galaxies* themselves — it took them eight years. *Metaplace* lives on in the work of the developers it inspired.

And I still get occasional fan mail for *My Vineyard,* requests to bring it back. To this day, the Facebook page for it has a quarter million people following it. It closed in 2013. Five years later, the most recent post asking for it to come back, as of today, April 27th, 2018, was three days ago.

This is not a *memoir*. That would mean memories, on the shelf.

No, this is a *manual*.

It's a long road.

You had better start building now.

Index

About the Author

Raph Koster is a veteran game designer who has been professionally credited in almost every area of the game industry. He's been the lead designer and director of massive titles such as *Ultima Online* and *Star Wars Galaxies*; a venture-backed entrepreneur heading his own studio; and he's contributed design work, writing, art, soundtrack music, and programming to many more titles ranging from Facebook games to single-player games for handheld consoles. Koster is widely recognized as one of the world's top thinkers about game design, and is an in-demand speaker at conferences all over the world. His book *A Theory of Fun for Game Design* is one of the undisputed classics in the games field and was recently revised for a 10th anniversary edition. In 2012, he was named an Online Game Legend at the Game Developers Conference Online. Visit his blog at **www.raphkoster.com**.

CPSIA information can be obtained
at www.ICGtesting.com
Printed in the USA
BVHW011358170222
629335BV00005B/98